D1120349

E
474.61
.P75
1996

BEFORE ANTIETAM:

THE BATTLE FOR
SOUTH MOUNTAIN

John M Priest (signature)

By

John Michael Priest

Foreword by
Edwin C. Bearss

OXFORD UNIVERSITY PRESS

New York   Oxford

Oxford University Press

Oxford   New York
Athens   Auckland   Bangkok   Bombay
Calcutta   Cape Town   Dar es Salaam   Delhi
Florence   Hong Kong   Istanbul   Karachi
Kuala Lumpur   Madras   Madrid   Melbourne
Mexico City   Nairobi   Paris   Singapore
Taipei   Tokyo   Toronto

and associated companies in
Berlin   Ibadan

Copyright © 1992 by John Michael Priest

First published in 1992 by White Mane Publishing Company, Inc.,
P.O. Box 152, Shippensburg, PA 17257

First issued as an Oxford University Press paperback, 1996

Oxford is a registered trademark of Oxford University Press

All rights reserved. No part of this publication may be reproduced,
stored in a retrieval system, or transmitted, in any form or by any means,
electronic, mechanical, photocopying, recording, or otherwise,
without the prior permission of Oxford University Press.

Library of Congress Cataloging-in-Publication Data
Priest, John M., 1949–
Before Antietam : the battle for South Mountain / by John Michael
Priest ; foreword by Edwin C. Bearss.
p.   cm.
Originally published: Shippensburg, PA : White Mane Pub. Co.,
© 1992.
Includes bibliographical references and index.
ISBN 0-19-510712-8 (Pbk.)
1. South Mountain, Battle of, 1862.   I. Title.
[E474.61.P75   1996]
973.7′336—dc20   96-2125

1 3 5 7 9 10 8 6 4 2

Printed in the United States of America

Acknowledgements

As with any work of this nature, it would be very difficult to express in order of importance all of the individuals and institutions whose knowledge and resources made its completion possible. I will, therefore, thank each of them as they come to mind.

Timothy Reese of Burkittsville gave me some of the primary sources about Fox's and Turner's Gaps. He also took me on my first real tour of South Mountain Battlefields.

My colleague, Bill Hilton, as in *Antietam: The Soldiers' Battle,* freely loaned me books from his private library.

Paul Chiles and Ted Alexander from Antietam National Battlefield willingly opened their files and made many of the Ezra Carman papers available to me as well as *The National Tribune.*

Dr. Richard Sauers of Harrisburg, Pennsylvania lent me a typed transcript of the William Bolton Journal and took me to the Military Order of the Loyal Legion of the United States (MOLLUS) Library in Philadelphia which resulted in the verification of a rare Confederate account about the signal station at Urbana, Maryland.

The curator and the staff at the MOLLUS Library are tremendous individuals. They readily made their manuscripts and books available for research, in particular, a few of General John Gibbon's letters. Many thanks to them all.

Dr. Jay Luvaas of the United States Army War College graciously took me on an extensive walking tour of Fox's and Turner's Gaps. I could not understand the battle until I stepped into those hallowed fields, which now are threatened by development.

George Brigham of the Frederick County Historical Society provided me with some excellent civilian accounts of the battle and further explained the terrain. He also provided me with several unique maps.

Mike Musick and his colleagues at the National Archives opened the door to a small but extremely valuable collection called the Antietam Studies.

The Manuscript Division at the Library of Congress contains the Ezra Carman Collection and Antietam Manuscript. There are some very interesting letters contained within those volumes. The Samuel Gilpin Diary is also located there.

The Special Collections Department at Duke University as well as the Southern Historical Collection at the University of North Carolina, Chapel Hill, contain many superb letters and diaries, too numerous to list here. The staffs are very friendly and very helpful. I look forward to visiting them again.

John Frye from the Western Maryland Room in the Washington County Free Library gave me access to the David Lilley Collection and patiently fielded questions about the weather and the hours for sunset and sunrise during the battle.

The microfilm room at the C. Burr Artz Library in Frederick contains a collection of *The New York Tribune*, the Markall Diary, and a comprehensive set of the Frederick County census records.

Dan Toomey, Maryland author, graciously provided me with a complete copy of Dr. Lewis Steiner's rare report of the Confederate occupation of Maryland.

Dr. Richard Sommers and his knowledgable staff at the United States Army Military History Institute in Carlisle Barracks allowed me to research in their vast manuscript collection. The book stacks at the USAMHI are a veritable gold mine of information. I also wish to thank Michael Winey and his staff in the photograph division at the Institute for enabling me to sift through their holdings.

I wish to extend my deepest thanks to John S. Derbyshire, John W. Kiely, and Robert Ulrich for allowing me to use letters from their personal collections.

As always, my special thanks goes to my wife, Rhonda, and our family for their patience and support.

Foreword

A Long Hot Summer: The Tide Turns

June 25, 1862, was just another bleak day for Jefferson Davis and his generals. To most people it seemed that their Confederacy was about gone "up the spout." The only good news from any military front in the more than five months that had passed since Col. James A. Garfield had defeated Rebel forces led by Brig. Gen. Humphrey Marshall on January 10 at Middle Creek, in eastern Kentucky, had come from Virginia's Shenandoah Valley. There, Maj. Gen. Thomas J. Jackson, better known as "Stonewall," in a brilliant campaign, had outwitted and outfought formidable Union columns led by three political generals—Nathaniel P. Banks, John C. Frémont, and James Shields. But elsewhere the news had been consistently grim all year.

On this very day, Gen. Robert E. Lee, not yet the commanding figure soon to be known as "Marse Robert" to his admiring soldiers, had watched as men of Maj. Gen. George B. McClellan's powerful Army of the Potomac flexed their muscles on either side of the Williamsburg Road. In a little-known engagement at King's Schoolhouse, McClellan's troops closed to within six miles of downtown Richmond. Had McClellan seen through Lee's bold plan to seize the initiative by calling "Stonewall" Jackson from the Valley to join with three of Lee's divisions to assail the Army of the Potomac's Fifth Corps north of the Chickahominy at daybreak on the 26th?

Elsewhere, wherever President Davis looked, the situation was equally bleak. Across the Appalachians, in the Confederacy's heartland, there was no comfort for Southerners. Union forces of Maj. Gen. Henry W. Halleck's "Army Group," having captured Memphis and Corinth, Mississippi, held West Tennessee, much of Middle Tennessee, and the northern tier of Mississippi counties. One of Halleck's armies, Maj. Gen. Don Carlos Buell's Army of the Ohio, thrusting eastward from Corinth, Mississippi, and Athens and Decatur, Alabama, threatened Chattanooga. At Tupelo, Mississippi, some 50 miles south of Halleck's headquarters, Gen. Braxton Bragg, soon to become a Davis favorite, had only recently replaced Gen. P. G. T. Beauregard as leader of the Confederate Army of the Mississippi. Bragg, a stern disciplinarian, was reorganizing the army that had fought at Shiloh and suffered through the siege of Corinth.

Uncle Sam's deepwater navy, aided by Maj. Gen. Benjamin Butler's soldiers, had underscored the Union's power afloat. Masonry forts and a divided and ineffective use of their infant navy had been disastrous for the South. Entering the

Mississippi, the Union warships had captured New Orleans, the South's largest city, and had ascended the mighty river as far as Vicksburg. The river ironclads and rams had moved down the Mississippi and were operating on White River as far upstream as Devall's Bluff, Arkansas.

Union forces in the trans-Mississippi had exploited their Pea Ridge victory. Maj. Gen. Samuel R. Curtis' columns had pushed deep into northeast Arkansas, occupying Jacksonport and thrusting to within 45 miles of Little Rock. A strong force of whites and Native Americans in blue was assembling on the Texas Road at Baxter Springs, Kansas, ready to carry the war into the Cherokee Nation. And in the far-off Rio Grande country, Texans who in March had occupied Albuquerque and Santa Fe had been checkmated at Glorieta Pass later that month. Abandoning an expedition that had once promised so much, the battered and disillusioned mounted riflemen were well along on their way back to San Antonio.

At numerous points along the South's Atlantic and Gulf coasts, Union amphibious commands had scored successes. The North Carolina sounds were controlled by Yankee gunboats, while enclaves had been seized and strengthened at Roanoke Island, New Bern, and Fort Macon. On the South Carolina coast, the Port Royal area had been in Union hands since early November 1861, and Fort Pulaski, at the mouth of the Savannah River, had surrendered on April 11, after a short bombardment. In East Florida, the Yanks held Fernandina and St. Augustine, and in West Florida, where until May 9 they had been confined to Fort Pickens and the western end of Santa Rosa Island, they now were in possession of Pensacola Bay and its navy yard. These enclaves gave the North a number of advantages. The ports and anchorages enabled Union warships to tighten the blockade, while reducing the number of harbors open to Confederate blockade runners and commerce. They provided staging areas for attacks on nearby Confederate cities such as the one directed against Charleston in mid-June. The South Carolina Sea Islands became the site of the Port Royal Experiment, where thousands of blacks were settled on abandoned plantation lands.

But all this was about to change. Beginning on June 26 at Mechanicsville—day two of the Seven Days' Battles—General Lee's army boldly attacked units of McClellan's Fifth Corps posted behind Beaverdam Creek. Other battles followed, McClellan lost his nerve, and, by the morning of July 2, the Army of the Potomac had retreated into a fortified camp at Harrison's Landing on James River, 26 miles southeast of Richmond. Coincident with the fight at Mechanicsville, the War Department in Washington constituted the Army of Virginia to be led by brash Maj. Gen. John Pope, called in from the West. The core of Pope's army—charged with shielding the Nation's capital and advancing overland to McClellan's support—were the three corps that "Stonewall" Jackson had baffled and befuddled during his Valley Campaign.

With two powerful armies in the field and a new General-in-Chief—Henry W. Halleck—in Washington, General Lee could not rest on his laurels. The man who, when called to command on June 1 had been derisively dubbed by critics and cynics as "Granny Lee" and the "King of Spades," retained the initiative. The reorganized and redesignated Army of Northern Virginia was soon on the march. "Stonewall" Jackson's corps was detached and positioned at Orange to hold the line of the Rapidan and guard the key Gordonsville railroad junction. Lee, with Maj. Gen. James Longstreet's corps, remained on the southeast approaches to Richmond to watch McClellan's army.

General Pope, by the end of the first week of August, was in the field and his three corps converged on Culpeper. On the 3rd, McClellan had been ordered to evacuate his fortified Harrison's landing camp and redeploy the Army of the Potomac from the Peninsula north to Aquia Landing and Alexandria on the Potomac. If the Federals successfully effected this concentration of these two great armies along the Rapidan-Rappahannock line, their overwhelming numbers would insure victory in the next "On to Richmond" campaign.

To further strengthen their armies for the anticipated decisive campaign, the Lincoln government pared down commitments in other areas. Maj. Gen. Ambrose E. Burnside was recalled from North Carolina and ordered first to Old Point Comfort and then to Fredericksburg. He brought with him large numbers of Ninth Corps soldiers who had captured Roanoke Island and had seized other key points on the North Carolina sounds. Also joining him were some of the soldiers who in mid-June had threatened Charleston, the citadel of rebellion, from the Port Royal enclave. Union strength in western Virginia was also to be drastically pared to bolster the northern Virginia buildup. Halleck in mid-August ordered the Kanawha Division to be assembled at Parkersburg preparatory to movement by rail to Washington.

Well before the Union effected this strategic combination, the situation had changed drastically. On August 9, "Stonewall" Jackson took advantage of the failure of General Pope's corps commanders to coordinate their marches and employed superior numbers to batter General Banks' corps at Cedar Mountain. Then, in the face of Pope's continued advance, Jackson and his three divisions retired and took up a defensive stance south of the Rapidan. On August 15, General Lee, satisfied that McClellan was withdrawing from the Peninsula, used the "ironhorse" to rush Longstreet's corps to Gordonsville. Maj. Gen. D. H. Hill with several divisions remained in the Richmond area to insure that McClellan's retrograde was not a feint.

Lee hoped to trap Pope's army between the Rapidan and the Rappahannock. But the Federals were alert to their danger, and, when the Confederates crossed the Rapidan on a broad front on August 20, Pope won the race to the Rappahannock. The armies confronted each other from opposite sides of the north-south reaches of the Rappahannock, as Pope successfully countered Lee's attempts to force a crossing. A daring August 22-23 night raid by Maj. Gen. James E. B. Stuart's cavalry on Pope's Catlett's Station headquarters resulted in the capture of more than 300 prisoners and Pope's despatch book, featuring detailed data as to his strength, dispositions, and designs; and referencing expected reinforcements and identifying their whereabouts. This information proved invaluable to General Lee. He now knew that he must find a way promptly to compel Pope to abandon the Rappahannock line, otherwise the arrival of two of McClellan's five corps in northern Virginia and the march of Burnside's Ninth Corps from Fredericksburg would give the Yanks sufficient manpower to overwhelm him and make their position impregnable. Lee did not choke.

Long before daybreak on August 25, Jackson, with three divisions, departed Jeffersonton and headed north. Nightfall found his corps bivouacked at Salem. Next morning the long column turned east, passed the Bull Run Mountain via Thoroughfare Gap, and at dusk struck the Orange & Alexandria Railroad—Pope's lifeline—at Bristoe Station. On the 27th, Jackson's people seized Manassas Junction, a major enemy depot, and routed one of McClellan's brigades that had been rushed westward by rail from Alexandria.

General Lee, accompanied by Longstreet's corps, had marched from Jeffersonton on August 26, taking the route pioneered by Jackson. Maj. Gen. Richard

Anderson's division was left behind to keep Pope's attention focused on the Rappahannock.

Pope had arrogantly announced to his soldiers five weeks before:

> Let us study the...lines of retreat of our opponents, and let our own
> to take care of themselves. Let us look before us and not behind. Suc-
> cess and glory are in the advance. Disaster and shame lurk in the rear.

But now, with Jackson astride the railroad and in possession of Manassas Junction, Pope was compelled to look to his rear.

On August 26, Pope, now reinforced by the Third and Fifth Corps of the Army of the Potomac and two Ninth Corps divisions, planned to carry the fight to the Confederates west of the Rappahannock. Jackson's march and unexpected Bristoe Station appearance caused Pope to change plans. Ignoring Lee and Longstreet, Pope, on the 27th, redeployed his army to face northeast and directed the columns to close on Manassas Junction, where he expected to find and overwhelm Jackson's corps. But when Pope entered Manassas Junction on August 28, he found Jackson gone. Pope—mistakenly concluding that Jackson was east of Bull Run at Centreville—ordered five of his six corps to converge there. Pope reached Centreville with two corps only to find that the division of Confederates that had been there earlier was gone. At 7 p.m., the sounds of battle to the west rolled in and now Pope knew Jackson's whereabouts.

By midday on the 28th, Jackson's corps was in position and resting behind an unfinished railroad grade parallel to and north of the Warrenton Turnpike. Late in the afternoon, Jackson was apprised that a Union division had turned into the Warrenton Turnpike and was marching east toward Centreville. Jackson, although he knew that Lee and Longstreet were still west of Thoroughfare Gap, determined to assail the Union column. Otherwise all of Pope's army would soon be east of Bull Run, on commanding ground, and positioned to be rapidly reinforced by additional divisions of the Army of the Potomac known to be arriving at Alexandria from the Peninsula. Jackson correctly reasoned that an attack on the force passing across his front would draw the belligerent Pope back west of Bull Run and set the stage for a decisive battle on the next day with the reunited wings of Lee's army.

The two-hour fight at Brawner's Farm was bitter, a tactical standoff—the outnumbered Yanks held their ground until well after dark—but brilliant strategic thinking on Jackson's part. Pope, having pinpointed Jackson, had five of his six corps in motion on the morning of the 29th. Unable to fathom the Confederates' battle plan, Pope assumed that Jackson would retreat to escape his converging columns. Jackson had no such idea, and his three divisions posted in double line behind the abandoned railroad grade confidently awaiting the oncoming Yanks.

Meanwhile, a blunder on the part of the Federals allowed Longstreet's corps to pass through Thoroughfare Gap. By noon General Lee was on the field, and Longstreet's corps was in position at a right angle to Jackson's people. Longstreet's four divisions formed north and south of the Warrenton Turnpike and faced east. From 7:30 a.m. till dusk, Pope's divisions made repeated attacks on Jackson's veterans. But they were piecemeal and uncoordinated, and gains were soon nullified by Confederate counterattacks. About dusk, John Bell Hood's division of Longstreet's corps made a forced reconnaissance east to Groveton before pulling back.

Although Pope should have known better, he claimed in a telegram to the War Department that after "a terrific battle...with the combined forces of the enemy, which lasted with continuous fury from daylight until dark...the enemy was driven from the field, which we now occupy." At noon on August 30, a Saturday, Pope, unable to divine Lee's intentions and full of self-confidence, ordered a vigorous pursuit of the enemy. The advancing Yanks found Jackson's three divisions, battered but unbowed, still holding the line of the unfinished railroad. Assailed by soldiers of Irwin McDowell's and Fitz John Porter's corps, Jackson called for help. After checking the Union surge with artillery whose enfilading fire shredded their ranks, General Lee unleashed Longstreet's five divisions (R. H. Anderson's having arrived during the night after a hard march up from the Rappahannock). Jackson's corps had been the anvil and now Longstreet would be the hammer. And what a sledgehammer! Surging forward, spearheaded by Hood's division, Longstreet's Confederates, in savage fighting, successively drove Union forces from three positions. The Yanks, however, with their blood and grit bought sufficient time for Pope to escape disaster. By dark, the Federals had retreated across Bull Run.

Sunday, the last day of August, brought torrential rain. Pope, on reaching the commanding ground at Centreville, was reinforced from Alexandria by the Army of the Potomac's Second and Sixth Corps. These more than made good his losses, and Pope's self-confidence returned. But the administration now had doubts about Pope.

General Lee, although injured by a fall on the 31st, was unready to yield the initiative now that he had the bulge on Pope. Despite roads turned to ribbons of mud by the downpour, Lee sent Jackson's corps and Stuart's cavalry north up the Sudley Road, across Bull Run, and onto the Little River Turnpike. By daybreak on September 1, Jackson was positioned to outflank Pope's Centreville line and astride the Little River Turnpike that pointed like a dagger at Fairfax Court House well to the Yanks' rear.

Pope, with Washington's blessing, abandoned his Centreville position and continued the retrograde. About 4 p.m., units of the Third and Ninth Corps covering the Union columns retreating via the Warrenton Turnpike clashed with Jackson's corps at Chantilly (Ox Hill). The fight was bitter, waged at short range, and interrupted by a violent thunderstorm. Jackson was checked, the North lost two generals—Isaac I. Stevens and Philip F. Kearny—who had shown great promise, and darkness found Pope's battered and disillusioned army streaming back toward the Washington defenses.

General McClellan had remained in Washington when the Second and Sixth Corps rushed out to Centreville, a general without an army. On September 2, Pope ordered his beaten but not routed Army of Virginia to pull back into the Washington defenses. In the week beginning August 27, the Federals had lost 1,724 killed, 8,372 wounded, and 5,958 missing for a total of 16,054 casualties, more by 1,000 than McClellan had lost in the Seven Days' battles. He had also lost the confidence of the Lincoln administration, while many of the soldiers had lost confidence in themselves.

Confronted by the crisis in leadership, President Lincoln, despite guarded reservations and over the objections of Secretary of War Edwin M. Stanton and Secretary of the Treasury Salmon P. Chase, ordered General McClellan to take command of the retreating columns. Accompanied by his staff and escort, McClellan rode out into the Virginia countryside. "Little Mac," as he was called by the troops, was admired and respected by the veterans in blue. Word that he had been restored to command and was with them spread like wildfire and buoyed up sagging morale. General Pope was left without a command, and on September 6, he was ordered to proceed to St. Paul, Minnesota, to assume command of the

Department of the Northwest, where an uprising by the Sioux that had erupted along the Minnesota River on August 17 had caused grave concern.

In the days immediately following the arrival of the defeated armies back in the Washington area, the Army of Virginia, in existence only nine weeks, was consolidated with the Army of the Potomac. The First, Second, and Third Corps of the Army of Virginia were redesignated, respectively, the Eleventh, Twelfth, and First Corps of the Army of the Potomac. McClellan, between September 2 and 7, was at his best. Tired, footsore, and exhausted soldiers were fed, rested, and resupplied. McClellan was omnipresent. A superb horseman, he looked and acted like a leader. Morale soared, and the rank and file again believed in themselves.

General Lee, although he had drubbed the Yanks, recognized that it would be suicidal to attack them once they had retreated within the fortifications that in the 13 months since First Manassas had been thrown up covering the approaches to Washington. On checking with his generals, Lee totaled his casualties in the Second Manassas Campaign and found that the Army of Northern Virginia listed 1,481 killed, 7,627 wounded, and 89 missing for a total of 9,197. His troops had captured 30 Union cannon and 7,000 prisoners. The arrival of D. H. Hill's and Lafayette McLaws' divisions from Petersburg and Richmond on September 2, to be followed on the 6th by Brig. Gen. John G. Walker's division from Richmond, enabled Lee to more than make good battle losses suffered during the previous week.

Lee could not rest on his laurels. He would not assail the Federals in their prepared Washington defenses, but he must retain the initiative so boldly wrested from the foe. He knew that the tide had also turned against the North in the Heartland of the Confederacy, as well as in the trans-Mississippi. His victories, as well as successes gained by Confederate generals west of the Appalachians, were having important repercussions in Europe, particularly in Great Britain. In London, Lord Palmerston's government was seriously considering a diplomatic initiative. Her Majesty's government would offer to mediate between North and South, and if the Lincoln administration refused, consideration would be given to extending recognition to the Confederacy.

Lee also knew that the farms and plantations of the Virginia counties adjacent to Washington, having felt the hard hand of war, could not long support his army, while across the Potomac the fertile farms of Maryland and Pennsylvania beckoned. There were Marylanders in the Army of Northern Virginia, and these people reminded Lee that "a despot's heel was on thy shore," and his troops, if they crossed the Potomac, would be welcomed as liberators.

General Lee, who in three months had shown himself to be a daring and innovative strategist, made his decision—Cross the Potomac he must. From the Chantilly area, where he had concentrated his army on September 2, Lee started his long gray, grim but tattered columns toward Leesburg the next day, marching by way of Dranesville. Beginning on the 4th, when the first cavalry splashed and D. H. Hill's infantry waded across the Potomac at White's Ford, through the 7th, when the rear guard crossed, the Army of Northern Virginia left the Virginia shore and entered Maryland. Lee, plagued by his August 31 fall, in which he had injured his hands and had placed them in splints, crossed in an ambulance. By September 6, the Confederates occupied Frederick, and Stuart's horse soldiers fanned out and established and manned roadblocks at Poolesville and other points on roads leading southeast from the line of the Monocacy toward Washington. Signal corps personnel atop Sugarloaf Mountain likewise kept a sharp lookout for approaching Union columns.

By Sunday, September 7, McClellan had accomplished the impossible—a badly defeated army had been reorganized and readied for the field. Knowing little of the enemy's whereabouts or plans, McClellan put the army into motion as it marched out in search of the foe. Besides looking for the Confederates, McClellan also had the mission of protecting the Nation's capital and covering Baltimore. The army, on taking the field, was organized into three wings—the right, center, and left. General Burnside with the First and Ninth Corps, the former led by Maj. Gen. Joseph Hooker and the latter by Maj. Gen. Jesse Reno, marched on the right by way of Leesborough and Brookville, en route to the National Road. Maj. Gen. Edwin V. Sumner with the Second Corps and Brig. Gen. Alpheus S. Williams' Twelfth Corps, in the center, took the Rockville Turnpike, and Maj. Gen. William Franklin, with the Sixth Corps and Maj. Gen. Darius Couch's Fourth Corps division, traveled the River Road on the army's left. Cavalrymen from Brig. Gen. Alfred Plesanton's command were out in front—their task to find and drive in Stuart's horsemen. McClellan accompanied Sumner's wing. General Banks remained behind, charged with the defense of Washington.

Nightfall on Tuesday, September 9, found McClellan's army camped:

> Burnside's wing at Brookville, Sumner's wing on the Rockville Turnpike, at Middlebrook; Franklin's Sixth Corps at Darnestown and Couch's division at the mouth of Seneca Creek; and the field army's reserve—Brig. Gen. George Sykes' division...at Rockville.

Lee's crossing of the Potomac caused consternation in the North. The occupation of Frederick cut off strong Union garrisons at Harpers Ferry and Martinsburg, in the lower Shenandoah Valley, from direct communication with Washington. There was "tremendous excitement" and evidence of panic in Harrisburg, Hagerstown, and Baltimore. Streets were crowded with anxious people, militia turned out, and the less stalwart prepared to flee. On the 8th, to reassure Marylanders, General Lee announced:

> The people of the Confederate States have long watched with deepest sympathy the wrongs and outrages that have been inflicted upon the citizens.... We know no enemies among you, and will protect all, of every opinion. It is for you to decide your destiny, free and without constraint. This army will respect your choice, whatever it may be.

Not only in Virginia but everywhere else the Union tide that had surged irresistibly in the fourth week of June had turned. Not since 1812 and Napoleon's retreat from Moscow had there been such a dramatic change in the fortunes of war. To many people, both in the Union and in western Europe, it appeared that the Confederacy was about to become a new nation to be honored and recognized by the world community.

General McClellan's defeat and loss of face in the Seven Days' battles and the mid-June repulse at Secessionville on South Carolina's James Island had caused Mr. Lincoln's War Department to reevaluate its commitment of manpower on the South Carolina Sea Islands and on the North Carolina sounds. The redeployment of General Burnside and his Ninth Corps from the sounds to Virginia's tidewater resulted in the small force left behind to hold key enclaves adopting a defensive stance and relying on the navy to keep them supplied. Maj. Gen. David Hunter, at Port Royal, to send troops to Virginia, abandoned his James Island campaign aimed at Charleston to concentrate on the defense of Port Royal. To partially make good his loss in manpower, he organized a regiment of African Americans.

In western Virginia's Kanawha Valley, Maj. Gen. William W. Loring's Confederate troops took advantage of the redeployment of Brig. Gen. Jacob D. Cox's Kanawha Division to reinforce Pope's Army of Virginia to take the offensive. Loring advanced from Giles Court House and, on September 13, the day that a soldier in the 27th Indiana—near Frederick—found the "Lost Order," occupied Charleston.

Out in the South's Heartland, General Bragg and Maj. Gen. Edmund Kirby Smith, through hard and fast marches, one battle, and numerous skirmishes, had scored successes that rivaled Lee's in Virginia. Kirby Smith, in the four weeks since leaving Knoxville on August 16, had bypassed and isolated a large Union division holed up in Cumberland Gap; routed an army at Richmond, Kentucky, on August 30; entered the Bluegrass region; captured Lexington and Frankfort; and by September 10 was within seven miles of the Ohio River and Cincinnati. Bragg's columns departed Chattanooga on August 21, and had outmarched and outfoxed Buell and his Army of the Ohio.

On Sunday, September 14, McClellan's and Lee's armies fought bitter battles for the possession of the South Mountain Gaps, and "Stonewall" Jackson's columns, having converged on Col. Dixon Miles and his 12,000 defenders of Harpers Ferry, opened fire from three directions from cannon emplaced on Maryland and Loudoun Heights and Schoolhouse Ridge. That same day, deep in Kentucky, Bragg's vanguard attacked the Union garrison holding the Green River bridges at Munfordville. Bragg's troops were repulsed, but his army was nearby and Buell's columns, mistakenly believing Nashville to be Bragg's goal rather than Louisville, had been outdistanced by the Confederates. On the 14th, Buell's army was at Bowling Green, 40 miles southwest of Munfordville. On September 17, the day that the two major eastern armies battled at Antietam, the Munfordville garrison, more than 4,000 strong, surrendered to Bragg and it seemed that the Confederates must win the race for Louisville.

At Vicksburg, on America's greatest river, Union forces had also been rebuffed. On July 1, Uncle Sam's deepwater fleet and river gunboats controlled the Mississippi from its source to its mouth—except for the three-mile reach at Vicksburg. The Vicksburg Confederates stood tall during the last days of June and the first three weeks of July, and on July 24 Union naval power recoiled. Farragut's ocean-going ships dropped down to Baton Rouge and New Orleans and the river ironclads and rams chuffed upstream to Memphis.

The Confederate August 5 attack on Baton Rouge misfired. Undaunted, the Rebels occupied and fortified Port Hudson, giving them command of the 240 miles of the Mississippi between Vicksburg and Port Hudson, along with the mouth of Red River. Maj. Gen. Earl Van Dorn next concentrated most of the troops who had battled the Yanks at Baton Rouge, the Vicksburg defenders, and thousands of recently exchanged prisoners at Holly Springs in northern Mississippi, ready to take the offensive against Maj. Gen. Ulysses S. Grant's Army of the Tennessee. Already, on September 13, Maj. Gen. Sterling Price and his Army of the West had advanced from Guntown and had seized Iuka, on the Memphis & Charleston Railroad, 25 miles east of Corinth. Price, by this bold movement, had positioned his army to either cross the nearby Tennessee River and march on Nashville, as urged by Bragg, or cooperate with Van Dorn in a converging attack on Corinth.

In the three months since the fiery bantam Maj. Gen. Thomas C. Hindman had taken charge in Arkansas there had been a 180 degree change in fortunes.

By vigorous enforcement of conscription and impressment laws, he had fielded a new army. The Union force that had once threatened Little Rock had turned aside and was now confined to the Helena enclave. The Union column that had thrust deep into the Cherokee Nation was back in Kansas, its commander under arrest. Hindman's field army crossed the Boston Mountains and, in cooperation with the Indian Territory Confederates, was bracing for a return to southwest Missouri and then "On to Fort Scott."

At sea, *Alabama*, a vessel destined to become the war's most famous commerce raider, had been commissioned in the Azores on August 24, and on September 18, one day after Antietam, she captured and burned her first prize.

On the political front, there were also major concerns for the Lincoln administration. Beginning with Maine in September, the voters would be going to the polls. The war having turned sour, there were fears that in many states the voters would take out their frustration on Republican stalwarts, on both the national and state levels.

John Michael Priest, in his *Antietam: The Soldiers' Battle*, captured and fired the enthusiasm of the reader with his moving story of the combat experiences of junior officers and the rank and file and their thoughts on that terrible day in September 1862, when the sun seemed to stand still. He did this, insofar as possible, by allowing the soldiers in blue and gray, all long dead, to tell their stories through letters, diaries, newspaper articles, etc. Priest has a talent for winnowing the grain from the chaff and weaving it together to enable his readers to better know and appreciate the hell through which these soldiers passed. He sees the Civil War soldiers much as Ernie Pyle saw the GIs of World War II. Too bad that John Michael Priest did not personally know any of these people and their experiences that he describes so vividly.

John Michael Priest looks back in *Before Antietam: The Battle for South Mountain*. His focus is again on the soldiers of the Army of the Potomac and the Army of Northern Virginia in the hectic days immediately before Antietam. Those were heady days for General Lee and his lean and hungry veterans who had crossed the Potomac and carried the war into Maryland. To counter the invasion and turn back this threat to the Nation's capital, Union columns, again led by General McClellan, took the field. A crisis in the war was at hand. Not only in Maryland but everywhere along the 1,000-mile frontier from the Chesapeake to the Indian Territory, the forces of the Confederacy were in ascendance.

Mr. Priest employs the research and writing skills that, honed in *The Soldiers' Battle*, earned the plaudits of reviewers to detail the troops' marches, bivouacs, and skirmishes during the critical days following Lee's September 4-7 crossing of the Potomac and culminating in the Sunday, September 14, fight for the South Mountain Gaps. This story is moving and dramatic, and sets the stage for Antietam, the South's true "High Water Mark." So it is "On to South Mountain."

EDWIN C. BEARSS

List of Maps

MAP LEGENDS

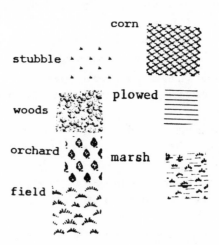

List of Photographs and Illustrations

Most of South Mountain Battlefield is privately owned, such as the Gaber Farm, and the O'Neil and the Haupt Farms. When touring the area, please, stay on the public roads. There are not many photographs of the three mountain passes because the fields have become much more wooded or overgrown than in 1862.

Table of Contents

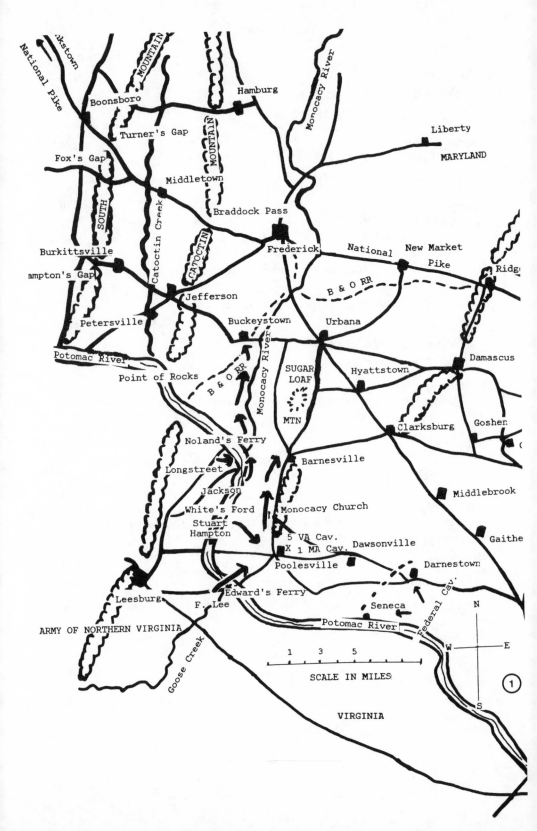

MAP 1: Situation—September 5, 1862.

Chapter One

SEPTEMBER 5, 1862

THE BUGLER IN the 9th Virginia Cavalry sounded "to horse" at 3:00 A.M. Lieutenant Colonel Richard L. T. Beale joined his regiment in the road which led to Leesburg and waited—and waited. Closely packed columns of infantry clogged the road and forced the cavalry to halt within a mile of the town to await further instructions. Without them, the 5th Virginia Cavalry, at the head of the brigade column, could not move and the orders did not appear to be forthcoming. By the time Brigadier General Fitzhugh Lee's brigade (the 5th, 4th, 3rd, and 9th Virginia Cavalry) did advance, Beale's troopers had eaten their breakfasts of roasted corn and fresh apples.[1]

The soldiers had to wait for Major General Jeb Stuart, who commanded the Army of Northern Virginia's cavalry division, while he, with characteristic disregard for the time, rode into town to meet with General Robert E. Lee.[2] Lee started the war council with his two corps commanders, Major Generals James Longstreet and Thomas J. Jackson, without waiting for Stuart. Officially, the Confederate government desired to "relieve the people of Maryland from the tyranny from which they were enchained."[3] The general's intelligence sources had optimistically informed him that 20,000-25,000 Marylanders would join his army. The state, with its untouched ripening fields, would also provision his starving soldiers, who, by general order, had to pay for all their forage and sustenance. (The threat of court-martial and hanging, during the early stages of the campaign, coerced a large number of his troops to comply.) The Army of Northern Virginia had to prove to the Marylanders that it was upon their soil to liberate and not to pillage.[4]

Jeb Stuart took along several of his staff officers, one of whom was the

1

gigantic Prussian, Major Heros Von Borcke. The entourage found the three
generals in the home of one of Leesburg's most prominent citizens, whose
name Von Borcke did not record. While Stuart busied himself in the council,
Von Borcke and the other officers ambled across the street to the home of
a crippled elderly gentleman, whose name Von Borcke also forgot. The old
man was confined to a huge cane chair. He heartily invited the Confederates
to enjoy an early dinner. Never ones to refuse an opportunity to indulge
themselves, they eagerly accepted—a scene they would repeat several times
before the ensuing campaign ended.[5] Like their idol and mentor, Stuart, they
tended to satisfy their personal needs before those of their men and the lower
ranking officers.

Leesburg had become an open town to the Confederates, whose citizens
knew the Army of Northern Virginia was fighting a war for survival. The
townspeople, despite the deprivation forced upon them by the constant warfare which swirled through Loudoun County, opened their doors, their arms,
and their kitchens to the ragged Confederate soldiers.[6] Private John S. Shipp
(Company G, 6th Virginia) summed up the devastation quite succinctly in his
diary when he scribbled, "We are now close to Leesburg...pass through quite
a pretty country but nearly depopulated."[7]

Leesburg was an oasis in the middle of a wasteland. The soldiers, who
had learned from experience how to panhandle, took advantage of every situation. With many of them unshod, and subsisting on green corn and apples,
the promise of any change in diet was too tempting to ignore.[8] Second Lieutenant William A. Johnson (Company D, 2nd South Carolina) and a comrade
insisted that they could not rudely refuse any meal offered to them. While
in Leesburg, the people wined and dined them like their own sons.

One morning, the two famished soldiers breakfasted at five houses on
the same street. Starvation had taught them that gluttony was its own reward.
Being "gentlemen" by rank, and possibly upbringing, they flirted with every
woman and girl they encountered, and left the town with memories more
pleasant than that of any previous campaign.[9]

Jackson's Corps and part of Longstreet's had risen before dawn and marched, very slowly, toward White's Ford, which was about five miles northeast
of Leesburg. They traveled in parallel columns, with Longstreet's being slightly
north of Jackson's.[10]

Colonel Bradley T. Johnson's brigade (the 21st, 42nd, and 48th Virginia,
and 1st Virginia Battalion) reached the ford sometime between 9:00 A.M. and
10:00 A.M.[11] The day long crossing evolved into a martial festival. Without
exception, the regimental bands hailed each regiment with patriotic airs, in
particular, James Ryder Randall's "Maryland! My Maryland!"[12]

Private John Worsham (Company F, 21st Virginia) paid little attention to
the cold water as he slipped down the steep bank of the ford into the Potomac
River and waded toward the half mile long sandy island which divided the
river, midstream, into two branches. The prospect of freeing Maryland's fertile soil from Yankee domination helped allay his discomfort.[13]

Bradley T. Johnson, a Marylander, rightfully led Jackson's Corps into his homeland. He and many of his men sincerely believed their presence would lure thousands of secret secessionists into the Army of Northern Virginia.[14]

Sergeant Samuel D. Buck (Company H, 13th Virginia) could not explain the festive atmosphere which accompanied the march out of Virginia. The rank and file laughed as if they were going to a ball. The picnic like atmosphere started to wane when the regiment, which led the brigade, halted on the Virginia side of the river and started to strip down for the fording.[15]

Brigadier General Alexander R. Lawton chose Brigadier General Jubal Early's brigade (the 13th, 25th, 31st, 44th, 49th, 52nd, and 58th Virginia) to lead his infantry division across the state line as a goodwill gesture to the Marylanders, whom he believed they were liberating.[16] Early's younger brother, Samuel, an ambitious captain upon his staff, shared Lawton's optimism. In his zeal to see the brigade across the Potomac with all due haste, he led the regiment's officers in a charge against their own men. They herded the partially naked soldiers into the water like cattle.

The moment young Sam Buck headed toward the water's edge, his father, who watched over him like a nanny, rode up and pulled him onto the back of his horse. While he crossed dry shod onto the opposite shore, he listened to his comrades ruthlessly cursing Captain Early for not giving them time to remove their shoes. Many of them knew they would drop along the roadside with raw and blistered feet.[17] As he neared the Maryland side of the river, he heard a number of the men join in with one of the bands on the bank in another chorus of "Maryland! My Maryland!" Those soldiers, like himself, had shrugged off Captain Sam Early's stupidity for what it was, an inflexible sense of duty.[18]

Private William A. McClendon (Company G, 15th Alabama), in Colonel James A. Walker's brigade, marched immediately behind Early's regiments, and he clearly saw the Virginians fording ahead of them. Colonel Walker allowed the Alabamians and the Georgians in his command to halt and disrobe. They peeled off their shoes, socks, trousers, and drawers, the latter of which had become a much cherished luxury item in the army.[19] The veterans quietly rolled their cartridge and cap boxes in their clothes and cheerfully slipped into the river with their pants and shoes held above their heads. McClendon, who had envisioned the Potomac as some kind of impassable torrent, felt quite relieved by the seemingly placid water. The Alabamians carefully wove a path across the waist deep, slippery bottomed river. Not a single man lost his footing and went under, and the regiment calmly redressed on the Maryland shore. It gave the Rebel yell, and leisurely strolled up river toward the Monocacy River.

"Nobody seemed to be in a hurry," McClendon noted with some understatement.[20]

Jeb Stuart, who was quite busy trying to ascertain what to do with his cavalry brigades, did not overexert himself either. He failed to provide the infantry with an adequate cavalry screen. While he occupied himself about Army Headquarters, Jackson's Corps approached White's Ford under the protection of Company H of the 4th Virginia Cavalry. Captain Robert L. Randolph and First Lieutenant Alexander D. Payne guided their small command away from the rest of Fitzhugh Lee's brigade during the early hours of the day. The cavalrymen, a number of whom were shoeless, splashed across the Potomac ahead of the struggling foot soldiers to thinly reconnoiter their flanks.[21]

The plodding infantrymen turned north along the Chesapeake and Ohio Canal, which they followed for four miles to where the Monocacy passed under it and emptied into the Potomac. Cutting east, across a bridge over the canal, they marched on to the pike which led to Frederick.[22]

Simultaneously, Brigadier General John B. Hood's division was fording just north of Jackson's old division. The men, having worked up a sweat during the dawn march from Leesburg, found the river bottom slippery and the water downright chilly.[23] The artillerists, to keep their caissons and limbers from floundering in the badly rutted river, dismounted from their seats on the ammunition chests and waded alongside their guns. The incessant churning of the men, horses, and wagons through the water raised the river's depth above its normal two and one half feet.[24] Near the island in the middle of the ford, the water rose over the horses' bellies.[25]

Not every Southerner felt overjoyed with the liberation of Maryland. Private James Steptoe Johnston, Jr., (Company I, 11th Mississippi), Colonel McIver Law's orderly, immediately noticed the absence of enthusiastic Marylanders on the other shore. He complained in a letter to his fiancée, "I cordially confess that no one could be more desirous of getting out of this State than I...for from the very moment we put our feet on Maryland soil, our blood was chilled. Instead of an outburst of overflowing joy, at the sight of their deliverers, not one solitary soul had come to the River bank to see us cross or welcome us to the soil." The Confederates had stumbled into the Garden of Eden after the Fall.[26]

Colonel William D. DeSaussure (15th South Carolina) refused to participate in the invasion. He vehemently asserted that he had enrolled in the Army of Northern Virginia to defend the South within its own borders and he would not wage a war of aggression against the North. At that point, Lieutenant Colonel George W. James (3rd South Carolina Battalion), whose regiment was attached to DeSaussure's, sprang forward and denounced him as a coward. As James led the combined regiments into the river, DeSaussure reluctantly took his place at the head of the column.[27]

General orders issued at Leesburg barred the majority of sick, wounded, and barefoot men from entering the Promised Land and diverted them northwest, with the wagons, toward Winchester.[28] The directive greatly reduced the Army's combat strength. The hundreds of shoeless infantrymen who swarmed about the stalled cavalrymen south of the town alarmed Second Lieutenant Robert T. Hubard (Company G, 3rd Virginia Cavalry). He had never seen so many stragglers before. Without exception, each of them had a disability or a hospital ticket. The lieutenant, who was not on provost duty, helplessly watched squads of soldiers rip off their shoes and throw them away.[29]

Having seen Brigadier General James Kemper's brigade dwindle by what he described as "hundreds of muskets," Private Alexander Hunter (Company A, 17th Virginia) bitterly griped, "This idiotic proclamation cost us ten thousand men.... From first one cause and then another, the regiments, brigades and divisions had dwindled into one-half of the strength which they carried to Manassas."[30]

The war had exhausted Corporal James B. Painter (Company K, 28th Virginia). When rumors circulated throughout the camps that there would be no quarter given in the next engagement, he grumbled that he did not care to fight under either the "Black Flag" (no quarter) or the "Red Flag" (the Confederate battle flag). Being barefoot, he stayed with the supply wagons and did not ford the Potomac.[31]

Discontent among the ranks affected the officers also. On September 4, orders went out to arrest any officer who was absent without leave or who straggled. Consequently, a number of competent officers were sent to the rear of their commands. On September 5, Captain James C. Marshall (Adjutant, 14th North Carolina), having overstayed a twenty-four hour leave to visit relatives in a neighboring regiment, reported to his colonel, who had received a copy of the "straggling" order from Lee's Headquarters. The captain saluted as he calmly approached his friend, Colonel Risden T. Bennett.

"I am twenty-four hours late," he said.

"Yes," Bennett replied, "General Lee has anticipated you."

The response took Marshall by surprise. He apparently had no knowledge of the arrest order.

"What do you mean?" he blurted.

"Read that order lying on the table."

The captain scanned the document and smirked. Knowing the regiment had drawn picket duty, a chore he detested, he tossed the order back on the table and smugly informed his colonel, "Being under arrest, I will remain in camp."

"No," Bennett said, returning the grin, "I shall take you along. Your position will be at the tail end of the regiment, and you, being under arrest, will be an ornament to its tail."

The object of a thinly concealed barb, James C. Marshall reluctantly entered Maryland as the victim of his own jest.[32]

Similarly, Lieutenant William N. Wood (Company A, 19th Virginia) had fallen awry of his commanding officer, Colonel John B. Strange. During the night march to Leesburg, Wood, because of reduced numbers in the ranks, commanded Companies A and I. The companies plodded along very slowly in the pitch darkness, unable to see where they were going and unable to keep track of each other. As the regiment prepared to go into camp near Leesburg, Colonel Strange ordered the lieutenant to report immediately to his tent.

The colonel curtly confronted the young officer as he stepped up to his quarters.

"Lieutenant, did you not hear the orders about straggling?"

"I did, sir," Wood responded.

"One of your men," the colonel said, "has just been discovered ahead of his company. Consider yourself under arrest."

"All right, sir," the lieutenant replied in disgust. (He could not help it that one man had outdistanced everyone else which made the entire command appear like malingerers.) Returning to his men, Wood believed the matter closed.

The next morning (September 5) the regimental adjutant awakened him before reveille. When the colonel once again requested Wood's presence, the young officer impertinently growled, "Present my compliments to the Colonel and inform him that I question his right to put me under arrest for the offense mentioned, and therefore, decline to resume my duties, and demand a court of inquiry."

When the 19th Virginia waded into the Potomac, William N. Wood triumphantly shuffled behind his men, under arrest and gave a whoop as he stepped into Maryland.[33]

Nobody seemed safe from arrest. By the time the Army of Northern Virginia had arrived at Leesburg, Brigadier General John B. Hood had run afoul of a superior officer, whom he did not regard as such. During the Battle of the Second Manassas (August 28-30, 1862), the Texas Scouts in Hood's old brigade captured several new and fully equipped Federal ambulances, which he accordingly distributed among the regiments under his command. On August 31, as the march began toward Maryland, Brigadier General Nathan Evans, who had temporary command of Hood's division, ordered Hood to reassign the ambulances to his own South Carolina brigade. Hood refused to comply on the grounds that the booty rightfully belonged either to his division or to the entire Army.

Evans placed Hood under arrest and immediately referred the matter to Major General James Longstreet, a Regular Army comrade from prewar days. Longstreet, who was suffering from a severely chafed heel and who had to stomp about with one foot carpet slippered, was in an evil mood when he received Evans' complaint.[34] He, in turn, told John Hood to report to Culpeper, Virginia to await the formal reading of the charges before him.

When Robert E. Lee heard of the incident, he tried to mediate what could have devolved into a militarily dangerous situation. There were enough rumors floating around about disabled or wounded staff officers that he did not have to add to them. Longstreet was allegedly "wounded" and, Lee had both of his hands in splints, as the result of an accident on September 1. The soldiers subsequently believed that Lee had been shot in battle.[35] He could not afford to lose another general officer, particularly one of Hood's calibre. The Texas Brigade was fiercely loyal to General Hood and would possibly mutiny if "their" general was court-martialed. Lee countermanded Longstreet's directive by removing Hood from command and placing him at the rear of his division, while allowing Evans to distribute the Yankee ambulances as he desired.[36]

Petty jealousies and misunderstandings plagued the Army of Northern Virginia. On September 4, Major General Thomas J. Jackson placed Major General Ambrose P. Hill, a former West Point classmate, and the commander of his Light Division, under arrest for allowing the rear of his column to straggle en route to Leesburg. The two men never resolved their differences and nurtured strong dislikes for each other until their deaths.[37]

Jeb Stuart's cavalry division did not move out until 2:00 P.M. Diverting in two directions, two of the three brigades bypassed Leesburg on alternate routes. Stuart did not deploy his cavalry in a wide arc to the east and to the northeast, to protect the flanks of Jackson's and Longstreet's lurching infantry columns. Instead, he inserted Brigadier General Wade Hampton's cavalry brigade (1st North Carolina Cavalry, 1st South Carolina Cavalry, Cobb's Legion, and Hampton's Legion) into their line of march. Stuart and his officers, along with most of the division's artillery, struggled through the Potomac at White's Ford with Hampton's command. Fitzhugh Lee's four regiments, unhindered by the swearing infantrymen, rode off toward Edwards' Ferry, about seven miles south of White's Ford.[38]

Colonel Thomas Munford (2nd Virginia Cavalry), who had just been promoted to brigade command that morning, was in charge of the rear guard.[39] His personal dislike for Stuart bordered on hatred and he did not conceal his opinion of the dashing cavalier. The colonel described Stuart as a self-centered, self-indulging fop, who jealously guarded his command and who did not want to share any of the plaudits concerning it with anyone else.[40] Thomas Munford considered it no accident that his brigade, which had driven Cole's Maryland Cavalry from Leesburg the day before, had received the dubious honor of protecting the rear of Lee's Army from the Army of the Potomac's advance units. His command (2nd, 7th, and 12th Virginia Cavalry), numbering under three hundred troopers, found themselves in a potentially self-destructive situation.[41]

At White's Ford, the cavalry and its artillery lost two hours in the crossing. The delay gave Major Heros Von Borcke and some of his fellow officers time to relax on the island in the middle of the river, and observe the invasion. The big Prussian, ever the Confederate propagandist and gallant gentleman, sat astride his mount enthralled by the procession as it splashed by him.

"It was indeed a magnificent sight," he wrote, "as the long column of many thousand horsemen [an overly generous estimate] stretched across this beautiful Potomac. The evening sun slanted upon its clear placid waters and burnished them with gold, while the arms of the soldiers glittered and blazed in its radiance."[42]

The Union cavalry across the river did not know exactly where the Confederates were nor did they particularly care.[43] They had not had a good summer and the fall did not look much better. Private William B. Baker (Company D, 1st Maine Cavalry) dejectedly wrote home, "....We have been whipped and driven to the Potomac twice and now if Jackson [Thomas J. Jackson, C.S.A.] does not attack us I fear the Southern Confederacy is established.... I know not what Jackson had in his noodle but it is all over for the present and we poor insignificant bodies can look back only with regret. Our men are sick and tired of such doings and don't care a farthing how the thing is settled."[44]

Brigadier General Alfred Pleasonton, the Federal cavalry division commander, having the 1st Massachusetts, 8th Illinois, and 3rd Indiana Cavalry at his disposal, ordered them across the Potomac in an arc that fanned west and south from Darnestown, Maryland.[45] The three regiments left Darnestown around 11:00 A.M. to patrol very cautiously from Seneca Creek (four miles to the southwest) to Poolesville (eight miles to the northwest).[46]

Their instructions were to locate and report on the Confederate activities along the Potomac and not to engage the troops. Rumors reached the 3rd Indiana that the Rebels were crossing at Noland's Ferry (about sixteen miles beyond Darnestown) and Colonel [Scott] Carter sent Companies E and F to investigate the report.[47] Late in the afternoon, the squadron (two companies) pressed just beyond Poolesville, opposite Edwards' Ferry, and ran into the 4th Virginia Cavalry, which was screening the advance of Fitzhugh Lee's brigade. The small Confederate regiment charged and scattered the Federals without inflicting any casualties.[48]

Private Samuel J. Gilpin (Company E, 3rd Indiana Cavalry) discreetly noted in his diary, "We were forced to fall back...and did so," apparently, without firing a shot.

Having not fed themselves or their mounts in twenty-four hours, the Westerners did not feel up to a firefight. They retreated back through Poolesville and arrived in Darnestown around 9:00 P.M.[49] They did not have an opportunity to share their intelligence with any other patrols in the vicinity.

Around 4:00 P.M., Captain Samuel E. Chamberlain (Company B) and his motley squadron of the 1st Massachusetts Cavalry, having spent the entire morning on a scout along the Potomac from Seneca Creek to just below Edwards' Ferry, wearily rode into Poolesville.[50] The New Englanders, exhausted from a seventeen day grueling boat ride from South Carolina and a forced march from Washington, D.C., resembled rabble in their threadbare and tattered uniforms. Their service in the Deep South had forced them to adopt lighter clothing and they had not had enough time to acclimate to the colder Maryland evenings, which this fall were unusually bitter. Because their baggage was still on the transports in the Potomac, many of the New Englanders remained on active duty without stockings or boots. They had no shelter halves, either.[51]

Their played out horses did not look much better.[52] Seasick and dehydrated from the long voyage below decks, they wobbled unsteadily, and painfully on Maryland's stone paved pikes. Like their riders, they had not been given enough time to adjust to the inhospitable climate or to the rough terrain. A few of the mounts were shod on their forefeet; most had no shoes at all, because the Army discovered that horses did not need to be shod to walk on South Carolina's sandy soil. By September 5, three days after their arrival in Washington, Maryland's crushed limestone roads had disabled a large proportion of the regiments' mounts.[53]

As the squadron, which contained members from Companies A through H, passed through the village, the civilians coldly stared at them. When the regiment exited to the western side of Poolesville, the people darted into the street behind them and constructed makeshift barricades of stones and debris to block the Yankees' line of retreat should a fight break out.[54] The one hundred Federal troopers, who were armed for the most part with Colt pistols and breech loading Smith carbines, soon discovered that the Smith's India-rubber cartridges seldom fired.[55] They were in no shape to take on the 5th Virginia Cavalry, which, while fording the Potomac, saw them and then attacked them. A running skirmish involving swords, carbines and pistols stampeded the Yankees back into the village.[56] The bewildered Northerners, unable to see through the swirling dust, clattered into the obstacles which unhorsed almost fifty percent of them. Within a few minutes, the Confederates dispersed fifty-two of the Yankees and captured forty-eight, nine of whom were wounded. While they hastily disarmed their prisoners, including the mortified Captain Chamberlain, the Virginians tallied their losses—three killed and four wounded. Much to their disgust they discovered that many of the Yankee mounts were unshod.[57] [Refer to Map 1]

The 5th Virginia Cavalry continued northeast for another six miles, where it joined the 4th Virginia Cavalry in bivouac for the night. The routed troopers of the 1st Massachusetts Cavalry, in the meantime, kept running east, under the impression that they had lost fifty men to a numerically superior force.[58]

Private Otis D. Smith (Company F, 6th Alabama), who was near the tail end of Major General Daniel H. Hill's division, halted with his regiment on a bluff overlooking the Potomac. It was almost sundown, and the private, who had quit school teaching the previous year because of dyspepsia, used the time to observe the natural beauty which abounded across the river from him. The distant hills appeared golden brown and autumn had begun to tinge the trees. Rich looking farm houses and richer looking fields spread across the landscape to the horizon in a mouth watering tapestry.

Colonel John B. Gordon's (6th Alabama) sonorous and erroneous bombastic oration distracted Otis Smith for a few minutes. As they stood on the high river bank, across from the Maryland shore, Gordon insisted, according to the private, "We were especially honored in being the first troops to cross the Potomac. Our names would go resounding down the corridors of time, our deeds be perpetuated in song and story. Our crossing the Potomac, rivaled only in the past by Washington and his heroes crossing the Delaware, could furnish subjects for the patient painter's canvas, inspiration to the sculptor's chisel. Future generations should rise up and call us blessed to the end of time..."

At the Biblical inference that he might be somehow kin to the Blessed Virgin Mary, Smith forgot the rest of Gordon's remarks. Resounding Rebel yells echoing off the river banks finally marked the end of the colonel's speech. The 6th Alabama fell in with the rest of Rodes' brigade and marched down to the river singing "Maryland! My Maryland!"

The encroaching darkness overshadowed the water and made it much colder than during the day, dampening the Alabamians' enthusiasm somewhat. The preceding troops had deepened the river bed to three to four feet by churning through it, and the current, which rolled swiftly through the newly created swells, tugged hard against the struggling infantrymen, who used all of their energy to hold their accoutrements above their heads. An occasional splash denoted another man going under. "Maryland! My Maryland!" literally washed away before they ever reached the state's shore.[59]

Not everyone attempted to sing his way across the Potomac in D. H. Hill's division. Colonel Bryan Grimes (4th North Carolina, George B. Anderson's brigade) dismounted and tried to walk around his horse to lead it down to the river when the animal kicked him with a well aimed hind leg. While not specifying exactly where the steed struck him, the colonel was too incapacitated to ride a horse or to walk. He jolted into Maryland in an ambulance.[60]

Meanwhile, the remainder of Fitzhugh Lee's cavalry brigade, followed by Wade Hampton's command, arrived in Poolesville shortly after dark, where they loitered for an hour to enjoy the people's hospitality.[61] The villagers gave the Confederates an overly enthusiastic reception. Several young men, two of whom operated general stores, immediately sprang to horse and joined the army. The two shopkeepers opened their businesses and offered their entire stock in exchange for Confederate scrip. The troopers bought them out—boots and shoes going first. The officers, in particular Major Von Borcke, burdened themselves with cigars, lemons, and pocketknives.[62]

Throughout the entire frenzy, the civilians plied the soldiers with questions regarding their troop strengths and destination.[63] Their legalized foraging completed, the two brigades moved out toward Barnesville. Fitzhugh Lee's two remaining regiments joined the 4th and the 5th Virginia Cavalry regiments in that village that evening and Stuart, with Hampton's cavalry, filed into the lush fields two miles southwest of them.[64]

Elsewhere, the Confederate forces were encountering confused reactions from the Marylanders. Many, like James S. Johnston of the 11th Mississippi, having seen no one upon crossing the river, and very few along the roadside following the invasion, complained bitterly about it.

He scrawled, "After moving some distance into the country and the report had gotten abroad that we were men like unto themselves (save the dirt) a few over bold individuals actually came to the road side [to] look at us, and finally some of them made bold to display a little secession proclivities, but every thing was done in such a distrustful and timid manner that we were soon convinced that 'secesh' in Maryland was as near an humbug as anything of the day."[65]

Hood's fractious Texans shared the same experience. Captain George T. Todd (Company A, 1st Texas), while being amazed by the tremendous quantities and the low prices of food stuffs in Maryland, bitterly resented the way most of the Marylanders treated him and his men. As the regiment passed through Buckeystown, which he mistakenly recollected as Greencastle, Pennsylvania, the women lined the streets to jeer at and insult his men. For the first time the Texans heard the insult, "dirty rebel." For the most part, the Texans controlled themselves, despite the fact that the women further taunted them by wearing small Union flags pinned across their chests. One lanky fellow, however, could not resist the urge to retaliate.

As Todd's company came abreast of the women, this particular individual called out, "This is Hood's Texas Brigade, and they are noted for storming and taking all Breast Works that carry those colors."

The women, some of them probably blushing, maintained their posts while the laughter of the entire 1st Texas rolled down the street into their faces.[66]

The Confederates had claimed their first moral victory while subtly knowing that they never had a chance of winning Western Maryland to their cause. In the days which followed they would remember that the cold waters of the Potomac were nothing compared to the icy reception they received in the state.[67]

The uncertainty of how they would be treated, drove many to break ranks and beg at farms along the roadside. Sergeant Edward Moore (Poague's Virginia Battery) and several members of his crew luckily stumbled onto a secessionist family who invited their unexpected guests to supper that evening. The family greatly reinforced their beliefs of a general uprising among the Marylanders.[68]

Usually the Marylanders accepted Confederate currency for eggs and butter, but nothing larger, if they had an option. They collected the Confederate scrip out of curiosity and in some cases fear of reprisal.[69]

Alabamian Otis D. Smith and his regiment stumbled along the Chesapeake & Ohio Canal in the dark for two miles until they came upon a small grocery store and a canal boat loaded with flour and bacon. Fences disappeared and fires sprang up everywhere as the regiment disintegrated and overran the boat.

While his comrades ransacked the barge, Smith went into the grocery store where he found the shopkeeper besieged by filthy soldiers. The man's eyes nearly burst from their sockets and stood out starkly against his livid face as the soldiers helped themselves to his stock and paid for it all in Confederate scrip. By the time Smith got to the front of the line, some fifteen minutes later, nothing of any consequence remained upon the shelves.

"Money, money everywhere and not a cent to spend," he thought to himself.

Elbowing himself through the mob, Smith passed up crackers, cheese, cans of candles, even tobacco. Instead, he yelled at the shopkeeper for salt. The harried and frightened civilian disappeared into his back room and reappeared within a minute with a half a bushel of salt.

The quantity left the starving Southerner nearly speechless. When he finally got his voice back, he gasped, in disbelief, "That for a quarter?"

"Oh," the Marylander retorted in a trembling but deprecating tone, "when you empty this, I will bring you another half bushel."

Smith feverishly filled his entire haversack with the condiment and tendered his filthy shinplaster paper quarter to the store owner, who accepted it with disdain. Undaunted, the Confederate stepped outside to pack his booty somewhat more compactly.

Unfolding his handkerchief, he carefully placed as much salt as it could accommodate in the center of it. He then, very meticulously, tied it off, being careful to leave enough of the corners protruding for him to use them for their natural purpose. Being the company cook, he had a moral obligation not to contaminate the salt, therefore, he never blew his nose in the middle of the handkerchief—only in the corners.[70]

Captain George T. Todd of the 1st Texas wryly recollected that his men preferred to purchase their goods rather than pilfer them, particularly when ordered not to steal. He tongue-in-cheek noted their camps were alive with quacking ducks and clucking chickens for about one week.[71]

With the exception of light skirmishing, the Northerners had no significant encounters with the Confederates that night. Private Samuel J. Gilpin (Company E, 3rd Indiana Cavalry) entered in his diary, "After some complaining to Colonel Carter for his treatment, we were in our saddles and off. Spent the night in skirmishing, chasing Reb cavalry and being chased in return. Advancing and retreating."[72]

There were no substantial Union troops north of the capital. General Pleasonton was still trying to expand and augment his very thin cavalry screen around Washington and Baltimore. It was not the right time to spark a general engagement.

The closest Union infantry was still in the District of Columbia and the surrounding area. The last campaigns of the Peninsula, Second Manassas, and Chantilly had left the Federal Armies ragged, dirty, disorganized, and disillusioned. The rank and file did not want to pursue the Army of Northern Virginia anywhere.

"....we looked veary bad being Lousey, Durty & Allmost naked & worn out," Captain James Wren (Company B, 48th Pennsylvania) lamented, "...I took my Boots of[f] this morni[n]g for the first time in 15 days & when I puled them of[f] it took the bark of[f] the frunt of my feet & they Blead & was very painfull for a little while."[73]

For many of the regiments, the story was the same. The surgeon of the 77th New York, George T. Stevens observed that packing up to move on the next campaign would be virtually effortless because the men had little more than themselves and their personal equipment to carry.[74] Private David Thompson (Company G, 9th New York) regretted parting with his bulky Sibley tent for the more cramped dog tent. He griped that wherever a person touched the side of the tent during a rain storm, the muslin duck cloth leaked.[75] Even with two people in a single tent, it became nearly impossible not to touch the sides somewhere.

In the 30th Ohio, which was camped nearby on Upton Hill, Private Edward E. Schweitzer (Company I) would have been glad to have slept under the cover of anything. He still had not forgotten the wet cold mud he had slept in en route to Washington.[76]

Things were just as bad in the I Corps. For instance, only one regiment in Colonel William A. Christian's brigade, the 26th New York, received blankets and tents upon arrival in Washington.[77] The Federal army was a shambles.

President Lincoln's Army was, again, undergoing a metamorphosis. In an attempt to preserve Washington from Confederate assault, following the most recent defeat at Manassas, the armies of the Union had retired to the protection of the forts which encircled the capital.

To effect this remodeling, the Army of Virginia, Major General Ambrose Burnside's North Carolina Expeditionary Force, the Army of the Potomac, and the Kanawha Division from Ohio were merged to form a single and allegedly cohesive force. It also absorbed a large number of nine-month regiments from Pennsylvania which were enrolled in August to bolster the Union army's rapidly depleting rolls.[78]

The average soldier had no faith, either in the military organization as it currently existed, or in the calibre of the general officers of the army. Private William B. Baker (Company D, 1st Maine Cavalry) curtly summarized the entire situation when he told his family, "Many of our officers are political men and will not help one another if they can help it.... They [the men] are not discouraged but would fight like tigers today. Just give them a leader in whom they could put confidence."[79]

On September 2, Major General George B. McClellan, who failed so miserably in the Peninsular Campaign earlier in the year, became the commander of the newly amalgamated Army of the Potomac. Spirits rose somewhat among the ranks, for he had earned a reputation among the men for studied caution. He was a man who did not rashly commit men to battle at severe loss of lives and he knew how to conduct a well planned retreat. Even his appointment to high command could not control the panic and confusion which reigned in the streets of Washington.[80]

No one, including the brigade or division commanders of the Army knew what to expect. Brigadier General George G. Meade (Pennsylvania Reserves) dejectedly penned the day before:

> We came here under orders from McDowell (in whose corps we are), who directed us to march from Fairfax Court House to Arlington. Since reaching here we have had no orders of any kind, and we cannot tell where we are going, though I presume we will take post somewhere in the vicinity of the city, for its defense.... Our division, the Reserves, is pretty well used up, and ought, strictly speaking, to be withdrawn, reorganized, filled up with recruits, and put in efficient condition.[81]

The Army of the Potomac licked its wounds while the Southerners invaded Northern soil. The citizens of Frederick, Maryland, knew far more about the location of the Army of Northern Virginia than the Federal Army. Around midnight, Surgeon Charles E. Goldsborough, who was left in charge of the telegraph at the Hessian Barracks in Frederick, received the following message from Harpers Ferry, Virginia, "Lee's Army will enter Frederick tomorrow. Any property that you do not want to fall into the hands of the enemy had better be destroyed. Our communications will soon be destroyed. [Dixon] Miles, Commanding."

Goldsborough immediately ordered the drummer to tap out the "Long Roll." Around six hundred convalescents assembled on the common and presently hobbled off under the direction of Assistant Army Surgeon C. P. Harrington toward Gettysburg, Pennsylvania. They took two wagons which were filled with medical supplies. They torched the remaining quartermaster and hospital stores.[82]

From the roof of her home on West Patrick Street, Miss Katherine S. Markall watched the panic in the street below her. "Federals burning their stores & 'skedadling' [sic]...Saw the sick from the barrack hospital straggling, with bandaged heads & co. towards Pa. & was greatly excited."[83]

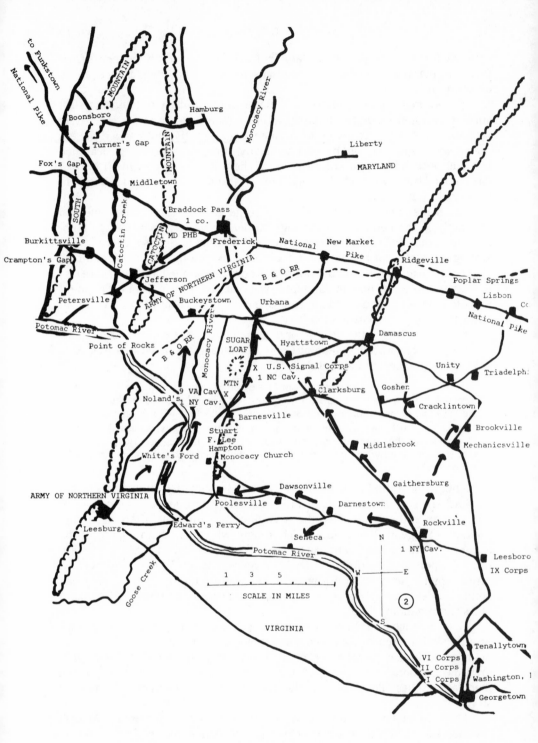

MAP 2: Situation—September 6, 1862.

Chapter Two

SEPTEMBER 6, 1862

SHORTLY AFTER DAWN, the 5th Virginia Cavalry paroled Captain Samuel Chamberlain (Company B) and his forty-seven troopers from the 1st Massachusetts Cavalry.[1] Not long after, the Virginians mounted and followed Hampton's brigade, which had taken the lead under Jeb Stuart's personal direction, on the road which led through Barnesville and around the southern base of Sugar Loaf Mountain.[2] The day before, during their approach to the mountain, the Confederates had passively observed signalman A. H. Cook frantically wigwag news of their approach to another Federal station.[3] The Rebels, noticing no further transmissions from the Federal observation post, rode along as if on an afternoon jaunt, protected only by a small point guard under Captain Thomas Ruffin (Company H, 1st North Carolina Cavalry).

Simultaneous with the Confederate advance, Lieutenant Brinkerhoff "Brink" Miner and his orderly A. H. Cook (U.S. Signal Corps) decided to return to Sugar Loaf and re-establish communications with the station at Seneca, Maryland.[4] As the 1st North Carolina Cavalry approached the eastern flank of the mountain, a courier and a headquarters orderly, who was carrying the campaign's dispatches, recklessly galloped past the North Carolinians and disappeared around a sharp bend in the road. Within seconds, the two found themselves startled by the equally surprised two man Union signal detachment, which stumbled into them from the opposite direction. The quick witted Lieutenant Miner and Private Cook realized they were outgunned and immediately drew their revolvers. Glancing over his shoulder Miner shouted, "Come on, men, here are the rebels."[5]

In the bloodless scuffle which followed, the courier wheeled about and

Lieutenant Brinkerhoff "Brink"
Miner, U.S. Signal Corps.
BROWN, *THE SIGNAL CORPS, U.S.A.*

escaped, while the Yankees snatched the orderly's mount by the reins and raced off with him.
The courier, pulling to an abrupt halt when he
rode into Captain Ruffin's advance guard, gasped
the alarm. They immediately gave chase. Finding only traces of the Yankees' tracks in the
road, the North Carolinians blindly thundered
toward Urbana with Stuart and the rest of the
command close behind. The captain and his
men rode four miles down the road before they
caught up with the Yankees. [Refer to Map 2]

They captured Cook, who was picketing the
missing orderly and two horses in front of a
roadside farmhouse. While part of the detachment disarmed the private, several others kicked in the door to the house and bolted inside.

A young woman's screams, followed by
loud scuffling, then more shrieks resounded through the open front door as
the dirty troopers dragged the semi-clad "Brink" Miner outside. The Yankee's
acquaintance, an attractive girl of about sixteen, followed him into the yard
and cried uncontrollably while they frisked her boyfriend.

The North Carolinians yanked several documents from the lieutenant's
clothing just as General Stuart galloped into the confusion. Sliding from the
saddle he anxiously asked, "Are the dispatches all right? Are the dispatches
all right?"

A soldier pointed to the orderly's horse with the unopened dispatch sat-
chels across the saddle.

Turning to the humiliated Yankees, Stuart chirped, somewhat sarcastically,
"Good morning, gentlemen. I am very happy to see you."

Lieutenant Miner replied, "Good morning, General, we are sorry we cannot return the compliment."

"Oh, well," Stuart responded with a laugh, "it is the fortune of war, you
know."

After personally frisking the lieutenant, he issued orders for his troopers
to treat the two prisoners well. He then mounted and rode off.[6] Besides net-
ting some papers of negligible importance, Stuart captured a complete set of
wigwag instruments which he promptly turned over to his own signalmen.[7]

While Stuart's cavalry was moving out toward Urbana, Alfred Pleasonton's troopers continued to scout the banks of the Monocacy and the fords
in the vicinity of Poolesville with small patrols.[8] Their presence on the hills
along the Confederate right made those portions of the Army of Northern
Virginia which were on the Maryland side of the river very uncomfortable.
The possibility of the Army of the Potomac cutting the forces of Robert E.
Lee in two at Edwards' and White's Fords and taking it from the rear apparently
occurred to Brigadier General Robert Rodes, whose brigade had been one of

the last in D. H. Hill's division to cross the river the previous evening. He sent out scattered patrols from his brigade (3rd, 5th, 6th, 12th, and 26th Alabama) to discourage the Yankee videttes from getting too close to the army's column.[9]

In the meantime, hundreds of famished Confederates scrounged the countryside west of the Monocacy for food. Privates J. M. Polk and Jim Astin (Company I, 4th Texas) staggered to a farm house which was about half a mile from their line of march. Uncertain about how they would be treated, they knocked on the door and nervously stepped back to see what would happen. Presently, a woman came to the door.

Could they have breakfast? Polk asked. He explaining they had not eaten for two days and were very hungry. The lady compassionately invited them in and sat them down at her kitchen table. They gorged themselves on buttermilk, butter, and coffee until they felt they were too fat to walk.[10]

Maryland did not seem as hostile to those Confederates who, having marched all night, forded the Potomac that morning.[11] For the most part, the soldiers of the 12th Virginia (Parham's brigade) fell in love with the beautiful countryside and admired the well maintained flour mills which lined their five mile long route from White's Ford to Martinsville.[12]

Some of them, however, were too footsore to pay attention to anything but their blistered feet and the crushed stone pike on which they walked. Private George S. Bernard (Company I, 12th Virginia) slung his waterlogged boots over his rifle barrel, determined never to wear them again. Following Second Manassas, he unsuccessfully tried to replace his worn out brogans by stripping a deceased Confederate of his shoes. His conscience, however, stopped him as he untied the shoelaces and struggled with the dead man's foot. Despite the derisive comments of his comrades, he vowed to go barefoot rather than defile a corpse.

Later that day (August 31), as the regiment assembled to move out, his friend, Private Nathaniel "Nat" Osborne (Company E), himself barefoot, gave Bernard a fine looking pair of high Blucher boots. The private thanked his comrade for his generosity and asked what he should do with them if he acquired another pair. Osborne said he could return them.

George Bernard, as he took his place in the column and prepared to march deeper into Maryland, could hardly wait to give the boots back to Osborne. Stiff and as unyielding as the Prussian for whom they were named, they pinched his feet so badly that after the first half mile out of Manassas, he decided to march without them. He wore them only at night to keep his feet warm, and once, when crossing the Potomac. (He believed the unbending leather soles would protect his feet from sharp rocks.)

When the regiment stepped out and the boots began to sway heavily from his rifle barrel, he reminded himself that he had given his word. The boots had to go back to the original owner. He still hoped to break them in before they broke him down.[13]

The verdant farms awed James Steptoe Johnston, Jr. (Company I, 11th Mississippi), who informed his fiancée, "The genral appearance of the country is very refreshing as the soil has never been trampled down by men & horses;

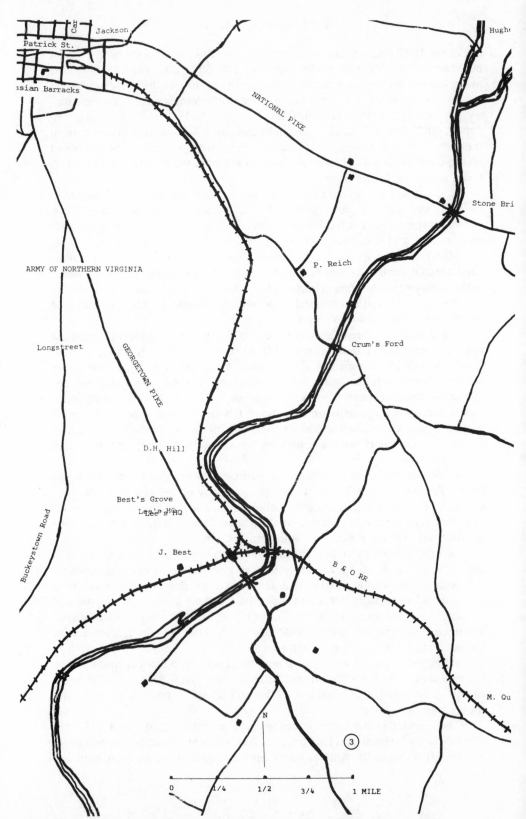

MAP 3: September 6, 1862. Confederate presence around Frederick, Maryland.

the fences are unburnt and corn fields and orchards unpillaged, as they have been in the greater portion of this state [Virginia]. The products of the soil was abundant and cheap, and the people seemed hardly to realize that there was a war."[14]

He could not have been more wrong. At 10:00 A.M., the war came to Frederick.[15] Doctor Pat Heny, having relieved Doctor Charles Goldsborough as the officer of the day, plopped himself onto one of the chairs on the veranda of the Hessian Barracks (South Market Street).

Turning to Goldsborough, he sighed in his thick Irish brogue, "Bejabbers, Chuck, wouldn't it be a purty piece of work for us to destroy all that property and have no Lee put in his appearance at all?"

No sooner had the words left his mouth than a lone, butternut clad Confederate cavalryman clattered up to the veranda steps. He leveled his carbine at Heny, who stood up to greet him.

"I demand the surrender of this post in the name of General Lee and the Confederate States of America."

The confused Irishman turned to his friend, Charles Goldsborough, and asked, "What had I better do?"

Goldsborough frankly responded, "If you was prepared to defend the place tell the man so; if not, surrender it."

Facing the horseman, he hurriedly spat, "Then I surrender, sir."

The Rebel, smiling, told the officers on the porch that he belonged to Elijah White's company of border cavalry. He added the advance of the army would be coming up soon and the Yankee officers should stay on the hospital grounds until the provost guard arrived.

Heny recovered his composure by the time the Southerner left the grounds to join his comrade on South Market Street. "The haythen would have shot me in a moment without a bit of scruple, I do believe, I really do believe, so I do," he gasped, "and a mean trick it was to point a rusty old blunderbuss at a gentleman that's niver harmed him in his life, so it was; and divel the bit would I lament if he fell dead in the first fight, the baste."

His friends laughed him into an embarrassed silence. Shortly thereafter the Confederates placed a guard and a battery of light artillery on the hospital grounds to protect the place. The Yankee officers reconciled themselves to their house arrest.[16]

Meanwhile, the officers on Longstreet's staff celebrated their crossing as if at a garden fete. Precisely at 10:15 A. M., Captain Osmun Latrobe of Georgia noted the time and "Took a *long* drink" of medicinal whiskey. He also mistakenly believed that Longstreet had gotten his entire Corps into Maryland.[17] Unlike Jackson's Corps, which had gotten as far as Three Springs and Buckeystown, some nine miles south of Frederick, Longstreet's was strung out from Buckeystown, to just south of Leesburg. There was about a thirty mile spread between the head and the rear of the column.[18] John B. Hood's division (Law's and Wofford's brigades) and Nathan Evans' Independent Brigade were just beyond Buckeystown. The rest of the Corps, excluding John G. Walker's division and part of Kemper's brigade, bivouacked somewhere between there and the C & O Canal aqueduct at Cheek's Ford.[19]

At White's Ford, Brigadier General Joseph Kershaw's regiments (2nd, 3rd, 7th, and 8th South Carolina) stripped to the skin and plunged into the river like boys at a swimming hole. With their pants held above their heads, they splashed each other with their free hands, and shouted, and cursed their way into Maryland.

"We needed a good washing of our bodies, but wading in the water did us no good in that direction," Lieutenant William A. Johnson (Company D, 2nd South Carolina) recalled.

The line soldiers of the 2nd South Carolina, pragmatists that they were, did not allow patriotic sentiment to obscure their vision. At first, like Lieutenant William A. Johnson, they thought the local citizenry had not greeted them at the ford because no one had told them of the invasion. The South Carolinians encountered only one person within five miles of White's Ford. As they marched over the plundered canal boat, which the 3rd Alabama had capsized the day before, they stumbled upon a freed black man, who was taking the towpath south toward Washington. The Confederates left the man alone, but not before suggesting that one of the men in Company D take him along as a companion for his slave, George.

Shortly thereafter, the regiment struck the main highway. The limestone dust caked their uniforms and the sweat began to trickle in streams down their faces. With every mile they became more filthy and evil smelling. Lieutenant Johnson could feel the perspiration roll down his socks into his shoes.

As the South Carolinians tramped along the pike, more and more civilians gathered in clusters along the western side of the road to gawk at them. Some were on horseback or in carriages; most were afoot. Out of pity, many removed their shoes and handed them to the barefoot soldiers as they swaggered by them. Years later, the ever observant Lieutenant Johnson bitterly remembered, "We were not long in finding out that the Potomac was as far north as the Southern Confederacy extended, and that we were in as much of an enemy's country as if we were in Pennsylvania."[20]

Despite the order to the contrary, straggling became a terrible problem. Officers as well as enlisted men dropped along the roadside to sleep or staggered into nearby farms to forage. While many of the Marylanders professed to be "secesh," they proved Yankee enough to sell their produce to the starving Confederates.

"As for taking our money," Mississippian James S. Johnston complained, "they would let us have as much of little things such as butter and eggs as they could afford to give and take the money for a curiosity...."[21] The Confederates, hungry as they were, did not let their political beliefs interfere with their survival.

Few men, including officers, refrained from begging. In some instances, such as that of the 1st and 4th Companies of the Washington Artillery (Louisiana), an officer and some enlisted men, working as a squad, systematically ferreted out breakfast. Lieutenant William M. Owen and his chums, Corporals

E. I. Kursheedt and George "Bliffkins" Montgomery, found the Marylanders along their circuitous route very hospitable and, allegedly, overt sympathizers to the Confederate cause. They provided him and his comrades with plenty to eat.[22]

General Robert Rodes' cavalry chasing patrols merely trotted two miles east, watched the Federal cavalry videttes melt out of sight, then turned about and marched back to their bivouac. Otis Smith of the 6th Alabama and a comrade quietly slipped away from the rear of the column to forage.

Cutting cross country, they stumbled upon a one room school house. Smith, the former school teacher, entered the building to interrogate the school master, a venerable old fellow of about seventy. The teacher, who was as frightened as his pupils, stared silently at the two ragged and unkempt Rebels.

Smith ordered the children to surrender their lunches. Within a minute every one of the twenty-five to thirty "urchins"—as Smith contemptuously referred to them—had plopped their baskets and pails down in front of the two ruffians and scurried back to their quivering school master. As the two soldiers hunkered down and started to selectively pick the tastiest morsels from their informal buffet, the sound of pounding hooves echoed through the open door.

A quick glance up the road which passed in front of the school house caused Smith and his comrade to drop their plunder and run. Skedaddling as fast as their feet could carry them, the two foragers vainly tried to outrun the dust enveloped cavalry squadron as it thundered past the school. All the while the teacher and his brood stood outside and jeered, "Run, Rebs, run, the Yanks will catch you!"

As the horsemen sped by Smith and his friend, leaving them in the settling dirt and pelting them with clods kicked up by the horses, the two men noticed the troopers wore Confederate uniforms. Minutes later, as their breathing returned to normal, Smith's friend gasped, "Well, you played Hades, didn't ya!"

Exasperated because they had lost a fine meal to the shenanigans of some cavalrymen who wanted to race on a level road, Otis Smith did not bother to reply. The dejected soldiers trudged back to their regiment in silence.[23]

The Federal cavalry, which Rodes had so feared that morning, amounted to nothing more than scouts from the 3rd Indiana Cavalry, who were heading back to Clarksburg. Companies B, C, D, and E of the 1st New York Cavalry met them there around 10:00 A.M. Having left three fourths of their regiment in Middlebrook, those two squadrons completed their forced march from Rockville only to find themselves going into the field immediately.[24]

They spread themselves thin, in small squads, south along Seneca Creek and northwest toward Hyattstown. While Company E of the 3rd Indiana Cavalry picketed their unsaddled mounts, the rest of the regiment and the 8th Illinois Cavalry trotted southwest toward Poolesville. The 1st U.S. Cavalry completed the screen by fanning out east to Brookville to protect the Baltimore & Ohio Railroad.[25]

The 1st New York Cavalry, unlike the Hoosiers, did not hesitate to engage the Confederate patrols which were sent after them nor to chase down stragglers. Throughout the day, Sergeant John Haggarty (Company B) and his few troopers herded in disillusioned Rebels. At one point, near Sugar Loaf Mountain, from which Jeb Stuart's newly acquired signal equipment busily jerked to and fro, a combined force of about twenty men from Companies D and E, under the command of Lieutenant William K. Laverty, clashed with Captain Thomas C. Waller's Companies A and I of the 9th Virginia Cavalry, which were left behind to guard the mountain.[26] As the Virginians charged the New Yorkers, whom they almost surrounded, they cut off two of the Yankee troopers, who were a considerable distance out on the flank. Their dust caked uniforms giving them some kind of butternut appearance, Privates Almon Decker (Company E) and Michael Dunn (Company D) joined the Rebels. At the first opportunity, the two shot ahead of the Confederates and rejoined their regiment on the retreat to Clarksburg.[27] [Refer to Map 2]

Roving Federal scouts did not deter Jeb Stuart from his triumphant ride into Frederick by way of Urbana. Very shortly after his troopers recovered his dispatches and confiscated the Federal signal apparatus, the general and Wade Hampton sent the latter's brigade quartermaster ahead of the column to gather forage for the command.

The young officer, who was wearing a dark blue tunic, stopped at the home of an elderly, rich farmer on the northern side of the village. The man met him at the gate to his yard and invited him in. The quartermaster politely declined, requesting, instead, corn for his brigade.

The Marylander frankly informed the trooper that he had none to spare, but concluded, "The war must go on, the Government must be kept up, horses must be fed, and so I must let you have the quantity you ask for." Turning to one side, he called for two of his slaves and ordered them to load up the corn.

The two men moved out in a hurry while the old man faced the quartermaster with a self-satisfied air. He beamed. "Well, my friend, let me know where I shall deliver this corn, and I will have it taken right to the spot, as I am a man that goes for accommodating the Government."

The soldier twisted and pointed toward the column of dust approaching the edge of the village.

He grinned. "I see the command moving up now, and will gallop down and ascertain where General Hampton will locate the camp."

The farmer exlaimed, "Stop! Stop! What? Who? What General Hampton?"

"General Wade Hampton of South Carolina; it is his cavalry you see yonder. It's him you agreed to feed."

"But I can't, I can't," the old man protested. "I got no corn to spare; circumstances alter cases. Go to my neighbor Johnston. I ain't got none to let go. If I let anymore go, my stock will suffer."

"Ah! My fellow, I have you now," the officer insisted. "The corn must come, the contract must be fulfilled."

The Marylander, realizing he had given his word, scratched his head in defeat. "Well, I be drotted if this ain't taking a fellow by the nap without letting him know anything about it."

The corn was delivered by the time the brigade had unsaddled.[28]

As Hampton's brigade fanned into the fields west of the village, Jeb Stuart, with Von Borcke and Captain William W. Blackford, rode to the center of the town to the home of a Mr. Cockey. The general departed for Frederick, leaving instructions for both officers to establish headquarters in the yard. Von Borcke was then to meet him at Jackson's quarters, wherever they might be.

The remainder of the staff rode up and picketed their horses with their saddles on. The major and the captain directed their orderlies to pitch their tents in Mr. Cockey's garden, then told the black servants to start cooking, a task which the aristocratic Von Borcke thought they were best suited to perform.[29]

The day had not gone well at all for Thomas J. "Stonewall" Jackson. Early in the morning he mounted a powerful gray mare, which a Marylander had given him the day before. He merely touched its flank with a spur. The horse's eyes flashed and its nostrils flared. Rearing up on its hind legs, it fell backward on top of Jackson, then rolled off him. Jackson lay on his back for over half an hour, until he recovered his senses enough to turn the command of the Corps over to his brother-in-law, D. H. Hill.

Bruised and sprained, the general refused to go near the beast again. He rode to Frederick in an ambulance. Assistant Inspector General Henry Kyd Douglas and Lieutenant J. G. Morrison commandeered the gray and kept her for racing.[30]

During the morning and the forenoon, Jackson's Corps arrived in and around Frederick in the face of exceedingly light opposition. The 14th New Jersey, guarding the B & O Railroad Bridge over the Monocacy River at Monocacy Junction, south of Frederick, retreated east toward Baltimore, allowing D. H. Hill's, Lawton's, A. P. Hill's, and the leading elements of Longstreet's Corps the freedom to occupy the place. Similarly, Captain W. T. Faithful evacuated his company of the 1st Maryland, Potomac Home Brigade west toward Jefferson. Destroying those supplies which he could not carry or ship by rail to Pennsylvania, he abandoned about six hundred sick and wounded men to Bradley T. Johnson's brigade.[31]

Jackson, Lee, and Longstreet set up their tents near Best's Grove, about one and one half miles south of the city along the Urbana Road. A large apple orchard flanked the eastern side of the road, and an oak grove and a very large cornfield covered the western side, almost to the city.[32] Lee and Longstreet camped in the grove, and Jackson quartered himself across from them.[33]

Curious civilians started to pry about Headquarters, trying to get near the three generals. Lee and Jackson retired to quarters, explaining that their injuries and pressing military matters forced them to do so. They left the limping James Longstreet to contend with the inhabitants of Frederick.[34] Lee's first order appointed Bradley T. Johnson's brigade the provost guard of Frederick and made the city off limits to all without passes. He also forbade looting.[35]

The invading troops, however, operated under the proven axioms, "First come, first served" and "Finders—keepers; losers—weepers." The 21st Virginia, while leading Johnson's brigade down Market Street, in passing by the railroad depot near the corner of All Saints' Street, happened upon several boxcars, which were loaded with watermelons. John Worsham (Company F) joined the frenzied dash for the melons. Each man quickly shouldered one and slipped back into the column for the march to the Fair Grounds on the eastern side of town.[36]

Kershaw's brigade wandered into Best's Grove near dark. The officers positioned their regiments in the northern edge of the woods, across from a large apple orchard, with instructions for the men to remain in formation until ordered to change. The command, Lieutenant William Johnson (Company D, 2nd South Carolina) recalled, lasted until it was heard, at which point every South Carolinian who had a knapsack stripped it off then bolted into the orchard across the road or into the cornfield near the grove. More ravenous than the locusts of Egypt, they pilfered apples and corn.

Fires crackled in the darkness as the starving infantrymen shucked the corn cobs before shoving them into the hot ashes. They were careful to leave one or two layers of husks against the kernels to keep the corn from burning. Similarly, they gorged themselves on green apples, straight from the trees, or sliced them for stewing.[37] Severe cramps and diarrhea took their toll.

"...too much Maryland hospitality" complained Private Otis Smith (Company F, 6th Alabama) left his stomach in open rebellion and forced him to spend a great deal of time purging his digestive system.[38] He was not alone.

Illness disabled the Union soldiers as well. Lieutenant Curtis Pollock (Company G, 48th Pennsylvania), who was exhausted from the morning's eight mile march from Washington to Leesboro, Maryland, wrote to his mother, "Many of the men are sick with diarrhea and I have a touch of it...." He counted himself fortunate when the IX Corps remained in camp to organize itself while the rest of the army took up the march again.[39]

Major Von Borcke (Stuart's staff) left Urbana around 1:00 P.M., before he had a chance to eat dinner or to introduce himself to the flirtatious women who had invaded their bivouac. Leaving Captain Blackford to tend to them, he took the pike north to Frederick.[40]

Not finding Stuart at Best's Grove, he continued into the city. The boarded up houses of the Unionists silently protested the drunken revelry in the streets. A mob caught sight of the major in his plumed hat. Men and women alike thronged around Von Borcke and insisted, despite his protests, that he was either Stuart or Jackson. The street filled with civilians. Women thrust bouquets of flowers at him. Again and again he swore that he was not the person they thought he was, but the crowd followed him down Market Street to Patrick Street. [Refer to Map 3]

To escape them, he dismounted about the middle of the first block of West Patrick Street and strode into the City Hotel. He found himself in the smoke obscured saloon on the ground floor, which happened to be filled with beer drinking Germans. Von Borcke, suspecting that their alleged secessionism was a sham, let them chat, rather than he. One insisted the Army of Northern Virginia mustered 300,000 men. Another boasted how he expected the surrender of Baltimore or Washington any day. As the conversations grew louder, the general consensus developed that the Confederates could recruit another 30,000 soldiers over the next couple of days. Weary of their thinly veiled sarcasm and their incessant questioning, the major left and rode back to Urbana.[41] Nearby, at Monocacy Junction, the newly commissioned, but not sworn in, Second Lieutenant Samuel Buck (Company H, 13th Virginia) ruefully scratched in his diary that he honestly expected the Maryland men to rush to "the Cause." They did not do so, he concluded, because the Army of Northern Virginia was not much to look at.[42]

The civilians wanted to see generals, not the average, evil smelling infantryman.[43] Throughout the day, they swarmed around Robert E. Lee's Headquarters. At one point, several young ladies shamelessly threw themselves upon his neck, covering him with hugs and kisses until, red faced and blushing, he begged for mercy.[44] Once again, he ordered his sentries to turn back civilians. Stuart, however, despite an unbecoming altercation with Captain Elijah V. White, attempted to share his brief afternoon at Best's Grove with the ladies only.[45]

The incident began when Stuart ordered White and his band of independent cavalry to return to Loudoun County. The captain protested on the grounds that he was a Marylander by birth and that he had fought as hard as any man would upon his native soil.

Stuart decided to take issue with the cavalryman for the sake of asserting his authority.

Stuart tried to trap White into bragging that he had fought better than anyone, including Stuart and Lee himself. "Do you say you have done as much as any man, for the South?" Stuart coyly replied.

"No, sir," White said, realizing that Stuart wanted to verbally fence with him. "I did not say that; but I have done my duty to the South as a soldier, so far as my ability extends, as fully as anybody."

"You did say you have done as much as any man," the general countered.

"I did not say so," White told him.

The argument continued until Stuart finally commanded White to go back to Loudoun County to watch for flanking Federal forces from the direction of Dranesville, Fairfax Court House, and Washington, D.C.

The captain refused to comply and demanded to see General Lee, to which Stuart coolly said, "Come along, I'll go with you."

The general calmly strode into Robert E. Lee's quarters as if he lived there, leaving the captain at the tent flap. Presently, Lee met the captain at the entrance to headquarters and asked him what he wanted. White politely tendered his request and the commanding general told him to wait a short while until he could interview him.

With each passing minute, White became more and more distraught with rage until tears welled up in his eyes. As they started to course down his face into his mustache and beard, Jackson emerged from the tent and asked him what the problem was. The captain's response took Stonewall by surprise. Jackson said he had heard Stuart tell Lee that White had requested the transfer to Virginia. The partisan leader was so angry that he could not answer.

"Captain White, I think I can understand your feelings," Stonewall Jackson continued with genuine compassion, "for I once was situated just as you are now. During the Mexican War I was ordered to the rear just as a battle was about to take place, and I knew of no reason why I should be so unjustly treated; but I obeyed, and it so happened by doing so I had an opportunity to acquire distinction that I never could have had at the front. And Captain, my advice to you is to obey orders, no matter how unjust they may be. We are poor, short sighted creatures at best, and in the very thing that seems hardest for us to bear, Providence may have hidden a rich blessing for us. Go, Captain, and obey orders."

Stuart came out and called the still silent captain to his side.

"Captain," Stuart began mockingly, "did you say you was a Marylander?"

"Yes, sir."

"Ah! I didn't know that," the general lied. "General Lee wants you."

Lee, who knew his officers and staff better than they thought he did, removed Elijah White from his cavalry commander's immediate control and placed him directly under his own supervision. White and his partisans were to scout toward Harpers Ferry without engaging the enemy and report directly back to Lee in person.[46]

The captain won his round and left Stuart to play the cavalier with the ladies. In the meantime Colonel Thomas Munford and his small brigade were still covering Longstreet's column near Leesburg.[47]

Following a brief midday halt, the long, straggling lines which clogged the pikes from Edwards' Ferry and White's Ford slowly got under way again. Private George Bernard (Company I, 12th Virginia) felt a twinge every time he recalled the trek from Martinsville to the Monocacy. "...it looked to a man in the ranks as if our officers supposed we were not ordinary flesh and blood," he complained years later, "....and night coming on we were pushed ahead, to go how far no one knew." The miles seemed to extend forever. The exhausted soldiers repeatedly craned their necks to see if the head of the column was filing off into some distant field for a bivouac. It never happened. As the evening wore toward midnight, George Bernard (Company I), Dick Davis, Sydney Jones, and Billy Pucci (Company E, 12th Virginia) decided they had marched enough for one day.

Deliberately straying from the road, they happened upon a straw rick, about fifty yards west of the column. They ripped off their gear and nestled down for the night in comfort. A few minutes later, the glow of hundreds of fires danced and fluttered in the darkness and one of Bernard's comrades pointed in astonishment at them.

"Look yonder, boys! The command is going into camp! Suppose we get up and join them?" he suggested.

"No, no," Sydney Jones groaned in relief, "I would not move from this comfortable place, as tired as I am, if my great-grandmother were up there at those fires. I propose 'camping' here to-night."

No more discussion ensued. The four fell off to sleep without any difficulty.[48]

While the Army of Northern Virginia force marched its soldiers across the Potomac River, Major General George B. McClellan's reorganizing troops very slowly stumbled north from Alexandria, Virginia. By dark Brigadier General Jacob Cox's Kanawha Division of the Army of the West had proceeded beyond the northern suburbs of Washington, D.C.[49] The rest of the army, which had been expecting to stay put for several days, did not start to march until late in the afternoon.

The VI Corps led the second contingent. Scheduled to depart just before sunset, the battle worn soldiers sullenly packed up their meager possessions. Major General William F. Smith's division took the advance and crossed the Long Bridge into Washington, where it turned northwest on 7th Street. Curious civilians gathered on the sidewalks, having been awakened by the tramping and shuffling of thousands of feet. When asked where they were going, the weary soldiers generally mumbled, "We are going to meet the Rebels."[50]

The 49th New York's historian boasted , "...the Confederate Army had made its way into Maryland, and the Army of the Potomac was hot on its trail." The Federals were moving north and they were overburdened. In their haste, the I, II,and VI Corps generals did not issue orders to lighten the army's equipage or baggage.[51]

In the cool night air, many of the overheated men collapsed under the weight of their knapsacks. Their heaving bodies littered the pavement and sidewalks at every "breathing" stop. In the 49th New York, no amount of tugging and prodding could rouse the skulkers to their feet. By the time the column reached Tennallytown, a few hours after midnight, less than three fourths of its effectives remained in the ranks.[52]

Private Charles S. McClenthen (Company G, 26th New York, I Corps) ruefully recalled that the four days of rest in Washington had debilitated more than rehabilitated the veterans in his regiment. They now had to carry the new shelter halves and blankets which they received upon arriving in the capital. The inactivity had relaxed their hardened muscles, and the increased weight of their knapsacks made the straps cut deep into their shoulders. The regiment moved out late at night behind II Corps, which trailed VI Corps. The veteran New Yorkers suffered like recruits under their new luggage.[53]

As the Yankees lurched northward after it, the Army of Northern Virginia enjoyed a much needed respite from hard marching. Officially, Robert E. Lee's men, under penalty of court-martial, stayed to their camps and left Frederick unmolested. Colonel Bradley T. Johnson's brigade and camp provost details could not catch all of the men who slipped into the city and the troops knew it.

The 19th Virginia visited Frederick in squads. Lieutenant William N. Wood (Companies A and I) got a supper from a secessionist home which sported a small Confederate flag for every family member.[54]

Sergeant Edward Moore (Poague's Virginia Battery) returned to camp well fed and content. He meandered in, reconciled to the fact that no army punishment from the provost guard could diminish the joy he had experienced that day. Nevertheless, he felt quite relieved to find that the overwhelming numbers of foragers neutralized the effectiveness of the limited numbers of camp police.[55]

Similarly, Private John Worsham (Company F, 21st Virginia) waddled back into the Frederick fair grounds gorged on enough food to stuff six men. The moment he rejoined his regiment, he was ordered to brigade headquarters.

Fears of imprisonment and execution lingered in his mind until he stepped up to the adjutant general, who greeted him with a smile and told him to report to the chief surgeon at the Federal hospital. Worsham was to obtain a list of all the Yankee injured and write a parole, in duplicate, for each.

Much relieved, the private walked back to his company and packed his belongings in his blanket roll. He considered himself better off than most of his comrades. His kit, which consisted entirely of captured Yankee goods, included an oilcloth, a blanket, rubber cloth, haversack, wool socks, and, the most precious of all, jean drawers. They went most places with him, lest he "lose" them to a forager.

The Federal surgeon very cordially introduced himself and handed Worsham a list of seven hundred names. The doctor also handed him a lamp, pen, and ink before he escorted him into the hospital dining room. John Worsham cleaned off the table while his host explained that the room's size made it most suitable. The private, knowing that he had one thousand four hundred slips to fill out, plopped into a chair and set to work.[56] He had a long night ahead of him.

It also seemed endless at first to James S. Johnston of the 11th Mississippi. He had ridden quite a distance into the countryside to forage for delicacies. He finally came upon an elderly woman, Mrs. Dorsey, and her very attractive daughter, both of whom insisted they had just given all the food they could spare to the cavalry squad which was still hanging around their barn. A glance at the young lady convinced Johnston that there were delicacies of a better sort to be had. He parked himself on an upended barrel on their front porch and started chatting with both of them.

After a while, the young lady noticed how uncomfortable the soldier was becoming and invited him inside to sit at their table. She brought him all the apple butter and milk they had left. Johnston said he had not eaten in forty-eight hours and was "hungry much." "...I really spent a pleasant evening with quite a pretty and agreeable young lady," he wrote apologetically to his fiancée Mary M. Green.[57] Maryland seemed more hospitable to him than it had before.

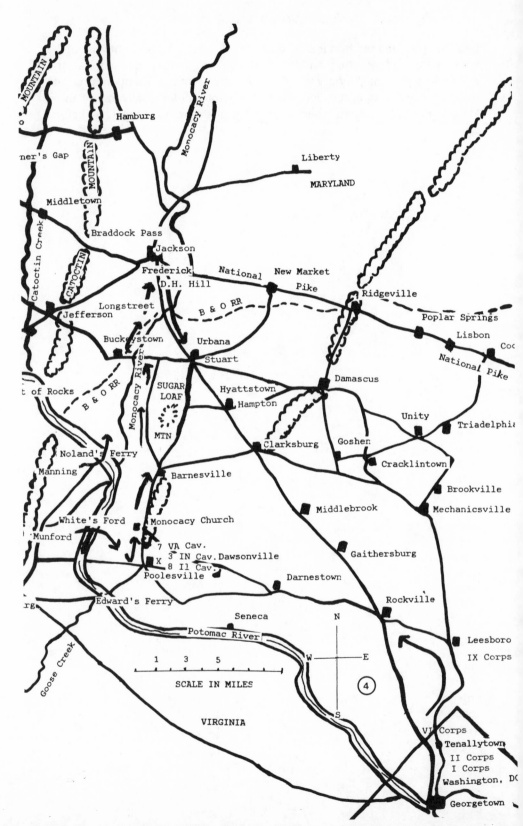

MAP 4: Situation—September 7, 1862.

Chapter Three

SEPTEMBER 7, 1862

MIDNIGHT FOUND Colonel Thomas Munford, his small brigade (2nd, 7th, and 12th Virginia Cavalry), and Chew's Virginia Battery fording the Potomac at White's Ford. The river seemed quite wide to Private George Neese (Chew's Battery). As he crossed the four hundred yards from Virginia to Maryland, he estimated the river's depth at two and one half feet—just the right height to soak a tall man's inseam and a short fellow's navel with cold water.[1] Depositing two videttes in Poolesville, the column moved all night and arrived in Urbana during the early hours of the morning.

About twenty-one miles east of Edwards' Ferry, the Union VI Corps staggered to a halt south of Tennallytown.[2] It was about 1:00 A.M. Hundreds of sleeping men from the 49th New York cluttered the sidewalks of the capital and the roadside beyond the city. The regiment resembled a small company more than a regiment. Those few who arrived at the predawn bivouac collapsed in a stupor, too exhausted to wake up.[3] Other regiments fared somewhat better. Captain Peter A. Filbert (Company B, 96th Pennsylvania) stoically wrapped his hands around a fresh cup of coffee and realized that he felt "tolerable." His intuition, refined by months of campaigning, warned him of another hot, dust choked day, which he accepted as a matter of course.[4]

The regiment's colonel, Henry L. Cake, nearly touched off a riot that morning when he passed the word to his gasping Pennsylvanians to surrender all of their excess baggage to the quartermaster and to strip to light marching order. It was bad enough they had had to repack their new uniforms and great coats the day they left Washington, but they had to ditch their knapsacks as well. The rank and file loudly refused to comply. The frustrated quartermaster fetched the colonel to quell the disturbance.

31

Colonel Cake reminded his veterans of their previous record: they had fought the enemy on Southern soil within sight of Richmond, Virginia. During that time, they had lost more than one hundred thirty casualties on three battlefields, and now they were going home to fight. Further, he boasted, the 96th was the only regiment going into the fight in light marching order. Professionals that they were, the Pennsylvanians reluctantly turned their baggage over to the quartermaster.

Nevertheless, someone groused so loudly about the command that it reached division headquarters before the day was much older. Major General Henry Slocum, who believed some subordinate officer had usurped his authority, galloped into Company A and demanded, "What are you doing with your baggage and knapsacks?"

"Stripping for a fight," an enlisted man growled.

"Where?" Slocum shot back.

"When we catch them," the soldier retorted. "Can you tell us?"

"No!" the general exclaimed. "But it is a good idea! There is nothing to complain of in it, and we will make it an order and strip the whole division."[5]

Colonel Cake's initial command rippled beyond the division and spread throughout the entire army.[6] While the infantry bedded down for several hours' sleep, Alfred Pleasonton's cavalry screen made its first successful strike against the Confederate cavalry. Acting on his own initiative, Colonel John Farnsworth, the brigade commander, decided to prove there were few Rebels in Poolesville. Early in the morning, he personally led four companies (two squadrons) each from the 3rd Indiana and the 8th Illinois Cavalry on an insane dash into the village. The flamboyant colonel spurred his mustang full tilt down the main street, well in advance of his men, and, in quick order, captured every Confederate in the place. Both troopers of the 7th Virginia Cavalry, one of whom was mounted, surrendered without firing a shot. The Westerners returned to Darnestown gloating in triumph. After General Pleasonton complimented them for doing business "on their own hook," they settled down for a day of reading mail and writing letters.[7] [Refer to Map 4]

The Federal cavalry never probed the Confederate flanks enough to accurately ascertain their strength or troop locations. Instead, the troopers relied on the New York papers for their intelligence reports. Private Samuel Gilpin (Company E, 3rd Indiana Cavalry) casually wrote in his diary, "Today's paper reports 40,000 Confederates at Frederick; they [the Rebels] seemed much pleased."[8]

The Confederate army was still dragging itself across the Potomac. Colonel Van Manning's brigade (3rd Arkansas, 27th, 46th, 48th North Carolina, and 30th Virginia) entered Maryland at Noland's Ferry, a few miles north of the mouth of the Monocacy River. Once again, "Maryland! My Maryland!" echoed along the river banks. Once again, the Marylanders greeted their supposed "liberators" with contemptuous silence and passivity.

"We had," Lieutenant John Sloan (Company B, 27th North Carolina) sarcastically scrawled, "evidently crossed at the wrong ford."[9]

In Best's Grove, south of Frederick, the Washington Artillery (Louisiana) bivouacked on either side of Major General James Longstreet's quarters.[10] Captain Charles Squires (1st Company, Washington Artillery) shrugged off "stories" that the enlisted men had seen Stonewall Jackson sitting on a fence picking lice out of his clothing. He had not changed his slouch hat, coat, pants, or boots since First Manassas in July, 1861, which prompted Squires to jot in his diary that Jackson's wading of the Potomac and the other streams in Maryland had done nothing to improve his appearance.[11]

Jackson stayed in his tent most of the morning, trying to nurse his sore back, which a couple of young Baltimore belles had sprained again during the previous evening. As he hobbled toward his tent, they sprang upon him from their carriage and, literally, clung to his neck for several minutes until he pleaded for mercy. Mistaking his genuine discomfort for flirtatious gallantry, the two young women retreated, giggling, to their carriage and bid their driver leave.[12] Dawn found the general in too much pain to attend morning services.

At the hospital in Frederick, Private John Worsham (Company F, 21st Virginia) did not get to sleep until daylight. By then he had put a very large dent in his seven hundred Union parole receipts. As the first light darted into his room, the exhausted soldier stretched out on a bench and dozed off.[13]

While he slept, hundreds of Confederates roamed the city to purchase supplies. Many, like Lieutenant William M. Owen (Washington Artillery) and his crew of foragers, bitterly complained about the closed and empty shops, and the stripped fields which greeted them. They eventually found an allegedly sympathetic grocer who opened his store to them in hopes of garnering Federal greenbacks as his competitors had earlier. The Louisianans loaded up with coffee, sugar, Scotch, champagne, and other "spirits," which the lieutenant euphemistically dubbed "essentials." The shopkeeper lost his temper when the Southerners paid him off with several hundred dollars in Confederate scrip. One of the soldiers replied that the "shinplaster" money would be backed by gold in New York after the Confederates razed Maryland.[14]

The shops which stayed open sold out quickly because their prices were so low. Coffee went for thirty cents a pound, tea for two dollars a pound; bacon sold for seventy cents per pound. The soldiers bought everything imaginable— spool cotton, sewing silk, ladies' shoes, and calico dresses for their womenfolk at home. Some Frederick residents displayed their Confederate sentiments cautiously. A number of them informed Captain Greenlee Davidson (Letcher Artillery, Virginia) they feared reprisals by their Unionist neighbors once the Army of Northern Virginia, which they thought was on an extraordinarily big raid, recrossed the river. The captain erroneously believed what he needed to believe—once the Marylanders realized that the Confederates were in their state to stay, they would unreservedly flock to the Southern cause.[15]

For many of the soldiers, however, Frederick had become an inhospitable city of close mouthed, sullen people, whose shops, for the most part, had been suddenly "bought out." Lieutenant William A. Johnson (Company D, 2nd South Carolina) and a comrade wrangled passes to town in the hopes of abandoning their debilitating green apples and corn diet. Discouraged by the virtually abandoned streets and the barred stores whose doors were adorned with "Sold Out" signs, the two tramped the streets until noon without any success. They could not tolerate the "Yankee" arrogance of the place. The lieutenant even had greenback Federal money in his pockets.

The dejected pair walked as far as the apple orchard on the J. Best farm when they decided to take a short cut back to their camp. Following the northern border of the orchard they came to a path which cut diagonally through the trees to the eastern side of the house.

Some heavily laden apple trees immediately outside of the backyard fence lured them toward the main house. Famine overruled their pride as Johnson and his friend bombarded the tree branches with sticks and rocks. Scurrying among the fallen apples like schoolboys, they feverishly filled their haversacks with them.

"Halt! Halt!" echoed menacingly behind them.

The lieutenant and his comrade instinctively took off running. Fearing they had fallen prey to a Yankee squad, they never bothered to look back. The foot falls of their pursuers grew louder and faster, followed by the ominous clicks of two rifle hammers going to "Full Cock." The two refugees glanced over their shoulders to face their executioners and abruptly halted—relieved. Three Confederate sentries moved in on them with leveled weapons.

Lieutenant Johnson's reassuring smile evaporated as the corporal of the guard informed them that their regiment, the 3rd Arkansas, had strict orders to guard the house because it was General Daniel H. Hill's Headquarters. The Arkansans had just arrived from the C & O Canal. They were "dumb enough" to actually obey all their officers and to take all of their orders seriously. The corporal, the South Carolinians noted, seemed quite "stuck up" with his own authority as he explained that his detail had to protect the orchard. The corporal angered the two foragers further by arresting them and marching them into the back yard with about fifty other poachers.

William Johnson and his newly acquired "friends" vehemently swore and protested their confinement. The more sullen they got, the more pleased the three greenhorns seemed to become with themselves, and the more bothersome the prisoners became. Within a very short time a woman stomped up to the back door and glared at the Rebels in the yard.

"You nasty, dirty rebels!" she shouted, "I'm going to make General Hill put you in the cow lot."

The men followed her quaking right index finger to the manured pen west of the yard.

"You shant stay in my backyard." She threw her arms up above her head in exasperation.

"Amen!" the soldiers impudently shouted at her back as she rushed inside. The repulsive odor of cow manure drifted over them. They vowed to a man they would neither surrender to an irate Yankee woman nor to those "Arkansas Immigrants."

Shouts of, "Never! No, Never!" reverberated above the cursing behind the house.

When Major John W. Ratchford, Hill's adjutant general, came to the door and told them the woman had ordered the general to confine them to the cow lot, the veterans told him they would resist being moved, particularly since a Yankee had demanded it.

Ratchford calmly informed the men he did not blame them for being angry then quietly slipped inside the house, whereupon the prisoners openly dared their guards to stop them. Bolting the fence en masse, they stripped the trees clean of fruit and stampeded, unmolested to their camps.[16]

The men of the 14th North Carolina resented the condescending attitude of so many of the Marylanders. When the regiment left Buckeystown for Monocacy Junction that morning, the civilians gaped at the filthy veterans as they shuffled down the pike.

"They look hard; clothes in rags," gasped one.

Another observed, "Half of them are barefoot; have not even dirty uniforms."

"No uniforms at all," marveled a third.

"But just look at their guns," someone else interjected, "ain't they bright and polished, and don't they glisten in the sun?"[17]

A number of Confederates, including enlisted men, brought slaves with them to perform their menial labor. Others, as in the case of Ned Haines, personal servant to Private John Dooley (Company A, 1st Virginia), were sent from home to take care of the family's sons who were in the service.

Ned Haines, who had been by his side at First Manassas and throughout the Peninsula Campaign, caught up with him at Monocacy Junction. Ned not only brought letters from home but also a pair of well fitting shoes. The aging slave promised to care for Dooley as much as he had for his father before him.[18]

Ned knew he was a slave and, apparently, had become accustomed to it because it was the only life he knew. Few of the soldiers realized how completely professional they had become, despite their occasional blatant disregard for protocol and authority. Their shared hardships had bonded them to their comrades far tighter than any overt patriotism. For those who doggedly stayed in the ranks on the Maryland side of the river, soldiering had become their profession and their master.

Private George Bernard of the 12th Virginia hobbled several painful miles before he caught up with his regiment, which went into bivouac in a wheat field three miles south of Frederick. He tripped and winced his way across the stubble toward the camp and had barely begun talking with others of Company I when his comrade, Jim Nash, asked him if he would like a pair of shoes. Nash plucked Bernard off his feet before he could reply and carried him a few yards further to Captain Samuel Stevens, the regimental quartermaster. Stevens issued Bernard the last pair of shoes he had purchased in Frederick that day. They fit so perfectly that the private felt he could wear them to a ball.

Bernard returned to his friends, who immediately besieged him with requests for his old pair. He gladly surrendered his "iron soled" boots to Billy Price only after Price swore he would take care of them and return them to Osborne of Company E, when, and if, he ever saw him again. The Blucher boots outlived the pledge, and most of the men who wore them in rapid succession over the next few months.[19]

The men depended upon their comrades as much as they had their mothers. They shared a childlike distrust for authority and seldom hesitated to defy it or mock it when they could do so with impunity.

The ever observant Lieutenant William Johnson (2nd South Carolina) frankly observed, "Orders from our Generals to respect rail fences, cornfields and orchards were a useless waste of thought and paper, simply because orders from our stomachs beat orders from our officers all to smash." Further, he rationalized, "...with us rank and file soldiers the world or prosperity would never know us, hence we were not very particular about our 'reps'. We knew that all we got out of the war would be what we got in it."[20]

The enlisted men had a reason to scoff at officers, in particular cavalry officers, who had earned reputations for hoarding the luxuries of the countryside for their personal use. Jeb Stuart and his officers in Urbana were living "high on the hog" while their enlisted men scrounged the countryside for food. Stuart's host, Mr. Cockey, whose attractive niece Anne Cockey was visiting from New York, invited the general and his party to dinner. The officers accepted.

They passed the afternoon singing and flirting with the genteel women of the village. Stuart, the unabashed womanizer, immediately started to concentrate on their host's New York relative, whose outspoken Southern sympathies earned her Stuart's sobriquet, "The New York Rebel."

After dark, under a very romantic full moon, the general suggested a promenade. According to etiquette, the ladies chose their partners and strolled down the village's main street in the direction of Hyattstown. They halted on the hilltop at the edge of town, at the eastern end of the tree lined lane which led back to an abandoned female academy. The two story, rectangular building sported a veranda on each floor. At his first glimpse of the stately building, Stuart exclaimed to Von Borcke, "Major, what a capital place for us to give a ball in honour of our arrival in Maryland! Don't you think we could manage it?"

His staff, who generally did not invoke his ire by disagreeing with him, unanimously endorsed his suggestion. Von Borcke immediately started making arrangements for the impromptu affair. He had to see to cards of invitation, lighting, decorations, and music.[21]

While Stuart made plans for his party, some of the officers and enlisted men of Louisiana's Washington Artillery had a celebration of their own. Lieutenant Owen and his foragers guzzled the whiskey and wine they had purchased in Frederick earlier that day, until they were thoroughly drunk. Years later, the lieutenant whimsically recalled that the champagne flowed like water. He and his cohorts bedded down in a stupor.[22]

In all likelihood they enjoyed their revelry some distance from army headquarters. General Thomas J. Jackson, who had not gone to morning service because his back hurt him too much, decided to go into Frederick for evening services in the local Presbyterian church, where Dr. John B. Ross, a friend of his, served as pastor. Shortly after dark he limped into an ambulance, and with Lieutenants J. G. Morrison and Henry Kyd Douglas as his escort, he rode toward Frederick. They had barely started before Jackson asked Lieutenant Douglas if he had gotten them a pass. When the young inspector general responded that he had not requested one because he did not feel the general and his party needed a pass, Jackson recited Lee's order concerning them, then sent Douglas back to Assistant Adjutant General E. F. Paxton to receive one.[23] Few enlisted men could fault Jackson for circumventing protocol or regulations.

That same day, the VI Corps, leading the rest of the Army of the Potomac, left Tenallytown between 4:00 P.M. and 6:00 P.M. on a northwesterly route toward Rockville. With all the regiments stripped down to light marching order, they covered a leisurely six miles in three and one half hours before settling down for the night.[24]

While they slept unmolested, so did the general whose name usually struck a fearful chord in Union veterans. The Presbyterian church in Frederick did not have an evening service; therefore, Lieutenant Douglas escorted General Jackson to the Reformed Church to hear a sermon from the lieutenant's old friend, Dr. J. M. Zacharias. Jackson dozed off shortly after the sermon began. Lieutenant Douglas musingly watched the general's brown felt hat drop from his lap onto the floor and his chin onto his chest in a very profound sleep. The nap lasted through the remainder of the service, including the closing prayer, in which the loyal Dr. Zacharias asked for God's blessing upon President Abraham Lincoln. The reverend wasted his patriotic gesture upon the general, who did not awaken until the church organ droned out a very low bass note at the end of the service.[25]

With the exception of an hour's halt south of Frederick, Colonel Thomas Munford's command, including Chew's Battery, had been in the saddle over fourteen hours since crossing the Potomac around midnight. As they left the outskirts of the city they watched the 38th North Carolina trying to demolish the big iron railroad bridge over the Monocacy River.[26] The infantrymen did not particularly care to destroy the structure, which simply amazed them. Many had never seen such an architectural masterpiece before. Private James W. Overcash (Company G, 6th North Carolina) admired the bridge so much that he described it in a letter to his father. It was "...the best RR bridge that I ever saw. There was no wood about it."[27]

Munford's troopers arrived in Urbana several hours later. Stiffened and sore, they limped into camp for the night, uninvited to and, unaware of Stuart's plan for a ball.[28] The brigade needed all the sleep it could get, because the general had a special assignment for it.

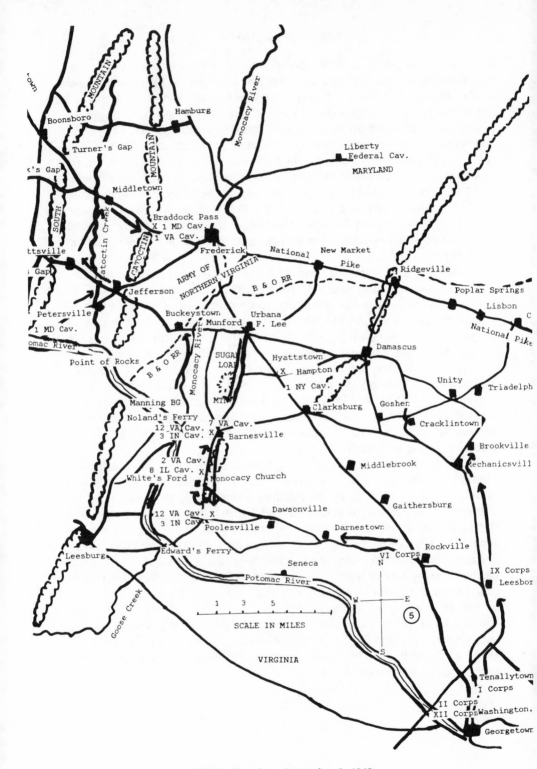

MAP 5: *Situation—September 8, 1862.*

Chapter Four

SEPTEMBER 8, 1862

THOMAS MUNFORD'S CAVALRY left Urbana during the early morning, under direct orders from General Stuart to drive the Federals from Poolesville.[1] Captain R. P. Chew's battery rolled along with the exhausted cavalrymen to provide fire support should they encounter the Yankees in force.[2] The 12th Virginia led the column, followed respectively by the 7th Virginia, Chew's guns, then the 2nd Virginia Cavalry.[3]

Colonel Munford boasted of his marksmen in the 2nd Virginia, "I had a great many mountaineers who could kill a running deer with their rifles or cut off a wild turkey's head and if well posted it was not safe for any man, especially an officer to come within range of their guns. It was a *cruel kind of fun,* but it was war, and they would *enjoy the practice.*"[4] He left them in Barnesville to cover his line of retreat, while the rest of the command moved south toward the Potomac.[5]

At the same time, General Alfred Pleasonton had sent his cavalry in a wide arc designed to protect the infantry, which was just north of Washington, and to observe any further Confederate movements into Maryland.[6] Colonel John Farnsworth, who commanded his own regiment, the 8th Illinois Cavalry, and the 3rd Indiana Cavalry, rode into Poolesville for the second time in as many days. The 3rd Indiana, which led the advance, stumbled into the point of the 12th Virginia Cavalry on the northern edge of the town and drove them toward the main body of their cavalry which was supporting Chew's Blakely gun and one howitzer from a hill about one mile to the north.[7]

Private George Neese (Chew's Battery) hurriedly rolled with his gun into position in front of the woods which crowned the hill on its northern side as the Federal cavalry maneuvered into column of fours. The two guns quickly loosed several rounds at the 3rd Indiana as its black hatted troopers drew their sabres to charge. One well placed shell scattered the Westerners, who retreated to the town.[8] First Lieutenant Robert Chapin (Company M, 2nd US Artillery) wheeled his two guns to within half a mile of Chew's Battery and returned fire from the low ground east of the Barnesville-Poolesville Road.[9] The accuracy of the Northern artillerists both amazed and frightened Chew's gunners. After the first two shots, their shells fell right into the Confederate battery. Private Neese could not explain the tremendous improvement in the Yankees' marksmanship since they left Virginia. He swore he had never seen such fine shooting before. He thought he would never leave the place alive.[10]

While Lieutenant Chapin checked the Confederate artillery with superior fire, the 3rd Indiana Cavalry executed a flanking movement to the east and north of Munford's position. While part of the regiment prepared to assault Munford's left from a hill on that flank, the rest of the command slipped farther north to cut off the Rebels' retreat along the Barnesville Road.[11] The counterstrike took Munford's command by surprise.

George Neese saw the large cavalry detachment, which seemed more like two or three regiments to him, sweeping toward the battery along the Barnesville Road.[12] Simultaneously, Sergeant Major James H. Figgatt, whose regiment, the 12th Virginia Cavalry, was protecting the battery from the northeast, glanced to his left only to find the rest of the 3rd Indiana swooping down the hill from that flank.[13]

Colonel Munford panicked. Galloping into Chew's section, he excitedly screamed at the captain, "Cut loose from your pieces!" Captain Chew very calmly refused to comply and countermanded the order by telling his men to stick by their guns.

Carbine and pistol fire suddenly cracked to the rear of the battery as the two Virginia cavalry regiments spurred into action. The 7th Cavalry, with drawn sabres, charged pell mell into the Yankees which pressed the command from the rear while Colonel Asher Harman (12th Virginia Cavalry) tried to wheel his eighty-three-man regiment to face the balance of the 3rd Indiana. A high stone wall temporarily thwarted what might have been a brilliant maneuver.

The Virginians held off the Union counterattack with their inferior sidearms while volunteers threw a section of the fence down to allow them to sortie against the Federals. A portion of the Westerners gave way while another section of them swept in behind the Confederates.[14] Cavalrymen in both uniforms swirled around the gun crews, who were nervously trying to limber up.[15]

The Virginians suffered severely in the melee. Before they could untangle, the 12th Cavalry lost eight men, two of whom were killed.[16] Captain Charles T. O'Ferrall (Company I) raised his pistol and squeezed the trigger in the face of a Yankee sergeant as the noncom brought his sabre down upon the captain. O'Ferrall's pistol misfired—the cap exploded but did not ignite the powder. The sergeant's sabre snapped the captain's right arm about three inches above the wrist. The cavalryman frantically tried to strike O'Ferrall from the saddle. As O'Ferrall dodged from one side to the other to keep from being wounded again, Sergeant Major Figgatt came to his rescue. Figgatt delivered a glancing but powerful sabre blow to the Yankee soldier's head and neck which unhorsed him and enabled O'Ferrall to escape.[17] Sergeant Samuel Morgan and Private John Colbert (both Company A) died near the guns.[18] Captain S. B. Myers, commanding the other cavalry regiment, lost two wounded before they cut their way out of the mess.[19]

The confused artillerists, in the huge cloud of dirt and dust which engulfed their position, could not sort out the combatants.[20] With the 7th Virginia slashing a path through the Union line, the equally befuddled Indianians wove between the moving limbers to escape and left the battery unmolested.[21] As the 3rd Indiana halted to regroup, the 12th Virginia pulled out to cover Chew's unprotected Blakely gun from the flank and rear.[22] The Northerners had taken a good drubbing themselves. Not counting Lieutenant Henry Wright (Company D, 3rd Indiana Cavalry), whose horse caught a round through the shoulder, they had sustained eleven casualties, one of which was mortal.[23] [Refer to Map 5]

The battered 12th Virginia wrapped around the flank and the rear of Chew's Battery and successfully held back the desultory counterstrike of the 8th Illinois Cavalry, which took the field after the 3rd Indiana retired from the fighting.[24] Company D of the 8th Illinois became entangled in a long range cavalry engagement with the sharpshooters of the 2nd Virginia, who had rushed from Barnesville. The Virginians drove the cautious Yankee cavalry back just before dark.[25]

Neither regiment suffered any loss during this fracas, damaged pride excepted. Colonel John Farnsworth boasted in his report that his troopers chased Munford's Southerners three miles to Monocacy Church before Confederate fire superiority and the darkness caused them to retire from the field.[26] Private Samuel Gilpin of the 3rd Indiana, who had become engaged in the ballyhoo around Chew's Battery, mistakenly scratched in his diary, "They [the Confederates] really outnumbered us greatly. Had they known our number, we might have been made."[27] According to George Neese of Chew's Battery, Munford's cavalry retired about one mile before preparing for a stand across the Urbana Road. The artillerists unlimbered, facing south, for an attack which never materialized.[28] The reported "spirited encounter" of the 8th Illinois occurred on paper but not in fact. Their only casualty, Charles Wilhelm, broke his collar bone when his horse stumbled and threw him. They returned to Poolesville before dark to report a "paper" victory.[29] [Refer to Map 5]

Thomas Munford's cavalrymen were not the only ones who found themselves in a difficult situation. The self-proclaimed "Captain" Edward S. Motter and fourteen troopers from the 1st Virginia Cavalry did not take kindly to the icy reception they received in Middletown. The adopted Virginians, most of whom came from Middletown Valley, including the captain, spent several hours at Samuel D. Riddlemoser's house on Main Street. Flaunting their military prowess, they loudly boasted they were hunting for Cole's Maryland Cavalry (U.S.A.). As they left the secessionist's home, the cavalrymen caught sight of an American flag flying from the second floor window sill of George W. Crouse's house.

The captain, with several of his soldiers, stormed up the steps, heading for the front porch. George Crouse's daughter, seventeen-year-old Nancy, with her friend, Effie Titlow, right behind her, darted out of the door into the path of the Confederates. Miss Crouse defiantly asked what they wanted.

"That damned Yankee rag," Edward Motter snarled as he tried to brush past her.

The young woman dashed into the house, ahead of the Rebel, fired a quick retort at him and raced upstairs. Ripping the flag from its staff, she draped it across herself and ran down to the open door, where she blocked the soldier's path with her body.

Motter ordered her to surrender "that damned Yankee rag." She adamantly refused.

Drawing his revolver, Motter cocked it, placed it against her temple, and threatened to kill her if she did not surrender the colors.

Relying upon the chivalry which officers were supposed to uphold, she boldy replied, "You may shoot me, but never will I willingly give up my country's flag into the hands of traitors."

With the muzzle against her temple, Motter again commanded Nancy to surrender the flag. Realizing that he would probably kill her, the young woman quite sensibly handed her colors over to the soldier. He tied it around his horse's head and mounting up, rode off with his comrades toward Frederick.

Shortly thereafter, Captain Charles H. Russell (Company I, 1st Maryland Cavalry) and his fifty man patrol operating on a swing from Harpers Ferry through the valley to Petersville, Jefferson, and Middletown, trotted into the town. Miss Crouse frantically directed the column toward Braddock Pass. The Yankees thundered a few miles east on the National Pike and, struggling up the steep road to the Pass, reached the summit. A few hundred yards east of the crest, south of the road, they spied a cluster of horses outside of John Hagan's Tavern.

Captain Russell ordered a charge. The Confederates heard them coming. Before the Yankees reached them, they mounted and the race was on. The chase ended one and one half miles from Frederick. In the bloodless melee, the intrepid Union soldiers nabbed fourteen of the Confederates and nine horses. Captain Motter escaped.

From his position on the city's outskirts, Russell could, with field glasses, get a safe view of the Confederate bivouacs. He saw few wagons and hardly any tents. Content with his catch for the day, which included John Hagan's son and two deserters from Company H of the 1st Maryland Cavalry—

Privates James Wheeler and Joshua Fluharty—he decided to ride back to Harpers Ferry.[30] [Refer to Map 5]

The rest of the Army of Northern Virginia awoke to a new day, alive with the prospects of justifiable plunder. The cold and relatively unpolluted Monocacy River cleared Lieutenant William Owen's (Washington Artillery) alcohol induced headache in minutes.[31] Many enlisted men, like Private John Shipp of the 6th Virginia, merely enjoyed having all of the water they could drink risk free.[32]

The well bred Private John Dooley (Company A, 1st Virginia) attempted to visit his former Jesuit professors at the Jesuit Novitiate on East Second Street. As he neared the rectory, Father Parece, S. J., met him just outside the front door and heartily welcomed him inside. The priest, who had only spoken one time to the young Confederate when he was a freshman at Georgetown before the war, amazed Dooley with his recall. The priests treated the grimy infantryman to a hot bath, with soap, fresh clothes, and, above all, a set of clean underwear. John Dooley had stepped into heaven on earth and he savored every second of it.[33]

Many foragers, had not heard or had disregarded Robert E. Lee's proclamation to the people of Maryland, which Colonel Charles Marshall of Baltimore had prepared for distribution that day. Colonel Bradley T. Johnson, who commanded the city's provost guard, read the order to the citizens of Frederick and jubilantly proclaimed:

> It is right that you should know the purpose that brought the Army under my command within the limits of your State, so far as that purpose concerns yourselves. The People of the Confederate States have long watched with the deepest sympathy the wrongs and outrages that have been inflicted upon the citizens of a Commonwealth, allied to the States of the South by the strongest social, political and commercial ties. They have seen with profound indignation their sister State deprived of every right, and reduced to the condition of a conquered Province. Under the pretense of supporting the Constitution, but in violation of its most valuable provisions, your citizens have been arrested and imprisoned upon no charge, and contrary to all forms of law; the faithful and manly protest against this outrage made by the venerable and illustrious Marylander, to whom in better days, no citizen appealed for right in vain, was treated with scorn and contempt; the government of your chief City has been usurped by armed strangers; your legislature has been dissolved by the unlawful arrest of its members; freedom of the press and of speech has been suppressed; words have been declared offenses by an arbitrary decree of the Federal Executive, and citizens ordered to be tried by military commission for what they dare to speak. Believing that the People of Maryland possessed a spirit too lofty to submit to such a government, the people of the South have long wished to aid you in throwing off this foreign yoke, to enable you to again enjoy the inalienable rights of freemen, and restore independence and sovereignty to your State. In obedience to this wish, our Army has come among you, and is prepared to assist you with the power of its arms in regaining the rights of which you have been despoiled. This, Citizens of Maryland, is our mission, so far as you are concerned. No constraint upon your free will is intended, no intimidation will be allowed. Within the limits of this Army, at least, Marylanders shall once more enjoy their

ancient freedom of thought and speech. We know no enemies among you, and will protect all of every opinion. It is for you to decide your destiny, freely and without constraint. This army will respect your choice whatever it may be, and while the Southern people will rejoice to welcome you to your natural position among them, they will only welcome you when you come of your own free will.

Robert E. Lee, General Commanding[34]

Further, Bradley Johnson added, "Let each man provide himself with a stout pair of shoes, a good blanket, and a tin cup. Jackson's men have no baggage."

They did not have much else either. Dr. Lewis H. Steiner of the United States Sanitary Commission, having listened to the Colonel's boast, quietly wrote in his diary, "If ever suicide were contemplated by any one, it must be by those civilians who proposed to attach themselves to Jackson's corps."[35]

The Confederates' seasoned appearance had a negative effect upon their potential volunteers. "Oh! They are so dirty!" a respectable Frederick woman wrote. "I don't think the Potomac River could wash them clean; and ragged! there is not a scarecrow in the fields that would not scorn to exchange clothes with them.... I saw some strikingly handsome faces though; or rather they would have been so if they could have had a good scrubbing."[36]

An anonymous informant for the New York *Times* described the Confederates more graphically when asked whether the Army of Northern Virginia recruited many men in Frederick:

> Not many in Frederick, but about five hundred came in from Baltimore, Anne Arundel, Montgomery and Carroll Counties, and some from Baltimore City. After seeing the character of the army and the life which the men lead, many of them refused to join, and were getting home again.... They acknowledged that they had been to Frederick, but after seeing and smelling it, had concluded to return home.... I have never seen a mass of such filthy, strong-smelling men. Three of them in a room would make it unbearable, and when marching in column along the street the smell of them was most offensive.... Their sympathizers at Frederick have been greatly disappointed in the character of the army, and most of them are now as anxious for them to disappear as they were for them to come.[37]

Doctor Charles Goldsborough and the other doctors at the Hessian Barracks admired the discipline of the Confederate infantry. Despite their wretched appearances, the harsh discipline, and their general state of fatigue, he respected the line soldiers.[38]

The lack of recruits did not diminish the Confederates' love for Maryland's rich fields nor did it deter them from pursuing other military objectives in conjunction with aggressive foraging. Throughout the day, the engineers and assorted volunteers from different infantry commands drilled blasting holes into the stone piers which supported the railroad bridge over the Monocacy, south of the city. Some of the men, particularly the soldiers of the 4th Texas, seemed to enjoy the demolition work. Their chaplain, the Reverend Nicholas A. Davis, reveled in the thought that it "...must have cost [the Marylanders] thousands of dollars."[39]

The thunder of the occasional blasting annoyed others, because it disturbed the tranquility of their day. Private William A. McClendon (Company G,
15th Alabama) enjoyed the warm pleasant weather and the carefree atmosphere too much to pay any particular attention to anything else. "We did
not know and cared less about what the enemy was doing," he later wrote.
"We only knew we were near Washington City...."[40] Even General John Hood's
hard working Texans knocked off their hammering and drilling to periodically
raid chicken coops and barnyards for food.[41]

While the Army of Northern Virginia stripped Frederick of poultry, Jeb
Stuart's staff officers in Urbana spent the day preparing the deserted female
academy for their gala affair. Von Borcke sent hand written invitations to the
local gentry while enlisted men swept and aired out the dusty building. By
evening bouquets of roses and the battle flags from Brigadier General William
Barksdale's brigade (13th, 17th, 18th, and 21st Mississippi), decorated the walls
of the main hall like those of an ancient manor. Stuart and his officers, with
their ladies on their arms, stepped out to "Dixie" behind Colonel William H.
Leese (18th Mississippi), his staff, and the 18th Mississippi's excellent band.
They entered the hall amidst applause. The tallow candles which illuminated
the hall cast a romantic glow about the building.[42]

While they prepared to dance, Colonel Van H. Manning's fatigued brigade
(27th, 46th, 48th North Carolina, and 30th Virginia), minus the 3rd Arkansas,
which was on provost duty near Monocacy Junction, dragged itself into
Buckeystown. Having spent the better part of the day en route from the
Potomac, they needed their rest.[43]

Simultaneously, the 17th Virginia (Kemper's brigade) caught up with the
rest of its brigade around Monocacy Junction.[44] After three days the Army
of Northern Virginia finally was pulling itself together for a deeper drive into
Maryland.

Meanwhile, the Army of the Potomac lurched northeasterly toward
Frederick but at a pace which defied logic. The VI Corps started marching
at 7:00 A.M., moved a leisurely three to six miles and bivouacked about one
mile or so beyond Rockville. Several hours later, around 6:00 P.M., the corps
moved forward again and camped about four miles below Darnestown. In
all, the soldiers covered about eight miles that day.[45]

The IX Corps did not move until 6:00 P.M. It also trudged eight miles
throughout the night toward Brookville, where it arrived around 1:00 A.M.
the next day.[46] Cavalry videttes fanned out across the B & O Railroad and
picketed the area around Franklinville and Liberty, effectively cutting the
Army of Northern Virginia off from Baltimore.[47]

The Maryland countryside left an indelible impression upon Private
William Baker (Company D, 1st Maine Cavalry). His squad spent the early part
of the day scouting for a "lost" squad of cavalry, which they found. He was
more than willing to return to camp for the evening in Brookville.

"There is a small collection of houses and a few stores, just enough to
give the place a name," he later informed his mother. "Why out in Virginia

if there is two houses, a few Negro huts, a pig pen, and a stack of hay they call it a village and consider it quite a place. We are once more on Union soil and among friends, and I assure you it seems good to march through a country which has not been made desolate by war. Then the smiling faces which greet us as we pursue our wearisome, dusty march reminds one of home...."[48]

The smiling faces of the young ladies of Urbana must have reminded the Confederate officers at Stuart's ball of home too. As the officers and their companions entered the dancing area, each man unsnapped his sabre and leaned it against the wall.[49]

Von Borcke, having assumed the duty of Master of Ceremonies, selected a polka to open the affair, and boldly proclaimed Miss Anne Cockey, the "Queen of the Ball." As he stepped forward with outstretched arms to sweep her away, she deliberately eluded him and quickly informed him that she did not dance round dances.

A fellow officer advised the Prussian that in the United States, particularly in the South, respectable young ladies occasionally waltzed and then only with their brothers or first cousins. Etiquette further required them to reserve reels and other such dances for strangers. The quick thinking Von Borcke immediately ordered the band to strike up a quadrille.[50] Within minutes, the ladies proclaimed the party a complete success.[51]

While the Confederate cavalry staff danced at an event which inspired romantic memories, Major Alonzo W. Adams led five companies of the 1st New York Cavalry on a reconnaissance toward Hyattstown. Approaching from the southeast along the Clarksburg Road, the Yankee cavalry halted on the hill south of the valley in which the village lay.

Halting on the crest, Major Adams dramatically pointed his sabre toward Wade Hampton's few videttes, who occupied the town. He called out, "Boys, I am going to drive those rebels out of that place, will you follow me?"

The New Yorkers responded with a cheer. Starting at a trot, they broke into a gallop as they reached the edge of Hyattstown. Screaming like Indians, they shot or rode down several of the Confederates. Sergeant Roland Ellis personally brought in two fully equipped and mounted privates.[52] Moments before his capture, the Confederate officer who commanded the detachment dispatched a courier to Urbana.

Content with their victory, Adams' New Yorkers reined to an abrupt halt before rounding the curve northwest of the town. They retired back to Hyattstown. The major sent a few pickets from Company B to the top of the hill with instructions to patrol the road where it passed between a thick cornfield on the western side and a dense woods, on the eastern flank.[53] Sergeant Abraham Westbrook, and Privates Bartholomew Besley, John R. Burd, and Henry C. Wilson (all Company B), while riding to the hilltop on the Urbana Road, just north of Hyattstown, spooked Wade Hampton's exhausted outpost again.[54]

At the same time, the dust covered orderly raced the four miles to Stuart's headquarters. Dismounting in the yard of the female academy, he clattered into the main hall and loudly blurted the alarm. Small arms fire, echoing loudly into the hall, punctuated his report. The band crashed to a halt.

For a few minutes pandemonium dominated the ball as officers rushed to their weapons and yelled for their horses. The mothers called for their children.

Jeb Stuart and his staff calmly mounted and galloped to the front.[55] As they rode away, Captain Blackford tried to allay the women's fears. They need not leave, he assured them. It was only a night attack on a picket post—nothing serious.[56]

Around 9:00 P.M., Sergeant William H. Beach (Company B, 1st New York Cavalry) and his small detachment quietly rode down the Urbana Road into the southern side of Hyattstown to relieve Sergeant Westbrook and his scouts. Rapid hoofbeats approaching from the north brought the column to a halt as Private Henry C. Wilson (Company B) clattered up to the sergeant. He was hatless and his voice trembled with excitement. He had used all his ammunition in a hot firefight. The Confederates were hiding in the cornfield at the top of the road on the left and Beach and the squad had better not go up there. Wilson insisted that they would be ambushed at close range. Sergeant Westbrook and Privates Besley and Burd were trapped in the shade of the woods opposite the cornfield.

Sergeant Beach, knowing that Wilson was a very reliable man, heeded the private's advice despite the fact that he had not heard any shooting. As the column started to ascend the hill north of the town, he carefully noted how the moon cast a dark shadow from the trees on the right almost to the middle of the road. He ordered his troopers to file into the dark and to proceed with caution.

Beach stayed in the road, trying to draw fire. Half way up the hill, Confederate skirmishers opened fire upon him from behind the high rail fence which bordered the cornfield. No less than twelve rifle balls zinged past the sergeant's head. Not waiting for the enemy to reload, he, his squad and the three other men put spurs to their horses and bolted west. Their mounts instinctively nosed the top rails off the fence along the opposite side of the road, and jumped it into the woods. There was no sense taking on infantry.[57]

By the time Stuart arrived with Captain John Pelham's horse artillery, Colonel Laurence S. Baker and his 1st North Carolina Cavalry had secured the area. Nevertheless, the general, after placing Pelham in battery, formed the rest of the brigade in line, and charged the New Yorkers, who, having no artillery, retired beyond range. Throughout the evening, Confederate skirmishers and their artillery harassed the Federal position from the hill north of the town.[58]

Stuart and his officers left their subordinates to hold the Northerners in check while they rode back toward Urbana to resume the party. The fact that it was close to midnight did not alter the general's plans for a good time.[59]

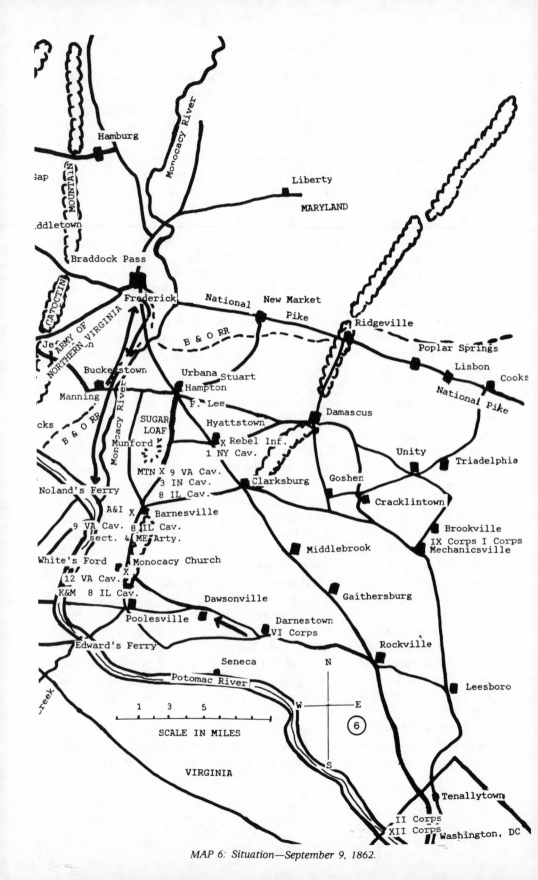

MAP 6: *Situation—September 9, 1862.*

Chapter Five

SEPTEMBER 9, 1862

STUART AND HIS CAVALIERS, except for Pelham's battery, returned to the female academy in Urbana some time between midnight and 1:00 A.M.[1] The general immediately reassured the anxious civilians who were still clustered about the place that his troops had everything under control. Ordering the band to strike up some lively dance melody, he dispatched his junior staff officers to round up the young ladies who were no longer present, and within half an hour, the hall became a scene of great merriment. The dancing continued until just before dawn.[2]

Captain Blackford, who had stolen the attractive Miss Cockey away from the fumbling Von Borcke when the dancing resumed, positioned himself by the main entrance to the hall with the young belle by his side. They had not been there long when the tramp of heavy boots distracted Anne Cockey's attention away from him. Clasping her hands together in front of her, she screamed. The startled dancers gathered about the door.

Ambulance crews were carrying casualties from the Hyattstown skirmish into the upper rooms of the academy. The ladies hurried to assist the few wounded, staining their white dresses with the soldiers' blood.[3] Von Borcke and Blackford escorted the distraught "New York Rebel" into the fresh air. In one of the ambulances they found a boy whose tunic was saturated with blood from a shoulder wound. Miss Cockey, while valiantly attempting to staunch the blood flow, fainted in front of the two officers. They abandoned the injured soldier for a minute or two to tenderly revive the young lady. They futilely tried to talk her into going home.

"I must do my duty first," she weakly insisted before she returned to the young soldier's side.[4] The casualties, though few, and not too serious, successfully monopolized the ladies' attention. For a brief time they had deprived their officers of "quality" companionship. The wounded Rebel under Anne Cockey's care cried like a child and piteously begged her to tend to him personally, exclusive of everyone else. With a pained smile, he volunteered to get shot any day to be treated by such surgeons as he had that morning.[5]

While Stuart's officers lost their ladies to enlisted men, Major General Lafayette McLaws' Confederates in Frederick began to stir in hopes of finding breakfast. Many of them were quite content to scrounge from the nearby farms and to drink the fresh water. Private Alfred N. Proffitt (Company D, 18th North Carolina) bragged to his brother, "We are encamped on a steep hillside without tents.... We have plenty to eat and good water. The prospect of health is good.... I am now in Maryland and enjoying myself finely...and not much to do.... I haven't taken off my clothes since I left home and it will take some scrubbing to get them clean. I wished you had the chance to wash them for me."[6]

A large number of men, among them Corporal William W. Sherwood (Company F, 17th Virginia), took advantage of the bright, warm day. He wrote in his diary, "myself and Some more of us went to the [Monocacy] river and had a fine bath. we then Came back and laid about in the Shade."[7]

Many curious civilians decided to use the quiet day as an excuse to descend upon the Headquarters of the Army of Northern Virginia. Late in the morning, Katherine S. Markall, her friends Jennie Myers, Alice Lanahan, Fannie Ebert, Annie Fout, and a gentleman friend, whom Miss Markall referred to as Bob, escorted Mrs. Douglas, the mother of Thomas J. Jackson's assistant inspector general, Henry Kyd Douglas, into camp to visit her son at Army Headquarters. They met Longstreet first and gave him a bouquet of flowers as a remembrance. Mrs. Douglas also wrangled an interview with the taciturn Jackson, who invited her to stay overnight and prolong her visit with her son. She declined. Douglas refused to disturb Lee for his mother.

Lee overheard the lieutenant. Stepping outside his tent, he apologized for the officer's bad manners with a mock reprimand then graciously added, when out of earshot of her son, "but, Mrs. Douglas, it is the only time I ever knew your son to fail in the performance of his duty, as General Jackson can testify." The women in the group insisted upon shaking Lee's hands, both of which were bandaged to the finger tips.

"Touch them gently, ladies," he politely warned them. They did.

Having accomplished what she desired, Mrs. Douglas decided to return to Ferry Hill, near Shepherdstown, Virginia. Henry Douglas, Jackson's devoted aide, deeply appreciated the kindnesses shown his mother. He also astutely noted how each of the generals behaved himself. While Lee and Jackson stayed in their tents most of the time, Longstreet affably received guests throughout the day.[8]

Many of the Confederates, however, realized they had overstayed their welcome in Maryland. When William Johnson of the 2nd South Carolina and his comrade arose and donned their tunics that morning their friends descended upon them like locusts and quickly divided the booty which the pair had brought back from Frederick the previous evening. Just as quickly they pulled the story of an inhospitable Northern girl and her free servant out of Johnson. Her well dressed black maid had left an indelible impression upon them. Johnson's friend abusively expressed their shock at the liberated Maryland attitude toward the race which this particular group of South Carolinians thought to be socially and morally inferior. The soldiers around him heartily agreed with his remarks. In their minds, Maryland was no place for a decent white man.[9]

In the meantime, General Alfred Pleasonton's Federal cavalry began to harass Wade Hampton's men at Hyattstown, Colonel Thomas Munford's rear guard at Monocacy Church, and Captain Thomas C. Waller's detachment of the 9th Virginia Cavalry in the Barnesville area.[10] The second battalion of the 1st New York Cavalry, under Major Alonzo Adams, charged into Hyattstown once again, where it overran a slow moving squad of Confederate infantry. (The New Yorkers lost one man and one horse in the fight—both severely wounded.)[11] [Refer to Map 6]

At the same time, the 12th Virginia secured the crossroads at Monocacy Church while the rest of the brigade fell back toward Sugar Loaf Mountain. Waller's squadron (Companies A and I) of the 9th Virginia Cavalry picketed Barnesville and the approach road to the eastern base of the mountain.[12]

Once again, the 8th Illinois Cavalry, supported by the 3rd Indiana Cavalry and Captain O'Neil Robinson's 4th Maine Battery (both on its right flank), sallied north of Poolesville to probe the Confederate positions.[13] The regiment spread out in reverse order, with Company A on the extreme left, near the Potomac, Company K near the Poolesville Road in the center, and Company B on the extreme right along the Barnesville-Gaithersburg Road.[14] Two miles north of Poolesville, Captain Elon J. Farnsworth's squadrons (Companies K and M) charged the 12th Virginia Cavalry, which picketed the road below Monocacy Church. Caught by surprise, Colonel Asher Harman ordered his outgunned regiment to wheel into line to meet the Federals head on. A huge cloud of dirt obscured the attacking troops from view. Sergeant Major James Figgatt (12th Virginia) recalled seeing only dust as the regiment, with drawn pistols and bared sabres, slammed into the two companies of the 8th Illinois. The melee abruptly ended several minutes later when Yankee bullets toppled one of the Virginian's mounts in the road. As the two forces attempted to untangle, several riders and horses stumbled over that dead horse, including Captain John Ford (Company C, 12th Virginia), who went down with a leg wound. The regimental guidon also disappeared in the pile up. In the confusion, most of the regiment escaped to the woods northeast of the crossroads, leaving the Federals in control of the field.

The Illinois cavalrymen snatched up the fallen Confederate guidon and gathered in their captives. They brought in one captain and seven enlisted men, one of whom was mortally wounded. They left one Confederate fatality upon the field, while suffering no losses themselves.[15]

As the Union soldiers regrouped, the 12th Virginia Cavalry slipped away toward Sugar Loaf Mountain, leaving Captain Thomas Waller of the 9th Virginia Cavalry to hold Barnesville against the right wing of the 8th Illinois. Captain Elisha S. Kelley's squadron (Companies B and E) furiously struck Waller's squadron (Companies A and I) just southeast of Barnesville. Corporal George M. Roe's mount, "Lamkins Billy," bolted uncontrollably into the town and through a group of four startled Confederate troopers, who had gathered in the street to oppose the Federal advance. Roe, with his pistol drawn, managed to wheel his frenzied horse about behind the Rebels, who had turned around to pursue him. The corporal brazenly ordered the four men to surrender. One of them reached for his service revolver. A bullet through the Reb's mouth dropped him dead in the road and the corporal nervously held the other three at bay for about five minutes until Captain Kelley and the rest of the squadron came up to relieve him.[16]

The Federals pushed the Confederates about two miles north of Barnesville. The fleeing Virginians halted twice to return fire but to no avail. During one of the two halts, Captain Kelley (Company E, 8th Illinois) rode down Lieutenant Cassius Williams (Company A, 9th Virginia). With his revolver drawn, Kelley boldly trotted up to the Virginian, who was snapping off rounds at the Federals swarming around him, and told him to give up. Williams refused to do so, aimed at Kelley, but did not fire quickly enough. Kelley shot Williams through the body, and he toppled to the ground with a perforated liver and abdomen.[17]

The chase continued as far as the eastern base of Sugar Loaf, where Waller and his Virginians, reinforced by the rest of the 9th Virginia Cavalry, which had just arrived from New Market, turned and pushed the two Federal companies back to Barnesville.[18] They ran into the rest of the 8th Illinois Cavalry, a couple of companies of the 3rd Indiana Cavalry and a section of Robinson's battery (4th Maine). Once again, Companies B and E of the 8th Illinois Cavalry deployed into the open ground northeast of the town as skirmishers. As they cautiously advanced, mounted, against the Virginians, the artillerists fired two rounds over their heads. The first one fell in the middle of the 9th Virginia and scattered them like quail; the second, however, dropped short and ripped off the nose of Private Solomon Jewell's (Company E) horse. Content with having fought the good fight, both sides settled down to observe each others positions for the balance of the day.[19]

Once again, the Confederate cavalry lost not only ground, but men and horses, neither of which they could spare. In addition to mortally wounding Lieutenant Williams, the Yankee troopers inflicted twenty-four more casualties—five wounded and nineteen captured—in the brief engagement.[20] Samuel Gilpin of the 3rd Indiana Cavalry, was not actively engaged in the skirmishing, but wrote, "We have taken thirty or forty prisoners, one of them a Hoosier lieutenant. I believe there was none killed of our party."[21]

For once, during the war in the East, it seemed as though the Federals were gaining the upper hand; General Alfred Pleasonton, commanding the

Army of the Potomac's cavalry division, mentioned every little skirmish in his report and meticulously kept a body count, the standard by which the armies gauged their victories. In his official report, the general bragged "...we lost not a man or a horse."[22] He overlooked Solomon Jewell's mutilated horse.

While the rear guard was fighting for its survival around Sugar Loaf Mountain, General Jeb Stuart, Major Heros Von Borcke, and Captain William W. Blackford and the rest of the Confederate cavalry staff planned to spend the rest of the day at Mr. Cockey's estate in Urbana. They slept late that morning and had to rush the regimental flags back to their respective infantry commands. Stuart ordered Von Borcke, whom he persistently treated rather condescendingly, to see to that task immediately, because the regimental commanders wanted their standards returned without any further delay. Stuart then rode to Frederick to briefly hang about headquarters, where he flirted with Miss Katherine Markall and her friends.

To complicate matters, the village doctor issued a formal luncheon invitation to the general and his Prussian aide. The general looked forward to an afternoon of cigars and civil conversation, during which time he intended to tease Von Borcke about his thick Teutonic accent and his halting English.[23]

Farther to the south, starting about 9:00 A.M., the Federal VI Corps inched its way forward from Darnestown, proceeding very cautiously behind its cavalry screen. The men rather enjoyed the leisurely four- to six-mile walk.[24] It took them the better part of the day—about six hours—to reach Dawsonville. They spent two of the six hours resting in a large woods just northwest of Darnestown, where Bartlett's brigade (5th Maine, 16th, 27th, and 121st New York, and 96th Pennsylvania) formed in line of battle and advanced in a demonstration of force against Confederate forces which turned out to be non-existent.[25]

The soldiers meticulously took stock of every farm they passed. John Conline (Company E, 4th Vermont) fell in love with the well maintained fields and fences, which the Confederates left unmolested. The comfortable looking farm houses, generally surrounded by large trees, left him with a pastoral impression of Maryland which he never forgot.[26] Fences were there to be burned and crops to be harvested without any genuine fear of reprimand or reprisal. The further the Federal Army got into Maryland, the more ravenous it became. Experienced officers like Captain Jacob Haas (Company G, 96th Pennsylvania) allowed their "boys" that afternoon to "get lots of corn and potatoes" from a large cornfield near Dawsonville, while he, following a bath and a change of clothes, invited himself to supper at a nearby farm house.[27] Perceiving himself as the liberator of Maryland from the Southern scourge, the average rank and file Federal soldier believed he had the right to help himself freely to whatever he wanted within the State as a token of gratitude in payment for his devotion to the Union.[28]

Private William B. Baker of the 1st Maine Cavalry, serving with the IX Corps, discussed the matter more honestly. In a letter to his mother, he wrote, "...you would be surprised to see how quick, after halting we get up a lunch.

In half an hour the boys will make fires, cook apples, make coffee, and fry pork.... Green corn has been very plenty where we have marched and we have helped ourselves freely. It comes rather hard for some of the boys to pass nice orchards well ladden with fruit and cornfields without just walking in and being quite free but they have come to know we are among friends."[29]

At least one IX Corps' division commander attempted to stop the wanton looting of the Maryland countryside. Shortly after 6:00 A.M., on the heels of his Second Division, which had just left Leesboro, en route to Brookville, Brigadier General Samuel Sturgis issued an order holding all company captains under his circle of authority responsible for any pillaging done by the enlisted men.

"[They] ware not allowed to go into aney Fruit or other gardains," Captain James Wren (Company B, 48th Pennsylvania) complained after he received the directive some three and one half hours later.

Sturgis personally enforced his order by trooping the division column shortly after it reached Wren's brigade.[30] A general out of sight was a general out of mind, however, and once he was gone, the soldiers helped themselves to the bountiful fields of Maryland undisturbed.

The newly arrived recruits of the 35th Massachusetts, which had joined its brigade the day before, had all learned the fine art of foraging. An unidentified member of the regiment with typical New England understatement later bragged, "We began to understand the saying, that an army moves upon its stomach."[31]

For many of the Federals, their gluttony had disastrous after effects which literally left many of them writhing on the ground. Private William A. Roberts (Company K, 45th Pennsylvania) recalled how his comrades, because their allegedly rapid marches had put them too far ahead of their provision train, liberally raided cornfields, orchards, and potato patches to fill their empty stomachs. While still on the "quick march," they fell out for a few moments to start small fires over which they quickly roasted the outside of the corn. Leaving the inside of the kernels cold and raw and the outside crisped, they faithfully fell back into formation and ate their meals on the march. The only quick marching the IX Corps did that day came from the resultant cramps and diarrhea from their "green" provisions. Roberts very discretely alluded to their misfortune when he wrote, "One can imagine the effect of such food on an empty stomach."[32]

The IX Corps covered itself with more dust than glory. The regiments, depending upon their position in the column, marched eight to twelve miles that day in about ten hours, hardly indicative of a forced march.[33] The corps, with the exception of the Kanawha Division, veterans of the Western Virginia campaign, had spent most of its time in North Carolina on garrison duty. It had not, for the most part, become hardened to excessive marching except on the parade ground.[34] Of the twenty-three regiments in its first three divisions, excluding the Kanawha Division which had seen some action in Western Virginia in 1861, at least six of the regiments (17th Michigan, 45th and 100th Pennsylvania, 9th New Hampshire, 35th Massachusetts, and 16th Connecticut) had never been in combat at all and had just recently joined their respective brigades.[35]

Chroniclers of the march through Maryland complained about the dust and the heat, which at the end of the column became increasingly intolerable and suffocating.[36] Typical of an army which was traveling in friendly territory, the column lurched and stalled to regroup or reroute itself. One of the men in the 35th Massachusetts groused that the untried civilian could not appreciate the discomfort of marching with bruised feet in a closed column alongside of a road which was occupied by slowly rolling wagons or artillery and which was flanked on the far side by another wheezing column of infantry.[37]

Blatant straggling plagued the IX Corps as much as it did the rest of the Army of the Potomac, and in some cases, the liberal cordiality of the Marylanders along the route encouraged it. Men worked the fields as if there were no war. Women and children leaned in doorways or out of windows to cheer the men onward.[38] Civilians met the passing soldiers at the gates to their yards and farm lanes to hand out lemonade, cakes, pies, bread, liquors, and fruit, many of which later proved debilitating.[39] Regiments, fragmented and scattered, further delaying advances.[40] Others, like the 30th Ohio (Kanawha Division) merely waited their turn at Leesboro and did not get under way until 3:00 P.M.[41]

All things considered, the IX Corps did as well as could be expected under the circumstances, which in its case were far from desirable. Lieutenant Matthew J. Graham (Company F, 9th New York) noticed, "Thousands went plodding along the road apparently entirely uncontrolled." He tried to preserve the honor of the IX Corps by concluding, "the disorganized ones were judged to have been portions of Pope's command, which had not yet recovered from the demoralization [which was] the result of the severe campaign [Second Manassas] through which they had just passed."

He praised his colonel, Edgar A. Kimball, for not allowing the 9th New York to become "contaminated by this loose example." A heavy guard was posted every morning and throughout the day to keep the 9th in formation. No one was allowed to fall out unless ordered to ride in an ambulance by one of the surgeons. Consequently, at least until after it reached Frederick, the regiment lost no one to straggling.[42]

Back in Urbana, where Stuart and his staff enjoyed hospitable conversation and fine cigars with the village doctor upon his veranda, a fourteen-year-old vagabond Indian boy entertained them with his tame squirrel. At one point, the boy tried to sell Von Borcke the animal. He almost convinced the major to take him along as a "servant." Stuart, a veteran of Plains warfare, advised the Prussian against such a move. Indians, the general stated, as a whole were incorrigible thieves, and the boy would make a very poor servant.[43] The war seemed so very far away.

Late in the afternoon, the staff heard the rumbling of artillery in the direction of Sugar Loaf Mountain and just before dark, a report came in from General Fitzhugh Lee's brigade (1st, 3rd, 4th, 5th, and 9th Virginia Cavalry) about the brisk skirmish near Barnesville. Not ones to be disconcerted over a minor scrape, this time, Stuart and his coterie moved from the doctor's residence to Mr. Cockey's, where, in exchange for a serenade performed by the general and company, they spent the evening, surrounded by fair ladies and genteel people.[44]

What he heard was the 4th Maine Artillery trying to quiet the bothersome Rebel skirmishers of Thomas Munford's and Fitzhugh Lee's brigades who were harassing the Federal troopers around Barnesville.[45] In one instance, a Confederate cavalryman attempted to ride down Private S. S. Boon (Company B) of the 8th Illinois Cavalry, who was on picket alone. Boon killed him and triumphantly rode into camp with the man's saddled horse.[46]

At Hyattstown, dismounted North Carolinian troopers slipped along the fence rows bordering the Hyattstown-Urbana Road to snipe at the pickets from the 1st New York Cavalry at long range. John Pelham's Virginia horse artillery occasionally sent a harmless round hurtling their way causing, as Sergeant William Beach (Company B, 1st New York Cavalry) said, an "annoyance."[47]

An annoyance was, perhaps, the best way to describe the Maryland Campaign for those who had been engaged in its little scraps and skirmishes. Men were not getting killed wholesale, but piecemeal. Individuals were lost in seemingly senseless engagements.

After dark, Colonel Van Manning's brigade (3rd Arkansas, 27th, 46th, and 48th North Carolina, and the 30th Virginia) started south with its division along the Monocacy River toward the aqueduct which it was supposed to demolish. (Their day had not begun well. Very shortly before they entered Frederick that morning, around 10:00 A.M., they had a run in with a Federal cavalry patrol which cost Company B of the 27th North Carolina two men, captured.)[48] As it arrived at the aqueduct some twelve hours later, the division came under fire from a handful of pickets from the Potomac Home Brigade (Maryland), who seriously wounded Captain G. T. Duffy (Company B, 24th North Carolina) in the spine, before the Yankees escaped. Much to the division commander's rue (Brigadier General John G. Walker), the masonry work on the aqueduct proved too solid to tear apart with the tools which they had at their disposal.

"...it was found to be virtually a solid mass of granite. Not a seam or crevice could be discovered in which to insert the point of a crow-bar," Walker complained. His men had marched more than thirteen miles to accomplish nothing. Turning his command about, he marched them back in the dark toward Buckeystown. They bivouacked about two and a half miles west of the Monocacy.[49]

The viciousness of the skirmish around Sugar Loaf gnawed at Elisha Kelley's conscience. Sometime before evening, the Illinois officer visited the mortally wounded Lieutenant Cassius Williams of the 9th Virginia Cavalry. Finding him in a farmhouse near Barnesville, Kelley apologized to Williams for shooting him. Cassius Williams politely, but matter-of-factly, answered, "I refused to surrender, and I would have shot you if I could have fired first."[50]

In retrospect, the lieutenant had stripped their war of all illusions. They knew that the struggle in Maryland was going to be one to the death or to exhaustion, whichever came first.

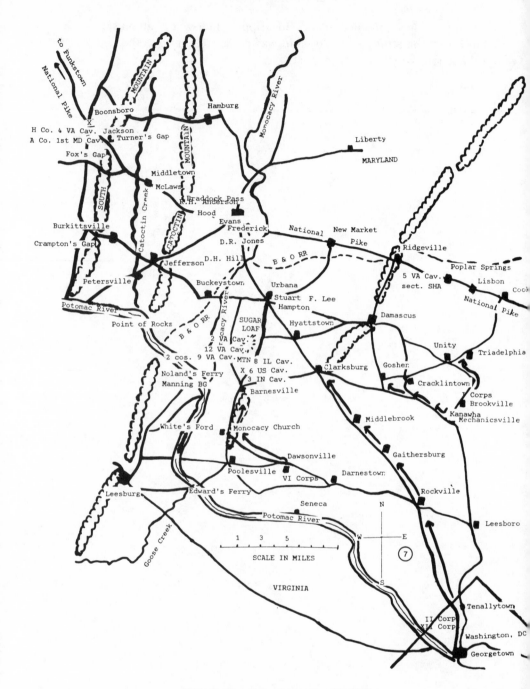

MAP 7: Situation—September 10, 1862.

Chapter Six

SEPTEMBER 10, 1862

THE CAVALRY SKIRMISHING around the southern perimeter of Sugar Loaf Mountain, which had started during the late afternoon of the previous evening, continued into the morning hours. It prompted Colonel John Farnsworth, commanding the 8th Illinois Cavalry and the 3rd Indiana Cavalry to request reinforcements from General Alfred Pleasonton.[1] Upon receipt of the order, he dispatched Captain William P. Saunders with his 6th U.S. Cavalry to dislodge what he believed was a numerically superior force from the wooded slopes of the mountain.[2]

With Fitzhugh Lee's mounted brigade in support, Thomas Munford's dismounted troopers, without the 7th Virginia Cavalry, which had been pulled out early that morning with orders to report to Stonewall Jackson, put up a determined resistance despite their inferior numbers. The tenacious Munford curtly brushed the affair aside as "Sharp Skirmishing."[3]

Lieutenant Colonel Richard L. T. Beale (9th Virginia Cavalry), who estimated the Confederates were outgunned three to one, nervously watched Colonel William H. F. "Rooney" Lee, his commanding officer, post Captain Oscar M. Knight's squadron as dismounted skirmishers on the regiment's flanks. The colonel, whose cousin commanded the brigade, carefully deployed the two companies behind logs and trees while the remainder of the regiment stayed mounted. Lee had chosen Knight's squadron for the detail because his two companies were the only ones armed with carbines. When Knight saw the superior Federal forces on the low ground in front of him, he realized his post of honor could very well become his final one. He suddenly became more aware of his bad leg and decided, at the first opportunity, to excuse himself from the field.[4]

Back in Urbana, Jeb Stuart and the division's staff calmly received the news of the Federal pressure at Sugar Loaf Mountain. Brushing it aside as "a sharp but unimportant skirmish," they spent the day resting.[5] Munford and Knight, knowing very well that they were all that stood between the Army of the Potomac and Robert E. Lee's columns at Frederick, did not consider it an "unimportant skirmish."[6]

Unknown to any of the forces struggling for the mountain and the Confederate signal station at the top of it, Robert E. Lee had issued Special Orders No. 191. Lee intended to capture Harpers Ferry and defend the passes along South Mountain. The Army of Northern Virginia was leaving Frederick and heading west. Major General A. P. Hill's division broke camp before sunrise and by 3:00 A.M. it was marching north toward Frederick.[7] Brigadier General Alexander R. Lawton's division started after him, followed by Brigadier General John R. Jones' division, the wagon trains, and the Reserve Artillery.[8]

Jackson and his staff reached the intersection of Market and Patrick Streets in Frederick about sunrise, well ahead of his corps, only to find them alive with curious civilians. The general shocked his assistant inspector general, Henry Kyd Douglas, when he publicly asked his corps engineer for a map of Chambersburg, Pennsylvania. He further enquired of several of the people who surrounded him if they could provide him with strategic information concerning distances to various villages and the road system which wove them together. The effect upon them was immediate, and almost ludicrous. Lieutenant Douglas could see their faces reflect their astonishment as each one gradually became aware that the great Stonewall Jackson had stupidly given away his army's destination.

While the column and most of his staff turned to head west on Patrick Street, the general pulled Henry Douglas aside to confide in him. Informing the young officer of Lee's plan to take the Federal garrisons at Martinsburg and Harpers Ferry, Virginia, he quietly asked him what he knew of the fords along the Potomac between Sharpsburg and Williamsport, Maryland.[9] It did not occur to Douglas, as he and Jackson rode up Market Street toward Second Street, that the Army of Northern Virginia had failed in its campaign to win Maryland to the Confederacy and that Lee was retreating with his army while he could.[10]

For the moment, Jackson wanted to pay his respects to the Reverend Dr. John Ross, who lived on the northern side of West Second Street, directly across from Record Street. He and Douglas halted in the road in front of the parsonage where the pastor's slave told them the doctor had not awakened yet. Douglas was about to ring the doorbell when the general stopped him. Jackson hastily scratched the following on a piece of dispatch paper: "Regret not being permitted to see Dr. and Mrs. Ross, but could not expect to have that pleasure at so unseasonable [an] hour. T. J. Jackson, September 10, 1862, 5 1/4 A.M."

Handing the note to the slave, the pair turned their horses to the left and rode to Mill (Bentz) Alley where they wheeled south. They joined the column on the western side of Carroll Creek and moved west, down West Patrick Street.[11]

Once again the people of Frederick displayed their dual loyalties as the Confederates worked their way through the city. Captain Greenlee Davidson (Letcher Virginia Artillery) bitterly recalled, "Some few of the people cheered us and a great many ladies welcomed us by waving handkerchiefs and flags, but a large proportion of the people looked sullenly upon us."[12]

A few, like Mrs. Mary A. Quantrell, who operated a private school from her home on the southwestern corner of Patrick Street and Mill (Bentz) Street, decided to take a more patriotic stance. Gathering her daughter, Virginia, and five of her students about her, she snatched up a small Union flag and moved out onto her doorstep. With a defiance born of ignorance, she gave the flag to her daughter, who waved it from side to side. A number of the Confederate enlisted men yelled at the girl to drop the colors. When she refused to comply, an angry Rebel lieutenant stepped forward with his sword drawn and struck the fluttering cloth from her hands. As he marched out of sight, "Virgi" raised the colors again.

Presently, a Confederate officer rode up to Mrs. Quantrell and the children and advised her to desist. Her patriotic response impressed him. He brought his mount up onto the pavement next to her porch, and promised no one would molest them while he remained there. The mood of the marching troops changed briefly. Several units cheered as they moved past her. The officer gallantly saluted Mary Quantrell and her stalwarts before he departed and said, "To you, madam, not to your flag."

Moments after he disappeared into the surging column, a squad of embittered enlisted men surrounded her. A milling group of her neighbors, Henry Nixdorff, William and Nicholas Fleming, A. E. Gittinger, J. C. Hardt, and Mrs. Abbott, who were standing across the street, helplessly watched the infantrymen yank the flag from her hands. The soldiers maliciously snapped the staff in several places and hurled the pieces onto the sidewalk. Replacing the torn flag with a bigger one, she continued to flaunt the colors, unmolested.[13]

An hour or so later, when Lawton's division entered the city, clusters of citizens still lined the roadside to gawk at the Confederates. Private William A. McClendon (Company G, 15th Alabama), who loaded himself down with several empty canteens, straggled from his regiment to fill them from Mrs. Barbara Frietschie's clear spring. It was located less than thirty feet southeast of Carroll Creek, where it crossed West Patrick Street. While filling them, he overheard a cavalryman exchanging compliments with a young woman, whom he had obviously known from before the war.

"Why, John," she exclaimed as the crusty soldiers passed, "how can such a dirty, filthy set of soldiers defeat the neatly dressed boys of the Army of the Potomac? Such clothes! All ragged and filthy."

Her friend, who patiently listened to her with one leg thrown casually over the pommel of his saddle, calmly drawled, "Bessie, we don't put our best clothes on to kill hogs." The crowd along the street enthusiastically applauded and McClendon used the distraction to slip back into the ranks, feeling quite proud of his tattered uniform.[14]

The spring attracted scores of the thirsty Rebels. A great many of them flopped on the doorstoops which lined the pavement on both sides of the street. Henry Nixdorff and E. A. Gittinger marveled at the spunk of the venerable Barbara Frietschie. Throughout the Confederate occupation, she flew a bunting National flag from one of her attic windows, an act which drew no particular attention.

During the withdrawal, the ninety-six-year-old Unionist generally stayed indoors avoiding the exhausted Confederates who plopped down on her stoop while their comrades brought water to them from her spring. Occasionally, with her muslin kerchief draped around her shoulders, she ventured outside in her closed bonnet and black satin dress to scold the veterans on her porch for their unpatriotic conversations.

Insisting she could tolerate them drinking her spring water but would not brook disloyal speech, she finally chased them off with her cane. Henry Nixdorff remembered the elderly dame could be "kindly when the occasion called for it."[15]

The grimy Confederates generally accepted the pro-Union displays with light hearted effrontery. Lieutenant William M. Owen (Washington Artillery) enjoyed the holiday spirit as if he were at home at a parade. Regimental colors bobbed up and down in military rhythm and the martial music from the regimental bands echoed smartly through the streets of the town. Ignoring the faces which were pressed against the window panes to stare at them, he tried to concentrate upon the clear, blue sky and the ladies who waved their handkerchiefs at the troops as they passed. He sarcastically noted that the civilian men who huddled together along the route appeared cool or, more correctly, timid, as if they were afraid to express themselves.

The artillerists, marching in front of their limbers and caissons, decided to make the most of the day. Lieutenant Frank McElroy (1st Company, Washington Artillery) struck up a merry song and the men followed in chorus.[16] They too took careful notice of the blatant Unionism. At one point along Patrick Street, Lieutenant Owen fixed his gaze upon a "buxom" young woman, whose dancing black eyes, also, attracted his attention. Having pinned a small Federal flag across her ample chest, she quite naturally attracted several solicitous remarks from the ranks.

One of the enlisted men cried aloud, "Look h'yar, Miss, better take that flag down; we're awful fond of charging breast-works." Down the line, the same old joke rippled as each succeeding regiment's wag took up the repartee until the column reverberated with laughter and howls.[17]

Brigadier General Joseph Kershaw halted his South Carolina brigade on South Market Street just below the Patrick Street intersection, while Brigadier General Howell Cobb, the temporary commander of the division, deliberately accosted a large group of men and boys who had assembled on the northwest corner of the street. Riding up to the sidewalk, Cobb, the former United States Secretary of the Treasury, clenched his mouse colored slouch hat in his fist and bitterly denounced the group as Union men and Southern haters. Comparing the dust brown rags his men wore to their fine civilian attire, he swore his soldiers would return after they whipped the Yankee army and jail every one of them.

The civilians laughed at him and mockingly applauded his foolishness while the Confederate soldiers silently ignored the entire affair. Dr. Lewis Steiner (U.S. Sanitary Commission) penned in his diary that the general was "A drunken, bloated blackguard...."[18]

Reining his mount to the left, the general led his column west on Patrick Street with the men of Frederick trailing him on the northern sidewalk. As he continued his march, all the while spouting bombast, more and more civilians crowded the pavement to laugh at him. Ladies poked their heads out of their second story windows to watch the folly and the men of the 2nd South Carolina duly noted each one of them. Try as he could, Lieutenant William Johnson (Company D) never saw the comely Yankee girl whom he referred to as "the Sphinx."

As the Confederates neared the top of the hill west of Mill Alley, a girl, whom Johnson judged to be about fourteen or fifteen years old, leaned out of her upper floor window (on the south side of the street) and waved a Confederate flag at General Cobb. Spurring to a place immediately beneath the window, the general called out, "Sissy, you're the gal I'm looking for."[19]

Turning in the saddle toward Kershaw's command, which was standing in the road not thirty feet from him, he yelled for "his boys" to give her three cheers. He repeated the order, "Three more, my boys!" and again, "Three more!"

When he noticed the "Yankee" civilians were not joining in his tribute, the general turned sour. Gazing at the sullen crowd on the sidewalk, Cobb shook his fist at them.

"Oh you damned long-faced Yankees! Ladies, take down their names and I will attend to them personally when I return."[20]

He failed to notice how quiet his own soldiers remained. The civilians cheered the girl. The South Carolinians nervously eyed the mob along the street, feeling quite uncertain as to how they were going to behave. A door slammed behind Lieutenant Johnson, startling him. Simultaneously, a man threw open a window in the house and called from his upper floor, "Who is that speaking over there?"

The man who had shut the door in leaving the house shouted back, "That is Howell E. Cobb, Secretary of the Treasury under Buchanan."

In the meantime, the general pulled his hat down over his head and galloped away with the cheers of the crowd at his back. They had thoroughly enjoyed the sideshow. A lanky private in Company B of the 2nd South Carolina, unable to restrain himself, jerked his slouch hat from his head and in mockery of the general waved it wildly above his head.

He screeched, "Now, boys, three cheers for me; I'm a general too!"

MAP 8: September 10, 1862. Jackson's route through Frederick, Maryland.

Men collapsed on the street, writhing with laughter. Joseph Kershaw, having witnessed the entire farce, guffawed so violently he nearly fell from the saddle. Shouts echoed in the streets as men, boys and, soldiers tossed their hats and caps high into the air.

Several minutes later, the officers regained control of their troops and the infantry continued its march. Once again, "Maryland! My Maryland!" reverberated down the street as everyone, including the people of Frederick, joined in the merriment.[21] [Refer to Map 8]

The column of Confederate troops seemed endless. Major General Lafayette McLaws' division, followed by Major General Richard H. Anderson's division led the corps' advance through Frederick. Brigadier Generals John B. Hood's division and Nathan Evans' brigade (both of which were under Evans' command) and David R. Jones' division followed, respectively.[22] The head of Longstreet's Corps did not get moving until 10:00 A.M.[23] The lumbering wagon trains and the army's reserve artillery, having preceded Longstreet's men on the road to Catoctin Mountain necessarily slowed the troops which were decamping behind them. The soldiers did not grouse about the leisurely pace. They faced the day much as they had any other.

The corps uncoiled very slowly. The officers, pursuant to orders, deliberately formed their men in columns of four to stretch out the regiments and convince the Federal spies in the city that the Army of Northern Virginia was extremely large.[24] Consequently, it was late in the day before Colonel William A. Parham's brigade (6th, 12th, 16th, 41st, and 61st Virginia) moved out at the rear of Richard H. Anderson's division. Private George Bernard (Company I, 12th Virginia) recorded in his diary that the regiment left camp around 2:00 P.M.[25] Brigadier General James Kemper's brigade (1st, 7th, 11th, 17th, and 24th Virginia) did not leave its bivouac at Monocacy Junction that day.[26] D. H. Hill's division remained in Frederick as the rear guard of the army.

The extended marching order of the Army of Northern Virginia made it look much larger than it was. Stretched out in a line which Captain Charles Russell (Company I, 1st Maryland Cavalry, U.S.A.) estimated to be twenty miles long, it left an indelible impression of superior numbers upon the minds of many of the people in Frederick.[27]

Corporal William Sherwood (Company F, 17th Virginia), whose brigade formed the rear guard of the division, filled his stomach with an exotic breakfast of bread, coffee, and mackerel, and felt too refreshed to worry about any rumor or order which filtered down through the ranks. He shrugged off a camp story about fighting in Baltimore and quietly prepared three days' rations. He believed the Army of Northern Virginia was going to carry the war into Pennsylvania.[28]

John Dooley (Company A, 1st Virginia) strolled the three miles into Frederick to bid adieu to his Jesuit friends at the Novitiate on Second Street. Fathers Maguire and Ward and Dooley's former classmate, Jack Davis, found themselves in an awkward situation. Federal medical officers, having been captured with the hospital on September 6, dropped by to speak with

Father Ward, who apparently had Southern sympathies. They wanted the priest to exert his influence upon the Confederate commanders to obtain medical supplies for their wounded. Father Ward tried to excuse himself from the situation by insisting he had to be "equally polite" to all and, by implication, could not take sides.

Jack Davis, much to Dooley's chagrin, politely informed his friend that he was a Federal man and that he wanted a passport to Baltimore. The overly sensitive John Dooley felt hurt by Davis' Unionism. He tried to behave cordially, but when Jack Davis, the consummate gentleman, offered him some clothes, Dooley declined. He returned to camp confused—torn between Jack's kindness and his own pride.[29]

The farther west the Army of Northern Virginia marched the more Unionist the people became. The leading brigade of Jackson's Corps reached Middletown around 10:00 A.M. Nestled in a rolling valley between Catoctin and South Mountains, about one-third the distance between Frederick and Hagerstown, the small village reminded Captain Greenlee Davidson (Letcher Virginia Artillery) of Lexington, Virginia.

There the similarities ceased. Locked houses, closed stores, and virtually deserted streets coldly greeted the Confederates, who by now had no illusions. These people did not want to be liberated. The disillusioned Captain Davidson described the atmosphere of the town and the Catoctin Valley in a letter to his father.

He wrote, "It has the reputation of being the bitterest abolition hole in the state."[30]

Stonewall Jackson and his staff entered the town, half a mile ahead of the column. Two little girls, with their hair tied back in red, white, and blue ribbons, burst from their house and raced to the curbstone as the officers rode by. Laughingly, they waved small Union flags at Jackson and then turned their backs upon him as he doffed his hat in a polite salute.

With a smile of resignation upon his face, he looked back upon his staff and admitted, with classic understatement, "We evidently have no friends in this town."[31] While the horsemen rode down the street, the girls' frightened mother hurried the children inside amidst the cheers of the approaching infantry.[32] Middletown was a ghost town in the middle of a veritable Garden of Eden.

While the Confederates pursued their course toward South Mountain, the Army of the Potomac continued to inch its way closer to the Confederate rear guard. The IX Corps spent the day at Brookville to enable all of its regiments to catch up with it and to let the I Corps pass through en route to Triadelphia, which was about four miles due north.[33]

The IX Corps' troops used the halt to bathe in the canal which ran through the town.[34] It also gave them ample time to loot the nearby farms of green corn, potatoes, and peaches.[35]

Brigadier General George G. Meade's brigade of Pennsylvania Reserves (I Corps), for the most part had left the Maryland farms alone. Sergeant Archibald F. Hill (Company D, 8th Pennsylvania Reserves), who admired the verdant farms, solemnly recalled, "To leave the ranks and attack any of the orchards was a thing strictly forbidden, and consequently unsafe."

He had seen only two men break ranks during the day, both incidents occurring just before dark. In the first instance a plump Pennsylvanian inadvertently knocked a hornet's nest from an over burdened apple tree by jerking an apple from one of its branches. The hornets nearly killed him before he could clear the fence and spring into the road. They stung him over the eye, in the nose, and several times in his scalp before he outran them.

The second incident happened when the 8th Pennsylvania Reserves bivouacked next to a farm lane for the evening. Sergeant Hill left his sick messmate to fill his empty canteen with milk, and stumbled across Meade, who was riding up the lane toward the main house.

Spying a peach tree, the general commanded one of his mounted orderlies to guard the tree while he continued to the farmhouse to ascertain how many pickets were needed to protect the property. When Hill returned from the barn several minutes later, he saw the cavalryman leaning forward in the saddle helping himself to the peaches. Meade also happened upon the orderly.

"What are you about there?" Meade nastily demanded.

The alarm jolted the orderly.

"Why, you thief!" the general exploded.

The cavalryman looked confused.

"You mercenary villain," Meade continued. "I set you to guard that tree, and—and—you—" The general spurred his horse up to the soldier. "I'll cut your head off!"

With his sword slashing above his head, Meade dashed upon the enlisted man and slapped him several times upon the back of the neck with the flat of the blade. The defenseless cavalryman tried to tuck his head, tortoise like, between his shoulder blades. He moaned pitifully as he tottered from one side to the other in the saddle.

The general momentarily gained control of his emotions and tried to sheathe his weapon. He hesitated again. Anger rolled across his face. Seizing the sword by the blade he menacingly shook the hilt in the terrified soldier's face. As the sentry dodged and howled again, the general screamed at him, "Confound you! I can scarcely keep from murdering you!"

The irate general returned his sword to its scabbard. An audible sigh escaped from the sentry when he heard the metal hilt clink against the top of the sheath.

"Oh, you deserve killing!" Meade snarled, and the soldier groaned.

"Don't you think I ought to kill you?" Meade asked.

He glared wrathfully at the soldier through his wire rimmed spectacles. Getting no reply, he demanded, "Say!"

"Yes, sir," came the feeble reply.

Meade suddenly wheeled about and trotted away from the quaking orderly. In the moonlight, Archibald F. Hill thought he detected a faint smile across the general's mouth.[36] He had had his sport and had exerted his authority in a manner which would feed the rumor mills for a considerable length of time. Perhaps being aware of his reputation as an irascible, quick tempered "snapping turtle," Meade wanted to reinforce that image.

The Army of the Potomac was starting to slowly envelop the Army of Northern Virginia within the confines of Frederick. Major General Joseph Hooker's I Corps concentrated itself in the vicinity of Triadelphia, six miles north, by back roads, from Brookville, where the bulk of the IX Corps camped.[37] Brigadier General Jacob Cox's Kanawha Division, one of the best disciplined divisions in the corps, was in the lead seven miles to the northwest at Goshen.[38] The II Corps and the newly constituted XII Corps, had gotten as far as Clarksburg, about five miles west of the Kanawha Division.[39] The VI Corps covered thirteen miles that day. Passing by way of Dawsonville on the Darnestown Road, the corps started to file into camp in the woodland south of Barnesville as early as 3:00 P.M.[40]

The muggy weather and the overcast sky drained the men of their energy. The now reeking Captain Jacob Haas (Company G, 96th Pennsylvania), remembering the refreshing bath of the day before and the clean clothes into which he had foolishly changed, grumbled out loud in his diary, "Terrible march."[41] The exhausted men tended to spook easily. When the column marched past a nearby farm, the roosters all stopped crowing. The silence cut Sergeant Robert S. Westbrook (Company B, 49th Pennsylvania) to the marrow.[42] The oncoming night did not allay his tensions, either.

At 7:00 P.M., two hours after arriving in camp, Jacob Haas found himself in charge of the VI Corps' picket outposts. He did not relish the task because the Rebels were within earshot and gunshot of his line.[43] An occasional shell made the sentries more skittish.[44] The captain nearly panicked when four loose horses, probably from the cavalry videttes in the area of Sugar Loaf Mountain, stampeded into his men and disappeared to the rear.[45]

The fighting around the mountain continued noisily throughout the afternoon and a little into the night. Captain William P. Saunders, commanding the 6th U.S. Cavalry with his two artillery pieces and the 8th Illinois and the 3rd Indiana Cavalry, had failed miserably to dislodge Thomas Munford's two Virginia regiments and the one squadron of the 9th Virginia Cavalry from the mountain's wooded slopes.[46] Private Samuel Gilpin (Company E, 3rd Indiana Cavalry) summarized the situation better than any official report of the action.

"Our artillery," he wrote, "could silence their guns but our dismounted cavalrymen could make little headway up the steep mountain sides. There were a few killed and wounded on both sides and at night, matters stood about the way they had been on the night previous."[47]

Using the darkness and Munford's pesky skirmishers on the hillside to cover his moves, Brigadier General Fitzhugh Lee retired his brigade from the field and headed north toward New Market. Lieutenant Colonel R. L. T. Beale (9th Virginia Cavalry) retired, feeling good about the day's work.[48] Munford with

his two remaining regiments, the 2nd and the 12th Virginia Cavalry, felt abandoned.[49] His small force of under 475 troopers was expected to hold a
corps at bay.[50]

The fighting had gained neither side any advantage. The Federals failed
to take the mountain and all the shooting had resulted in two Federal
casualties—one killed, and one wounded.[51] [Refer to Map 7]

While Brigadier General Alfred Pleasonton's cavalry pawed the ground
around Sugar Loaf Mountain, Lieutenant Colonel Stephen W. Downey (3rd
Maryland, Potomac Home Brigade) with a nineteen-man escort under the command of Second Lieutenant Francis Shamburg (Company A, 1st Maryland
Cavalry) was on a long range reconnaissance out of Kearneysville, Virginia,
a small village about eighteen miles southwest of Boonsboro.[52] Around dusk
they accidentally rode into a dangerous situation.

As his patrol approached Boonsboro from the southeast along the
Boonsboro Pike, they missed Lieutenant Alexander D. Payne (Company H,
4th Virginia Cavalry) and his small squad of the Black Horse Troop (about
10 troopers) as they passed through the town hunting for provisions while
en route to Hagerstown. The Yankees' unintentional prey, according to the
victims, appeared to have been two Confederate officers who were riding
unescorted into the town from the east.

Against General Jackson's advice, Lieutenant Henry Kyd Douglas, along
with Colonel S. Bassett French, decided to follow Lieutenant Payne and his
small cavalry screen into Boonsboro. Douglas, who had lived in the Boonsboro-
Sharpsburg area his entire life, insisted on acquiring information about the
fords along the Potomac. (He later wrote that he desired "incidentally to see
some friends" who resided in Boonsboro.) Colonel French, while not desir-
ing female companionship, desperately needed a well cooked meal and some
other refreshment. He rode ahead of Douglas into Boonsboro to get their
supplies.

While the Black Horse troopers kept going toward the end of town, Colonel French dismounted at the corner of Main Street and the Boonsboro Pike.
Tying his horse outside, he lumbered into the United States Hotel to order
his supper. (The establishment, which was located on the southeastern corner of the intersection, was run by a rabid Union sympathizer.) French found
Private Bernard P. Green (Company H, 4th Virginia Cavalry) and two other
troopers in the general store, which operated in the hotel lobby.

Henry Douglas and the courier who accompanied him were preparing
to join the colonel when the squad of the 1st Maryland Cavalry stampeded
into town and took them on the flank. Douglas heard the loud pounding of
hooves coming from the south along the Boonsboro Pike. Moments later he
was startled as the Yankees thundered around the corner, in column of fours,
with their pistols blazing. Bassett French's horse toppled into the street—
dead—before the colonel could get to it. Dodging bullets which thudded
through and into the walls, he followed a black freedman into the hotel's cellar
and at the man's insistence, hurled himself into an evil smelling pile of filth,

which he later discovered was a rubbish pile.

The courier and Douglas instantly wheeled their horses about and pulling their revolvers from their holsters, cracked off a couple of rounds at the Yankees who pursued them east toward the main camp of the corps, which was about a mile distant. A bullet knocked Douglas' fine gray hat with its ostrich plume from his head. Resisting the urge to stop and retrieve it, because the plume had been a gift from a lady friend in Frederick, he dug his spurs into his mount and kept on going.

Simultaneously, Private Green dashed out of the hotel and groped for his horse's bridle, which he discovered was entangled around the animal's feet. Freeing the reins, he hurled himself into the saddle, and spurred his mount west along Main Street in pursuit of Lieutenant Payne. Belligerent citizens took potshots at his back as he raced past their homes.[53]

As his horse climbed toward the crest of the first hill immediately east of town Henry Kyd Douglas caught Jackson's attention. The general, who was walking his mount toward the town, stopped swinging his hat in his free hand, sprang onto his horse and galloped back toward John Murdock's house, where the head of his column was swaggering off the road into the fields to the north.

Private Thomas W. Latimer (Company F, 1st Virginia Cavalry) dashed up to Douglas and his courier and pointed out that the Federal charge had stalled in the pike. The Yankees, who saw Colonel Bradley T. Johnson's brigade (21st, 42nd, 48th Virginia, and 1st Virginia Battalion) approaching on the National Pike from the hillside east of Murdock's, reined to a sudden halt.[54]

Unaware of the infantry which were approaching them from the rear, Douglas and his two comrades yelled for their "nonexistent" troopers to follow them. The three charged recklessly at the Marylanders, who turned tail.[55]

In the meantime, Lieutenant Alexander Payne, having rallied his ten men around a red brick house on the edge of the town, began to order his men inside when one of his soldiers reminded him that Jackson had ridden in advance of his corps and was probably going to be captured. Hoping the dust cloud in the road concealed their approach, Payne ordered his troopers to horse. They turned about and charged the Yankees from the west. Colonel Downey's men, caught between two fires, dashed as madly as the thick limestone dust of the road would permit out of town toward Sharpsburg.

Douglas joined Payne and his company and chased the Marylanders several miles. During the pursuit, the Confederates killed one of Lieutenant Shamburg's troopers, wounded and captured three others, and unhorsed Colonel Downey, who managed to secure another mount and escape despite a slight head wound.[56]

(It was a miracle that the many potholes in the limestone road injured no one in either party. The neglected and poorly maintained Boonsboro Pike was not in any shape for madcap cavalry chases.)[57] [Refer to Map 9]

When the sweating cavalrymen returned to Boonsboro, they found Bassett French emerging from the hotel in a most disturbed state. Foul smelling and besmeared with decomposing refuse, he presented anything but an admirable

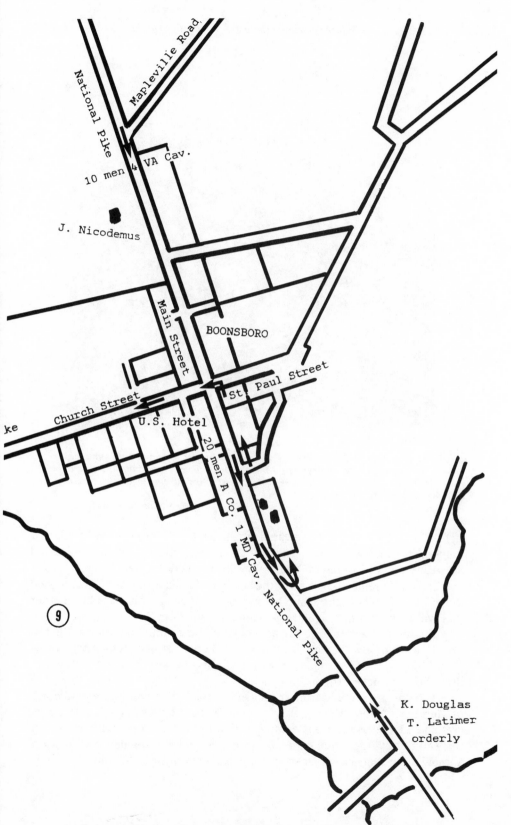

MAP 9: September 10, 1862. Cavalry skirmish in Boonsboro, Maryland.

Boonsboro, Maryland in 1862
This view is from the western end of town looking east toward South Mountain.
The wagons in the picture are on the National Pike. The prominent house on
the right is where the Black Horse Troop rallied before rushing to Jackson's rescue
on September 10, 1862.

FROM BROWN, *THE SIGNAL CORPS, U.S.A.*

sight. Grateful to be alive, he rewarded the black man's loyalty with a ten dollar Confederate note, which even then was an empty gesture when one considered the real value of Confederate currency in any Federal state.[58]

Captain Greenlee Davidson of the Letcher Virginia Artillery, who witnessed the affair, laughingly informed his father, "...poor French. I doubt whether you will ever find him again in advance of our lines."[59]

The weary Lieutenant Douglas recovered his crumpled hat from the National Pike along with Francis Shamburg's kepi. Just over the eastern brow of the hill, west of Murdock's home, he found General Jackson's gloves in the road and picked them up also.

As he dismounted in front of Jackson's tent, which was in the field north of Murdock's house, the general, in a somewhat condescending voice, congratulated Douglas upon his escape and upon his fast horse. The lieutenant respectfully handed the general his gloves, which he had not missed. Somewhat embarrassed, Jackson grinned and went into his tent.[60]

Private Green of the 4th Virginia Cavalry not too long afterward met Jackson and some of his staff as they rode into the town to ascertain what had happened.

The enlisted man boldly approached the general.

"General," he said, "we drove them out."

"That was good," the general answered somberly.

"General, we captured some," Green boasted.

"That is better."

"...And killed and wounded other[s]," the cavalryman continued.

"That is better still."

Before either man could say anything else, Colonel Bassett French charged up to them.

"General," he gasped, "was it not a gallant thing in the small squad of the Black Horse to charge so large a force and save you from capture?"

"Very gallant, Colonel; very gallant," Jackson patiently responded.

"General, how would you have felt if the Yankees had captured you?"

"Very bad, Colonel," Jackson responded in half jest, "especially if they had found me in a dark cellar with a negro standing guard over me."[61]

The day ended with the Army of Northern Virginia heading west, toward the Blue Ridge Mountains and, according to many of the enlisted men, toward Pennsylvania. The Army of the Potomac, while not nipping at the Confederates' heels, was getting uncomfortably close. Lee had time and George B. McClellan on his side. Lee knew how McClellan thought. He had fought and defeated him on the Peninsula earlier in the year, and had assessed the disorganized condition of the Army of the Potomac at the time. He did not feel threatened by McClellan. In a meeting the day before with Brigadier General John G. Walker, one of his division commanders, Lee sarcastically mentioned, "He [McClellan] is an able general, but a very cautious one." Later, in retrospect, Walker reported, "The advance of the Federal army was so slow at the time we left Fredericktown as to justify the belief that the reduction of Harper's Ferry would be accomplished and our troops concentrated before they would be called upon to meet it."

Lincoln accused McClellan of having the "slows." Fearing he might not have enough men to overpower the Army of Northern Virginia, the general considered asking for more troops "at the risk," he wrote, "of being thought slow and overcautious."[62]

MAP 10: Situation—September 11, 1862.

Chapter Seven

SEPTEMBER 11, 1862

IT WAS CLOUDY at daybreak, and it looked like it would rain.[1] That did not discourage Private William B. Baker (Company D, 1st Maine Cavalry). Following a breakfast of boiled mackerel, potatoes, buttered biscuits, applesauce, hard bread, and coffee with fresh milk, he and two other New Englanders grabbed a ten quart pail and raided a grape arbor along the brook which flowed through Cracklintown. Not satisfied with filling the pail, Baker tore off his hat and filled it also with the choicest clusters he could find.

When he got back to camp he gorged himself on grapes. Then he wrote a letter to his sister describing his foray. "They're as big as common crab apples and make excellent sauce," he bragged. "It is beginning to rain and I am glad of it. Hope it will rain enough to lay the dust. What do the people at home think of this war and [what] do they think of it going to amount to in the long run? Just let a fellow know."[2]

About eight miles northwest of Cracklintown, at Damascus, Adjutant Charles J. Mills (2nd Massachusetts), busied himself with a letter to his mother. While writing from under the cover of his India rubber blanket, which dripped water sporadically upon his paper, he tried to reassure her that he was being fed as well as could be expected under the circumstances. His mess finished off the chickens they had acquired the night before with a breakfast stew. He commented, it "only wanted onions to make it perfect." He still had a touch of the dysentery which he explained, "I have given up trying to cure it for the present.... When, if ever, we stop, I shall take it in hand." It disturbed him far less than his mother's intermittent letters.

"I have only received two letters from you, and a mail has just come without one. I wonder where they are. My semi-weekly advertisers have come with satisfactory regularity."[3]

The rain turned out to be sporadic in most of the area and it did not lay the dust. It dampened the soldiers' clothes enough to make them heavier.

While the Federals slowly got under way, D. H. Hill's division, the last organized Confederate infantry at Monocacy Junction, arose before daylight and in the words of Orderly Sergeant James Shinn (Company B, 4th North Carolina), "we left camp with the rising sun for parts unknown to us."[4] Covered with the powdery dust kicked up by the head of the column, they entered Frederick at an early hour where the people received them coldly. All of the stores and houses were shut. Curious citizens peeked furtively at the Confederates from their upstairs windows. Private Calvin Leach (Company B, 1st North Carolina) recalled that a few ladies waved Confederate flags at them as the soldiers passed and "a few rosy lips showed some signs of pleasure at seeing us," Sergeant Shinn recorded. "I thought the people looked rather long faced to have much sympathy with the South," he concluded.[5]

Surgeon Lewis H. Steiner somberly followed Hill's corps. Their superb discipline and their above average band reflected tight leadership. They marched much faster than either Longstreet's or Jackson's corps, which convinced Dr. Steiner the Federals were not far behind.[6]

Up ahead, at Middletown, the civilians cooly received Longstreet's Corps. Captain Greenlee Davidson, who had unsuccessfully tried to buy provisions for himself and his messmates wrote home, "The lands are in the highest state of cultivation and every farm has a barn almost as large as Noah's Ark. But strange to say, none of these magnificent barns, or roomy smokehouses contain neither corn nor meat.... It is true that a considerable number of the houses were deserted, but where I found the owners at home, they all told me they had nothing to sell. It is perfectly evident that the people of this section of the State are as hostile to us as if we were north of [the] Mason and Dixon line."[7]

Private James S. Johnston (Company I, 11th Mississippi), Colonel Evander McIver Law's orderly, bitterly protested the Marylanders' hostility. He wrote to his fiancée "[the]...traders [traitors] closed their doors by the time we were a days march of them. In some towns the Ladies display themselves for the Union and said that the dirty crowd we had along, had better go home and leave them alone. Our soldiers, in every case, treat them with respect and would only laugh at their talk about 'the Union.'" As an afterthought, perhaps to reassure his beloved of his loyalty to her and to equate feminine pulchritude with secessionist proclivities, he added, "The ladies *around* Frederick are quite pretty, but towards Hagerstown, being almost entirely Dutch, they were *tidy* but *exceedingly homely*."[8]

For the most part, the enlisted men in the Army of Northern Virginia religiously obeyed the orders against pillaging, once they reached Middletown. The provost guard left two ragged corpses swinging from trees along the roadside east of the town, just beyond Braddock Pass. According to the civilians who witnessed the incident, the two men had been caught stealing apples.

The Confederates who saw the two soldiers turning ugly in the sunlight refrained from their usual raiding and left the valley virtually untouched.[9]

The frightened citizens religiously obeyed General Jackson's order to shut all of their stores to his troops.[10] That did not stop the ladies from emulating the heroic Nancy Crouse. Several of them stood along the roadside with the Stars and Stripes draped across their chests.[11] The seemingly never ending stream of Confederates astonished one little old lady who, as the men marched by her, gasped in awe that she "did not think there was so many men in the world."[12]

The army divided when it reached Middletown. Jackson's Corps continued over South Mountain toward Hagerstown. Longstreet's Corps followed after it without Major General Lafayette McLaws' division, which took the southern road from the center of Middletown toward Burkittsville. With considerable understatement, John S. Shipp scribbled in his diary that the few people he encountered were strong Unionists.[13] The townspeople bragged to the gritty, dirt caked Confederates how the village had voted 60-40 in the last district vote in support of the Union.[14]

Colonel William Parham's undersized brigade (6th, 12th, 16th, 41st, and 61st Virginia) covered only four miles that day. Being the division's rear guard, the men contended stoically with the gagging dust cloud which the division wagon train churned up as it rumbled slowly down the pike toward Burkittsville.[15]

While the infantry lumbered along the main pikes on the way to Harpers Ferry, Virginia, and Hagerstown, Maryland, Jeb Stuart's Cavalry division started to retire from its Urbana-Hyattstown-Sugar Loaf line. The day did not begin well for Colonel Thomas Munford's 2nd and 12th Virginia Cavalry. Brigadier General Winfield Scott Hancock's 5th and 6th Maine, 43rd New York, 49th and 137th Pennsylvania Infantry in conjunction with Colonel John F. Farnsworth's 3rd Indiana, 8th Pennsylvania, and 8th Illinois Cavalry started their advance from Barnesville at 6:00 A.M.[16]

The newly created cavalry brigade split into two groups. The 8th Illinois Cavalry took a roundabout way along the eastern base of the mountain toward Hyattstown while the other two regiments swung around to the west.[17] Hancock's infantry deployed into battle line as far back as Barnesville, sent out skirmishers, and advanced very slowly toward Sugar Loaf as support for the 8th Pennsylvania Cavalry and the 3rd Indiana Cavalry.[18]

The infantry, trying to maintain their dressed battle lines, necessarily slowed down their cavalry screen, who, being without artillery support, inched toward their objective.[19] At 9:00 A.M., the VI Corps' skirmishers started to ascend the western slope of the mountain, well ahead of their main body of troops, where they engaged Colonel Thomas Munford's dismounted troopers of the 2nd Virginia Cavalry, whom they mistook for infantry.[20] A section of the Stuart Horse Artillery under Second Lieutenant Daniel Shanks commanded the approaches to the signal station and fired effectively enough to keep the Federals from directly approaching those roads.[21] [Refer to Map 10]

The fighting, which both sides exaggerated to heroic proportions, consisted mostly of noise with little if any noticeable results. The skirmishers of both armies exchanged rounds for the better part of two to three hours without inflicting any casualties.[22] Private Samuel Gilpin (Company E, 3rd Indiana Cavalry), who was part of the cavalry screen, tersely entered in his diary that the Rebels discharged their weapons and fled some time before the main body of the VI Corps arrived at the base of the mountain.[23]

The Confederates were fighting more among themselves than with the Yankees. The trouble started with Jeb Stuart and his staff, who were still enjoying the company of the Cockey girls in Urbana. Stuart dispatched Major Von Borcke early in the day with orders to pull his cavalry brigades back toward Frederick. Sometime after 9:00 A.M., Von Borcke rode into Munford's position at Sugar Loaf with orders for the colonel's two undermanned regiments to assume the rear-guard of the army.[24]

Munford argued that Stuart's orders conflicted with Jackson's. While shoving his written directives from Jackson in the Prussian's face, the colonel asked him to explain the matter to Stuart.

"Oh, Colonel," Von Borcke exclaimed, "vood you no run & ze the general. He is no way long off."

Munford agreed to ride along with the major only to learn that Stuart was still in Urbana, some five miles northeast of Sugar Loaf. Von Borcke, having grown quite uncomfortable in his rain soaked saddle, squirmed more noticeably as he and Munford neared the Cockey house. He reined aside with the colonel, out of earshot, and begged, "Oh, Colonel, vill you be so good as to zey to ze General that you understand me but not ze order? He so much laugh at me. I do not like it so much." Munford agreed to play the game.[25]

When Stuart explained to Munford how he, as commander on the field, could overrule Jackson's orders, the colonel had to obey. Disgruntled, Munford rode back to his dismounted troopers and ordered them to pull out.[26] About 11:00 A.M., Brigadier General Fitzhugh Lee's 3rd, 4th, and 5th Virginia Cavalry with Lieutenant James Breathed's section of the Stuart Horse Artillery retired through Urbana, en route to New Market. Brigadier General Wade Hampton's cavalry brigade (1st North Carolina, 2nd South Carolina, 10th Virginia, Cobb's Legion, and Jeff Davis Legion) followed them soon, headed toward Frederick.[27]

By then, Munford's command had withdrawn to the hilltop northwest of Hyattstown in Hampton's former outpost. The 8th Illinois Cavalry promptly occupied the signal station atop Sugar Loaf Mountain, dismounted, and fired a carbine volley into the air to signal their victory.[28]

By noon, Hancock's main infantry force had arrived at the base of the mountain.[29] Shortly thereafter, Companies B and G of the 96th Pennsylvania were sent forward as pickets and the VI Corps settled down for the rest of the day.[30]

The Federals, however, did not give the Confederate rear-guard any respite. Around 1:30 P.M., videttes from the 1st New York Cavalry caught the attention

Hyattstown, Maryland
This woodcut shows a glorified version of the 1st New York Cavalry's final charge
against the village on September 11, 1862.

STEVENSON, *A HISTORY OF THE FIRST VOLUNTEER CAVALRY*

of Munford's cavalry and Lieutenant Daniel Shanks' artillery section. Two rounds sent the New Yorkers scattering for higher ground beyond their range. Major Alonzo W. Adams hastily reformed his column, and waited for Major Marcus Reno with his squadron of the 1st United States Cavalry to join his command. Using Reno's men as a reserve, he directed Captain William H. Boyd and 1st Lieutenant James Stevenson of Company C to lead the charge.

When the Federals got close enough to see that the Rebels had mounted and were standing in column in the road in Hyattstown, they drew their sabres and charged. The Confederates turned and ran to the cover of their guns while the Yankees, who had worked themselves into a frenzy, blindly galloped into an abandoned village. Regaining their senses when the Rebel guns fired, the Yankees hastily fell back to Clarksburg where a chance artillery shell killed one horse and left the rider in a dazed heap.[31] [Refer to Map 10]

The Federals won the field without pressing their objective. Captain Robert P. Chew's Virginia battery, which was unlimbered in the road, three miles south of Urbana, pulled out before Munford's cavalrymen had a chance to catch up with it.[32]

The echoing carbine fire from Hyattstown prompted General Stuart and his staff to bid hasty adieus to their ladies. The women panicked and screamed that they feared retaliation from the Yankees. Mr. Cockey, who did not desire to be treated as a sympathizer, mounted and rode off with the Confederate staff officers. They departed in a cloud of dust, leaving their belles to face the dastardly Yankee cavalry, who they erroneously assumed were in close pursuit. Ten minutes later, Munford's exhausted troopers rode through Urbana on the way to Monocacy Bridge, two miles below Frederick.[33]

While the Confederate cavalry and the advance units of the Army of the Potomac sparred ineffectually with one another, the rest of McClellan's huge army continued to deploy, like the outspreading tentacles of a squid around its prey. The Kanawha Division of the IX Corps moved out around 6:30 A.M. Moving north from Goshen, it covered the twelve miles to Damascus, then reached Ridgeville by nightfall where it bedded down.[34]

The rest of the corps started to move out between 7:00 A.M. and 9:00 A.M. By late in the afternoon, the entire command was spread out between Ridgeville and Hyattstown.[35] The Pennsylvania Reserves, which were leading the I Corps, bivouacked around Poplar Springs, about four miles southeast of Ridgeville, on the National Pike.[36] Brigadier General John P. Hatch's division camped another two miles down the pike at New Lisbon and Brigadier General James B. Ricketts' command spent the night at Cooksville two miles further to the southeast.[37]

The men of the I Corps never forgot the rich farms which lined their route of march. "All the farmers stayed at home and attend to their farms," Private Lyman C. Holford (Company A, 6th Wisconsin) noted with astonishment. "The consequence [is] that instead of weeds as high as a man's head, we find corn, tomatoes, potatos, tobacco, fruit of all kinds, and rich grain, and haystacks."[38]

The 5th Virginia Cavalry, with John Pelham's section of artillery, had visited Poplar Springs the day before.[39] The detachment had been turned loose from Stuart's Horse Artillery and Fitzhugh Lee's brigade to secure fresh mounts for the light artillery. One of the participants in the raid, who years later still kept his identity anonymous, sadly recalled the heartache that Captain James S. Oden, the battalion quartermaster, and his party visited upon the defenseless farmers. He remembered that the bulk of the inhabitants were German immigrants or of Teutonic stock who spoke with a barely intelligible English-German dialect.

At one farm, three very "strapping women," upon seeing the Confederates approaching, locked their house, armed themselves with pitchforks, and formed a defensive formation in front of the barn. Captain Oden detailed a squad to make a feint of breaking in the house door. The women immediately set after the thieves with their pitchforks at the "charge bayonets." The moment they abandoned the barn door, another detachment of Rebels slipped inside and stole the Germans' four fine horses. The Confederates rode away with the women bitterly cursing at them in a language which they did not understand.

Shortly thereafter, when the Rebels tried to lead away a family's only two horses, the entire family—men, women, and children—clung to the horses' necks and pleaded pitifully with the soldiers to spare their beloved pets. The tears of these helpless civilians struck the Confederates deeply. "Such scenes as this were far more trying to our men than those in which resistance was met with," the pillager wrote. He took the time to swap his broken down iron gray for a strong bay. He later excused his "acquisition" with the following explanation, "A cavalryman of Stuart's command, in those days, was as ready for a loose trade as a Methodist minister, and as they all owned their animals there was nothing to prevent them from following their intention in that direction."[40]

The marauders, despite the fact they paid for everything they took in cash, did not ease the hatred they bred in the hearts of the Marylanders with whom they came in contact. According to Sergeant Major E. M. Woodward (2nd Pennsylvania Reserves), whose brigade occupied Poplar Springs, the Rebels left the farmers destitute of the horses which they needed to work their farms.[41] Despite some assertions by the local citizenry that the cavalry had been very civil to the townspeople and had merely inquired if the farmers had seen any Yankees about, most of the local people groused loudly about how the "liberating Army" had paid for whatever they stole in worthless Confederate currency and even more worthless quartermaster's orders.[42]

Further to the south, where the Confederates no longer exercised any influence, the II Corps trudged into its camp. The 8th Ohio deployed as skirmishers on Walter's Plantation, near Clarksburg, where it ran into Federal cavalry who told them something must be brewing at Harpers Ferry, Virginia. Sixteen-year-old Sergeant Thomas F. Galwey (Company B, 8th Ohio) shrugged their theories off as rumor. He grumbled in his diary about seeing Brigadier General John Sedgwick, who commanded the Second Division of the corps, and that he was "crusty as usual."[43]

The XII Corps arrived in Damascus and halted there while the IX Corps passed through. Adjutant Charles Mills (2nd Massachusetts) took the time to keep his mother abreast of the army's condition. He wrote, "...it [Maryland] is paradise compared with Virginia. The country is far more beautiful also. Moreover, things seem to be conducted with some system, unlike [John] Pope's style of doing things. Instead of marching one long column on the road, with constant halts, we have five or six parallel ones, and accomplish our march much more quickly and easily."[44] While the Union infantry bedded down for the night, the Federal cavalry continued to reconnoiter what they assumed were the Confederates' flanks. The 1st New York Cavalry, flushed with its "victory" at Hyattstown, received orders in the evening to move west toward Barnesville. In a chilly, persistent rain, they marched into the early hours of the next day. According to Sergeant William H. Beach (Company B), the regiment picked up a battery of light artillery on the way to the front.[45]

At dusk, Captain James Abraham and his independent West Virginia cavalry company sloshed into New Market, twelve miles northwest of Poplar

Springs, and inadvertently scattered several videttes from Fitzhugh Lee's brigade, who retired west without firing a shot.[46] No sooner had his soaked troopers begun to prepare their dinners than an aide from Major General Ambrose E. Burnside ordered them to remount and proceed to the general's headquarters.

The lieutenant and his company responded immediately. The general commanded Abraham and his troopers to escort one of his headquarters' orderlies to Major General Joseph Hooker, who commanded the I Corps. The lieutenant, who knew the road well from his prewar travels, did not relish the rain drenched ride to Poplar Springs.[47]

The steady rain which fell that evening seemed to preoccupy the soldiers more than the threat of battle. The storm stretched from Frederick to Washington, D.C., where the V Corps was preparing to advance. Private John L. Parker (Company F, 22nd Massachusetts) grumbled years later how the rain made his wool blanket too heavy to carry but did nothing to break the humid, close air or lay the choking dust in the roads.[48] Miles away in Ridgeville, Private Edward Schweitzer (Company I, 30th Ohio) wrote in his diary that his head and feet got "pretty wet" in the day long march from below Damascus.[49]

The Army of the Potomac, despite its renewed vigor since George McClellan assumed command, was composed of a considerable number of untried troops. Twenty of the regiments on active service had been in uniform for less than two months. Adjutant Charles J. Mills of the veteran 2nd Massachusetts complained, "The 13th New Jersey and 107th New York are new. In point of numbers they are certainly an acquisition, as the whole Brigade was only 1500 before, and these Reg'ts amount to about 2000. But as the Colonel of the New Jersey Reg't. told Colonel [George L.] Andrews yesterday that they had never been drilled in loading and firing, and have done nothing but march since they left home, I do not imagine they will prove very valuable auxiliaries on the field."[50]

The fact that so many of the green regiments had never handled their weapons before became evident as the campaign continued. The 35th Massachusetts seemed to exemplify what could go wrong with rifle muskets in unfamiliar hands. During the afternoon, in Damascus, Private Frederick F. Blakely shot off the forefinger of his right hand when his weapon accidentally discharged.[51] Numbers did not mean strength in battle, which this new regiment would prove in the near future.

A disconcerting animosity existed between the eastern and the western regiments of the IX Corps. Brigadier General Jacob Cox had to earn the respect of the elitist eastern officers. They considered his Ohioans as little more than undisciplined militia. At Ridgeville, the general sent out the 6th New York Cavalry to picket the front and ordered his infantry to bivouac in line of battle rather than "en masse" as expected by the corps commander, Jesse Reno.

Around dusk, Reno galloped into the 23rd Ohio as it prepared to bed down. He found the men helping themselves to a local farmer's straw. Lieutenant Colonel Rutherford B. Hayes (23rd Ohio) and the brigade commander, Colonel Eliakim Scammon, stood by watching the men rob the farmer.

Outraged, Reno lashed into the Ohioans. "You damned black sons of bitches!" he spat. Who was their colonel, he demanded.

Rutherford Hayes boldly stepped forward and said he had the honor of commanding them. Reno demanded an explanation for the men not bivouacking en masse and for the looting.

The colonel told the general to see General Cox if he wanted the troops' formation explained. He also suggested the general contact the quartermaster to settle the matter with the straw's owner, provided he were loyal.

Reno calmed down and again asked Hayes to identify himself, which he did. Hayes deliberately requested the general do the same. Not wanting to be "shown up" by an upstart westerner, Reno reminded Hayes they were in a loyal state and were forbidden to loot.

Rutherford Hayes, having little respect for Reno's Regular Army attitude, snorted, "Well, I trust our generals will exhibit the same energy in dealing with our foes that they do in the treatment of their friends."

What did the colonel mean by that remark? the general demanded.

Nothing, the colonel retorted.

The corps commander galloped away with the Ohioans' cheers for their colonel echoing off his back.[52]

Across the Catoctin Mountains, west of Frederick, the Confederate Army of Northern Virginia continued to push westward. McLaws' division spent the night on the Burkittsville-Middletown Road, east of Crampton's Gap at South Mountain.[53] R. H. Anderson's division was in Pleasant Valley along the western base of South Mountain. The rest of Longstreet's Corps stretched from Boonsboro to Funkstown, west of Turner's Gap at South Mountain.[54]

Jackson's Corps, without D. H. Hill's division, which was camped at the eastern base of Turner's Gap, had taken the first left hand road from Boonsboro and marched crosscountry to Williamsport.[55] His command crossed into Virginia and that evening camped astride the B & O Railroad line, northwest of Martinsburg, Virginia.[56]

Robert E. Lee was pulling his army out of Maryland and neither the Yankees nor his own men knew it. To do this, he had to surround Harpers Ferry and eliminate the Federal garrison there so it would not have a chance to cross the Potomac northwest of his line of march and trap his army in Maryland. McLaws was to envelop Harpers Ferry from the east and Jackson was to take it from the northwest. Brigadier General John G. Walker's division, which had spent the day in battle line south of Frederick on the Point of Rocks Road, was to take it from the east.[57] Except for Lee's division and corps commanders, it seems no one guessed what the commanding general was intending to do. Many supposed that if the Army of Northern Virginia was going to invade Pennsylvania, Harpers Ferry would have to be captured to protect Lee's line of supply across Maryland to Winchester and Martinsburg, Virginia.

Captain John C. Gorman (Company B, 2nd North Carolina) best reflected the perspective of the rank and file when he recalled, "Little did I think, as I stood that night on picket duty on the mountain [Turner's Gap, South Mountain] that in a few short days a battle would be fought on the very spot I stood on."[58] The campaign thus far had seemed more like a leisurely excursion than an invasion.

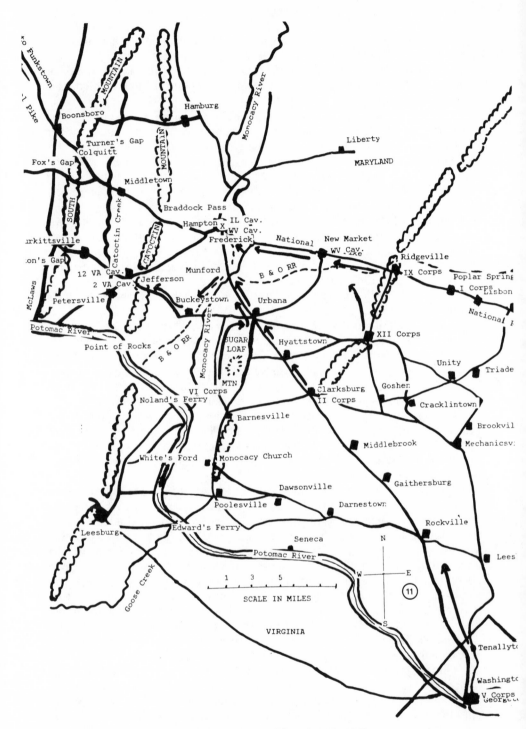

MAP 11: Situation—September 12, 1862.

Chapter Eight

SEPTEMBER 12, 1862

LIEUTENANT JAMES ABRAHAM and his independent company of West Virginia cavalry wandered onto a Mr. Burdette's farm near Poplar Springs not too long after midnight. The lieutenant, who had met Burdette a year or two before the war, suggested to Burnside's aide that they leave the men at the bottom of the hill, below the springs, while they rode up to Major General Joseph Hooker's quarters.

Arousing the Marylander from his bed, the lieutenant, true to the form of a good line officer, requested and received shelter for his troopers before they proceeded any further. With his men sheltered from the torrential rain, the two officers rode to the top of the hill into Hooker's bivouac.

They found the general asleep in his wall tent. Abraham felt that it was too small for a man of Hooker's military stature. The lieutenant, who idolized Hooker, was taken aback somewhat when the general arose, lit his own candle and greeted the two in his nightshirt. Abraham eyed Hooker from head to foot—nearly six feet tall, about 180 pounds, smooth, ruddy face, grey hair, soft blue eyes—he thought to himself that the general, "in fact...possessed but few of the visible characteristics one would naturally look for in a soldier...." Following more or less informal introductions, the IX Corps staff officer informed General Hooker of General Burnside's desire to lead the army on the following morning [September 12].

"Tell General Burnside," Hooker growled, "that I issued my orders in Washington City five days ago which were to govern the movements of my troops to this place, fixing their time of arrival here, and the heads of the columns came in within ten minutes of the time designated. I this evening issued orders to govern their march tomorrow, and shall not change them; they move at nine o'clock. Tell Gen. Burnside that if he wishes the advance to put his troops on the road before I get up and say to him, that we will strike the enemy's videttes at the Monocacy, will have a brush with Stewart's [sic] cavalry about Frederick City, a nice little fight at South mountain and hell on the Antietam."

At that, the two officers stepped out into the pouring rain, rejoined their troopers at the base of the hill, and started their long ride back to Ridgeville. Lieutenant Abraham never forgot what he assumed was the general's premonition about the days which followed.[1] He had no way of knowing that both Hooker and Burnside had already received intelligence that the Confederate infantry had left Frederick and that only their cavalry remained behind to picket the mountain ranges.[2]

While Abraham's Independent West Virginia Cavalry rode through the heavy rain to relay General Hooker's comments, the Army of Northern Virginia was arising to another day of marching. Longstreet's corps of two divisions continued its trek at daylight. Leaving their camp a few miles below Funkstown on the National Pike, they headed for Hagerstown.[3]

Early that morning Longstreet's cavalry escort, the 1st Virginia Cavalry, under the command of Lieutenant Colonel L. Tiernan Brien, approached Funkstown on the National Pike.[4] The lead squadron of the regiment drew their sabres as they approached the village and inadvertently flushed some young boys from along the roadside, who raced for their lives into town, screaming, "The rebels are coming! The rebels are coming!"[5]

Their shrieks brought Mrs. Angela Davis to her front steps. She and her neighbors looked down the street as two mounted, sabre bearing Confederates came into view, paired off to opposite sides of the road and faced each other. Seconds later eight to ten men from the first squadron in the column, brandishing their sabres in the air, spurred their horses into a gallop and charged into the town. Thundering to a halt in front of Mrs. Davis' house, they leaped from their saddles and called for her neighbor by name. His brother, who was in the 1st Virginia Cavalry, had told his comrades to pay their respects.

The Confederates had barely quieted themselves when the main body of the regiment started into town. Mrs. Davis marvelled at Lieutenant Colonel Brien's fine uniform and his superb charger. The well dressed and completely accoutred cavalrymen contrasted sharply with Brigadier General Robert Toombs' threadbare infantry who followed them.

Dressed mostly in butternut, and wearing battered slouch hats, which according to Mrs. Davis, "looked worse than those worn by the darkies," they carried everything they owned over their shoulders in blanket rolls. Many were barefoot and others were nearly so, with their toes poking through the holes in their worn out shoes or the tears in their dirt encrusted socks.

"Poor, brave, uncomplaining men," she wrote, "I felt so sorry for them."[6]

All day the Confederate column moved through Funkstown. The cavalry entered Hagerstown just before noon and dismounted on the Hagerstown-Williamsport Pike, three miles west of the city near the Fairgrounds and the B & O Railroad crossing.[7] The people of Hagerstown did not display the bitter anti-Southern sentiment that the Confederates had experienced between Frederick and Funkstown. The young ladies handed flowers to Lieutenant William M. Owen and his men as the Washington Artillery creaked and jolted through the town.

While passing through, the cannoneers scrounged through the local stores for waterproof clothing and dress patterns for their girlfriends back in Louisiana. The lieutenant, tongue-in-cheek, said they went shopping. One of his enterprising men discovered a store which was overstocked with bell crowned beaver hats. When he showed up with his crew wearing one of the old fashioned beavers, the battery raided the store and bought out the proprietor's supply. The long naps on the back of the top hats would keep their necks dry and they sported them proudly despite their unmilitary appearance.[8]

There were decidedly pro-Union displays in the streets of the city as well. As Colonel Joseph Walker's South Carolina brigade passed Hager's Store, a group of young ladies gathered in the doorway to flaunt their patriotism in the Rebels' faces. Their leader, a very attractive girl, about sixteen years old, waved a big Union flag to and fro and taunted the passing Confederates with, "Why don't you fight under this flag?" One of Orderly Sergeant Frank Mixon's soldiers (Company E, Volunteers from Gregg's brigade) shouted back, "Hagerstown, Hager's Store, Hager's daughter—hurrah for Hager!" With that, the rest of the regiment gave the girls a rousing Rebel Yell.[9] The Confederate rank and file conducted themselves with a dignity which inspired compassion.

In Funkstown, Mrs. Davis pitied them so much, in spite of her strong pro-Union convictions, that she put buckets of water with several tin cups at her front door. She watched the men continuously dip into the buckets and return the cups. Occasionally she tried to comfort them with feigned cheerfulness and she told the soldiers she was from New York and not a Rebel sympathizer. Nearly every time she asserted herself, the Rebels shouted, "Boys, this lady says she is a Yankee," before turning to her and asking her if the water was poisoned and if she would sample it first. Usually she tasted it to prove her honesty.

The Confederates, many of them young men who had learned to distrust kindness from the hands of their enemies, repeatedly asked her why she bothered to be so nice to them when she did not support their cause. Mrs. Davis justified her humanitarianism with the Biblical injunction, "because my Heavenly Father has taught us to give a cup of cold water even to our enemies." This attitude strained the chivalrous chords of one officer's heart. Riding up to Angela Davis, he demanded a cup of water from one of the enlisted men. The man explained, as he handed the water to the officer, "A 'Yankee' lady is giving us the water."

The "gentleman" hurled the cup to the pavement. "If that is so," he blustered, "I won't drink a drop of it!" As he dug his spurs into his horse and dashed off, the embarrassed enlisted man tried to soothe Mrs. Davis. He said the fellow was drunk and he hoped she would not be offended.[10]

The Union sympathizers in the area went so far as to try and coax the blacks who were traveling with Lee's army into desertion. Private John Dooley of the 1st Virginia, having gone into bivouac with his command on the Hagerstown-Williamsport Pike, sent his manservant Ned to Hagerstown to forage for some supplies for himself. The slave met an abolitionist woman who tried to cajole him into running away. Ned, who had no desire to be liberated, played along with her and her family. Burdened down with bunches of grapes and other delicacies, he returned to John Dooley later in the afternoon.

"Massa John," he exclaimed, "they couldn't fool me. I knows too much about them abolitionists; dey gits a feller to go 'long with 'em and then lets him shift for hisself." The old man laughed at his own insight. What could a freedman do anywhere, once he was freed? He was still considered a third, or at the best, a second class person who had no legal rights under the law.

Ned paused a moment to regain his composure, then continued with a seriousness born of genuine love, "Massa John, it wouldn't do for me to leave you here, for if you gits wounded or anything happens to you, who goin' to take care about you an' tell the folks at home when you are well?"[11]

Many of the soldiers of the Army of Northern Virginia had no one to watch out for them except themselves. Private Calvin Leach of the 1st North Carolina scratched in his diary that the exertion from marching over South Mountain at Turner's Gap and the hot weather coupled with no water ration caused considerable suffering.[12] Corporal William W. Sherwood (Company F, 17th Virginia) phrased it more bluntly. He wrote, "...we began to go up the blue ridge and it was a very tiresome march."[13]

While Longstreet's corps secured Lee's northern flank at Hagerstown, Lafayette McLaws' and Richard H. Anderson's divisions continued to push west toward Harpers Ferry. By the end of the day, McLaws' command of four brigades stretched from one mile below Brownsville, Maryland (one mile southwest of Crampton's Gap) to the base of Maryland Heights, southeast of Harpers Ferry.[14]

As ordered, Stuart's cavalry division effectively masked the rest of the army's movements across the mountains. Thomas Munford's brigade with Chew's battery started toward Jefferson from Frederick early in the morning. The column moved very slowly and did not finish the twelve-mile ride until just before dark. It camped for the night near Jefferson.[15]

The Federal army did not waste any time renewing its pursuit of the Confederates. It was raining rather heavily when the IX Corps took to the road from Ridgeville to New Market between 7:00 A.M. and 8:00 A.M.[16]

Cox's Kanawha Division reached New Market shortly before 11:00 A.M., at least an hour ahead of the rest of the corps. Jesse Reno, the corps commander, and several other officers from the three remaining divisions, joined Cox in front of a tavern along the limestone paved National Pike. Cox stood behind them to eavesdrop on their conversation. His infantrymen's easy, swinging step with weapons balanced properly at the shoulder did not go unnoticed. He listened proudly to his peers involuntarily comment upon the professional carriage of his Westerners. The unfortunate enmity between him and his commanding general, which sprang from the Colonel Hayes' incident, disappeared.[17] Rather than slow down the division's advance, Reno halted the other commands to allow the Kanawha Division and its wagons to maintain the lead of the corps.[18]

Brigadier General Samuel Sturgis' division wheezed into New Market around noon after what some of the men in the 51st Pennsylvania (Ferrero's brigade) considered a very laborious march. The rain, which ended soon after their arrival, left the roads slippery and treacherous. The men of the 51st Pennsylvania felt they were wearing more of the road than they considered proper.[19] When the clouds cleared, the sun came out with a muggy vengeance. While the division rested for two hours in New Market to let Brigadier General Isaac Rodman's division take the National Pike ahead of it, the roads turned into caked mud and then dust. "Never saw such a hot sun," Private James Pratt (Company H, 35th Massachusetts) pithily complained to his wife.[20]

He seemed to forget there were more important things to notice about the Maryland countryside than its muggy September afternoons. An American flag which sported red, white, and blue ribbons from the top of the staff greeted Captain James Wren (Company B, 48th Pennsylvania) and his company as they neared the bank of the B & O Railroad, east of the village. When the thirty-nine-year-old captain looked closer, he discovered a "verey fine young lady" and three of her friends were waving the colors at the regiment from the railroad bank. Company B gave her three cheers and the "Tiger"—mating growl of approval—as they passed. "New Market is a fine little town," James Wren concluded.[21]

A few miles to the southeast along the National Pike, Joseph Hooker's I Corps fell drastically behind schedule. The heavy rain undoubtedly contributed to the delay. John Reynolds' Pennsylvania Reserve Division took to the Pike at 10:00 A.M., one hour behind its assigned time.[22] Brigadier General Rufus King's division, at Lisbon received its marching orders at 10:00 A.M. but could not move out until after division inspection which delayed the advance until noon.[23] When the division did get under way, it did so at an extremely slow pace. Brigadier General John Gibbon's western brigade (19th Indiana, 2nd, 6th, and 7th Wisconsin) drew the rear guard of the column, with the 6th Wisconsin getting stuck with provost duty. That slowed the steps even further.[24] Corporal George Fairchild (Company C) groused about the entire affair in his diary.

"Our fun," he sarcastically penned, "was to hunt up stragglers and play the rogues march for them."[25]

The division covered nine to eleven miles that day in nine hours of marching.[26] Brigadier General James Ricketts' division of Hooker's corps marched nine miles to the vicinity of Strawtown and went into bivouac in the fields which, according to the local people, the Confederates had abandoned the day before. In the early afternoon, they heard the distant rumble of artillery and knew there was trouble ahead and they were not going to be part of it.[27]

Wade Hampton, whose cavalry brigade drew the rear guard for Jeb Stuart's cavalry division, scattered his videttes as far as the western limits of New Market. His command of one hundred fifty men consisted of North Carolinians, South Carolinians, Mississippians and Alabamians from four of the brigade's five regiments.[28] Cobb's Legion (Georgia) and the brigade's wagons passed through on the National Pike around noon, about the same time that Hampton's pickets caught sight of Lieutenant Abraham's company of West Virginia cavalry as it led the IX Corps advance through New Market.[29] The general personally conducted the withdrawal toward the high ground immediately west of the substantial stone bridge across the Monocacy River. Leaving a small picket detachment on the hills on the opposite side of the river, Hampton pulled the rest of his command to the lower ridge west of the bridge and put a section of Captain J. F. Hart's South Carolina artillery on either side of the pike.[30] As an added precaution, he detailed a small party of saboteurs to set black powder charges in the bridge. Since they were not equipped with drilling equipment, the troopers set the fused charges along the sides of the road, next to the bridge's walls.[31]

The time seemed to drag on forever. As was their custom, Stuart and his staff officers had decided to spend their leisure hours in comfort. Following a cursory inspection of the stone bridge position, Stuart, Fitz Lee, Wade Hampton, William Blackford and the rest of the generals' staffs rode back into Frederick to dine with Miss Katherine S. Markall and her family, at the home of the prominent secessionist lawyer, Mr. William J. Ross. William Blackford, whose father had lived with the Rosses before the war, while he was in law school, recommended the lawyer's home to Stuart. They could count on fine food and gracious female companionship there.

The entourage did not enjoy their brief ride down East Patrick Street. The dour citizens stood silently in front of their closed up houses and shops and stared coldly at the Rebels as they passed through. A few brave souls ventured forth to ask what Von Borcke recalled were "ridiculous questions."

A flurry of activity from the roof of a third-story house along Patrick Street distracted Von Borcke from carefully scanning both sides of the street. He saw a pro-Union man frantically signalling what Von Borcke later assumed were the approaching Federal troops with a large national flag. The major immediately posted two sharpshooters on the sidewalk across from the house and sent word to the gentleman to cease and desist or be shot. The civilian, whom Von Borcke did not identify, instantly complied. He and his flag rapidly disappeared from the house top. The officer quietly joined the rest of the staff at the Ross house for lunch.[32]

About two blocks to the south, just east of Market Street, the Confederate surgeons, who had shared quarters with the Federal surgeons at the old Hessian Barracks, joined their adversaries for relaxing conversation from the second floor porch of the east wing of the barracks. Doctor Charles E. Goldsborough grudgingly watched the Confederate officers liberally help themselves to the Federal hospital liquor cabinet and could not help but reflect upon the tremendous social gulf which separated the rank and file Rebels from their superior officers. The surgeons were much better cared for than the enlisted men.

Goldsborough felt sorry for the Rebel line soldiers who lived in such filth and who rooted for food like animals. He hated the cruel, overbearing discipline he saw meted out to the private soldiers for the slightest infractions while general officers cavorted about the streets drunk without reproach. For a week, he and his comrades had heard nothing of the Federal army. While the Confederate surgeons drained the hospital's liquor supply and passed the time in idle chatter, he wondered if the Army of the Potomac would ever come to their reprieve.[33] Goldsborough had no way of knowing that while the doctors lounged about on the porch, James Abraham's West Virginians were closing in upon Wade Hampton's videttes.

The West Virginia cavalrymen flushed the Confederate vidette outpost from the high ground east of the stone bridge around noon.[34] As they chased the Rebels across the Monocacy and up the opposite crest toward Hart's artillery, a couple of the Rebs touched off the powder charges on the bridge. Explosions thundered along the river bank. Pieces of powder kegs shot into the air, and the acrid stench of burned powder lingered in the heavy cloud of smoke which engulfed the river bottom. Seconds later when everything settled down, the disappointed Confederates, who were secure behind Hart's readied battery, could see the stone bridge blackened but still standing.[35] Lieutenant Abraham, rather than gallantly ride into the Confederate artillery and Wade Hampton's rear guard of one hundred fifty men, whom he saw preparing to meet his attack, wisely decided to cut off his pursuit and directed his cavalry to the crest of the much higher eastern bank of the river.

Abraham did not have to wait long for further directives. Colonel Eliakim Scammon, commanding the Kanawha Division's lead brigade (the 12th, 23rd, and 30th Ohio), joined the lieutenant minutes after he regrouped his company. Before Abraham could deliver a report, Colonel Augustus Moor, with Captain Frederick Shambeck's company of Chicago Dragoons (later Company C, 16th Illinois Cavalry) in tow, blundered into the conversation before either of the other officers could decide upon a course of action.

Moor, who had seniority over Scammon, ordered the two cavalry companies to cross the bridge and take the Confederates in a frontal assault. The West Virginians were to spread out to the left and attack the Rebels on the flank while Shambeck's Westerners, in column of fours, were to drive a wedge through the Confederate center. Abraham protested. A sturdy post and rail fence bordered both sides of the road on the western bank. The rails were too tightly morticed to be rapidly torn down.

Moor leaned forward in the saddle. "This colonel's eyes," Abraham sarcastically recollected, "were so badly off that he could not see the enemy's guns...."

Without another moment's thought or hesitation, Colonel Moor sent the two companies recklessly careening down the slope, with the Illinois troopers in the lead. Abraham's West Virginians lost precious momentum as the head of the column crashed into the southern fence along the road and dismounted to pry it apart. Abraham happened to look up as Shambeck's men rounded a sharp bend and foolishly tried to climb the first low ridge to get at the Confederate guns which were west of it. A single blast of canister sent the cavalrymen reeling in confusion back to the bridge.[36]

In Frederick, Doctor Charles Goldsborough noticed the puff of smoke and abruptly got to his feet as the report of the cannon echoed seconds later into the "L" created by the two barracks buildings. Two more puffs followed by louder bursts caught everyone's attention. The Federal surgeons, correctly surmising that the bigger guns were Federal, could not conceal their relief.

The Confederate doctors, who saw the Yankee army was approaching, matter of factly admitted it was time for them to leave Frederick. Taking long pulls from the Northerners' "medicinal" whiskey, they shook hands with the Federals, then said goodbye. Hurriedly packing up, they mounted and disappeared down Market Street west of the barracks.[37]

Two and a half miles away, west of the stone bridge, Lieutenant Abraham and his West Virginians stubbornly tore down at least three fences in an effort to gain a peach orchard on the Rebels' southern flank.[38] In their excitement, they did not recall the scream of the two Federal shells which sailed over the ground north of the National Pike. A section of Captain Seth J. Simmonds' Kentucky Battery, consisting of a twenty-pounder Parrott gun and a twelve-pounder Napoleon, pulled up seconds after the ill fated charge began, unlimbered and responded with counter battery fire.[39] Unable to withstand the much heavier Federal guns, and with the Yankee cavalry in the orchard on their flank, the Confederates withdrew their guns and their cavalry toward town. They pulled out slowly and in good order, indicative of excellent command control and discipline.

Abraham and his West Virginians calmly dismounted in the orchard to await orders and infantry support. Rather than remain idle, they helped themselves to the peaches, a good many of which they harvested.[40] [Refer to Map 12]

The Federal artillery continued to shell the farm land to within a mile of the city's limits. It inflicted no casualties upon the Confederates who remained mounted, with their section in battery. The Yankee gunners intentionally provided cover fire for the infantry which arrived at the river sometime around 1:00 P.M. or 1:30 P.M.[41] From his home in Frederick, Jacob Engelbrecht counted off each of the reports as they echoed west from the river. When the twenty-second roar faded away, he checked his watch. It was 2:00 P.M.[42]

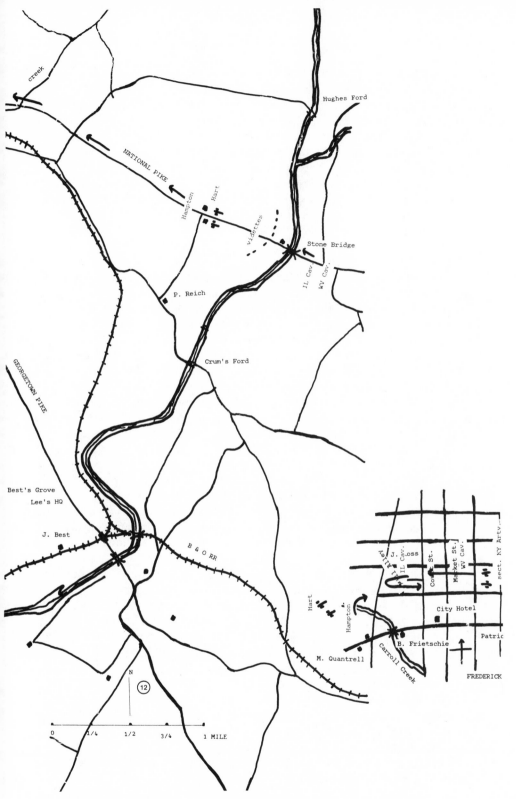

MAP 12: September 12, 1862. Cavalry skirmish in Frederick, Maryland.

The 23rd Ohio, Colonel Scammon's front regiment, crossed the bridge and advanced up the pike. The 12th Ohio, followed by the 30th Ohio, crossed the river by a ford half of a mile north of the bridge. The 30th Ohio deployed to the right of the 23rd Ohio, which had gone into line north of the pike, while the 12th Ohio flanked south below the bridge, under the cover of the western bank of the hill nearest the bridge and went into line on the southern side of the pike, immediately opposite the left flank of the 23rd Ohio.[43]

Once in formation, the brigade calmly waited for Colonel Moor and Captain Schambeck's cavalry company to escort Captain Simmonds' artillery section down the road until it also came abreast of the line.[44] Colonel Benjamin F. Reno and a couple of orderlies from Company G of the 1st Maine Cavalry, cautiously followed the overly ambitious Moor.[45] Jacob Cox, the division commander, rode with them.

Behind them, Moor's brigade deployed without him. While he was trying to "play soldier with cavalry," as Lieutenant Abraham put it, the 28th Ohio moved into line behind the 12th Ohio. The 11th Ohio went into column of four in the road to support the cavalry, and the 36th Ohio flanked half a mile to the right, beyond supporting distance of the front line.[46]

The battle unfolded like a grand parade in slow motion. From Frederick near the Hessian Barracks, Doctor Goldsborough watched the Union columns straighten like graceful, long dark blue ribbons across the fields on either side of the pike.[47] Shortly after they advanced, Simmonds' two guns unlimbered at the first place they could alongside the road and opened fire upon the Confederate cavalry and Hart's two pieces, which, having retired a little bit closer to town, halted, faced about and went into battery on both sides of the road less than half a mile away from the Federals. In the quick exchange of rounds, Simmonds' first shot disabled one of the Confederate's pieces, killing two horses and three men. The Rebels quickly withdrew their troops and both pieces into town, moving west on Patrick Street.[48] An orderly galloped to the Ross house and interrupted the officers' pleasant afternoon. Fitz Lee and Hampton left first. Stuart remained behind to command the troops in the street.[49]

Goldsborough, automatically assuming the Federal infantry would immediately pursue them and that the Confederates had abandoned the city, ran down Market Street to the Patrick Street intersection. To his chagrin, he found a Rebel officer calmly sitting astride his horse and staring down East Patrick Street. The officer, who sported a full, sandy colored beard, noticed Goldsborough from the corner of his eye and motioned the doctor to his side.

"You are a Federal surgeon, are you not?"

"Yes," Goldsborough replied.

"Tell your commanding officer," the Rebel said firmly, "that we have treated your friends kindly while in possession of the city, and we will expect your army to do the same toward those who sympathize with our cause."

The doctor, who knew the rules of "civilized" warfare, boldly told the officer he could not deliver a verbal message but he would convey the request if it were in writing.

The officer surly informed him he had no time for such a formality and if he heard of any hostile actions against the secessionists, he would be in a position to retaliate. Apparently, Goldsborough did not seem overly frightened or impressed because the officer felt obliged to inform him that he was Jeb Stuart. Still unimpressed, the surgeon turned away from the general and started down Patrick Street toward the eastern suburbs of the city.[50]

In the meantime, the Rebel cavalry disappeared around the bend in the National Pike where the eastern branch of Carroll Creek intersected the road from the north. Unable to ascertain their position, Colonel Benjamin F. Reno, acting as the headquarters liaison officer for his older brother, Major General Jesse Reno, told Colonel Moor to hold back his cavalry until he and his two orderlies could scout the terrain. The colonel halted his advance.[51]

At that point a young corps staff officer, whom General Cox did not know, rode up to him between the two brigades and impetuously exclaimed, "Why don't they go in faster? There's nothing there!"

The general turned, rather nastily, toward the impudent officer and asked, "Did General Reno send you with any order to me?"

"No," the aide insubordinately replied.

"Then," Cox retorted, "when I want your advice I will ask it."

Taken aback by the general's effrontery, the officer galloped toward the front, where he accosted Moor and repeated the same spiel. The colonel erroneously assumed that the corps commander was displeased with his performance and to the amazement of everyone around him, ordered the two cavalry companies to charge into Frederick.[52]

Colonel Benjamin Reno and his orderlies rode about five hundred feet into the field north of the National Pike where he could look down Patrick Street. He spied the Confederate rear guard falling back toward Market Street. Simultaneously, he glanced over his shoulder to the left and caught Moor, with drawn sabre, leading Schambeck's Illinois Cavalry, then Abraham's West Virginians, full tilt, in column of four, along Patrick Street. By the time Reno realized what was going on, the column had thundered past him. He yelled at his orderlies to follow him and they spurred their mounts into a futile gallop to try and catch up.[53]

Cox, having lost sight of the headquarters aide, did not realize what was happening. All he saw was the dust of the column, followed closely behind by Simmond's Napoleon field piece and the twenty-pounder Parrott.[54]

(Jacob Engelbrecht, the civilian who had so meticulously counted the number of artillery shots fired that day, saw far more of the action than most of the participants. Shortly after the artillery ceased fire, he went to the roof of the V. S. Brunner warehouse near the railroad depot, and observed the action with a pair of opera glasses.)[55]

Brigadier General Wade Hampton sent one hundred ten of his troopers out Patrick Street, while he remained behind to oversee the ambush. Placing Captain Hart's section in the road immediately west of the Patrick Street-Mill Alley intersection, he turned the command over to Colonel M. C. Butler

(2nd South Carolina), who was moving his column of forty men south on Mill Alley. As soon as the troopers cleared Patrick Street, Butler ordered Captain Joseph F. Waring (Company F, Jeff Davis Legion) to right about face the men, which placed Captain John Meighan (Company C, 2nd South Carolina Cavalry) at the head of the column. From the warehouse roof top, Jacob Engelbrecht breathlessly watched the Confederates, through his opera glasses, draw their sabers and pistols for an ambuscade which he could not prevent.[56]

Moor and Schambeck's Illinois cavalry company blindly clattered down Patrick Street toward Mill Alley.[57] Frightened pedestrians, among them Doctor Charles Goldsborough, fearing they would be ridden down, frantically scrambled for cover. By the time he recognized that a gray haired colonel was leading the charge, Captain Seth Simmonds' artillerymen had unlimbered both guns near the corner of South Carroll and Patrick streets and were preparing to give fire. The doctor hesitated a moment before trying to force a locked door which opened onto the sidewalk. When he heard pounding hoofbeats further down the street, followed by shouting and a staccato of pistol shots, he panicked. Throwing his back into the recessed doorway, he tried to melt into the door and stood there motionless, too scared to move.[58]

The Confederates at Mill Alley heard the Federals long before they reached the street corner. Private David B. Rea (Company C, 1st North Carolina Cavalry) glanced around the corner and snatched a quick look at the portly Colonel Moor, whom he noted was mounted upon a splendid black horse. At the same time, a little girl leaned out a window across the street to wave her white handkerchief at the colonel.

Whirling his sabre above his head, Moor shouted, "Come on, boys, come on, let's give 'em hell!"

Seconds later, Hart's artillerists fired canister into the head of the Yankee column. Then Lieutenant John Meighan's cavalrymen sprang at it as it crossed the intersection. Firing and slashing as they went, the Confederates took the Yankees by surprise.[59] Pistol shots cracked loudly down the street, which stirred Stuart's officers from the Ross house. As William Blackford and Heros Von Borcke frantically mounted up to escape, a civilian opened fire upon them from a second story window with a shotgun. The buckshot barely missed Von Borcke and Wade Hampton, who was nearby.[60] Too rattled to return fire, the two staff officers tried to spur away when one of the ladies sprinted through the fire to hand Blackford a plum cake in a sack, which he unceremoniously threw across his saddle as he rode away.[61]

The fighting at the intersection, while vicious, did not last long. A South Carolinian tried to strike Moor down with his sword but the colonel, who proved surprisingly agile, struck the blade aside then wrung it from the Rebel's grasp. Moor raised his sword to crush the Carolinian's skull, when the soldier spurred his horse into the colonel's and ducked. The blow missed the Southerner and threw Moor off balance, and before he could regain his posture, the Rebel grabbed him by the collar and jerked him from the saddle. The colonel thudded solidly upon the cobblestones and his command streamed rearward in a panic, with the Confederates whooping and hollering right behind them.[62] Their cries preceded them down the street. Transfixed in the doorway, Doctor Goldsborough watched the Yankee formation disintegrate. The Illinois troopers crashed into Abraham's West Virginians. Unhorsed soldiers scrambled madly for garden walls and alley ways. They took any available route of escape.

Sergeant Edward Hollister (Chicago Dragoons) feverishly tried to outrun a Rebel, who was trying exceedingly hard to slash him from behind. Every time the enemy thrust at him, the sergeant seemed to be one hoof beat ahead. As he came abreast of Goldsborough, the Southerner tossed his saber aside, and drew his pistol. Taking deliberate aim, he shot the sergeant in the back. Hollister, who had been standing in the stirrups, fell to the street dead, only a few yards away from Goldsborough.[63]

Colonel Benjamin Reno and his two orderlies having just caught up with the tail end of Moor's column near Market Street tried to wheel their horses to the rear. Reno's animal balked. Repeated tugs could not force it to run. The ring from the Martingale bridle had gotten caught in the horse's bit, and hurt its mouth. It refused to move.

Four shots, in rapid succession, zinged past the colonel. He tried to return fire but his pistol merely clicked. Dismounting, he turned his horse up a nearby alley, then ran sixty to seventy feet down the street, looking for a way out. With the Confederates getting much closer, he scaled an eight-foot high board fence and threw himself into a backyard flower garden and a small orchard.

Bolting into the house through the back door, he walked into the front room, where he frightened the three ladies who lived there. After he introduced himself as a Yankee, one of the women rose to open the front door.

"Madam," he gasped, "please, don't open the door."

The Rebel cavalry dashed past the house, startling her further. Saying that he did not wish to be captured, Reno told the women that he would go back out the rear door into the garden, which he did.[64]

The Confederate pursuit did not last long. During the rout, one of the Yankee cavalrymen knocked down the number four man on the twelve-pounder Napoleon. The stunned artilleryman did not release his grip on the lanyard as he fell. The blast rattled windows and shook houses along the street, knocking both Yankees and Confederates to the pavement. At least eight Federal soldiers crashed to the ground with their horses.[65] Lieutenant Charles P. Achaff (Company F, 11th Ohio Infantry) disappeared almost entirely under his horse. What the survivors could see of him told them that he was dead as well and they made no attempt to retrieve him.[66]

In their haste to escape, the remaining Illinois cavalrymen stampeded into the gun and overturned it into the ditch along the northern side of the road. While the Confederates retreated toward the far edge of town, the Fredericktonians reappeared on the streets to assess the damages. Doctor Goldsborough very carefully checked over Sergeant Edward Hollister's body.

The surgeon recovered the soldier's watch, New Testament, and revolver. He checked the weapon. The cylinder still contained six rounds and was cold. It had not been fired. The doctor shook his head in disbelief. He could not understand why Hollister did not use it.[67]

Captain Schambeck lost three other men dead, four captured, and twelve wounded, including himself, none of whom he reported as casualties. Similarly, Lieutenant James Abraham tallied his losses. John Elliot was dead.

"Adolph Eberhart had his leg shot off," the lieutenant later wrote.[68]

Five or six others received slight wounds, and the Confederates captured one sergeant and three enlisted men.[69] The Federals retrieved their two artillery pieces. The Confederates had not been able to get close enough to capture the twenty-pounder's team, which they would have needed to haul both guns away. In the melee, they gunned down five of the six horses belonging to the twelve-pounder.[70] Despite their failure to capture the artillery, the Rebels successfully drove the Yankees from Frederick. They also won the casualty game. With two dead and five wounded or missing, they came out ahead.[71] [Refer to Map 12]

Abraham summarized the fiasco succinctly when he recalled, "I have never been able to understand how any one lived between the two fires...." In reference to the unfortunate Colonel Moor, who was then riding his horse toward Middletown under a Confederate escort, the lieutenant musingly added, "...I never knew him to play soldier with cavalry again, he having evidently convinced everyone else, if not himself, that he was not a success with troops on horseback."[72]

The 11th Ohio, being the support regiment for the cavalry column did everything it could to catch up. It took the regiment half an hour to run into the suburbs of Frederick.[73] As the wheezing infantrymen got to within a few hundred yards of Frederick, Lieutenant Colonel Augustus H. Coleman (11th Ohio) halted the regiment to formally deploy it for battle. Breaking from column of four to column of division (two companies on front), he ordered the regiment to fix bayonets. He positioned himself on the front center of the first division to lead his troops quite dramatically into Frederick.[74]

To the right of the National Pike, Lieutenant Colonel Rutherford B. Hayes (23rd Ohio) got his regiment hopelessly lost in a huge cornfield east of the city.[75] While his Ohioans floundered around, the 12th Ohio, on his left flank, deliberately assaulted the peach orchard to its front.

Private Samuel Compton (Company F), who had begged for permission to be relieved from wagon guard so he could take part in the liberation of Frederick, followed his company headlong into the neatly spaced trees. He recalled that the men sort of took a "detour" into the orchard. Unable to resist the tree branches which were so laden with fruit that they nearly touched the ground, Private Americus "Tub" Keyes (Company K) called out, "Break ranks! Charge for the peaches."

The men obeyed immediately. Before long the trees were filled with blue coated soldiers. One of them fell out of his roost and opened his scalp upon his bayonet.

"First blood," Tub Keyes shouted. "Fall in."

The Ohioans suddenly dropped out of the branches as Second Lieutenant Robert B. Wilson (Company F) timidly walked in on them. "Forward," Keyes commanded.

Once again the companies bolted forward, without their lieutenant, who meekly trailed after them. When they approached a second, much larger orchard, the wag, Tub Keyes again ordered the men to, "Halt. Charge for the peaches."

The enemy could wait. Samuel Compton fondly remembered the taste of those peaches sixty years later. They still made his mouth water.[76]

Farther to the right, the 11th Ohio started to straggle. Overheated soldiers chucked their knapsacks aside as they trotted past the scene of the earlier fighting.[77] The corpse of a Confederate artillerist, who had lost the top of his skull to a shell fragment, lingered unpleasantly in Private Martin L. Sheets' (Company A) mind.[78] As the command continued along Patrick Street their well intended charge fizzled into an embarrassing crawl. The panting soldiers collapsed by squads along the pavement, too fagged out to continue running.[79]

To the north, where Market Street intersected Seventh Street, the 36th Ohio, which had strayed way off course, rounded the corner and came running through town to drive off Confederate cavalry, which was no longer there.[80] Instead, the loyal citizens, freed at last from Southern control, flooded the streets. Federal flags sprouted from the second story windows. Cakes, pies, fresh water, peaches, every type of conceivable delicacy showed up along the streets. The civilians' enthusiasm went beyond the reasonable limits of propriety.[81]

Women, overflowing with adoration, snatched begrimed soldiers from the line of march and kissed them.[82] An elderly German woman who weighed in at two hundred pounds, literally snatched Company F's Lieutenant Wilson (12th Ohio) off his feet. Wrapping her arms about his waist, she lifted him off the ground in a bear hug and nearly shook him into unconsciousness, while his men cheered her. Once she let go, the lieutenant received orders to place Company F on provost duty with instructions to round up deserters and womanizers, a duty which his men did not relish because it took them away from the huge quantities of food on which the troops around them gorged themselves.[83] Besides policing other soldiers, they had to police their own. When an extremely attractive young lady sprang from the roadside and blurted she could kiss the entire regiment, a grisly old sergeant unabashedly stepped forward with the suggestion that she start with him. She hurriedly declined and retreated into the throng on the sidewalk.[84]

The regiments seemed to pour into Frederick from every quarter.[85] Clean up began immediately. Soldiers of the 11th Ohio found their Lieutenant Charles Achaff (Company F) beneath his dead horse, gasping for air, but otherwise unhurt. They pried him free and he walked away from the spot as if nothing had happened.[86]

Colonel Benjamin Reno, who found his horse in a nearby front yard after the skirmish, rode into the Patrick Street-Market Street intersection, where he discovered a corner building filled with wounded or sick Confederates. Realizing he was probably the only healthy Yankee in that end of town, he called out to any of the Rebels who might hear him, "Just keep quiet; our troops are coming up, and will see that you are taken care of." Wheeling his horse about, he started down East Patrick Street where he encountered Colonel William Steere at the head of his regiment, the 4th Rhode Island (Harland's brigade, Rodman's division). He informed the colonel of the "hospital" and continued to ride down the street while the colonel detached a company to guard their prisoners.[87]

Shortly thereafter, Colonel Reno came across General Burnside, commander of the right wing of the Army of the Potomac, and his brother, Jesse Reno. Company G of the 1st Maine Cavalry protectively surrounded the two officers. Jesse Reno, having believed the "eyewitness" reports of his brother's fast running orderlies, seemed pleasantly surprised that Benjamin was not among the dead.[88]

At the generals' appearance, the people of Frederick went berserk. Surgeon Lewis Steiner joyously wrote in his diary, "...the citizens, with enthusiastic eagerness, devote themselves to feeding the troops and welcoming them to their houses, as their *true* deliverers from a bondage more debasing than that of the African slave."[89]

Within the half hour, around 5:00 P.M., General Pleasonton's cavalry division with the 1st New York Cavalry and the 12th Pennsylvania Cavalry entered the city on the Urbana Road, only to discover the town secured by the IX Corps' infantry.[90] Everywhere they went, people thrust food, American flags, or themselves upon the troopers. Samuel Gilpin of the 3rd Indiana Cavalry scratched in his diary, "...[we] were getting in the middle of all this flag waving, singing, shouting, joy, and caresses."[91] With few exceptions, the troopers never forgot the overwhelming gratitude of the Fredericktonians.[92]

Some men, however, being more perceptive of the effects of war on the populace harbored darker remembrances. Private Charles M. Smith (Company E 1st Massachusetts Cavalry) in a letter to his parents, described Frederick as "a large city but pretty well ransacked by the rebs."[93] An officer with the 6th U.S. Cavalry, Captain James S. Brisbin, had grown tired of the war and the senselessness of it all. Deep inside he harbored a genuine compassion for the Confederate soldiers, whom he knew were so destitute and hungry.[94]

While the cavalry column pushed into the town to the suburbs around south Market Street, the rest of Brigadier General Isaac P. Rodman's division struggled over the fences and through the cornfields one-half mile southeast of the city, between the B & O Railroad and the National Pike. Colonel Harrison Fairchild's brigade got bogged down in the tall corn. With darkness coming on it was impossible to tell where the individual regiments were among the stalks, except where their colors bobbed fitfully up and down. The brigade (9th, 89th, and 103rd New York) moved to the rocky knoll overlooking the railroad depot and went into bivouac.[95]

Brigadier General Samuel Sturgis' division occupied the high ground on both sides of the stone bridge where the National Pike crossed the Monocacy. James Nagle's brigade (2nd Maryland, 6th and 9th New Hampshire, 48th Pennsylvania) held the high hill top west of the river.[96] The 35th Massachusetts, from Colonel Edward Ferrero's command (51st New York, 51st Pennsylvania, 21st and 35th Massachusetts), wandered into a cleared straw field north of the bridge, plundered the straw stacks, and bedded down for the night.[97] On the high meadows, east of the river, the rest of the brigade went into camp surrounded by the rubbish of the Confederates who had occupied the area before them. Rumors filtered through the 21st Massachusetts that Stonewall Jackson's corps had bivouacked in the vicinity to which one of the regimental wags wryly commented that the Confederates' "graybacks" (lice) were commingling with their Federal "cousins."[98]

As the rest of the IX Corps settled down, Brigadier General Orlando Willcox's division passed down the National Pike, to Market Street, where it split. The 79th New York marched a mile or two north of the city to go on picket.[99] Colonel Thomas Welsh's brigade (8th Michigan, 46th New York, 45th and 100th Pennsylvania) stretched from the western outskirts of the city to its eastern suburbs. Private Frederick Pettit (Company C, 100th Pennsylvania) found only dead horses along the roadside and houses filled with sick and wounded Rebels. The regiment went into camp somewhat relieved that it had not seen the "elephant."[100]

While the IX Corps settled down for the evening and squads of soldiers stole into the city to enjoy the hospitality of the people, the II Corps, having spent the bulk of the day on the march finally went into bivouac around Monocacy Junction. Sixteen-year-old Thomas Galwey of the 8th Ohio marvelled at the golden brilliance of the setting sun as it reflected off the windows of the city. He had seen few places to rival its majestic beauty.[101]

As General Sedgwick's division swung into camp near the Junction, the 19th Massachusetts fell into close formation alongside the Georgetown Road to listen to the "riot act." Aware that Robert E. Lee had issued a proclamation against looting, the regimental adjutant read off an order prohibiting foraging. In the middle of the declaration, Lieutenant John P. Reynolds' black servant, Henry Johnson, hove into sight with an earthen crock of butter tucked under each arm. Grinning at the officers of Company D while they furtively hand signalled him to dodge for cover, he deftly took the hint and eluded the regimental staff. "The officers managed to make good use of the butter," the regimental historian recalled from a veteran's wry perspective. "It was too much of a luxury to part with orders or no orders."[102]

The II Corps had picked up quite a few new regiments, particularly in Brigadier General William French's division. The men, having never seen the "elephant," looked forward to battle with an eagerness born of their ignorance.

One of the soldiers, Private John Weiser (Company G, 130th Pennsylvania) wrote home to his parents, "...Sometimes we was within One mile of the Enemy but could not overtake them they being fast afoot and accustomed to running.... Some of the Critters have been taken prisoners today. I do not Know how many I seen on the Road as we were resting...."[103] Having never been in combat, the private had not learned to respect his adversaries.

The VI Corps did not set any speed records again that day. The corps left the base of Sugar Loaf Mountain at 9:30 A.M. in a thick fog which covered the troops with a fine mist. By 5:00 P.M., it had gotten as far as Urbana after following a circuitous route of eleven miles.[104]

It filed off the Georgetown Road just northwest of Urbana around 5:00 P.M.[105] The men viewed the day through lackluster eyes. Captain Jacob Haas (Company G, 96th Pennsylvania) grumbled in his diary about the cloud cover and the fog which followed the rain. He then jotted down that he sent a letter with a $20.00 check to his wife.[106] His close friend, Captain Peter Filbert of Company B, unable to ignore the "beautiful" stream which the regiment had trailed for the last two miles, stripped down and bathed in its refreshing water, despite the fact that others were drinking from it.[107] Drum Major Montreville Williams (3rd New Jersey) noted that the regiment went on picket and that the "boys," who had marched twelve to fourteen miles that day "slept well."[108] The XII Corps got as far as Ijamsville—a day long trek of eleven miles.[109] With all of the sleeping, straggling and looting, the march from Washington, D.C., for the most part seemed like a lark.

President Lincoln did not like the Army of the Potomac's rate of march. In reference to General McClellan, he complained to his cabinet, "He can't go ahead—he can't strike a blow. He got to Rockville, for instance, last Sunday night, and in four days, he advanced to Middlebrook, ten miles, in pursuit of an invading enemy. This was rapid movement for him."[110]

While the Army of the Potomac concentrated around Frederick, Jeb Stuart and his rear guard slipped to the summit of Catoctin Mountain at Braddock Pass, where the National Pike crossed the Blue Ridge west of the city. Leaving the Jeff Davis Legion at the pass with a section of Hart's battery, the general and the rest of the Wade Hampton's brigade rode down into the valley and camped around Middletown. David Rea of the 1st North Carolina Cavalry described the town as a "dingy mountain hamlet."[111]

The night seemed all the more bitter because of the cold reception the Confederates received there. Stuart and his close knit staff quartered themselves in a comfortable farmhouse. They "shared" Captain William Blackford's plum cake with the captain and generally enjoyed themselves.[112]

Shortly before Hampton's men settled in for the night, Colonel Munford's isolated 2nd and 12th Virginia Cavalry and Chew's battery rode sleepily into Jefferson. Weary from the twelve-mile ride, they found very little to comfort them. Private George Neese (Chew's battery) never forgot the sour expressions upon the civilians' faces. The women appeared distant and cold. As they passed through en route to a bivouac closer to the mountain, the tired artillerist noticed a brief flicker of white in a nearby window pane. A young woman ever so cautiously waved her handkerchief at the Confederates as they rode by. She had her back turned so that her neighbors could not clearly see her secessionist demonstration.[113] Winter nights were never so cold as Western Maryland's loyalty to the South.

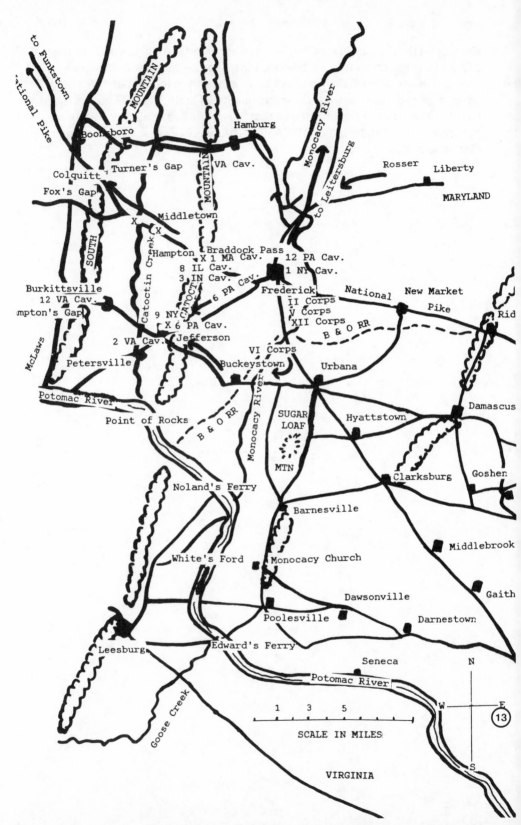

MAP 13: Situation—September 13, 1862.

Chapter Nine

SEPTEMBER 13, 1862

THE ARMY OF THE POTOMAC began the morning as typically as it had all the previous ones—with a cavalry reconnaissance to its front and flanks. McClellan ordered Alfred Pleasonton to send his cavalry division in three directions to probe Robert E. Lee's rearguard. Colonel Andrew T. McReynolds' brigade (the 1st New York and 12th Pennsylvania Cavalry), with a section of Lieutenant Peter C. Hains' Company M, 2nd U.S. Artillery proceeded north on the Emmitsburg Road.

The men were dirty and fatigued. Having left their tents and baggage in Washington at the beginning of the campaign, they had not changed their clothing in eight days. They were also traveling on short rations. Privately, Sergeant William H. Beach (Company B, 1st New York Cavalry) suspected that the Confederates were making a move toward Pennsylvania.[1]

Pleasonton also detached the 6th Pennsylvania Cavalry (Rush's Lancers) to scout toward Jefferson, a village six miles southwest of Frederick.[2] They left Frederick around first light without any infantry support. Pleasonton obtained General Burnside's permission to send the 3rd Indiana, 8th Illinois, and 1st Massachusetts cavalry regiments out at the same time. They proceeded rather cautiously along the National Pike and around 9:00 A.M. reached the base of Catoctin Mountain, about four and a half miles west of Frederick.[3]

One section each of the 2nd U.S. Artillery from Hains' Company M and Captain James M. Robertson's combined battery B and L accompanied them.[4] They came under fire from Hart's Washington South Carolina artillery which was in the road not too far below the crest at Braddock Heights.[5]

A single shot brought the column to a halt. Lieutenant Hains and Captain Robertson immediately rolled their four guns into battery to the left and the right of the road.[6] The gunners cranked down the elevation screws on their two bronze Napoleons and two three-inch Ordnance Rifles to reach the top of the ridge.[7] Their rounds, while providing moral support for the cavalry, did not hit their intended targets. Their shots struck the mountain side well below the Confederate artillerists.[8]

Captain Hart's South Carolinians did not set any gunnery records either. The 3rd Indiana Cavalry, leading the advance, halted in the road, which brought the 8th Illinois Cavalry and the 1st Massachusetts Cavalry to a full stop in the Pike. The Confederates' solid shots whizzed harmlessly overhead.[9] Captain Casper Crowninshield, commanding the regiment, ordered his troopers to dismount. The New Englanders quietly lowered themselves to the ground with their horses' reins in their hands.[10]

Charles M. Smith of Company E recalled with amazement, "Sept. 13th was the first day I ever heard the shell whistle about me." It was a day filled with novelty. Abandoned Confederate corpses lying motionless along the roadside and in adjacent cornfields haunted him. Days later they appeared in his letter home more like mirages than human beings. He never said what killed them but merely that they had died.[11]

Although the regiment had never been under direct artillery fire before, it behaved quite well.[12] Adjutant Charles Francis Adams (Company H, 1st Massachusetts Cavalry), who had to exchange his worn out horse for another in Frederick, put the spurs to his new mount as the first report from Hart's battery echoed across the valley toward the city. He felt disgusted because his baggage, in particular his towel, toothbrush, and soap, remained in his used up horse's saddlebags, and he had a sinking feeling that he had parted company with them forever. When he caught up with the regiment and saw that it was dismounted and resting along the roadside he quietly slipped into its ranks. The occasional Rebel shots which fluttered harmlessly overhead reminded him of the time the regiment came under indirect fly-overs on James Island. One or two of the rounds came disagreeably close but he decided to tough it out.[13] Everything seemed to slow down.

The artillery fire awakened Heros Von Borcke of Stuart's staff, who was trying to spend a pleasant morning away from the war at a farm house near Middletown. The major awakened the general and within minutes they rode off to inspect the situation at Braddock Heights.[14] They left the 1st North Carolina, 2nd South Carolina, 10th Virginia, and Cobb's Legion of Wade Hampton's brigade on the ridge east of Middletown as a reserve.[15]

Stuart arrived very shortly after the Federal cavalry made its appearance in the valley east of Catoctin Mountain. He behaved hesitantly, almost confused.[16] The general did not consult with either Captain Hart, who had immediate command of the artillery at the pass, or Lieutenant Colonel W. T. Martin, whose regiment (Jeff Davis Legion) was strung out along the crest to support the guns, before assuming overall command.[17]

Unable to ascertain how many Federal troops he faced or whether it was a reconnaissance or the entire Army of the Potomac, Stuart sent a courier back for the rest of Hampton's command.[18] The 1st North Carolina dismounted and fanned out along the crest south of the National Pike as sharpshooters, alongside Colonel Martin's Mississippians, while the rest of the brigade formed the rear guard.[19] They hurried rather needlessly. The Federals seemed to walk into the conflict as if they had time on their side. They did.

Private David Rea of the 1st North Carolina, from the eastern side of the mountain, stared in awe at the strong Federal cavalry column as it came within range of Hart's gunners. From his post, he watched the artillerists repel what seemed like several half hearted cavalry attempts to gain the base of the mountain. Eventually, the Federals spread out to both sides of the Pike and dismounted to advance as skirmishers.[20]

Stuart never rode beyond the wooded crest of the mountain. Without personally surveying the terrain, he dispatched a mountain howitzer and its crew under the direction of Von Borcke to the north along the ridge. The Prussian and his small command charged headlong from the National Pike into the dense undergrowth on its flank. While the artillerists fought the brush with swords and their bare hands, the soldiers on both sides settled down to watch the artillery volley ineffectually at each other.[21] [Refer to Map 13]

The cannonading reverberated as far east as Mount Airy eighteen miles away. Private Lyman C. Holford of the 6th Wisconsin distinctly heard the individual reports of the guns from his regiment's bivouac in New Market. He calmly wrote in his diary that he would not be the least bit surprised if the army had another fight with the Rebs very soon. After all, they were said to be on the Maryland side of the river.[22] First Lieutenant Isaac Hall (Company D, 97th New York) and his men patiently listened to the distant rumbles of the artillery duels along the Catoctin from their division bivouac near Mount Airy. The reports rolled through the air at sporadic intervals, a great deal like the rumors which said that the Rebels were retreating.[23]

While the opposing batteries seemingly competed to see which gunners could overshoot the other, the Army of the Potomac ever so cautiously began to move. The VI Corps started to uncoil itself at sunrise. Winfield Scott Hancock's (6th Maine, 43rd New York, 49th, and 137th Pennsylvania, and 5th Wisconsin) and Colonel William Irwin's (7th Maine, 20th, 33rd, 49th, and 77th New York) brigades, leading the advance, crossed the Monocacy east of Buckeystown and continued west over the covered railroad bridge above the B & O Railroad. The command halted for an hour in the apple and peach orchards near the Monocacy flour mills then moved into a meadow which Sergeant Robert Westbrook of the 49th Pennsylvania, mistakenly, believed was on the Thomas Farm.[24] Brigadier General W. T. H. Brooks' 2nd, 3rd, 4th, 5th, and 6th Vermont regiments marched about four miles farther southwest to Adamstown.[25] The remainder of the corps moved out sometime between 10:00 A.M. and noon. Eight miles separated them from their advance units and their officers did not set any speed records while trying to get them there.[26]

Word of the fight near Braddock Pass came to Army Headquarters east of Frederick long after the echoes of the first artillery exchanges died away. Brigadier General Isaac P. Rodman's two-brigade division of the IX Corps took to the road sometime between 10:00 A.M. and 11:00 A.M.[27] Colonel Edward Harland's command (the 8th, 11th, and 16th Connecticut, and the 4th Rhode Island) marched at the "common time," west on the National Pike, heading to the relief of Pleasonton's cavalrymen.[28] Church bells accompanied the strains of church choirs, which celebrated the city's liberation.[29] Once again, the pro-Unionists thronged to the streets to rejoice. Colonel Harrison S. Fairchild's brigade (the 9th, 89th, and 103rd New York), which slowed its rate of march to impress the civilians with their expertise at drill, arrived at the western end of Frederick.[30] As the applause of the hundreds of enthusiastic civilians dissipated, a courier from the 6th Pennsylvania Cavalry galloped into the brigade with a report that the Lancers had cornered some Rebels in an orchard near Jefferson.[31] General Rodman immediately ordered Colonel Harland to detach the 9th New York, without its battery of Dahlgren boat howitzers, to the cavalry's assistance.[32]

At this time McClellan did not have any idea what was going on beyond his skirmish posts and along the eastern base of Catoctin Mountain. Consequently, he moved only as much of his army as he deemed necessary to carefully probe Lee's flanks. Therefore he moved his army just far enough to prepare for a defensive strike should the Army of Northern Virginia attempt to dislodge him.[33]

The remainder of the IX Corps was either approaching Frederick or still in its camps along the Monocacy east and southeast of Frederick.[34] Sykes' division of V Corps Regulars and the II Corps stayed in their camps southeast of the city near Monocacy Junction.[35] The I Corps remained at New Market to await further instructions. The leaderless XII Corps was just arriving upon the field in the vicinity of Crum's Ford about three fourths of a mile below the National Pike.[36]

The 27th Indiana in Brigadier General George H. Gordon's brigade led the advance for the XII Corps. Companies F and A (on the left and the right, respectively) forded the Monocacy at Crum's Ford sometime between 10:00 A.M. and 11:00 A.M., about the same time that Rodman's division uprooted itself and marched toward Frederick. The two companies advanced in skirmish formation northwest, parallel to and north of Crum's Ford Road. As they neared the intersection with the Hughes' Ford Road, which crossed the National Pike one-fourth of a mile to the north, the two companies halted to allow the IX Corps troops to advance into Frederick.

The infantrymen instinctively flopped down in the grass, relieved that they had encountered no Rebels. The regiment was not ready for its first engagement. Privates John Campbell and David B. Vance, Corporal Barton W. Mitchell, and Sergeant John M. Bloss (all Company F) went to the ground within arms reach of each other in the shade of an overgrown tree line. To Bloss' right, Private William H. Hostetter and the rest of Company A followed suit.

While they were lying there, Bloss struck up a conversation with Mitchell. Bloss happened to glance over the corporal's shoulder and saw Vance reaching out with his left hand to grab what appeared to be a long yellow envelope.

"What is that paper laying there in the grass?" Bloss asked the corporal.

Forty-six year old Corporal Mitchell did not hear him but David Vance, to Mitchell's left, who was the corporal's junior by twenty-six years, did.

Vance, who had already snatched up the envelope, read the address aloud, "General D. H. Hill, Commanding...."

"Hand it to me," Bloss demanded.

Vance passed it over Mitchell to Bloss. As he did so, two cigars fell out onto the ground next to Mitchell. The corporal snatched them up immediately and stuck one in his mouth.

"I know what this is," Mitchell chirped while striking a match.

He started to enjoy the smoke as Bloss read the envelope.

The name "D. H. Hill" immediately attracted the sergeant's attention. Opening the envelope, he read the communiqué out loud.

"Special Orders, No. 191, HDQRS. Army of Northern Virginia, September 9, 1862...." he muttered, as the enlisted men in his immediate area gathered around him. The names, "Jackson," "Longstreet," "McLaws," and "D. H. Hill," jumped out at him as he continued. "Boys," John Bloss blew through his teeth, "this is an important paper if genuine. I will take it to Captain Kopp."

Mitchell returned the untouched cigar to Bloss who refolded the envelope and tried to restore it to its original condition.

William H. Hostetter (Company A), the left flank of his company, and David Vance (Company F) watched Bloss leave Mitchell to enjoy his cigar, and walk back to the reserve picket, which was about one hundred yards to the rear of their line. The sergeant showed the envelope to Captain Peter Kopp, who quickly read the letter and without losing a moment, escorted the sergeant to Colonel Silas Colgrove, the commander of the 27th Indiana.

"Colonel," John Bloss said, as he handed the envelope up to Colgrove, who had not had time to dismount, "this dispatch I have just found is important, if true."

Before the colonel could look at the papers, Brigadier General Nathan Kimball, whose II Corps brigade was nearby, rode up to the three soldiers. Kimball glanced at Bloss, his nephew by marriage, then took the envelope from the colonel's hands and read it himself. Without saying a word, he turned about and rode off toward Division Headquarters. Colonel Colgrove followed him immediately.[37]

The two arrived at Brigadier General Alpheus Williams' quarters only to find him absent. They encountered the division's Acting Adjutant General, Captain Samuel E. Pittman and turned the document over to him for inspection.

Pittman, who had been a teller at the Michigan State Bank in Detroit before the war, scanned the handwriting and the authorizing signature at the end, "R. H. Chilton, Assistant Adjutant-General." He recognized Chilton's handwriting. As a paymaster in the United States Army in the 1850s, Chilton had cashed quite a few checks at Pittman's window.

Saying that the order really came from the headquarters of the Army of Northern Virginia, he started to draft a note to McClellan's adjutant general when General Williams, who had just arrived, stopped him. Williams commanded the captain to personally deliver the Special Orders to the commanding general.[38]

The artillery duel between the Rebels at Braddock Pass on Catoctin Mountain and the Yankees' regular artillery in the valley to the east had grown monotonous. Wade Hampton's troopers felled trees and left them along the roadside. When the Federals forced their position, which the rank and file knew was inevitable, they intended to barricade the National Pike to slow down their advance.[39] They had nothing to fear from the Yankee gunners, who had increased the elevation on their pieces and persistently overshot the mountain.

Von Borcke's artillery finally cut their way onto an open plateau on the Federal right front. As the gun unlimbered and wheeled into battery, the major seriously studied the enemy's position, which was some fifteen hundred feet below him. His men cheered in derision and hurled their kepis in the air as each Yankee round whizzed harmlessly over their heads. Their flippancy turned to awe as the Yankees seemed to put more troops into the field. "The valley beneath, stretching away from the immediate base of the mountain, was literally blue with Yankees," Von Borcke recalled.[40]

With the first artillery shot that morning, the well drilled troopers of the 3rd Indiana Cavalry and the 8th Illinois Cavalry peeled off the road by twos— the 3rd to the south of the road and the 8th to the north.[41] Von Borcke's crew scattered the 8th Illinois a couple of times within two hours. The major enjoyed watching the mounted soldiers scurrying about for safer positions.[42]

Eventually, the 3rd Indiana rode into the place immediately in front of Von Borcke's post.[43] The 8th Illinois countermarched to the south side of the road, where in the face of extremely inaccurate fire, three-fourths of the command dismounted and prepared to skirmish up the mountainside.[44]

The 3rd Indiana did the same. The troopers, in a superb display of professionalism, counted off by fours.[45] Every fourth man held the reins of the first three, who dismounted, unsnapped their carbines and prepared to advance in open order (one man every six feet).[46]

The Yankee skirmishers disappeared into the brush and trees at the base of the steep mountainside, which caused Von Borcke no small amount of distress. The minute the enemy moved out of his line of sight, the major sent an orderly after Stuart with his request to retreat.[47]

The Confederate skirmishers immediately north and south of the National Pike found themselves harder pressed than Von Borcke. From their position below the eastern crest of the mountain they could see what seemed like an entire division of Yankee infantry moving slowly down the Pike from Frederick in column of fours. Their column extended as far as some of the dismounted troopers of the 1st North Carolina could see.[48]

Lieutenant Charles Francis Adams of the 1st Massachusetts Cavalry quietly watched the lead regiment of the infantry column march up to a position in the pike to the right rear of his men.[49]

The 11th Connecticut led Colonel Harland's untried brigade (the 8th, 11th, and 16th Connecticut, and the 4th Rhode Island) to the relief of the cavalry.[50] The foot soldiers nonchalantly plopped down on their haunches to keep the horsemen company. Adams politely informed a captain near him that the Rebels had perfect range on the road.

The words had barely left his mouth when a solid shot whirred through the brush just above his head, skittered across Lieutenant William H. Forbes and Captain Caspar Crowninshield of the 1st Massachusetts Cavalry, who were lying down not thirty yards behind him, and smashed into a mixed file of sitting cavalry and infantrymen.[51]

Private Charles M. Smith (Company E, 1st Massachusetts Cavalry) gaped in horror as the cannon ball plowed through the four men near him. It smashed the legs of three infantrymen and grazed the boot of one of the Massachusetts' troopers who happened to be sitting between them. Smith had never seen men wounded in such a manner before. The poor fellows, he sadly informed his parents, lost their legs.[52] That single shot forced Harland's brigade of more than 1,900 men to deploy.

Pressured by overwhelming Yankee infantry support, Von Borcke became more nervous with every minute that Stuart took to materialize. The general finally showed up. He gave the gunners permission to retire their piece toward Middletown. Then he dismissed the reforming Yankees below him as merely two brigades. When Von Borcke told him that cavalry skirmishers had just moved into the brush and trees below them, Stuart refused to believe him.

Rifle fire crackled to the right and a little bit to the rear of the two officers. Von Borcke loudly tried to force his point of view upon the general, but to no avail. Finally, Stuart rebuked him.

"Major," the general shouted, "I am quite sure those shots came from our own men, who are firing at far too great a range; ride over there at once and order them to reserve their ammunition until they can see the whites of the Yankees' eyes."

Despite the fact that he knew he was probably going to be killed, the major obeyed.[53]

The shooting on the right came from the skirmishers of the 1st North Carolina, who literally did "see the whites" of their enemies' eyes before firing. The steep hillside forced the 3rd Indiana Cavalry to crawl on their hands and knees toward the Confederate lines. The North Carolinians killed one Indianian and wounded two more in what seemed like guerrilla tactics.[54] Private Oliver H. Trestor (Company D, 3rd Indiana Cavalry) threw himself over what everyone thought was an abandoned fence. The Rebels, who were hiding behind it, promptly killed him before running from the field.[55]

Jeb Stuart's stubbornness nearly cost him his obedient aide. As Von Borcke neared the right flank where he assumed the 1st North Carolina still remained, he heard the brush rustle in a thicket close by him. He delivered the general's command in a very low voice only to see a Yankee push his way through the branches nearby. At the same time, a bullet chipped the bark off the tree behind him, inches from his skull.

Wheeling his horse in a semi-circle, the Prussian spurred away in the opposite direction as more Federal skirmishers emerged into the clearing around him. Returning to his original position, he and Stuart, who with bullets cutting the leaves around them finally believed the major, galloped across the open ground toward the safety of Middletown Valley. The rocky mountainside was almost as difficult as the Yankee bullets to contend with. Stuart sent the word along the line to retreat.[56]

It did not take much for Hampton's cavalrymen to comply. Hart's battery disappeared over the crest of the mountain with the first small arms exchange. It retreated in full sight of the Yankee skirmishers. The 1st North Carolina Cavalry and the Jeff Davis Legion, after obstructing the road in several places with felled trees, followed the guns as quickly as they could.[57]

It was 2:00 P.M. The fighting which had started at first light had lasted over eight hours.[58] Two regiments from Hampton's small cavalry brigade and one battery had kept four Yankee guns, more than 1,900 infantry, and three cavalry regiments at bay without losing a single man. On the other hand, despite their poor marksmanship, they had wounded six Yankees—three of them seriously—and killed one in a rather sharp skirmish.[59] [Refer to Map 13]

While the Yankee cavalry dislodged Wade Hampton's troopers from Braddock Pass, McClellan pored over "Special Orders 191," which Pittman delivered to him before noon. Instantaneously, Army Headquarters came alive. Orderlies and aides scurried back and forth acting as if they had something important to do. Someone muttered something about the rapid movement of the army and a nearby civilian, sensing that it spelled impending danger to the Army of Northern Virginia, slipped away to bring the word to the Confederate rear guard.

Simultaneously, General McClellan wired President Abraham Lincoln one of the finest wartime fictions ever produced:

> I have the whole rebel force in front of me, but am confident, and no time shall be lost. I have a difficult task to perform, but with God's help will accomplish it. I think Lee has made a gross mistake, and that he will be severely punished for it. The army is in motion as rapidly as possible. I hope for a great success if the plans of the rebels remain unchanged. We have possession of Catoctin. I have all the plans of the rebels, and will catch them in their own trap if my men are equal to the emergency. I feel I can count on them as of old.... Will send you trophies....[60]

"Little Mac," as his men referred to him, did indeed have all of Lee's plans and the bulk of the Rebel army was in front of him. "Special Orders 191" gave McClellan more than he needed to know, but the most important parts (paraphrased) were:

1.   All sick and non-ambulatory men would proceed to Winchester. All others would catch up with the army as it moved.

2.   General Jackson would pass by Middletown, move toward Sharpsburg, cross the Potomac, secure the B & O Railroad near Martinsburg, and cut off the Federals as should escape from Harpers Ferry.

3.   General Longstreet would take the same road to Boonsboro and halt his command there with the reserve, supply, and baggage trains.

4.   Generals McLaws' and R. H. Anderson's Divisions would follow the same route as Longstreet, turn off at Middletown on the route to Harpers Ferry, and take Maryland Heights to capture the Federal garrison at Harpers Ferry by Friday (September 12).

5.   General Walker's Division would cross the Potomac at Cheek's Ford, and take Loudoun Heights by Friday morning, if practicable. He would assist McLaws and Jackson in capturing escaping Federals.

7.   D. H. Hill's Division would form the rear guard of the army.

8.   General Stuart would detach a squadron of cavalry to accompany Generals Longstreet, Jackson, and McLaws. The main body of the cavalry would bring up the rear of the army and gather up stragglers.

9.   Jackson, McLaws, and Walker would rejoin the army near Boonsboro or Hagerstown once their objectives had been achieved.[61]

Although he did not know the exact size of the Army of Northern Virginia, McClellan knew what Lee intended to accomplish with it. At the time he wrote his message, the general did not have possession of Catoctin nor was his army in motion "as rapidly as possible." He piddled around at his quarters for almost three hours before notifying any of his field commanders of his find. Why he delayed so long has never become a matter of record, but Colonel Ezra Carman of the 13th New Jersey speculated that the general thought the orders were a clever hoax which the wily Lee had deliberately planted where he would find them.[62]

The "Little Napoleon" of the Union Army at this point demonstrated that he was a Napoleon in his own mind, rather than one in fact. A quick review of his dispatch to Lincoln illustrates that he was not going to assume any fault for defeat but that it would fall directly upon his troops. He would only catch Lee in his own trap if the Union Army was "equal to the emergency."[63]

His army, while eager, was not prepared to pursue the Confederates. It would not initiate any type of action without authority from above. Orders to march did not leave McClellan's headquarters until after 2:00 P.M. They did not reach either Pleasonton's cavalrymen or the lead elements of the IX Corps until around 3:00 P.M.[64]

By then the 3rd Indiana, 8th Illinois, and the 1st Massachusetts cavalry regiments had crossed Catoctin Mountain and were attempting to envelop the Confederates' flanks in Middletown Valley. The 1st Massachusetts Cavalry broke over the hilltop on the National Pike and galloped down the western side of the Pass when incoming artillery fire from a section of Confederate artillery, on the high ground immediately east of Middletown, brought it to a stumbling halt in the base of the valley.[65] The New Englanders filed into the fields south of the road and advanced in line until they reached the eastern side of the third of five ridges, where, safe from the Confederate artillerists, they maneuvered into column of fours.[66] To their right, across the road, a couple squadrons of the 3rd Indiana and the 8th Illinois regiments dismounted in skirmish order, while the rest of the two regiments remained in the road as support. The four guns, Lieutenant Peter C. Hains' Company M and Captain J. Robertson's Companies B and L (both 2nd U. S. Artillery), rolled into battery to assist them.[67]

Once again the Federals ran into some of the 1st North Carolina's dismounted cavalry and a section of Captain Hart's Artillery.[68] Colonel Laurence S. Baker's cavalrymen kept the Yankees' heads well below the crest of the ridge. A portion of Captain Thaddeus Siler's (Company K) squadron occupied the upper floors of houses along the eastern edge of the town. They put up a "very stubborn resistance" Private Charles M. Smith of the 1st Massachusetts Cavalry complained.[69]

The North Carolinians were buying time for the rest of Hampton's brigade which was escaping to the steep hill west of Catoctin Creek.[70] General Stuart sent the Jeff Davis Legion farther west on the National Pike to secure Turner's Gap at the Mountain House.[71] Volunteers were setting powder charges on the covered wooden bridge which spanned Catoctin Creek in the valley to their front as Stuart and the ever present Von Borcke rode into Middletown to inspect their skirmish line. They were not ready for what they saw—the fields on both sides of the National Pike were blue with Federal soldiers.[72]

The 1st Massachusetts Cavalry burst over the ridge into the sights of Hart's gunners, who promptly limbered up and prepared to retire.[73] Across the pike, the dismounted Westerners rose up and advanced steadily against the hard pressed North Carolinians.[74] Their fire struck down Captain Siler of the 1st North Carolina Cavalry. A rifle ball shattered his left thigh. He refused to leave the field.[75]

General Stuart allowed the artillery section to retreat but refused to give the order to the cavalry. Federal shells exploded in the streets and burst over the hill east of town with increasing accuracy. The skirmishers of the 3rd Indiana and the 8th Illinois Cavalry regiments started to press Colonel Baker's 1st North Carolina from the left flank and the front.[76] To the right (south) the ill conceived charge of the 1st Massachusetts stampeded over itself as the regiment ran headlong into fences and ditches. Horses balked and riders took "headers" over the top rails when their mounts pitched them from their saddles. Squads dismounted to tear the fences apart, only to run into more rows.[77]

Von Borcke, who wanted to get away from the fracas alive, knew better than to advise Stuart that it was time to pull out. He watched helplessly as the North Carolinians started to take hits, and the situation became more and more untenable. The Prussian never forgave Stuart for needlessly sacrificing brave men so he could reassert his own bravado.

"There was no necessity whatever, here, for the safety of the main body, to sacrifice a smaller command, for we might have withdrawn with honour long before the enemy's fire had so cruelly thinned our ranks," Von Borcke complained.[78]

When the general finally ordered the retreat, he created a rout. Panicked North Carolinians mounted their horses and raced down the main street of Middletown trying to escape the plunging fire of the Federal artillery. Only the severely wounded Captain Thaddeus Siler (Company K) and his squadron remained behind to conduct some semblance of an orderly withdrawal.[79]

The appearance of another section of Federal horse artillery thundering down the pike hastened the captain and his men along much faster.[80] Sharpshooters' rounds zinged past their ears. Buckshot from scatter guns, which irate civilians fired at them from second story windows, hurried the Rebels along. Horses pitched into the road dead, disabling and wounding their riders. By the time Siler's men caught up with Von Borcke on the western slope of the last hill where it descended to Catoctin Creek, their own troopers had set fire to the bridge. It burned furiously. Hot embers touched off fires in a nearby barn and machine shop, filling the entire valley with flames and acrid smoke.

Von Borcke clattered across the bridge to the opposite bank moments before the span collapsed. Captain Siler and his men forced their horses into the shallow stream and forded to safety. Once across, they rejoined the rest of their brigade on the crest of the steep hill to the west to await the Federal counterattack.[81]

Meanwhile, the Yankees' two Western regiments mounted up and prepared to take Middletown by direct assault. The disgruntled 1st Massachusetts Cavalry limped onto the National Pike and belatedly formed in column of fours to back up the charge. The men were angry and verbally abusive about the entire fiasco.

With sidearms at the ready, the 3rd Indiana and the 8th Illinois galloped into town, firing in every direction. Adjutant Charles Francis Adams of the 1st Massachusetts Cavalry, having lost his writing materials in the regiment's ill-fated attack against drainage ditches and fence rows, listened apprehensively to the rapid staccato of small arms fire and fully expected to run into serious opposition. The New Englanders, who rode into the village with their carbines unsnapped and their revolvers unholstered, found themselves assailed on all sides by the jubilant women of Middletown. Waving handkerchiefs and pitchers of cool water greeted the astonished Yankees. In the distance, rifle and pistol fire reverberated through the streets like fireworks on the fourth of July.

The quick witted Charles Adams later informed his mother, "In vain I looked for Rebels, nary one could I see and at last it dawned on me that I was in the midst of a newspaper battle—'a cavalry charge,' 'a sharp skirmish,' lots of glory, but n'ary reb."[82]

The 1st Massachusetts arrived too late to nab any Rebels. The 3rd Indiana and the 8th Illinois snatched up three prisoners with no losses to themselves.[83] They also gobbled up all the buttered bread which the Middletown ladies offered them, leaving none for the troops which followed.[84]

Presently, Captain Horatio Gibson's section of the 3rd U.S. Horse Artillery

(Companies C and G) rolled down Main Street to the first ridge west of the town. While the cavalry regrouped in Middletown out of sight behind the guns, the two guns went into position and exchanged rounds with J. F. Hart's section of Blakely guns and Captain Thaddeus Siler's dismounted troopers on the next hill, about one thousand yards farther west.[85] The North and South Carolinians held their ground long enough for the rest of the brigade and its supply wagons to escape. Their mission accomplished, they slipped down the National Pike, taking all of their wounded with them. The 1st North Carolina had three men captured and eight more wounded, among them Captain Siler.[86] [Refer to Map 13]

Eventually, after the firing ceased to the front, Pleasonton's cavalrymen got moving. Colonel John F. Farnsworth, acting upon a tip from the local people, sent Major William H. Medill (8th Illinois) with a mixed squadron of the 8th Illinois and Companies E and F of the 3rd Indiana Cavalry to the south on Marker Road. They had orders to keep an eye on the Confederate wagon train which the townsfolk said was heading south along that road. The four companies set off at a rapid pace after the train.[87]

The rest of the brigade hurried west on the National Pike. Passing through the smoke filled valley, which they considered one of the most beautiful they had ever seen, they forded Catoctin Creek and pressed forward.[88] Three miles out of Middletown, the Yankees halted on the crest of a steep hill about one mile east of South Mountain.[89] The sight of a lone Confederate cavalryman, who was standing in the Bolivar Road-National Pike intersection in the valley, several hundred yards below them, stopped the Yankee brigade like a brick wall.

The regimental and brigade officers scanned the National Pike with their field glasses as far as the base of South Mountain. Several more cavalry videttes came into view farther along the road. On the eastern slope of the mountain, the Yankees spotted a battery.

The officers conferred and debated. The sun seemed to be getting lower in the west, near the top of the mountain. Before too long, the shadows would not be in their favor. The sunlight nearly blinded them now as it glared in their eyes. Finally the officers concluded that an advance was not in their best interests. The three regiments went into bivouac on the hill, in full sight of the Rebel pickets and braced themselves for a cold night during which the temperatures would drop into the mid-thirties.[90]

While they settled down, General Pleasonton arrived upon the field. Not satisfied with the lack of intelligence, he sent companies D, E, and M of the 8th Illinois Cavalry and a detachment from the 3rd Indiana Cavalry north of the National Pike to probe the perimeter of the Mississippians of the Jeff Davis Legion. Skirmishing broke out between the dismounted troopers.[91] Within short order, the Southerners shot down five Westerners. Private Daniel Snyder (Company E, 8th Illinois Cavalry) died in the fighting. Two troopers in the

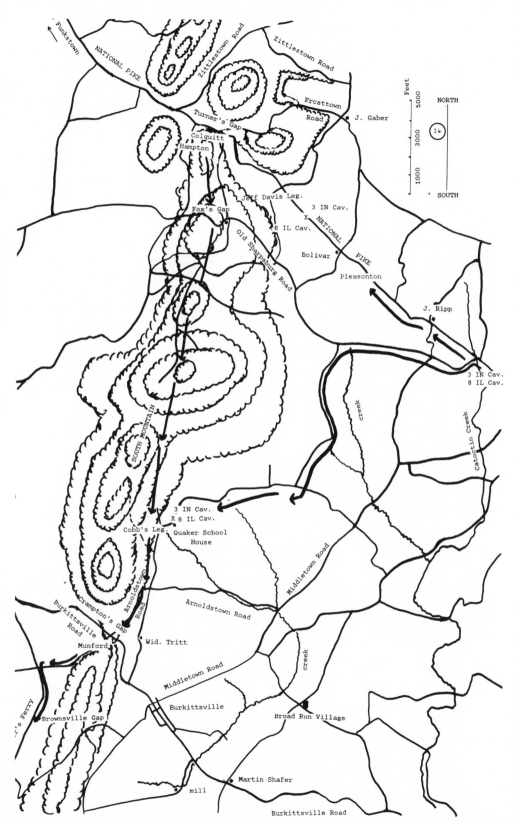

MAP 14: September 13, 1862. Skirmishing at Middletown, Maryland, and at Quaker School House.

3rd Indiana, and Privates E. S. Woods (Company M) and S. G. Eggleston (Company D), both of the 8th Illinois Cavalry, came off the field wounded—the latter seriously. The bullet which smashed into Eggleston's thigh severed his artery. The surgeon arrived in time to save his life but Surgeon Abner Hard could not repair the leg well enough to restore its full use to the private. The Westerners saved face, however, by not leaving the field empty handed. Private A. P. Thoms brought in two prisoners.[92]

The fighting around Middletown became the focal point of the initial Federal push against the Army of Northern Virginia's rear-guard. Two other actions also occurred simultaneously with the fighting along the National Pike. Early in the morning, while he was executing his defense of Braddock Pass, Stuart sent a courier along the western base of Catoctin Mountain to Hamburg, some six miles to the north. He ordered Fitzhugh Lee's 3rd, 4th, and 9th Virginia Cavalry to probe the Federal right flank, in an attempt to turn it.[93]

The reduced command, which had been enjoying a quiet day at the eastern base of the mountain, moved out toward Frederick in accordance with the instructions, about ten miles southeast of its camp. The famished troopers of the 9th Virginia Cavalry, having not eaten for two days, did not relish the idea of going on a fishing expedition. Just north of Frederick, the 4th Virginia Cavalry, with the 9th Virginia in support, attacked the rear of the 1st New York Cavalry, which, in conjunction with the 12th Pennsylvania Cavalry, and a section of Company M, 2nd U.S. Horse Artillery, were also scouting for them. A brief fracas occurred with nominal casualties. The Virginians captured a few Yankee troopers and two ambulances, and the 1st New York came away with a number of Rebel cavalrymen. General Fitzhugh Lee, realizing that he could not turn the entire Federal army, discreetly retired to the base of the mountain with his booty. The brigade fell into battle line and remained near their horses well into the night.[94]

The Confederate prisoners provided the Federal brigade commander, Colonel Andrew McReynolds, with the information he desired to know. Robert E. Lee intended to invade Pennsylvania. With that intelligence, the colonel continued to lead his column northward on the Emmitsburg Road, rather than pursue the Virginia cavalry along a parallel road.[95]

Late in the afternoon, following an incident at a farm house, in which Quartermaster Ezra H. Bailey (1st New York) snatched a carbine from a trooper in order to ferret out a sniper, the cavalry approached the outskirts of Emmitsburg.[96] Captain William H. Boyd (Company C), the adventurous Lieutenant Ezra Bailey, with another captain and a small escort rode into the town alone. Their dust covered uniforms and the dimming light of the day made them appear like Confederate cavalry.

Riding up to the hotel, they were received most cordially by the hotel manager, who addressed them as Confederate officers. The wily Captain Boyd noted the error immediately and without flinching informed the fellow that he—Brigadier General Fitzhugh Lee—and his staff would be quite honored to accept the gentleman's hospitality.

The hotel manager opened his finest bottles of liquor and following exchanges of amenities asked the officers what they wanted. A good camp ground for their brigade was the reply. The southerner escorted them to an excellent meadow. On the way, the secessionists filled the street, while the pro-Union people shut their shutters tight. The Marylanders did not catch on to the ruse until the head of the column entered the town. By then it was too late. They returned to their homes angry.[97]

The 9th New York Infantry arrived at the base of Catoctin Mountain, one mile east of Jefferson, sometime between noon and 1:00 P.M.[98] The 6th Pennsylvania Cavalry (Rush's Lancers), in column of fours in the Jefferson Pike, patiently let the infantry come up behind them before their commander informed the New Yorkers that they had some Rebels cornered in an orchard not too far away.[99] To the west, at the top of the ridge, Corporal John H. E. Whitney (Company B) and Lieutenant Matthew J. Graham (Company F) saw what appeared to be a Confederate battery in the road. They knew that there had to be infantry support nearby.[100]

As the Lancers, with the 9th New York behind, stepped out, Captain R. P. Chew's Virginia Battery calmly limbered up and pulled away unmolested. Private George Neese, having heard the artillery roar and seen the muzzle flashes from Braddock Pass, four miles to the north, felt relieved that the captain had decided retreat. As they headed north on the road to Middletown, he hoped they would not be cut off from Stuart's forces in the valley.[101]

Captain Thomas B. Holland (Company D) and the dismounted marksmen of the 2nd Virginia Cavalry secured the gap east of Jefferson. Colonel Asher Harman took his 12th Virginia Cavalry toward Burkittsville three and one half miles to the west.[102] As the Federal column approached, the 2nd Virginia's sharpshooters took cover in a tangled ravine and waited.

While the Lancers ascended the steep road which cut across the ravine at right angles, Colonel Edgar Kimball deployed the 9th New York infantry. Company B went to the left of the road and Companies C, H, and I to the right. The movement attracted the Virginians' attention. Private Charles F. Johnson of Company I distinctly heard six shots in rapid succession whistle past.[103]

At the same time, Captain Holland and a handful of his mounted Virginians charged into the head of the Lancers.[104] The Pennsylvanians scattered, leaving one of their men in the Southerners' clutches.[105] The three New York companies on the right tore headlong into the tanglefoot and the trees. Struggling through the ravine, they finally reached the mountain top.

Staring through sweat stung eyes, the panting Northern infantrymen spied Captain Holland and his troopers in the open ground about one thousand yards in front of them. A shot echoed loudly through the trees from the left.[106] At the same time Corporal J. H. E. Whitney saw a corporal in his Company B scramble through the brush after a Confederate vidette, who eluded him.[107]

A dispatch rider caught up with the column at the same time and ordered the rest of the regiment into the woods to the left of the road.[108] Private Sam

Marsh (Company I) brought in a treed Rebel who had taken a post there to observe the Yankee cavalry.[109]

The three companies on the right pushed their way through a huge corn-field which Private Charles Johnson swore was about one mile long. As they came into open ground where the ridge sloped down to Jefferson, they saw the rest of their regiment emerging into the open in line of battle. The New Yorkers gaped at the verdant meadows to the west and to the north—ten miles of nodding grain fields, orchards, and neatly marked off farms.[110] Lieutenant Matthew Graham said that the valley below "...stretching away to South Moun-tain lay exposed like a vast painted canvas." From where he stood, he could see several houses in Middletown in flames. He could also see counter bat-tery fire from the ridge west of the village and squads of cavalry (Pleason-ton's) along the National Pike.

Company K brought the regiment's six-gun battery up the road and the line advanced without any opposition into Jefferson.[111] Company I under Lieutenant Frank Powell remained on picket on the northern flank.[112] The people of the village invited the Yankees into their homes. Stacking their weapons in the streets, the weary soldiers gorged themselves on milk, butter, and fruit. Shortly after this most of the enlisted men and officers eased themselves to the road and fell asleep. In the background, miles away, the sounds of the Confederate bombardment at Harpers Ferry reverberated ominously across the valley.[113]

The Confederates at Brownsville, a mile south of Crampton's Gap, on the western side of South Mountain did not remain idle. General Lafayette McLaws placed two brigades under the command of Brigadier General Paul Semmes. While Pleasonton was forcing Catoctin Mountain and the 1st New York Cavalry and the 6th Pennsylvania Cavalry were probing the northern and southern flanks of the Army of Northern Virginia, Semmes' brigade (10th and 53rd Georgia, and 15th and 32nd Virginia) moved to the mountain top immediate-ly east of Brownsville and occupied Brownsville Gap. Next the general split Colonel William Parham's brigade (6th, 12th, 16th, 41st, and 61st Virginia) from Richard H. Anderson's division and scattered it along the ridges to the north. The 6th and the 12th Virginia arrived at Crampton's Gap around 3:00 P.M. The 16th Virginia moved to Solomon's Gap, about one mile north-west of Crampton's Gap on Elk Ridge, and the 41st Virginia spread out to the south toward Brownsville Gap.[114]

General George B. McClellan slowly mobilized the rest of the IX Corps and part of the VI Corps. Not one to needlessly risk his soldiers' lives, he assumed a "wait and see" posture. Colonel William Irwin's brigade (20th, 33rd, 49th, and 77th New York, and the 7th Maine) of William F. "Baldy" Smith's division, VI Corps left Buckeystown about the same time that the 9th New York started its assault against Jefferson Gap. Irwin halted his brigade at the eastern base of the mountain and detached two regiments—the 20th and the 33rd New York—to ascend the mountain. Like the 9th New York, which had scaled the same heights, they got entangled in the undergrowth while the rest of the command marched up the pike in close support. They were also awed by the beautiful panorama from the western ridge of the mountain.[115]

By 3:00 P.M., the head of Colonel Irwin's column reached Jefferson.[116] Once again the civilians flooded the main street and opened their hearts to the veterans of the VI Corps. The men slowly marched through the village, taking their time and absorbing all the natural beauty—the pretty girls.[117] Their approach awakened the 9th New York, who sullenly watched them pass. Lieutenant Matthew Graham (Company F) noted how filthy and ragged the VI Corps troops were and attributed their weather beaten appearance to hard marching.[118]

The only ones who did any hard marching that day were Colonel William Irwin, who commanded the brigade, and an unidentified trooper from the 6th Pennsylvania. While the 33rd New York advanced about one mile west of Jefferson, they ran into the ever watchful Captain William Holland (Company D) and his detachment from the 2nd Virginia Cavalry. They were holding the Petersville-Jefferson intersection.[119] Colonel Irwin, following the example of the lone trooper dashed ahead of his men. The cavalryman, firing his revolver in one hand and carbine with the other whooped and hollered as he rode down a lone Confederate vidette, who turned about and surrendered. Colonel Irwin galloped past him, pistol in hand and brought in three more Rebel cavalrymen.[120] [Refer to Map 13]

Captain Holland immediately ordered his Virginians to withdraw. They fell back to Burkittsville and Crampton's Gap just as Stuart's supply train started to ascend the pass from the northeastern approach.[121] Captain Chew's horse artillery, having found itself cut off by Major William Medill's mixed detachment from the 3rd Indiana Cavalry and the 8th Illinois Cavalry, got to within a mile of Middletown before turning back on the Burkittsville-Middletown Road. They ascended the gap, just ahead of the 2nd Virginia Cavalry. When they got to the summit where the two roads which crossed the Pass intersected, the guns went into position in the crossroad.[122]

Two miles to the north, they could see the two Yankee squadrons winding their way along the country road which parallelled the mountainside and ran into the northeastern approach road about one mile from the Burkittsville Road. The Northerners did not seem to be in too much of a hurry. It was getting late in the day. The sun was shining bright over the crest of the mountain; it threw dark shadows among the trees on the eastern slope. With only an hour or so until sunset, the Yankees slowed their pace.

From its position immediately north of the Quaker School House, where the road turned southwest before running along the base of the mountain, the point of Major Medill's Yankee cavalry column saw the sunlight glinting off the barrels of Captain Chew's bronze guns. A second look confirmed that the Confederate wagons were creeping up the mountainside and that there was too much Rebel cavalry in the area to mess with.[123] Wade Hampton's brigade had arrived behind the train and was trying to follow it to the safety of Crampton's Gap.[124]

Major Medill and his officers concurred. They did not really need the wagon train. A winding, rock strewn ravine, bounded on both sides by a worm fence, cut westward and uphill to the same road which the Confederate cavalry had used not a minute or two before. The Yankees decided to turn up the short cut and double back to their regiment at the National Pike.

Everything went well until Company F of the 3rd Indiana, which was the tail end of the column, filed into the ditch. Colonel Pierce M. B. Young wheeled Cobb's Legion around and sent it galloping against the Yankees' left flank.[125] Captain G. J. Wright (Company D, Cobb's Legion) pulled his company away from the rest of the command.[126] The Rebels, with their pistols cracking and their swords bared, caught the Yankee detachment by surprise. Young came in from the south and Wright from the north.[127]

Major William Medill (8th Illinois) brought his troopers to a halt. Without a moment's loss, a number of men jumped to the ground and started to rip apart the worm fence between them and the Reb cavalry. Simultaneously, the troopers to the rear loosed a disorganized volley to the south and the front.[128] Captain Wright toppled to the ground with a wounded arm.[129]

Private Charles Dawson (Company F, 3rd Indiana Cavalry) and his comrade, Private Thomas, leveled their carbines, simultaneously, at Colonel P. M. B. Young. Dawson drew a bead on the colonel's chest and squeezed the trigger when the Rebel was less than ten feet away. His carbine misfired. A second later, Thomas fired. The shot smashed Young's leg and killed his horse, which sent both plummeting to the ground.[130] Carbine and pistol shots rent the late afternoon air. Bullets seemed to come in from every quarter. Nearly every man around Privates Dawson and Thomas was hit. Neither one understood how they survived it.

Rebel cavalry were everywhere. Swords were used freely. Four troopers from the 3rd Indiana Cavalry received head and shoulder wounds. A pistol shot pierced Samuel Cross' lungs and another felled Private Thomas' mount. Before he had a chance to gain his feet he received a glancing sabre blow across his left shoulder, which temporarily disabled him. Another Rebel trooper crushed Corporal J. Harvey Williamson's (Company F, 3rd Indiana Cavalry) skull with a sabre strike. The corporal fell heavily to the ground within arm's reach of Private Dawson, who in the confusion did not recognize the casualty as his friend.[131] Corporal Charles Plopper (Company A, 8th Illinois Cavalry) rode away from the fighting mortally wounded. George Bowes (Company F, 8th Illinois) went down with a bullet in his bowels.[132] Sergeant Joseph Lewis (Company E, 3rd Indiana Cavalry) and Sergeant G. B. Barksdale (Company D, Cobb's Legion) shot at each other at the same time. Barksdale dropped into the ravine dead with a bullet in his heart. Lewis fell across him also with a hole through his heart. Nearby lay Lieutenant James F. Marshall (Company D, Cobb's Legion)—another fatality.[133]

The fighting ceased when the 3rd Indiana Cavalry and the 8th Illinois Cavalry cut their way through the Confederates and escaped toward Middletown. The Georgians rounded up their five prisoners and their casualties and started to leave the field. They allowed Private Charles Dawson (Company F, 3rd Indiana Cavalry) to bid farewell to Harvey Williamson. A quick glance at the corporal's glazed eyes beneath his bloodied face told Dawson that he could do nothing for him. "...he was too far gone to speak or notice anything," Dawson later informed his girl friend.[134] As he rode off with his captors, a few of them bludgeoned Private F. B. Wakefield (Company G, 8th Illinois Cavalry) with their swords and left him for dead in the road.[135]

Once again, both sides claimed victory. The 8th Illinois lost one killed, eight wounded, and one captured. The 3rd Indiana counted three dead, eight wounded, and five missing. Twenty-six casualties within a few minutes did not exactly sound like winning. The Georgians trotted away from the fight with thirteen losses—four dead, nine wounded, and several stray horses.[136] They had saved their wagon train from a nonexistent threat and in the process had gained nothing for it other than the attention of Colonel Thomas Munford and his cavalry at Crampton's Gap. [Refer to Map 14]

As the first sounds of the engagement echoed up through the Gap, Munford ordered Captain Chew to train his three-gun battery upon the road to his left front. Wade Hampton immediately dispatched a rider with a Confederate flag to prevent a slaughter. He arrived about a minute before George Neese's number four man was going to pull the lanyard.[137]

The artillery stayed in position until dark, when it retired to the western base of the mountain and went into bivouac.[138] Colonel William Parham's infantry brigade stayed at the three gaps in the area overnight. They were all that was between the Army of the Potomac and the remainder of Lafayette McLaws' and R. H. Anderson's divisions near Harpers Ferry.[139]

About the time that the 3rd Indiana and the 8th Illinois Cavalry were conducting their cavalry attack against "superior" numbers in Middletown, the IX Corps was receiving its marching orders. Brigadier General Jacob Cox's Kanawha Division broke camp west of the Monocacy and started the advance around 3:00 P.M.[140] It had to catch up with Colonel Edward Harland's brigade (8th, 11th, and 16th Connectictut, and 4th Rhode Island), which had trailed Pleasonton's cavalry over Catoctin Mountain toward Middletown. Brigadier Generals Samuel Sturgis', then Orlando Willcox's divisions followed very slowly.[141]

The jubilant citizens of Frederick stalled the advance for a considerable length of time. The regiments halted frequently to enjoy the city's hospitality. At one point, relatives of George Washington halted Jacob Cox and his staff and invited them into their home to look at several of the first president's personal artifacts. The officers reverently gathered around a case containing the general's Revolutionary War uniform for several minutes before marching west.[142]

In Frederick, hundreds of civilians cluttered the streets to cheer and throng General McClellan and his staff. At one street corner, Colonel Edward Ferrero halted his brigade (51st Pennsylvania, 51st New York, 21st and 35th Massachusetts) and dressed ranks to pass them in review for the commanding general. When they marched out, the recently mustered 35th Massachusetts sang out with "Marching Along" and "Old John Brown."[143] The 21st Massachusetts faced by the right flank and tried to present arms to the women and children who were waving handkerchiefs and flags at them. The corps commander, Jesse Reno, rode up on the regiment and curtly ordered Colonel William S. Clark to get his people moving. Facing left, the regiment advanced with the brigade as far as Mill Alley and Patrick Streets, where everyone halted again.[144]

The infantry, for no apparent reason, plopped down on the curbs for two hours.[145] When the 35th Massachusetts stopped in the road to relax, a couple of the old hands advised them, "Save your breath, boys; you'll need it ahead there!" The embarrassed soldiers never sang on the march again. A sense of foreboding came over them. They recalled how earlier that afternoon, when the regiment marched down to the Monocacy River to fire its Enfields for the first time, how the nipples broke off when the hammers struck them and how some of the minié balls, being too small, barely cleared the muzzles by ten feet before plunking into the water.[146]

In the meantime, the rumor mongers were at work. Very shortly after the 21st Massachusetts sat down along Patrick Street, word reached them that an old lady who lived nearby had waved a Union flag at the Rebels as they passed through the town. General Reno and his brother Benjamin reined their horses to a halt in front of Private James Stone (Company K). The private saw the general dismount in front of his company, and leaving the reins with his brother, walk up to the house across the street.

The general knocked. A little old woman came to the door and he disappeared inside with her.[147] Moments later, he emerged from the house with the old lady as his escort. Stuffing the bunting flag which he had in his hand into his saddle bag, he told his brother he had offered Mrs. Frietschie money for the flag but that she had refused.[148] With that they rode off and Ferrero's brigade followed.

McClellan fought a deliberate and a too well calculated war. His marching orders traveled too slowly for a man who wanted to crush the Confederate army in its own trap. The rest of the IX Corps did not leave its bivouac along the Monocacy until after 6:00 P.M., about a quarter of an hour before dark.[149] When Orlando Willcox's division reached Frederick, Samuel Sturgis' men marched again. They crossed Catoctin Mountain at 11:00 P.M.[150] Colonel Edward Ferrero's soldiers hated the night march. They stumbled over the piles of crushed limestone which the Marylanders had left in the road to mend it.[151] The soldiers of the 21st Massachusetts never forgot the sights which greeted them as they neared Middletown. In the moonlight, they saw two dirty Rebels swinging from a tree about one hundred feet from the National Pike. Civilians coldly informed them that they had been hanged for pilfering apples. The Yankees left the two rotting corpses dangling in the night air and proceeded to loot every chicken coop, pig pen, and apple orchard in the area.[152] Sturgis' division swung into a field on the eastern side of Middletown and settled down for an uneasy night.[153]

The Kanawha Division had reached Middletown by dark and had gone into camp along Catoctin Creek.[154] Samuel Compton (Company F) and his comrades from the 12th Ohio never forgot the inspirational beauty of Middletown Valley from the overlook on the western side of Braddock Pass. Sixty years later he fondly remembered it with the same exhilaration.[155] Others preferred to recall the natural beauty of the young women in the village. As the 11th Ohio tramped through Middletown, John Manning nudged his friend, J. Hammer "Hamer" Smith (both of Company B), and nodded in the direction of a woman and a cavalry sergeant. She coquettishly toyed with a small American flag which dangled from the trooper's sword.

"Say, Hamer," Manning sighed, "I would not mind getting a little wound if I could only have that black-eyed girl to nurse me."

Smith nodded in agreement as if to say "wishful thinking." Neither of them understood at the time how close John Manning would get to his dark eyed beauty.[156]

Orlando Willcox's exhausted soldiers did not get beyond Braddock Pass that evening. It took his division six hours to march four miles.[157] At least five of his eight regiments had never seen combat, much less hard marching.[158] Private Frederick Pettit (Company C, 100th Pennsylvania) thought that the regiment had marched "some distance," and William A. Roberts (Company K, 45th Pennsylvania) complained that a large portion of his outfit were debilitated with severe diarrhea.[159]

Diarrhea did not curb the men's appetite in the least. While they might not have developed the veterans' nose for battle, the new soldiers had developed a nose for finding food where it was not. The 17th Michigan, which did not halt until nearly midnight, did not waste any time in feeding itself.

Private David Lane (Company G), having just stacked his musket with the rest of his company, overheard Second Lieutenant Christian Rath ask, "Where's John Coneley?"

A murmur rippled through the company. He could not be found, came the response. More than likely, he was out on "a private expedition."

"Well," Rath demanded, "then send me the next best thief; I want a chicken for my supper."

The men soon procured a bird for their lieutenant as well as an abundance of fruits for themselves. The ease with which they learned how to steal astonished David Lane. He brushed it aside as an hereditary trait.[160]

Willcox's division had to slow its pace to wait for the 79th New York, which, having been sent on picket duty the night before, did not return to Frederick until after the army had left. The lieutenant colonel halted the regiment on the outskirts of town, reformed ranks, and calling all the drummers to the front, strutted the regiment through. The inexhaustible residents, mostly attractive women and children, appeared along the streets and in upper story windows dressed in red, white, and blue. They cheered the regiment all the way to its bivouac west of the city.[161]

Brigadier General Isaac Rodman's division also halted west of Catoctin Mountain to wait for a stray brigade. Colonel Harrison S. Fairchild's brigade (9th, 89th, and 103rd New York) stumbled into Frederick before 11:00 P.M., less one squad from the 9th New York which was left on duty, by accident, at Jefferson.[162] The brigade arrived in Frederick in time to prevent a jail break by the Confederate prisoners.

Around 11:30 P.M., inmates in the Frederick County jail set fire to the building. Sheriff Michael Zimmerman started to haul the office furniture outside. Captain William G. Barnett and Second Lieutenant James Horner (both of Company B) of the 9th New York, who took "French leave" and did not go on the Jefferson expedition, saw the flames shooting out of the roof and reacted quickly. Horner stayed to remove the jail's furnishings and to fight the fire. Barnett raced to the regiment's bivouac of the night before and by chance happened to find Lieutenant Colonel Edgar Kimball and the regiment which had bedded down less than half an hour before.

The colonel sent the captain back with three companies. They arrived about the same time that the sheriff and Lieutenant Horner started to open the cell doors and herd the gagging prisoners into the jail yard. Barnett posted road guards on the streets to surround the prison pen and at the same time placed sentries on the high walls around the court yard. Another detachment of the New Yorkers fought the fire in vain. The wooden interior of the jail went up like a match. The stone outer walls contained the fire. Those three worn out companies of the 9th New York, having marched twenty-five miles that day, got no sleep that night.[163]

By 10:00 P.M., the bulk of the Army of the Potomac had settled in for the night. The VI Corps covered an area from Buckeystown to Adamstown to Jefferson.[164] The I Corps, II Corps, XII Corps, and Brigadier General George Sykes' division of the V Corps bedded down around the eastern side of Frederick. Major General Darius N. Couch's IV Corps division occupied Licksville, south of Buckeystown. As usual, the Federal cavalry provided a thin screen. The 1st Rhode Island Cavalry covered the fords south of Point of Rocks on the Potomac. The 6th U.S. Cavalry scouted as far as a mile or so beyond Jefferson, and Colonel John Farnsworth's brigade was bottled up about two miles east of Turner's Gap.[165] The average distance covered by any corps that day was about seven miles.[166] None of the infantry forces were within easy striking distance of any of the three passes along South Mountain.

The Confederates were not in much better shape. Brigadier General Paul Semmes' two brigades of some 1,114 men stretched about one mile, with half of the troops at the top of Crampton's Gap.[167] During the retreat from Middletown, Stuart sent a courier to Major General Daniel H. Hill at Boonsboro, stating that he was being pursued by two brigades of Federal cavalry and that he needed an infantry brigade to assist him.[168] Hill sent Colonel Alfred Colquitt's (13th Alabama, 6th, 23rd, 27th, and 28th Georgia), and Brigadier General Samuel Garland's brigades (5th, 12th, 13th, 20th, and 23rd North Carolina), with Captains John Lane's North Carolina and J. W. Bondurant's Alabama batteries toward Turner's Gap, about two miles east of Boonsboro. Only Colquitt's command ascended the steep National Pike to the Mountain House. By the time he got there, Stuart had already sent most of Wade Hampton's brigade south toward Crampton's Gap.[169]

Colonel Colquitt and his aide, Lieutenant George D. Grattan (Company C, 6th Georgia) met Stuart at the head of the Jeff Davis Legion on the west side of the mountain below the gap. The officers ordered their men to the side of the road to allow the cavalry to pass. Simultaneously, Alfred Colquitt and the lieutenant rode off to the roadside for a conference with General Stuart.

The general told the colonel there were no troops following him except cavalry and Colquitt's infantry would have no trouble holding the gap. Colquitt responded by requesting two companies of cavalry for picket duty but Stuart declined. Stuart rode down into Boonsboro, and Colquitt was left to hold the eastern base of the mountain with his brigade of 1,400 men.[170]

Not very long after, the civilian who overheard General McClellan's officers boast that the army was on the move arrived on the other side of the gap and delivered his information to Stuart. The general immediately sent a rider to General Robert E. Lee's Headquarters, which were in Hagerstown, some fifteen miles away.[171]

Stuart and the Mississippi cavalry also ran into Colonel Thomas Rosser with his 5th Virginia Cavalry and Captain John Pelham and his section of artillery. Rosser, who was returning from his horse gathering expedition north of Frederick, had tried to rejoin Stuart near Middletown earlier in the day but realized he could not get through the superior numbers of Federal troops on the National Pike. Consequently, he turned north along South Mountain for several miles, then turned west. Crossing the mountain, he headed south toward the place where he assumed Stuart was retreating and met him in Boonsboro.

For reasons undisclosed to Colonel Rosser, Stuart ordered the 5th Virginia Cavalry and Pelham with his two guns to occupy Fox's Gap one mile south of Turner's Gap.[172] He never bothered to inform General D. H. Hill, the infantry division commander in the area, about the deployment of those troops on the right. Nor did he tell him of the existence of the Old Sharpsburg Road.[173]

Lee received Stuart's message from a scout shortly after dark. It reported that the Federal Army was advancing in solid ranks toward the base of South Mountain. He lost valuable time in considering the predicament before calling Major General James Longstreet to his quarters. Longstreet, who found him studying a map, listened to the commanding general's report. When Lee asked him for his suggestions, Longstreet proposed he and D. H. Hill pull back across the Antietam at Sharpsburg, because the next day would be too late to advance to Turner's Gap. Lee told Longstreet to send his command to Turner's Gap, except one brigade, which was to guard the trains at Hagerstown.

"The hallucination that McClellan was not capable of serious work seemed to pervade our army even to this moment of dreadful threatening," Longstreet bitterly complained.

Lee decided the pass at Boonsboro had to be held until Harpers Ferry surrendered. Consequently he informed Jackson, McLaws, and D. H. Hill of the situation by couriers. Hill had to defend Turner's Gap and McLaws was to expedite the capture of Harpers Ferry, then move to Sharpsburg to rendez-vous with Jackson. Further, Longstreet's supply train guard was to keep an eye out for Governor Andrew G. Curtin's Pennsylvania militia which were said to be moving on Hagerstown from Chambersburg.

He further ordered Stuart to keep communications open with McLaws near Maryland Heights. He was also to delay McClellan's advance as long as possible.[174] Stuart considered the former order more important. He had no intention of wasting his time at Turner's Gap.

The IX Corps infantry at Middletown did not know what to expect the next day either. General McClellan had not issued any orders to Jacob Cox, the division commander in the area, concerning operations for the next day. Instead, General Pleasonton, leaving his cavalrymen in bivouac on the high ridge east of Turner's Gap, met Cox at his quarters. After requesting an infan-try brigade for the next morning, he stipulated they had to depart at 6:00 A.M. Further, since he and Colonel George Crook had served together in the Old Army, he wanted his comrade to lead the detail.

Cox, who never thought that either of his brigade commanders would object, said he would comply. Colonel Eliakim Scammon got wind of the ar-rangement and did not hesitate to confront his commanding officer with a complaint.

Scammon, himself a regular army officer before the war, reminded Cox that by the division's custom, the two brigades alternated the lead of the col-umn. It was his brigade's turn the next morning.

Cox tried to back out of the argument by saying that he had extended the privilege to Crook as a courtesy to Pleasonton. Scammon insisted upon the division lead as a point of professional honor to which Cox agreed as long as Scammon remained determined about the matter.

After Scammon left his quarters, Cox hunted out Pleasonton. He found him in George Crook's tent. Cox retracted his original decision, with the ex-planation tendered him by Scammon. Alfred Pleasonton tried to argue that as senior officer in the field he had the right to choose not only the command-ing officer of the detail but the troops involved as well.

Cox reasserted his authority by immediately issuing the order for Scam-mon to take the advance.[175] It was a decision which neither one would regret.

Chapter Ten

SEPTEMBER 14, 1862

FOX'S GAP
9:00 A.M.—Noon

Colonel Alfred Colquitt, commanding the Confederate infantry brigade at Turner's Gap, anxiously watched the campfires on the hillsides and in the valleys east of his position steadily mushroom in numbers until it became obvious that Stuart had erred in his estimate of the strength of the opposing force. The colonel realized that the Yankees had gathered more than two cavalry brigades between him and Middletown. While it was still dark, he sent a courier to Major General Daniel H. Hill in Boonsboro, informing him of the situation. As a colonel, he needed confirmation from a higher authority before he could take action.[1] While he was waiting, he deployed his brigade for action. The regiments marched east on the National Pike to a point 850 yards from the Mountain House. The brigade assumed a defensive posture just beyond the first bend in the road, east of the serpentine farm lane which branched northeast from the Pike. A gully, caused by erosion, and bordered by a stone wall on the eastern lip, ran southeasterly out of the woods on the southern spur of the mountain into the road.

Three-fourths of the 28th Georgia (about 225 men) filed into the woods north of the gully. The rest of the regiment (about 75 men), together with the 23rd Georgia (about 300 men) on its right behind the stone wall, continued the line to the National Pike. The balance of the brigade (the 6th and 27th Georgia, and 13th Alabama), averaging some 250 effectives per regiment, extended the line another 750 feet to the right, through the deep wooded ravine on the eastern side of the mountain. Alfred Colquitt did not have to be a

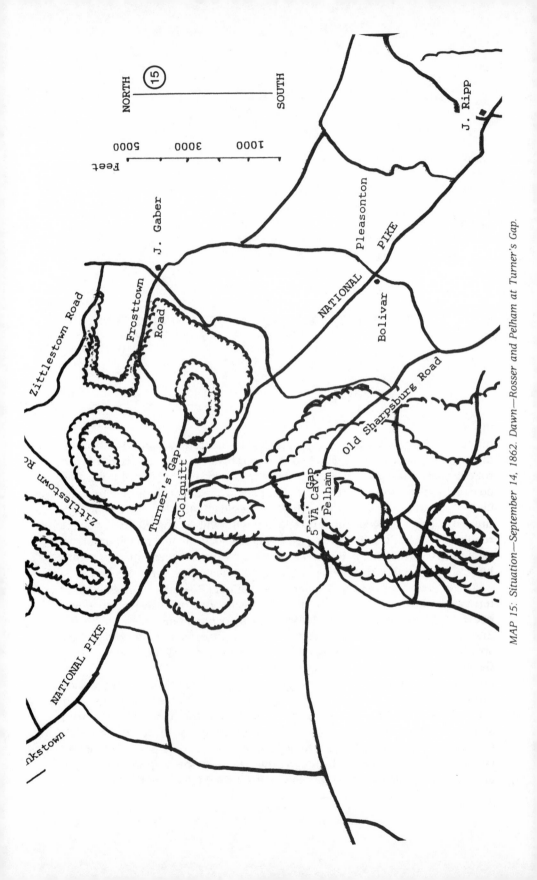

MAP 15: *Situation—September 14, 1862. Dawn—Rosser and Pelham at Turner's Gap.*

mathematician to realize that he needed more men to defend the pass.[2]

D. H. Hill, Stonewall Jackson's brother-in-law, and his aide, Major John Ratchford, arrived at the Mountain House before daylight to study the situation for themselves. The glowing fires in the distance reaffirmed Colonel Colquitt's earlier report. Hill rushed a courier down the mountainside to fetch his four remaining brigades (G. B. Anderson, Garland, Ripley, and Rodes) in his command. He and Ratchford then sought out Alfred Colquitt for a personal reconnaissance of Turner's Gap.[3]

After inspecting Colquitt's position, Hill, Ratchford, the colonel, and the colonel's staff returned to the Mountain House. While the general and Ratchford quietly trotted south along the wood road, which skirted the eastern brow of the mountain from the Mountain House to the Old Sharpsburg Road, Alfred Colquitt, Lieutenant George Grattan (Company C, 6th Georgia), his aide, and the rest of his staff started to cook breakfast.[4]

Three-quarters of a mile along the ridge, Ratchford and Hill heard men's voices and the rumbling of wagon wheels reverberating through the trees where they believed the Old Sharpsburg Road crossed the mountain at Fox's Gap. Unable to see who was crunching about in the woods to their front (south) and flank (east), the two officers assumed the people making the racket were Federals and they decided to return to the National Pike.[5]

Unknown to either of the officers, what they had heard was Captain John Pelham's two guns and Colonel Thomas Rosser's 5th Virginia Cavalry advancing into position along the wood road at Fox's Gap. John Pelham stationed himself where he could best utilize his section while Tom Rosser's Virginians dismounted and took cover behind the stone wall which bordered the wood road immediately north of the Old Sharpsburg Road intersection. Pelham placed his artillery section in the northwestern corner of the first rectangular cleared field north of the pass. From that position, he could control the entire length of the Old Sharpsburg Road down to the school house where the road split and another wood trail forked west toward the mountain crest some two to three thousand feet southwest of the pass.[6] Below him, to the east, he could see a great deal of Federal activity. [Refer to Map 15]

The Northern artillery, on the high ground west of the Bolivar Road intersection at the National Pike, went into battery with the rising sun to their backs. Captain Horatio G. Gibson's six three-inch rifles (Companies C and G, 2nd U.S. Artillery) and Lieutenant Samuel N. Benjamin's Regular battery of six 20-pounders (Company E, 2nd U.S. Artillery) could sweep not only Turner's Gap but Fox's Gap as well.[7] They opened fire with a single shell several minutes after daylight.[8] It was more of a wake up call than a directed shot. The Federal artillerists advised the Confederates that their troops were up and moving. They provided moral support for the Yankee cavalry scouts who had just started to probe the valley west of Bolivar.[9]

Several hundred yards south of the Pike, D. H. Hill and Major Ratchford came across P. Hartley's cabin, which was in a small clearing on the western side of the wood road. Hartley, with his children huddling close about him, met the Confederates in his front yard. Major Ratchford, who was wearing a blue greatcoat which he had captured at Seven Pines earlier in the year, approached the mountaineer to ask what he knew about the Federal positions when Hartley interrupted him.

"The road on which *your* battery is," Hartley butted in, "comes into the valley road near the church."

Ratchford and the general quickly realized that the farmer had mistaken them for Yankees. They played the game accordingly.

"Are there any rebels on the pike?" Hill asked.

"Yes; there are some about the Mountain House."

"Are there many?" Hill continued.

"Well, there are *several*," Hartley guessed with definite understatement, "I don't know how many!"

"Who is in command?" Hill pressed.

"I don't know," Hartley shrugged.

Without warning that solitary Federal shell from the Yankee artillery "whirpled" through the blinding morning sky and crashed through the trees over their heads. One of Hartley's young daughters screamed in terror. Hill, who had a daughter at home who was about the same age, tried to soothe her with a few kind words, then spurred north with Ratchford.[10]

Four miles farther east, on the eastern bank of Catoctin Creek, General Jacob Cox, commanding the Kanawha Division, deliberately arose and breakfasted early. At the same time, Colonel Eliakim Scammon fed his brigade (the 12th, 23rd, and 30th Ohio) and got it moving. He joined Cox promptly at 6:00 A.M., just as Alfred Pleasonton's gunners opened fire against the Confederates at South Mountain.[11] The 12th Ohio led the march, followed by the 23rd Ohio and then the 30th Ohio.[12]

The two officers crossed Catoctin Creek well ahead of their men and started to ascend the ridge to their front when a lone officer, standing by the roadside, startled Cox. The general, who recognized him as Colonel Augustus Moor (28th Ohio), spurred up to him immediately and asked him how he got to Middletown.

The graying Colonel Moor told his friend that following his release the previous evening he had walked from the western side of South Mountain. "But where are *you* going?" Moor asked.

Cox told him that Scammon was going to support Pleasonton in a reconnaissance.

"My God! be careful!" Moor gasped before catching himself. "But I am paroled!"

He turned his back to the general, unwilling to violate the conditions of his honorable release.

Jacob Cox did not need any further warning. He wheeled his horse about and galloped back to Eliakim Scammon. Promising to bring up George Crook's brigade, he continued back to Middletown. As he passed every regimental commander he warned them to be prepared for any type of action. Personally, he was not sure what was ahead.[13]

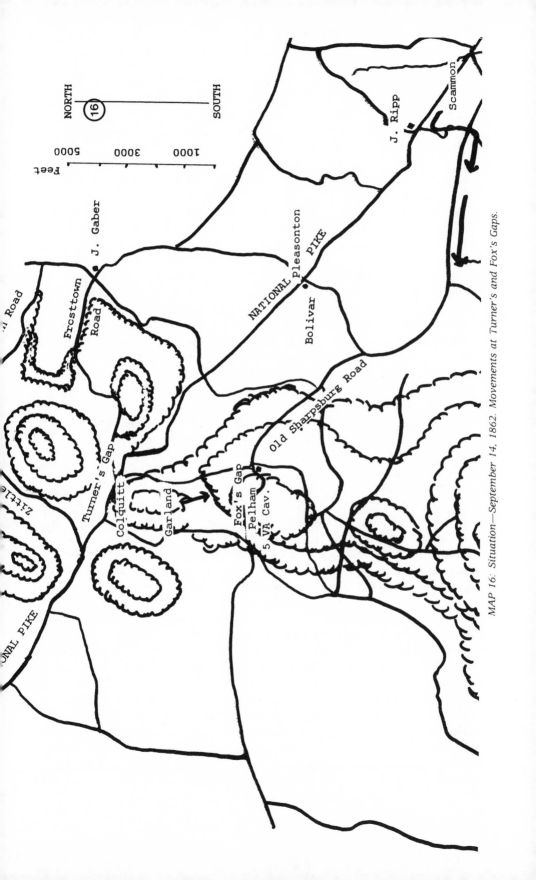

MAP 16: Situation—September 14, 1862. Movements at Turner's and Fox's Gaps.

Brigadier General Samuel Garland arrived at the Mountain House as the first rays of sunlight rose over the eastern hills onto the crest of South Mountain. Lieutenant George D. Grattan (Company C, 6th Georgia) never took his eyes off the immaculately attired general. The lieutenant anticipated the meeting because the general had recently become engaged to "a very dear friend" of Grattan's. Colonel Colquitt rose from his breakfast and politely asked Garland to dismount and join them, which he did, while his men filed by and stacked arms.[14] They waited there for further orders.

Shortly thereafter, D. H. Hill and his aide arrived at the Mountain House.[15] The division commander halted momentarily to study the Federal deployment in the valley to the east. What he observed distressed him.

The Yankees had the jump on him. Scammon's Ohio brigade was slowly moving south on the back road which led from the cut off at J. Ripp's to the Old Sharpsburg Road.[16] The Ohioans did not set any speed records. The undulating Old Sharpsburg Road became much steeper as it climbed South Mountain west of Mentzer's Saw Mill. Their column slowed down to a lurching crawl, and the regimental officers halted the men frequently so they could recover their wind.[17] [Refer to Map 16]

D. H. Hill directed Garland to march south and secure Fox's Gap at all costs. The Army of Northern Virginia's ammunition train, at the western base of the mountain, could not fall into the Yankees' hands. The North Carolinians had to hold the pass at the expense of their lives.[18] The extremely narrow, undulating, and rutted wood road slowed their advance as they stumbled south.[19] The 5th North Carolina under Colonel Duncan K. McRae led the column at the double quick in column of fours with the other regiments behind. The heavy woods along their eastern flank sheltered their advance from Captain Seth Simmonds' section of twenty pounders and General Alfred Pleasonton's artillery. They were busily shelling Captain John Lane's Georgia Battery, which had gone into battery in the open ground on the plateau west of and above the 23rd and the 28th Georgia regiments.[20] Around 8:00 A.M., minutes before Garland's brigade reached Fox's Gap, where the Old Sharpsburg Road crossed the wood road at the Wise Farm, Captain John Pelham (Stuart Horse Artillery) rose in the stirrups, to emphasize the drama of the moment. He told his gunners, "Men of the Horse Artillery, the safety of General Lee's wagon trains and the security of the whole army depend on our holding off the enemy until help can arrive. We must hold on at any cost. Now, to battery!"[21] A single artillery piece opened fire, which alerted the North Carolinians to the possibility that they might have started their advance too late.[22]

That first round, a case shot from the bronze Napoleon, alarmed the Federals as much as it did the Confederate infantry who were converging upon the Gap. The shell, failing to explode, bounded down the road. It sent the Yankee infantry to cover on the left side of the road opposite the school house.[23] The 12th Ohio, Scammon's lead regiment, immediately doubled back on itself and filed into the western end of Mentzer's field, below the line of

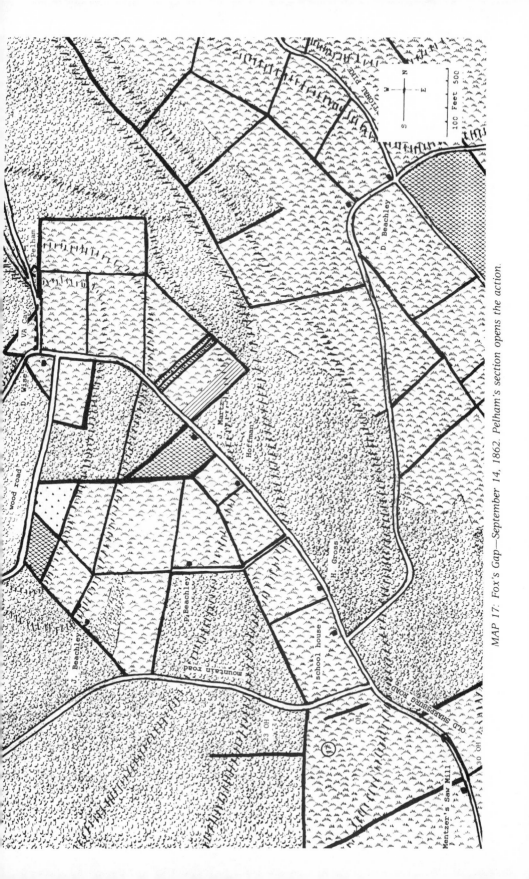

MAP 17: *Fox's Gap—September 14, 1862. Pelham's section opens the action.*

sight of the artillerists.[24] Colonel Rutherford B. Hayes, commanding the 23rd Ohio, the next regiment behind the 12th Ohio, diverted his command to the south and pushed it into the dense woods southeast of the schoolhouse.[25] The 30th Ohio, bringing up the rear of the column, halted to await further instructions.[26] [Refer to Map 17]

Pelham's shot had bought precious time for Garland and his small brigade of less than one thousand men. After conferring with Colonel Rosser (5th Virginia Cavalry), Garland hastily deployed his troops along a very tenuous twenty-five-hundred-foot front which paralleled the crest of the mountain.[27] Having rushed south of the Old Sharpsburg Road, the 5th North Carolina, the general's southernmost regiment, veered off to the east, where the wood road made a sharp turn west. With a dense laurel woods and a hedge row on its right flank, it took cover on the eastern edge of a cornfield along a broken down stone fence. The 12th North Carolina (92 men) supported it from the ridge road, about two hundred feet to its rear. The 23rd North Carolina placed itself behind the stone wall on the eastern side of the road and occupied the line for about two hundred fifty feet. The western edge of that stubble field, which was bordered on all sides by stone walls, continued for about another one hundred yards to the north where a stone wall, approximately six feet high and about four feet wide at the base separated it from a belt of woods which extended five hundred feet farther north. A small three-acre field, dotted with oak and pine stumps finished out the Confederate position to the Old Sharpsburg Road. Daniel Wise's farm house, a crude, small cabin, with a basement, was situated in a one-acre triangular field which dropped very sharply down the western side of the mountain. Across the road, on the western slope, was another triangular one-acre field backed by dense woods. Across the road from the rectangular field, northeast of the house, two more large cleared fields continued the line for about one thousand feet. A seemingly impenetrable forest and laurel thicket bordered the Confederate position on the south and the west. Garland had no troops between the left flank of the 23rd North Carolina and the Old Sharpsburg Road intersection. The excellent stone walls which bordered both sides of the wood road from the stubble field to the crossroads had no troops to defend them.

The 20th North Carolina went into line north of the Old Sharpsburg Road behind the stone wall which bordered the wood road on the east. Two hundred fifty yards farther to its left, the 13th North Carolina stacked its rifles along the wood road and stared into the woods along the eastern slope of the mountain.[28]

Captain J. W. Bondurant's Alabama battery of four guns rumbled down the road and swung into the stubble field in front of the 23rd North Carolina. Private John Purifoy, one of the artillerists, felt uneasy about the situation. The infantry had stacked its weapons in the woods, west of the wood road, on the lip of a depression just below the western crest of the mountain. They had no pickets out which Purifoy could see. Leaving their caissons and limbers in the road, the artillerists rolled their four guns

(3 three-inch rifles and 1 Napoleon) by hand to the ridge line about one hundred yards to the east.[29]

Private Purifoy recalled, with understatement, "...it was an unusual thing to put artillery in position without pickets or videttes."[30]

Captain Bondurant, in placing the guns so close to the stone walls on their northern and southern flanks, did not leave the gunners enough room to maneuver them. From where he was on the right, John Purifoy could not see any of the men from the 5th North Carolina who were in the cornfield immediately opposite his post.[31] In spite of the high stone wall on their left flank, the artillerists still managed to get a clear view to their left front to the vicinity of the Gross farm.[32]

The Federals, who occupied the lower ground, had a more difficult time ascertaining the locations of the two Confederate batteries. Colonel Scammon's three Ohio regiments wasted about half an hour before they took any decisive action against the mountainside and the well concealed Rebels. "Old Granny" Scammon, as his men referred to him, did not budge until his division commander, Jacob Cox, arrived upon the field to supervise the front lines.[33]

At the same time, Colonel Scammon and James Abraham's Company of West Virginia Cavalry ferreted out Colonel Hayes (23rd Ohio). His troops were halted on the brigade's left flank in a westerly running ravine parallel to the mountain road, which branched off from the Old Sharpsburg Road. Instructing Hayes to keep his regiment in the woods as much as possible, Scammon also ordered him to flank and overrun the artillery section which he suspected was on the mountainside somewhere to their front (west).

Omitting the "what," Colonel Hayes blurted, "...if I find six guns and a strong support?"

"Take them anyhow!" Scammon insisted.[34]

"All right then," the colonel shouted as he turned to his men, "we'll take them anyhow." With his eyes glistening, he decided to make the most of the moment.[35]

Hayes asked for a cavalry screen and received Sergeant A. B. Farmer and a handful of James Abraham's troopers.[36] He then proceeded to untangle his regiment so it could advance.

In moving by the flank to get off the Old Sharpsburg Road, the colonel inadvertantly faced his regiment by the rear rank, which placed the shorter men in the back line. In preparing to move out, he brought them to "attention," faced them south then ordered them to march out by the right flank. Company A fanned out to the west as skirmishers. Company F spread out in skirmish order to the south and Company I covered the northern (right) side of the column as it moved out. Instead of following the mountain road, the seven remaining companies kept well south of the road where the ground became higher and let Company I scour the lower position along the road and the ravine.[37] It did not take long for the Ohioans to get lost along the high knoll on the southern end of the position. The dense woods, the rock outcroppings, and the steep acclivity slowed their pace considerably.

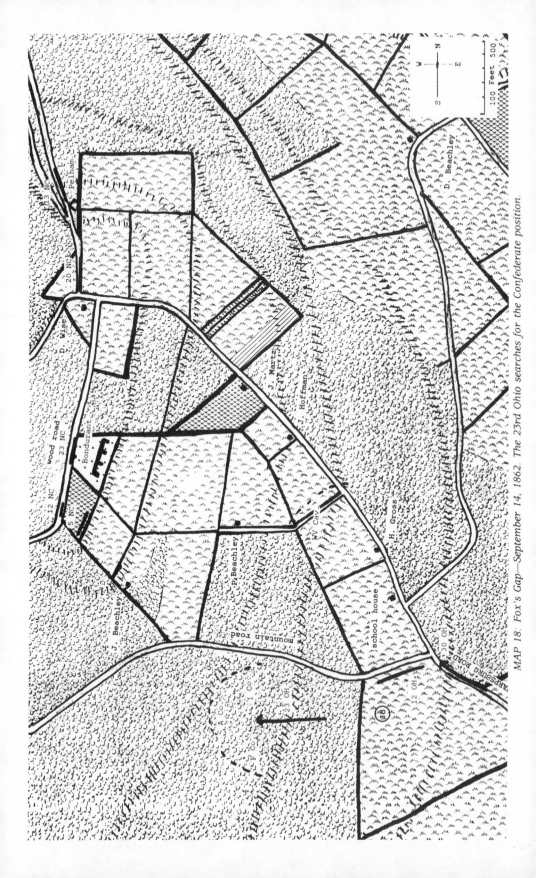

MAP 18: Fox's Gap—September 14, 1862. The 23rd Ohio searches for the Confederate position.

Shortly after the 23rd Ohio disappeared farther into the woods, Colonel Scammon dismounted the rest of the West Virginia Cavalry and sent them northwest along both sides of the Old Sharpsburg Road. Being uncertain of the battery's location, they moved out cautiously, without any intention of starting a general engagement on their own.[38]

Private John Purifoy (Bondurant's Artillery) and his crew members caught sight of the dismounted cavalry first. He recalled that the battery had been in position sometime between half an hour to an hour when his crew noticed a few men stealthily moving about the fields northeast of their guns. Recognizing their Yankee uniforms, he anxiously recalled that they seemed content with attracting and keeping the gunners' attention rather than engaging them in combat.

Captain Bondurant dispatched an artillerist to find General Samuel Garland. Without any infantry pickets to his front, he felt vulnerable to capture. A few minutes lapsed when the fellow returned empty handed. Another runner took off at a trot and the gunners tried to make themselves inconspicuous.[39] Lieutenant James Abraham (West Virginia Cavalry), satisfied that his men had successfully flushed Confederate skirmishers back to the woods on the top of the mountain, sent a messenger back to Colonel Scammon and General Cox, then ordered his men to take cover and to await reinforcements.[40] [Refer to Map 18]

Word of the position of the Confederate battery reached Jacob Cox about the same time that General Jesse Reno arrived on the field. Reno, having brought with him one of the local farmers, ordered Companies A and F of the 12th Ohio to follow the civilian to a point directly opposite the guns. They were to capture the battery by assault.[41] As the two companies set out on their forlorn hope, Cox sent Company F from the 30th Ohio, northwest, on either side of the Old Sharpsburg Road to relieve the cavalrymen.[42]

Captain Bondurant's messenger faithfully reported the situation along the Old Sharpsburg Road to an officer in one of the two regiments along the southern end of the wood road. The officer, being of junior rank, refused to take it upon himself to respond to the crisis. Frustrated, the artillerist started back toward his battery.[43] He had no way of knowing that he had barely missed his brigade commander and Colonel Duncan K. McRae (5th North Carolina) as they went into the cornfield south of Bondurant's battery to reconnoiter that flank.

General Garland and the colonel rode through the cornfield, and stepping over the dilapidated stone fence to the left of the 5th North Carolina, walked their horses about another forty to forty-five feet into the open field in front of their troops.[44] Another stone wall ran north to south along the hill and their front. A belt of laurel and small trees, stretching north from the denser woods and the thickets on their right, dominated the ridge opposite that stonewall. From their vantage point, the two officers could scan most of the terrain within a two-thousand-foot radius from the southeast to the northeast.[45]

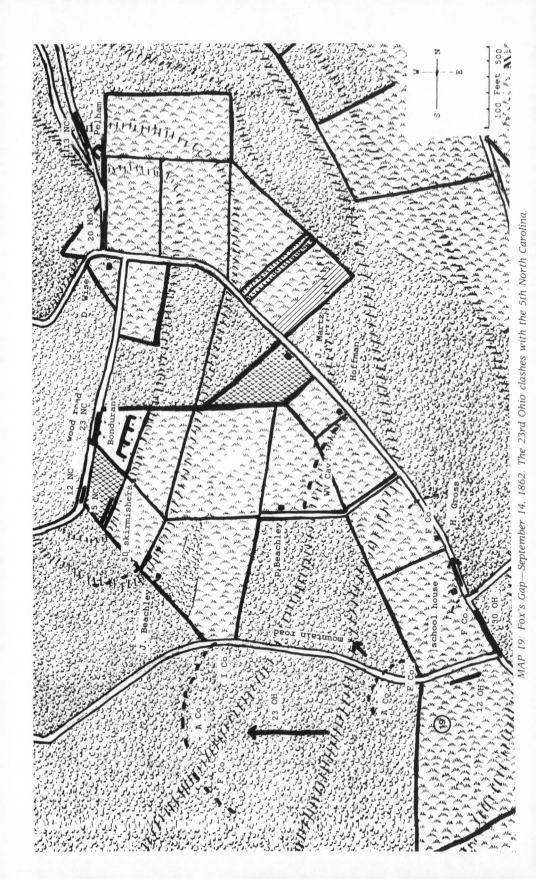

MAP 19: Fox's Gap—September 14, 1862. The 23rd Ohio clashes with the 5th North Carolina.

Not very long after they started their surveillance, both officers noticed movement along the mountain road to the southeast. Colonel McRae called for fifty skirmishers from the 5th North Carolina to sweep through the woods to their right front in an attempt to flank whoever it was moving about down in the hollow.[46] The two officers had no idea how close the Federals were to their position. The thick undergrowth and closely packed trees forced part of the 5th North Carolina to file to the left until some of the line cleared the woods on the right flank.[47]

Company I of the 23rd Ohio, which was entangled in the woods along the mountain road, did not see them coming. The soldiers of the 23rd North Carolina, from their elevated position on the wood road along the mountain's summit, helplessly watched the two lines converge.[48]

On the opposite slope southeast of the Confederate position, Colonel Rutherford B. Hayes (23rd Ohio) saw them also and responded immediately. Halting the regiment, he faced them by the rear rank. He centered himself on the regiment to deliver a "brave up" talk, as Company F retired to the battle line.

With his eyes shining, he said, "Now boys, remember you are the 23rd and give them Hell. In these woods the rebels don't know but we are 10,000; and if we fight, and when we charge yell, we are as good as 10,000 by God." He wheeled his horse about. "Give them Hell! Give the sons of bitches Hell."[49] The regiment stumbled down the rocky heavily wooded slope toward the mountain road.[50]

By then, the two skirmish lines had collided with one another. Companies A and I of the 23rd Ohio methodically herded the North Carolinians back toward the cornfield near the top of the mountain.[51] Private Robert B. Cornwell (Company A) coldly went about his work as if he were stalking game. He loaded, and fired fourteen rounds at the backs of the Rebels. He bragged, "...if some of them didn't do execution it is not my falt for I had a good rest [for] all but 2 shots." His company killed at least eight of the enemy before the 23rd Ohio came to its assistance.[52] [Refer to Map 19]

As the first reports of the rifle fire echoed up the mountain side, Samuel Garland yelled at Colonel Duncan McRae to bring up the rest of the 5th North Carolina. The woods on its right disrupted the regiment's formation. Filing to the left, it came to front in the open field below the brow of the hill in a slight hollow. Reforming, it marched up to the belt of woods which dominated the next rise of ground. By the time the North Carolinians had gotten beyond the far side of the woods, the 23rd Ohio had crossed the mountain road into the open ground to their right front.

The Confederates delivered a telling volley into the startled Ohioans which staggered their advance. The fighting quickly evolved from an uncertain firefight to a desperate shootout. The lines consolidated as the officers recalled their skirmishers and the men settled down to do some wholesale killing. Colonel Hayes gave the Rebels no respite. With bulldog tenacity, he ordered

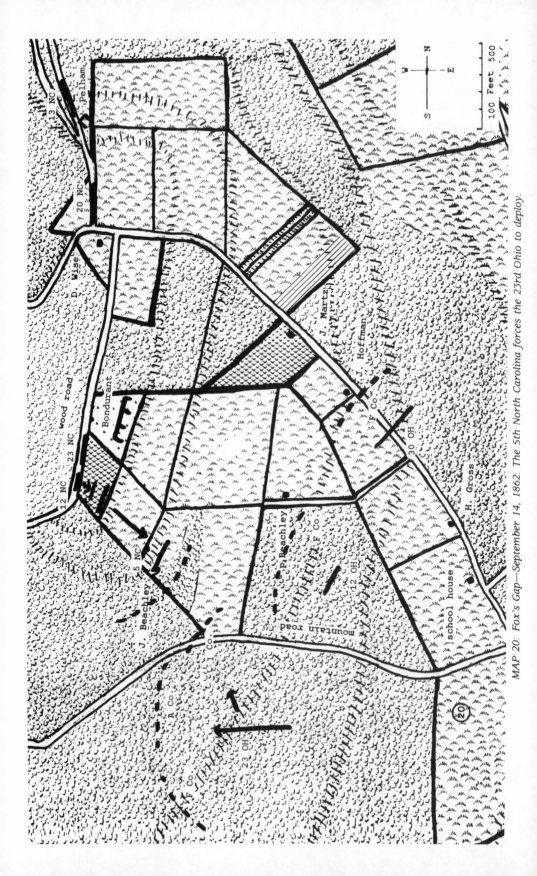

MAP 20: Fox's Gap—September 14, 1862. The 5th North Carolina forces the 23rd Ohio to deploy.

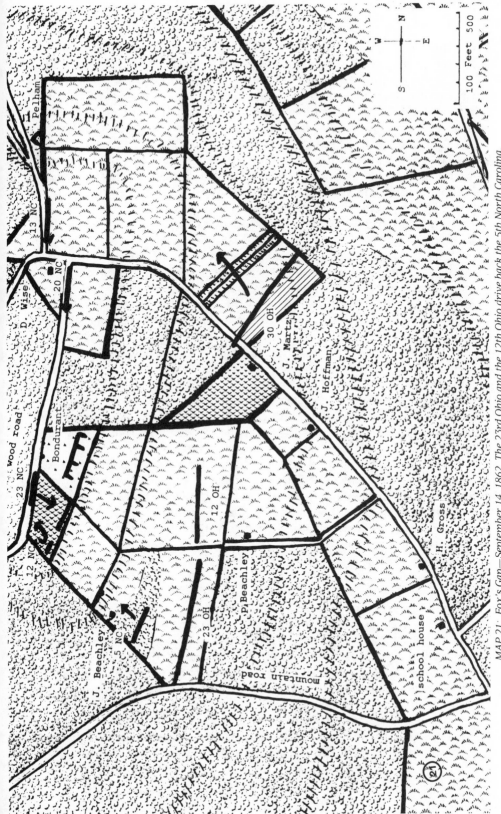

MAP 21: Fox's Gap—September 14, 1862. The 23rd Ohio and the 12th Ohio drive back the 5th North Carolina.

his line to move out. The 23rd Ohio's bugler sounded the "Charge."[53] The Ohioans yelled and hollered as they surged forward, and scattered the untried conscripts on the right flank of the 5th North Carolina. Their sharpshooters took cover behind the stone wall on the Rebels' right flank and opened fire. Their shots whistled into Captain Bondurant's artillerists, wounding three of them, among them John Purifoy, who was stationed at the southern most gun.[54] [Refer to Map 20]

When Garland saw the North Carolina conscripts burst from the woods and head into the hollow east of the cornfield, he sent for the 12th North Carolina.[55] Captain Shugan Snow of Company I, who had recently been promoted from private to company then regimental command, boldly led his company sized regiment to the eastern edge of the cornfield, where they halted to deliver a volley.[56]

Another Federal line, farther to the north and more extensive than that of the 23rd Ohio emerged from the woods on a northwesterly course. Companies A and F of the 12th Ohio, thanks to their reputable civilian guide, crossed Peter Beachley's lane directly below the muzzles of Bondurant's battery. As the two companies brought themselves to face west, the rest of their regiment crossed the farm lane and went into line on the left. The right companies fired a volley to the left front which knocked down several North Carolinians as they fled through the woods toward the cornfield near the crest of the hill.

At the same time, the 30th Ohio came into front, north of the Old Sharpsburg Road, on the right of the 12th Ohio.[57] The 12th North Carolina, caught in a crossfire from the skirmishers to their right, left and front, fired wildly at the newly arrived Ohioans, then fled from the field.

Samuel Garland spurred up to the 23rd North Carolina, along the wood road, and ordered Colonel Daniel H. Christie to advance into the northern end of the cornfield to the left of the 5th North Carolina's rattled conscripts.[58] Without waiting to see them deployed, Garland galloped north on the wood road to bring his two remaining regiments, the 13th and the 20th North Carolina, onto the field.[59]

In the meantime, the left wing of the 5th North Carolina retired a short distance then stubbornly held its ground.[60] Lieutenant Colonel Hayes (23rd Ohio) frantically reformed his line before the men became too carried away by the impetus of their own attack. The Confederates' musketry suddenly increased in volume as they fought it out toe to toe. [Refer to Map 21]

The North Carolinians put up a determined resistance. They were buying time for the rest of the brigade while Duncan McRae of the 5th North Carolina departed to chase after the remainder of his command. He managed to rally his rattled right wing at the cornfield and bring them back to the wall.

While McRae attempted to save his regiment from further disgrace, General Garland, who was on his way back to the cornfield, passed Bondurant's battery and yelled for the gunners to fire and then retire north. The artillerists heard him and several line officers from the 12th North Carolina screaming at their routed soldiers to regroup.[61]

The infantry officers managed to bring part of the regiment under control. Those men of the 12th North Carolina who stayed upon the field retreated north to join ranks with the 13th North Carolina as it crossed the Sharpsburg Road.[62]

Garland did not wait for the battery to fire. Continuing southeast, he rejoined Colonel McRae in the cornfield.[63] Almost immediately, a bugler behind the belt of woods below their position blew the "Charge." The 23rd Ohio was rushing the 5th North Carolina again.[64] The general suggested to McRae that he recall his regiment and he sent a runner off immediately with the command. The outgunned 5th North Carolina, under Colonel McRae's instructions, withdrew as quickly as possible to the rear. While the Rebels scrambled through the hollow, heading back toward the cornfield, McRae told Garland he suspected the Federals, who had collected a superior force in the woods to their front and right, intended to turn his right. He further advised the general to shell the eastern part of the field to expose the Yankee position. Garland said the Yankee sharpshooters had forced the battery to quit the field and rode off to the left of the line.[65]

By then, the 23rd Ohio had gotten to the stone wall one hundred yards east of the 5th North Carolina and the 23rd North Carolina.[66] There the Ohioans ran into a deadly barrage. The Rebels picked off officers with unnerving accuracy. Captain John W. Skiles (Company C) went down with a shattered arm. Captain Abraham A. Hunter and Lieutenant James Naughton (both Company F) fell wounded as did Lieutenant Ritter.[67]

When the Ohioans rushed into the woods, Colonel Hayes dismounted and ran after them. Seconds after the regiment reached the clearing on the opposite side, when he was standing about twenty feet behind his line, a bullet smashed his left arm just above the elbow. It carried away half of the bone, leaving a ragged wound in the back of his arm. The impact staggered him, but he would not fall. Believing he had been hit in the artery, he cried for an enlisted man to tie off the blood flow with his handkerchief.[68] Nausea and the blood loss forced him to lie down to regain his composure.[69]

Four canister rounds, in delayed succession, added a new but very short lived dimension to what had been an infantry engagement. Captain Bondurant ordered his guns to fire by the right oblique, which placed the pieces in column. He could only fire one gun at a time. Consequently, each crew fired its piece in turn, limbered up, and pulled north along the wood road toward Daniel Wise's cabin.[70]

Those four bursts startled Colonel George Crook's brigade (11th, 28th, and seven companies of the 36th Ohio) as it filed into the ravine east of Peter Beachley's house. The 11th Ohio was on the left, in the woods. The 28th Ohio held the open ground in the center, and the seven companies of the 36th Ohio extended the line to the right to the Old Sharpsburg Road near J. Martz's house.[71] [Refer to Map 22]

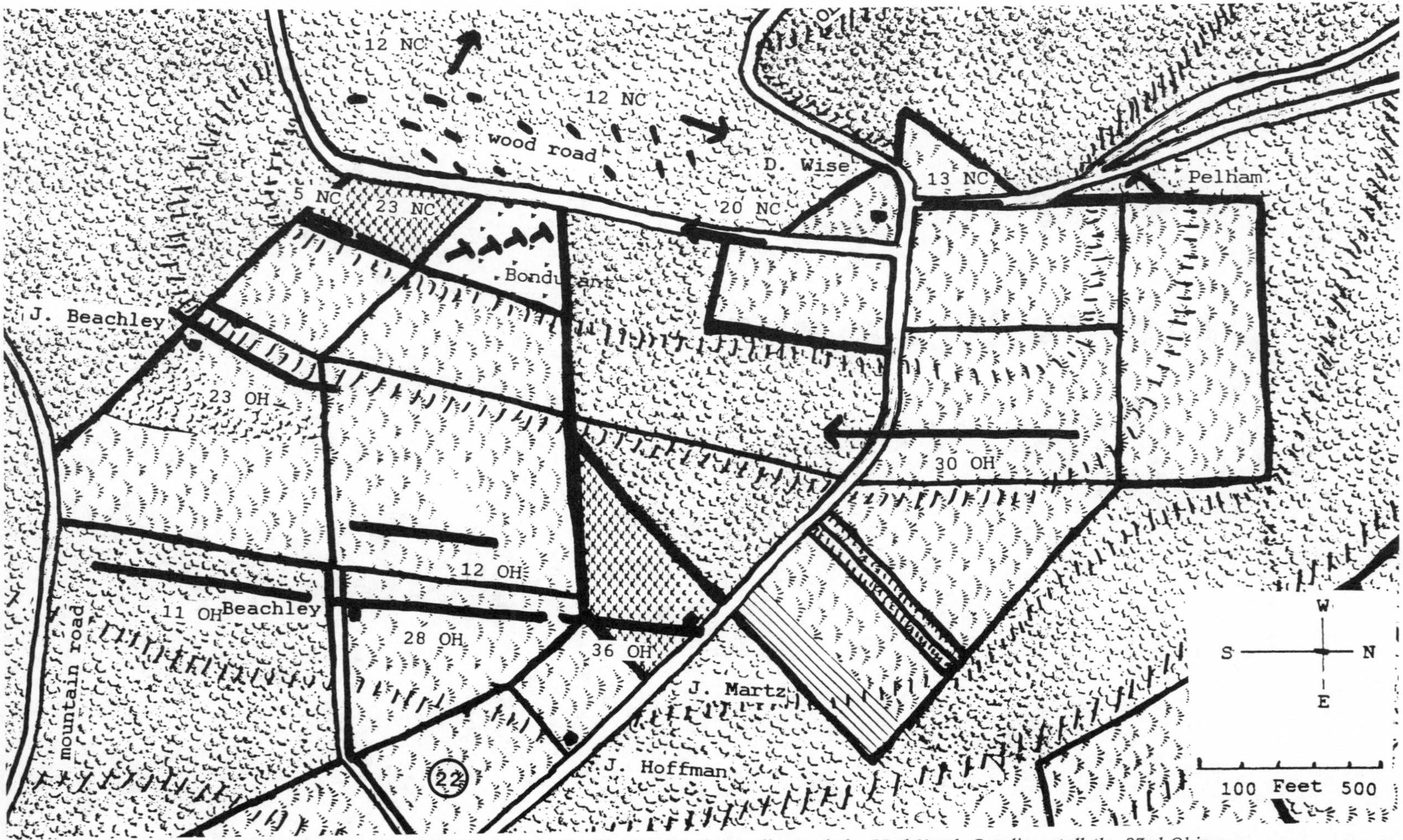

MAP 22: Fox's Gap, September 14, 1862. The 5th North Carolina and the 23rd North Carolina stall the 23rd Ohio.

Chaplain William W. Lyle (11th Ohio), who took shelter in the ravine on the far left of the line, became more frightened with each burst of canister. It troubled him that men were going to die on the Lord's Day. He recalled how sweetly the birds sang that morning at Middletown and how the dew dripped gently from the grass and the trees and gave everything a natural sparkle as the morning's sun trapped them in its brilliant eastern glare. Before the regiment left Middletown, he managed to gather a "few who loved prayer" and they shared the 86th Psalm. "Bow down thine ear, O Lord, hear me: for I am poor and needy.... In the day of my trouble I will call upon thee: for thou wilt answer me." It comforted him as the canister clattered through the woods to the west.

While the regiment rested in the woods, Quartermaster Sergeant M. H. Wilson arrived with the latest mail from home. Lieutenant Colonel Augustus Coleman (11th Ohio) allowed him to distribute the letters. The chaplain cherished every word he received, in particular the letter from his friend Professor James McEldowney, who reminded him that, "Under the protection of Heaven we know you are safe, as even the hairs on your head are numbered."

Frightened as he was, the chaplain spent several minutes in fervent prayer, contemplating repeatedly that despite his circumstances he was not forsaken by his God. "... [as] I tried to rise to the full appreciation of those precious words," William Lyle wrote, "I felt as much, if not more, of heaven and of heaven's peace, than I remember ever to have enjoyed...."[72] He realized that many of his moral charges would be dying on the fields to the west.

While the 11th Ohio read its mail, Bondurant's Rebel guns rolled through the rest of Garland's brigade as it deployed for battle. Samuel Garland intercepted the 13th North Carolina on the wood road west of Wise's field.[73] Spying Company F of the 30th Ohio in extended order north of the Sharpsburg Road, the general surmised that the Yankees were attempting to turn his left flank.[74] He immediately sent the 13th North Carolina into Wise's field, where the stone wall which enclosed it and the thick woods on its eastern and southern sides afforded them the greatest protection. At the same time, he sent the 20th North Carolina farther south. The regiment went into line behind the stone wall along the western edge of the stubble field formerly held by Bondurant's Battery. The thick woods separated its left flank from the 13th North Carolina's right.[75] The men hunkered down behind the stone wall and the road bank to await what they knew was inevitable.

On the left, about the same time that the 23rd Ohio forced the 5th North Carolina toward the cornfield on the top of the hill, the 13th North Carolina advanced fifty yards into Wise's field.[76] The 30th Ohio, in response to the Confederates' movement to its left, filed across the Sharpsburg Road into the woods below the North Carolinians and connected with the 12th Ohio in Beachley's mow field. As the regiment executed the movement, Company F attempted to file south with it. Part of the company had gotten into the woods

Brigadier General Samuel Garland, C.S.A.
Killed in Action, September 14, 1862.
COURTESY OF THE OLD SOUTH MOUNTAIN INN,
TURNER'S GAP, NEAR BOONSBORO, MARYLAND

opposite Wise's field when the Rebel skirmishers, in conjunction with Bondurant's battery, opened fire.[77] The North Carolinians, who could see the skirmishers from Company F who had not crossed the road yet, singled them out. The Ohioans dove for cover along the stone fence on the northern side of the Sharpsburg Road and went no farther.[78] As they did so, Captain J. Lane's Georgia artillery opened fire from the high ground more than one mile away, north of the National Pike, which killed and wounded several of their men during that first encounter.[79]

Despite their casualties, the Ohioans pressed into the woods to push the North Carolinians toward the top of the mountain. General Garland and his staff, refusing to leave Wise's field, stayed near Lieutenant Colonel Thomas Ruffin, Jr. (13th North Carolina) despite the increased volume of fire to their front.

"General," Ruffin ventured, "why do you stay here? You are in great danger."

"I may as well be here as yourself," Garland replied rather curtly.

"No," Ruffin argued, "it is my duty to be here with my regiment, but you could better superintend your brigade from a safer position."

At that instant a minié ball thudded into Ruffin's hip. Knowing that he had no field grade officers to replace him, he leaned over to Garland and asked the general to find a field officer for his regiment should his wound incapacitate him. Samuel Garland turned and yelled something at an orderly. A bullet tore into his chest and he toppled from the saddle. In the racket, Ruffin did not know that the general was down until he heard Garland moaning and saw him writhing on the ground.[80] While an orderly sped away to give Colonel McRae command of the brigade, Garland's staff snatched up the dying general and carried him north along the wood road toward the Mountain House [South Mountain Inn].[81] (They left him on the front porch of the inn.)[82] McRae hurried to the left of his line to survey the situation. Finding

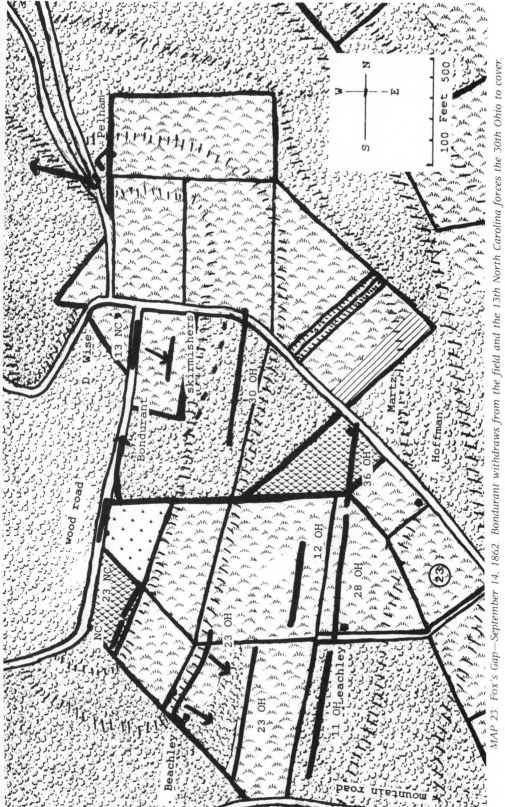

MAP 23: Fox's Gap—September 14, 1862. Bondurant withdraws from the field and the 13th North Carolina forces the 30th Ohio to cover.

Captain Halsey, Garland's assistant adjutant-general, he dispatched him toward the Mountain House with a request for more troops from D. H. Hill, stating that he did not have enough men to hold the Federals back.[83]

In the meantime, the fighting to the south increased in volume. The strong willed Colonel Hayes of the 23rd Ohio refused to relinquish command of his regiment, inspite of his disabling injuries. Several of his soldiers retired from the stone wall back to the woods, which convinced the colonel that his regiment was ready to break. Hayes stood up and stopped a sergeant as he wandered past him.

"I am played out," the noncom complained, "please, sir, let me leave."

Hayes, who had used his sword as a prop, momentarily pointed it toward his wound. "Look at this," he snarled, "Don't talk about being played out. There is your place in line."

The disappointed soldier skulked back to the stone wall while the colonel lay down again.

He found himself next to a wounded Rebel.

"You came a good ways to fight us," Hayes said.

The Reb asked him where he was from.

"I am from Ohio."

"Well, you came a good ways to fight us," the Confederate quipped.

The conversation lapsed into an uncomfortable silence. Finally, Hayes gave the Rebel his wife's name—Lucy—and a message for her, should he die. As he finished his message, a soldier ran up to Hayes and shouted that he thought the enemy was trying to turn his left flank. He ordered Captain James L. Drake to wheel back his Company H and the company next to it.[84] In the tumult the rest of the regiment gave way and retreated back to the belt of woods on the rise of ground behind them. Colonel Hayes, weakened from blood loss and intense pain, remained on the ground, semiconscious.[85] Bullets from both sides zinged over his head and thudded into the ground around him for fifteen to twenty minutes. When the feared Confederate counterstrike never developed, Major James Comly ran through the fire to ask Hayes if he meant the entire regiment. No, the colonel gasped, but let it stand. At that the major ran back to the woods, leaving the colonel between the lines.[86] [Refer to Map 23]

On the right, the 12th Ohio and the 30th Ohio bellied up the hill doing everything they could to stay below the sights of the two North Carolina regiments in the cornfield to their left front. They had no idea that Bondurant's battery had left the field and that another regiment—the 20th North Carolina—had gone into line behind the stone wall along the ridge. The two regiments remained prone and let the 23rd Ohio absorb the Rebels' ammunition.[87]

Colonel Hayes regained consciousness. Painfully raising his head to look about, he realized he was alone. He loudly pleaded, "Hello, 23rd men! Are you going to leave your colonel here for the enemy?"

Six volunteers dashed from the cover of the woods, offering to take the colonel wherever he wanted to go. Their presence, however, attracted too much fire. As Hayes weakly commanded them to return to the regiment, the small arms fire picked up again. Minutes later, Lieutenant Benjamin W. Jackson (Company C) scrambled through the clearing and dragged the colonel back to the woods. The lieutenant laid him down behind a log and went back to the firing line.[88]

The musket fire died away as quickly as it began. As the regiment cautiously edged its way across the open ground back to the stone wall, Lieutenant Jackson returned to Colonel Hayes and started down the hill with him toward Peter Beachley's house, where the surgeons had established the division's field hospital.[89] Lieutenant Robert B. Wilson (Company F, 12th Ohio) remembered seeing the colonel wandering to the rear with his arm in a sling.[90]

About that time, the soldiers of the 12th Ohio, with the 30th Ohio on its right in the woods, crawled on their hands and knees to the cover of the stone wall on the brow of the hill.[91] From where he lay, Private Samuel Compton (Company F) heard the Confederate officers shouting commands at their men. The orders resounded clearly. The private estimated that they were just over the crest, some sixty feet away—too close—too close.

His officers, also, must have thought they were within easy striking distance of the North Carolinians. The order rippled down the line to charge. The instant the men gained their feet the command to "lie down" echoed overhead. The glint of sunlight reflecting off the leveled muskets of the 23rd North Carolina sent Samuel Compton and his comrades to the ground. As the smoke cleared from the front of the 23rd North Carolina, they believed they had cut down the entire Yankee regiment. (Their volley dropped a handful of the Ohioans.)[92] The Westerners did not want to make another attempt to dislodge the Rebels from their seemingly impregnable position.

The sun beat down upon the sweating troops. The ground heated up. The stones in the wall started to lose their natural coolness. Some of the officers, including Colonel Carr B. White (12th Ohio), plugged their canteens into their mouths with increasing frequency. The pungent smell of army whiskey occasionally stabbed at the enlisted men's nostrils and brought with it a foreboding that they would have to rely upon themselves for direction in the ensuing engagement.[93] The heat also brought out an unwanted intruder. A mountain rattlesnake slithered out from under the stone wall and quietly started to wind its way across the prostrate enlisted men. The men froze, allowing the reptile to stay on its course, unmolested. The snake continued crawling from man to man until one fellow snapped. Jumping to his feet, he killed the snake (probably with his rifle butt) and threw himself to the ground before the Rebs had a chance to pick him off.[94] Sharpshooters still pinged minié balls off the rocks over their heads.

While the Ohioans lay on the slope, Colonel Scammon sent an orderly after Captain James R. McMullin's 1st Ohio Independent Battery, which was still at the low ground around Mentzer's Mill. McMullin refused to send a

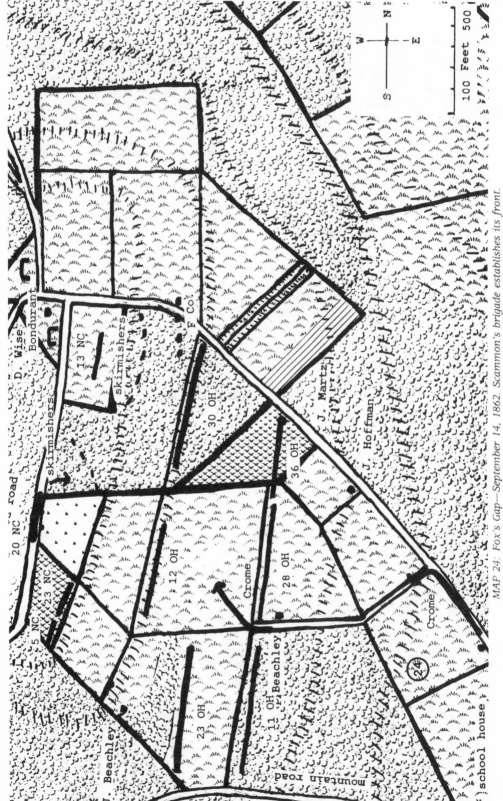

MAP 24: Fox's Gap—September 14, 1862. Scammon's brigade establishes its front.

section back to the mountain. The position was too dangerous, he protested. "Old Granny" Scammon did not know what he was talking about. When the aide told the captain that the section would be supported by the 12th Ohio, McMullin consented. He sent Lieutenant George Crome and his two ten-pounder Parrotts.[95]

The two artillery limbers struggled up the steep and narrow Old Sharpsburg Road toward Peter Beachley's farm lane.[96] Crome's artillerists got as far as the farm house, where they unlimbered the field pieces and manhandled them toward the prone infantry along their right front. The gunners laid their shoulders to the guns and pushed them through Lieutenant Robert B. Wilson's Company F on the right of the 12th Ohio.[97] [Refer to Map 24]

Crome's rifled guns fired their first canister rounds into the 20th North Carolina. In quick order, another ear shattering report, followed by the hail like staccato of cast iron shot hammering the stone wall, echoed loudly above the scattered sniper fire. In response to the increased pressure, Colonel Alfred Iverson (20th North Carolina) sent Captain James B. Atwell (Company B, 20th North Carolina) and his skirmishers into the woods between the 20th North Carolina and the 13th North Carolina. As they neared the Yankees' right flank, one of Crome's (1st Ohio Battery) Parrott rifles splattered the stone wall along the wood road with an accurate canister round.[98] Atwell's skirmishers, despite the presence of Company F of the 30th Ohio in the same woods on their left, took deliberate aim and began to gun down Crome's Yankee artillerists. Within short order, they methodically dropped four of the six gunners.

Infantrymen from Lieutenant Robert Wilson's company of the 12th Ohio recklessly stood up and attempted to man the abandoned gun. Two more gunners rapidly hit the ground. Private Charlie James collapsed when a minié ball bored through his leg.[99] Seconds later, another bullet smashed the Number One man's right hand when he stepped up to the muzzle of the gun to ram the charge down the bore. As the rammer clattered to the ground, George Crome scurried around the outside wheel.[100] Grasping the rammer, he stepped up to the muzzle of the piece and rammed the canister round down the tube. Running to the left side of the trail, he frantically sighted the gun and stepped back, clear of the wheel, to give the command to fire. A volunteer corporal from Company C of the 12th Ohio, holding the lanyard, nodded to the lieutenant and turned his head aside. The command resounded briefly above the solitary pair. The lanyard snapped the friction primer. As the gun roared and recoiled, George Crome fell with a musket ball in his breast. "It was a tragic scene that I shall never forget," Robert B. Wilson mournfully remembered.[101]

The Confederate skirmishers attracted rifle fire from Company F of the 30th Ohio, which was hiding in the woods on their left. Captain James Atwell left the field in the arms of his men—mortally wounded. They did not have enough soldiers to take the guns or to repel the Yankees supporting them.[102] As the Confederates retreated back to the wood road, the three Federal

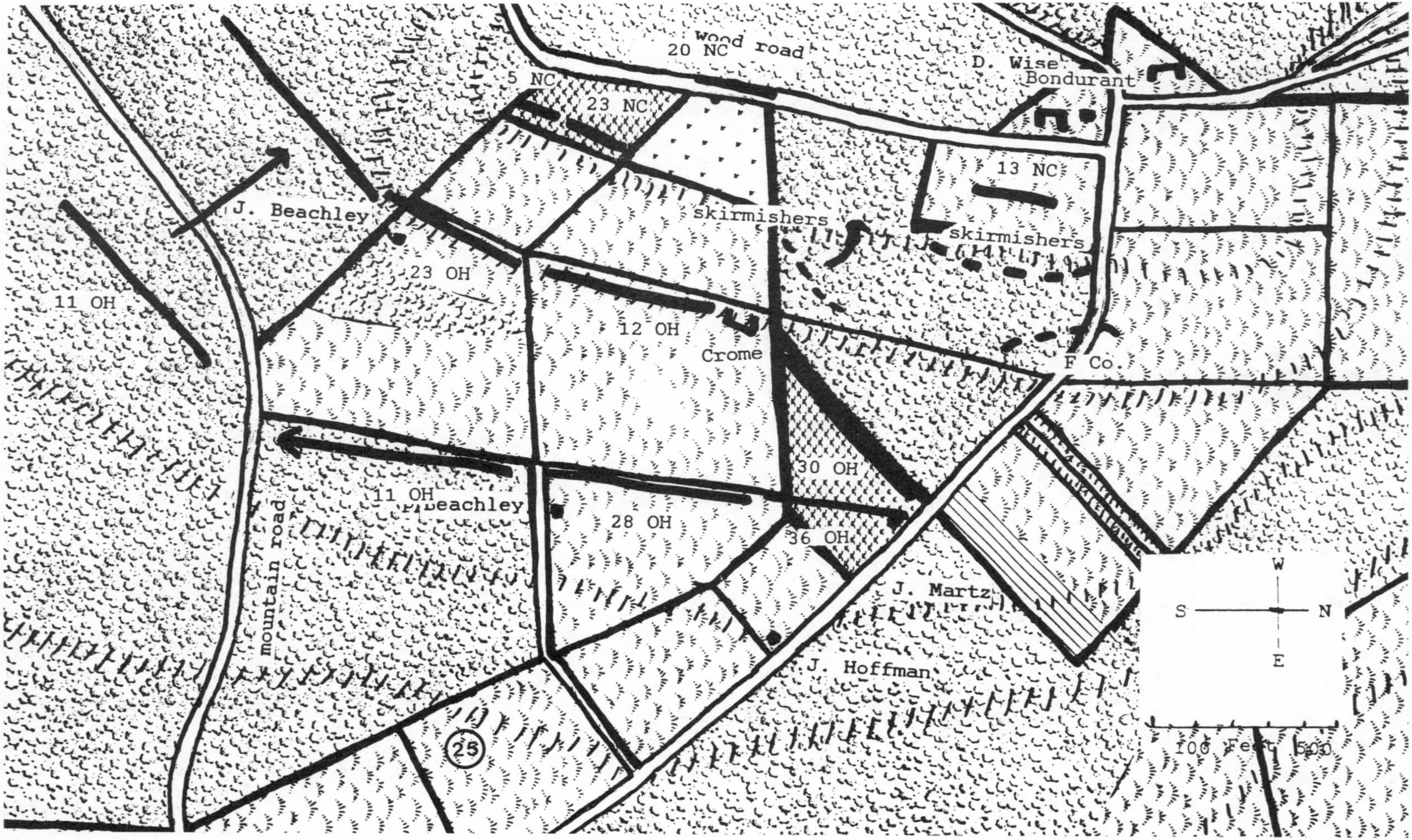

MAP 25: Fox's Gap—September 14, 1862. The skirmishers of the 20th North Carolina silence Crome's artillery section.

regiments below the crest furtively prepared for close combat. When the order came along the stone wall to fix bayonets, steel clinked ominously upon steel.[103]

On the far left of the Federal line, the 11th Ohio, under orders to attract the Rebels' attention and to deliberately draw their fire, crashed into the woods on the 23rd North Carolina's right front. Colonel Christie's (23rd North Carolina) main line and some stray skirmishers in the woods to the south fired into the Ohioans and forced them back upon the left of the 23rd Ohio.[104] Once the 11th Ohio rejoined the line, the infantrymen of the 23rd and the 12th Ohio regiments, upon command, gave a prolonged cheer and sprang en masse over the wall.[105] [Refer to Map 25]

The moment Colonel Daniel H. Christie (23rd North Carolina) saw the Yankees burst into his line of sight, he realized they would envelop his left flank. He screamed at Adjutant Veines E. Turner to find General Samuel Garland, and apprise him of his situation. The lieutenant raced away on foot to deliver a message to a general who, unknown to him, was bleeding to death on the front steps of the Mountain House.[106] He had barely passed behind the rear of Colonel Alfred Iverson's 20th North Carolina when his own regiment and the 5th North Carolina, in the cornfield to the southeast, volleyed once into Eliakim Scammon's two regiments and into the flank of the 11th Ohio.[107]

The dense laurel on the 5th North Carolina's right flank destroyed the 11th Ohio's formation. Lieutenant Colonel Augustus H. Coleman (11th Ohio), an ostrich plume bobbing jauntily from his Jeff Davis hat, valiantly reformed what he could find of the regiment, and pushed them farther west, toward the wood road where it turned west, behind the Confederate lines.[108] While his men struggled with the terrain, the 23rd Ohio stormed toward an opening in the stone wall between the right of the 23rd North Carolina and the left of the 5th North Carolina.[109] At the same instant, part of the 12th Ohio struck the North Carolinians from the northeast, while the rest of the regiment surged forward against the 20th North Carolina, which was along the wood road.[110]

Neither the 5th North Carolina nor Colonel Daniel Christie's men (23rd North Carolina) had time to reload before the Ohioans savagely pitched into them with their bayonets. The 5th North Carolina, Captain Thomas M. Garrett commanding, scattered to the rear before the 23rd Ohio reached it. Colonel Christie needlessly screamed for his line to retreat. The sun glinting off the onrushing line of steel shouted louder than he could. Most of his regiment bolted like jumped game toward the wood road.

Adjutant Veines E. Turner of the 23rd North Carolina missed the bulk of the regiment as it leaped and stumbled through the laurel on the mountain's western slope. Not realizing that most of the soldiers had retreated, he continued, with his distressing message, toward the regiment's former position. Colonel Duncan McRae of the 5th North Carolina, the acting brigade commander, whom he found stranded near the 13th North Carolina along

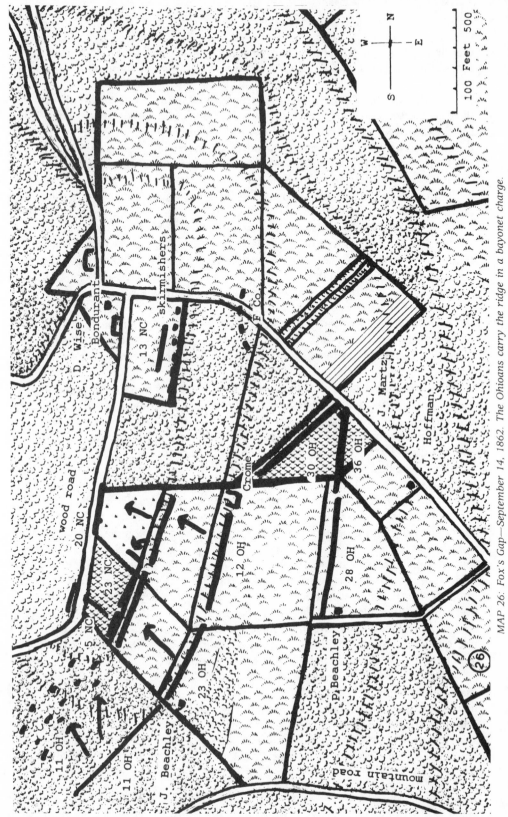

MAP 26: Fox's Gap—September 14, 1862. The Ohioans carry the ridge in a bayonet charge.

the wood road, east of Wise's field, had nervously informed him that, because he had neither staff officers nor a horse with which to contact General Hill, there would be no reinforcements.[111]

The startled adjutant rushed back to the cornfield and nearly collided with the Ohioans as they surrounded Company E of the 23rd North Carolina, which, in the suddenness of the attack, had not gotten the word to withdraw.[112] Bare muzzles clanged against leveled bayonets around the stone wall as the melee devolved into a killing frenzy. Private Charles R. Stevens (Company A, 23rd Ohio) hastily dispatched three of the Confederates before they could surrender. Nearby Sergeant Major Eugene Reynolds (23rd Ohio) and several Ohioans went down from bayonet thrusts.[113] [Refer to Map 26]

On the right, the 20th North Carolina waited until the 12th Ohio got to within fifteen feet of the wood road before it fired. A number of the Ohioans in Company E crumbled in the blast. A minié ball smashed into the forestock of Corporal Leonidas H. Inscho's rifle, driving splinters into his left hand. Frightened by his wounding, he madly dashed to the safety of the stone wall.[114] Unwilling to die from multiple stabbings, most of the North Carolinians turned their backs and scrambled into the woods behind them.[115] The Westerners, their adrenalin charged bodies too excited to calm down, split into two wings to respond both to the fleeing Confederates to their front and to the trapped North Carolinians (23rd North Carolina) on their left.[116]

Corporal Leonidas Inscho (Company E, 12th Ohio), who had huddled below the lip of the wall to examine his rifle and his hand, suddenly realized that the men on his left had abandoned him. He quickly poked his head over the wall only to find himself face to face with a Rebel captain. The plucky Ohioan, with more bravado than brains, leaped up, snatched the officer by the collar, and demanded he surrender. The officer refused and leveled his revolver at Inscho's face. The corporal grabbed the revolver by the barrel and forced it skyward. The officer's finger convulsed on the trigger and the gun fired.

Inscho jerked the weapon from the Confederate's grasp. The North Carolinian repeatedly pelted the Ohioan in the face with his bare fists, as the corporal struggled to haul him head first over the three-foot high stone wall. Bracing his right foot against the stones, the corporal jerked the captain off balance and landed him flat on his back on the eastern side.

Picking up the Rebel's revolver, the corporal boldly jutted his head above the wall. A short distance away, he spied five more Southerners behind a laurel tree. Pointing his weapon at them, he demanded their surrender and much to his amazement, four of them did. As they threw their rifles to the ground and stepped out into the open, the fifth man advanced toward Inscho with his rifle primed. Swearing that he would never surrender, he leveled his piece at Inscho. There was a report and a small puff of smoke. The bullet splattered against the stone wall as the agile Yankee ducked down behind it. The soldier turned to run away. Inscho stood up and icily dispatched him with the remaining five shots in the service revolver. With the muzzle still smoking, he turned upon his five prisoners and ordered them to the rear. They complied.[117]

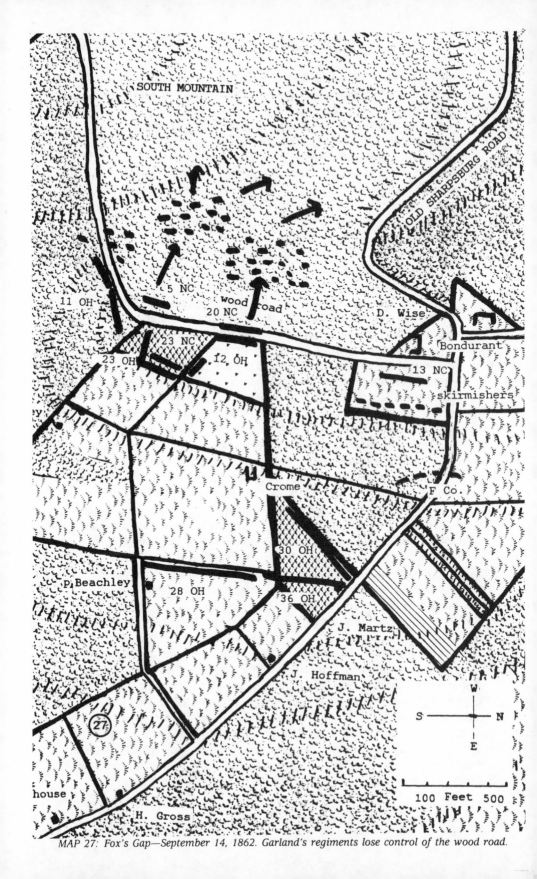

MAP 27: Fox's Gap—September 14, 1862. Garland's regiments lose control of the wood road.

To the right of the line, the remaining companies of the 12th Ohio's right wing viciously fired into the back of the rest of the 20th North Carolina as it crashed through the woods on the western slope of the mountain. Captain Lewis T. Hicks (Company E, 20th North Carolina) listened to the bullets snap the branches and leaves off the trees above his head as he and his company half ran and half fell down the steep mountainside.[118] Samuel Compton of the 12th Ohio, in the ecstacy of the chase, mistakenly assumed that the Confederates he saw topple from sight were the victims of his company's marksmanship.[119]

In his fury, a Yankee deliberately gunned down Assistant Surgeon William W. Jordan (23rd North Carolina) while he tended to the wounded too close to the firing line. His dear friend, the 23rd's Adjutant V. E. Turner sadly watched him fall before he escaped to the safety of the woods.[120]

Farther to the north, Lieutenant Wilson of the 12th Ohio saw one of his men lunge at a young Carolinian who had already raised his hands to surrender. The quick thinking officer snatched the man's rifle by the barrel before he completed his strike. The quaking Yankee infantryman disappeared into the woods to continue the pursuit while the captain attempted to pry some intelligence from the equally shaken Confederate. When asked for his regimental number, the "handsome bright looking" fellow, Wilson recalled, stunned him by telling him. Wilson forgot the state, though he never forgot the number. Unwittingly he had captured a stray from the 12th North Carolina.[121]

The impact of the Ohioan attack forced the Confederates to abandon their wounded. The Yankees bagged an estimated two hundred prisoners with that charge.[122] Some of the Ohioans attempted to alleviate the suffering of the injured. Samuel Compton stumbled across a teenager who was sitting upright against a tree along the wood road. He pleaded with Compton for some water. Unable to refuse, despite his own short supply, the private handed his canteen to the boy. The wounded soldier snatched it from Compton's hand and feverishly drained it.

As he handed it back, Compton shook the canteen. When he realized it was empty, a violent shiver snaked its way down his spine. It was bad luck to go into combat without any water.

"Won't you take a message to my mother?" the Confederate gasped. "Tell my mother it's her fault I'm here."

Before Compton could ask his name, the Carolinian slumped over dead. Having no time for sympathy, the private disappeared into the woods where most of Scammon's brigade and the 11th Ohio foolishly thrashed about like the "beaters" in a stag hunt.[123] [Refer to Map 27]

While the 11th, 12th, and 23rd Ohio regiments forced the mountain crest at the points of their bayonets, their casualties began to limp and stagger to the field hospitals at Beachley's and along the Old Sharpsburg Road. Chaplain William Lyle (11th Ohio) had just given directions to the ambulance crews in the ravine east of Beachley's and was starting to return when the 23rd North Carolina volleyed into the 23rd Ohio. The musket balls whizzed and zinged over the quaking chaplain's head, showering him with snapped twigs and clipped leaves. Throwing themselves behind some protective looking rocks, William Lyle and his attendants listened apprehensively to the spent balls pattering against the rocks. When the cheers of the three Ohio regiments reverberated through the woods, the hospital team made its way to the Beachley farm house.

Chaplain Lyle had not been there long when George, the regiment's black contraband, wandered in with Corporal Charles James (1st Ohio Independent Battery) slung over his back.

"Why! is that you, Charley?" William Lyle called in amazement as he recognized his friend from Troy, Ohio. "Where are you wounded?"

"Oh, it's only a flesh wound," Charley managed weakly. "Wouldn't have left, only couldn't stand. The lieutenant was wounded too. We peppered them, though!"

A preliminary examination revealed that the ball had gone through his leg and had done a tremendous amount of damage to it. The chaplain helped him into the farm house and turned him over to Assistant Surgeon Andrew C. McNutt. Several hundred yards to the north, Surgeon J. Frank Gabriel (11th Ohio) set up his table in the Hoffman house. Ambulances started to crowd into Beachley's lane and the day seemed to drag on forever.[124]

On the western slope of South Mountain, the three Ohio regiments became lost in the thick mountain laurel. Once they became entangled in the intertwined branches, briars, and closely packed oaks and chestnuts, they lost all their bearings. The frightening noises of their own men floundering through the dense forest on their flanks resounded loudly from every quarter. Squads of men wandered aimlessly about, trying to rejoin their commands and jumping with fear at every sound. The deeper they probed down the mountainside, the more lost they became. After penetrating the woods for about a quarter of a mile, Colonel Carr B. White (12th Ohio) ruefully discovered he was alone.[125]

Samuel Compton found him aimlessly wandering about in search of some bodies to command.

"Say, Compton," the colonel shouted with surprise, "I'm lost. Where is the old 12th?"

"I know where about 150 are," Compton replied matter-of-factly.

"Take them to me quick," the colonel blurted.

Sam Compton hesitated. Noticing the colonel had two canteens slung over his shoulder, he asked, "Give me a drink of water?"

Carr White swung one of them to the private who instantly uncorked it and put it into his mouth. He spat out the first mouthful faster than he swigged it. Gasping for air, he heard the colonel laughing at him.

"You prohibitionist," White mocked him, "taking down whiskey like an old toper."

"Colonel," Sam Compton sputtered, "be a gentleman, give me a drink of water!"

"I would if I had it. The other is brandy."

As Compton escorted the colonel uphill toward the wood road, he shed all the patriotic illusions he had ever harbored to explain the many Federal defeats in the East.[126] Unfortunately, a good many of the line officers in the 12th Ohio were drunk.[127]

Farther to the south, forty men and two officers of the 11th Ohio were fighting a private war of their own. In their frenzied pursuit of the North Carolinians they got cut off from the main body of the regiment and found themselves engaged with scattered clusters of retreating Confederates.[128] Farther behind them, near the wood road, the right wing of the regiment stalled just inside the wood line and took cover from the overshots from the cornfield

Colonel Carr B. White of the 12th Ohio. Like many of his line officers on September 14, 1862, he was drinking hard liquor during the battle of Fox's Gap.

USAMHI

east of them.[129] The attack against the 23rd North Carolina sapped the 23rd Ohio of its combat effectiveness for the day. The morning's fighting cost the regiment more than one hundred men in killed, wounded, and missing— among them, the colonel and seven company officers. Unable to press the attack, the regiment bellied down in the cornfield among the casualties of the 23rd North Carolina to wait out the day.[130]

To the north, the 13th North Carolina, with a fragment of the 12th North Carolina, was backed by Bondurant's battery. They stopped the Federal assault around Wise's cabin. The artillerists placed their guns within a semicircle, facing south and southeast, behind the stone wall which encircled the house.[131] The 13th North Carolina faced east, between the stone walls bordering the wood road.[132]

Bondurant's artillerists opened fire immediately upon the 11th and the 12th Ohio regiments as they blundered into the woods south of their position. Case shot burst among the trees and canister clattered through the branches overhead, forcing the Yankees to remain prone on the leaf covered ground.[133] To the east, in response to what appeared to be intensified Confederate pressure, Captain Seth Simmonds' (Kentucky Artillery) detached Lieutenant Daniel W. Glassie's section of ten-pounder Parrotts to back up the 30th Ohio. Using prolonge ropes, the sweating artillerists hauled their 1500 pound rifled tubes into the cornfield, west of the Hoffman house and south of the Old Sharpsburg Road. They went into battery in front of the prone

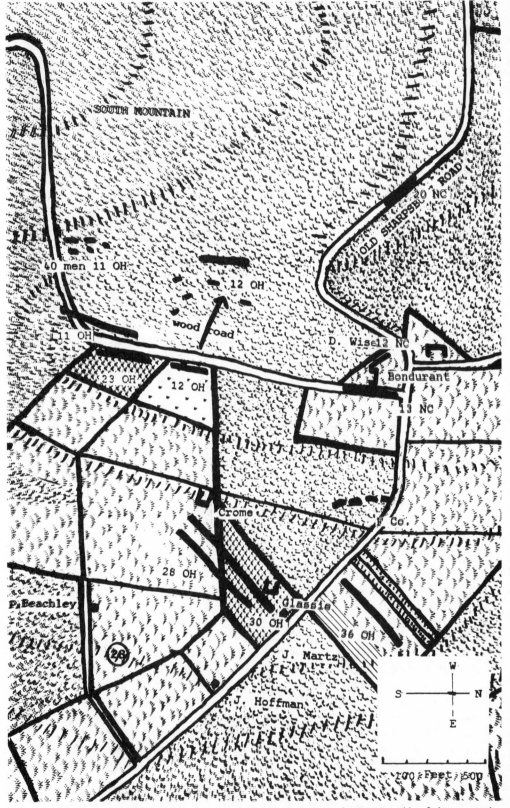

SOUTH MOUNTAIN

OLD SHARPSBURG ROAD

20 NC

40 men 11 OH

12 OH

wood road

11 OH

D. Wise 12 NC

Bondurant

23 OH

12 OH

13 NC

Crome

F Co.

28 OH

P. Beachley

Glassie

30 OH

36 OH

28

J. Martz

J. Hoffman

W
S — N
E

100 Feet 500

MAP 28: Fox's Gap—September 14, 1862. The Ohioans get lost on the western side of the mountain.

Ohioans.[134] Simmonds' Kentuckians intended to direct their guns to the north and the northwest in an attempt to silence Bondurant's Alabamians and the Georgian artillerists on the spur north of the National Pike.[135]

It took time to manhandle the guns into position, and the 30th Ohio did not want to move into action without softening up the Confederates first. Private Joseph E. Walton (Company I, 30th Ohio) clearly recalled that the regiment, when ordered to charge into the woods to its front, did not respond.[136] General Cox, who realized the longer his men remained idle, the longer it would take to get them moving, did not want to lose the initiative or the ground he had so dearly won in the last attack. He sent the 36th Ohio from George Crook's brigade to file north across the Old Sharpsburg Road on the right flank of the 30th Ohio. As the 36th inched its way up hill to extend the main line, he ordered the 28th Ohio into the cornfield behind the 30th Ohio, as support.[137]

Meanwhile, remnants of the 20th and the 23rd North Carolina regiments with their commanders, Colonels Alfred Iverson and Daniel Christie, respectively, had meandered as far as the Old Sharpsburg Road, where it wound its way down the western side of the mountain. They rallied around Colonel Duncan McRae, their brigade commander, who intercepted them there. McRae had not been able to reach D. H. Hill because he did not have any mounted couriers present, and had lost contact with the rest of his brigade.[138] The relative lull, excepting Bondurant's harassing artillery practice, should have spurred him to do something. Instead, he waited to reorganize his position and to ascertain what was going on around him. He knew the 13th North Carolina, under the command of the wounded Colonel Ruffin, still held the crest with Bondurant's gunners. McRae had lost contact with the remains of the 5th North Carolina. He did not find out until after the action that Captain Thomas M. Garrett's small contingent from the 5th North Carolina manned the southern stonewall which bordered Wise's garden.[139] He was not sure what the Federals were doing.[140] [Refer to Map 28]

Unknown to him, Colonel Charles Tew, commanding his own 2nd North Carolina and the 4th North Carolina from G. B. Anderson's brigade, was approaching the wood road intersection from the Mountain House. The colonel halted his two regiments just before they reached the clearing on the northwest corner of the Old Sharpsburg Road and sent Captain Edwin A. Osborne (Company H, 4th North Carolina) ahead on a reconnaissance. The captain jumped over the stone wall along the wood road at the corner of the first field north of the Old Sharpsburg Road and, following the rail fence which ran east from that point, tried to work his way down the mountain. The sharpshooters of the 36th Ohio, who were hiding in the ravine north of the Hoffman house caught him in the open. Their shots pocked the stone wall behind him and sent him barrelling back over the wall into the wood road. He reported to Colonel Tew that they were at the front.[141]

Charles Tew, in the meantime, had scanned the woods south and southwest of his position. Smoke clung to the trees ·in a suffocating fog.

Bullets occasionally zinged into his line from the right rear. He yelled for Captain John G. B. Grimes (Quartermaster, 4th North Carolina) to return to the Mountain House with a plea for more men. The young man ran past his regiment, past his dear friend, Colonel Bryan Grimes. The colonel, who had severely injured his leg when the Yankees shot down his horse, momentarily forgot his intense pain as his stare followed the captain along the wood road until the woods seemed to swallow him up. He never saw Captain Grimes again. No one did. He simply disappeared.

Bryan Grimes, however, had to defend his small sector of the field with an undersized regiment of less than 175 men.[142] The stubborn colonel posted his best marksmen along the stone wall with orders to pick off any Yankee who foolishly exposed himself.[143]

Along the ridge road, the wounded Colonel Ruffin became aware that the small arms fire on his right flank had dwindled. The relative silence made him feel uneasy. He sent his adjutant, First Lieutenant Jasper Fleming, south along the wood road, to reconnoiter the situation and to report back to him.[144] As he did so, Lieutenant Daniel W. Glassie's section from Simmonds' Kentucky battery went into battery in the cornfield on the opposite side of the woods, east of his regiment.

Their high pitched shells screamed over the wood road and made the Confederate position on the top of the hill, behind the 13th North Carolina too dangerous for Bondurant's left section. Several minutes into the barrage, the captain ordered those two guns to move farther to the northwest to the one acre field across the road from Wise's cabin.[145] As they did so, Adjutant Fleming staggered back to the 13th North Carolina and told Colonel Ruffin he had no friendly troops on their right flank. They were surrounded.[146]

The Yankee artillerists overreacted to the situation in front of them. In their zeal to get their pieces up the mountainside, they had spilled the water buckets beneath the gun carriages, which they did not discover until they loaded their first projectiles. Counterbattery fire came hurtling in from Captain J. Lane's Georgia Battery, which was on the spur north of the National Pike, forcing them to handle their pieces too fast. Within minutes, the barrels started to overheat.[147] Jacob Cox put them on the hillside to buy time for his scattered infantry division, which was attempting to regroup on both sides of the wood road, about 600 yards south of Wise's cabin.

The 11th Ohio and the 12th Ohio, in reforming in the woods, had become intermixed.[148] Samuel Compton of the 12th found about 180 of his regiment in line, facing north, with their right wing near the wood road.[149] Some of the 11th Ohio, including Lieutenant Colonel Augustus Coleman, had worked their way into the middle of the 12th.[150] A very small portion of Company A (23rd Ohio) fell in somewhere in the line also. Private Robert B. Cornwell and his close friend, Josh Barnes (both Company A) joined them, both anxious to renew the fight.[151]

Along the Old Sharpsburg Road, Glassie's two rifled guns fell ominously silent. Having no water to sponge the sparks out in the tubes, the Kentuckians reluctantly abandoned their section.[152]

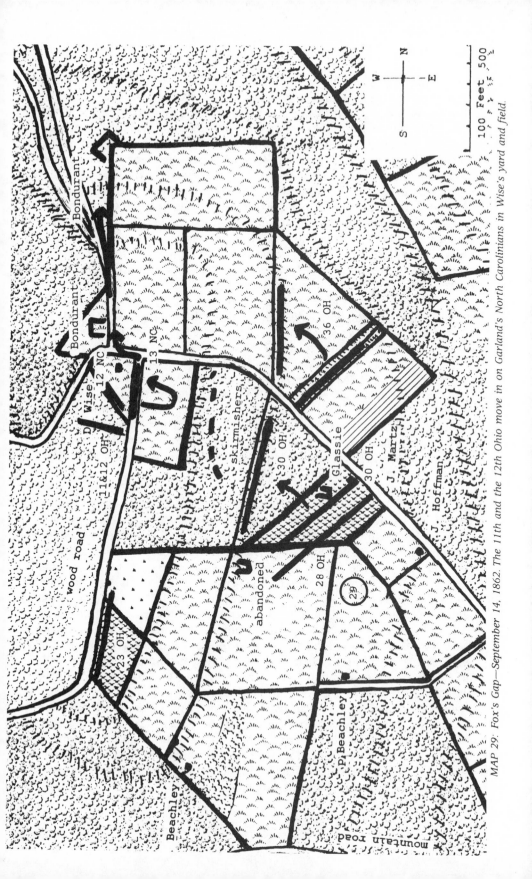

MAP 29: Fox's Gap—September 14, 1862. The 11th and the 12th Ohio move in on Garland's North Carolinians in Wise's yard and field.

As they retreated, the Ohio regiments southwest of the cornfield made a concerted rush against the Wise house and the woods east of it.[153] Colonel Thomas Ruffin saw them coming and tried to escape north along the wood road, where he ran into rifle fire from the 36th Ohio, which forced him back toward his original position.[154] The 2nd and the 4th North Carolina fired by the right oblique into the 30th and the 36th Ohio regiments.[155] Across the field from them, Private Andrew Wykle (Company K, 36th Ohio) saw his brother James topple over, wounded. He suddenly regretted having run away from home to enlist because their parents had refused to sign their consent.[156]

Ruffin's left flank had barely reached the wood road-Old Sharpsburg Road intersection when the 11th and the 12th Ohio regiments struck Wise's farm and enveloped its small yard. The rest of Bondurant's battery limbered up and escaped north to the position formerly held by Captain John Pelham's horse artillery section.[157] [Refer to Map 29]

Colonel Thomas Rosser and his 5th Virginia Cavalry, having evacuated their morning position with John Pelham's two guns shortly after the 2nd and the 4th North Carolina regiments arrived upon the field, went into line behind the stone wall on the western side of the wood road.[158] As the firing increased near Wise's, Rosser galloped down to Colonel Duncan McRae, whom he found along the Old Sharpsburg Road with the remnants of the 20th and the 23rd North Carolina regiments. At McRae's request, Rosser lent him a mounted courier who sped off to Major General D. H. Hill with the first news he had received from that sector in more than an hour and a half. Rosser then asked the colonel to retire his two regiments north, across the road, to the hill behind them, to support Pelham's two field pieces.[159] They complied without attempting to contact the 13th North Carolina.

As they retired through the woods west of the 2nd North Carolina, which was on the hill above them, they exposed the regiment's flank and rear to Federal fire from around Wise's house and yard.[160] Thomas Ruffin tried breaking his 13th North Carolina to the rear (the west) only to find the woods in that direction swarming with Ohioans. Left with no option but the aged axiom that "the best defense is an offense," he gave the command to charge the 30th Ohio's skirmishers, who had advanced into the woods to his front.[161] The suddenness of his attack stunned the Westerners. Driving the Yankees almost to their guns, the Rebels halted and turned tail as the colors of the 30th Ohio, followed by the rest of the regiment, swarmed around Lieutenant Daniel W. Glassie's two abandoned Parrott guns and charged toward the woods.[162] The retreating Rebels returned fire and spattered Company G with good effect. A single minié ball, boring through C. Chamberlain's right shoulder, imbedded itself in 18-year-old Hiram Mushrush's right shoulder and felled both men instantly. (Mushrush's wound healed, but he could never raise his arm as high as his shoulder.)[163] Across the road, Andrew Wykle (Company K, 36th Ohio), who was unable to reach his wounded brother because of the intense musketry, dove for cover behind a rock and waited for the rest of the regiment to advance to his assistance.[164] His brother would have to wait it out with the rest of the casualties.

Back at Wise's cabin, the situation had become untenable. The 11th and the 12th Ohio regiments flanked the handful of North Carolinians in Wise's garden and a desperate hand to hand melee ensued over the colors of the 5th North Carolina. Captain Thomas M. Garrett of the 5th North Carolina ordered his color guard to advance east toward the regiment's left flank when the Ohioans charged the fence row. The color bearer, marching steadily along the wall, defiantly waved his colors from one side to the other in a bold attempt to rally his regiment.[165]

From the perspective of Lieutenant Colonel Augustus Coleman (11th Ohio) and his squad, the Confederate and his color guard seemed to materialize from behind a cluster of chestnut sap-

Lieutenant Colonel Augustus Coleman of the 11th Ohio. Coleman, who almost lost his life to a bullet in the head on September 14, 1862 at Fox's Gap, was killed on September 17, 1862 at Antietam.
FROM THE 34TH ANNUAL REUNION OF THE ELEVENTH OHIO

lings near the garden. When the Yankees were about forty paces away from the Confederates, a shot rang out from nearby and one of the color guard dropped to the ground. Coleman profanely yelled at the color bearer to halt and surrender his flag.[166] Other Ohioans joined in and screamed for him to give up.[167] The Rebel abruptly stopped, then deliberately turned and fired his pistol.[168] The bullet snapped off part of the white feather which Coleman wore in his Army hat. J. Hammer Smith (Company B), who was standing not ten feet from Coleman, inadvertently ducked as the upper half of the feather fluttered delicately to the ground.[169]

The Rebel turned to run away, when two minié balls hit him simultaneously—one in the shoulder and the other in the head. At least five other rounds struck his corpse before it thudded to the ground.[170]

Before anyone in the 11th Ohio realized what had happened, Private Henry W. Hoagland (Company F, 12th Ohio) leaped over the wall, and pulled the flag from the dead Rebel's hands. Augustus Coleman demanded the flag. The private, much to the disgust of his lieutenant, R. B. Wilson, complied. The battlefield was no place for a personal dispute. The lieutenant never forgave the colonel for his selfishness.[171]

The Ohioans continued to press the outnumbered North Carolinians back, despite their stubborn resistance. Shortly after the flag incident, the Confederates wounded and captured Lieutenant Robert B. Wilson, who managed to break away and then capture his captors.[172] Their musketry mortally wounded Captain William W. Liggett (Company H, 12th Ohio) as he attempted to storm the garden wall with his section of the regiment.[173] Nearby, J. Hammer Smith (Company B, 11th Ohio) kneeled by the body of his wounded comrade, John Manning . As Smith returned to the line, he never realized the seriousness of his friend's injury.[174] A load of buck shot brought down Joshua Barnes and Robert Cornwell (both A Co., 23rd Ohio) at the same time. A pellet bored into Cornwell's right thigh, striking the artery but not severing it. The two lay on the ground, close together, each trying desperately not to bleed to death.[175]

The Yankees fought the Confederates valiantly for the possession of Wise's one acre plot of ground. When a Rebel soldier popped up along the stone wall in front of Private John Hammond of the 11th Ohio, the hearty Westerner snatched the surprised fellow by the collar and jerked him over to the Yankee side of the lines. (Three days later, Hammond was killed at Antietam.)[176] Near the middle of Wise's wall, the 12th Ohio stumbled upon a North Carolinian whom they had killed as he was crossing the stake and rider on top of the stone fence. He died facing west, with his arms extended and the palms turned up. His mouth hung open in a haunting gape. When Samuel Compton of the 12th Ohio found him, some wags had pulled the Rebel's opened haversack around to the front of his body. They shoved a biscuit in his mouth and had folded his cold fingers around one in each of his hands.

As the Ohioans crossed west to the safety of the woods on the other side of the wood road they shouted insults at his corpse.

"Say Johnnie, you're a hog!"

"You need ice not rations where you are going!" another taunted.

"Was that gal good lookin' that baked them are Biskits?"

The catcalls faded from Sam Compton's mind as he hunkered down behind the stone wall in the southeastern corner of Wise's yard. By then, the bullets were flying thick from the north and from across the wood road.[177]

As the 5th North Carolina crossed the Old Sharpsburg Road west (behind) the 2nd and the 4th North Carolina regiments, which were still on the wood road north of the Gap, it became apparent to Colonel Charles C. Tew (2nd North Carolina) the Yankees were cutting him off. To worsen matters, the 36th Ohio's skirmishers, in moving against Bondurant's section in Wise's yard, were trying to envelop the two regiments from the north. Bondurant gave the order for his command to retreat north toward the security of the section in Pelham's old position. Captain John C. Gorman (Company B, 2nd North Carolina) bitterly lamented, "Men [were] falling at every few steps."[178] Orderly Sergeant James Shinn, also of Company B, noted in his diary, "The fight now became a bushwhacking affair. The Mt. was very rugged & the Laurel & other bushes very thick. We fell back but little at a time...."[179]

When Charles Tew retired his command to the north, Colonel Thomas Ruffin and the 13th North Carolina made their dash toward Wise's house.[180] Their retreat turned into a rout as the North Carolinians ran the gauntlet

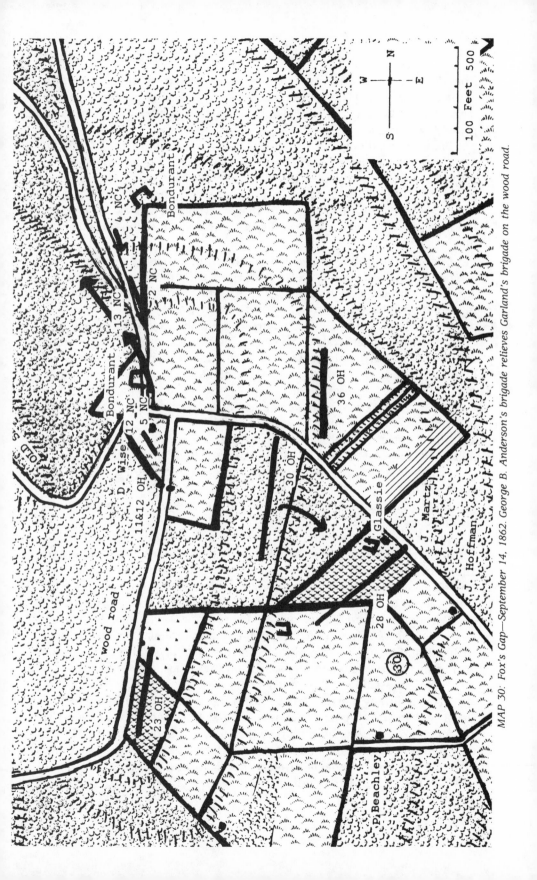

MAP 30: Fox's Gap—September 14, 1862. George B. Anderson's brigade relieves Garland's brigade on the wood road.

from the gate at the northwestern corner of the field to the wood road, north of the Old Sharpsburg Road. The Ohioans calmly picked off his men as if they were at a Sunday shoot, seemingly oblivious to the scattered rounds which pelted their position.

Frame Ripley (Company H, 12th Ohio), who was next to Samuel Compton (Company F), diligently zeroed in on the fence gate as the Rebels tried to cross the road. Within a few minutes, he had killed seven men.[181] Inside the garden, in full view of the Confederates, Francis M. Underwood (Company G, 11th Ohio) calmly loaded and shot at every man who popped into his line of sight. Presently, his messmate John B. Roberds, stumbled out of the laurel behind him.

Coolly turning about, he called to John to come closer.

"This is the best place you ever saw!" Frank exclaimed as John came near.

At that instant, a Confederate, wearing a white blanket over his shoulder, made a dash for safety from a thicket in front of them.

"Now watch, John," Frank said matter-of-factly, "and see him tumble!"

Underwood quietly raised his rifle to his shoulder, sighted in, breathed easy, and squeezed the trigger. The cap burst. The rifle roared. It recoiled solidly into his shoulder. Through the sulfuric cloud, they saw the Confederate fall—lifeless—to the forest floor.

"There," Frank said with a great deal of satisfaction, "that is the *fourth* one I have landed just there!"

The bullets buzzed about their ears too thickly to suit John Roberds. He told Frank they would be killed if they stayed there any longer.

"Oh," Underwood gasped with amazement, "I never thought of that! I guess we had better get back a little!"

Rather sheepishly, the two retreated to the safety of the woods to wait out the engagement.[182]

At one point the situation became desperate. Trapped members of the 13th North Carolina tied their handkerchiefs to the points of their bayonets and poked them above the stone wall on the eastern side of the wood road. An officer, whom Samuel Compton mistook for Colonel Hayes of the 23rd Ohio, leaped to his feet in full view as the Rebs stood up to surrender.

Waving his sword, he screamed, "Cease firing!"

When the Yankee rifles fell silent, the North Carolinians pulled up their weapons and loosed a rattling volley. The officer threw himself behind the wall as the bullets flattened themselves on the opposite side.

"Give 'em Hell, boys!" he cried.

In the following minutes, few of the erring Rebels escaped. The slaughter sickened Samuel Compton.[183] Colonel Thomas Ruffin and his survivors did not intend to stop running until they got to the Mountain House.[184] While they stampeded north, the 2nd and the 4th North Carolina regiments rallied around Bondurant's Alabama Artillery. [Refer to Map 30]

Simultaneously, D. H. Hill at the Mountain House heard the firing increase in tempo toward his right flank, and rode down the wood road to the rear of the 2nd North Carolina, where he rallied the 12th and the 13th North Carolinas. The general galloped up to Colonel Ruffin, and while shaking his hand, exclaimed that he had given the regiments up for lost and did not understand how either of them had escaped. Calming down, Hill blurted, as a queer afterthought, how glad he was to see McClellan's whole army to his front. Ruffin's face twisted in an expression of disbelief. How could Hill, with his small force, rejoice at facing an army twenty fold greater than his? Hill, quickly interpreting the colonel's puzzled face, explained himself. He, at first, thought the action along his sector was a feint by part of the Army of the Potomac. He believed the main part of McClellan's forces were going to break through farther to the south and cut Lee's main army off from Jackson at Harpers Ferry. The explanation did not allay Ruffin's fears about being overwhelmed by superior numbers but it did clarify why the gap had to be held until the Federals were fought to a standstill.

Firing broke out to the northeast, where the northern slope of the ridge descended to the National Pike. Skirmishers from the 36th Ohio accidentally stumbled upon the right flank of Captain William M. Arnold's (Company A) skirmishers from the 6th Georgia and a firefight erupted on the mountain side.[185] Once again, Hill spurred back to the Mountain House. Detaching Captain Thomas H. Carter's two twelve-pounder mountain howitzers from his Virginia battery, which was in position across the road from the inn, he ordered them south to assist his battered infantrymen.[186] While the two light guns rattled down the mountain road on their rickety carriages, the general rounded up teamsters, cooks, couriers, and a number of his dismounted staff and rushed them south to assist the artillery.[187]

They went into battery on a rocky knoll just west of the wood road and about seven hundred yards north of Wise's cabin.[188] Facing southeast they fired several case shot at the Federal skirmishers. The artillery bursts sent Company G of the 36th Ohio to cover down the hill, below the line of sight. The Ohioans left the mortally wounded Private Henry J. Gibbons on the field. He bled to death within half an hour. Sergeant George Bartmess went down with a serious wound through his leg below the knee. Acting Corporal John Silken and Privates Charles R. Delong, Warren M. Walter, and Peter Hockinbury turned tail and ran from the field. Private Hall disappeared during the action, and never returned to the ranks.[189] On the right, Captain William M. Arnold's sharpshooters peppered Company K as it tried to flank the mountain howitzer section. The Federal company lost six enlisted men killed and fourteen wounded in a short time and retreated back to its original line.[190] From near the Hoffman house, General Jacob Cox saw the Confederate cooks and headquarters' staff massing behind the guns and assumed they were going to attack his right (northern) flank.[191]

Convinced he was facing a much larger force than his own, and fearful of committing his battle weary infantry to the woods north of the Old Sharpsburg Road, Cox ordered his troops to retire to their original positions

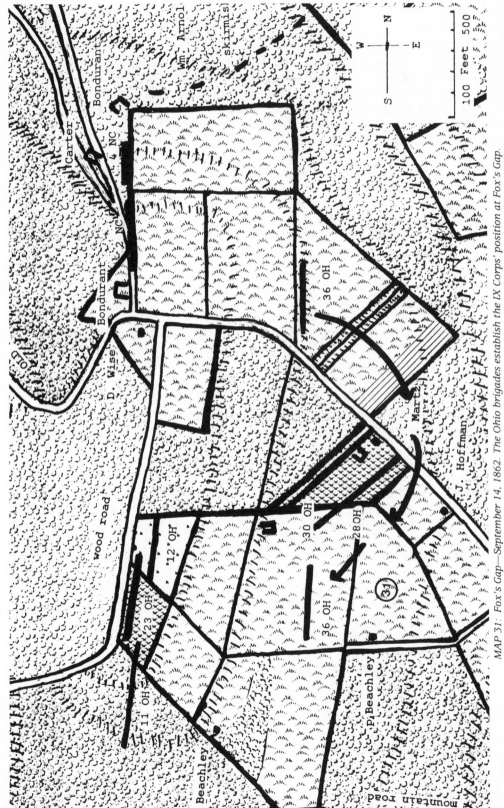

MAP 31: Fox's Gap—September 14, 1862. The Ohio brigades establish the IX Corps' position at Fox's Gap.

parallel to the wood road.[192] The 30th Ohio held the right, in the western edge of the cornfield above the Hoffman house, with its right flank on the Old Sharpsburg Road. The 28th Ohio went prone behind them. The 12th Ohio retired to the field south of Wise's field where it initially encountered Bondurant's Alabama Artillery. The 36th Ohio rested on the hillside below it, just above Beachley's house. The 23rd Ohio and the 11th Ohio finished the line out to the left, with their left flank resting in the woods southeast of the wood road.[193]

It was noon. Cox's troops had seen enough battle and had achieved their initial objective. They had turned the Confederate right. He had contracted his lines to await the arrival of the rest of his corps.[194] [Refer to Map 31]

Chapter Eleven

SEPTEMBER 14, 1862

A relative silence—a general cessation of the constant roar and clatter of small arms fire—settled over the battlefield as both sides slowly re-established their positions north and south of the Old Sharpsburg Road. During the forenoon, at approximately 10:00 A.M., Brigadier General Roswell Ripley's brigade (44th Georgia, 1st and 3rd North Carolina), followed by Brigadier General Robert Rodes' 3rd, 5th, 6th, 12th, and 26th Alabama regiments left their camps near Boonsboro and started east toward Turner's Gap. Ripley's men, having spent the previous evening standing and sleeping in formation, did not feel up to the march. (The 4th Georgia left Ripley's brigade during the morning to guard Hamburg Pass, northeast of Boonsboro.)[1]

Private Calvin Leach (Company B, 1st North Carolina) grumbled in his diary about having to march with half cooked rations in his haversack. Halfway up the mountain, the regiment halted with the brigade to ditch its knapsacks. To the southeast, cannon roared ominously. Again, Leach found reason for complaint. While the soldiers loaded their weapons, the private lost the New Testament which a friend had given him.

A steady column of wounded men snaked its way down the National Pike, indicating the severity of the fighting. The residents of the Mountain House clattered down the road alongside them. Leach particularly noticed the tears streaming down the frightened civilians' faces. He recalled how that same family, which had seemed so happy to see them as they crossed the gap two days before, had waved the Confederate flag at the column as it passed. Before the column renewed its trek to the summit, the wary Rebels stared at Garland's dismounted staff officers as they carried his corpse down the steep road toward Boonsboro.[2] To the southeast, they listened to the blasts of artillery fire reverberating off the mountain top.

Bondurant's battery, in the field north of Wise's cabin, deliberately pounded the Federal troops with canister as they attempted to realign themselves along the mountainside. The charges sailed over the prone Yankee lines, and plowed up the ground behind them. The ricochetting cast iron balls "...cut long furrows in the sod, with a noise like the cutting of a melon rind," General Jacob Cox vividly recollected.[3]

During the preceding half hour to forty-five minutes, Captain John Lane's pair of twenty-pounder Parrotts and three ten-pounder Parrotts, on the plowed knob north of the National Pike and Captain Thomas Carter's ten-pounder Parrott at the Mountain House had also focused their attention upon the rest of the IX Corps as it approached the valley from Middletown. They had engaged Seth Simmonds' twenty pounders and Lieutenant Samuel N. Benjamin's heavy battery of the 2nd U.S. Artillery, which had gone into action on the small spur one-fourth of a mile northwest of the Bolivar intersection.[4] The Rebel gunfire whined over General Orlando Willcox's division of the IX Corps as it crested the ridge east of Bolivar.[5]

Colonel Thomas Welsh's brigade (46th New York, 45th and 100th Pennsylvania), leading the division, came under fire immediately. Welsh threw the 100th Pennsylvania along the southern side of the National Pike with orders to skirmish west to secure Cox's right flank from a suspected Confederate infantry attack. The rest of the division went into line along Bolivar Road. Colonel Benjamin Christ's brigade (28th Massachusetts, 8th and 17th Michigan, 79th New York, and 50th Pennsylvania) moved south, behind the heavy batteries to see what developed. Welsh's two remaining regiments started to advance north along Bolivar Road, heading for Mount Tabor Church.[6]

Captain Gabriel Campbell (Company E, 17th Michigan) studied his watch. It was 11:30 A.M. Having never been under fire before, he seemed intent upon committing to memory his supposed time of death.[7] The lingering image of the Kanawha Division's knapsacks lying alongside the road west of Middletown reminded Adjutant Lewis Crater (50th Pennsylvania) of the serious work which lay ahead of the regiment. The Rebel shells, which burst threateningly overhead, did not allay his fears. He watched his men intuitively load and cap their muskets as they moved under the cover of the hill to the west.[8]

Private Frederick Pettit (Company C, 100th Pennsylvania), whose company held the regiment's right flank along the National Pike, anxiously advanced with his comrades to within half a mile of Lane's battery. When they passed the intersection of the school house lane and the Pike, the artillery barrage intensified. The shells burst thick and fast amidst the extended formation. Company C broke formation and rushed into the drainage ditch along the southern bank of the road. Shortly thereafter, a staffer from General Burnside ordered them to retire to the left.

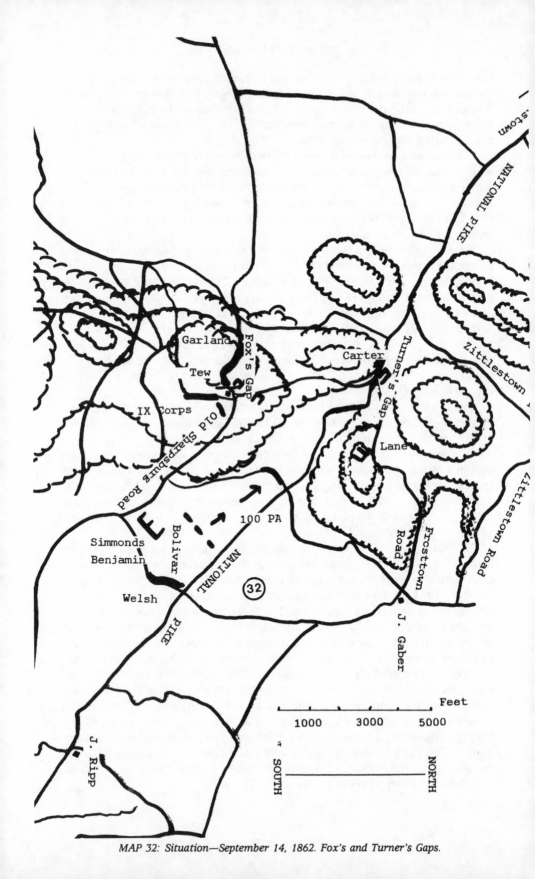

MAP 32: *Situation—September 14, 1862. Fox's and Turner's Gaps.*

The incoming artillery rounds seemed to accelerate with their pace as the men ran back toward the school house road. The Confederates cut down one of the fleeing Pennsylvanians before they disappeared into the woods between the Federal and the Confederate batteries.[9] Unknown to them, the rest of the division had advanced toward the relief of Cox's division at Fox's Gap.

The Confederate batteries, in addition to delaying the IX Corps' advance and forcing it to deploy, also provided cover fire for the rest of D. H. Hill's division as it arrived at Turner's Gap. Shortly after noon, while Bondurant's gunners kept the Yankees ducking, D. H. Hill started shifting what he could find of Garland's command and Colonel Charles C. Tew's (2nd North Carolina) two regiments. They anchored their left flank on the Old Sharpsburg Road, just west of the artillery.[10] They needed reinforcements desperately, and some were on the way.

At the top of the mountain, General Ripley halted his brigade in battle line on the eastern edge of Turner's Gap, north of the National Pike. Calvin Leach of the 1st North Carolina wrote, "...I could see the Yankees in a line of battle and their artillery placed firing on us and our artillery was in position playing on them."[11] Below them the 100th Pennsylvania probed the base of the mountain.

While Ripley's brigade stood to arms, Robert Rodes' Alabamians moved east on the National Pike, past its left flank. Turning north, on the mountain road which wound to the top of the spur toward Lane's battery, the Alabamians relieved General George B. Anderson and his two remaining regiments (14th and 30th North Carolina).[12] Anderson immediately filed his command behind Ripley's, which was still standing in place, onto the wood road and headed south to connect with the 2nd and 4th North Carolina. Ripley did not put his men on the march behind him.[13] At the same time, the rest of Orlando Willcox's division (IX Corps) continued to consolidate its position on the mountain's eastern slope. Its shuffling attracted the attention of Lane's Confederate artillerists near Turner's Gap. [Refer to Map 32]

Lane's Georgian gunners changed the direction of their fire from Bolivar Road to the Old Sharpsburg Road. They laid down a fire barrage which harassed the Federal right flank. Their shells alarmed Companies B, D, and I of the 36th Ohio as they staggered up the Old Sharpsburg Road while returning from picket duty along three byroads in Middletown Valley.

The wheezing Ohioans gaped at the line of wounded which stumbled down toward the refreshing stream at Mentzer's sawmill. Squads of dejected Confederates, many of them also wounded, hobbled past too. Undaunted, the three companies joined their regiment in the field southwest of the J. Martz cabin to endure the pounding. Not too long afterward, shell fragments wounded six more men.[14]

Shrapnel pelted the farm houses like hail against a window pane. In the yard of the Peter Beachley house, Dr. A. C. McNutt and Chaplain William

W. Lyle of the 11th Ohio sat up Private Andrew F. Thompson of Company F to extract the musket ball which had passed through both of his lungs and lodged in his shoulder. McNutt probed the wound, located the ball, and was preparing to extract it when a projectile hissed close by behind them and exploded a short distance away. The surgeon finished his operation and bound up the wound. (Thompson died twenty-four days later.)

Chaplain Lyle tried to keep the ambulances, which clogged the farm lane, moving down the mountain. The artillery fire stunned the drivers. Lyle and Assistant Surgeon McNutt, during a momentary lull, pleaded with the frightened hospital assistants to move their wagons to safer ground. Several tense minutes lapsed before the wagoners reacted to the two officers' entreaties. As the wagons creaked down the lane, the Confederate batteries renewed their barrage with fury.[15]

The gunners had a much more tempting target than the ambulances at which to lob shells and solid shot. The wagons just happened to be in the wrong place at the wrong time. Captain Asa M. Cook's 8th Massachusetts Independent Artillery and Colonel Benjamin Christ's brigade slipped and stumbled up the Old Sharpsburg Road. The 79th New York led the column, followed by the 17th Michigan, the 8th Michigan, and the 50th Pennsylvania.[16]

Volunteers from the 79th New York shouldered two cannon from Cook's Battery into the small plowed strip of ground in the open field north of the Martz cabin.[17] Cook directed the two twelve-pounder Napoleons to open with shell upon Lane's Georgians, whom they could see on the knoll across the National Pike gorge to their right.[18] While he did so, the 79th New York moved south by files into the field near the western edge of Hoffman's property.[19] To the rear, Colonel William H. Withington diverted his untried 17th Michigan to the right, into the woods northeast of the New Yorkers.[20] The other regiments (8th Michigan, 50th Pennsylvania, and 28th Massachusetts) marched up the road in column behind them.

To the south, Colonel Welsh advanced his two regiments (46th New York and 45th Pennsylvania), in line up the hill parallel to Christ's column. He halted in Hoffman's field, west of the house and within sight of the 79th New York and Martz's cornfield. The untried Pennsylvanians peeled off their knapsacks and lay down.[21] The 46th New York continued the line to the left for another four hundred feet.[22]

Up ahead, the section from the 8th Massachusetts Independent Artillery loosed their first two shells at the Georgia battery to the north. Within three minutes, six more rounds whirled through the air. One of the guns, disabled during the barrage, fell silent. Cook ordered the crew to retire the piece and sent word back for another to advance from the column of caissons in the Old Sharpsburg Road. As the relief crew struggled with their piece up the road, and the other crew tried to manhandle theirs away, Bondurant's Alabamians (near Wise's) unloaded canister upon the unsuspecting artillerists.[23]

Eighteen-year-old Private Frank A. Keene died where he stood. Privates Franklin Adams, Arthur D'Arcy, Lewis Francis, and Sidney Mellen went down in the blast—two of them mortally wounded.[24] Asa Cook yelled for the rest of his battery to retreat in column of caissons while his surviving artillerists bolted into the woods behind their guns and took cover.[25] The ensuing scramble clogged the narrow road. The panicked drivers tried to wheel their cumbersome caissons around to drive them off the field. It created a traffic jam which stalled the ambulances from Beachley's lane.[26]

The Confederate artillery fire caught the 46th New York and 45th Pennsylvania on the flank. Private William A. Roberts (Company K, 45th Pennsylvania), who had never been under fire before, marvelled, from his prone position, at how easily the canister shredded the trees across the road into pulp.[27]

Cook's New Englanders had barely escaped to the woods when the Alabamians switched to solid shot. Their rounds bounded over the crest of the hill and sailed wildly down the Old Sharpsburg Road. Captain Gabriel Campbell (Company E, 17th Michigan) patiently watched his company file into the woods north of the deep cut in the road. As the last man cleared the road, he turned toward the commotion up the hill from him. Several solid shot bounded down the road. One passed within arm's length of the captain and plowed into the company behind him.

"There was a scramble up the sides of the ditch and out of range," he recalled.[28]

The shot bowled over eight soldiers in the 8th Michigan and scattered the regiment to the rear.[29] When the shells from Lane's Battery joined in the barrage, they created more confusion. The frightened Westerners slammed into the 50th Pennsylvania, which was deploying into the field behind them. Their blanched faces and terrified expressions disturbed the veteran Pennsylvanians, who had never known their comrades to show the "white feather" before.[30]

They had barely cleared the road when a few cavalrymen clattered down upon them, screaming for the infantrymen to make way for the artillery. They caught the 100th Pennsylvania between the high road banks near the Gross farm and sent it scurrying into the woods north of the road. A shell fragment struck Andrew Lang (Company C) on the hip and temporarily disabled him. His comrades grabbed him and pulled him out of the way. Seconds later, Cook's caissons rumbled down the road past the breathless Pennsylvanians who were trying to reform in the woods, which continued to shudder with each shell burst.[31]

Across the road, General Willcox rode into the panicked soldiers and tried to rally as many as he could.[32] He shuffled the 50th Pennsylvania into the cleared ground about five hundred feet east of the Henry Gross house. He faced them and the 28th Massachusetts north, parallel with the road and ordered them to hold their ground.[33] In the meantime, First Lieutenant Horatio Belcher (Company G, 8th Michigan) rounded up about one hundred men from his command and started back up the Old Sharpsburg Road toward the sounds of the firing. The gutsy lieutenant, unable to find his division or brigade commander, reported to General Cox who dispatched him and his orphans to the far left of his line, on the slope south of Peter Beachley's.[34]

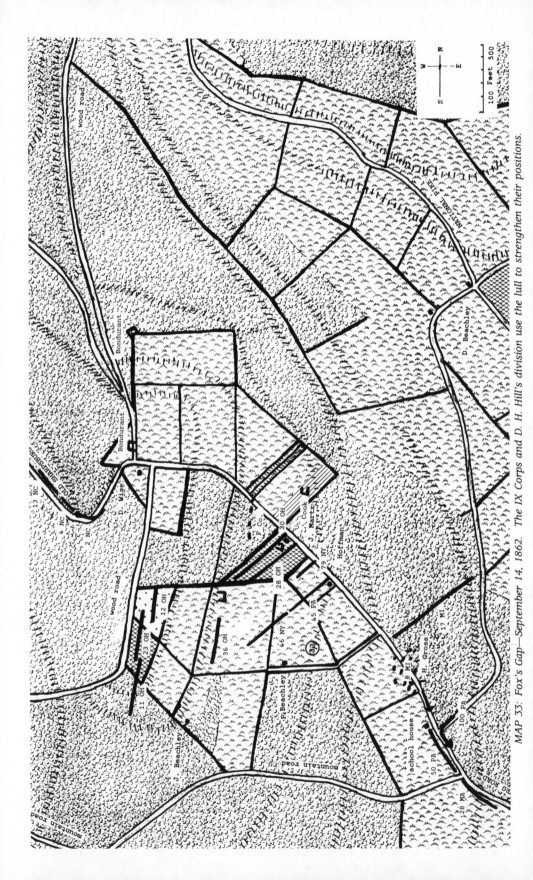

MAP 33: Fox's Gap—September 14, 1862. The IX Corps and D. H. Hill's division use the lull to strengthen their positions.

The officers of the 100th Pennsylvania ordered the men to fix bayonets. The soldiers expected to make a charge when they were sent back down the mountainside toward Bolivar. Filing down the road, they wearily countermarched toward Mentzer's saw mill, away from the fighting.[35] [Refer to Map 33]

The plunging artillery rounds continued to saturate the area. The stretcher bearers around the Hoffman house dropped their injured men near the surgeons and headed for cover. William Lyle helplessly watched an unexploded case shot cut a disabled man in half, seconds after his helpers had laid him in what they assumed was a safe spot.

A piece of the hot iron tore away part of Dr. J. Frank Gabriel's white coat as he operated upon a wounded man in Hoffman's farm yard. Shortly thereafter, another piece slapped him lightly in the leg, while a third fragment whizzed under his horse. Chaplain Lyle's servant and then his horse bolted down the mountain side in haste. After what seemed like hours, the ambulances managed to get to the Old Sharpsburg Road and to the safety of the valley east of the mountain.[36]

Adjutant Lewis Crater (50th Pennsylvania) swore that the soldiers were packed into the farm yard shoulder to shoulder. Off to the left, he stared at the yellow sulfuric clouds from Bondurant's guns. He also saw the yellowish puffs of smoke from Lane's guns. The Pennsylvanians instinctively went to ground with each discharge of Bondurant's Battery then rose with "mechanical precision" after the projectiles hurtled down hill. Unable to return fire, Crater believed Willcox had placed the regiment there to draw the Confederates' attention.[37] He was wrong. The Confederates had singled out the division while it tried to consolidate below the Kanawha Division.

"...The shells," Jacob Cox vividly noted, "which skimmed the crest and burst in the tree-tops at the lower side of the fields made a sound like the crashing and falling of some brittle substance, instead of the tough fibre of pine and oak."[38] A little farther up the mountainside, General Willcox galloped up to the left flank of the prone 17th Michigan, which had taken cover in the woods north of the road.

"Is this my Michigan?" he yelled.

Captain Gabriel Campbell of Company E nodded.

"Form into line," Willcox ordered.

The regiment, having been in service only since August 21, presented an inviting target to the Confederate gunners.[39] Their high crowned, ostrich plumed Jeff Davis hats and new frock coats contrasted sharply with the kepis and soiled fatigue blouses of the veterans around them. As the 700-800-man regiment filed across the road, Private David Lane (Company G) noticed the men had tucked their white gloves into their coat pockets instead of wearing them.[40]

Once the men cleared the road, Colonel William Withington fronted them and marched them up hill in line of battle over the prone 79th New York, which was still facing south by the flank. The regiment lay down in Martz's cornfield, where the green troops put their faces to the ground, and waited out what seemed like an unending bombardment. The time conscious Gabriel Campbell (Company E, 17th Michigan) glanced nervously at his pocket watch. It was only 1:00 P.M. The case shot from Lane's battery snapped the leaves from the cornstalks until they literally blanketed the prostrate soldiers. The regiment started to take casualties.[41]

Near Hoffman's, Chaplain Lyle of the 11th Ohio diligently continued to console the wounded and to treat their injuries. He anguished over their physical and their spiritual sufferings. Sometime during the Confederate barrage, one of the Michigan casualties called him aside.

"Can't you do something for me? Oh, this is awful!" he moaned.

The chaplain ripped open the boy's blood saturated tunic and shuddered. The soldier had a dreadful wound in his chest. Lyle quietly told the boy that he was probably going to die.

The young man's eyes riveted upon the chaplain's as he realized what he had just heard. "Then I am lost. I must go to hell!"

"Why are you lost?" Lyle asked.

"O! I have sinned against God—I have resisted the spirit—I have been a very wicked boy—I am lost! I am lost!"

The chaplain tried to console the forlorn soldier with the reassurance of salvation through Christ for whom he could look for mercy.

The dying soldier refused to believe him, and repeatedly asked, "What shall I do?"

Once again Lyle told him to believe upon Christ.

"Are you a chaplain?" the young man queried.

"Yes."

"Will you pray for me?"

"Yes, I will, comrade," Lyle replied. "Let me put this wet cloth on your wound first."

As he washed the blood away, the preacher asked the fellow if he wanted a little wine. Getting no response, the compassionate chaplain knelt by the infantryman and again attempted to convey the message of salvation through faith in Christ. William Lyle reassured him he was precious in God's sight, despite his sinful life, and that Christ had suffered death upon the cross for him. Unable to convert the soldier, he left him alone and wandered off to tend to more of the casualties. As he walked away, attendants propped the boy in a more comfortable position.[42]

The Confederate artillery fire veered east, walking toward the Bolivar Road. Bondurant's battery ceased fire. Brigadier General George B. Anderson, having arrived upon the field from the Mountain House with his two remaining regiments (14th and 30th North Carolina), decided to make a reconnaissance on the slopes to the east of the wood road. He sent the 30th North Carolina, under the command of Colonel F. M. Parker, into the open to develop the Yankees' position.[43] The Yankees got the jump on them instead.

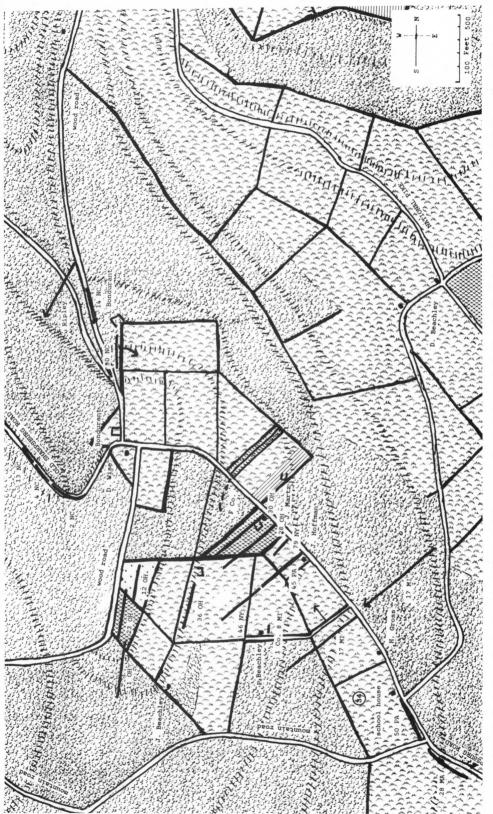

MAP 34: Fox's Gap—September 14, 1862. D. H. Hill prepares for his left grand wheel and probes the Federal lines along the Old Sharpsburg Road.

Skirmishers from Company F of the 30th Ohio, in the woods east of Wise's field, opened on them.[44] A number of men pitched to the ground, wounded.[45] Down at the Hoffman farm, Lieutenant Colonel David M. Morrison of the 79th New York noticed the Rebel advance. Ordering his regiment to its feet, he faced the line by the right flank and double quicked it up to the low stone wall between the Hoffman and the Martz farms. The Confederates melted back into the safety of the woods beyond the mountain crest as the New Yorkers approached the left flank of Cook's abandoned section. While the 79th New York went prone behind the stone wall, content that it had thwarted a serious Confederate counterthrust singlehandedly, the North Carolinians regrouped along the Old Sharpsburg Road, west of the wood road.[46] They left fifteen or more men upon the field, wounded or missing.[47]

An all too brief lull settled over the field as the recoiling 14th and the 30th North Carolina regiments joined forces with the left of the 2nd, the 4th, and the 13th North Carolina regiments and pushed them farther west.[48] John Lane's Georgia Battery continued to plop shells into the IX Corps at Fox's Gap. In the meantime, General Ripley's three regiments started to arrive along the wood road.[49] The Confederates quickly retired west, down the mountainside, out of the Yankees' line of sight and pushed rather unsteadily south toward the Old Sharpsburg Road. The laurel and the rock outcroppings became more threatening than any of the Federals opposite them. [Refer to Map 34]

"We...marched on the top of the mountain keeping even with the enemy going over rocks and cliffs and some of the worst places I almost ever saw," Calvin Leach of the 1st North Carolina lamented.[50] The brigade suffered no casualties.[51]

As Ripley's people relieved what was left of Samuel Garland's brigade, the head of Brigadier General David R. Jones' division arrived in Boonsboro. The command covered fourteen miles in a grueling three and one half hours.[52] Private John Dooley (Company A, 1st Virginia) took the time to look at his watch. It was 2:00 P.M. As the column continued through the town, it passed an ambulance bearing Samuel Garland's stiffening body. Dooley stared at the wagon as it creaked west toward Hagerstown. A bystander mumbled that the fighting was desperate and that the Yankees had wounded General Robert E. Lee. Rumor had it he was in an ambulance with his arm in a sling. The news saddened the infantry while they advanced into battle.[53]

Colonel Joseph Walker's South Carolina brigade (1st, 2nd, 5th, and 6th South Carolina, 4th South Carolina Battalion, and the Palmetto Sharpshooters), followed respectively by Brigadier Generals Richard B. Garnett's (8th, 18th, 19th, 28th, and 56th Virginia), and James L. Kemper's brigades (1st, 7th, 11th, 17th, and 24th Virginia) got as far as the Pleasant Valley Road, when a courier from their corps commander, James Longstreet, diverted them south.[54] When the end of their column cleared the National Pike-Boonsboro Pike intersection, Colonel George T. Anderson's Georgia brigade (1st Regulars, 7th, 8th, and 9th Georgia) and Brigadier General Thomas Drayton's brigade (50th and 51st Georgia, 15th South Carolina and 3rd South Carolina Battalion) passed, heading

Lampert

Ripley

SOUTH MOUNTAIN

13 NC

4 NC

2 NC

OLD SHARPSBURG ROAD

30 NC

wood road

14 NC

Bondurant

Bondurant

D. Wise

11 OH

23 OH

12 OH

J. Beachley

36 OH

30 OH

1 Co. 8 MI

p. Beachley

46 NY

17 MI

28 OH

45 PA

J. Mart

79 NY

17 MI

J. Hoffman

35

mountain road

school house

50 PA

H. Gross

28 MA

100 PA

ey

W

S

N

E

100 Feet 500

SBURG ROAD

MAP 35: Fox's Gap—September 14, 1862. The lull in the battle prior to the big assault.

up the mountain.[55] Longstreet, with Brigadier Generals John B. Hood's and Nathan Evans' commands, was not too far behind.

Back at Fox's Gap the incoming Rebel shells neutralized any effective maneuvers by the Northern infantry. Asa Cook's Massachusetts gunners hugged the wooded hillside and made no attempt to recover their pieces. Across the road, the infantry molded themselves into the ground and tried not to get hit. "...This fire lasted some 2 or 3 hours," Private John Palmer (Company G, 36th Ohio) jotted in his journal, "the enemies shells bursting around us, and over our heads...."[56] To Private William A. Roberts of the 45th Pennsylvania it seemed more like five hours.[57]

The Confederates tended to concentrate their fire upon J. Martz's cornfield where the IX Corps had put an unusually large number of troops. The 28th Ohio was lying under the cover of the rail fence which bordered the woods east of Wise's field. The 30th Ohio was prone behind them.[58] To its rear the 17th Michigan stretched across the cornfield in a north-south line.[59]

The 100th Pennsylvania, after having been sidetracked toward Bolivar, was halted and countermarched back toward the mountain. The regiment, under General Willcox's personal orders, hurled itself to the ground near the school house at the base of the mountain. The men were too fagged out to continue. A large portion of their regiment was strung out, exhausted along the valley and the Old Sharpsburg Road. The shells flew "thick and fast" as Private Frederick Pettit described it, but the Pennsylvanians were too close to the ground to be hit.[60] Shortly thereafter, the regiment marched west and went into line in Martz's cornfield.

Rather than watch his regiment get whittled away before he had a chance to commit it to battle, Colonel William Withington (17th Michigan) ordered his Michiganders to their feet. When the corn leaves fell away from their uniforms, they appeared to materialize from the earth. The colonel ordered the men to retire to the woods, which were across the road to their right rear, and form in column of battalions with the left wing behind the right wing.

The untried troops obeyed the command as well as could be expected. Companies and wings became impossibly mixed when the Yankees dashed across the road into the cover of the woods. Captain Campbell of Company E fell in with his men to see what was going to happen.[61] He did not have long to wait.

As a line officer he had no idea that General McClellan, Burnside and Pleasonton had decided to send Willcox's division on a sweep north from Fox's Gap to silence the Confederate batteries at Turner's Gap.[62] At 3:00 P.M., as prearranged, the bugler in the 17th Michigan sounded "Attention." Captain Campbell, feeling something significant was about to happen, noted the time.[63] [Refer to Map 35]

To the west, Confederate reinforcements struggled toward the Old Sharpsburg Road. D. H. Hill personally directed Colonel George T. Anderson's Georgians and Brigadier General Thomas Drayton's brigades onto the field. Riding up with "Tige" Anderson and Thomas Drayton, he found General Ripley in the Old Sharpsburg Road. Hill ordered Ripley to extend his line and George B. Anderson's farther to the right (west) until they came in contact with Colonel Thomas Rosser's dismounted 5th Virginia Cavalry and Captain John Pelham's artillery section. He explained that "Tige" Anderson's Georgians and Drayton's brigades were coming upon his left flank. He needed room to put them into the line. Once they formed, Ripley, who would assume command of the four brigades, was to left wheel up the mountainside and drive the Yankees from the crest. Without waiting for the two new brigades to arrive or to advise either Colonel Rosser and Captain Pelham of the intended move, the four officers went their own directions. Ripley returned to his two brigades. Anderson and Drayton reported back to theirs. Hill returned to the Mountain House to await the arrival of Robert E. Lee and James Longstreet, both of whom had set up their headquarters east of Boonsboro.[64]

At 3:00 P.M. Nathan Evans' South Carolina brigade (Colonel P. F. Stevens, commanding) started up the mountain on the National Pike with John B. Hood's division on the road behind it. Hood, who was still under arrest from his argument with General Evans, rode at the rear of his former command.

When he neared the foot of the mountain, Hood watched the Federal artillery shells burst on the hill to both sides of the Pike. He heard, "Give us Hood!" reverberate from the bobbing column as it wound up the road. As he got closer to the base of the mountain, he noticed General Lee and his assistant adjutant general, Colonel Robert H. Chilton, standing next to a fence along the roadside. The colonel approached Hood and handed him a note which informed him that Lee wished to talk to him. Hood dismounted and walked over to Lee.

"General," Lee began somberly, "I am just upon the eve of entering into battle, and with one of my best officers under arrest. If you will merely say that you regret this occurrence, I will release you and restore you to the command of your division."

"I am unable to do so," the stubborn Hood replied, "since I cannot admit or see the justness of General Evans' demand for the ambulances my men have captured. Had I been ordered to turn them over for the general use of the Army, I would have cheerfully acquiesced."

Lee repeated his request that Hood apologize.

Hood refused.

"Well," Lee said, partly out of respect, but more so because of necessity, "I will suspend your arrest till the impending battle is decided."[65]

John B. Hood quickly remounted his horse and galloped toward the head of his command. Hat in hand, in a salute to his troops, he spurred past his men. Their cheers temporarily drowned out the roar of the exploding Yankee shells.[66]

By then Longstreet had recalled the rest of David R. Jones' misguided division. Walker's, Garnett's, and Kemper's brigades lost more than an hour trooping along the Pleasant Valley Road, which ran parallel to the base of the mountain.

Captain Henry T. Owen (Company C, 18th Virginia) grumbled that the men marched about two miles before turning east on the Old Sharpsburg Road. From that intersection the division clumped another mile. Heavy artillery fire echoed from the top of the mountain and what Captain Owen believed were occasional stray shots plunked to the ground near the line. The command to deploy had barely rippled through the regiments when they were counter-manded and the column right about faced and headed back down the road to the Pleasant Valley Road.[67]

The three brigades finally arrived at the National Pike by way of the Boonsboro Pike around 4:00 P.M.[68] Kemper held the left flank, Garnett the center, and Walker the right flank. The division extended about one mile, from north to south, in double ranks, along the road. The 18th Virginia (Garnett's brigade) was in the center of the formation. The regiment fronted east, facing a small white brick cottage with a tiny fenced in yard. A splendid oak grove, near the house, attracted Captain Henry T. Owen's (Company C) attention.

The order "Load!" echoed down the line. The Virginians sprang their ramrods, rang them down the bores, and snapped caps to clear the barrels. They frightened the uninitiated civilians in the area.

A bareheaded man in his shirt sleeves rushed through the front door of the cottage and dashed around the corner of the house before Captain Owen, who was standing by the front gate, could react. The captain caught sight of him as the fellow leaped the back fence and hightailed it toward South Mountain.

Very shortly, the front door to the cottage opened again. A bonnetless woman, with a child in her arms, walked very cautiously up to the gate. Her bloodless face, ashen blue lips, and glazed eyes reflected her intense fear. She fumbled for the gate latch but could not find the strength to lift it. She tried to ask Owen for assistance, but her voice failed her. The child in her arms whimpered like a scared puppy, trying very hard not to cry.

Owen, who feared she would collapse, opened the gate for her, and gently touching her on the arm, softly insisted, "Come this way, madam."

As he approached his line with her, he ordered the men to open ranks. The company promptly and silently stepped back to let her pass. When they got to the opposite side of the road, he said, "Madam, take that path," his hand pointed toward the cow trail over the small knoll to the west, "and escape to the rear."

She did not understand him. "Oh, tell me where I must go to be safe," she pleaded.

"Take that path," he repeated, "and flee over the hills to your neighbors and may God protect you."

The regiment started to march north. The captain turned away from the regiment and trotted up to his company. Major George Cabell (18th Virginia), who had witnessed the incident from the head of the regiment, rode up to him and asked if Owen remembered the frightened look on the woman's face. (It would haunt Henry T. Owen for many years.)[69]

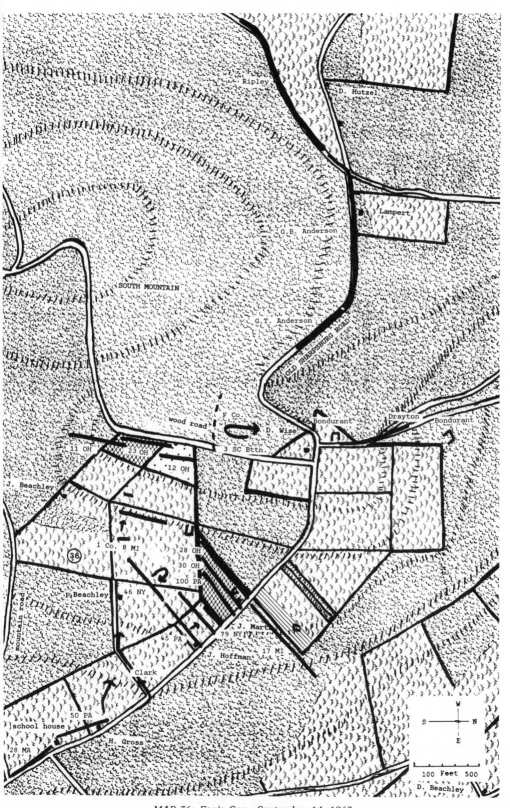

MAP 36: Fox's Gap—September 14, 1862.
Ripley begins the grand maneuver and Drayton is left to hold the wood road.

To the southeast at Fox's Gap, Roswell Ripley waited until "Tige" Anderson's brigade connected with his left, then advanced his column by the right flank west until it came to the intersection of the Old Sharpsburg Road and the crossroad near D. Hutzel's. At that point, some one thousand yards west of the wood road, he diverted his command south.[70] At the time he started his maneuver, Drayton's brigade had not come up yet. "Tige" Anderson's Georgia regiments and Ripley's left regiments were still in the Old Sharpsburg Road more than nine hundred feet from the wood road when the lead regiment of Drayton's brigade arrived near the top of the gap.[71] As the firing broke out behind them, Ripley's men continued south onto the byroad and left Drayton's men to their fate. The general dispatched a courier toward the Mountain House with a message for D. H. Hill. "...he was progressing finely," Hill bitterly recollected, "...to the rear of the mountain on the west side."[72]

Shortly before 4:00 P.M., Thomas Drayton had inadvertently run into an attack which had been planned to drive away a far superior force. As he approached the Old Sharpsburg Road intersection, the field became silent.[73] He ordered Captain Daniel B. Miller and his Company F from the 3rd South Carolina Battalion southeast across the ridge to ascertain where the Federals were. The skirmishers pushed as far south as the edge of the woods below Wise's field, where they spied some of Cox's Ohio skirmishers. The company immediately turned about and headed back for its brigade.[74] The men did not get away undetected. The Yankee pickets alerted their officers, who in turn passed the word to their division commander, Jacob Cox.

Cox sent word to Lieutenant Horatio Belcher's detachment from the 8th Michigan to rush forward to the position formerly held by J. W. Bondurant's Alabama Artillery.[75] While the regiment moved out by the flank, the 46th New York, on the left of the 45th Pennsylvania, believing it was to join in the movement, took off on a tangent behind it. Lieutenant Colonel Joseph Gerhardt (46th New York) did not advance very far before General Willcox recalled the regiment to its original position.[76] The regiment fell back. The 50th Pennsylvania, under orders from Willcox, advanced uphill toward the far left of the line.[77] It drew fire from Lane's persistent Georgians north of the National Pike. Two or three gaps appeared in the lines as the two regiments stumbled up the slopes toward their objective.

The incoming rounds struck the stone wall along the eastern edge of Martz's cornfield and knocked the stones off above the heads of the prone 79th New York.[78] In the meantime, General Willcox had galloped down the hill toward Mentzer's Saw Mill where he ran into General Jacob Cox and Brigadier General Samuel Sturgis' division which had just arrived upon the field. It was around 3:30 P.M. Jesse Reno immediately detached Captain Joseph E. Clark's four-gun Company E, 4th U.S. Artillery, up the Old Sharpsburg Road to secure the left of Jacob Cox's line.[79] [Refer to Map 36]

At the same time, Samuel Sturgis ordered his aide-de-camp, Captain William C. Rawolle to fetch Captain George W. Durell's Company E, Pennsylvania Light Artillery, and send it to the top of the mountain to stop the enfilading artillery fire from across the National Pike.[80] The officer galloped away, but too late to prevent the general advance which McClellan had planned.

Back at the wood road, Drayton deployed his brigade. The 3rd South Carolina Battalion spread south in a wide arc into the "L" shaped woods south and east of Wise's field.[81] The rest of the brigade (15th South Carolina, 50th and 51st Georgia) went into line along the stone fence bordering the wood road north of the Old Sharpsburg Road and Bondurant's battery. About fifty intrepid Rebels, running under the cover of their own artillery's plunging fire, raced across the open ground toward Asa Cook's abandoned artillery pieces. Leaping over the rail fence which separated the two upper rectangular fields, they continued on to the high stone wall on the eastern edge of the lower pasture. From there, a few of the stalwarts scrambled over the wall and darted ahead another four hundred feet into the deep gulch which cut across their front. A third dash of about two hundred fifty feet brought them to the cordwood stacks which bordered the woods directly behind the deserted artillery section. They popped off harassing shots into the trees above the heads of the Michiganders, who were cowering on the hillside a short distance below them, then retreated back to the secure stone wall of the lower field.

The bullets pattering the tree bark reminded Captain Gabriel Campbell in Company E of the 17th Michigan of hail striking a tin roof. The men stripped off their knapsacks and piled them behind the second rank. They fixed bayonets. Campbell looked at his watch for the seventh time that day. It was 4:00 P.M. The regiment stood up. At the command, "Forward," the men clambered up the slope. When they cleared the wood stacks and broke into the open ground, they let out a lusty cheer. Almost as quickly, the Confederates behind the high stone wall fired a volley into the regiment.[82] Men pitched to the ground, among them a fifteen-year-old drummer whose leg was shattered.[83] Four of his comrades fell out and tenderly carried him off the field.[84]

To the southwest, skirmishers from the 3rd South Carolina Battalion shoved into the "L" shaped woods which enclosed Wise's field. Tearing down a large portion of the dilapidated rail fence which marked the eastern edge of the field, the South Carolinians pushed into the woods to pressure the 28th Ohio. The Ohioans retired before the Rebels got near them, and the 30th Ohio moved into their position near the southeastern corner of the woods.[85] The Ohioans did nothing to provoke an incident.

Behind them, along the stone wall west of Hoffman's, William Todd (Company B, 79th New York) saw gaps appear in the 17th Michigan's steadily advancing line. Presently, Willcox galloped up to Lieutenant Colonel David Morrison of the 79th and commanded him to take the woods to his front. General McClellan personally desired it.

Gallantly unsheathing his sword, the colonel yelled for his regiment to stand up and charge.

"Is this your regiment?" Willcox blurted rather incredulously as he scanned the command with a glance.

"Yes, General," Morrison replied, "but if you will give me more men we'll take the battery."

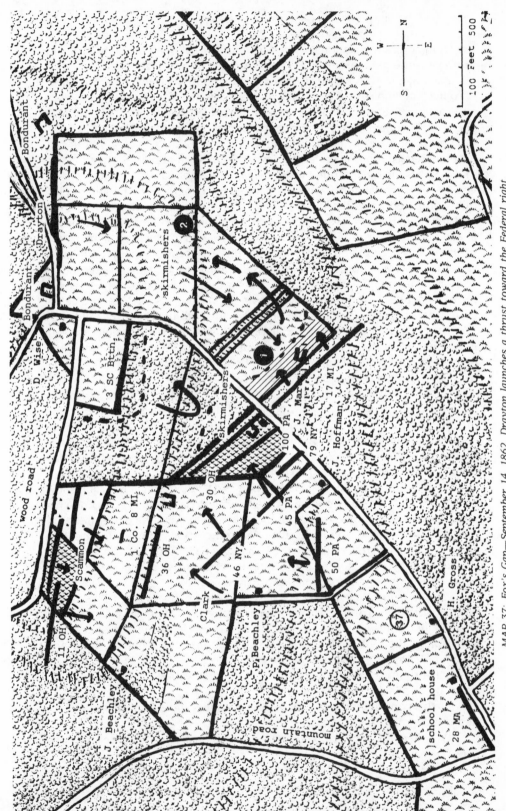

MAP 37: Fox's Gap—September 14, 1862. Drayton launches a thrust toward the Federal right.

"No," Willcox insisted, "I'll send another regiment. Yours is too small."[86]

Riding away toward the 45th Pennsylvania and the 46th New York, he left the embarrassed colonel with his stalled regiment.

Private Eugene Beague (Company G, 45th Pennsylvania), who was lying with his company close to the Hoffman house, mentally blotted out the scream of the incoming rounds. The field suddenly became ominously silent. He stared in horror at the surgeons and their attendants who seemed to gather around with their threatening knives, saws, and probes like vultures waiting for their prey to collapse. General Willcox galloped up to Colonel Thomas Welsh, the brigade commander, and, after briefly speaking to him, spurred on to the 46th New York, south of the regiment. Lieutenant Colonel John I. Curtin (45th Pennsylvania), who was mounted behind the center of the regiment, called out, "Attention, battalion! Shoulder arms. Forward, guide center, March!"

As the last company officer echoed the command, the line stepped out. Companies A and K, the flank companies, armed with Springfield rifle-muskets, sprinted into Martz's cornfield. The line followed them closely. Passing through the 79th New York, which was falling back, the Pennsylvanians stepped over the low stone wall and pressed into the corn. Lieutenant Colonel Curtin's horse balked, refusing to jump the wall. The distance increased between him and his regiment. The colonel dismounted, tossed the reins over the horse's neck, and slapped the animal on the flank. The horse galloped down hill, away from the fighting, and the disgruntled Curtin crawled over the wall after his troops.

About halfway into the field Confederate picket fire spattered the 45th Pennsylvania and the 46th New York to its left. Through the open woods, they could see the Rebels retiring before their two skirmish companies. Every now and then the South Carolinians halted to return fire before turning away to escape. As the Pennsylvanians and the New Yorkers crawled over the rail fence and the prone 30th Ohio, they saw the Confederates scrambling for their lives over the rail fence on the western side of the woods.[87] [Refer to Map 37]

By then the 17th Michigan leaped into the hollow across the road, northeast of the 45th Pennsylvania. Under this natural cover, they returned several volleys into the stone wall to their front. They cut down most of the Rebels. While the smoke drifted away, the Michiganders climbed out of the depression and charged the wall.[88]

From the plowed knoll, about one mile to the north, Major General Daniel H. Hill stood near Captain Lane's Georgia battery as the 17th Michigan, the 45th Pennsylvania, and the 46th New York advanced to the attack. They appeared to swing out of the woods like an inverted "V" with the apex pointed toward the northwest. Hill ordered Lane to direct his fire toward the advancing Yankee formation. To his disgust, Lane's rounds appeared to miss their mark. "His firing was wild," Hill recalled years later.[89]

The Michiganders and their comrades were less critical of Lane's gunnery practice. The high stone wall foiled the 17th Michigan's brilliant

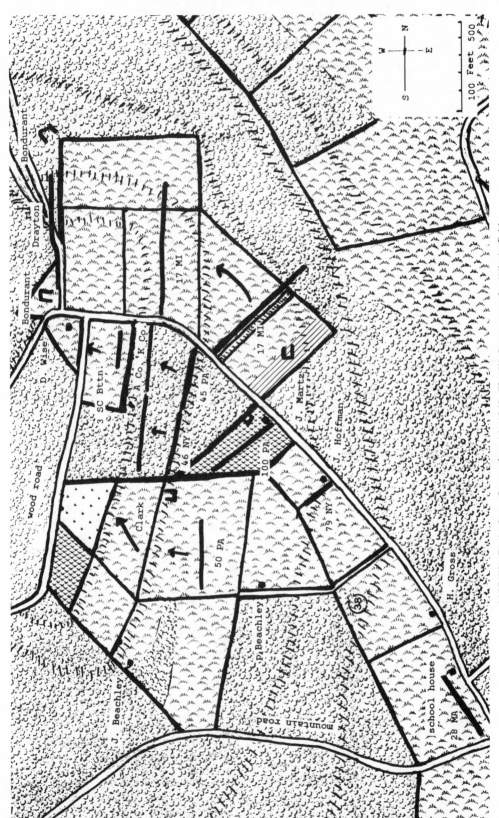

MAP 38: Fox's Gap—September 14, 1862. The IX Corps assaults Wise's field.

bayonet charge and brought it to a halt. The disgruntled Westerners crawled over it, despite incoming rifle fire from the stone wall along the wood road, and reformed their lines preparatory to another assault. A large number of their men were sprawled out over the ground behind them.[90] While they moved forward, Lane's barrage wildly plastered the ground along their front. The regiment halted at the rail fence which divided the lower field from the upper field and tried to fight it out.[91]

To the south, Companies A and K of the 45th Pennsylvania retired to their main line just as Lane's shells started snapping off the tree tops above their heads. Unexploded projectiles plowed furrows in the ground close to the line. The Pennsylvanians seemed to waver. Having never been under fire before, a good many of them panicked and started to shoot wildly with their Harpers Ferry muskets at anything which moved to their front.

"Steady, boys, keep cool!" Colonels Welsh and Curtin warned them.

The firing increased in tempo until nearly the entire regiment had shot away its first rounds. As the smoke drifted above the tree tops, the Confederate artillerists to their front and right sighted in on it and dropped several more shells and some canister into the woods.

"Cease firing!" the line officers screamed at the tops of their voices.

Andrew Bockus (Company G, 45th Pennsylvania), an old hunter and one of the regiment's best shots, who was standing near Private Eugene Beague, upon hearing the command, impudently muttered to himself, "Don't care a damn! I saw a Johnny!"

Within a minute Beague heard Colonel Curtin call out, "Forward to the fence!"

The Pennsylvanians, with part of the 46th New York to their left, crashed through the woods and took cover behind the partially destroyed rail fence. Across the stump dotted Wise's field, they saw the 3rd South Carolina Battalion level its muskets across the top of the stone wall. The Carolinians volleyed, many of their shots going too high. The Pennsylvanians returned fire with their Springfields and Harpers Ferry Muskets. The .69 caliber muskets, having been converted to percussion weapons from flintlocks, were loaded with buck and ball loads. They packed a tremendous wallop when discharged—so much so that many of the men swore they killed at both ends.[92] [Refer to Map 38]

The 45th Pennsylvania started to take casualties. Canister from Bondurant's battery shredded the trees to pulp and splintered the fragile rail fence along their front. Lieutenant George D. Smith, Colonel Thomas Welsh's assistant adjutant general and Lieutenant James M. Cole (both from Company I) died in the fighting. Private Eugene Beague of Company G watched two of his closest friends go down in quick order. Portly and amiable George Brewster, with whom he had chatted at breakfast that morning, was dead, as was the muscular Henry Fenton, with a bullet in his heart.[93]

The regiment closed ranks to the left; the regimental front began to shrink. As it did, the 17th Michigan, its own line thinned by increased small arms fire from the wood road and from artillery rounds, crossed the Old Sharpsburg Road, south, and joined the Pennsylvanians' right flank. By the time the regiment had advanced into the woods, it had pushed the 45th Pennsylvania deeper into the forest. Once again, Captain Gabriel Campbell (Company E, 17th Michigan) obsessively checked the time. It was 4:30 P.M.[94]

While the three infantry regiments struggled for control of Wise's field, another Federal battery had strained into position. Captain George W. Durell's Company E, Pennsylvania Light Artillery of ten-pounder Parrotts went into position between and around Cook's two abandoned guns in the field north of J. Martz's cabin. The artillerists split their fire between the knob north of the National Pike and the wood road on the ridge to the west.[95]

Durell's Pennsylvanians aggravated rather than diminished the situation. They kept up an almost continuous fire against Lane's Georgians. The incoming Confederate rounds made effective Yankee infantry maneuvering nearly impossible. The shells splintered the tree tops behind the battery, showering them with branches and leaves. At one point a single shell lopped off two large tree limbs, one of which knocked Captain George Durell to the ground. His men helped him to his feet. He was bruised and dazed, but otherwise unhurt.[96] In the cornfield across the road, Private Joseph E. Walton (Company I, 30th Ohio) hugged the ground with his company near Seth Simmond's unmanned artillery section. Frightened by the unrelenting musketry, he later remembered that it was one of the severest "musketry drills" he saw during the entire war.[97]

While the smoke of the battle rose unabated from the wood road and Wise's field, both armies attempted to feed more troops into their respective front lines. General Ripley and his three brigades did a great deal of marching and countermarching in the laurel thickets on the western side of the mountain. In moving by the flank down the crossroad west of the wood road, the general ordered Colonel "Tige" Anderson to move his command by the left flank and head uphill toward the mountain crest. While Anderson's main line floundered about in a southeasterly direction, the right wing of the 1st Georgia Regulars, under the command of Captain Richard A. Wayne (Company E), which had not received the command to change direction, continued south. The colonel meandered about the mountainside, trying to find some sense of direction.[98] The dense laurel thickets and the interlacing branches overhead obstructed his vision in all directions. The deeper he took his command into the woods the more lost he became. Finally he halted the brigade and sent a runner through the woods to find Captain Wayne and his skirmishers.[99]

Roswell Ripley flanked his brigade by the right, deeper into the woods.[100] As he did so, he lost contact with "Tige" Anderson, who was supposed to be on his left flank, and with Brigadier General George B. Anderson, who was supposed to be on his right flank. Rather than halt and call in his brigades, Ripley continued to wander about the mountainside until he out distanced both of his wings.

George B. Anderson halted his brigade somewhere on the western slope and detached the 4th North Carolina on a reconnaissance to the south. Colonel Charles C. Tew (2nd North Carolina) ordered Captain Edwin A. Osborne (Company H, 4th North Carolina) and his men to the front as skirmishers. They were to probe the mountainside as cautiously and as silently as possible.

"Our progress was necessarily very slow, as the woods were very dense and the ground very rugged and mountainous," Osborne recollected. The regiment inched its way south, beyond the Federal left flank, all the while increasing the distance between it and the brigade.[101]

On the eastern side of the mountain, General Sturgis' division of the IX Corps started to climb into position behind Orlando Willcox's men. Colonel Edward Ferrero's brigade (51st New York, 51st Pennsylvania, 21st and 35th Massachusetts) led the division onto the field. The walking wounded and the stretcher bearers limped and stumbled down the road to greater safety. Above the casualties' moans and pleas for water, the untried men in the 35th Massachusetts fixed their startled glances upon a four-man stretcher team which was carrying a severely injured boy away from the battle. The crippled drummer screamed at the top of his lungs, "Forward, boys, forward! We're driving them! Don't let this scare you; give 'em hell! They can't stand cold steel!"[102] A little farther on in the road, the stretcher bearers carried him past the 21st Massachusetts. One of the New Englanders asked him how things were going at the front. He screamed back, "The 17th is doing bully!"[103]

The 51st Pennsylvania filed off the Old Sharpsburg Road into the field in front of Durell's battery and laid down while the gunners directed a concentrated fire at Lane's battery.[104] The 51st New York went to the ground in the woods behind Durell's guns. The men grumbled loudly about having to leave their knapsacks piled by companies in the thickets. Too much like Second Manassas, they groused, where they set them aside and never got them back. Bugler Robert West (Company H, 51st New York) slung his rubber poncho and his army blanket over his shoulder, determined not to go without either of them.[105] The 35th Massachusetts, a new regiment with about eight hundred men, went prone in Martz's cornfield.[106] The 21st Massachusetts was in line around the Hoffman house.[107] Moments after the 21st hit the dirt, two shells whistled harmlessly overhead.[108] Lane's battery, under increased pressure from Durell's battery ceased fire and withdrew from the fight.[109]

The firing continued unabated in Wise's field. Bullets clipped through the woods and zinged dangerously close to the prone Yankee lines. One of them killed Private Henry H. Cleveland (Company K, 35th Massachusetts), who was lying next to Sergeant Frederick Merserve.[110]

The longer they "rested" there, the more uneasy Private James M. Stone (Company K, 21st Massachusetts) became. The surgeons, who had set up shop around the Hoffman house, left their trademarks littering the grounds all about the place. Piles of severed arms, legs, feet, and hands dotted the hillside within a good toss of each of the operating tables. Having never seen a field hospital before, he lost all interest in seeing one again.[111]

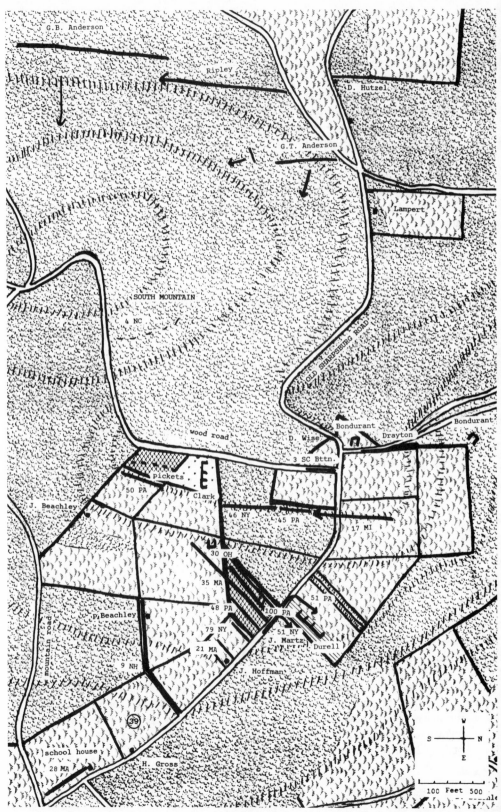

MAP 39: Fox's Gap—September 14, 1862. The rugged terrain destroys D. H. Hill's ill conceived left grand wheel.

Not too far away, Second Lieutenant Albert A. Pope (Company I, 35th Massachusetts) found himself daydreaming about Middletown and the six chickens he had stolen that morning to make soup. He also fondly recalled the superb lunch he and First Lieutenant William Hill (Company I) had taken with a Yankee woman and her two "very fine daughters." "Best meal I've had since leaving home," he wrote.[112]

While they were lying there, Brigadier General James Nagle's brigade climbed the Old Sharpsburg Road to reinforce Ferrero. Nagle had only two regiments with him—the 9th New Hampshire, a new regiment of nine hundred men, and the 48th Pennsylvania. (The 6th New Hampshire and the 2nd Maryland were detached on picket duty along the National Pike.)[113]

The 48th Pennsylvania, his veteran regiment, filed by the left from the Old Sharpsburg Road into the lower end of Martz's cornfield. Lieutenant Colonel Joshua K. Sigfried (48th Pennsylvania) halted his soldiers next to the nearly six-foot high stone fence on their left flank long enough for them to strip off their knapsacks. Scores of walking casualties pushed and shuffled through their line, trying to escape the shooting along the wood road.

Before they got under way, a squad of dirty Rebels ambled past Company G. One particularly tall North Carolinian attracted Captain Oliver C. Bosbyshell's attention by craning his long neck, as if trying to fit it for a horse collar, to stare at all the people who surrounded him.[114] [Refer to Map 39]

At the urging of a frantic headquarters orderly, the inexperienced Colonel Enoch Q. Fellows (9th New Hampshire) sent his regiment at the double quick past Henry Gross' house to Peter Beachley's farm lane. Corporal Hiram S. Lathe (Company F) raised his leg to climb out of the road onto the bank when a spent minié ball slammed into his knee joint and dislocated it. His brother James hastily pulled out his pocket knife. Dropping beside Hiram, he extracted the ball. He bound the leg up and started carrying his brother down the hill to a field hospital while the regiment continued down the lane.

"Halt! Front!" rang out over the regiment.

The New Englanders responded quickly, only to find themselves facing down hill, with their backs to the Rebel bullets. The officers dismounted, a sure sign there was serious work ahead.[115]

"Fix Bayonets!"

The line rattled ominously as the rookies unsheathed their sabre bayonets and attached them to the muzzles of their weapons. Nineteen-year-old Private Daniel E. Hurd (Company G) tried to forget the face of the wounded man he saw at the base of the mountain—his first one. He had his eye shot out. The sight drained the young private of his romantic notions about war.

"About face, forward, charge bayonets."

The men faced by the rear rank. Stray rounds cut the air about them. The New Englanders' mascot, a five-year-old black boy, Jokum, whom they had literally picked up in Washington, shrieked, "Guess I'd bettah git out o' heah fo' I gits hurted!" Goading his mule about with his bare feet, he barrelled downhill.[116] Daniel Hurd swallowed the lump in his throat and started in the opposite direction with his regiment.

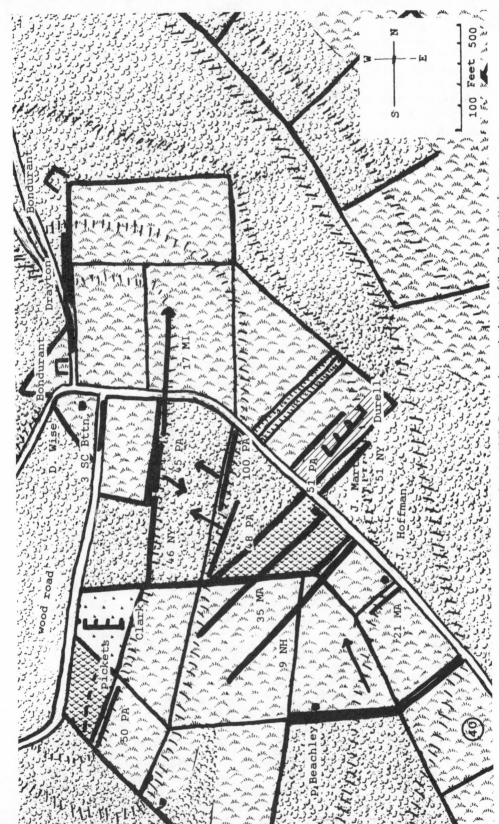

MAP 40: Fox's Gap—September 14, 1862. Drayton bears the brunt of the Federal attack.

"Bullets from the enemy were whistling just above our heads and were not particularly agreeable music," he recollected.[117] A ball struck Lewis W. Aldrich (Company I) in the hip. Dropping his rifle, he clamped both hands over the hole and dropped to the ground, damning the Rebels as he fell. Seconds later, a round bored through Herbert N. Streeter's right hand. Quickly switching his weapon to his left hand, he strutted over to his captain. Waving the bloody hand in the officer's face, the boy, with genuine sincerity, exclaimed, "See there! Now what shall I do?"[118] The company pressed on without him.

Meanwhile, the Yankee musketry across Wise's field started to subside. The 45th Pennsylvania asked for relief because it was running out of ammunition. Colonel Welsh ordered the 100th Pennsylvania forward. The "Round Heads," so nicknamed because of their Calvinistic origins, slipped through the 45th's ranks while they melted back to the cornfield. Taking their posts at the rail fence, the exhausted replacements leveled their Springfield riflemuskets and fired at will.[119] General James Nagle, upon seeing the movement to his front, ordered the 48th Pennsylvania forward.

The coal miners from Pottsville, Pennsylvania, after they piled their knapsacks on the northern side of the stone wall, fronted again and charged farther up hill into the smoke blanketed corn.[120] A solid shot thudded into the ground and bounced. Captain James Wren (Company B) watched the twelve pound cast iron ball slowly roll toward his company. One of the enlisted men ran out into the field and, in jest, stepped on the shot to stop it.

"[He] was so seveirly Jarred that he had to be taken to the Hospitle," the captain scratched in his diary.[121]

The impetuous 9th New Hampshire noticed the commotion to its front. From its position it appeared as though a line of Confederates had risen up from the stone wall and broken to the rear. A shell burst among Company E. Fragments hurled Privates Moses Paul and Henry Simpson to the ground. The burst plucked Corporal Lysander Mayo and Private Luther Hurlburt off their feet. Mayo picked himself up and went back into the attack. The private, who was severely injured by the flying clods of dirt and whose body was wrenched and jarred by the concussion, remained motionless in the field. The officers quickly closed ranks and urged their men forward.

"See the rebels run!" one of the recruits screamed.

Colonel Enoch Fellows, his straw hat conspicuously bobbing with each step in the confusion, also noted the swaying cornstalks. "Charge and cheer, boys! Yell, boys!" he croaked.

They did, with a vengeance. More stray rounds thudded into their line before they reached the stone wall. Charles A. Judkins (Company A) helplessly watched his uncle, Joel Judkins and a friend, Charles W. Glidden, suddenly disappear from the line on either side of him. Captain Leonard H. Pillsbury momentarily turned about and snapped, "Charlie, take care of Uncle Joel." The boy helped his uncle, whose thigh was shattered, to his feet and limped with him down the slope.

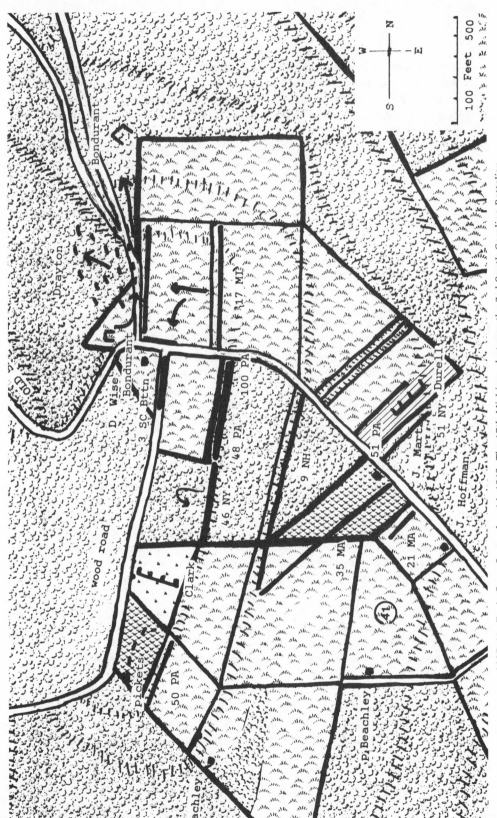

MAP 41: Fox's Gap—September 14, 1862. The 17th Michigan destroys the 3rd South Carolina Battalion.

As the high stone wall materialized before them, the New Englanders in-stinctively shed their excess equipment. Without stopping, they struggled to free themselves of their blanket rolls, and knapsacks, which they left scattered in their rear. A large number of them stupidly hurled their haversacks and canteens aside. They did not want anything to keep them from glory![122] [Refer to May 40]

The stone wall shattered whatever formation they had left. "...We climbed [it] as best we could," Daniel Hurd recollected.[123] The regiment stumbled through the cornfield, ironically chasing its own men.

In the meantime, to leave room for the replacement troops which were coming onto the field, the battered 17th Michigan flanked to the right. It crossed the Old Sharpsburg Road and entered the lower field through the bar gate in its southeastern corner.[124] Bondurant's battery, in response to the movement, loosed one poorly aimed volley at Wise's field, then limbered up. The 48th Pennsylvania, having just gone on line to the left of the 100th Pennsylvania, heard a solitary shell scream through the air north of the Old Sharpsburg Road. One of Durell's gunners landed a shot square on the Napoleon, dismounting it. The frightened Confederate gunners dragged the disabled piece behind their limber in a desperate attempt to escape north on the wood road when the Pennsylvanian artillerists killed one of their horses. The Alabamians retreated to the far end of their line, near Pelham's original post and went into battery without any ammunition.[125] The cheers and taunts of the Yankee infantrymen followed them down the road.[126]

Without Bondurant's artillery support, Thomas Drayton's brigade could not remain upon the wood road. His northern most regiments (50th and 51st Georgia, and 15th South Carolina), having fought with the ferocity of a division, melted away from the double stone walls in front of the 17th Michigan. The 3rd South Carolina Battalion was trapped in the wood road east of Daniel Wise's cabin.[127] It was getting very shadowy. The sun was well below the top of the mountain, making it seem prematurely dark. Less than an hour of daylight remained.[128] Twice in the last hour and a half, Major William G. Rice (3rd South Carolina Battalion) advised Lieutenant Colonel George S. James that the regiment could not maintain its position. He warned the stubborn colonel that the command inevitably faced death or surrender. James ignored him. Their rate of fire had dwindled to almost nothing.[129] When the 17th Michigan left wheeled to finish off the South Carolinians trying to cross their front to the wood road, a bullet struck George James in the chest. Seconds later, as the 17th Michigan mopped up, a minié ball dropped Major Rice as well.[130] The Confederates had had enough. Some tried to scramble over the three-foot high stone wall behind them, but the Yankees shot them in their backs.[131]

Lieutenant Colonel Joshua Sigfried (48th Pennsylvania) noticed the 46th New York retiring from the battle. The New Yorkers, with their cartridges nearly expended, pulled back a short distance to regroup and to allow the fumbling 9th New Hampshire time to assume their place on the left of the 48th Pennsylvania.[132] [Refer to Map 41]

Colonel Sigfried dispatched the unflappable Captain James Wren and his Company B out to the left front, into the southwestern end of the woods to reconnoiter the western slope of the mountain. The main line of the regiment went prone while Wren extended his men in open order and crashed into the forest.[133] On the right the 100th Pennsylvania and the 17th Michigan continued to pepper the wall along the wood road.[134]

Some of the panting soldiers from the 9th New Hampshire spotted Wren and his Pennsylvanians climbing over the fence at the far side of the woods and mistook them for Confederates.[135] Their inexperienced officers feared that their personal chance to win martial glory was escaping across their left front. Rather than fling the command into a possible ambuscade, Colonel Enoch Fellows (9th New Hampshire) and his staff rallied it behind the rail fence in Martz's cornfield.[136] The New Hampshire volunteers planned to soften up the opposition a little before giving them the proverbial "cold steel." Not everyone understood why the regiment halted.

Private Daniel Hurd of the 9th New Hampshire complained, "Part of our regiment saw someone to fire at, no doubt, but I didn't....You must remember that 900 men strung out in double file would reach some distance...the enemy...were not in sight of where our part of the regiment were at that moment."[137]

The Rebels, however, had a good view of the Yankee left flank. Captain Edwin A. Osborne of the 4th North Carolina and his intrepid company of North Carolinians had gotten close enough to the wood road to see the cornfield on the southern end of the Federal line and the adjacent plowed field north of it. The captain glanced rather quickly at the standing corn and the casualties who littered the field, then fixed his stare upon Captain Joseph Clark's battery.[138] The four ten-pounder Parrotts, which were facing north, made tempting prizes.[139] The captain ran back toward the regiment to report his find.[140] Unfortunately, he did not notice the Federal pickets from the 50th Pennsylvania who were peering through the corn from the opposite side.[141] Private George Bogardus (Company H, 50th Pennsylvania), ran to Captain Clark, who then started to face his battery across the road. He also informed Major Edward Overton (50th Pennsylvania). Within a minute an orderly galloped off to get reinforcements.[142]

West of the wood road, Captain James Wren and his skirmishers from the 48th Pennsylvania blundered into Captain Edwin A. Osborne and his skirmishers from the 4th North Carolina, who were screening the approach of George B. Anderson's North Carolina brigade.[143] The Pennsylvanians instantly snapped off a few rounds at the Rebels, which sent them to cover. The North Carolinians returned the fire.[144] Their miniés clipped the leaves off the branches above the coal miners' heads. The sudden burst of small arms fire, followed by the hostile zips of near misses and the dull thuds of rounds striking trees, rattled the 9th New Hampshire. Without waiting to identify their targets, the eight-hundred-sixty odd "fresh fish" brought their rifles to the shoulders, aimed, and jerked triggers.[145]

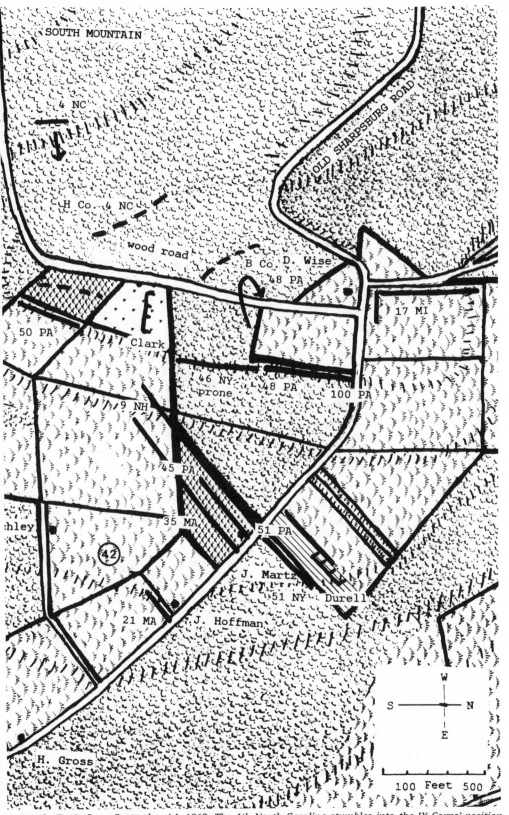

SOUTH MOUNTAIN

4 NC

OLD SHARPSBURG ROAD

H Co 4 NC

wood road

B Co D. Wise
48 PA

17 MI

50 PA

Clark

46 NY
prone

48 PA

100 PA

9 NH

45 PA

35 MA

·hley

42

51 PA

J. Martz

51 NY Durell

21 MA

J. Hoffman

H. Gross

W
S — N
E

100 Feet 500

MAP 42: Fox's Gap—September 14, 1862. The 4th North Carolina stumbles into the IX Corps' position.

The 46th New York, hearing the thunderous report, dove to the ground and stayed there.[146] The Pennsylvania skirmishers received the full impact of the well intended volley. "...The Branches of the trees [fell] down on us like the falling of wheat before the seith," James Wren recollected. Visions of Second Manassas, where his men were caught between two fires, flashed through the captain's mind. He screamed for Company B to "rally to the right and left, from the center, double quick, to the rear!" The skirmishers did not wait upon formalities. They ran for their lives back toward Wise's field. "I wanted to mak[e] the Battle Line before thay Could Load & fire again on us," Wren wrote in his diary.[147]

By the time the company reached the eastern side of Wise's field, no more Confederate resistance remained along the wood road. The men went prone on both flanks of the 48th Pennsylvania and, with the other regiments of the line, patiently waited to see if the Confederates were going to pursue them or not.[148]

General George B. Anderson, leaving the rest of the brigade under cover farther down the mountainside behind him, personally rushed the 4th North Carolina forward to the skirmishers' support.[149] He also adopted a "wait and see" posture. [Refer to Map 42]

Similarly, Colonel "Tige" Anderson, whose brigade was somewhere to the northwest, had no intention of running from the Federals. Neither did he intend to take on the entire Yankee army on his own. His courier to Ripley, Captain James G. Montgomery (Company K, 1st Georgia Regulars), whom he had sent off for what seemed to him like a long time before, finally reported back to him, with bad news and no orders. The captain had found Roswell Ripley and his brigade marching about the woods more than four hundred yards southwest of his position. "Tige" Anderson could not wait for orders which he would never receive. In response to the firing off to his left front, he changed his direction of march to the northeast. Colonel William J. Magill deployed the left wing of his 1st Georgia Regulars in that direction as skirmishers.[150] George Anderson responded to the situation at hand and did not operate according to any preconceived strategy.

On the opposite side of the ridge, the Yankees, sensing that something had to be done, assaulted the stone wall. The mismanaged 9th New Hampshire led the attack. The smoke had barely cleared after its volley, when the soldiers crawled over the rail fence above Martz's cornfield and charged into the woods. The right wing passed through the 48th Pennsylvania at Wise's field. The left wing picked up the shaken 46th New York. As the New Englanders broke into the open ground, they dragged in the 45th and 100th Pennsylvania and the 17th Michigan.[151] No one anticipated the carnage between the stone walls along the wood road. Private Frederick Pettit (Company C, 100th Pennsylvania) and his comrade John P. Wilson could not cross over the corpses and the wounded who were piled on top of one another.[152] Some of the New Hampshire soldiers climbed over the fence near the southwestern corner of the field where they ran across the dead North Carolinian who

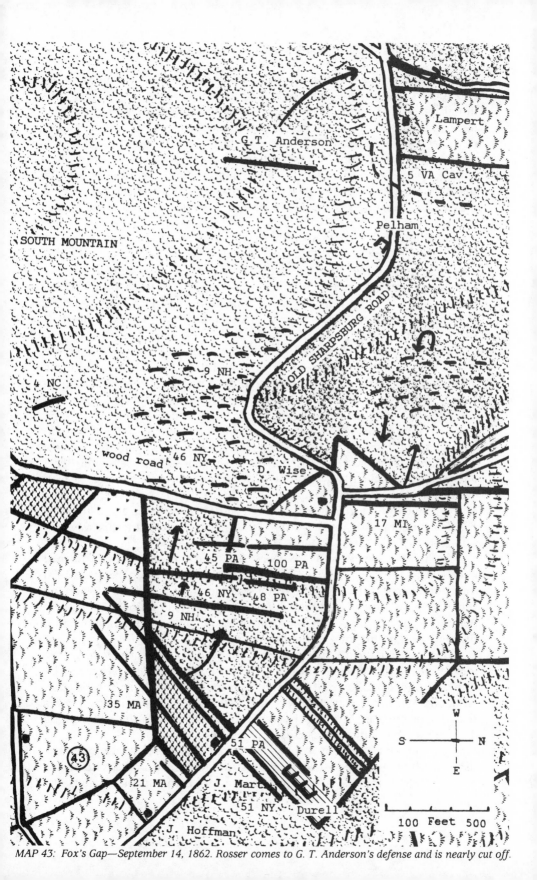

SOUTH MOUNTAIN

G. T. Anderson

Lampert

5 VA Cav

Pelham

9 NH

4 NC

OLD SHARPSBURG ROAD

wood road   46 NY

D. Wise

17 MI

45 PA   100 PA

46 NY   48 PA

9 NH

35 MA

(43)

51 PA

21 MA   J. Mart...

51 NY   Durell

J. Hoffman

W
S — N
E

100 Feet 500

MAP 43: Fox's Gap—September 14, 1862. Rosser comes to G. T. Anderson's defense and is nearly cut off.

had been killed while crawling over the wooden rider. The biscuits in his hands and mouth had disappeared. He still straddled the fence—eyes open and mouth agape. The unobservant rookies shouted at him as they went over the top and shrugged off his silence as bad manners.[153]

Everywhere, squads of men halted to stare. Only the 46th New York, the 9th New Hampshire, and the 17th Michigan went down the western slope as units.[154] The woods were dark. The setting sun filtered eerily through the trees. The laurel thickets disrupted their formations. The regiments fragmented into squads. Here and there they captured a few wounded and exhausted Confederates.[155]

Adjutant W. F. Shellman (8th Georgia), who rounded up several of Drayton's survivors, reported back to Colonel "Tige" Anderson. The Yankees, he gasped, had turned Drayton's right flank. In order to avoid being cut off and destroyed, Anderson ordered his brigade to file by the left and reform in the Old Sharpsburg Road. By some miracle the Georgians reached their objective and reformed near the crossroads from which they had jumped off from more than an hour earlier.[156]

The flashes of small arms fire, stabbing in the darkness of the woods, attracted the attention of Rosser's Virginia cavalry videttes and Pelham's horse artillery section. The intrepid captain ran his guns down to the Old Sharpsburg Road east of Anderson's column. Rolling them into battery, the gunners loaded with shell and opened upon the Federals who swarmed through the woods.[157] The artillery fire screamed into the forest and lit up the mountain with blinding flashes. Sergeant George L. Wakefield (Company G, 9th New Hampshire), having thrown himself to the forest floor seconds before the Rebel gunners snapped their lanyards, heard the reports of two field pieces, "which seemed to shake the very mountain."[158] The four Yankee regiments started to retire quickly, dragging their prisoners with them.[159] Once again, the time conscious Captain Campbell of the 17th Michigan referred to his watch. It was 6:00 P.M.[160] [Refer to Map 43]

As the sweating Pennsylvania, New York, and Michigan troops reformed and filed to the rear of Wise's field, Colonel Sigfried (48th Pennsylvania) marched his regiment up to the stone wall along the wood road. Again, he sent Captain Wren and his Company B to the left front to probe the flank.[161] Before leaving, the captain insisted that everyone on the left flank hold their fire until he and his men returned safely.[162]

One hundred twenty-five yards into the woods, the Pennsylvanians ran into the 4th North Carolina. The Northerners opened fire, then retreated. The North Carolinians followed them, and dragged the rest of their brigade (2nd, 13th, and 30th North Carolina) with them.[163] The Pennsylvania coal miners reloaded on the run. The Rebel yell reverberated through the encroaching darkness as the Confederates closed in for the kill.[164]

A minute or two before Wren's men stirred up the firefight, Colonel Harrison Fairchild's brigade (9th, 89th, and 103rd New York) from Isaac Rodman's division climbed the hill east of the southernmost cornfield and deployed.[165]

The 9th New York went on line immediately behind Clark's battery on the eastern side of the stone wall which paralleled the ridge from the south side to the "L" shaped woods around Wise's field. The 103rd New York lay down in line on the left, anchoring it along the stone wall at the southeastern corner of the cornfield. Two companies of the 89th New York connected with its right, and the rest of the regiment was arranged in column in a northwesterly line, when the North Carolinians launched their attack.[166]

Wren and his men of the 48th Pennsylvania halted about eighty yards west of the wood road long enough to turn and discharge their weapons before splitting to both flanks and rallying with their regiment. The captain was attempting to tell Colonel Sigfried that the Confederates were only seventy-five yards away when a Confederate color bearer led the charge into the open.[167] The 2nd and 13th North Carolina regiments broke across the wood road and made for the cornfield, which they thought was unoccupied. The second they saw Clark's battery they gave their yelping battle cry and opened fire with a rattling volley, shooting by squads as they came into the road.[168] Lieutenant Colonel Edgar A. Kimball (9th New York) ordered the regiment to hit the ground.[169] The 103rd New York stampeded part way down the hill, heading for the safety of the woods behind it.[170] Private Charles Johnson (Company I, 9th New York), who was standing on the extreme left of his regiment, while listening to the minié balls zing high over his head, helplessly watched the 103rd break to the rear. For a minute or two he thought the brigade had broken.[171] To his left, where two companies of the 89th New York had come into line, no firing occurred. They stayed down behind the stone wall, while the rest of their regiment attempted to get on the field. The Rebel rifle fire nearly scattered them too. Their commander, Major Edward Jardine, leaped onto the wall where the four fields joined on the hillside, and screamed, "Eighty-ninth New York, what in hell are you about! Continue the movement!"

As the two left regiments moved back into position, the Confederates bolted across the wood road toward the cornfield and Clark's battery. The 89th New York let them get to within a few feet of the line before rising up and cutting them down like mow grass.

The Regular artillerists leaped to their rifled pieces, which were shotted with double canister. Seconds later, Captain John Gorman (Company D, 2nd North Carolina) remembered, "...like a thunderbolt from a cloudless sky, comes the booming of cannon, and the whole earth in front of us seems torn up by grape and canister."[172] The brilliant flashes of the muzzles followed by the ear shattering report of each gun as it was discharged in sequence brought a brief, unearthly silence on that end of the field.[173] Presently, the 89th New York moved out through the corn to mop up.[174] Lieutenant Colonel Edgar A. Kimball of the 9th New York speedily led the right wing of his regiment by files through the field behind Joseph Clark's battery and disappeared into the brush to the north to secure the flank.[175]

As the smoke cleared, the frightened New Yorkers realized that the

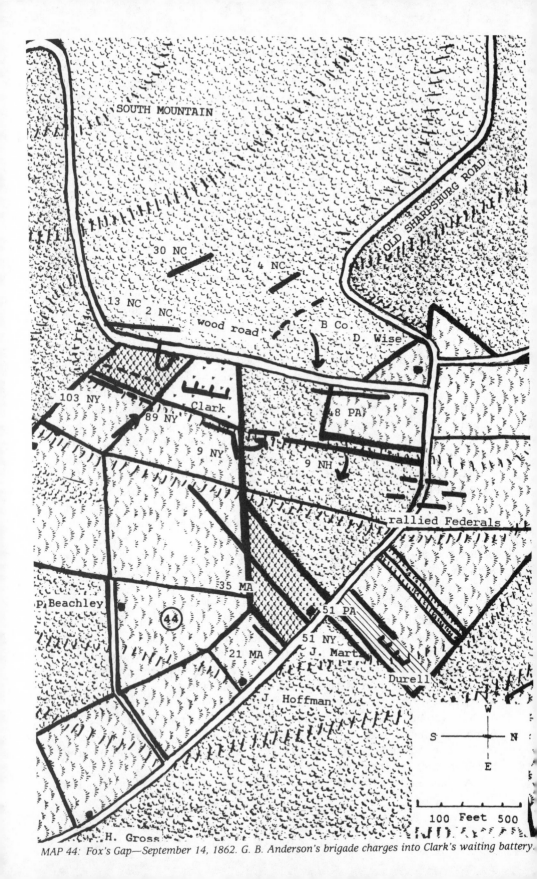

SOUTH MOUNTAIN

OLD SHARPSBURG ROAD

30 NC

4 NC

13 NC 2 NC

wood road

B Co.

D. Wise

103 NY

Clark

89 NY

9 NY

48 PA

9 NH

rallied Federals

35 MA

P. Beachley

(44)

51 PA

51 NY

J. Mart.

21 MA

Durell

J. Hoffman

W

S — N

E

100 Feet 500

H. Gross

MAP 44: Fox's Gap—September 14, 1862. G. B. Anderson's brigade charges into Clark's waiting battery.

troops on their right had started firing and that only dead, dying, and wounded Confederates remained behind.[176] "...We lay down upon the field with the dead lying all around us," David Thompson sadly wrote his friend, Elias, "& the angry shots upon the opposite hill sounded in our ears—a different lullaby from any that I had before heard."[177]

To the north the fighting evolved into a violent fusillade. James Wren's skirmishers retired again to the regiment but anchored themselves on the left of the line rather than on both flanks as the 4th North Carolina opened fire. Their muzzle flashes followed by the rain of bullets zipping overhead unnerved the unfortunate 9th New Hampshire, which was standing to arms to the left rear of the 48th Pennsylvania.. A large number of the New Englanders, having just reloaded, responded in a volley into the backs of the Pennsylvanians, then, by impulse, broke to the rear.[178] Lieutenant Colonel Joshua Sigfried's well drilled veterans ducked down behind the stone wall along the wood road as the recruits' minié balls passed well above them. Quickly recovering themselves, part of the regiment prepared to give fire while some of their officers and enlisted men ran back to the eastern edge of Wise's field and bullied the New Englanders back into line along the rail fence.

Back at the wood road, the front rank of the 48th Pennsylvania kneeled and the rear stood up to shoot over them. The men were badly shaken and very angry for having gotten caught between two lines of fire. Quite a few of the rattled men, much to their embarrassment, shot away their ramrods into the stone wall on the western side of the road.[179] During the following twenty to twenty-five minutes, the Pennsylvanians expended the better part of their regulation forty rounds. The Yankees banged away at the shadows, cutting down tangle foot and riddling a great many trees, but hitting very few of the enemy. The 4th North Carolina stubbornly matched the Federal musketry round for round.[180]

To the northeast, George Durell's artillerists clambered over the rail fence behind their battery to man their guns. The dirt from the sweet potato patch, which they had been pilfering with bare hands, clung to them as they loaded with shell and plastered the woods across the ridge. They had plenty of room to work. Shortly after the battery opened on Drayton's men, Asa Cook's New Englanders rushed into the battery, recovered their long-silent cannon, and rolled their two guns away to the rear.[181] [Refer to Map 44]

While the 48th Pennsylvania and the 4th North Carolina slugged it out, the 9th New Hampshire returned to the fence on the eastern side of Wise's field. Lieutenant Colonel Herbert B. Titus methodically chewed out each company as he trooped the line. The normally proper and religious officer seemed to glare right through each man as he chided them. Sergeant Franklin J. Burnham (Company E) never forgot what the colonel growled, when he stopped to dress down his company.

"And I have a word to say to this company, too," he fumed, with his voice rising in pitch as he continued, "I know you are green and haven't had much drill and discipline, but there is one thing you do know, and that is that you must obey orders; and though I am a Christian man at home...." He lapsed into a Biblical chain of epithets which shocked his men, who had never heard him swear before. "Don't you ever fire a gun again, nor change your position, without orders."[182]

Several minutes after dark, around 6:30 P.M., the firing ceased, when the Northerners realized that they were not receiving any incoming rounds. Unknown to them, George B. Anderson's North Carolinians (2nd, 4th, 13th, and 30th North Carolina) had quit the field by moving west, down the mountainside to the crossroad where they had last seen Roswell Ripley and his Georgia brigade.[183] It came as no surprise that they could not find them.

In filing northeast to engage the Yankees at the wood road, Anderson's men crossed Ripley's front. The befuddled general, whose skirmishers in the ebbing light could vaguely discern some commotion east of his brigade, assumed that the troops were Yankees. He promptly marched his brigade north along the crossroad and left the field without contacting either of his brigade commanders.[184] Once again, the mountain top became ominously silent.

The 6th New Hampshire and the 2nd Maryland from Welsh's brigade finally arrived, following a couple of hours of duty along the National Pike.[185] The weary regiments in Wise's field retired into the woods behind them. The 48th Pennsylvania returned to Martz's cornfield. Part of the regiment recovered its knapsacks and lay down for a cold night's sleep.[186] The men could not light fires because they would disclose the regiment's position to the Rebs. The officers took roll. Captain James Wren of Company B lost three men— missing.[187] Another eight were wounded.[188]

Wren and his men captured quite a few of the 13th North Carolina's knapsacks. They were loaded with booty. "[they had] all Kind[s] of Little articles such as rasor, photegrafs, Bibels with som[e] very fine motos on the margons of them," the captain boasted. He stole a Bible from one of them, then gave orders for his soldiers to change their shirts, socks, and drawers from the Southerners' supply.

They saw no harm in it. Ironically, many of the captured knapsacks were theirs which they lost at Second Manassas. The Pennsylvanians stripped in squads of six to eight men, a move designed to keep them from getting caught with their pants down should the Confederates counterattack.[189]

To the northwest, in the one-acre field at the wood road intersection, Michigander Gabriel Campbell and a small detachment of his men from the 17th Michigan tried to sort out their wounded from among the Confederate casualties. Within a short time they had gathered in what they believed were most of the regiment's wounded. As the Yankees headed toward the gate in the southeastern corner of the field, the captain noticed what appeared to be an unarmed squad of Rebels climbing into the opposite corner of the field. At first he thought they were trying to succor their own injured. He quickly noticed they were looting the dead of both armies.

The Rebels also picked up discarded rifles. They fired a couple of them. Campbell yelled at them to cease and desist. They swore at him. Realizing that he could serve his country better in active service rather than as a prisoner of war, the captain slipped through the gate into the Old Sharpsburg Road.

As his hand touched the cross bar, General Orlando Willcox, who was mounted, accosted him. Who did that firing? the general demanded. Rebs, the captain replied. They were picking up arms and probably preparing for a rally. At that the general wheeled his horse about and sped down the hill. The captain cautiously continued down the road behind him.[190]

Willcox ordered Colonel Edward Ferrero and his brigade to the front. The colonel ordered the 35th Massachusetts, the largest regiment (800 men) in his brigade, forward as skirmishers.

Colonel Edward A. Wild (35th Massachusetts) stood up and yelled, "Throw off your packs!"

The New Englanders struggled to shuck their cumbersome knapsacks. Sergeant Frederick Merserve (Company K) could not pull his off his back. He was grateful for it later on, after the battle ended, when the regiment could not find their knapsacks.[191]

"Fix bayonets!" Wild commanded.

Steel clanked against steel. The regiment faced to the west and double quicked toward Wise's field. Passing over the prone regiments which reformed in the woods, the New Englanders climbed over the stone fence into the wood road.[192] Colonel Wild swore at the column and ordered it into the woods. As they started the flank movement, a shot rang out. One of the men collapsed in the road. Instantly, a squad of the New Englanders lunged at a group of wounded Southerners who were propped up against their knapsacks. When they threw their hands up and pleaded for mercy, they received it.[193]

Second Lieutenant Albert A. Pope (Company I) never saw such a thick woods. The dead and wounded lay in piles throughout the place. He hated stepping over them and walking through their blood.[194] The woods fragmented the regiment into squads of confused soldiers, none of whom really knew what they were doing.

"Company A!"

"Company B!"

The officers, in a vain attempt to reform their lines, sounded more like a brigade than a regiment.[195] They would have awakened any sound sleeper. As it was, they alerted George T. Anderson's Georgians of their advance.

Lieutenant H. D. D. Twiggs (Company D, 1st Georgia Regulars) and Lieutenant G. B. Lamar, Jr. of Company F, in charge of his skirmishers, reported to him in the lower end of the Old Sharpsburg Road. The colonel saw the Yankees crossing the road up hill and east of him and decided to leave the field. Leading his men by the left oblique, he cut northeast through the woods in an attempt to intercept the rash New Englanders.[196]

The 35th Massachusetts turned back before it advanced too far down the slope. The right wing stopped at the cart path which ran northwest off the wood road. Discarded canteens and haversacks littered the path. The men

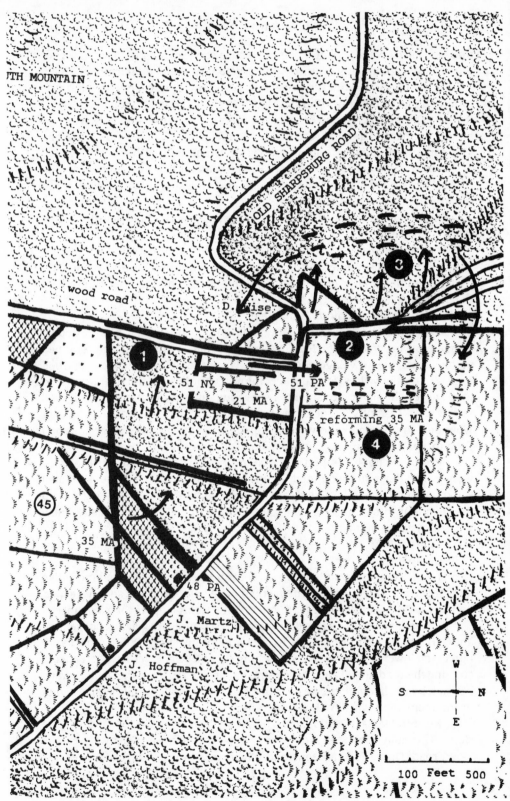

TH MOUNTAIN

OLD SHARPSBURG ROAD

wood road

D. Wise

1

2

3

51 NY   51 PA

21 MA

reforming 35 MA

4

45

35 MA

48 PA

J. Martz

J. Hoffman

W
S ——— N
E

100 Feet 500

MAP 45: Fox's Gap—September 14, 1862.
The 35th Massachusetts gets lost in the dark on the hillside west of the wood road.

halted and their officers ordered them back to the wood road, unaware that the Georgians were halted a short distance beyond and waiting to capture them.[197]

While the untried men of the 35th Massachusetts disappeared into the woods on the western slope of the mountain, the rest of Colonel Edward Ferrero's brigade marched up the Old Sharpsburg Road toward Wise's field.[198] They could not believe the carnage which surrounded them. Captain William Bolton (Company A, 51st Pennsylvania), in glancing to the north along the high stone fence which the 17th Michigan had taken with the bayonet, spied a gory heap of at least Confederate casualties.[199]

At the wood road intersection, Colonel Ferrero filed the two lead regiments along the stone wall—the 51st Pennsylvania on the right, and the 51st New York to the left. The 21st Massachusetts finished out the formation by lying down behind them.[200] Following the single shot into the 35th Massachusetts, Ferrero issued an order for the regiments to hold their fire until the Confederates came into the open.[201]

General Jesse Reno followed the brigade up the hill. His medical director, Doctor Calvin Cutter, and two orderlies—Alexander H. Wood and Martin Ficken (Company L, 6th New York Cavalry)—escorted him. He had no idea of the battle situation to his front. Near J. Hoffman's, he stopped Private A. B. Counnel (Company F, 30th Ohio) and, pointing to the right, north of the road, asked him what troops were to the front. The private, who was heading down the mountain with his company's empty canteens, and who had not seen the 35th Massachusetts deploy, replied that there were no Federal troops in that area. They were all to the left of the road. Rebels were in the woods. The general rode on without saying anything.[202]

About one hundred yards farther west he and his escort came upon Captain Gabriel Campbell of the 17th Michigan who was meandering down the road, trying to rethink what he had been through that day. The general seemed absorbed in meditation. He rode about half a length in front of his escort. The captain stopped to observe Reno's activity.[203]

Meanwhile, about half of the 35th Massachusetts emerged, in disorganized squads, from the woods north of the wood road intersection. Their officers were herding them east, over the stone fence into the field, then south across the rear of the rest of the brigade as Reno approached the crossroads. The inexperienced regiment started to form behind the 21st Massachusetts. The rest of their men fumbled about in the woods trying to get back to their lines.[204] Soldiers still called out as they tried to sort out the shadows. As Companies A, F, D, and I of the 51st Pennsylvania cleared the Old Sharpsburg Road, Captain William Bolton happened to glance back toward Wise's field. In the darkness he saw a dancing glimmer of a light. The stupid 35th Massachusetts, he thought, was trying to post sentries by using a lantern for a guide.[205] [Refer to Map 45]

They were gathering in their lost recruits who were filtering back into the regiment. General Reno, who had entered Wise's field, let his horse

Major General Jesse Reno, IX Corps, Commanding.
Killed in Action, September 14, 1862.
COURTESY OF THE OLD SOUTH MOUNTAIN INN, TURNER'S GAP,
NEAR BOONSBORO, MARYLAND

walk slowly toward the road, leaned forward in the saddle to observe the movements of the Pennsylvania skirmishers. He paid no attention to the stragglers passing over the wood road or through the field. Surgeon Cutter and Private Martin Ficken were riding at his side when they startled a rookie from the 35th Massachusetts who was walking into the field through the gate in the northwestern corner.

"Rebel cavalry!" the soldier screamed as he wheeled about and aimed his musket at the general.

"Don't fire!" Ficken yelled a second too late.

The weapon flashed in their faces.[206] Immediately, six rifle shots rang out from the small field northwest of the wood road intersection. Gabriel Campbell quickly glanced over that way. In the darkness, he saw what appeared to be Rebel soldiers falling in behind the fence along the wood line.[207]

The bullet glanced off Jesse Reno's scabbard and into his chest, just below his heart.[208] The general tottered in the saddle and feebly dismounted. Turning to Martin Ficken, he gasped that he was wounded, and he feared badly. The startled orderly quickly ran back through the brigade and returned with a blanket. At the same time, his other orderly, Alexander Wood, returned from the woods on the west side of the ridge. One of the orderlies grabbed the reins of the horses and started leading them off the field. The surgeon, remaining orderly, and two or three enlisted men laid the general on the blanket and struggled with him down the Old Sharpsburg Road.[209]

Captain Campbell stopped the orderly leading the horses.

"What happened?"

"Reno is shot," he replied as he passed by.

The four men with the general paused in front of the captain, and immediately enlisted his aid. He supported the middle of the blanket from the right side. In the darkness, Campbell could not discern the general's features, but he seemed to be pale. No one spoke.[210] In the background, along the wood road, a rapid volley flashed along the tree line.[211]

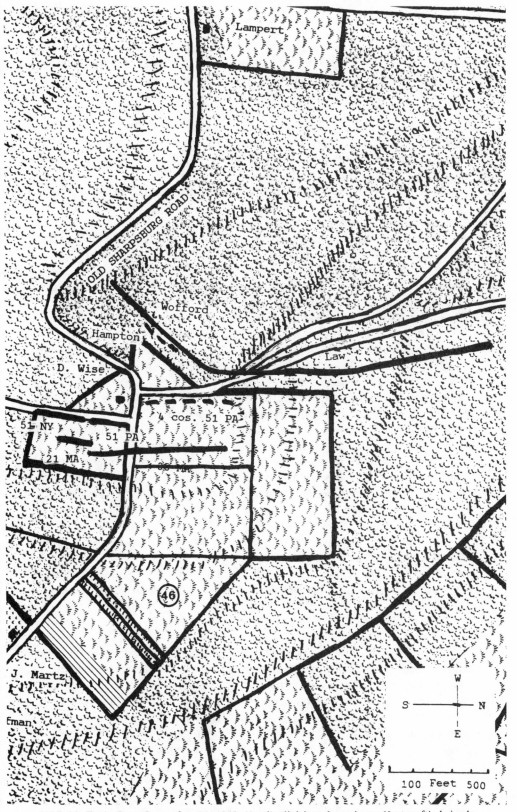

MAP 46: Fox's Gap—September 14, 1862. Hood's division closes in on Hartranft's brigade.

The five men slowly and tenderly carried the general as far as the woods east of Wise's field. There, they transferred him to a waiting stretcher. He looked up at them gratefully. Before the hospital attendants bore him away, General Orlando Willcox dismounted by his side.

"Willcox," Reno gasped, "I am killed. Shot by our own men."[212]

He did not speak again until he was laid down under the oak across the road from the school house below Henry Gross' place. (It was already night. His staff ordered Alexander Wood and Martin Ficken to say nothing about what they had seen to anybody.)[213]

Back at the wood road, Colonel Edward Ferrero's brigade became involved in a vicious firefight with Brigadier General John B. Hood's division very soon after Reno's wounding. Hood's two brigades ran into George T. Anderson and his Georgians along the wood road north of the right flank of the 35th Massachusetts as it retired from the woods. Hood placed Anderson on his left.[214] Hood personally led the Texas Brigade (18th Georgia, Hampton's Legion, 1st, 4th, and 5th Texas) and Colonel Evander M. Law's brigade (4th Alabama, 2nd and 11th Mississippi, and 6th North Carolina) along the western side of the wood road until they were northwest of Wise's field.[215]

As Hampton's Legion neared the one-acre field north of Wise's cabin, a call went out for three volunteer skirmishers. Privates Henry Brandes, Elliott Welch and George B. Gelling (all Company H) ventured forth with a lieutenant. Coming to the edge of the woods, they saw a line of Yankees (Companies A, D, F, and I, 51st Pennsylvania) moving in the open across their front. The four Rebels opened fire, then retreated into the woods.[216] They took cover while the rest of the division, which had advanced into position just west of the wood road, fired a "murderous volley" into the forming Yankee line.

The four Pennsylvania skirmish companies north of the Old Sharpsburg Road saw the muzzle flashes and went to the ground without any time to spare. Before the Confederates could reload, the Pennsylvanians returned the volley. Most of their shots went too high and they inflicted nominal casualties.[217]

The Rebel bullets slammed into the 35th Massachusetts before it could reform. Colonel Edward Wild went down with a shattered left arm along with several men.[218] The regiment responded immediately. Its fire lit up the night sky, as the men shot into the backs of the 51st Pennsylvania. Every regiment along the front hit the dirt.[219]

"Cease firing!"

"Fire! fire!"

"Cease firing!" echoed back and forth between officers of the various companies. Finally, the 51st Pennsylvania threatened to cut down the leaderless New Englanders. (In the initial confusion after Colonel Wild's wounding, the regimental staff lost time in an attempt to find Sumner Carruth, the lieutenant colonel. He was lost somewhere.) Captain Stephen H. Andrews (Company A) finally assumed command and took the regiment back into the woods east of Wise's field.[220] By then the fire had slackened off enough to allow the 51st

New York to get into the fray. Musketry rattled on for another fifteen minutes. The Yankees ceased fire when they realized they were not getting shot at.[221] [Refer to Map 46]

When the field grew quiet, Colonel John Hartranft of the 51st Pennsylvania recalled all of his skirmishers except Company A. Captain William Bolton posted his company in the wood road north of the Old Sharpsburg Road. The carnage he found between the two walls not only appalled but misled him. He thought his men had personally done tremendous damage to the Confederates along the wood road. He had no way of knowing that the Rebels lost less than thirty men in the final firefight.[222] He could, however, fairly estimate his regiment's and the brigade's casualties. Their bleeding bodies littered the area. Edward Ferrero's brigade lost more than one hundred fifty men during the forty to forty-five minute confrontation.[223]

While standing in the wood road, Bolton had time to reflect upon the day's events. Dead Confederates, their stiffening corpse held upright by the unyielding stone wall, still aimed their weapons with glassy concentration at the troops in Wise's field. Others had perished with the torn cartridges clenched in their hands—struck down while trying to load. He estimated that there were at least one hundred twenty-five bodies between the walls of the lane. It was hard to tell. In some places, they lay on top of one another as high as the top of the wall itself.

The captain tried to find the words to sum up everything he felt at the moment. It would not be anything poetic. He wrote in his journal, "...pickets were soon established for the night, and from the groans and moaning of the wounded all night long, and lying right among the dead, we spent a cheerless, wretched, supperless night."[224]

The Confederates still held the western slope of the mountain and part of the wood road. The IX Corps had fought all day for nothing. The men of the 51st Pennsylvania had not captured the high ground nor defeated the Confederates, whom they outnumbered and had lost a general whom they loved. They had nothing to feel elated about.

Chapter Twelve

SEPTEMBER 14, 1862

TURNER'S GAP

At 3:00 A.M., the Federal drummers beat reveille. It echoed along the east bank of the Monocacy while General Joseph Hooker's I Corps roused itself from a comfortable bivouac.[1] No one seemed in a particular hurry. It was the typical start of another McClellanesque day: leisurely breakfasts of hard crackers and coffee beneath a clear sky. Sergeant Archibald F. Hill (Company D, 8th Pennsylvania Reserves) spoke for many of his comrades when he recalled how the men bedded down the previous evening little suspecting they were going anywhere the next day.[2] The clear and cool morning relaxed the men. When the sun came up at 5:49 A.M. the men still remained in camp.

> "Dear Emma," began Private James H. McIlwain (Company G, 11th Pennsylvania Reserves),
> "This is Sunday and we are laying resting at this place having traveled on a heavy march evry day last week.... we dont know what minute we may be called to Arms. This is a beautiful Country and it is a great pity that the troops of either Army Should invade and destroy the beautiful farms which are full of every kind of fruits most of which are ripe or nearly So but the Old Saying is those that dance must pay the fiddler. So the Secessionists of Maryland were the whole cause of this invasion It is pitiful to See the women and children leaving their homes and fleeing for the Union Army to protect them. The Rebels where ever they find Union people they take evry [sic] thing they have—rob their Orchards destroy their Corn and Kill their Cattle They Say that we done in this way when over in Virginia they intend to do the Same in Maryland and Penna. I hope they will have a warm time in Penna.... Kiss the children for me and my love to yourself.
>
> I remain your
> Husband
> James H. McIlwain"[3]

He had hardly folded the letter and addressed it when a distant cannonading echoed across the fields from the west. First Lieutenant Samuel W.
Moore (Company B, 90th Pennsylvania) looked at his watch. It was 6:00 A.M.[4]
The drummers rolled out the Assembly. Within half an hour, the I Corps was
packed up and converging upon the National Pike.

General George G. Meade's Pennsylvania Reserve division started the
corps' advance within the hour.[5] Brigadier General Rufus King's division
followed the Pennsylvanians. Their columns blocked the road. For more than
an hour General James B. Ricketts' division impatiently stood by and watched the rest of the corps pass. At 8:00 A.M., the division finally gained the road.[6]
By then Meade's soldiers had arrived in Frederick.[7]

National flags, full sized and miniature, and white handkerchiefs fluttered
from nearly every window sill and door jamb when Brigadier General Truman
Seymour's veterans (1st, 2nd, 5th, 6th, and 13th Pennsylvania Reserves)
tramped through the quiet city streets. Sergeant Major E. M. Woodward (2nd
Reserves) craned his neck a little to glance up at the shuttered windows on
either flank. Here and there, he detected the slats opening cautiously so the
people inside could furtively follow the regiment up the street. A few souls
ventured into their doorways, still in their white night clothes, which the
sergeant major, at that early hour, mistook for "neat, snowy white," street
clothes.[8] By the time the civilians fully realized that the Yankees were in their
city again, the head of the column had passed the western edge of the town.
As usual, the Federals did nothing to quell the enthusiasm of the civilians who
thronged their line of march as the last brigade in Meade's division, Colonel
Albert Magilton's, headed out West Patrick Street.

Ladies stood in the doorways with buckets or glasses of cold fresh water,
and begged the thirsty soldiers to break ranks for some refreshment. The
veterans did not hesitate to step out and share a few seconds with them. The
women inundated the Yankees with overflowing kindness and flattery.

Archibald Hill of the 8th Reserves coyly recollected, "I can't for the life
of me tell what made me so thirsty that morning; for I must have stopped
a dozen times for a drink of water." The fact that each glass came from the
hand of a woman obviously had nothing to do with his intense thirst.[9]

The patriotic demonstrations only increased in intensity as the rest of
the I Corps marched into the town. The mild elation at seeing so many fresh
Federal troops in their city turned into deafening cheers.[10] "Little children
stood at nearly every door, freely offering cool water, cakes, pies, and dain-
ties," Major Rufus Dawes (6th Wisconsin) remembered. "The jibes and insults of the women of Virginia, to which our men had become accustomed,
had here a striking contrast in a generous and enthusiastic welcome by the
ladies of Frederick City."[11] "God bless the loyal women of Maryland," Colonel William F. Rogers (21st New York) joyously agreed.[12]

Once in a while, however, a "vinegar faced old man or an old woman"
reminded the Yankees of Maryland's dual loyalties.[13] Brigadier General John
Gibbon, commanding a brigade in Rufus King's division, became acutely aware

of the state's divided loyalties. Having spent the last two nights on the front porch of Dr. Shipley, a family acquaintance, he carefully noted how the doctor's niece adroitly avoided any type of contact with the Northerners. The general suspected both he and she were secessionists and she was a "rabid" one. He observed, "...nearly all the pretty girls are hot rebels, whilst all the old dried up & ugly ones are in favor of the Union! Rather a hard case I think!"[14]

The Fredericktonians, while dispensing water and pastries, did not open their stores and shops to their liberators. Forty-three-year-old Lieutenant Isaac Hall (Company D, 97th New York) and a large number of the enlisted men hastily read each chalked "Sold out" and "Closed up" sign. They irreverently joked about the town folks' real motives for not throwing their businesses open to them. They felt it had little or nothing to do with honoring the Sabbath.[15] Lieutenant Samuel W. Moore of the 90th Pennsylvania, while enjoying the bread and apples during the brigade's one hour rest, looked at his watch. It was a little after 9:00 A.M.[16]

Up ahead, the rest of the I Corps, behind the IX Corps, cautiously approached the top of Catoctin Mountain at Braddock Pass. Private Bates Alexander (Company C, 7th Pennsylvania Reserves) and his comrades surveyed the damage of the previous day's artillery skirmishing along the National Pike. Dead horses and splintered pieces from gun carriages and caissons littered the roadside on the winding ascent up the eastern slope. The Yankee enlisted men halted intermittently, in passing, to pick up and examine several of the large shell fragments, which they found strewn along their path, to determine which side had fired them. Showing them to their officers, they universally confirmed they were of English manufacture. Shattered trees, broken fence rails, damaged houses and barns, and an occasional furrow in the aging limestone pike attested to the severity of the Confederate artillery practice.

Private Alexander marveled at the destructive power of the shells. He took the time to examine an impressive barn close to the pike. A single fragment ripped away two of the gable's three upright supports and left the third swinging like a pendulum by a single nail through the gable's floor. Closer inspection revealed structural damage to the barn's huge, oak center beam as well. A little farther on, they came upon a burned barn, fired, as rumor had it, by a bursting shell. "...the artillery boys of both sides looked on and smiled as their guns continued the work of destruction," Bates Alexander lamented.[17]

The head of the Reserves reached the top of the mountain before 11:00 A.M. Puffs of artillery smoke, billowing bluish white in the distance along South Mountain, followed by the reports of the guns, attracted the Pennsylvanians' attention. "I think we could see three miles of pike from this place," Private Bates Alexander wrote.[18]

The fighting contrasted so sharply with the undulating, verdant valleys on both sides of them. Pennsylvanians from Company C of the 7th Reserves scratched their heads in amazement as they gathered around the picket fence surrounding a small house near the road. The Rebels, after chopping down the telegraph poles along the Pike, took the wires and meticulously wove them between the pickets around the entire yard. The children of the house quickly encircled the Pennsylvanians. There was a "big bundle of wire," they gleefully clucked, laying in the field down yonder.[19] Unable to stray too far from the column, the men rejoined their regiment. The children had not seen enough of war to grow tired of it.

Sergeant Major Woodward of the 2nd Pennsylvania Reserves, having experienced too much of it, took grim satisfaction in the destroyed rear chest from one of the Washington Artillery's caissons, which he mistakenly assumed to be a casualty of Saturday's skirmishing.[20] They did not linger but continued their march to the west.

Behind them, the rest of the I Corps continued to advance from Frederick. At 11:00 A.M., Rufus King's men crested Catoctin Mountain.[21] The division rested for a few minutes to gain its breath after the steep climb. Colonel William F. Rogers (21st New York), whose brigade led the column, solemnly contrasted the dried pool of horses' blood in the packed limestone of the road bed with the pastoral images and sounds of Frederick, which lay in the valley to the east. Long, winding infantry formations, the muzzles of their burnished weapons gleaming in the brilliant sunlight, snaked their way forward for as far as he could see. In the distance, he distinctly heard a single bell toll the summons to church. Thoughts of home and of Sunday services crept into his mind and reminded him of the peace and sanctuary he had forsaken so long ago. Tears unexpectedly welled up in his eyes and rolled down his face.[22] He felt completely alone as the brigade resumed its trek down the mountain.

By noon a large crowd of curious civilians had followed the I Corps from Frederick to the overlook on the western side of Braddock Pass.[23] They stared in awe at the individual artillery reports from the batteries on the eastern slope of South Mountain, which was six miles away. "...every few seconds," wrote Franklin B. Hough, Duryea's brigade historian, "a puff of light blue smoke, a little white cloud suddenly appearing in the sky, and a report, showed the position and activity of the rebel batteries...and those of the union troops below."[24] The crowd remained at the Pass, mesmerized by the spectacle beyond them.

While they gazed safely at the grand panorama of a battle unfolding before them, Middletown Valley throbbed with military activity. The townsfolk turned out in their Sunday clothes along the route to stare at the dusty men. It seemed strange to see gentlemen of military age escorting women in public. In passing, the veterans mocked the plain clothed men by saluting them while they smiled at their lady friends.[25] Once again, the Unionists treated the newly arrived soldiers to whatever edibles they had left in their homes and stores. Milk, fresh water, fruit, and tobacco quickly exchanged hands.[26] A young lady stepped into the street and slipped a bouquet of flowers into Adjutant Augustus Cross' (2nd Pennsylvania Reserves) hands. They both blushed as their eyes met and the lieutenant marched away with his regiment. Meade's Pennsylvania division passed through the town to the western bank of Catoctin Creek around 1:00 P.M.[27]

Within minutes, fires dotted the hillsides and flat land along the creek and the aroma of freshly brewed coffee wafted over the valley.[28] From the appearance of things, the men did not believe they were going into action at all that day. They made no wagers in that regard nor did they care to speculate upon the matter, either.[29] One of the enlisted men ambled over to the surgeon of the 2nd Reserves and asked him to pull an aching tooth.

"Why, my dear boy, we are going into battle in a little while," the surgeon said.

"I know that," the soldier complained, "but who wants to go to heaven with a tooth-ache."[30]

While he worried himself over a minor disability, ambulances, loaded with the severely wounded soldiers from the fighting at Fox's Gap, jolted down the National Pike from the west. The music academy of Middletown and all of the churches opened their doors to the casualties.[31] The compassionate women of the town emptied their homes of pillows and bedding. They knelt next to the men who were bleeding to death in their streets and tried to comfort them with quiet words.[32]

At 2:00 P.M., Sturgis' division of the IX Corps started its approach toward the front. Filing down the National Pike, it took the side road (Marker Road) which forked to the south immediately west of Catoctin Creek.[33] Its advance cut off John Gibbon's western brigade (19th Indiana, 2nd, 6th, and 7th Wisconsin) in the eastern end of the town.[34] The front half of King's division forded the Catoctin below the burned bridge, and spread out to enjoy the afternoon as best as the men could under the circumstances.[35] The sudden flurry of activity panicked some of the civilians, who started to flee eastward. Their sudden exodus prevented Duryea's brigade (97th, 104th, and 105th New York, 107th Pennsylvania) from entering the town. They were caught up in a general advance which began without their commanding general. George B. McClellan and his staff had not yet reached Catoctin Mountain.[36]

While Samuel Sturgis diverted his division to the south toward the Old Sharpsburg Road, General Meade moved his Pennsylvanians west on the National Pike.[37] Staff officers and couriers galloped up and down the line with orders for the regiments behind them.[38] An impressive gaggle of men, women and children tagged along with the soldiers as well. They had never seen a battle before. They wanted to look at one close up and no one tried to turn them back.[39]

Truman Seymour's Pennsylvania Reserve brigade advanced as far as the crossroads at D. Beachley's, to within half a mile of Turner's Gap to support the 1st Massachusetts Cavalry, which was posted in the half mile long cornfield north of the Pike. Neither unit was in the place it should have been. Adjutant Charles F. Adams of the 1st Massachusetts Cavalry sarcastically referred to their present predicament as a "blunder." The New Englanders remained mounted in the tall corn watching their own heavy batteries exchanging salvos with Lane's Georgia Battery on the high ground northwest of the intersection. Except for a couple of "drop shorts," none of the projectiles fell close to the cavalrymen. "Here we sat on our horses for two hours," the lieutenant groused, "doing no good and unpleasantly exposed."[40]

Presently an orderly sent the infantry back to the Bolivar intersection. From his place in the ranks, west of the crossroads, Private Bates Alexander of the 7th Pennsylvania and Corporal Carmany watched Seymour's brigade double back by files along the right of the column.

"Was te heal doona se now?" the corporal growled in his thick Scottish brogue. ["What the hell do you see now?"]

Alexander did not reply.

They were not the only ones displeased with their current situation. Back in Middletown, General Burnside, on his way to the front, looked up General Marsena Patrick, who was commanding Rufus King's point brigade (21st, 23rd, 35th, and 80th New York) and informed him he would attend to his request for transfer as soon as the upcoming campaign ended. Patrick felt somewhat mollified by the general's response to his written request from the previous day, but he still considered General John Gibbon a "toady." Neither did he have any confidence in his division commander, Rufus King, who was waiting for a transfer himself. He strongly disliked King's successor, General John Hatch, who commanded the First Brigade (22nd, 24th, 30th, and 84th New York, 2nd U.S. Sharpshooters). The only brigade commander in his division he had no thoughts about was General Abner Doubleday.[41]

At 2:30 P.M., orders arrived from Washington, D.C., relieving King from command. He immediately turned the division over to Hatch and proceeded eastward on the National Pike to his cushy job with the Adjutant General's Office in the capital.[42] With his departure came the order to advance west on the National Pike.

Fifteen minutes later, McClellan, his staff, and his extensive cavalry escort (Oneida Cavalry, Companies A and E, 4th U.S. Cavalry) arrived in Middletown. They rode by General James Ricketts' stalled division and Lieutenant Samuel W. Moore (Company B, 90th Pennsylvania) quietly marked the time.[43] The general was going to the front to personally supervise what he believed to be the killing blow for the Army of Northern Virginia.[44]

THE BATTLE AROUND FROSTTOWN

Meanwhile, Meade's lead regiment double backed upon itself, turned north on the Old Hagerstown Road and cut off the civilians who had crossed the road into the fields between the Yankees and South Mountain.[45] Half a mile farther on, the division crossed the Mount Tabor Road intersection. Seymour's brigade led the deployment followed by Colonel Thomas Gallagher's (9th, 10th, 11th, and 12th Reserves) and Colonel Albert Magilton's brigades (3rd, 4th, 7th, and 8th Reserves).[46]

From the open knoll on the northern side of the National Pike, D. H. Hill

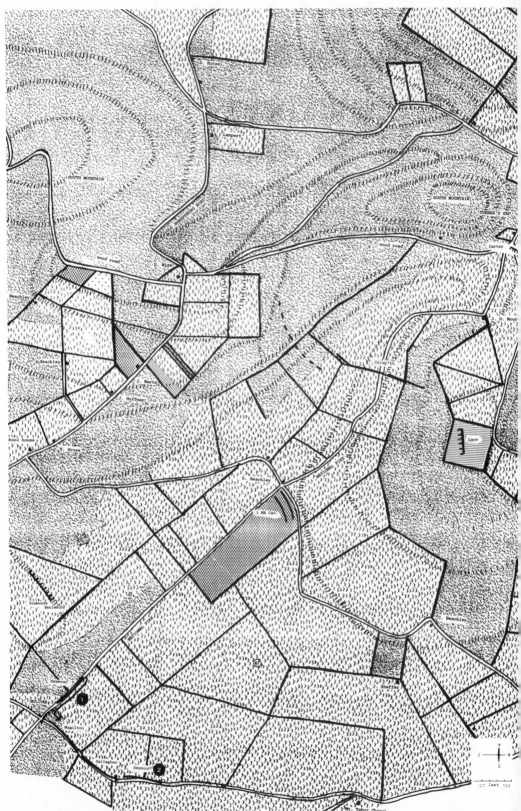

MAP 47: *National Pike Gorge—September 14, 1862. The Pennsylvania Reserves move into the valley.*

apprehensively watched the Yankees wend their way toward his vulnerable left flank. Having surveyed the ground with General Robert Rodes earlier in the day, he had sent Rodes with his five Alabama regiments (the 3rd, 5th, 6th, 12th, and 26th Alabama) to the Frosttown Road gorge. More than three-quarters of a mile separated Colonel Alfred Colquitt's brigade (13th Alabama, 6th, 23rd, 27th, and 28th Georgia) from Rodes' right flank. With the Yankee infantry outmaneuvering him and the heavy guns south of the Bolivar intersection mercilessly pounding the pass and Lane's battery, Hill sent a courier to Rodes requesting infantry support.[47] [Refer to Map 47]

Rodes received the message about the time that the Pennsylvanians entered the eastern edge of the gorge between the Frosttown Roads and the Zittlestown Road. Realizing that his small command (about 1200 men) was facing a division about three times its size, he reluctantly complied with the request and simultaneously asked for artillery support. While the 12th Alabama, his right regiment, filed south, the general deployed his brigade to cover more than a thirty-five-hundred-foot front.[48] The 6th Alabama, Colonel John Brown Gordon, commanding, started north toward the top of the gorge and the Widow Main's farm. The 5th Alabama, next in line, held the hillside south of her place. The 3rd Alabama and the 26th Alabama completed the formation in the vicinity of the N. Haupt and the J. O'Neil homesteads. None of the regiments, because of the dense woods on the left flank and the huge cornfield near the western cul-de-sac of the gorge, maintained any type of physical contact with the other.[49]

Lieutenant George W. Reed, Jr. (Company F, 5th Alabama) and his skirmishers spread out to the east toward a patch of wooded ground immediately south of the Zittlestown Road and about fifteen hundred feet to the right front of Colonel Thomas Gallagher's Pennsylvania Reserves brigade.[50]

As soon as the 12th Alabama reached the exposed field occupied by Captain John Lane's Georgia Battery with Rodes' plea for artillery, the captain sent one of his guns under a lieutenant to the left. Simultaneously, D. H. Hill, who realized that the Northerners were not going to attempt an assault up the steep hillside along his front, commanded Colonel Briston B. Gayle (12th Alabama) to volunteer skirmishers to watch the left flank near the Frosttown gorge.

Adjutant L. Gayle (12th Alabama) pulled out his roster of officers to find out whose turn it was for duty when the colonel impatiently snarled at him to "detail Lieutenant Park to command the skirmishers."

Robert E. Park (Company F), upon hearing his name, reported for his assignment. After selecting four men from each of the ten companies, he trotted with his detachment into the woods to the northeast and disappeared from sight.[51] In the meantime, Captain Lane's solitary gun rolled into the Frosttown Road near the easterly bend where the gorge begins its descent into the valley.[52] The gunner withheld his fire until the 7th Reserves, the second regiment from the end of Albert Magilton's command, reached the Frosttown

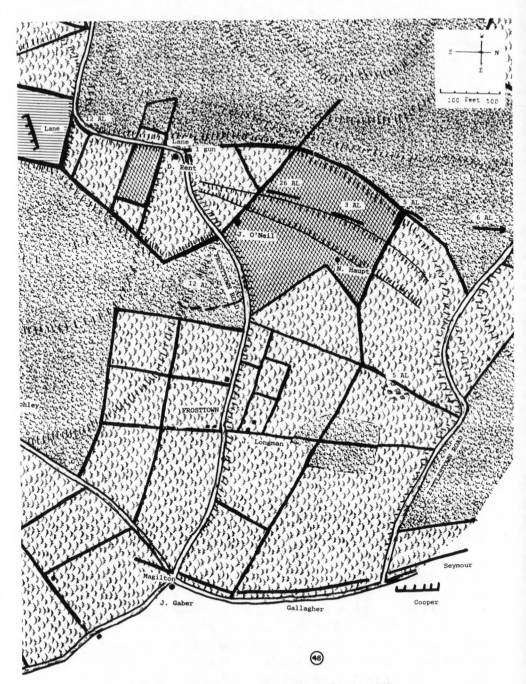

MAP 48: The Frosttown Road—September 14, 1862.
Rodes' division braces for the assault of the Pennsylvania Reserves.

J. Gaber's Farm along the Old Frosttown (Dalghren) Road.
COURTESY OF DUANE GLEASON

Road and the Old Hagerstown Road intersection. As the regiment passed in front of J. Gaber's house and barn, he opened fire with shell.[53]

Bates Alexander of Company C automatically turned his head toward the report in time to see the projectile burst over the top of the house while the company passed it to the right. George Hornberger ducked, but the concussion from the blast whirled him about like a top and threw him to the ground with several of his comrades. At the same time, two hysterical women, one of them carrying a baby, raced out onto the front porch of the frame log farm house. The unnerved Pennsylvanians, who were trying to reform, screamed at them to get into the cellar below the porch, which they probably did. (In the confusion, no one paid any particular attention to them.)[54]

The suddenness of the attack scattered the civilians, who, having kept pace with Magilton's men, were about five hundred feet away from the blast. "The effect upon the sightseers was magical," Sergeant Major E. M. Woodward (2nd Reserves) recalled with a certain amount of amusement, "they [were] breaking through our lines with wild screams, and knocking the boys around like toys." The men in the terrified herd unhesitatingly bolted the fence east of the road, leaving the women and children on their own. The children hurled themselves upon the ground, shrieking uncontrollably, while the ladies unceremoniously climbed the rails in their long skirts. The veterans thoroughly enjoyed watching them dangle from the fence posts by their petticoats and hoop skirts. "Never did we see a battle opened with such a prelude before, and it did us more good than all the harangues our generals could have delivered," the amused sergeant major wrote.[55]

The officers shouted at the line to move out. Bates Alexander found a new two-quart tin cup whirling about in the road between him and the man next to him. He snatched it up and pressed northwestward with his regiment.

Up ahead, to the left front, the color company, Company H, tramped west on the road. As Company C neared the barn on the right side of the road, another round whined through the air overhead. Crashing through a corner of the wagon house's roof, it slammed, unexploded, into the cow yard near the barn. Fresh manure sprayed out in a geyser higher than the barn roof and in all directions. The Pennsylvanians dodged the shower of flying manure as best as they could and followed the brigade into the open ground west of the Old Hagerstown Road.[56] The Confederate gunnery practice triggered a response from the Federals. The division double quicked into the fields north and south of the intersection. The move brought the 8th Reserves under the cover of a steep rise of ground south of the Frosttown Road, well below the line of sight of the Confederate gun on the mountain to the west.[57]

Captain James H. Cooper ordered his Company B, 1st Pennsylvania Artillery, which was accompanying Magilton's rear regiment, the 8th Reserves, forward to return fire. The four three-inch rifles passed behind the division, which had stepped west into the fields, and went into battery on a small elevation two thousand feet north of the Frosttown Road intersection.[58] The gunners shot a couple of rounds, and receiving no response, ceased fire.[59] Meanwhile, the Reserve division started to form line of battle parallel to the Old Hagerstown Road. It was about 3:30 P.M.[60] [Refer to Map 48]

Truman Seymour's regiments secured the right wing north of the intersection of the Zittlestown Road and the Old Hagerstown Road. The 1st Rifles (13th Reserves) under the command of Colonel Hugh McNeil fanned out to the front of the brigade as skirmishers. The 2nd Reserves, with two companies of the 1st Reserves on their right, formed about fifty yards to their rear. The remainder of the brigade (1st, 5th, and 6th Reserves, south to north, respectively) finished out the formation about another fifty yards back.[61]

To the southeast, opposite Seymour's left flank, but not connecting with it, Colonel Thomas F. Gallagher organized his regiments. The 9th Reserves held the extreme right, with the 11th in the center and the 12th on the left. The 10th Reserves went into line about seventy-five paces to the rear of the brigade.[62]

Colonel Albert L. Magilton's brigade (3rd, 4th, 7th, and 8th Reserves) completed the line. General Meade detached the 3rd Reserves north, for three fourths of a mile along the Old Hagerstown Pike, to cover the right flank of the army.[63] The 4th Reserves were on the right of the line. The 7th Reserves filled in the center in a plowed field, with its left flank resting upon the Frosttown Road. Across the road, the 8th Reserves, with a steep, heavily wooded hill to its front, finished out the formation.[64]

Colonel Magilton fronted his regiments to face west and gave the command to load. Private Bates Alexander (7th Reserves) prepared to charge his .69 caliber Harpers Ferry musket with his "special cartridge": a double load of powder, three pumpkin balls, and twenty-one buckshot.

Holding it up for all to see, he bragged, "Fellows, here she goes."

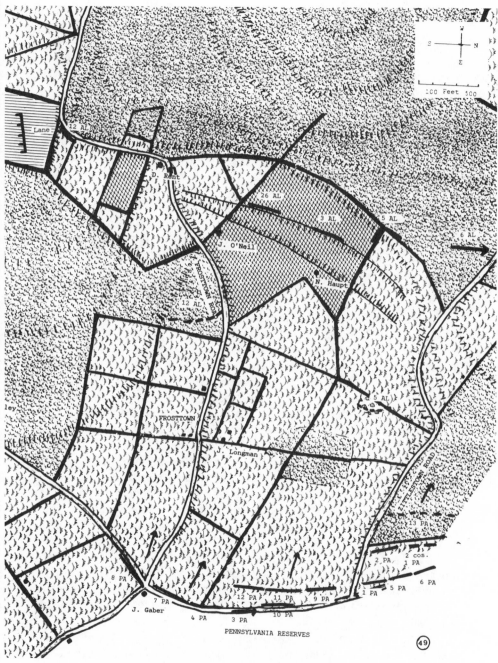

Lane

12 AL

D. Rent

26 AL

J. O'Neil

3 AL

AL

6 AL

FROSTTOWN ROAD

12 AL

N. Haupt

5 AL

FROSTTOWN

J. Longman

LITTLESTOWN ROAD

13 PA

8 PA

7 PA

J. Gaber

4 PA

3 PA

12 PA

11 PA

10 PA

9 PA

2 PA

1 PA

1 PA

2 cos.
1 PA

5 PA

6 PA

PENNSYLVANIA RESERVES

100 Feet 500

(49)

MAP 49: The Frosttown Road—September 14, 1862.
The Pennsylvania Reserves begin their attack.
(This action is simultaneous with the deployment shown on Map 55.)

As he rammed the cartridge home, his friends shook their heads in disbelief and told him it would burst the gun. The stubborn Pennsylvanian disagreed. "I was well prepared, loaded not quite to the muzzle," he clearly recollected years later.[65]

A little farther south, Sergeant Archibald Hill (Company D, 8th Reserves) eavesdropped upon a disturbing conversation between Lieutenant William M. Carter (Company B) and Captain Cyrus L. Conner (Company D).

"Captain, I think there will be a fight!" the lieutenant nervously exclaimed.

"No doubt there will," Connor replied matter-of-factly.

"Captain," Carter anxiously continued, "I know I shall be shot."

"Oh, nonsense!"

"But I will," the lieutenant insisted. "I am an unlucky mortal. I was shot while on the Peninsula almost the first chance I got—I was only wounded there; to-day I will be killed; I know it."

The captain was becoming impatient. The last thing he needed was an unstrung company officer. "Come now, lieutenant, it's only a foolish notion that has got into your head; get rid of it; cheer up; you will come out all right."

William Carter was not convinced. "I wish I could think so," he lamented. "I will fall doing my duty."

"I know you will do your duty, lieutenant," Conner answered as Carter returned to his post behind his company.[66]

Meade launched the assault at 4:00 P.M. Truman Seymour's brigade stepped off and pressed quickly along the wooded slope north of the Zittletown Road. Colonel Gallagher and his men followed at the right oblique, trying to close the gap between the two brigades. Albert Magilton's brigade tried to maintain the line but the steep hillside south of the Frosttown Road slowed it down. What Meade had originally intended to be a coordinated division assault broke into three separate actions.[67]

The 6th Alabama fell into line along the Widow Main's farm lane in front of her house about the same time that the 13th Reserves (275 men) reached the western edge of the woods some eighteen hundred feet to the east.[68] The Pennsylvanians, in sweeping past the 5th Alabama's skirmishers, who were in the gorge below their left wing, had gotten into the woods unobserved by either the 5th or the 6th Alabama. From their advantageous position, they cautiously examined Rodes' troop dispositions. Seymour halted his command and sent a courier back to Meade at the Old Hagerstown Road with word that he could brush the Confederates away from his front and take the Rebel left wing by the flank. Not too long afterward, around 5:00 P.M., Meade gave his approval.[69] [Refer to Map 49]

In the meantime, the 6th Alabama ran into opposition from an unanticipated source. Private Otis Smith (Company F), who had spent the better part of the day fighting his queasy stomach and weakened digestive tract, never forgot the bitter reception they received from the Widow Main. The obese old lady and her "white haired brood," as Smith described her family, blocked the door to her single room cabin and turned away every Alabamian who came to her for water. Glaring at them through her steel rimmed glasses she nastily referred to every one of the men as "Low down thieving rebels."

The dirty veterans cheered her lustily. Colonel John Gordon (6th Alabama) and his staff rode up to her to find out what caused the commotion.

Saluting her with his upraised kepi, he politely tried to lure her away from her door.

"My dear madam," he drawled, "fighting will begin in five minutes. Your life and that of your children are in imminent peril. You must leave here at once."

The obstinate old woman, with her hands on her hips, her eyes alive with anger, railed at the colonel, "I know what you want, you thieving Rebels, you want to get me out of my house and come and steal all I've got. I won't go there! I'll die fust!"

"Go it, old lady," someone crowed.

"Hold the fort!" another chimed in.

"Bully for you!" cheered still a third.

Stunned into silence for the first time, the proud John Gordon sullenly rode to another part of his line. His staff laughed at him and he did not appreciate it.

Otis Smith did not have time to see what Mrs. Main decided to do. Gordon sent his company down the wooded and tangled mountainside into the gorge on the regiment's southern flank.[70]

Meanwhile, in the valley, the 9th Reserves, on Gallagher's right flank ran into stiff resistance from Lieutenant Reed (5th Alabama) and his skirmishers who retired quickly to a stone wall which skirted the base of the mountain along the western end of the open field north of N. Haupt's cabin. They rejoined their regiment there, the left wing of which was moving to assist the 6th Alabama. A little farther to the south, in the cornfield, the 3rd Alabama fired a volley into the 11th Reserves when it crested the north-south ravine which crossed its front and took out more than thirty of the enlisted men and more than half of the regiment's commissioned officers.[71] Captain Evans R. Brady (Company K) and Lieutenant Walter F. Jackson (Company G) died in the blast.[72] Quartermaster Hugh Torrence (11th Reserves), Captain Everard Bierer (Company F), Captain Nathaniel Nesbit (Company E), and Lieutenant James S. Kennedy (Company D) went down with them.[73] Colonel Thomas Gallagher, the brigade commander, went to the rear with a musket ball in his right arm. On the way back, he passed the control of the brigade over to Lieutenant Colonel Robert Anderson (9th Reserves).[74] At the same time, the 26th Alabama, on the right of the 3rd Alabama, kept the 12th Reserves pinned in a firefight south of the Haupt house.[75]

General George Meade, riding a short distance behind the 10th Reserves, which was in his second line, initially refused to commit the regiment to battle. However, when the left half of the 5th Alabama broke to the north and the 6th Alabama slammed into the open field to his right, he assumed that the Confederates were turning his flank. He rushed Lieutenant Colonel

Adoniram Warner (10th Reserves) and his regiment on the double quick to extend his line and assist Seymour's troops.[76]

Colonel Gordon's 6th Alabama dashed into the woods east of the Main house and caught the 13th Reserves and their second line (2nd Reserves, and 2 companies, 1st Reserves) in the open field on the slope north of the Zittlestown Road. Their sudden fire staggered the 13th Reserves.[77] The 2nd Reserves hurried to its assistance and joined ranks with the 13th for the remainder of the engagement.

Wheeling his horse about, General Truman Seymour shouted to Colonel R. Biddle Roberts, "Can't your regiment take that height?"

Roberts responded by sending his regiment forward.[78] At the same time, Colonel William Sinclair (6th Reserves) detached Captains William H. Ent (Company A) and Charles D. Roush (Company B) with their companies to sweep the woods to the north and turn the Confederates' left.[78]

Captain John Lane's gun started to drop shells into Seymour's command from its position on the south spur along the Frosttown Road.[80] The left wing of the 5th Alabama, moving to the cover of the stone wall on the northern side of the large cornfield, opened fire upon Seymour's exposed left flank. As the 6th Alabama slipped back toward the Main farm, drawing the remainder of his Pennsylvanians after them, Truman Seymour decided to commit his last regiment, the 5th Reserves. As the regiment approached him with its well maintained formation, he hailed Colonel Joseph Fisher.

"Colonel," Seymour demanded, while pointing toward the gorge, "Put your regiment into that corn-field and hurt somebody!"

"I will, general," the colonel yelled back, "and I'll catch one alive for you."

The regiment cheered and wheeled south, across the Zittletown Road into the gorge. In very short order, they leaped the stone wall into the cornfield and snatched up Lieutenant George W. Reed (5th Alabama) and eleven of his men, whom they triumphantly herded back to Seymour.[81]

The fighting along the line became general. In the twilight, the smoke clung to the lower branches of the trees and settled in the gorge, making it difficult to see very far in any direction. The stone walls and the uneven ground disrupted formations and broke down regimental cohesion.

While Seymour's and Gallagher's brigades engaged most of Rodes' brigade, Lieutenant Robert Park (Company F) and his skirmishers from the 12th Alabama stalled the 8th Reserves, Albert Magilton's left regiment in the woods south of the Frosttown Road. The lieutenant posted his men behind the trees, bushes, and rock outcroppings which covered the hillside overlooking the low ground to the east. After cautioning every man to take careful aim and to be sure of his mark, he eyed the Pennsylvanians' beautifully aligned formation. The Yankee skirmishers cautiously approached his command in a "dense line." Their professionally maintained regiment, following them at the prescribed interval, appeared like a flowing, black ribbon across the farmland in front of them. His trained glance told the lieutenant he was not facing untried troops. He could hear himself breathe. His heart thumped violently within his chest.

When the Yankees crept into the tree line, Lieutenant Park let them get well within accurate range of his skirmishers. Suddenly, he screamed the command to fire. Flame slashed into the darkening woods. The Pennsylvanian skirmishers recoiled from the impact then raced back on their regiment. The Alabamians hastily reloaded and prepared for the inevitable counterstrike. The 8th Reserves pushed into the woods en masse. Again, the Rebels waited until the Yankees were too close to miss. The second volley brought down more than thirty of the Reserves and slowed their assault. Their officers swore loud enough for the Alabamians to hear.

"Close up," and "forward," bounced off Lieutenant Robert Park's back as he and his men slowly retired west. The Rebels fought from tree to tree and the Pennsylvanians, with equal tenacity, pushed them uphill.[82]

To the north, the 7th Reserves crossed the second fence row, while passing around J. Longman's farm. Several of the file closers dropped back to loot a peach tree near the farm house. Private Bates Alexander of the 7th Reserves plucked three of the peaches. Sticking one in his mouth and the others in his blouse, he ran after his men. As he did so, Lane's battery opened up on the division from the southwest. A solid shot landed between the feet of a file closer in the 4th Reserves, a short distance to the right. The impact hurled the man into a forward somersault and left him in a heap. Everyone assumed he was dead, but he hurriedly picked himself up and trailed after the other men.

On the right, the 4th Reserves lost its cohesion in several small ravines and the stone fences which cut across the field. However, the veterans did not get lost. Here and there, they rallied in some semblance of a line and advanced.

Bates Alexander's captain hurried his company into the Frosttown Road in files of two. As the men marched rather uncertainly up the lane, between the stone fences on either side, Alexander nervously watched his captain examine his column and the rest of the regiment on the northern slope of the gorge on his right. The captain seemed confused and uncertain as to whether he had done the right thing. In the excitement, the private did not remember hearing the rifle shots cracking and booming in the woods to the south.[83]

Lieutenant Robert Park and his stalwarts of the 12th Alabama stubbornly resisted every inch of ground. They were buying time in the face of insurmountable odds. The Yankees quickly shot several of his soldiers. Panic swept through his small detachment. At least six of his men broke and ran. Park swore at them, threatened them, and screeched unenforceable commands at their backs as they leaped and crashed through the woods toward the western side of the mountain. The fiery lieutenant refused to surrender.

To his front, he noticed a Yankee officer carelessly step out from cover. Park called to Sergeant Porter F. Myers (Company I), one of his best men, to bring the officer down. Myers stood up, aimed, and fired. A second later, he crumbled to the forest floor. Robert Parks ran over to his friend's side, and, pulling him up a little, he gave him a drink of water from his canteen. When

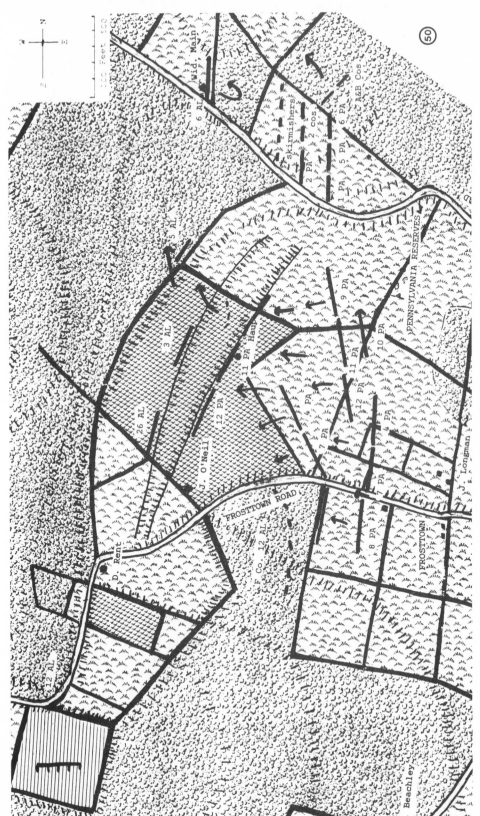

MAP 50: *The Frosttown Road to the Zittlestown Road—September 14, 1862.*
The Pennsylvania Reserves engage the Alabamians along the base of South Mountain.

50

he stood up to leave Myers, he realized he was surrounded. He found himself staring into at least a dozen rifle muzzles. He surrendered when ordered and started walking down the mountain, humiliated.[84] The Pennsylvanians, flushed with victory, continued to penetrate the woods further in an effort to catch up with the rest of their division. [Refer to Map 50]

To the north, the Reserves started to turn Rodes' flanks and break up his formation. The 9th Reserves expended its ammunition and retired from the field.[85] General Meade called back the 10th Reserves from the right. He rode up to Lieutenant Colonel Adoniram Warner.

"Go in and help our men in there," he exclaimed, pointing out the fence formerly held by the 9th Reserves.

The Pennsylvanians crawled over the stone wall and swung left into the cornfield, heading into the ravine. Part of the line volleyed into the hillside across from it as the men moved forward. One wing of his regiment held back, refusing to advance into the ravine. Riding into his men, Warner herded them into the depression.[86] On the left, the 11th Reserves and the 12th Reserves slammed into the 3rd Alabama and the 26th Alabama.[87] On the right, the 5th Reserves, with part of the 1st Reserves, crashed into the cornfield, driving the 5th Alabama into the skirmishers of the 6th Alabama, who had taken cover in the woods on the mountainside.

The O'Neil and the Haupt Houses as they appear today.

COURTESY OF MR. SPARKS

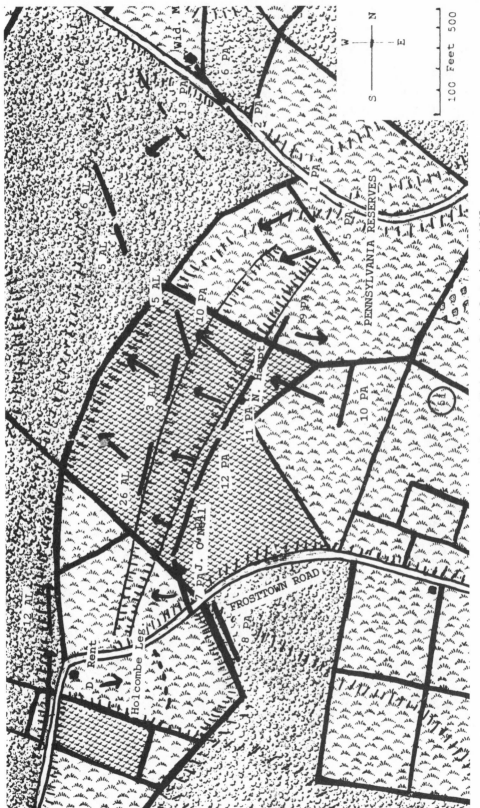

MAP 51: The Frosttown Road to the Zittlestown Road—September 14, 1862. The Pennsylvania Reserves push back Rodes' line.

Major Edwin L. Hobson (5th Alabama) managed to swing back the left wing of the 5th Alabama and work his way up the crest to join ranks with the 6th Alabama, which, under increased pressure from the 1st, 2nd, 6th, and 13th Reserves, quit the field around Main's and headed south. A single minié ball bored through Sergeant Thomas W. Hall's breast and thudded into the shoulder of his lieutenant, Archie Golson (Company G, 6th Alabama), shattering it. The mortally wounded officer stumbled away, leaving the severely wounded sergeant in the woods to fend for himself. Another bullet ripped away part of S. J. Jones' (Company G) left hand.[88] Private Otis Smith (Company F) had barely gotten into a comfortable position on the hillside when the 5th Reserves and Company K of the 1st Reserves, in extended order, broke through the corn. The Yankees' line extended well beyond each of the Rebels' flanks. Their line bristled with bayonets and their dark uniforms gave them a massive appearance in the fading light.

The Rebels, who were concealed behind trees and shrubs allowed the Yankees close to within one hundred yards before opening fire. The volley knocked over at least twenty men. Lieutenant John D. Sadler, and Privates Jeremiah Naylor and Peter Miller (all Company K, 1st Reserves) died in the skirmish. Lieutenant Henry N. Minnigh and several others were wounded.[89]

The Pennsylvanians recoiled to the edge of the field to close ranks. The Confederates reloaded then bolted like scared game up the hillside with the Pennsylvanians behind them. Every now and then, a man turned about to respond with a snapped shot. The Yankees splattered their backs with an overwhelming amount of small arms fire. The "pat-pat" of their lead balls against the rocks around the fleeing Otis Smith reminded him of hail slapping the ground.

Near the crest of the mountain, Smith and three of his comrades dove for cover into a hole which was flanked by huge boulders on either side and fronted by two large trees. The four Confederates kept the Federals at bay to their front, not realizing the rest of the Yankee line had swarmed around them.

"Come out of there or you will be gobbled up," an unseen Rebel called down to them from above.

The four had barely crawled into the brush behind them when shots at point blank range cut them down. The Pennsylvanians killed all of them except Smith, whom they left on the field to bleed to death from two serious wounds. As he lay there in a half swoon, he believed he heard the fire suddenly increase with tremendous fury.[90]

In the tumult, the 10th Reserves passed between the trapped right wing of the 5th Alabama and left of the 3rd Alabama. At the same time, to the south, the 11th Reserves and the 12th Reserves wounded Colonel Edward A. O'Neal (26th Alabama) and broke their formation. The Confederates scattered up the mountain, heading for the crest of the gorge.[91] While the left of the Gallagher's brigade, now under the command of Lieutenant Colonel Robert Anderson (9th Reserves), herded the 3rd Alabama northwest toward what was left of Rodes' brigade, it dragged the right wing of Albert Magilton's brigade into the fray.[92]
[Refer to Map 51]

The charge of the Reserves shattered their own formations and triggered a counterattack upon their left wing by Colonel Peter F. Stevens and his South Carolina brigade of about 550 men. Stevens had barely arrived with his five regiments (17th, 18th, 22nd, and 23rd South Carolina, and the Holcombe Legion) and Rodes' detached 12th Alabama before the Yankees swarmed into the gorge west. The Holcombe Legion quick marched toward the woods east of the Frosttown Road, moving in the direction of the firing where the 8th Pennsylvania was driving back the handful of skirmishers from Lieutenant Park's scattered command. The 23rd South Carolina almost connected with Rodes' right. The 22nd South Carolina and the 18th South Carolina continued the line to the north side of the Frosttown Road, leaving the 17th South Carolina to complete the hastily formed line to the south.

While the 12th Reserves, on the left of Gallagher's brigade, smashed into the right of the 3rd Alabama, the 7th Reserves and the right wing of the 8th Reserves, moving by the right oblique charged into the corn north of the road. Bates Alexander of the 7th Reserves followed his company into the action despite a strong temptation to "get lost" among the rustling stalks to enjoy his peaches.[93] A solid shot from Lane's gun several hundred feet to the southwest sent the right wing of the 8th Reserves into the cornfield on the downward slope along the northern bank of the road.[94] The left wing pushed the Holcombe Legion back.

Captain S. A. Durham (23rd South Carolina) advanced his regiment a short distance down the slope where he ran into the retreating Holcombe Legion and the 26th Alabama as they fled the field in the face of overwhelming Yankee troops. The captain quickly pulled his regiment back into the line on the left of the 22nd South Carolina, where he attempted to rally the remnants of the 26th Alabama. Federal troops continued to move through the corn toward the base of the mountain. Colonel Peter F. Stevens ordered a general advance into the gorge. The Rebels had almost reached the stone wall at the base of the mountain when the 7th Reserves and the right wing of the 8th Reserves broke into the open ground southwest of the cornfield. A handful of Southerners from their command reached the fence and opened fire upon the Northerners at under fifty yards. Their rounds ineffectively clattered through the cornfield behind the Pennsylvanians. The angered Yankees halted to reform. Screaming at the tops of their voices, they charged the wall before the Confederates could reload.

The Confederates frantically scrambled up the hillside to their three regiments, which peppered the Reserves as they crawled over the stone wall. Captain Cyrus Conner (Company D, 8th Reserves) and Lieutenant William M. Carter (Company B, 8th Reserves) were crossing it together when a bullet thudded into Carter's forehead and threw him onto his back—dead.[95] His premonition had come true.

A Rebel skirmisher to the north, about half way up the mountainside, deliberately propped his rifle on the top of a large boulder and squeezed off a

MAP 52: *The Frostown Road to the Zittlestown Road—September 14, 1862.*
On the right, Stevens' (Evans') South Carolina brigade fails to turn back the Pennsylvania Reserves.
On the left, the Confederates prepare their defense on the crest of South Mountain.

round. The bullet, which passed through and mortally wounded Private Geattings (Company H, 4th Reserves), also struck down Private Calvin S. Gay (Company H), who was climbing the hill behind him. The soft lead projectile penetrated Gay's leg below the knee and lodged in his calf. Refusing to quit the field, he staggered back into the fray.

Simultaneously, a minié ball struck Private Isaac D. Cory (Company H) in the chest, and plucked him off his feet. His comrades pulled his blanket roll and overcoat off to examine his wound. The ball fell out from the inside of his blouse, where it had stopped, leaving only a nasty bruise on his chest.

A bullet nicked Private George Woodruff's (Company H) wrist. His blood up, his face streaked with powder, he seemed demonic. When a comrade asked him where he was going, he spat, "After secesh blood and buttons!"

They went after the Rebels' "blood" with a vengeance. When the man who shot Geattings and Gay tried to scale over the rocks behind him, a fusillade of no less than thirty-six rounds thudded into his body. He collapsed in a bloodied heap.[96]

Farther to the left, along the bend in the Frosttown Road Company D of the 8th Reserves became separated from the rest of the regiment. The three South Carolina regiments (18th, 22nd, and 23rd South Carolina) stubbornly held onto their small portion of the mountain by fighting from rock to tree. While they kept the 7th and the 8th Reserves at bay, the 17th South Carolina moved east through a small field south of the Frosttown Road.[97] In the thick smoke the South Carolinians did not see the Yankees on their left flank.

The left wing of the 8th Reserves, having clawed and fallen its way up to the rocky ledge on the edge of the woods to the south, finally caught up with the rest of the command and went prone. The right wing of the 8th Reserves, having pushed back the left of Stevens' brigade, became separated from the rest of the regiment. In the general chaos the men on that end of the line accidentally flanked the 17th South Carolina as it pressed southeast, heading for the southern end of the Reserves' position. Unable to resist such an advantage, the Pennsylvanians poured a devastating fire into the Rebels. At a distance of under thirty paces, they could not easily miss. [Refer to Map 52]

"Poor Fellows!" Sergeant Archibald Hill (Company D, 8th Reserves) lamented, "I almost pitied them, to see them sink down by dozens at every discharge!"

The sergeant deliberately brought down a lanky Rebel who, with his side turned to Hill, was loading his gun. The South Carolinian collapsed between two large rocks. The 17th South Carolina retreated up the mountainside and the 7th Reserves and the 8th Reserves clawed after them, herding them in a northwesterly course toward the crest.

Sergeant Hill loped over to the left to check out his "kill." As the sergeant approached his prey, the Rebel painfully sat himself upright. "...I was convinced he was not dead yet," Hill recollected with some understatement.

When he asked the soldier if he was wounded, the Confederate mournfully nodded. Blood flowed copiously from the entry wound in his neck. The South Carolinian also pointed to a wound in the upper part of his left arm, just above the shoulder. (The round in passing through the arm had lodged in his neck.) Hill informed him he was a prisoner and turned him over to one of his own men to escort him to the rear before rejoining the fight.[98]

A little farther to the right, Private Bates Alexander (Company C, 7th Reserves) could not believe how quickly the South Carolinian opposition faded away. The Confederates dodged from tree to tree. The battle devolved into bushwhacking more than any type of "civilized" warfare. To Alexander's left front, he noticed a couple of Rebels who were squatted down behind a large rock and sighting in on the center of the regiment. Finding himself a short distance in advance of his own men, the private kneeled down in a small open spot and drew a bead on the two. He was anxious to try out his homemade cartridge.

The report deafened him. The recoil slammed him onto his back. Bates Alexander lay on the ground in a stupor. He thought a cannon ball had struck him on the right side, breaking his right shoulder and tearing away the right side of his face. It took him several minutes to regain his senses. By then, his regiment had passed around him and had gone further up the mountain.[99]

Stevens' South Carolinians could not withstand the pressure. In less than an hour his brigade of about five hundred fifty effectives had lost more than two hundred officers and men.[100] The 17th South Carolina left sixty one of its one hundred forty-one soldiers upon the field, among them Major R. Stark Means. Colonel Fitz W. McMaster (17th South Carolina), realizing that Means was not among his troops, sent four men after him. The major, who was crippled with a severe thigh wound, rather than risk their capture, sent them back. He expected to follow his father, Colonel John H. Means, who had died less than a month earlier at the Second Manassas.[101]

The 23rd South Carolina, on the brigade's right front, came out of the gorge with twenty-four fewer men than it went in with.[102] Captain S. A. Durham (Company H), who led the men into the fight, was among the wounded. When he fell, Captain D. R. McCallum (Company F) took over. In the uphill skirmishing, a Yankee put a bullet through his cap. Pointing the Yankee out, he directed Private Samuel Windham to drop the fellow but the Yankees got Windham instead. He limped away with a bullet wound. As the regiment regrouped in the encroaching darkness on the top of the mountain and attempted to rally on Rodes' right, Captain McCallum picked up Sergeant W. Priestly Colclough (Company K), who was ill with pneumonia, and carried him back into the woods to cover.[103]

On the regiment's right flank, the Federals killed Lieutenant Colonel Thomas C. Watkins (22nd South Carolina) and broke the regiment. They inflicted seventy-one casualties upon the South Carolinians before they reached the top of the ridge. Major Miel Hilton (22nd South Carolina) valiantly tried to rally the men three times but could not because the Pennsylvanians were pressing them too closely.[104]

By the time they came up on the right of Rodes' brigade so few remained in their ranks that Rodes referred to them as "some South Carolina stragglers."[105] Colonel John Gordon's 6th Alabama remained the only Confederate regiment intact upon the northern edge of the ridge. He could not hold out much longer against the overwhelming Federal numbers. The 26th Alabama on his right flank went to pieces and scattered when it lost its Colonel Edward A. O'Neal. The Yankees cut off the 3rd Alabama and the left wing of the 5th Alabama. The 6th Alabama with the right wing of the 5th Alabama started to fall back upon the 12th Alabama, which, having come upon the field with Stevens' brigade, had formed on the South Carolinians' left flank.[106]

To the northwest, the 13th Pennsylvania Reserves and Companies A, B, C, D, and E of the 6th Pennsylvania Reserves slowly forced the 6th Alabama south upon Rodes' main line. They drove the Rebels from one ledge onto the left flank of the 12th Alabama, which by then had been joined by a small portion of the 3rd Alabama.[107]

In the fading light, General Robert Rodes, Colonel Briston B. Gayle, and Lieutenant Colonel Samuel B. Pickens (12th Alabama) stood in front of their regiment, peering into the dark woods trying to ascertain what was going on below them.

"What troops are those?" Rodes asked.

"I don't know, sir, I'll see," Gayle anxiously replied. Staring over the rocks onto the hillside, he exclaimed, "My God, it is the Pennsylvania Reserves!"[108]

Hearing his alarm, one of the Yankees called out for him to surrender.

Gayle quickly drew his revolver and fired point-blank into the Pennsylvanians. "We are flanked, boys," he screamed, "but let's die in our tracks."

Seconds later, he perished as he desired, riddled by a dozen musket balls. Lieutenant Colonel Pickens reeled and fell to the ground with a bullet through his lungs. His men picked him up and carried him south toward the National Pike. The 12th Alabama and the 3rd Alabama gave way and started to retire from the field. The 7th Pennsylvania Reserves gained the hilltop opposite them and cut them down mercilessly. The Confederates returned fire. Colonel Henry C. Bolinger (7th Reserves) caught a ball in the ankle and Major Chauncey A. Lyman assumed command.

He was overwrought. Trooping the front of the regiment, pistol in hand, while the men shot their ammunition away in the darkness, he warned them, "...if any man attempts to run I'll blow his brains out."

Bates Alexander (7th Reserves) and the men within immediate reach of the major stepped aside and gave him plenty of room to carry on so foolishly. A bullet cutting through the brush near the private's right ankle temporarily took his attention away from his commanding officer.[109]

On the left, the sniping continued. Sergeant Archibald Hill of the 8th Reserves nearly bought the farm when he stumbled upon a huge Rebel who saw him first. The sergeant hurled himself behind a rock the second the Confederate fired. The bullet zinged off the stone above his head.

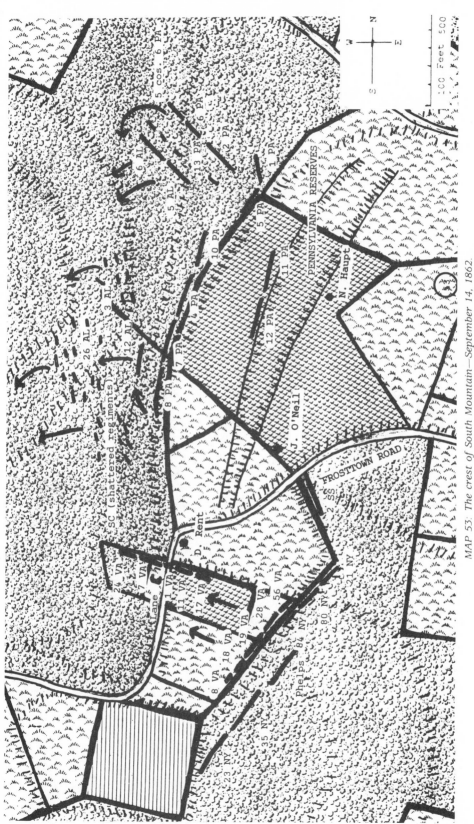

MAP 53: *The crest of South Mountain—September 14, 1862. On the left, Phelps and Patrick secure the woodline on the top of the mountain. On the right, the Pennsylvania Reserves turn Rodes' flanks and halt.*

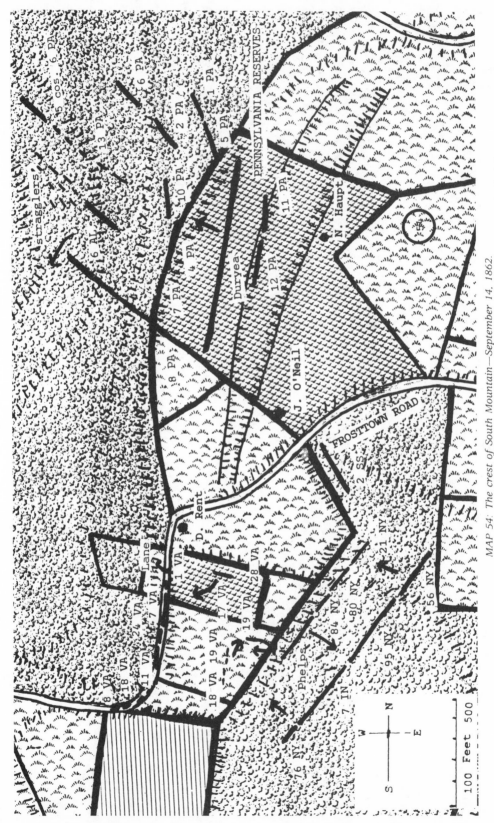

MAP 54: *The crest of South Mountain—September 14, 1862.*
On the right, Rodes' Alabamians quit the fight. On the left, the 76th New York repels the 19th Virginia.

Presently, the rest of the regiment arrived on the line with him. A minié ball struck Dave Malone (Company D) in the head. The impact slammed Malone flat on his back. His good friend, Archibald Hill helplessly watched him quiver and gasp for air until he died.[110]

Simultaneously the 13th Reserves and Companies A, B, C, D, and E of the 6th Reserves pushed further south. They brought the 1st Reserves, 2nd Reserves, 5th Reserves along with them on the left flank.[111]

Lieutenant Colonel Adoniram Warner (10th Reserves) and his regiment completed the line. Bringing up whomever he could find from his regiment, they crashed through the woods onto the ridge from the southeast.

The trapped portion of the 5th Alabama ran into Warner's men in an attempt to escape. Rifle shots stabbed into the darkness. Rebels pitched to the ground. Others threw their arms aside and surrendered. Those who could, broke to the west and the south, trying to get as far away from the front as possible.[112] [Refer to Map 53]

The 6th Alabama, the only regiment which remained intact in Rodes' brigade, reformed behind another rock ledge, allowing the 13th Reserves and the five companies of the 6th Reserves to get well within range. The woods thundered and flashed. The volley knocked down more than fifty Pennsylvanians. It stymied their advance and attracted the attention of a large number of stragglers whom General Rodes and Colonel Cullen A. Battle (3rd Alabama) were trying to rally. They fell in on Gordon's flank and started to enfilade the 6th Reserves, which then directed more of its fire upon them than upon Gordon's men.[113] Suddenly from the east, a fresh Federal brigade appeared along the crest.

General Abram Duryea's brigade (97th, 104th, and 105th New York, and 107th Pennsylvania), having just quick marched from the base of the mountain, arrived after dark. On the way, Duryea's men picked up about sixty prisoners. As they gained the crest, they passed around the exhausted 10th Reserves and drove whatever resistance which remained from the north ridge. Within a few minutes, the Rebels, who responded to their muzzle flashes, inflicted about twenty-one casualties.[114] [Refer to Map 54]

For the most part, the Yankees wasted their ammunition. Rodes' and Stevens' brigades were retiring south toward the National Pike.[115] The hour and a half of battle cost Rodes too many men: sixty-one killed, one hundred fifty-seven wounded, and two hundred four missing. The South Carolina brigade, involved for an hour or less, fared as badly: two hundred sixteen casualties—about seven men per minute.

Meade's Reserve division and Duryea's brigade, because they were attacking up hill, did not do as poorly as the Confederates. The fighting cost them four hundred thirteen men. A disproportionate number of them were line officers. The Confederates killed seven captains and lieutenants and wounded sixteen more.[116]

The regiments posted their pickets. Casualty clearing began at once. In the darkness, neither side had an exact idea of how deadly the contest had been. They only found fragments, as it were, scattered all over the mountainside and the gorge.

Private Otis Smith (Company F, 6th Alabama) lay on the ground too weak to walk. General Truman Seymour, whom the Alabamian mistook for John Reynolds, the division's former commander, rode up to him and asked him where the 6th Alabama's second position had been. Smith did not give him a satisfactory answer.

"You seem to be a pretty intelligent man to know so little, taking you for an officer," Seymour shot back.

"I am only a private, and know nothing," Smith snarled. "If I did, you think I ought to tell you?"

Truman Seymour smiled. Calling over his brigade surgeon, he ordered him to tend to Smith's wounds as best as he could. The doctor quickly wrapped Smith's two wounds and gave him a large swig of imported French brandy. Satisfied he had done his gentlemanly duty, Seymour turned to reassure Smith with a final request, "Is there anything else I can do for you?"

"Can't you send me to the foot of the mountain?" the Alabamian insisted somewhat groggily, "I don't want to die up here among the rocks."

The general summoned a stretcher crew and rode away.[117]

Private Bates Alexander (Company C, 7th Reserves) meandered down the Frosttown Road hoping to get some water to kill his thirst. Instead he stumbled across five disabled Confederates all lying quite close to one another. The private groped about in the darkness trying to determine the extent of their injuries. He grabbed the first one by the foot and carefully ran his fingers over the man's boot. A minié ball had smashed through his foot above the instep and exited through his heel. The boot heel dangled limply from the sole.

The second man, a young fellow named William H. Miller (Company A, Holcombe Legion), begged Alexander to prop up his broken leg with some stones to relieve his intense pain. A musket ball had snapped it in two below the knee. Two of the others were hurt too badly to walk but did not complain. They merely told Alexander not to step on them.

Off to his left, he heard someone groaning horribly.

"Who are you?" Bates Alexander cautiously asked, as he approached the noise.

"Oh, I am a Southern man, a rebel as you call us."

"How can you tell what I am?" the frightened Pennsylvanian asked.

"Oh, I can tell by your voice."

The private walked more cautiously toward him; he feared an ambush. "Are you one of those fellows who fight to the last, and are ready to stab or shoot when I may be close enough?"

"Oh, no, I couldn't shoot anyone if I wanted to, I am unable to move."

Alexander pulled his hammer on his weapon back to full cock as he moved by the Rebel's side. The Southerner valiantly suppressed his groans until

Alexander placed his hand upon the man's chest and asked him if he had any arms.

"No," the wounded man whimpered before telling the Yankee to feel his belt.

After frisking the man, Alexander let down his guard. The injured Confederate lay on his back across a large rock, with his feet dangling over the edge.

Alexander asked him where he was hit.

"I am shot in the back, and I don't think I will ever get well. I can't move my legs, they are numb all the way down."

The still suspicious Yankee wanted to know where the man had thrown his gun. He found it close by the rock—a carbine. Did the Reb have anything to eat? he queried.

"There is some poorly made bread in my haversack," the Reb told him.

Bates Alexander found it about three paces from the rock. He asked the Reb to swap it for some hard crackers because he wanted a change in his diet.

"Take it all, and welcome, for I don't think I shall ever need any of it."

The Pennsylvanian slipped four hard crackers into the Confederate's haversack in exchange for the bread. While trying to make small talk, he asked the Southerner to identify his regiment.

"I belong to the Holcombe Legion of South Carolina."

"How came you in the service," the Pennsylvanian quietly asked him, "are you a volunteer?"

"Oh, yes," the South Carolinian grimaced, " I was a student; most of the others had enlisted, and so did I. Now I am wounded nigh unto death, lying unattended on this rock."

"Is there anything I can do for you?"

"No, unless you bring me some water in my canteen."

The saddened Yankee placed the canteen along the rock, within reach of the dying Confederate. His arms were the only part of his body he could move. Bates Alexander placed a stone beneath the man's head and, bidding the man goodbye, walked off into the darkness.[118]

Not too far away, Captain Cyrus L. Conner (Company D, 8th Reserves) found a Confederate major in dress uniform huddled next to a rock. The ghastly wound in his thigh caused him too much pain for him to conceal.

"You are wounded, are you not?" Conner asked as he stepped up to the officer.

"Yes, in the thigh," the officer grimaced through clenched teeth, "and badly."

"May I inquire your name?"

"I am Major Means, of the Seventeenth South Carolina. May I ask you the same question?"

"I am Captain Conner, of the Eighth Pennsylvania Reserves."

"The—the—Pennsylvania Reserves!" he stuttered in his pain.

"Yes."

"Well, captain, your men fight like devils; they are driving our men up this steep mountain; I never could have believed it!" he exclaimed.

"Ah, major, there is blood in Pennsylvania as well as in South Carolina," Conner said with self-satisfaction.

"I am convinced of that," Means responded.[119]

Cyrus Conner left the proud Confederate to shiver alone in the cold night air. The regiment bagged fifty Confederates during their last charge—not bad for a day's work.[120]

Private Frank Holsinger (Company F, 8th Reserves) bedded down on the rocky ground without his blanket. Despite the freezing night air, he felt warm inside. He wrapped his blanket around a disabled Confederate with a shattered ankle. He could not leave the poor, quaking boy to freeze to death, alone on the mountainside. He could still hear the boy's tender thanks for showing him such great charity.[121]

The battle was over on the Pennsylvanians' end of the line and the men rejoiced over it. While their officer stumbled around in the woods trying to connect their regimental lines, a large number of the enlisted men handed out their blankets to injured Rebels.[122] Others, like Reuben W. Shell, the color bearer of the 7th Reserves, were glad to be alive.

"Dear father," he wrote a week later, "I do not care about getting into any more Battles."[123]

Lieutenant Colonel Adoniram J. Warner (10th Reserves) stretched out next to a large tree, too elated to sleep. Staring into the clear sky, he marveled how it seemed as if he could actually touch it. He did not, until that moment, realize how depressed he had been before the battle. "We had beaten the Rebs by sheer hard fighting," he recollected. He finally believed in the supremacy of the Union and its ultimate victory.[124]

The Confederates did not want to renew the battle in the northern end of the field, either. James Monroe Thompson (Company G, 6th Alabama) sadly recorded his small company's losses: eight men killed, one officer mortally wounded, six enlisted men wounded, and one missing. It was a terrible price for such a stubborn defense when one considered the company lost two pairs of brothers on the mountainside. John A. and Lewis M. Whetstone and Henry and John Carter were lying—dead—somewhere along the bloodied north ridge.[125]

THE BATTLE BETWEEN THE NATIONAL PIKE AND THE FROSTTOWN ROAD

To the south, the engagement, which had gotten under way shortly before 4:00 P.M., by 6:00 P.M. had increased in its fury.[126] Brigadier General Marsena Patrick and his four regiments, leading John Hatch's division, arrived at Mount Tabor Church around 3:30 P.M., where they encountered their corps commander, Major General Joseph Hooker. Having just deployed Meade's division by courier, he told Patrick to send out one regiment as skirmishers to cover their left flank on the southern side of the Frosttown Road gorge. Patrick passed the command to his first regiment, the 21st New York.[127]

Colonel William F. Rogers' New Yorkers (154 men) stripped off their knapsacks along the road. Three companies from each flank fanned out to the west, followed by the remaining four companies as a reserve.[128] The men moved out slowly across the rolling fields toward the foothill leading up toward the crest of the southern spur of the mountain—a distance of about eight hundred yards. Marsena Patrick turned his back upon the regiment and rode back toward the Old Hagerstown Road where he encountered Brigadier General John Hatch, the new division commander. As the New Yorkers headed west, instead of northwest toward the Frosttown Road, the general ordered Patrick to advance the rest of his brigade (the 35th, 23rd and 80th New York) to their support.

The impatient Patrick led the 35th New York forward, not giving the men time to remove their cumbersome knapsacks.[129] In his haste, he did not attempt to hold back the 21st New York, which continued to inch its way up the slope to the right. At intervals a man or two crouched down and scanned the rectangular patch of woods which extended west, up the mountainside toward the farm road which paralleled the Old Hagerstown Road and connected the National Pike with the Frosttown Road. Every moment they expected the wood line beyond that lane to erupt into a sheet of sulfur and flame. As they fanned out in their approach toward J. Sheffer's house, they flushed an elderly woman.[130] Running into the line, she grabbed an officer and frantically asked the New Yorkers where they were going.

"Only going up the hill," the officer replied rather sheepishly.

"Don't you go there," she cried out while waving the soldiers back with her hands. "There are hundreds of 'em up there. Don't you go. *Some of you will get hurt!*"

The dust encrusted Yankees grinned at her and silently slipped up the mountain to the lane north of C. Beachley's. Resting in the road, they glanced back at their support troops and wondered where they were. So did their brigadier, Marsena Patrick.[131]

Part way through the field east of Sheffer's the general noticed, much to his embarrassment, that his two remaining regiments had not yet left the Old Hagerstown Road. He left orders with Colonel Newton B. Lord of the 35th New York to extend his regiment (about 280 men) in skirmish order, advance to the ridge, and connect with the National Pike and the left flank of the 21st New York. Turning his back upon the 35th New York, he spurred back to the Old Hagerstown Pike and wasted time bullying Colonel Henry C. Hoffman's regiment, the 23rd New York, (about 280 men) into line of battle. The general then wheeled about, only to discover, with disgust, that Lieutenant Colonel Theodore B. Gates (80th New York) and his reluctant command still remained back at the Old Hagerstown Road awaiting specific instructions. After considerable "prodding," as Marsena Patrick grumbled in his diary, he finally got the 80th New York on line to the right of the 23rd New York.[132]

By then, around 5:00 P.M., Brigadier General James Kemper arrived at Turner's Gap with his small brigade (1st, 7th, 11th, 17th, and 24th Virginia), about four hundred men, ahead of Brigadier General Richard B. Garnett's brigade (8th, 18th, 19th, 28th, and 56th Virginia) and Colonel Joseph Walker's brigade (1st, 2nd Rifles, 5th, and 6th South Carolina, 4th South Carolina Battalion, and Palmetto Sharpshooters).[133] Kemper and his staff, with the brigade a short distance behind, rode north along the Frosttown Road to the northern edge of the small cornfield near the north-east bend in the road. As the command advanced in column of fours, Durell's Pennsylvania battery, which was on the open ground across the National Pike gorge, opened upon them with solid shot and shell. The Yankees pounded the road, disrupting the 1st Virginia, which was leading the brigade. For a minute or two, Private John Dooley (Company A) thought they would break.[134] A spent ten-pound shell struck Private John H. Daniel of Company H on the rump and hurled him about ten feet into the air, but did not seriously injure him. Dooley felt terribly helpless and frightened. The regiment had not loaded its weapons. The shells were splintering the big rocks in the woods on the left flank, showering the road with deadly shards.[135] One of the rounds burst in the 7th Virginia's lead company, killing one man instantly.[136]

Up ahead, James L. Kemper and his staff inadvertently came under fire from the 8th Pennsylvania Reserves, which was volleying into the 17th South Carolina to his left front.[137] He directed Captain John Beckham, his aide, to bring up the brigade, which was in the road about one hundred yards south of his position.

Returning to the column, the captain deployed the regiments for battle. The 17th Virginia (71 men) held the right of the line with the 11th Virginia (95 men) to its left. The 1st Virginia (23 men) held the center and straddled the Frosttown Road. The 7th Virginia (132 men) and the 24th Virginia (about 79 men) completed the formation in the woods west of the road.[138]

While marching through the open woods on the left of the road and across the open ground on the right, the regiments lost contact with each other. Colonel Montgomery B. Corse (17th Virginia) detached Lieutenant Francis W. Lehew and his Company B to the right front into the woods to engage the Federals whom he thought were there.[139] [Refer to Map 52]

By the time Marsena Patrick finally brought the 23rd New York and the 80th New York up to the rear of the 35th New York, he discovered a gap between the right flank of the 35th New York and the left flank of the 21st New York. Due to a misunderstanding of his orders, Colonel Newton Lord of the 35th New York extended his regiment as far as the National Pike, which left an interval of more than one thousand yards between it and the 21st New York.[140] The 23rd New York halted to support the 35th New York, while Patrick sent the 80th New York north along the farm lane, which parallelled the Old Hagerstown Road, to support Colonel William F. Rogers' 21st New York.[141] Leaving orders for the 35th to close on the left of his line and press north, he and his aide took off into the woods on the slope to reconnoiter his position.

Moving northwest through the woods, well in advance of the 21st New York, which remained in the road near C. Beachley's, the two officers accidentally rode into Lieutenant Lehew and his skirmishers from the 17th Virginia.

"Gray Coats!" the aide screamed.

The two officers wheeled their horses to the right and bolted east, down hill, while a scattered volley chipped the bark off the trees over their heads. Riding back to the 21st New York, he ordered it and the 80th New York to the front.[142]

While they advanced, Colonel Walter Phelps, Jr. brought his brigade (22nd, 24th, and 30th New York, and 84th New York [14th Brooklyn]) onto the road and deployed in battle formation without making contact with the 80th New York. General Abner Doubleday's brigade (7th Indiana, 76th and 95th New York, 56th Pennsylvania) followed in column of divisions (two company front) two hundred paces behind.[143] In his haste, Colonel Phelps pushed his brigade too far beyond the farm road only to find himself ahead of Patrick's skirmishers, who were on his flanks. He halted his men and sent one of his two aides back to General John Hatch, the division commander, to find out what he was to do next.[144]

The Virginians along the mountain crest took the initiative. The 24th Virginia, 7th Virginia, and part of the 1st Virginia moved onto the wooded slope on the left of the Frosttown Road. The rest of the 1st Virginia and the 11th Virginia moved to the northern border of the cornfield east of the road.[145] While examining his line, the general heard Lieutenant Lehew's party open fire upon General Patrick and his orderly. His line was incomplete. The Yankee artillery south of the National Pike gorge temporarily stalled Colonel Montgomery Corse and his 17th Virginia as it attempted to cross the stubble field south of the cornfield. The general dispatched Captain John Beckham to fetch the regiment.

Beckham put the 17th Virginia into position on the right of the 11th Virginia.[146] The move left a two hundred yard interval between the brigade's right flank and the wooded crest of the mountain. John Lane's guns, from a slight elevation of ground on the western edge of the cornfield, opened fire over the prone infantry into the Pennsylvania Reserves who were swarming the hillside and the gorge to the north.[147]

Brigadier General Richard Garnett's exhausted brigade (8th, 18th, 19th, 28th, and 56th Virginia), having halted at the Mountain House to regain its breath and reform, found itself short handed. Only four hundred officers and men remained in the ranks. The remaining half of the brigade lay along the National Pike and along the Boonsboro Pike too exhausted from nearly twelve hours of marching and countermarching to keep up with their comrades. After a few minutes, an orderly ordered them north along the Frosttown Road. The Virginians walked into the tail end of the Yankee plunging fire from across the National Pike gorge. The shells seemed to follow the brigade across the field as it diverted northeast toward the secure looking tree line on the horizon.

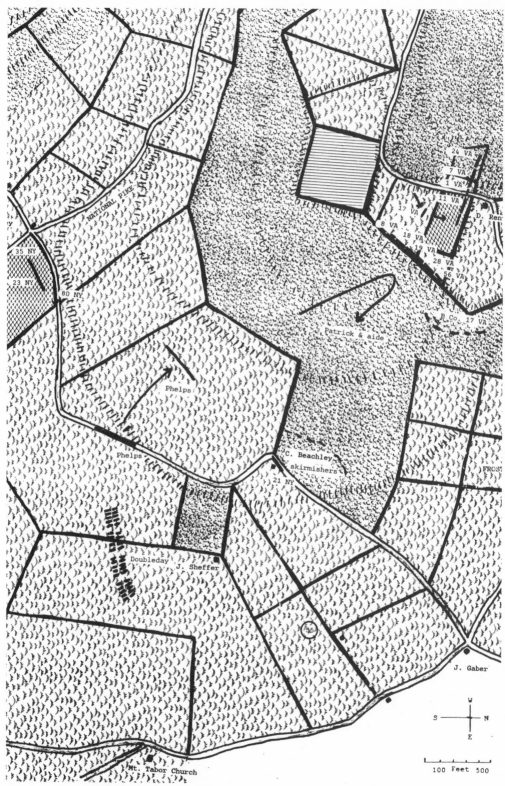

MAP 55: *The base of South Mountain northwest of Bolivar Crossroads—September 14, 1862. Patrick's brigade makes contact with Kemper's skirmishers.*

Captain Henry T. Owen (Company C, 18th Virginia), whose regiment was the next to the last in the column, almost lost his life to a chance round. The projectile burst over the broken down fence along the road a milli-second after he leaped over it. The horrendous concussion hurled the fence rails through the air like twigs and wounded four of the six men in his company. The two remaining men and the captain chased after the regiment and caught up with it at the rock ledge which ran through the tree line.[148]

Skirmishers melted into the trees to the left front, leaving the right of the brigade unprotected. The intrepid Captain John Beckham pulled the 56th Virginia (57 men) away from the head of the column and herded it toward the right of the 17th Virginia. The 28th Virginia (95 men) and the 19th Virginia (150 men) anchored themselves behind the stone wall which parallelled the crest and the wooded summit. An open field bordered by stone wall about fifty-four feet wide separated them from Kemper's brigade in the cornfield behind them. The 18th Virginia (81 men) and the 8th Virginia (24 men) extended the formation in a very thin line along the face of the woods to the southwest.[149]

The shadows became more pronounced in the increasing darkness. To the north, the fighting inched its way up the Frosttown Road gorge, where the Pennsylvania Reserves were pushing back Rodes' and Stevens' brigades. Bullets clattered through the corn over the heads of Kemper's prone men, making a noise like flushed game. The woods in front of Garnett's four right regiments boomed and flashed sporadically as the opposing skirmishers snapped off rounds at each other. [Refer to Map 55]

Curses and howls echoed back over the Confederate lines from the east, indicating the approach of a large Yankee force. The Confederate skirmishers wisely rejoined their regiments on the left of Garnett's troops without firing a shot.

The 21st and the 80th New York, in line from north to south, with typical Union bookish discipline, maintained as near a perfect skirmish formation as the terrain allowed. The steep, rocky, wooded hillside did not conform to the parade ground plain described in the drill manual. Every fifteen to twenty paces, the two regiments halted to realign themselves.[150] Their northwesterly route carried them through about one thousand eight hundred feet of woods, all of it up hill, and, at their rate of speed, probably required around forty-eight readjustments.[151] On their right, unnoticed, the 2nd U.S. Sharpshooters, operating under orders from General Hatch, cautiously scrambled up the hill on the southern side of the Frosttown Road, following almost the exact track taken by the 8th Reserves a short time before. (Hatch detached the sharpshooters from Phelps' brigade when he noticed, much to his ire, the 21st New York stray too far south of its original objective—the gorge to the north.)

Farther to the left, Colonel Walter Phelps, whose men had patiently waited until the 21st New York and the 80th New York cleared their line by ninety feet, urged his horse over the tortuous ground to within a short distance of the cleared ground beyond the woods. Finding he could approach the Rebels unobserved, he rode back to his regiments and ordered them to the front.[152] As he did so, General Patrick personally led the 21st New York and the 80th New York forward toward the left front of the 28th Virginia.[153]

With the line in motion, Patrick threaded his horse through the woods in a southeasterly direction down the mountainside. He passed behind Phelps' brigade (22nd, 24th, 30th, and 84th New York) to bring in the 23rd New York and the 35th New York, which had, once again, strayed too far to the left.[154]

For about five minutes, the pitifully small 18th Virginia (76 men), near Garnett's right flank, patiently rested. One of the enlisted men peeked over the rock ledge through a partially overgrown section of open woods on the regiment's right front.

"Major Cabell," he quietly drawled while pointing, "yonder is a Yankee."

George C. Cabell stared over the natural parapet to his front and sighted a lone Federal clumping around the large trees about two hundred yards off.

"Come in here and surrender, you blue bellied rascal, or by gum I will have you shot," he brashly hollered.

"He is coming," one of the Virginians crowed when the Yankee, unperturbed, stepped into the open fully armed.

Another Virginian chimed in, with a hint of surprise in his voice, "There is two or three Yankees down there coming this way."

"Whoee," a fellow nearby whistled through his teeth, "just look at em."

Captain Henry T. Owen of the 18th Virginia gasped at what he saw. A profound silence overwhelmed the Virginians. The extended line, which the apprehensive Owen overestimated at about a mile in length, steadily worked its way up the hill toward the crest. Behind it, to the southeast, Phelps' brigade, with the 84th New York (14th Brooklyn) on the right, moved up without seeming to break pace. The Virginians fired a panicky volley.[155] Their bullets rattled through the branches above the New Yorkers' head like hail, showering them with pieces of bark, twigs, and leaves.[156]

Their fire triggered a counter strike from Phelps' New Yorkers. General Hatch spurred his horse among them and, with a deafening shout, they charged the crest of the mountain. Passing over the skirmish line, the combined brigades quickly scrambled to within one hundred thirty feet of the rocky ledge at the edge of the woods.[157] Lieutenant Colonel Theodore B. Gates (80th New York), whose regiment was to the left rear, opened fire first. Seconds later, Walter Phelps' four regiments (252 men) came into position.[158]

Bullet for bullet, the Rebels slugged it out with the Yankees. Their volleys gouged holes in the Northern formation. Walter Phelps lost almost thirty-five percent of his effective strength in fifteen minutes. Convinced that he faced a much larger force, he decided to attack rather than get whittled away piece meal.[159] As he gave the command to charge, a bullet struck General Hatch in the leg. Despite his severe wound, he decided to remain upon the field.[160] By then Marsena Patrick arrived with the 35th New York and the 23rd New York.[161]

Their appearance spooked the 8th Virginia and the 18th Virginia. Captain Henry T. Owen of the 18th Virginia believed the Federals outnumbered them ten to one, but he was not going to stay around for a more exact count.[162] The two regiments, combined, sustained almost forty-five percent casualties.[163]

Unable to withstand any more of the beating, the Virginia brigade broke and ran. Clusters of men halted sporadically to return fire or to shout defiantly at their pursuers.[164] Part of the 19th Virginia retreated as far as a thicket about two hundred ten feet west of the wood line. The rest of the regiment and the survivors of the 28th Virginia ran to the rear and the cover of the stone wall on the eastern edge of the cornfield.[165] The New Yorkers hurled themselves against the eastern berm of the ledge below the Confederates' line of sight. Colonel Phelps, following the lead of the 80th New York and the 21st New York, ordered the 84th New York (14th Brooklyn) northeast along the edge of the woods so they could enfilade the cornfield in front of them.[166]

The men of the 21st New York lay down along the rocky ledge near the easterly bend in the Frosttown Road. On the right the New Yorkers watched the 11th Reserves envelop part of Rodes' Alabamians as they fled south under increased pressure from Truman Seymour's brigade. They marveled at the swiftness of the maneuver. The Pennsylvanians sprang upon the Confederates from a ravine and after a very brief struggle pulled off what Colonel William Rogers (21st New York) bragged was "one of the most brilliant little achievements of the war."[167] [Refer to Map 53]

The increased activity attracted the attention of Captain John Lane's detached guns northwest of the cornfield. Their muzzle flashes drew rifle fire from the 21st New York. Artillery men dropped to the ground. Each time the guns roared, the crews rolled them by hand back into the woods to reload. They managed to loose several rounds before the New Yorkers picked off too many of their men and silenced them.[168] In the poor light, they mistook Kemper's prone regiments for skirmishers.[169]

John Dooley (Company A, 1st Virginia), who had hastily loaded his rifle on the run, hugged the ground, trying not to get killed by the incoming rounds to which he could not respond. Beyond accurate range in the twilight, the Pennsylvania Reserves swarmed around and over the fences and the gorge to the north. He did everything he could to suppress his overwhelming desire to skedaddle.[170] No orders came down the line to return fire, but when they arrived to retreat to the Frosttown Road, he did not hesitate to comply.

Colonel Montgomery Corse of the 17th Virginia heard the firing on the extreme right roll closer. Most of it seemed to strike the eastern end of the cornfield. Without any targets to his front, he decided his men would ride it out.

The incoming rounds from the 80th New York proved too much. Colonel William Stuart (56th Virginia) crashed through the corn to Colonel Corse and breathlessly gasped that the right flank had collapsed. Quickly checking the left flank, Corse sadly noticed the rest of the brigade (1st, 7th, and 24th Virginia) had retired to a new position in the woods west of the Frosttown Road. After contacting Major Adam Clement (11th Virginia) on his left, he quickly and effectively retired the two regiments to the cover of the double stone walls along the Frosttown Road.[171]

On the right of the Confederate line, the 8th Virginia and part of the 18th Virginia (about 30 men) regrouped with Colonel Eppa Hunton. Fifty feet separated that part of the "line" from Captain Henry Owen and his twelve to fifteen men of the 18th Virginia. Sixty feet farther north he thought he detected a squad of about a dozen men. One hundred yards beyond, Major George Cabell of the 18th Virginia and General Richard Garnett managed to herd approximately one hundred more soldiers into the Frosttown Road.

Across the stubble field, the Yankees halted behind the eastern side of the stone wall along the woods' edge. Much to the amazement of the exhausted Henry Owen, the Yankees halted to "huzzah" and scream at them. The captain hoped for reinforcements to materialize in the night to drive the Yankees off. He also thanked the Federals for giving the scattered Rebel regiments time to regroup. It was considerate of them.[172]

Walter Phelps ordered his brigade adjutant to find Doubleday's brigade and bring it up.[173] The officer located the regiments a short distance below the crest of the ridge spread out in an impressive battle line more than one thousand feet long. The 76th New York (65 men) held the left of the line. The 7th Indiana (about 358 men), 95th New York (about 358 men), and then the 56th Pennsylvania (246 men) finished out the formation to the north.[174] The adjutant caught the 95th New York in the middle of a foraging expedition in a small cultivated field.[175]

"Our brigade cannot sustain itself much longer as we are nearly out of ammunition!" the brigade adjutant blurted. "For God's sake, to the front!"[176] At the call to fall in, Adjutant Edward L. Barnes (95th New York) and his scavengers chucked their turnips aside and rejoined their command.

Near the crest, the ascent became steeper. The adjutant dismounted and, like his regiment, pulled himself up the ledge by grabbing onto tree stumps and saplings. As the line neared the western edge of the timber and Phelps' and Patrick's combined brigades, a volley ripped through the darkness, seemingly in their faces. Abner Doubleday halted the brigade. The command to "fix bayonets" rippled through the ranks followed by the metallic clinking of metal upon metal. With a shout, the brigade bolted and stumbled through the darkness into Phelps' line, which fell back to replenish its ammunition.[177]

The Confederates in the cornfield stalled the Yankee counterattack at the three-foot high stone wall along the wood line. Following each of their volleys, they hurled themselves to the ground to reload. The fire seemed to begin with intermittent patters like a drizzle before bursting into violent, thunderous surges. Soldiers staggered from the ranks of the 76th New York. An insidious panic crept into the formation. The soldiers started to mill and bunch up like frightened cattle. Man-by-man the officers relayed the command to cease fire and the regiment finally calmed down.[178]

The volume of the incoming rounds and the extent of the muzzle flashes beyond the Rebels' flank indicated a very large Yankee force to their front. Lieutenant William N. Wood (Company A, 19th Virginia), whose part of the regiment remained in the cornfield with the 28th Virginia, patiently sat out the vicious crossfire from both flanks. The Union line along the regiment's right front, behind a stone wall, pounded the Virginians mercilessly.[179]

Colonel William P. Wainwright (76th New York) ordered his regiment to charge the Confederates' southern flank. The men did not respond quickly enough to suit Color Sergeant Charles E. Stamp (Company A). Angered by the muzzle flashes from the thicket south of the cornfield, and the regiment's sluggishness, he leaped the stone wall and valiantly rushed into the stubble field. He defiantly planted the colors in the ground about sixteen yards from the wall. Waving the line forward, he turned his head toward the woods and screamed, "There, come up to that!" A volley suddenly burst from the cornfield, stabbing the darkness with bolts of flame. A bullet thudded into Stamp's forehead. His body crumbled into the field, the flagstaff clenched in his dead hand.[180]

In the confusion a low murmur rising into a fearful cry traveled through the 76th New York. About a half dozen uninjured men broke formation, and headed rearward. The five remaining company officers rushed upon the demoralized men immediately. With threats of sabering them, they herded the soldiers into the ranks.

Climbing on top of the stone wall Captain George F. Noyes (76th New York), the brigade's officer of commissary of subsistence, tried to calm the panic by screaming, "Why, boys, what are you running for? We've beaten the enemy. Three cheers for victory."

Three feeble "huzzahs" echoed across the open ground. Colonel William Wainwright pranced his horse behind the line, ordering his men to fire low.[181] General Hatch, weakened from his injury, turned over his command to General Doubleday and was leaving the field by the left flank when the small arms fire slackened. From the clump of bushes to the front, the New Yorkers heard, "For God's sake, stop firing! You are killing your own men!"

Hatch overheard them and, as his last act upon the field, ordered a cease fire. The veterans, suspecting a ruse similar to one pulled on them at the Second Manassas, reluctantly complied.[182] The New Yorkers settled down and started to congratulate themselves over their victory, the silence being the only indication that they had achieved one.[183]

Remnants of the 18th Virginia and the 19th Virginia filed by the left flank into the open, fronted and double quicked, without a word of command to the southeast corner of the cornfield.[184] At the same time, someone in the cornfield ordered the left wing of the 19th Virginia to charge.[185] The 76th New York stared in disbelief as the Virginians dropped to their knees and volleyed from sixty feet away into their line. Colonel William Wainwright and his horse went to the ground together, the horse dead and the colonel shot through the arm. Tieing off his arm above the wound, he bawled out the command to fire. A second later, he drew his revolver and bitterly emptied all six chambers into the Confederates.[186]

On the right of the brigade, Adjutant Edward L. Barnes (95th New York), having delivered the command to fire by ranks to the regiment's right wing, climbed the stone fence northeast of the cornfield to better observe the effects. The first volley staggered the Virginians. He did not see the effects of the second one. A musket ball slammed into his left hip, throwing him backwards over the fence as his men loosed their second volley. Crawling dazedly to his hands and knees, then to his feet, he limped behind his men, refusing to leave the field.[187]

The shooting rolled across the cornfield to the north. Captain William Wood (19th Virginia) fell back with a portion of the left wing of the 19th Virginia and the 24th Virginia toward the Frosttown Road.[188] Unsupported Colonel John B. Strange and what remained of the 19th Virginia upon the field vainly tried to outgun the Yankees. Two volleys ended the scrap as quickly as it began. The colonel lay among his casualties—dead.[189] Both of the Sheppard brothers—Mell and Dan (Company B) and Tom Randolph with J. J. Christian (Company A) remained there too, never to carry arms again. James M. Brown (Company F) staggered away with a shattered arm, earning himself the cruel nickname "One-Arm Brown."[190] [Refer to Map 54]

While the 76th New York destroyed the 19th Virginia as a cohesive military unit, the scattered regiments along the Frosttown Road prepared for a counterattack which never developed. On the northern end of the line, the 17th Virginia fired away all of its ammunition.[191] On the southern flank, an enlisted man to the left of Captain Henry T. Owen of the 18th Virginia called out, "General Lee is up here and wants to see some of you officers."

Owen immediately sent a runner to the right who repeated the message to Colonel Hunton (8th Virginia) who ran over to the captain and asked for the general's whereabouts. They found Lee in the stubble field watching the progress of John Strange's suicidal attack. Lee, mounted upon his cherished Traveler, calmly ignored the bullets which sliced through the night air around him.

Colonel Hunton and the captain darted into the open and Owen snatched at Lee's reins, intent upon leading him from the field. The general stopped him.

Addressing the colonel, Lee asked, "Where is General Walker?"

"I don't know."

"Then who commands these troops here?" Lee continued.

"This is Pickett's brigade and [it is] commanded by General Garnett," Eppa Hunton nervously replied. "The enemy is driving us back."

"I will have reinforcements here in time to check them," the general reassured him. "Where is General Garnett? I want to send him a message to get these troops out of this place as quick as he can."

Pointing north, the colonel shouted, "General Garnett is up there to the left where that firing is going on."

The commanding general remained silent for about a minute, thinking. Finally, he coolly inquired, "How many men have you here with you?"

"About thirty or forty," Hunton guessed.

> Take all the men you have here and form a line back there in the road [the National Pike], facing toward the mountain. I have no troops out in that direction and I am afraid these rascally Yankees are going to try to flank us. If you hear any troops coming from that direction fire on them for you may know they belong to the enemy. There is a picket across the road at the gap to stop stragglers and a large number have been stopped there. Send down after them and strengthen your lines along the road over there.

As the general rode to the north to consult with Garnett, Hunton and Owen rounded up their thirty men and trotted down the Frosttown Road toward the National Pike.[192]

Meanwhile, the Yankees continued to shoot at a foe whom they could not see. For an hour they blasted into the blackness of the night.[193] Marsena Patrick grumbled in his diary how his men disgraced themselves by wasting their ammunition upon a nonexistent foe.[194]

Robert E. Lee began his withdrawal from the mountain shortly before 7:00 P.M. by which time his pledged reinforcements, Colonel Joseph Walker's South Carolina brigade (1st, 5th, and 6th South Carolina, 2nd Rifles, 4th South Carolina Battalion, and Palmetto Sharpshooters), rushed into action.[195] Captain Owen remembered seeing Colonel Walker stand in the stirrups while his command double quicked through the stubble field to the left of his patrol as it neared the Gap.

"By brigade, right wheel!" Walker cried out. "Forward, charge bayonet!" reverberated down the mountain before the men had barely executed the original order.[196]

Around 8:00 P.M., the South Carolinians stumbled into the left of the Federal I Corps as Colonel William Christian's (26th, 94th New York, and 88th and 90th Pennsylvania) and General George L. Hartsuff's (12th and 13th Massachusetts, 83rd New York, and 11th Pennsylvania) brigades from James Ricketts' division relieved Abner Doubleday's troops.[197]

While the brigade charged through the bloodied cornfield in the dark, Lieutenant Colonel John M. Steedman (6th South Carolina), whose men were closest to the Yankees, could not identify to which army they belonged.[198] He soon found out.

First Lieutenant James L. Goddard (Company F) 76th New York glanced over his shoulder as the regiment and the 7th Indiana retired east. He called Colonel William Wainwright's attention to the commotion in the cornfield behind him. The colonel responded immediately. He faced the regiments by the rear rank and marched them back up to the stone wall.[199] The South Carolinians did not recognize who was in front of them until they saw the stripes on their National colors.

The two sides volleyed simultaneously into each other. Three South Carolinians died in the furious moment. Uzzel Goodson (Company E, 6th South

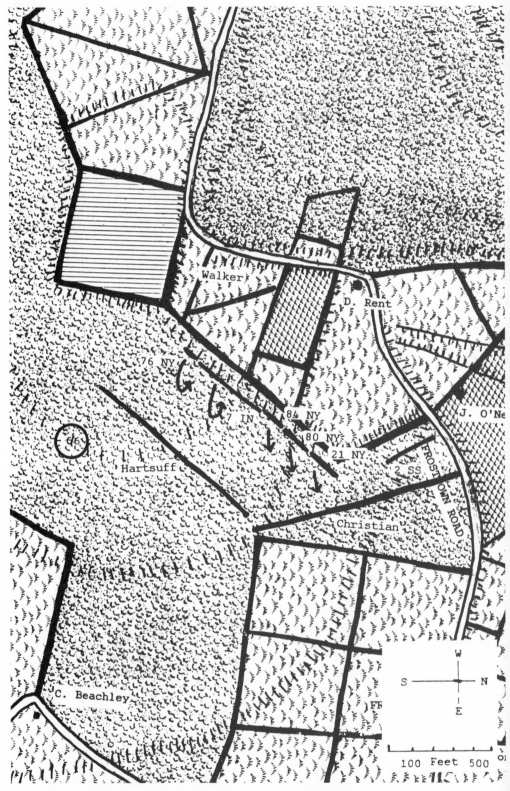

Walker

D. Rent

76 NY

7 IN

84 NY

80 NY

21 NY

2 SS

96

Hartsuff

J. O'Ne

FROSTTOWN ROAD

Christian

C. Beachley

FR

W

S ——————— N

E

100 Feet 500 0

MAP 56: The crest of South Mountain along the Frosttown Road—September 14, 1862.
Walker's South Carolinians make a final assault against the I Corps' troops.

Carolina) and twenty-eight others were wounded.[200] Their musketry sailed too high and plummeted into Ricketts' division as it scrambled up to the stone wall. It rattled the 26th New York on the right of the line as it relieved the 84th New York (14th Brooklyn).

The two regiments were cheering each other when the Confederates attacked.[201] In the dark, the men mistook the 80th New York, which was about one hundred feet to the right front as Confederates, and fired on them and missed. Lieutenant Colonel Theodore Gates (80th New York) promptly chewed out Lieutenant Colonel Richard C. Richardson (26th New York) and directed him to the correct part of the wood line.[202]

All along the brigades' front men dropped out with wounds. A ball struck Captain DeWitt C. Tomlinson (94th New York) in the back of the neck.[203] Another killed a private in the 12th Massachusetts as he struggled up the hillside.[204] Having lost four dead and nine wounded in such a short time the two brigades went into formation and shot into a virtually deserted field.[205] A few rounds came back in response. A spent bullet slammed into Colonel Richard C. Richardson's forehead and jerked him from the saddle, leaving a dent in his skull.[206] The left wing of his regiment wasted twenty cartridges in response.[207] [Refer to Map 56]

Colonel Joseph Walker's South Carolinians, along with most of Rodes' Confederates, except Colonel Alfred Colquitt's brigade, retired to the National Pike at the Mountain House and formed in an "L" facing north and east.[208] Stragglers and wounded soldiers cluttered the road all the way into Boonsboro.

Captain Owen and Colonel Hunton coaxed about thirty-six skulkers into their "volunteer" formation but had a terrible time trying to strong arm the others into compliance. The officers found themselves literally kicking each reluctant soul to his feet and shoving him along. The captain had collected a little more than a dozen men until he came upon one who would not budge. He futilely pleaded with the fellow to get up.

The stubborn enlisted man cast a determined look of defiance up at the captain.

"There's no use talking about it," he said matter-of-factly, "for I don't care a cent. I am barefooted."

Owen brushed aside the excuse. He recalled seeing the shoeless S. Weaver coolly and conspicuously rallying men along the Frosttown Road. His anger welled up to the killing point.

"I ain't had a mouthful to eat today," the skulker bitterly griped. "I have been a fightin' and a chargin', and a retreatin' ever since sunrise this morning and I believe I have fit over the best half of Maryland so I am done for today. Unless the Yankees come right here I ain't going to fool with them anymore tonight."

Henry Owen threatened to run the soldier through. The soldier deliberately rolled onto his back.

"Captain," he drawled, "you have heard my story and I am no longer useful as a soldier tonight. If you think it right to do so you can just stick your sword through me (placing his hand over his heart) right here."

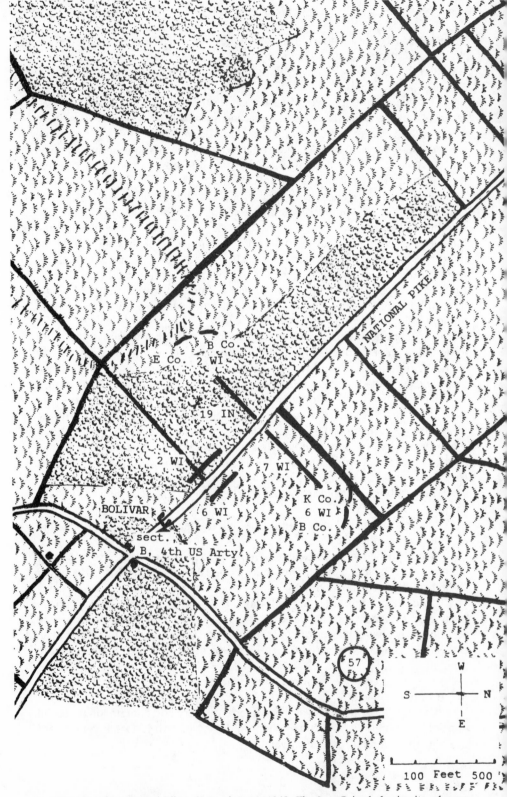

B Co.

E Co. 2 WI

19 IN

2 WI

7 WI

BOLIVAR

6 WI

K Co.
6 WI
B Co.

sect.,
B, 4th US Arty.

NATIONAL PIKE

57

W

S ——————— N

E

100 Feet 500

MAP 57: The National Pike—September 14, 1862. The Iron Brigade begins its advance.

The frustrated captain turned the man over to Colonel Hunton, who after several wasted attempts, left him alone.[209]

Both sides had fought themselves into a stalemate on the northern and southern flanks of Turner's Gap. The valley to the east, however, still crackled and roared with artillery and small arms fire, where Brigadier General John Gibbon's brigade (19th Indiana, 2nd, 6th, and 7th Wisconsin) attempted, rather belatedly, to punch through D. H. Hill's center.

THE BATTLE IN THE NATIONAL PIKE GORGE

General John Gibbon's Westerners spent the afternoon watching the battle from the hillside below the Federal heavy batteries. At 5:30 P.M., Gibbon set his brigade in motion.[210] The 19th Indiana and the 7th Wisconsin formed in line opposite each other. The 2nd Wisconsin and the 6th Wisconsin fell into double columns a short distance behind. When they reached the National Pike, Captain Rollin P. Converse (Company B) and Lieutenant John Ticknor (Company K) from the 6th Wisconsin fanned out to the right front of the 7th Wisconsin.[211] South of the Pike, Companies B and E from the 2nd Wisconsin moved out to cover the front of the 19th Indiana.[212] A section from Company B, 4th U.S. Artillery, under Lieutenant James Stewart, supported the advance from the road.[213] [Refer to Map 57]

As the brigade stepped out, the skirmishers ran into sporadic rifle fire from the half mile long cornfield north of the road.[214] (When the 1st Massachusetts Cavalry abandoned that position to support Meade's extreme right on the Hagerstown Road, Colquitt's skirmishers infiltrated it.)[215] They kept up a lively fire fight through the length of the field. The brigade went prone at the crossroads near D. Beachley's.

A shell from the gap exploded in the ranks of the 2nd Wisconsin, killing four men and severely wounding three. The regiments stood up and rushed into line. On the right of the road, Captain John B. Callis (Company B, 7th Wisconsin) recalled his skirmishers. The 6th Wisconsin, to the rear, moved to within one hundred twenty-five feet of the first line. South of the Pike, Colonel Solomon Meredith (19th Indiana) deployed nineteen-year-old Captain William W. Dudley and his Company B to cover the left flank of the column.[216]

At that point the left of the 19th Indiana came under severe rifle fire from sharpshooters in the upper floor of a cabin, some four hundred yards from the regiment's left front. Colonel Solomon Meredith of the 19th Indiana immediately called for fire support from Lieutenant James Stewart and his two Napoleons. Within a few minutes the gunners had sent three shells into the left side of the gorge. The first shot crashed through the second story of the cabin and sent the Confederates scattering for safer ground.[217] The brigade pushed back Colquitt's skirmishers on both flanks until they came within six hundred yards of J. D. Moore's farm house.

At the same time, Companies B and E of the 2nd Wisconsin came under fire from Captain William M. Arnold's (Company A, 6th Georgia)

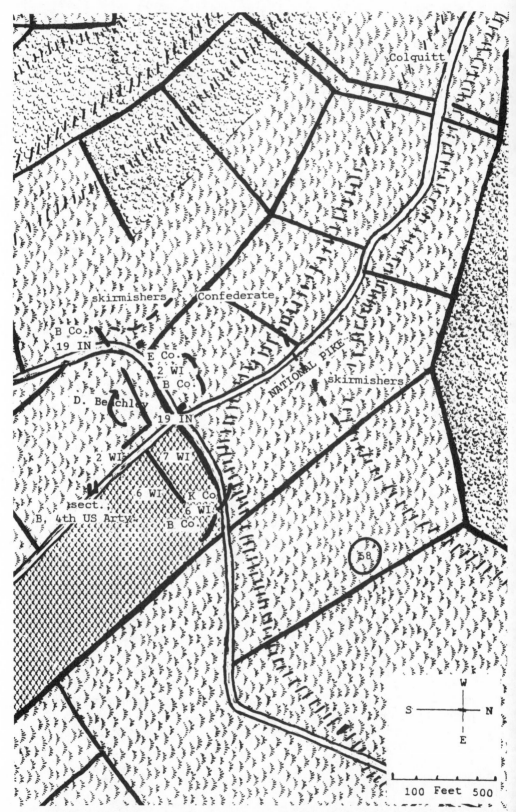

Colquitt

skirmishers   Confederate

B Co.
19 IN

E Co.
2 WI

B Co.

D. Beachley

19 IN

NATIONAL PIKE

skirmishers

2 WI   7 WI

6 WI   K Co.

sect.   6 WI

B, 4th US Arty.   B Co.

58

W

S ——+—— N

E

100 Feet 500

MAP 58: The National Pike—September 14, 1862. The Iron Brigade makes contact with Colquitt's skirmishers.

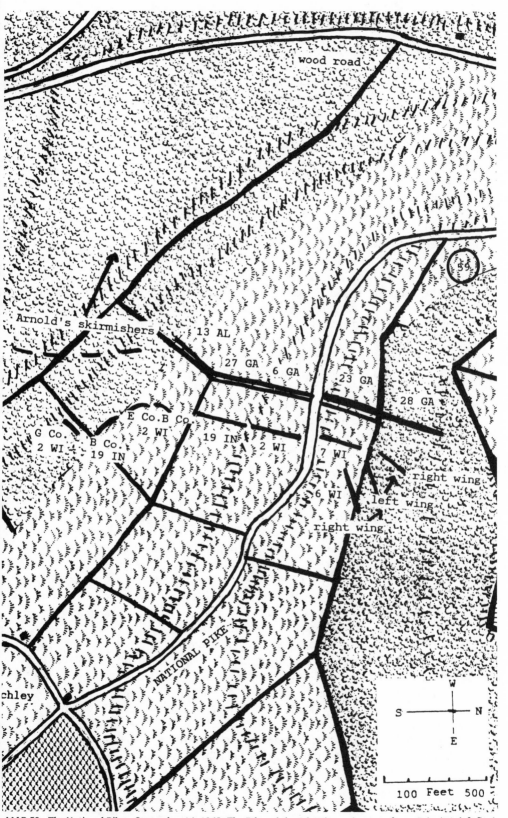

wood road

Arnold's skirmishers

13 AL

27 GA   6 GA

23 GA

28 GA

G Co.   E Co. B Co.
2 WI   2 WI   19 IN   2 WI   7 WI   right wing
B Co.   left wing
19 IN   6 WI
                                        right wing

NATIONAL PIKE

chley

W
S — N
E

100 Feet 500

MAP 59: *The National Pike—September 14, 1862. The 7th and the 6th Wisconsin try to force Colquitt's left flank.*

skirmishers. Colonel Meredith ordered Captain Clark with Company G to left wheel from the regiment and try to gain the Rebels' flank. The 19th Indiana (263 men) filed to the left, leaving room for the 2nd Wisconsin (341 men) to fill out the right flank to the Pike.[218] [Refer to Map 58]

On the right of the road, the 7th Wisconsin (337 men) got caught in the rough stony field southwest of the Moore house. The Wisconsin men halted and opened fire by the left oblique into the 23rd Georgia which was under cover of the stone wall running along the top of the ravine to their left front. Simultaneously, Captain John B. Callis, (Company B, 7th Wisconsin) swung his line to face the wall directly. In so doing, he unwittingly exposed the rear of his line to the 28th Georgia in the woods on his right flank. Captain Hollon Richardson (7th Wisconsin) dashed back to the 6th Wisconsin.

"Come forward, sixth!" he pleaded.

Lieutenant Colonel Edward S. Bragg of the 6th yelled, "Deploy column! By the right and left flanks, double-quick, march!"

The veterans maneuvered in the dark with machine like precision into battle line. The left wing of the regiment covered the 7th Wisconsin and the right wing extended into the open field beyond the right flank.

"Major!" Colonel Bragg hollered at Rufus Dawes, "take command of the right wing and fire on the woods!"

Dawes screamed, "Attention, right wing, ready, right oblique, aim, fire, load at will, load!"[219]

A sheet of flame, engulfed by a pungent sulfuric cloud, roared through the night against the black background of the woods. The smoke had hardly cleared before Colonel Bragg changed his plans. He moved the left wing by the right flank to a post behind the right wing.

"Have your men lie down on the ground," he called out, "I am going over you!"

Rufus ordered his line prone. The right wing passed over the left wing, halted and volleyed into the woods. Then it went to the ground and reloaded while Dawes brought his men, leap-frog fashion farther toward the front to deliver fire. Twice more the two wings stepped forward with drill field precision. The 7th Wisconsin lustily cheered their unique charge.[220]

Across the road Captain Clark's company enfiladed William M. Arnold's men on the flank and drove them back toward the wood road along the mountain crest. As they overran the Confederate position, they wounded and captured a captain from the 6th Georgia, and bagged the major of the 13th Alabama, a slow running lieutenant and eight enlisted men as well.[221] At the same time, the 19th Indiana and the 2nd Wisconsin pushed the 13th Alabama, 27th Georgia, and the 6th Georgia west toward the wooded hillside below the Mountain House.[222] [Refer to Map 59]

The 23rd Georgia stopped the 7th Wisconsin and the 6th Wisconsin cold about one hundred twenty feet from the stone wall. Corporal George Fairchild (Company C, 6th Wisconsin) staggered to the rear severely wounded. Nearby, his best friend, First Sergeant Ed Whaley writhed in agony from a mortal wound.[223] Men were dropping by the squads. George Miles (Company A), having gone into the fray with a death premonition, fell to the ground. His comrade behind him heard him gasp, "Tell my father I died doing my duty," before he expired. Private Philip Cheek (Company A) watched the colors of the 7th Wisconsin bob up and down time and again as the Rebels picked off the bearers. He wondered how anyone survived.[224]

The 6th Wisconsin succeeded in herding the 28th Georgia back to the stone wall on the left of the 23rd Georgia. Colonel Bragg ordered Major Dawes to deploy his wing on line with the right of the regiment and advance through the woods. Clawing and stumbling blindly up the hill they finally completed the formation and started to pour a rapid fire into the stone wall to their front.[225]

To the south, where the firing had stopped, the right wing of the 2nd Wisconsin right wheeled until it was parallel to the pike. Believing it was opposite the stone wall it volleyed blindly into the right of the 7th Wisconsin.[226] After ten minutes, the right wing, having expended all of its ammunition fell back. The left wing replaced it and shot away its ammunition also. The 19th Indiana then advanced its wings, in succession, to finish off what they thought were Confederates.[227]

The shooting gradually stopped. Around 9:00 P.M., Colonel Edward Bragg of the 6th Wisconsin ordered his men to cease fire when the barrels of their weapons became too hot to safely load them.[228] Captain John Callis (Co. B, 7th Wisconsin) also ceased fire. His men had no ammunition left. When General Gibbon was apprised of the situation, he ordered them to hold the mountainside with their bayonets.[229] No sooner had the field fallen quiet than a private in Company A of the 6th Wisconsin loudly blurted to David Noyes, "Captain Noyes, I am out of cartridges!" The 28th Georgia heard him and fired for several minutes into the Yankees to which the Westerners replied with equal vigor until mutual exhaustion silenced the lines again.[230]

Across from them Major Tully Graybill of the 28th Georgia, whose men had also shot away their rounds, mounted the wall and screamed defiantly, "Fix bayonets!" Receiving no reply, he sat down behind the wall to worry about those who mattered most in his life—his wife, and his dear children. He thought about the two bullet holes through his coat and thanked his Savior he was still alive.[231]

A deathly chill settled over the battle ground. The Yankees growled through powder stained and cracked lips about their empty canteens. Wounded and dying soldiers wailed pitifully in the darkness. The men callously bedded down, using the corpses of their comrades for pillows.[232] The three hours of combat had cost them dearly—thirty-seven killed, two hundred fifty-two wounded and thirty missing (an average of more than one man per minute). The 7th Wisconsin and the 6th Wisconsin accounted for seventy-five percent of them.[233] Only one officer died in the fighting. Captain Wilson Colwell (Company B, 2nd Wisconsin) remained upon the ground where he had led his

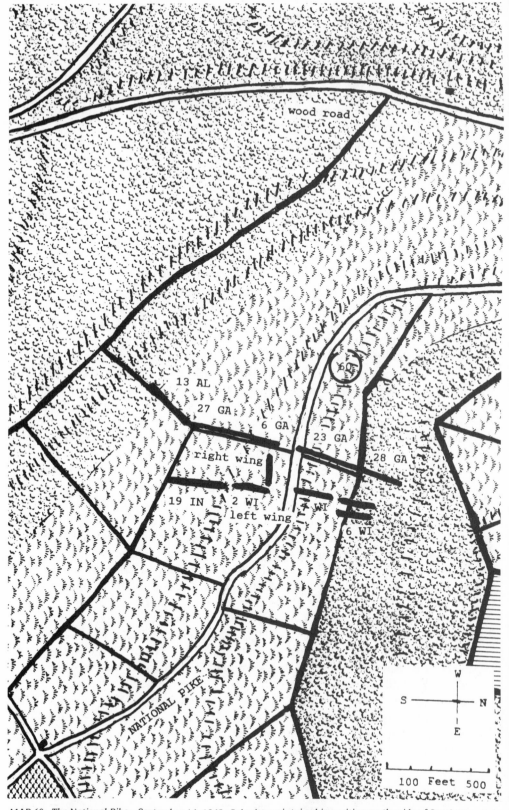

skirmishers so well.[234] By comparison, the Confederates fared much better: 109 killed, wounded, and missing.[235] [Refer to Map 60]

The Federal Army had won the tactical battle by forcing back the Army of Northern Virginia's flanks and by losing one hundred ten fewer men. Robert E. Lee won the strategic battle because he still held the gap at the National Pike.

Chapter Thirteen

SEPTEMBER 14, 1862

CRAMPTON'S GAP

Major General William B. Franklin's VI Corps, having spent the night on both sides of Jefferson, awakened a few hours before daylight. Pursuant to McClellan's orders, Franklin, with the assistance of Major General Darius Couch's division of the IV Corps, was to secure Crampton's Gap.[1]

At 2:00 A.M., a courier awakened Colonel Henry L. Cake (96th Pennsylvania) and delivered an order for him to advance his regiment, at dawn, toward Burkittsville. The colonel was promised the corps' headquarters escort, Captain Henry P. Muirheid's Companies B and G of the 6th Pennsylvania Cavalry, and a section of artillery as support.[2] The Pennsylvanians left for Jefferson at 5:30 A.M. without their cavalry screen or the guns.[3] Their advance set the rest of Brigadier General Henry Slocum's division into motion. The remainder of Colonel Joseph J. Bartlett's brigade (5th Maine, 16th, 27th, and 121st New York) followed behind the 96th Pennsylvania. General John Newton's brigade (18th, 31st, and 32nd New York, and 95th Pennsylvania) then Colonel A. T. A. Torbert's New Jersey brigade (1st, 2nd, 3rd, and 4th regiments) trailed slowly behind.[4] It took the division two and a half to three hours to shuffle the four miles from its bivouac near Buckeystown to the camp of Colonel William Irwin's brigade (7th Maine, 20th, 33rd, 49th, and 77th New York), which was one mile northwest of Jefferson.[5] Couch's division had not gotten on the road at all yet. It remained at Licksville, east of the Monocacy River.[6]

Franklin halted the VI Corps beyond Jefferson and ordered the men to set up camp while awaiting Couch's arrival.[7] He waited there for Couch until around 10:00 A.M. to 10:30 A.M. before again moving out.[8]

Keeping the same order of battle from the morning, the column picked up General William Smith's division as its tail.

The 96th Pennsylvania, this time with Captain H. P. Muirheid's two companies of cavalry (Companies B and G, 6th Pennsylvania Cavalry) in supporting distance, fanned out as skirmishers in front of the corps.[9] The regiment, unopposed, covered the four rolling miles between Jefferson and Burkittsville in about two hours.[10] "The enemy, however, did no[t] want to be 'felt'," Private Henry C. Boyer (Company A, 96th Pennsylvania) groused. "...A small squad of cavalry and one gun made up all the enemy we had in sight at any time..." until they reached the eastern base of South Mountain at Burkittsville.[11]

Captain Basil C. Manly's six gun battery and three regiments from General Paul J. Semmes' brigade of 422 men (53rd Georgia, 15th and 32nd Virginia) occupied Brownsville Gap, one mile south of Crampton's Gap. His fourth regiment, the 10th Georgia (206 men), picketed the Rohrersville Road at the western base of the mountain.[12] Colonel Thomas Munford's two cavalry regiments, and the 16th Virginia infantry from Colonel William A. Parham's brigade guarded the narrow Arnoldstown Road and the Burkittsville Road where it ascended the gap. The 2nd Virginia Cavalry (125 men), anchored the southern flank of the road through the gap. Eight companies of the 16th Virginia, in the center of the Confederate position, maintained a line behind the broken stone wall along the Mountain Church Road, which paralleled the base of the mountain. (Two companies secured the Burkittsville-Arnoldstown Road intersection at the summit of the pass.) The 12th Virginia Cavalry (75 men) extended the line on the left to the Arnoldstown Road.[13]

Two more of Parham's regiments, the 41st Virginia and the 61st Virginia were at Solomon's Gap on Elk Ridge, on the opposite side of Pleasant Valley about one mile west of Crampton's Gap. The rest of his brigade, the 6th and the 12th Virginia had retired to Brownsville before 10:00 A.M.[14] As they ascended the western side of the mountain, Captain R. P. Chew's three-gun battery passed the infantry in the road, headed toward Burkittsville. Behind them Lieutenant J. H. Thompson (Grimes' Portsmouth Virginia Artillery) struggled up the steep mountain with his section of naval howitzers.

The artillerists stopped for several minutes at the top of the mountain to catch their breath. Private George Neese (Chew's Virginia Battery) spied something which upset him deeply. In the distance, about three miles away, a dark, straggling wedge preceded by a thinner, black thread emerged from the folds in the ground west of Jefferson. They were Federals and their sheer mass betrayed their superior strength.

The five guns carefully rolled part way down the mountain on the Burkittsville Road until they were opposite the black church on the eastern slope of the mountain, where they unlimbered into battery.[15] They would have a long time to wait before opening fire.

Shortly before noon, the 96th Pennsylvania wandered onto the crossroads at Martin Shafer's, about nine-tenths of a mile southeast of Burkittsville. The

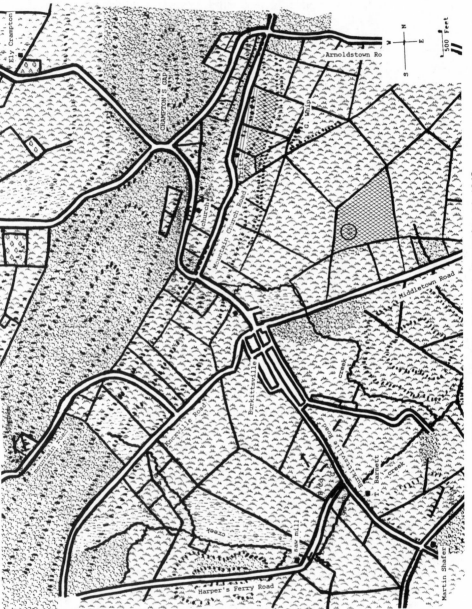

MAP 61: *Burkittsville, Maryland—September 14, 1862.*
Two companies from the 96th Pennsylvania make a reconnaissance into town.

regiment's cavalry escort slipped to the rear and out of sight as the infantry crested the hilltop overlooking the village. Diverging to the northwest, the Pennsylvanians slowly moved across the Burkittsville Road toward the Harpers Ferry Road which branched off toward the south some twenty-two hundred feet beyond the crossroads. Colonel Cake halted the regiment along the road. Company A trotted away from the left of the line to the sawmill at the western bend in the Harpers Ferry Road. Companies F and G dashed to the front toward the edge of the town. The rest of the regiment (about 350 men) went prone in the Harpers Ferry Road with its right on the Burkittsville Road. [Refer to Map 61]

First Lieutenant John Dougherty (Company F) stayed in the Burkittsville Road below the town with a dozen men while the rest of his company lay down in line along the crosstreet on the southeastern end of town. The remaining skirmishers fanned out in the field below the road.

When Major Lewis W. Martin joined him there a few minutes later, the two companies swiftly arose and rushed into the town. While Dougherty and Martin reconnoitered the Burkittsville Road to the bend in the road on the far edge of town, the infantrymen bellied down along both sides of the Middletown Road intersection, where it crossed the center of the village.[16]

Captain Jacob Haas' veterans in Company G left the ranks and broke into the houses along the main street which they looted indiscriminately. They scurried back to their company laden with milk, hams, and preserves.[17] At the time, they did not care whether the town was pro-Union or not.

Back near the Harpers Ferry Road, Colonel Henry Cake detailed Private Henry C. Boyer (Company A) to investigate T. Barnett's house, which was a short distance to the rear of the regiment. While stepping up to the front door, the private marveled at the spacious, trimmed lawn which surrounded the impressive brick house. South Mountain loomed ominously over his shoulder to the left rear.

The Confederates could see everything in the valley. The Yankees had no cover whatsoever. Boyer felt particularly alone as he pounded on the door. After what seemed like an interminable wait, a gentleman answered and requested an interview with Boyer's commanding officer.

The sickly young soldier, whose weak eyes generally kept him from serving in the line, quietly escorted Mr. Barnett down to Colonel Cake at the sawmill. Barnett begged Cake not to have a battle so close to the town. Most of the secessionists went across the Potomac when the war began. Only Unionists remained there.

The colonel, without any knowledge of the tactical situation along his front, quickly assured the civilian he had nothing to worry about. If the Southerners made any kind of stand, it would be along the base of the mountain and the stone wall which paralleled it.

The Confederates intended to fight the frightened civilian insisted. They had four thousand men, several hundred cavalry, and two cannons.

Major Lewis Martin, galloping in from the village, interrupted them. He tersely made his report. Dougherty was posted as ordered. The Rebels were ensconced behind the stone wall about one thousand feet from the edge of town and the colonel had a better view of the terrain than their own skirmishers. He was not sure how many Confederates held the mountainside.

As he blurted the last word an overly anxious orderly clattered into the group from the crossroads at the top of the hill behind them. Colonel Joseph Bartlett, the brigade commander, demanded a report.

Colonel Cake, who neither appreciated the aide's surliness nor put any great stock in Martin's attention to detail, deliberately wrote out Martin's and Barnett's stories. He tended to believe the civilian's strength assessment because the man would have seen the Confederates passing through the gap.

From the ridge behind the 96th Pennsylvania, the general officers and their orderlies calmly scanned the mountainside and the road ascending the gap. They spied one gun and a four-man mounted cavalry detachment which came nowhere near the alleged strength suggested by their reconnaissance.

Again the courier returned with a request for Colonel Cake to report to Martin Shafer's house, on the hill behind the regiment. The colonel spent several minutes there conferring with General Slocum, the division commander, his brigadier Colonel Bartlett, and their staff officers before returning to his regiment.[18] Considering they faced such a nominal force, Slocum and Bartlett agreed to probe the village and the gap with the Pennsylvanians.[19] The general, who probably believed Major Martin's assessment of the Confederate strength more than Colonel Cake's, brushed aside everyone's concerns by glibly suggesting the Confederates held the Burkittsville Road with four cavalrymen, two guns, and no infantry.

The Pennsylvanians scrambled over the rail fence along the Harpers Ferry Road and reassembled in the newly sprouting wheat field on the opposite side.[20] Captain Chew's battery and Lieutenant J. H. Thompson's guns countered their advance with a warning barrage.[21] The stunned Yankee infantry stopped. Their eyes responded to the five successive reports of the Confederate artillery pieces, and followed the hissing projectiles in their high trajectories over their heads toward the hill behind them. The bursting shells scattered the cluster of staff officers like flushed game.[22]

They fled to the shelter of the grove east of Shafer's crossroads, passing around Lieutenant Leonard Martin's Company F, 5th U.S. Artillery, as it wheeled into action on the crest of the hill.[23] The four ten-pounder Parrotts and two twelve-pounder Napoleons returned fire. Their rounds fell short of the mark, none of them striking anywhere near the guns on the mountainside.

The Confederate artillerists split their fire. Captain Chew ordered George Neese's crew to keep the Yankee guns preoccupied while the rest of the pieces hurled solid shot at the stalled Yankee skirmishers.[24]

Once again, the artillery pieces roared in succession. The shots plowed up the ground in front of the 96th Pennsylvania. Frantic commands echoed over the line. The veterans did not have to be told to take cover. Their instinct for survival sent them running pell mell back to the fence along the

Harpers Ferry Road. Leaping over the rails, the men hurled themselves to the reassuring dirt, intent upon riding out the shelling.

Private Henry C. Boyer (Company A, 96th Pennsylvania) mused, "...the Harpers Ferry Road was the dead line. The hint was taken." The Pennsylvanians did not intend to expose themselves to such accurate incoming fire.[25]

The Virginian artillerists stopped shooting almost as quickly as they had commenced. In their haste to neutralize the Federal threat, they disabled one of R. P. Chew's guns. The second shot violently recoiled the trail of George Neese's field piece into the steep bank on the western side of the Burkittsville Road which snapped a couple of the bolts on the carriage's mounting and disabled it. Having nothing to repair it with, the captain ordered the piece from the field.

Before the limber creaked away George Neese stopped momentarily to gaze across the fertile valley east of the mountain. The sun glistening off the bayonets and the rifle muzzles of the Yankee infantry reminded him of a rippling silvery sea. The Yankees, who outnumbered them so greatly, acted as if they were sneaking up on the mountain, unobserved. Their deliberate, overly cautious deployment reminded him of a lion trying to stalk a field mouse.[26]

Slocum's division did not intend to stalk anyone. He halted his command for lunch. Colonel Bartlett busied himself with the bulk of his brigade, which was lying down in the road which lead to Broad Run Village. While his men lounged in the afternoon sun, he rode down into the deep creek bottom which wove its way north, behind a knoll, to the Middletown Road.[27] General William F. "Baldy" Smith's division trickled into the Burkittsville area between 2:00 P.M. and 3:00 P.M., bringing corps commander William B. Franklin with it.[28] The troops went into bivouac.

Franklin, Smith, Slocum, Generals Winfield Scott Hancock, John Newton, and W. T. H. Brooks with their staffs assembled in Martin Shafer's grove, on the north side of the house, to enjoy some fine cigars and small talk. Presently, Franklin asked Slocum whom he wanted to lead the assault.

"Bartlett," Slocum tersely answered.

"Then send for Bartlett and let him decide," Franklin arbitrarily concluded, "he has carefully looked over the ground from the right, and General Brooks has done the same on the left, and as Bartlett is to lead the assault, let him decide."

Major H. C. Rogers, the division adjutant general, left to find Bartlett, whom he brought to headquarters within a few minutes. The generals leisurely continued their afternoon chat. It piqued Bartlett somewhat to think the general staff had nothing better to do.

Slocum asked him from which side of the road he would make his attack.

"On the right," Bartlett said, his voice betraying his astonishment.

"Well, gentlemen," Franklin interrupted, "that settles it."

"Settles what, General?" the confused Bartlett gasped.

"The point of attack," Franklin asserted.

Making no attempt to conceal his anger, Bartlett turned on Henry Slocum and demanded to know why the generals wanted his opinion when they had not included him in their discussions. The division commander coolly brushed aside the colonel's objection. The generals were equally divided as to which side of the road to strike from. Not too long afterward, when the other officers had left, the colonel asked Slocum what formation he wished the division to assume.

Slocum told him, "As General Franklin has allowed you to decide the point of attack, on the ground that you were to lead it, it is no more than fair that I should leave to you the formation."

Bartlett decided to deploy his five regiments in column of regiments on a two regiment front. With one hundred yards between lines it would cover a depth of fifteen hundred feet. He wanted the division to strike west, perpendicular to and north of the Burkittsville Road. The 27th New York would cover the charge as skirmishers and the division would not halt until it reached the crest of the mountain.[29]

While the Federal generals were deciding what to do about the Confederate situation, Rebel General Paul Semmes, at Brownsville Gap, south of Crampton's Gap, ordered the 10th Georgia to march from the Rohrersville Road to Colonel Thomas Munford's relief at the eastern base of the mountain.

At the same time, Munford sent for help. His courier reached Brownsville, about one mile southwest of the gap, before 3:00 P.M. Colonel William A. Parham immediately sent his two remaining regiments, the 6th Virginia (100 men) and the 12th Virginia (122 men), to Munford's assistance.[30]

The 10th Georgia trudged up the mountain and over the crest and started to deploy on the left of the 16th Virginia when Semmes countermanded his order, with a directive to go back up the mountain to the black meeting house in front of Chew's and Thompson's batteries.[31] The exhausted Confederates complied and ran into William A. Parham's Virginians as they descended the eastern side of the mountain. Parham halted the Georgians. Leaving two companies of Georgians at the church, the three regiments formed in a semblance of a line and headed back toward the eastern base of the slope.[32]

Captain J. R. Lewellen (12th Virginia), drawing his sword and waving it above his head, posted himself on the right front of his regiment and dramatically led it toward the low ground. Lieutenant Colonel Fielding L. Taylor, too ill to assume command, weakly staggered alongside of his men.[33] Two extremely footsore and shoeless veterans, John E. Crow and Billy C. Douglas (both from Company E) limped behind him, determined to give the Yankees a good show for the day.[34]

One mile to the south, at Brownsville Gap, Colonel Edgar B. Montague (32nd Virginia), commanding that sector, detached 200 of his 422 men to the bottom of the mountain. They spread out in a tenuous skirmish line north, until they connected with Munford's 2nd Virginia Cavalry. Averaging one

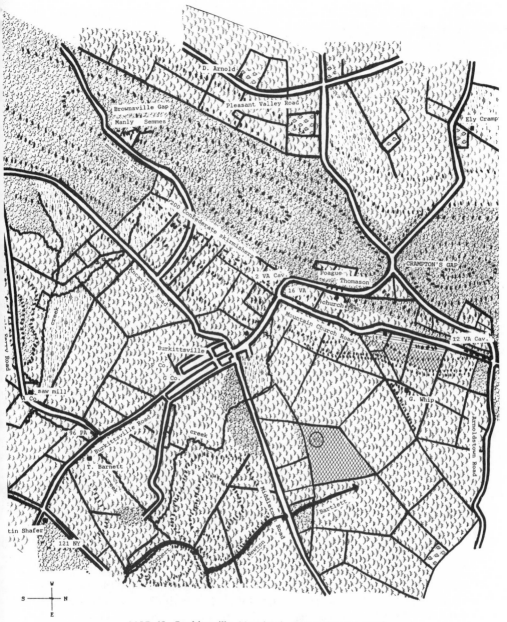

D. Arnold

Pleasant Valley Road

Brownsville Gap
Manly   Semmes

Ely Cramp

200 Confederate skirmishers

CRAMPTON'S GAP

2 VA Cav.

Poague
Thomason

Knoxville Road

16 VA

church

Mountain Church Road   Tritt

12 VA Cav.

Burkittsville

Berry Road

Co.
G Co.

G. Whip

Arnoldstown Road

saw mill

A Co.

96 PA

creek

Burkittsville Road

T. Barnett

Middletown Road

Bartlett

tin Shafer

121 NY

Topher

Newton Road

S — W — N
E

MAP 62: Burkittsville, Maryland—September 14, 1862.
Slocum's division of the VI Corps maneuvers for the grand assault.

500 Feet

man every twenty to twenty-six feet, they did not represent formidable opposition.[35]

Joseph Bartlett, meanwhile, according to his own plan, sent the 16th and 27th New York and the 5th Maine north through the ravine which intersected the Middletown Road about five thousand feet east of the Mountain Church Road. Bartlett wisely decided to leave the untried 121st New York behind near Martin Shafer's where it could not cause too much trouble. John Newton's and A. T. A. Torbert's brigades very slowly wound their way into the hollow behind Bartlett's men.[36] [Refer to Map 62]

Leaving the creek bed a short distance north of the Middletown Road, the 27th New York advanced on the oblique through an open field. It spread itself out at wide intervals and headed northwest through a large cornfield.[37] Passing through the corn, the Yankee skirmishers broke into the open and walked into shots from the base of the mountain from the pickets of the 16th Virginia and the 12th Virginia Cavalry. The New Yorkers worked their way to the stone wall in the hollow on the southeastern side of G. Whip's triangular field. Crawling over the wall, they swung west, through a thick clover field and pressed to the top of the hill along the heavily overgrown stone fence which ran north to south, connecting the Burkittsville and the Arnoldstown roads. There they became engaged at long range with the Confederates along the Mountain Church Road, some twelve hundred feet away. Color Sergeant William H. McMahon (Company G) went down with a bullet in his face.[38]

Three rectangular fields separated the opposing lines. The field nearest to the Confederates measured about two hundred feet from east to west. The middle field spanned around four hundred feet and the third, the one nearest to the New Yorkers, was around five hundred feet across. From the New Yorkers' position, the first field continued almost level to a rubbish covered fence row. The second field dipped into a swale which paralleled the mountain to the south. A second hedge-covered fence near the crest of the basin separated the last two fields. A cornfield, some three hundred yards wide and over one hundred yards deep, ascended the gentle slope toward the Mountain Church Road, which being on higher ground, stood out above the top of the corn.[39]

Colonel William Parham's newly arrived Virginians and Georgians, who descended the mountainside without seeing the Yankees, took cover behind the stone and rail fence sections which intermittently lined either one side or the other of the Mountain Church Road. The 10th Georgia anchored the left flank. The 6th Virginia was in the center and the 12th Virginia was to the south. Their arrival reinforced the 16th Virginia and increased the overall Confederate strength to 928 soldiers.[40]

The reports from Lieutenant J. H. Thompson's section of naval howitzers and Captain R. P. Chew's two rifled pieces, having moved to the crossroad at the top of the gap, roared violently. The mountainside trembled. Private George Bernard (Company I, 12th Virginia) in the Mountain Church Road

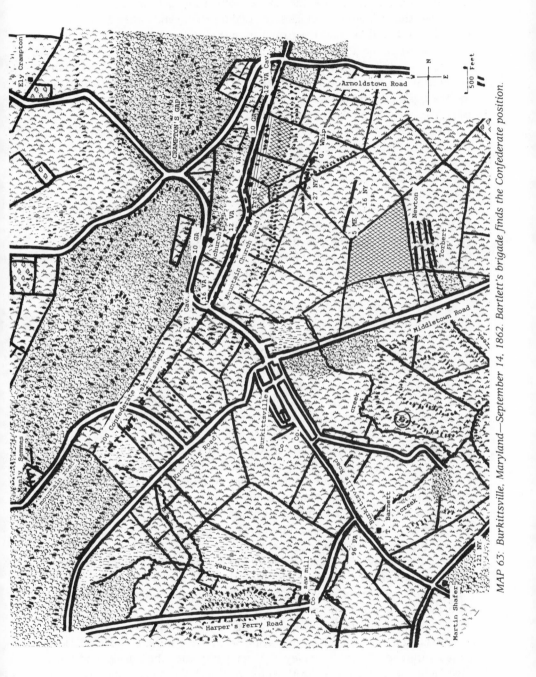

MAP 63: *Burkittsville, Maryland—September 14, 1862. Bartlett's brigade finds the Confederate position.*

ducked his skull behind the thick stones which formed the base of the fence row while the artillery projectiles screamed overhead and crashed into the rolling farmland well beyond their own infantry.

In short order, the skirmishers from the 16th Virginia scrambled back through the plowed field in front of Parham's men. Several rifle shots followed them across the fence to the right of the 12th Virginia.[41] The 16th New York (on the right) and the 5th Maine (on the left) rushed to the support of the 27th New York and formed a line behind it.[42]

George Bernard sheepishly raised his head above the stones which sheltered him and peeped across the open ground between him and the Yankees. Several flashes, followed instantly by puffs of white smoke, pocked the fence row about two hundred fifty yards away. These scattered shots soon escalated into a full scale volley.

The Rebels instinctively pushed themselves into the dirt. Minié balls picked up the freshly turned earth along the front of their line. Others zinged uncomfortably between the rails of the fence, barely inches above their quivering bodies. Bullets thudded into the trees and stumps or pinged off the rocks on the hillside behind them. The small arms fire swept over them like a sudden gust.

When it passed, the Virginians and Georgians, most of them unscathed, returned a devastating fire.[43] For almost forty-five minutes the opposing infantry hammered at each other, with the exposed Yankees suffering almost one hundred casualties.[44] Colonel Joseph Bartlett craned his neck over his shoulder looking for his supports. For some unexplainable reason, General Newton's four regiments (18th, 31st, and 32nd New York, and 95th Pennsylvania) were not moving forward to his aid. They remained near the eastern edge of the cornfield.[45] Their hesitation slowed up the New Jersey brigade in the ravine south of the Middletown Road. [Refer to Map 63]

Meanwhile, south of the Burkittsville Road, Colonel Henry L. Cake of the 96th Pennsylvania recalled Companies F and G from Burkittsville as Brigadier General W. T. H. Brooks' Vermont brigade quick stepped into the town to replace them. The Pennsylvanians rallied briefly along the Harpers Ferry Road then walked back to the creek bottom east of the road to lounge in the grass. They left Company A around the sawmill to their left front to protect the corps' flank. Colonel Cake quietly bellied down among his men, waiting for Company A to return from the sawmill on the Harpers Ferry Road. General Slocum dismounted along the line and crawled up alongside the colonel.

"Well," Cake lazily drawled, after exchanging amenities, "we have more than four cavalrymen and two guns before us."

"Yes," Slocum agreed, "we are going to have a fight."

Nodding in the direction of the ravine north of the Burkittsville Road, Henry Cake continued, "I see the Jerseymen struggling with the bushes and fence-rows, and the 121st [New York] seems restless." He paused momentarily." I am waiting for Captain [Lamar S.] Hay, who went to the mill toward Harpers Ferry. When he comes I presume you mean that we shall follow the 121st?"

"Well, no," the division commander replied matter-of-factly, "The 121st is not going. I have left it back to guard our prisoners, and you have done enough to-day."

The reports of Thompson's and Chew's artillery pieces changed Slocum's mind. The startled Pennsylvanians leaped to their feet and strained their necks to see where the shots fell. Presently, Company A quick stepped into line at the head of the regiment.

"Well?" Colonel Cake blurted.

"Well," Slocum snapped, "follow Torbert, and if you find anything to do, do it!"

By the time the regiment got moving, it had lost contact with the New Jersey troops. It caught up with them on the north side of the Middletown Road, where the regiments halted to form battle lines in the first open field west of the creek.[46] The 1st New Jersey fell in on the left and the 2nd New Jersey on the right. At a distance of one hundred fifty yards to the rear the 3rd New Jersey covered the 1st regiment and the 4th covered the 2nd regiment.[47] The 96th Pennsylvania finished out the formation.[48]

The newly arrived troops crowded John Newton's brigade northwest into the rear of the 16th New York and the 5th Maine. As they approached, Colonel Joseph Bartlett screamed, "Halt! Lie down!"

The 16th New York and the 5th Maine inched back from the fence row and disappeared in the dense clover in the hollow behind them.[49] The 32nd New York and the 18th New York (north to south) stepped over the two prone regiments and went into position along the rail fence. A few minutes later, the 31st New York and the 95th Pennsylvania (north to south) continued the line to the left.[50]

Musketry continued to pepper the stone wall. Occasional shells burst in the fields around the Yankees. Solid shot crashed through the cornfield east of Newton's brigade. In conjunction with the tall corn stalks, they disrupted Colonel Torbert's New Jersey troops as they came upon the field. The quick thinking officers of the 96th Pennsylvania obliqued their companies northwest to get them out of the field and harm's way.[51]

A solid shot smashed through Company K gutting Private Barney McMichael. Francis Boland, his best friend, dropped down beside him and cradled him in his arms. McMichael vomited blood with every painful breath. Boland uncorked his canteen and feverishly gave him swallows of water to clean his mouth and to ease his terrible thirst. The desperate soldier begged his comrade to tell his father how he died. Minutes later, McMichael bled to death. Francis Boland noticed they were alone. The regiment had gone in without them. It could keep on going for all he cared. He had to attend to more important matters than killing.[52]

To the south, the 4th Vermont, covering the advance of the rest of Brooks' brigade (2nd, 3rd, 5th, and 6th Vermont), came to an abrupt halt on the western edge of Burkittsville, near the northwestern corner of David Arnold's barn. A haystack to the left front hid the Vermonters from the 2nd

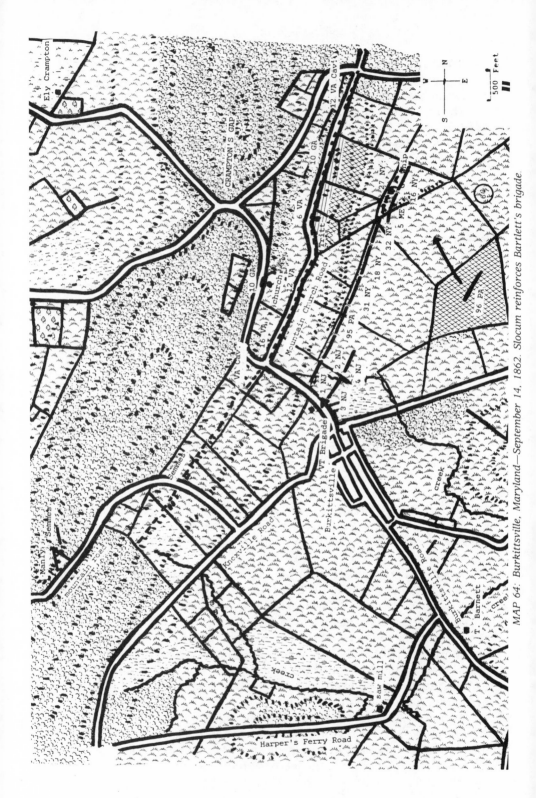

MAP 64: Burkittsville, Maryland—September 14, 1862. Slocum reinforces Bartlett's brigade.

Virginia's dismounted sharpshooters. As the rest of the brigade came to a stand-still in the road, Colonel Brooks and his cluster of aides trotted cautiously into the farm yard behind the barn. The long blue column provided the Rebels with an inviting target. Fire from unseen marksmen southwest of the town spattered the barn and the Michael Wiener house, on the northern side of the column.[53] [Refer to Map 64]

Across the road to the north, the 1st and 2nd New Jersey went into line behind a fence row on the left of Newton's line, which by then had gone prone in the dense clover. Joseph Shaw (Company H, 95th Pennsylvania), on their right flank, having retired with his company a short distance behind the stone wall which had protected them for almost half an hour, looked up to his left to the open space at the top of the gap. The Confederate artillery continued to belch death down into the valley. Rebel rifle balls zipped and whistled uncomfortably overhead. He groused, "Clover won't stop bullets like a stone wall or a hole to crawl into."

To the left a large number of the New Jersey boys leaped the stone wall which protected them.[54] Raising their fists, they foolishly taunted the Rebels to come out and fight. A sudden burst of small arms fire from the Mountain Church Road cut them down.[55] The New Jersey troops maintained their shooting for around twenty minutes.[56]

The 96th Pennsylvania, on the extreme right, reached the stone wall in the hollow on the southeastern edge of G. Whip's farm. Orders passed through the regiment to strip to light marching order then lie down. The men stored everything but their cartridge boxes, belts, cap boxes, bayonets, and rifles in the roomy lime kiln which they discovered near their flank.

Colonel Bartlett called out, "What regiment is this?"

Henry C. Boyer poked his head up. Their brigadier and a group of officers were prancing their mounts through the clover across from the regiment.

"The 96th," someone hollered back.

"By what good luck did you get here?" Bartlett continued.

"Walked!" the same fellow yelled.

Lieutenant John Dougherty and Major Lewis Martin leaped their horses over the stone wall and their regiment followed after them. Several paces into the luxurious clover the Pennsylvanians found the rest of their brigade by stepping on them. All the while shells burst overhead and solid shot scooped up the fields around them. Wheeling left, the regiment advanced steadily west and went prone in the clover fifty feet from the fence row. Rifle fire started to come in from the right flank at extremely long range.

Colonel Joseph Bartlett spurred his horse over to the dismounted Colonel Cake.

"We have no artillery and I have sent in vain to have a battery brought forward," he explained in desperation. "We can do nothing without it. If you will take the 96th into that field to the right and charge the wall it would be glorious work."

"Where is your regiment?" Cake demanded, in reference to the 27th New York.

"It has expended all its ammunition and is not available," the brigade commander explained.

"And the balance of the brigade?" Cake persisted.

"In the same condition," Bartlett curtly responded.

"You have expended all your ammunition a mile away," the colonel impudently snapped, "and have neither lost a man or killed one of the enemy."

Joseph Bartlett, whose wounded and dead had disappeared in the dense clover, lost his temper with the insubordinate colonel.

"You hear their passing bullets!" he yelled.

"Their rifles are better than ours," Henry Cake replied in a more respectful tone. Turning about he shouted, "Captain Lessig, bring the best rifle in your company."[57]

Presently, Private Edward J. Phillips (Company C) came forward with his rifle.

"Elevate for a mile and try the range of the skirmish line of the enemy!" the colonel ordered him.

The sergeant carefully adjusted his sights and elevated his rifle. Facing by the oblique, he aimed across the wide marshy ground toward the plowed field and the stone wall to the regiment's right front. When the weapon fired, Private Boyer craned his neck to follow the anticipated flight of the minié ball. It picked up dark earth in the plowed field about six hundred feet short of the Mountain Church Road.

"Put in a double charge of powder and try again!" Cake insisted.

The ball whistled closer but failed to hit the mark.

"Now load with a triple charge."

The third round still did not reach the wall. A groan rose from the prone Pennsylvanians. They did not like what was going to happen.

Facing the regiment, Colonel Cake called out, loud enough for all to hear, "Attention! The 96th will make this effort. That field [is] plowed as far down the slope as the water admitted, and on this side of the plowed ground, in point blank range of the enemy, we will be swamped and every man of us killed. You will see us decently buried."

With those words of encouragement, the officers began to check their men's accoutrements. In the event of a stand up fight, they were to pilfer the cartridge boxes of any man who went down and distribute the rounds to the survivors. After the first volley every weapon was to be checked to see if it fired. While the officers droned out the standard operating procedure, the field fell deathly silent.[58]

During the flurry of activity, Colonel Bartlett slipped south along the line to talk with Colonel Torbert of the New Jersey brigade. Being the officer in charge of the initial assault, Bartlett ordered Torbert to troop the line. The men were to cease fire, load, then prepare to charge.[59]

Stray shots still rang out across the open fields from both directions.

George Bernard of the 12th Virginia inadvertently exposed himself while trying to ram a cartridge down his rifle. Something jolted his right leg above the knee, sending a searing pain through his body. He frantically glanced at his leg. Blood gushed from the hole in it.

Bernard immediately pulled his handkerchief out and tied off his wound in an attempt to staunch the blood. He remembered the leather strap around his blanket roll, but discovered it lying too far to his left for him to reach it. He screamed at S. P. Branscomb, the next man on his left, to quit shooting and bind up his leg with the strap. Branscomb hastily applied the tourniquet then left Bernard on his own.

The wounded private flattened out. He wondered if the shooting would cease. He belatedly wished he had enough wealth to buy his way to the western side of the mountain and safety. A loud crackling noise snapped him back to the present.

Flames licked at the fence rails and the dry leaves not two feet to his left where Branscomb had just fired his last shot. The rolling smoke merely gave the Northerners a better target. When a bullet cut down Branscomb, Bernard decided to crawl to a safer spot. Digging his hands into the dirt, he started to tortuously pull himself south along the road toward Joseph H. Coleman (Company D).

His comrade screeched at him for, "God's sake not to come towards him," because he "would certainly be killed," because "the bullets were all coming there."

Dragging himself behind Branscomb, he inched his way next to P. T. Walton (Company I) to a point where the stone base of the wall seemed higher than elsewhere. The exhausted soldier felt relatively safe until he looked closely at Walton. The young man lay there with a bullet in his forehead. At that point, whatever sense of security remained abandoned him.[60] A short distance away, in Company C, two bullets killed Robert E. Eldridge and Private Mills as they lay beside Orderly Sergeant Hugh R. Smith. Sergeant W. W. Tayleure (Company E), one of the most esteemed men in the regiment, remained behind the wall, immobilized by a severe wound.[61]

South of the Burkittsville Road, the Confederate dismounted cavalrymen kept harassing the Vermont Brigade, which remained in the road awaiting orders to deploy. The intrepid First Lieutenant Abel K. Parsons (Company A, 4th Vermont) walked his horse around the barn to the open field on the western side then quietly returned to the general. John Conline (Company E) heard him tell Brooks the obvious: the woods on the mountainside were full of Confederates. Minié balls hissed harmlessly, but uncomfortably, overhead. General Brooks writhed uneasily in the saddle. Leaning toward Lieutenant Parsons, he tried to reassure himself and the men nearby. "I don't think there are as quite as many as all that," he said loud enough for the front company to hear.

He commanded the brigade to deploy at once. With the 4th Vermont in the lead, the regiments broke by companies to the left. Passing behind the barn and through the cow yard, they fronted in a large open pasture about three hundred yards away from the Rebels' dismounted cavalry. John Conline of the 4th Vermont ignored the shells because they were more noisy than harmful. Instead, he patiently scanned the field for at least ten minutes before any significant action occurred.

The Confederates, from the cover of a high stone wall, fiercely blazed away at the Yankees. From the top of Brownsville Gap, southwest of the Vermonters, Captain Basil C. Manly's single three-inch Ordnance Rifle and Captain M. C. Macon's two ten-pounder Parrotts pounded Burkittsville valley.[62] Ensign John T. Parham (Company C, 32nd Virginia), whose regiment waited in battle line to the right of the battery, watched the eight to ten shells plummet into the VI Corps troops on both sides of the Burkittsville Road when they quick stepped across the undulating farmland east of the mountain. The exploding projectiles seemingly gouged holes in their formations. The lines flowed around the holes like water around boulders in a swift flowing river. The ranks closed professionally and continued to surge forward. The amazed color bearer never saw so many Yankees in one place before. "It was a grand sight," he wrote, "I will never forget it."[63]

Around 5:30 P.M., the firing on the northern end of the field suddenly ceased. "Look yonder, boys!" a frightened member of the 12th Virginia screamed, "They are coming across the field!" "Fix bayonets, men! Fix bayonets!" rang out along the panicking line.[64]

The 3rd New Jersey and the 4th New Jersey regiments, at Colonel Torbert's command, charged as soon as their two front regiments, the 1st New Jersey and the 2nd New Jersey regiments stopped firing. Passing through the front line, the two rear regiments leaped the stone wall and dashed madly for the Mountain Church Road. The rest of the brigade jumped into the field behind them and followed them at one hundred fifty yard interval across the open ground. The 3rd New Jersey and the 4th New Jersey suddenly halted to allow the two rear regiments to leap frog over them.[65] A few token bullets pattered their line.

Sergeant John P. Beech (Company B) saw Samuel Hull pitch forward. For a brief second, he believed he saw the religious young man's lips quivering out a final prayer while he toppled to the ground. The men in the company loved Hull so much that they always volunteered to do his fatigue duty on Sundays to keep him from compromising his reverence for the day.[66]

On the right flank, immediately to the north, the red legged 95th Pennsylvania scrambled upright from the clover, followed by the 31st New York, and sprang across the rolling meadow. Seconds later, the 16th New York, 18th New York, 32nd New York, and the 5th Maine joined in the assault, converging left as they double quicked.[67] They left behind the 27th New York which had been called in from the skirmish line and was trying to reform.[68]

The 96th Pennsylvania, upon hearing the Jersey troops' cheers, braced itself for the attack.

"Attention! Forward! Steady now!" reverberated along the line.

Stepping in formation through the field to the next stone wall to their front, the coal miners fired a volley, checked their weapons, reloaded, and

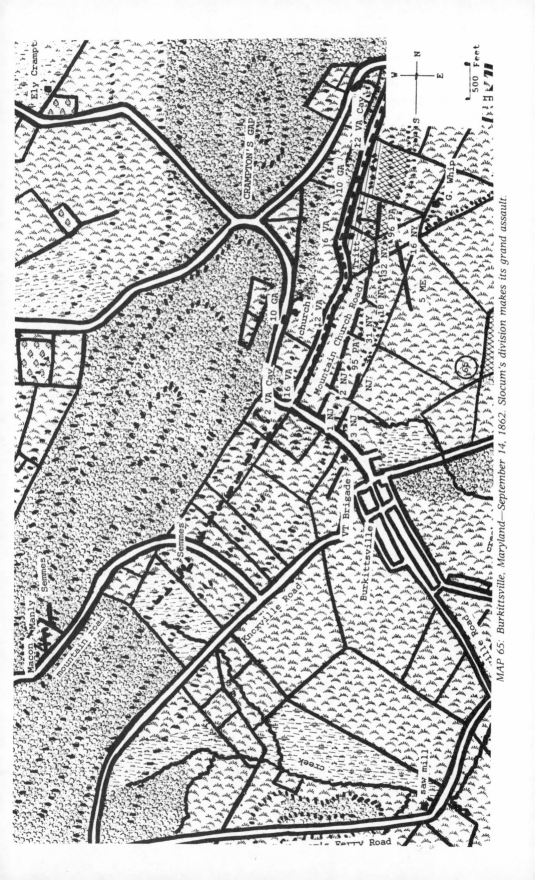

MAP 65: *Burkittsville, Maryland—September 14, 1862. Slocum's division makes its grand assault.*

climbed into the next field. Shells burst closely overhead. Minié balls zipped through the ranks with a peculiar "piffing" noise.

"Forward, double quick!"

A lusty cheer resounded rather emptily across the valley. Keeping well to the left of the swampy ground they were intended to charge through, the Pennsylvanians raced, heads down, through the shell spattered open ground to the next overgrown fence row. Volleying once, they reloaded before scrambling onto the crest. One hundred fifty yards of rich grass land which dipped into a gentle swale and was followed immediately by a cornfield, was all that remained between them and the Rebels. As the line quickly reformed and the regiment prepared to descend into the safety of the hollow, many of the enlisted men, among them Henry C. Boyer of Company A, suddenly realized they were alone. The eerie silence awed the 96th Pennsylvania. The solemn Yankees searched the fields to the left of their line. They saw no one. It seemed as if the New Jersey line had disappeared mid-charge. The veterans suddenly realized they were walking upright to their own deaths. Their past experiences told them the Confederates would hold their fire until they reached the open ground west of the corn. They suppressed their natural inclinations to quit the field and stoically marched into the low ground.

Colonel Cake sent the color bearer with one of their two regimental flags to the left of the line to identify them to the troops which were springing forward to their left rear. Officers ordered their men to fire at will only if they had targets. Panic took over as the regiment penetrated the corn. Rifles cracked rapidly—too fast to suit the company officers. As quickly as possible they ordered the men to "Trail arms." They complied, many of them with the ramrods still down the barrels of their pieces.

"Steady now! Forward, double quick!"

It seemed like seconds. Time clicked away faster than the men's minds could record it. Barely two steps clear of the corn, the Confederate infantry in the lane and on the hillside behind it volleyed. The 96th Pennsylvania shivered as if jolted by an electrical charge. Eighty-one of their men crumpled in the blast.[69] The regiment hurled itself into the tall grass.[70] The line officers fearing the collapse of their line boldly screamed at their men to charge.[71] The rest of the combined brigades obliqued to the right to follow them. [Refer to Map 65]

Nineteen-year-old Private James Allen (Company F, 16th New York) and his comrade, Private Richards, did not hear the command to right oblique. They found themselves alone in the plowed field in front of the stone wall, between the New Jersey Brigade and the rest of their own commands.

Richards gasped, "Hold on, Jim, what shall we do?"

"We'll charge them from behind that wall," the young Irishman replied.

Bracing themselves for their inevitable deaths, they charged the Mountain Church Road alone.[72] At the same time, the right of the line also desperately rushed the wall.

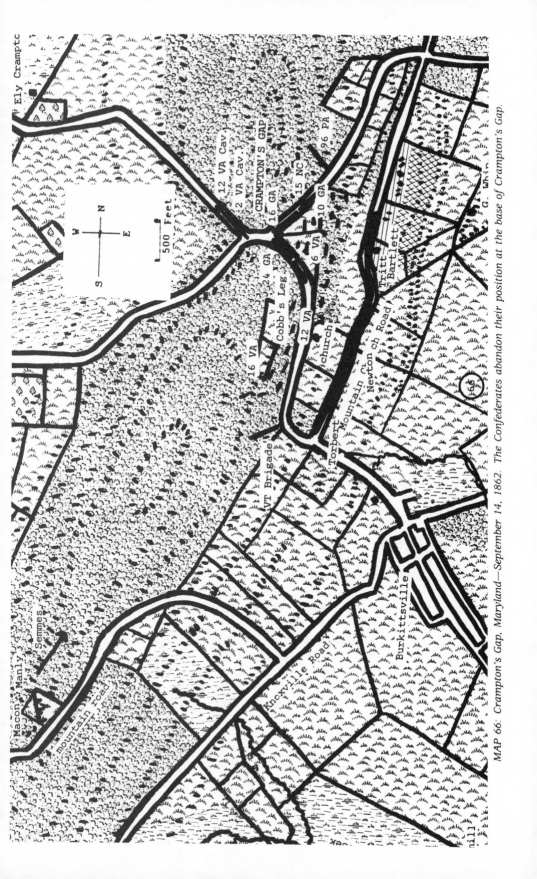

MAP 66: Crampton's Gap, Maryland—September 14, 1862. The Confederates abandon their position at the base of Crampton's Gap.

"Forward into the road and give them the bayonet," Henry Boyer of the 96th Pennsylvania heard, "it is death to all who hesitate now!"[73]

Companies C, A, and K bolted forward trailed after by Companies F and I then the rest of the regiment, excepting B Company which did not hear the command to join the attack. A bullet thudded into Lieutenant John Dougherty's chest, unhorsing him as he rode by Colonel Henry Cake's side. He fell too quickly for his friend to respond to his aid. Sergeant James Casey of Company F pried Dougherty's sword from his dying grasp and assumed command of the company. A minute later, when the regiment neared the stone wall, Major Lewis J. Martin toppled from the saddle with a musket ball in his head. Henry Cake ordered Adjutant George G. Boyer to carry the severely wounded officer from the field as quickly as possible. Martin died before he reached the rear lines and the colonel never forgave the hospital staff of his regiment for not following the line into battle.[74]

In the meantime, two of Brigadier General Howell Cobb's regiments, Cobb's Legion (248 men) and the 24th Georgia (292 men), arrived upon the field at the top of the gap. The peeved Colonel Thomas Munford, who had sent four couriers to the general and whose cavalry still tenuously held the flanks of William Parham's undersized brigade, placed the two regiments along the Burkittsville Road, with their left flank anchored on the Arnoldstown intersection at the crest. He then waited upon the general to arrive.[75]

Cobb, however, who reached Brownsville around 4:00 P.M., more than an hour earlier, had made no attempt to ascertain the situation. Around 5:00 P.M., he received Munford's first pleas for help and at that time decided to dispatch two regiments to his assistance. When William Parham's courier (from Crampton's Gap) reached him along with a runner from General Paul Semmes (at Brownsville Gap) and both insisted he send relief, he finally released his two remaining regiments, the 16th Georgia (368 men) and the 15th North Carolina (402 men).

Major Thomas S. McIntosh from division headquarters also intercepted him with a message from Major General Lafayette McLaws, who was at Maryland Heights. It ordered him to hold the gap at all costs even if it meant losing every man under his command. At that, the sluggish general, who never realized his rank entitled him to command all of the troops in the area, led those two regiments toward the pass.[76]

Many of the Confederates did not wait for the Yankees to reach the Mountain Church Road. The 2nd Virginia Cavalry, on the southern flank, and the 12th Virginia Cavalry, on the northern flank, mounted up and escaped up the Burkittsville Road and the Arnoldstown Road. They pulled the 16th Virginia (southern flank) and the 10th Georgia (northern flank) with them, leaving the 6th and the 12th Virginia infantry regiments to face Slocum's division.[77] [Refer to Map 66]

An amazed Private James Allen of the 16th New York and his messmate watched the Confederates stream from the wall. Flushed with their imagined military prowess the two scrambled over the stone wall and started across the Mountain Church Road. A bullet bored into Richards' left leg, dropping him in the road.

Allen dragged his friend to a nearby crevice in the wall. Giving him a drink from his canteen, Jim promised to return and take care of his friend if he pulled through all right.[78]

George Bernard of the 12th Virginia, having inched himself down to Lieutenant Joseph R. Manson of his company, begged him for a drink of water. The officer pulled him into his arms. Tugging his canteen around to his side, he strained to get some of the precious liquid into Bernard's parched mouth.

Someone screamed, "Our colors are gone!"

The lieutenant shot a glance along the line to the north. The flag had disappeared.

"Fall back! Fall back!" rang out over the 12th Virginia.

Those who could scrambled for their knapsacks, blanket rolls, and canteens and clambered up the mountainside toward a second fence on the edge of the woods.

"See yonder, boys!" a frightened Virginian hollered, "Cavalry!!"

The desperately wounded George Bernard panicked. He cringed at the idea of being trampled to death. He also saw himself dying from a savage bayonet thrust. His pulse quickened. He inadvertently gasped for air. The officer faithfully stayed by his side. Joseph Manson twisted his head toward the advancing Yankees, who halted about sixty feet away from him and dropped to their knees to volley at the retreating Virginians.[79]

Forty-six-year-old Doctor Thomas Newton (Company F, 6th Virginia), who was serving as a private, went down in the firing, severely wounded. Nearby, Assistant Surgeon Phil Baker (12th Virginia) quickly hurled himself into the saddle of his charger, "Bob Lee," and tried to escape before the Federals reached the stone wall. Spurring south, he ran into the advance of the 16th New York. In short order, he dismounted, slapped his horse on the rump and skedaddled up the mountainside after the rest of his regiment. Bullets ricocheted off the rocks around him as he climbed for safer ground. He reached the crest, he insisted, in a record two minutes, eleven and three quarter seconds. He deeply regretted the loss of his fine horse and his brand new saddle.[80]

Lieutenant Colonel Fielding Taylor (12th Virginia) fared far worse. When the Northern rifle fire mortally wounded him, enlisted men dragged him up the steep hillside toward the crest of the mountain. John E. Crow (Company E), who was struggling to pound a stuck ball down the muzzle of his fouled Enfield, jerked his ramrod from the bore and snatched up the colonel's gold headed cane. He shoved the cane six inches down the muzzle of his rifle, and trotted up the hill.[81] W. A. Shepard and "Berry" E. Stainback (both Company E) dove for cover behind the same tree, a rather ridiculous situation considering Stainback's excessive width. When the Federals poured over the stone wall, they both took off at a run to escape. Shepard, the lighter of the two, scaled the slope with much more ease. His overweight comrade, however, could not keep up.

As the fat Berry Stainback wheezed up the incline and continued to lose ground, his friend Sydney Jones (Company E) taunted him as he passed, "Hello, Berry! What's your hurry? Trying to *catch a train*?"

The exhausted soldier collapsed to await the inevitable. His messmate William C. "Buck" Johnson also surrendered, allegedly to continue sharing the blanket which Berry had rolled around his corpulent body.[82] A bullet ripped through E. Leslie Spence's neck and glanced downward into his side below the arm. The impact sent him crashing to the ground—paralyzed.[83]   Philip F. Brown of Company C was shocked to see blood trickling over the fingers of his left hand. He realized he could not move his arm. Crawling into the rutted Mountain Church Road, he prayed he would not be run over by any artillery.[84]

The Northerners at the stone wall had worked themselves into too much of a frenzy to pay any heed to the pleas of the Confederates who attempted to surrender. On the far left of the Confederate line, the 96th Pennsylvania slammed into the 6th Virginia.[85] A fierce bayonet fight broke out along part of the line. The Pennsylvanians swore they dispatched about one hundred fifty Rebels, when they had killed twelve. The Virginians wounded three of the color guard and killed both of the regiment's color bearers, Privates Solomon M. Minzi (Company C) and Charles B. Zeigler (Company H).[86] The Confederates bayonetted one of them at least twelve times. The other, who collapsed against the wall with a shattered left thigh, perished from a stab wound through his abdomen.

Colonel Henry Cake halted his command to reorganize it. He sent Lieutenant Samuel R. Russell of Company C back through the cornfield to bring up Captain Peter Filbert and his strayed Company B.[87] For several minutes, the Pennsylvanians halted to deliberately pick off the Rebels as they clawed their way up the mountainside in front of them.[88]

Of the one hundred officers and men the 6th Virginia carried into action, only thirty managed to get to the top of the mountain. Private John Shipp's small Company G lost a lieutenant and three enlisted men between the Mountain Church Road and the summit. When a bullet dropped the color bearer who was standing next to him, Shipp decided it was time to skedaddle.[89]

Below them, the Widow Tritt's small log cabin, surrounded by its own stone wall and out buildings, blocked the Pennsylvanians' advance.[90] Sharpshooters from Cobb's two Georgia regiments along the Burkittsville Road pestered the stalled 96th Pennsylvania.[91] A bullet slammed into Captain Jacob Haas' canteen, carrying away the cork and the mouth piece. The impact knocked him to the ground. He regained his feet in time to join the regiment as it flanked to the right and started to pass around the house. Another Confederate sent a ball by his head as he crawled over Tritt's fence. Angered, the captain attacked the house with his pistol drawn.

"I had him in tight papers," Jacob Haas crowed, "and took him prisoner."[92]

On the southern flank, toward the center of the Federal line, the rest of Colonel Joseph Bartlett's and General John Newton's brigades overwhelmed the Virginians. Their infantrymen poked their rifle-muskets through the rails over the heads of the wounded Confederates along the stone wall.

"Take care! Take care!" Lieutenant Joseph Manson (Company I, 12th Virginia) cried in vain as the weapons flared right over his head. "Wounded men! Wounded men! Don't shoot! Don't shoot!"

He frantically ripped the white handkerchief from George Bernard's wounded leg, tied it to a ramrod, and literally poked it in the New Yorkers' faces.

"We are wounded men! We surrender!"

"Get over the fence! Get over the fence!" the Federals growled.

Lieutenant Manson picked up the severely wounded Bernard and, with the help of one of the Northerners, heaved him over the top rail into the soft dirt on the opposite side. Manson then crawled over and picking the private up like a bride, started toward the rear with him. Behind them, Captain R. P. Chew's and Lieutenant J. H. Thompson's four remaining guns slammed their last four rounds down the mountainside before retiring.[93]

The fighting broke down into individual melees between the opposing armies and the rugged terrain. The Vermonters ran pell mell into the stone wall which the dismounted 2nd Virginia Cavalry had abandoned. For two to three minutes, the New Englanders stopped to fire into the Confederates' backs.[94] In the fading light and the increasing shadows on the eastern slope of the mountain, they killed Private James P. Abbitt (Company B) and wounded Lieutenant Thomas A. Tibbs (Company H) and one other man of the 2nd Virginia Cavalry.[95]

Crossing the stone wall, the Vermonters ran due west for about four hundred yards and penetrated the woods along the base of the mountain. A sheer rock ledge stymied their assault. Rather than skirt it to the right, where they would collide with the New Jersey Brigade, they started to scale it with their bare hands.[96]

Behind them, Colonel William Irwin's brigade (the 7th Maine, 20th, 33rd, 49th, and 77th New York) rushed to their support. They double-quicked from a belt of woods about five hundred feet south of Burkittsville.[97] A couple of shells from Manly's and Macon's rifled pieces at Brownsville Gap diverted them more toward the north.[98] The 33rd New York lost one man—wounded—to the artillery fire, the only casualty in the brigade.[99]

Cobb's Legion and the 24th Georgia, failing to notice the Vermonters, concentrated their fire upon A. T. A. Torbert's soldiers and stopped their assault for several minutes. The Confederates stubbornly contested every bit of hillside which cost the Northerners precious time.[100] To the north, Newton's and Bartlett's combined brigades stumbled to an halt along the stone wall, where they joined the 96th Pennsylvania to volley against Cobb's men who were on the higher road to their front and left.

By the time they got reorganized and moving, however, the Vermonters had gained the wooded mountain top south of the 24th Georgia and Cobb's Legion. The panting New Englanders halted in the darkening woods to regroup and catch their wind.[101] Soldiers from the scattered 16th Virginia skittered through the woods along their front moving west. The 4th Vermont veered south to cut off the shadows which crashed through the trees while the 2nd Vermont scrambled west over the mountain, headed for Pleasant Valley.[102]

Simultaneously, General Paul Semmes, under orders from Howell Cobb, double quicked his brigade (the 53rd Georgia, 15th and 32nd Virginia) north along the wooded ridge toward the Vermonters' flank. Less than half a mile away from their original position they ran into the fleeing 16th Virginia and the 4th Vermont which was close on their heels. "...we about-faced and went back as fast as we came," Ensign John Parham of the 32nd Virginia recalled. Retracing their steps back to the Brownsville Gap Road, the command filed down the mountain and formed a line across the Pleasant Valley Road, north of Brownsville to await the Federal onslaught.[103]

The 16th Virginia did not get away from the New Englanders, who descended upon them howling like demons. Encircled and with small arms fire slashing the darkness on all sides, most of the command surrendered. The 4th Vermont bagged Major Francis D. Holladay, the regimental colors, and seventy-four men.[104] Exhausted from the climb and by their sudden melee, the Yankees sorted themselves out, sent their prisoners to the rear, and sat down to rest for a few minutes.[105]

Behind them on the eastern side of the mountain, Colonel William Irwin's brigade crashed among the fallen trees, stumps, and boulders on that face of the mountain. They gained the crest in time to capture a couple of disgruntled Rebels and to claim a part in the struggle.[106]

The fighting on the southern flank further demoralized the rest of Colonel William Parham's Virginia brigade. The 3rd New Jersey and the 4th New Jersey regiments, having become entangled in the leapfrog assault across the open ground, slipped and scurried up the shale hill toward the Burkittsville Road.[107] They herded the frightened Virginians around both flanks of Cobb's two regiments, which held the upper end of the road.[108] When the 15th North Carolina (Cobb's brigade) reached the Burkittsville-Arnoldstown Road intersection at the top of the mountain, Cobb's Legion and the 24th Georgia abandoned their defenses. A friend of Private Tom Barrow's (Company B, Cobb's Legion) grabbed a Virginian by the arm and asked why he was hurrying so. He had no ammunition, the frightened soldier stammered, whereupon the Georgian slapped his cartridge box into the astonished fellow's hands and ran into the darkness himself. Nearby lay Sergeant Benjamin Mell (Company D, Cobb's Legion). He was dying alone in a pool of his own blood. He had just yelled for his friends to leave him and save themselves. Both regiments joined the stream of men running down the mountainside. They left behind their mortally wounded twenty-seven-year-old colonel, Jefferson M. Lamar.[109] The 4th New Jersey claimed him, his adjutant, who refused to leave his side, and ten other line officers as their prizes. In all Cobb's Legion brought four of twenty-two officers off the field.[110]

Acting upon Colonel Thomas Munford's advice, General Howell Cobb sent the 15th North Carolina and the 16th Georgia to take cover behind the stone wall along the Arnoldstown Road.[111] The wooded slope to the east and the low ground below the drop off east of the small plateau between the two crossroads swarmed with Federals. The general and his fifty-year-old brother-in-law, "Colonel" John B. Lamar desperately tried to rally their panicked men but to no avail.

The general snatched the regimental colors from a fugitive. A second later a heavy projectile, which he mistook for an artillery shell, jerked it out of his hands. Before he had time to recover, a round struck down his volunteer aide, John Lamar. The traumatized officer left the field with his dying brother-in-law.[112]

While the New Jersey brigade pressured the Confederate right flank, Newton's and Bartlett's brigades pushed toward the left flank and the center of the gap. The 16th New York anchored the left flank. The 18th, 32nd New York, and 5th Maine continued the line with the 96th Pennsylvania finishing out the formation on the right. The 31st New York, operating on its own accord was still along the Mountain Church Road and heading toward the Burkittsville Road intersection where Lieutenant Colonel Francis Pinto mistakenly thought he saw some of Irwin's men retreating. The 95th Pennsylvania was behind the brigades in support and the 27th New York still remained in the fields east of the mountain trying to reform.[113] In the increasing confusion and the deceiving shadows no one was sure where their own men were.

Jim Allen of the 16th New York on his individual foray reached the plateau in front of the 16th Georgia in time to see several skedaddlers crawl over the steep ledge a short distance east of the intersecting roads. He gave chase. Scaling the precipice a short distance in front of his regiment, he started across the open ground when a volley cut through the dark seemingly in his face. He hurled himself to the ground, and the bullets zinged well overhead.[114]

Behind him Lieutenant Colonel Joel Seaver ordered his regiment down. Most of the miniés passed through the tree tops at their backs. One nicked First Lieutenant William Walling (Company D) in the nose. As the blood trickled down over his cheek, he mused to himself, "O, God, the Lord, thou hast covered my head in the day of battle."[115]

Before the Confederates could respond, the 96th Pennsylvania, having crossed the Arnoldstown Road below the 15th North Carolina, came upon the 16th Georgia and the right wing of the 15th North Carolina from the rear.[116] Sergeant Andrew Anderson (Company K) shot the North Carolinian color bearer seconds before the Pennsylvanians fired into the backs of the two regiments.[117] The 16th New York fired into their fronts at the same time.[118]

It was too much punishment for the Rebels to take. A lieutenant from the 15th North Carolina stepped forward into the ranks of the 96th Pennsylvania to surrender lest he be killed in the slaughter he assumed would follow. The Pennsylvanians eagerly snatched him up as they bolted into the 16th Georgia where they captured the wounded Captain Augustus C. Thompson of Company G and forty other men, many of whom were not injured.[119]

While the Pennsylvanians reorganized themselves a short distance over the crest, the rest of the 15th North Carolina dashed around them, heading down the western slope toward the presumed safety of Pleasant Valley.[120]

A good many of them ran into an encircling detachment of five enlisted men from the 3rd New Jersey under the command of Acting Adjutant David Fairly and First Lieutenant Baldwin Hufty (Company E). In the ensuing firefight, the Confederates lost a few men to the Yankees' accurate rifle fire. The New Jersey soldiers captured four officers and a large number of men by the time the two lead regiments from the brigade arrived at the top of the mountain.[121]

Jim Allen (Company F, 16th New York) rose to his feet. Waving his arms, he screamed, "Up, men, up!" He charged the Confederates and singlehandedly brought in fourteen men and the colors of the 16th Georgia, which they had hastily tied to a sapling when a bullet cut the staff in two. Turning to the left, looking for support, he saw Lieutenant Colonel Seaver riding up the road toward him. After he ascertained what had occurred, Seaver rode down to the regiment and a few minutes later came back with an escort for the prisoners.[122]

While the rest of the Federal regiments halted long enough to catch their breaths, the 3rd New Jersey, the 4th New Jersey, and the 95th Pennsylvania rushed past the cross roads heading for a swale west of the crest.[123] They expected no opposition. A scattered volley from a handful of rallied Confederate infantrymen pelted the 95th Pennsylvania. A couple of men went to the ground, wounded. The Yankees fired back. The Rebel line, such as it was, dissolved. Private Joseph Shaw (Company H) watched the demoralized soldiers throw their rifles aside or try to break them on the surrounding trees. On the left (south), Corporal Joseph Lawton and Alfred Hoffman (both Company B) flanked the Southerners. Pointing to an officer who was trying to rally his men, Lawton and Hoffman drew beads on him and brought him down. A few more scattered shots kept the Confederates running even faster.[124]

Captain H. H. Carlton of Georgia with the six-pounder and twelve-pounder field pieces of his Troup artillery were in column on the next ridge in the southwestern extension of the Arnoldstown Road. They had been there for fifteen minutes patiently awaiting the Federal attack. They let the Northerners get to within one hundred yards before the six-pounder opened fire with canister.[125] It ripped through the 4th New Jersey, killing a number of men.

Adjutant Josiah S. Studderford of the 4th died instantly when a single canister ball gouged a terrible hole through his body.[126] The same blast rattled Colonel Joseph Bartlett, who believing the area secure, had nearly ridden into the gun.[127]

The Confederate gunners pulled the six-pounder back by prolonge, which allowed the howitzer's crew to fire. The round struck a cordwood

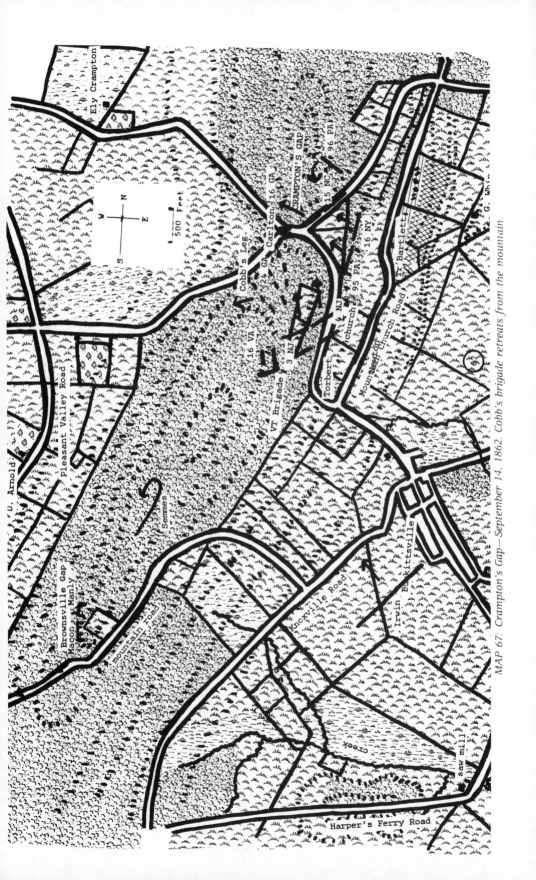

MAP 67: Crampton's Gap—September 14, 1862. Cobb's brigade retreats from the mountain.

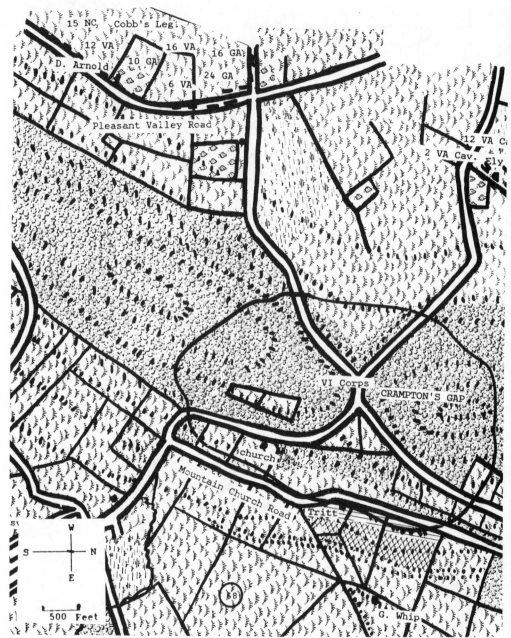

15 NC Cobb's Leg
12 VA   16 VA   16 GA
D. Arnold   10 GA
                     24 GA
            6 VA

Pleasant Valley Road

12 VA Ca
2 VA Cav. Ely

VI Corps   CRAMPTON'S GAP

church

Mountain Church Road
Tritt

W
S   N
E

500 Feet

68

G. Whip

MAP 68: Pleasant Valley, Maryland—September 14, 1862. Situation at dark.

stack near the 95th Pennsylvania and showered the men with splinters and wood chips. The Pennsylvanians opened fire to drive the guns off.[128] Private Bob Thomas of the battery collapsed with a bullet through both legs.[129] [Refer to Map 67]

Each gun fired twice more before the infantry pressure became too severe to withstand. As Fonny Johnson limbered up his twelve-pounder howitzer to pull it off, the axle broke on one side. The crew abandoned the piece, named "Jennie," in the road and escaped in the dark down to Pleasant Valley.[130]

With most of their ammunition gone, the Northern regiments halted, swearing under their breaths. In the distance, under the moonlight, they had seen the canvas of supply wagons in the valley west of the mountain. Without any cavalry support, they could not press their advantage.

The day had not been wasted. Privates David Polk (Company B, 95th Pennsylvania) and his friend Frank Sanders (Company F) picked up two battle flags in their charge over the crest.[131]

While Henry Slocum's division regrouped itself, the Vermont Brigade and Irwin's brigade from "Baldy" Smith's division worked their way into the cleared ground west of the gap. Surgeon George T. Stevens (77th New York) winced as he stepped over the Confederate casualties who cluttered the Burkittsville Road. On the way down the road, as it filed past the dismounted "Jennie," the 4th Vermont claimed its capture for the honor of the regiment.[132]

The Confederates had nothing to boast about. Thomas Munford and his two cavalry regiments secured the Rohrersville Road (northwestern end of the Burkittsville Road) in the vicinity of Ely Crampton's farm.[133] Farther south, on the Pleasant Valley Road, north of Brownsville, the scene was far from calm. General Jeb Stuart and his staff arrived from Maryland Heights to discover the Confederates in Pleasant Valley in a state of confusion. [Refer to Map 68]

Caissons and wagons cluttered the road. Hordes of disillusioned infantry stumbled around in the darkness. Major Heros Von Borcke (Stuart's staff) posted a strong provost guard across the road with orders to stop and reform any non-wounded stragglers. The staff officers then proceeded to the front to find Howell Cobb. It took them an hour to reach Brownsville and the David Arnold's farm.

General Cobb, recognizing the staff in the darkness, rode into the cluster and pleaded with the intrepid Stuart, "Dismount, gentlemen, dismount, if your lives are dear to you! the enemy is within fifty yards of us; I am expecting their attack every moment; oh! my dear Stuart, that I should live to experience such a disaster! what can be done? what can save us?"

Jeb Stuart graciously pulled the distraught Howell Cobb aside to console him. A few minutes later, both generals were reforming the infantry in the dark and placing what artillery they had present to prevent another Federal breakthrough.

Finally, Stuart turned toward his faithful Von Borcke.

"Major," he said with typical disregard of any previous intelligence,

"I don't believe the Yankees are so near at hand, but we must be certain about it; take two couriers with you, and find out at once where the enemy is."

The major did not appreciate the assignment. He expected to die at any moment, either at the hands of their own scattered pickets or at those of the exhausted Yankee skirmishers. Turning east on the Arnoldstown Road, the major got to within seventy yards of the Yankee camps. Their camp fires flickered all over the open, rolling fields on either side of him. In the dancing glimmer of a nearby fire, he saw the silhouette of a cavalry vidette in the road ahead of him. Without saying a word, he and his orderlies rode nearly a mile back to David Arnold's and reported to Stuart. By then, Lafayette McLaws with Colonel Alfred Cumming's brigade (8th, 9th, 10th, and 11th Alabama) had arrived and further strengthened the Confederate position in the valley.[134]

While the two armies bivouacked in Pleasant Valley and along the western base of South Mountain, the Yankee bandsmen started their gruesome task of fetching in the wounded and lining up the dead. They found plenty to do. Most of Howell Cobb's brigade remained near the summit of the mountain. He lost in captured 36% of his 1,310 effectives in less than one hour. The unfortunate Cobb's Legion left 62% of its men behind in Yankee hands.[135] Chief Musician Montreville Williams (3rd New Jersey) and his men labored until 1:00 A.M. the next morning trying to evacuate their own wounded before they bedded down on the rocky soil to get some sleep.[136]

They treated the defeated Rebs more humanely than the Confederates expected. A stretcher crew from General John Newton's brigade found the mortally wounded Thomas Newton (Company I, 16th Virginia) behind the stone wall along the Mountain Church Road. As they bore him toward the field hospital, a mounted officer asked him to which command he belonged. Newton told him, whereupon the Federal asked him his name and his home town.

"Why, that is singular," the officer blurted, "the name of my commander is General John Newton, of Norfolk, Virginia."

Before Newton could answer, the officer galloped off to ferret out General Newton.[137]

The two Northern soldiers who carried George Bernard of the 12th Virginia to the rear went to leave him in the dark on the cool grass of a nearby farm house. A kindly, middle aged man intercepted them before they could put him down. As they lowered Bernard to the ground, he heard the man assure him he would receive impartial treatment. He asked Bernard how he felt, and what would he like done for him. Before Bernard answered, the gentleman identified himself as the chaplain of the 5th Maine.

The dazed, weakened Virginian, without giving a second thought to the New Englander's prohibitionist proclivities, requested a dose of medicinal brandy. The chaplain said he could bring the Rebel tea but nothing stronger. Being in no condition to complain, Bernard accepted.

While he lay there, the Federal provost guard took Lieutenant Joseph

Manson (Company I) away to be herded in with the other unwounded prisoners. A stretcher crew carried Bernard into the farm house where a Federal surgeon and his hospital steward saw to him immediately. Bernard told the two men he feared the probing for the bullet.

"Show your grit," the steward quietly chided him, "Don't be alarmed."

The shamed Virginian clenched his teeth and groaned, "Go ahead, doctor!"

The surgeon quickly found the bullet, and deftly extracted it with less pain than his patient had originally imagined. The steward plopped the minié ball in Bernard's open palm.

"Put that in your pocket and carry it home," he said.

By then the chaplain had found him. The famished enlisted man guzzled the tea then looked around the room. He fastened his eyes upon Thomas Newton, and asked him how he had been captured.

A stony glance silenced him. The last he saw of the surgeon turned soldier, the fellow was carrying a rifle on the firing line. Bernard did not realize that the doctor was serving as an enlisted man.[138]

Thomas Newton did not want his presence known. His first cousin, John Newton, however, had his surgeon personally hunt him out and treat his wound. He ordered his relative removed to a private home in Burkittsville. Thomas Newton died there a few months later.[139]

A Federal soldier very compassionately walked the badly wounded Philip Brown (Company C, 12th Virginia) to a brick farm house about one mile behind the Northern lines. An elderly surgeon, at the Confederate's request, extracted the ball without administering any anesthesia. Brown watched the doctor make a two-inch incision in his upper arm. It took him five hard pulls with the forceps to extract the ball, which, in passing up the private's forearm and through his elbow, had gotten nearly flattened.

The exhausted private watched his blood splatter in every direction before the doctor deftly packed the wound with lint, at which point he passed out. The doctor brought him around by bathing his face in cool water. The doctor smiled.

"Young man," he said, "you stood the operation bravely, but you pinched my leg blue."

Still grinning, he handed the washed bullet with the flattened point, to Philip Brown. Brown's Yankee companion then fed him and tenderly bedded him down. Brown deeply appreciated the young soldier's charity.[140]

The day had been costly. Cobb lost 686 officers and men of 1,310 involved. The fighting cost Munford and Parham (including the 10th Georgia) 272 effectives of 928 officers and men engaged.[141] The terribly outnumbered Confederates took out 534 of over 9,000 Federals engaged.[142]

The weary Ensign John Parham (Company C, 32nd Virginia) summarized the day best when he curled up to sleep with his weapon beside him. He bitterly remembered it was "...the worst night I ever spent."[143]

Unlike the fighting several miles to the north, at Fox's and Turner's

Gaps, the Federals around Crampton's Gap had achieved their objective. They had driven the Confederates from the pass. The soldiers had won the battle but had, through no fault of their own, lost the opportunity to press their advantage and cut off the Confederates to the north at Boonsboro. Had McClellan not attempted to coordinate the attacks at all three gaps, but had allowed the VI Corps to press the advantage earlier in the day, the battle might have turned out differently. Darkness ended the battle and prevented either side from determining each others strengths and troop dispositions.

Chapter Fourteen

SEPTEMBER 15, 1862

CRAMPTON'S GAP

The cannonading resounded ominously for five miles up the valley from Harpers Ferry. In the first light, Captain William W. Blackford watched Colonel William Irwin's Northern brigade deploy in battle formation across the valley north of Brownsville.[1] The Yankees did not appear threatening. They moved very slowly, listening to the rolling thunder of the artillery.

By 10:00 A.M., they were within two hundred yards of Jeb Stuart's dismounted troopers, whom they found a short distance south of David Arnold's peach orchard and grape arbor. General Stuart with Captain William D. Farley and Lieutenant Chiswell Dabney rode up to Blackford, who was inspecting the position, and suggested that they raid the house for provisions.[2]

The four rode up to the two-story house and dismounted. Blackford quickly entered the house through an unlatched window on the ground floor. He lost no time in finding the pantry. Within minutes, he was handing meat, pies, cheese, and butter through the window to his accomplices. With bullets clipping through the trees around the house, the four settled down to enjoy a meal.[3]

Near Brownsville, the abandoned Major Von Borcke suddenly became aware of a brief foreboding silence. The guns at Harpers Ferry had ceased fire. In the distance, he heard shouts of joy emanating from the Confederate reserves closer to the Potomac River. It rolled up the Pleasant Valley Road in increasing volume until it reached the major. "Harper's Ferry has surrendered to Jackson!"

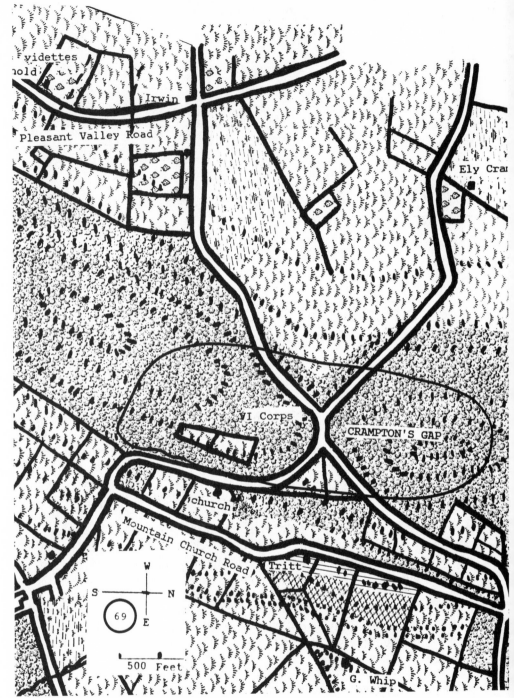

MAP 69: Pleasant Valley, Maryland—September 15, 1862. Situation during the morning.

Seconds later a panting orderly, reeking with sweat, pulled his lathered horse to a halt next to Von Borcke with the official news. Just as quickly, the major sent the courier forward to David Arnold's house.[4]

He arrived there about the same time the Federal skirmishers realized that something was going on. As he reported to Stuart, a lone Yankee mounted the stone wall two hundred yards north of the house.

"What the hell are you fellows cheering for?" he yelled at the top of his voice.

"Because Harper's Ferry has gone up, God damn you," one of the officers swore.

"I thought that was it," the skirmisher retorted before he disappeared behind the wall.[5]

With that, the VI Corps settled down for the rest of the day.[6] The Yankees meandered over the battlefield inspecting the aftermath of their previous afternoon's work. The men of the 49th Pennsylvania, while crossing the gap, passed around "Jennie," the twelve-pounder howitzer which the Troup Artillery abandoned. Sergeant Robert S. Westbrook (Company B) scoffed to think that the Rebels called it a cannon. Mounted on old cart wheels with a thin tube which resembled a stovepipe, the Pennsylvanians cracked jokes about it while they stumbled down the mountainside.[7]

Captain Jacob Haas (Company G, 96th Pennsylvania) retraced his regiment's approach around the Arnoldtown Road. The Confederates had killed one of his men and wounded eight more. The scores of Confederate casualties, most of them from the 16th Georgia and the 15th North Carolina, littered the immediate area, giving him a grim sense of satisfaction. Below him, in the fields east of the Mountain Church Road, his men were burying the regiment's dead.[8] [Refer to Map 69]

They would continue to lay more to rest as the day progressed. Time seemed to stop for the wounded. Private George Bernard of the 12th Virginia spent an unpleasant night propped against a sack of wheat, listening to the plaintive cries of the injured who filled every room in the house. At daylight the attendants put him and several other men upon the thinly strawed porch to give them some fresh air.

Starving as he was, he felt slighted when the hospital steward brought him a cup of weak lamb broth. Then he realized the Yankees received the same ration as they did.

"Indeed," Bernard observed, "we had been treated with so much kindness and consideration by all of the Federal soldiers, officers and men, with whom I had thus far come in contact, I had no ground for any complaint, but much cause for gratitude."[9]

Lieutenant John Gayle (Company C, 16th Virginia) felt the same way. During the morning, he and twenty other uninjured Confederates spent the morning burying their dead. Shortly afterwards, the captain received orders to report to General William Franklin's headquarters at Martin Shafer's house.

He found the general and his brigade commanders seated comfortably under the shade trees in the yard. The general invited the captain to sit down and enjoy some pleasant conversation. During their refighting of the battle, Brigadier General John Newton, who had located his cousin, Thomas Newton of the 16th Virginia, the night before, asked Gayle a lot of questions about Norfolk, the general's home town. The captain answered him politely then prepared to leave.

In rising, he told Franklin he had surrendered his prized pistol and sword to a Northern officer when he was captured. The general commanded an orderly to secure Gayle a mount and to accompany him to the regiment which brought him in and to retrieve his personal property.

The captain accepted the Yankee's kindness. When he surrendered at Appomattox in 1865, however, he still remained unrepentant of his secessionist ideology.[10]

FOX'S GAP

Several miles to the north, the victorious IX Corps spent a miserable night upon the battlefield around Wise's farm. The cold September air kept Captain Charles F. Walcott of the 21st Massachusetts awake. Shortly after midnight he heard someone, quite close to the regiment, crying for help.

The captain straightened his stiffening legs and briskly limped toward the voice. As he approached the injured man, he noticed a shadowy figure dart away from another man who was lying motionless upon the ground. He found Lieutenant Colonel George S. James (3rd South Carolina Battalion), who had lain upon the battlefield, feigning death, for several hours. He told Walcott he had tried to escape but could not. He was dying and knew it. He pleaded for help when the looter, whom Walcott had scared off, rolled him over to steal his watch. The New Englander covered the Confederate with a discarded blanket then gave him a swig from his pocket flask. Walcott sat down beside James. The colonel explained to his enemy how he had defied Colonel William D. DeSaussure (15th South Carolina) when the two regiments crossed the Potomac by calling the colonel a coward because he refused to wage war in Maryland. Now George James believed he was the only surviving officer in his regiment and he feared he had led most of his men to their deaths. (The Yankees shattered Thomas Drayton's brigade. They killed 49 officers and men, wounded 164 more, and captured an additional 176 effectives.)[11]

Not long after dawn, Captain Walcott posted a picket detachment under First Sergeant John F. Lewis (Company F). The sentries had barely started down the western side of the mountain when they stumbled into a stray Confederate patrol. The seven Rebels, who saw them first, took off at a run with the cries to halt echoing off their backs. Sergeant Lewis automatically brought his rifle to his shoulder and took careful aim. He cut down the Confederate sergeant in charge of the squad at less than fifty yards. The rest of the Confederates hurled their weapons to the ground before their sergeant's lifeless body thudded into the road. With their hands raised, they walked into the 21st Massachusetts' picket post and surrendered.

The astonished Yankees found their prisoners wearing knapsacks labeled "21st Mass." on them. The regiment had lost them at the Second Manassas. Lewis' men asked the Southerners what they had to eat.

"We have plenty of regular rations," the one Confederate bragged.

Lewis opened one of the haversacks and discovered six corn meal balls, covered with ashes. He did not particularly care for ashcakes. As he pulled his nose out of the haversack, he overheard a prisoner drawl, "We always liked your people well enough, but hated your government."[12]

A large number of the 35th Massachusetts, which had settled down in Wise's field, looted the haversacks of the Confederate dead for their quaint ashcakes. A few, expressing qualms about robbing the dead, abstained. Along the broken down stone wall east of their bivouac they found a large number of discarded knapsacks. Ignoring the North Carolinians who lay on their backs with their blackened faces grimacing at the morning sky, the New Englanders searched the abandoned blankets for lice before stealing them.[13]

Meanwhile, the troops began the laborious task of cleaning up after themselves. The 23rd Ohio started to inter the Confederate dead. Private M. Deady (Company I) found a stiffening Confederate officer with a piece of scrap paper pinned to his coat. The Federal reverently scratched the inscription, "H. Y. Hyers, Mad River Lodge, North Carolina," upon the crude head board and planted it at the end of the man's grave. He figured the officer had scribbled the note in his own hand to keep himself from becoming an anonymous corpse.[14] In the outbuilding near Wise's cabin, Captain Charles Walcott found two soldiers—one Federal, the other Confederate—who had killed each other in hand-to-hand combat.[15]

Private Eugene Beague (Company B, 45th Pennsylvania) and his friends gathered in their dead comrades and placed them in a neat row on the level ground in the cornfield west of J. Martz's cabin. They had twenty-one comrades to lay to rest. The Pennsylvanians wrapped their friends in their army blankets and lowered them into the trench they had dug for them.

Beague resented having to care for the Rebel casualties which had been left behind for them to decently bury. He had not expected to find so many bodies between the stone walls of the wood road. Their bodies literally blanketed the lane in heaps of two or three men. He consoled himself with the afterthought, "Our Harper's Ferry muskets with a good sized ball and three buckshot, at short range, had done fearful execution."[16]

Shocked members of the 9th New Hampshire, who in the daylight finally had a chance to survey the battlefield of the day before, could not believe what they saw. The Rebels were dirty and browned. Their poorly made gray uniforms looked more like short school boys' jackets. Many had no shoes. In one spot they came upon eighteen men in a pile.

Their twisted, blackened faces, contorted by death into ghastly grimaces and scowls, disturbed the new soldiers. One fellow succinctly wrote about the dead Rebels, "They are just the color of the ground, and so hard to be seen."

The hungry Yankees pilfered the Confederates' haversacks for what little food they had, including the foreign ashcakes. Others looted their pockets for souvenirs.[17]

Some men wandered the western side of the mountain to ascertain an approximation of the Confederate casualties. Sergeant Robert Smith (Company G, 48th Pennsylvania) obtained permission from his captain, Oliver Bosbyshell, to reconnoiter Wise's yard. In half an hour he returned with a body count of one hundred five dead Southerners.[18]

Overworked brigade surgeons methodically lined up their casualties in a macabre assembly line and started to work. Their matter-of-fact bedside manner fascinated Captain James Wren (Company B, 48th Pennsylvania). Mesmerized by their efficiency, he watched them set up four tables in the yard. The hospital attendants plopped a wounded man on the table nearest him. Another attendant followed and marked the soldier's wound with a piece of chalk. The surgeon stepped up with his saw and cut on the drawn line.

Fascinated by the human litter scattered about him, the captain decided to play a macabre matching game.

He wrote in his diary, "In Looking around in the yard I saw a Beautiful plump arm Laing which Drew my attention & in looking a Little [at] it and seeing another of the same Kind, I picked them up & Laid them together & found that thay a[re] a right [one] & one a Left Arm which Convinced me thay war of the one man." The surgeons did not bother to remove their patients' shoes and socks before amputating legs and feet and chucking them aside.[19]

Quartermaster Sergeant Joseph Gould (48th Pennsylvania), weaving past the surgeons, who were busy sawing away in the yard around Wise's cabin, went inside. He found a corpse with his face still pressed against a chinked hole in the cabin's wall. A bullet had slammed into his head while he peeked through the hole to observe the fighting. The air was heavy with the sickening smell of the Confederates' decaying bodies.[20]

West of the house, the Yankees laid out their own dead in a solemn line. A piece of paper with each man's name, company, regimental number, and state lay upon every body. Pioneers were digging a rough trench seven feet wide along the hillside. The practical Captain James Wren sadly jotted in his diary, "The troops feal desperat[e] towards the rebels as meney of them had brave Comrads whou stood in Line with them was now taking thear posision in ther Last Line."[21]

As the morning wore on and the dead Confederates continued to bloat in the sunlight, the burial crew from the 12th Ohio dragged their blackened corpses toward the ground level well in front of Daniel Wise's cabin. Rather than fight the rocky ground and the repulsive stench the Ohioans grabbed the Rebels by their belts and dropped them down the well. Daniel Wise walked over to them and ordered them to stop. (They walked away only to return the next day to finish what they had started.)

Lieutenant William J. Bolton (Company A, 51st Pennsylvania), whose men were wandering about examining the results of their previous day's work, wrote in his journal, "we came upon a dry well that was literally filled to the top with their dead."[22]

The IX Corps started to trickle down the Old Sharpsburg Road a few hours after daylight, leaving the field to the sightseers, the casualties, and the burial detachments.[23] Colonel Edward Ferrero's brigade got under way between 8:00 A.M. and 2:00 P.M.[24] The 51st Pennsylvania led the slow advance. All along the road, it happened upon many wounded Confederates, whom they left for the provost guard.[25]

Shortly before noon, the V Corps caught up with the brigade. In passing the 79th New York, a veteran of the 14th U.S. Regulars told Private William Todd (Company B, 79th New York) that his regiment had spent the day before in reserve. The twenty-two-year-old enlisted man mentally quipped how he wished he were in the Regulars.[26]

One of the veterans in the 21st Massachusetts, after staring down the battle worn soldiers in General George Sykes' V Corps division, which included two brigades of regulars and one of volunteers, as they filed past, blurted, "I don't see any difference in looks between regulars and volunteers."

A sergeant in the Regulars thrust his polished and spotless musket in the New Englander's face. He spat, "Here's where the difference comes in!"

The New Englander eyeballed the weapon a second and unabashedly retorted, "Yes, we use ours to fight with." Charles Walcott of the 21st Massachusetts said it was the best hit scored during the South Mountain fracas.[27]

The soldiers of the 79th New York were not in any mood to appreciate any sort of humor. William Todd counted fourteen Confederate bodies in the one corner of the crossroads. Nearby, the lone Rebel whom the Ohioans had left the day before astride the wood road wall still straddled it. Todd said the dead man was "curious" but he did not want to stay any longer to examine the spectacle.[28]

The untried 9th New Hampshire found the stiffening Rebel much more interesting. A gaggle of them scrutinized the man from top to bottom. A boy in Company E suddenly chirped, "That's the first rebel I've seen with a decent pair of boots on, and by thunder, if he ha'n't got up there to show 'em!"[29]

Captains James Wren and Henry Pleasants (Company C, 48th Pennsylvania) also meandered over Wise's field. Wren noted the corpse on the fence but offered no other comment about him. Instead, he busied himself counting bodies. In forty square feet he tabulated sixteen bodies. "Theas ware the finest set of Rebil soldiers I ever saw both in Mussel & in equipage." He and the other captain returned to their bivouac east of the field.

Presently, Billy Fitzpatrick, Pleasants' Irish valet, clumped over to the two officers. He seemed a trifle agitated.

Henry Pleasants asked, "Well, Billy, did you see them?"

"Trouth I did," gasped the Irishman, "but, Captain, isn't them men?"

The question took the officer aback. "Why?"

Fitzpatrick stammered, "By my soul every one of them has a third eye in his head."

Henry Pleasants roared with uncontrollable laughter.

"Billy," he coughed, "You saw that stone fence?"

"Yes, sir."

"Well," the captain continued as if talking with a child, "The enemy was behind it when we were engaged yesterday and in order to fire on us they had to take aim over the stone fence and consequently they got shot by our men somewhere between the shoulders and head and that is the reason so many of them is shot in the head."[30]

A rifle shot echoed with a sudden start upon the afternoon air. Private Greenleaf F. Jellison (Company C, 35th Massachusetts) plopped along the roadside with an accidental foot wound.[31] He was not the only self-inflicted casualty that afternoon.

The distraught Private Andrew Wykle (Company K, 36th Ohio) besides losing his brother—wounded—awakened in the morning between two very cold Rebel cadavers. He wandered back to his regiment, near Martz's cornfield where his messmate, William Rice, had coffee boiling. The regiment fell in before either one could drink his cup. While they stood at "rest arms," Rice absentmindedly began to crumble his hard cracker in his tin cup, with the muzzle of the weapon leaning against the inside of his elbow. His foot brushed back the hammer of his capped weapon.

The rifle fired. Andrew Wykle, scarred by the unexpected blast, helplessly watched his friend's brain spattered kepi sail more than ten feet into the air. The shock numbed him. He never heard Rice's body hit the ground. In his mind, the kepi repeatedly bobbed in the sky. "I never felt so bad in all my life," he recalled thirty-nine years later.[32]

A short distance down the mountainside, the 21st Massachusetts ran into one of Colonel Ferrero's aides. The mounted officer was herding in seven dejected Southerners whom he had surprised upon the back porch of a nearby cabin while on a private foraging expedition.[33]

Five hours later, the last units were still straggling after the rest of the column.[34] On the western side of the mountain, the 35th Massachusetts halted to study the natural beauty of the ripening valley south of Boonsboro and to enjoy a bull fight. In an adjacent field two young bulls—one black, and the other red—decided to square off against each other. The New Englanders named the black, "Mac," and the red, "Bob Lee." As the two butted heads and locked horns, the men could not help but compare the stubbornness of the contest with their own circumstances. They interpreted "Mac's" win as an omen on their behalf.[35] The IX Corps had time and George B. McClellan's cautiousness on its side. It halted three times before reaching the valley and the road to Rohrersville. The men believed they had lost every opportunity of catching up with the Confederates and that again they would escape.[36]

TURNER'S GAP

Sporadic skirmishing marked the predawn hours along the Frosttown Road. It was merely a sputtering finale to the exhausting evening of the day before. Lieutenant Colonel Philip J. Parisen (57th New York) dispatched eight men from each company forward as skirmishers. As they stepped forward into the pitch darkness of the wooded mountainside, Private Jacob H. Cole (Company A) stumbled and fell in between two rocks. He landed upon a Confederate. Unable to identify each other in the dark, they hurriedly exchanged compliments to find out who was talking to whom.

"Well, Yank," the Reb drawled, "there is no use for us to kill each other; let us make a bargain."

They agreed to become the prisoner of whichever army gained control of the ground.

When the sun broke through the trees and it became evident that the Rebel was a prisoner, Cole escorted him proudly back to the regiment's headquarters. The stunned nineteen year old received the cheers of his comrades and the shock of his life. He discovered his prisoner, standing at about six feet in height, towered a considerable distance above him.[37]

The dawn brought an audible shudder to the men of General James Ricketts' division, who having spent the night standing to arms with loaded rifles and fixed bayonets, did not anticipate the horror in the fields opposite them. The Virginians lay in heaps ninety feet in front of the Yankee line. A member of the 76th New York ventured onto the bloodied ground to inspect the havoc the regiment had wrought. He happened upon a seventeen year old Rebel who was playing opossum.

"Don't shoot! Don't shoot I'm your prisoner," he pleaded. The Yankee walked the boy back to General Hatch. All the while, the boy whined, "I told them I was a coward and couldn't fight, but they drove me up here, where I came near being killed; so I dropped, and crawled behind a stump and waited there all night."[38]

The civilians appeared upon the battlefield almost as soon as the Yankees occupied the ground. Ricketts immediately posted guards to keep them from walking off with discarded Federal property. Young John W. Long found a terribly wounded Confederate lieutenant, who was lying on his right side to keep the pressure off his riddled left arm. The boy counted eighteen bullet wounds in the man's arm between the elbow and the shoulder. Crossing in front of the cornfield where Garnett's brigade had been shot up, he quietly observed how the bullets cut off the corn stalks at about breast height. He also stooped over the body of Colonel John Strange (19th Virginia). A soldier told him the one and a half inch gash in the officer's chest came from a bayonet wound. Glancing toward the Yankee lines, he saw Confederate ramrods sticking out of the trees along the ridge. He surmised they were shot away as a last resort. Confederate scrip lay all about the place too, indicative of looting.

When Long picked up a discarded weapon and tried to leave the field with it, he was ordered to put it down. A soldier took it away from him before he could comply. The youngster ambled down the mountainside, heading for the National Pike gorge.[39]

Private Charles S. McClenthen (Company G, 26th New York) sniffed Colonel Strange's two canteens. One had water. The other contained whiskey. The Virginians, who were heaped in piles of three to four, seemed to have gotten confused in the dark and had huddled together like frightened children.

The New Yorkers picked over their bodies, searching for provisions. To their amazement, the haversacks were stuffed with biscuits, cold ham, and other delicacies.[40]

A little further to the north, the Pennsylvania Reserves, in the valley between the Frosttown Road and the Zittlestown Road, sent out men to determine how much damage they had done the day before. The gigantic Fred Green (Company D, 7th Reserves) sallied onto the hill in front of the regiment and came back with the severely wounded Major R. Stark Means (17th South Carolina), whom he unceremoniously left behind the center of the line. The men frittered away the time eating and chatting about the fight.[41]

Around noon, a Confederate surgeon came through the lines under a flag of truce. He wanted the bodies of General D. H. Hill and Colonel John Strange, both of whom he heard were dead. An armed escort took him down the Frosttown Road toward General George Meade's headquarters.[42]

Sergeant Bates Alexander (Company C, 7th Reserves) could not take his stare away from a grievously wounded Rebel who sat near his company. Sleeping, with his bloodied face lowered until his chin touched his chest, he at first appeared dead. A buckshot had marred both sides of his young face. The entry and exit wounds were directly in front of both of his ears.

In stark contrast, the unwounded Confederate surgeon, having found neither Hill or Strange sat disconsolately upon the ground with his hands clasped about his knees. His finely made gray coat contrasted sharply with the dingy tunics of the average infantrymen.

Lieutenant Harry Lantz (Company C) stood over him trying to pass the time as politely as he could.

"Well, Major," the sergeant overheard the lieutenant begin, "what do you think of Pope?"

"Pope sounded his trumpet too loudly, with his 'headquarters in the saddle,'" the major sarcastically shot back.

"Major," Lantz insisted, "you fellows may as well give in, we'll lick you anyhow in the end."

The surgeon abruptly turned his body away from the lieutenant and with his nose in the air sallied, "H'oh, that's just what we think of you."

Sergeant Alexander at first thought the Rebel was being foolishly arrogant then he realized the Confederates believed in their cause as much as the Federals did in theirs.[43]

BOONSBORO

While the I Corps awakened to a relatively calm morning, the II Corps took to the National Pike. The Federal cavalry trotted over South Mountain. The 8th Illinois Cavalry led the advance. Six companies under Colonel John Farnsworth remained on the National Pike. The remaining six companies cut across the mountain on the road which parallelled the ridge west of the Mountain House.[44]

At 10:00 A.M., the Federals ran into the dismounted skirmishers and the videttes of the 4th Virginia Cavalry, about one mile east of Boonsboro.[45] As they drew near to the Confederates, the dismounted troopers fell back and unmasked a battery of artillery. Its shells stymied the Yankee infantry and sent it to cover. The Rebels stalled them a second time then hastily withdrew toward Boonsboro as the Northern infantry fanned out to both flanks of the National Pike in battle lines.

Without warning, the infantry cleared the Pike to allow the six companies of the 8th Illinois Cavalry to charge the town. The 3rd Virginia Cavalry, under the leadership of Lieutenant Colonel John T. Thornton, charged into the Yankee cavalry. A bullet brought the colonel and his horse down together in a heap. The Virginians temporarily stopped the attack, but at a cost of one killed and fifteen wounded and missing.[46] Outgunned and outnumbered, the Confederates clattered down the Pike for the town's main street.[47]

The assault caught the 9th Virginia Cavalry along the curbs of Boonsboro, where the saddle sore troopers had dismounted to rest.

"Mount! Mount!" followed by the sharp staccato of pistol and carbine fire sent the troopers scampering for their horses. The 3rd Virginia Cavalry crashed into the lead elements of the regiment before the men managed to mount up. The pile up of frightened horses and equally scared men bottled up the National Pike.[48] Someone screamed for the 4th Virginia Cavalry, which was on the eastern edge of the town to charge, but in the confusion Colonel W. C. Wickham did not issue the command to his troops.

By some miracle, Lieutenant Colonel Richard L. T. Beale (9th Virginia Cavalry) extricated part of his command from the confusion and started it down the Boonsboro Pike toward Sharpsburg. In so doing, he pulled the cork out of the bottle. Bewildered horsemen stampeded in every direction they could to escape the Yankee column. Civilians complicated matters further by sniping at the Rebel troopers from the upper story windows of the houses lining both sides of the limestone road.

At the same time, General Fitzhugh Lee, with the 3rd squadron of the 4th Virginia Cavalry, collided with the rear of the regiment.[49] His cousin, Colonel W. H. F. Lee (9th Virginia Cavalry) screamed at his befuddled command to right about face and to stem the retreat.

The rear squadron of the 9th Virginia, hearing the command, attempted to comply, but was caught by the Federals before it completed the maneuver. The troopers could not see anything in the swirling limestone dust which engulfed their moving column.[50]

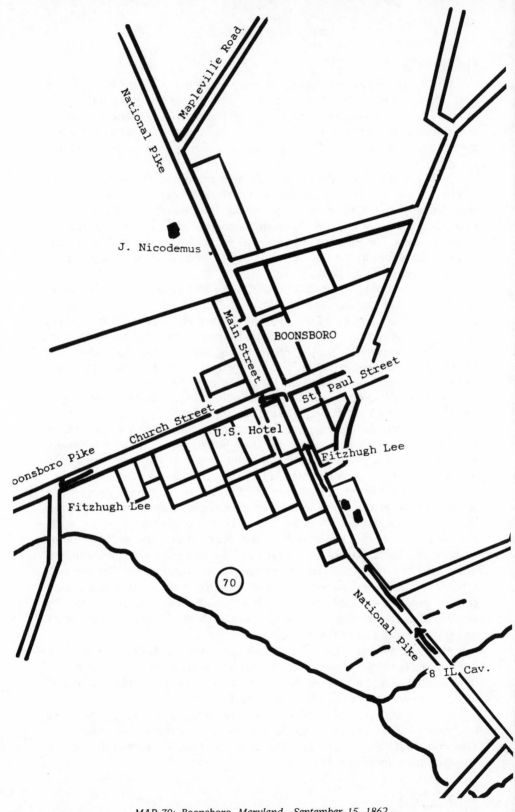

MAP 70: Boonsboro, Maryland—September 15, 1862.
Federal cavalry drives the Confederate rear guard from Boonsboro.

The 8th Illinois Cavalry plunged into the two fragmented Virginia regiments with a fury, while Yankee infantry tried to flank the Rebels from a cornfield along the southwestern side of the town. Colonel John F. Farnsworth of the 8th Illinois, having dismounted a Confederate cavalryman, rode the fellow down. Another Rebel trooper tried to cut the colonel down with a sabre thrust from behind when an enlisted man in Company B of the 8th Illinois plucked the man from the saddle with a pistol shot.

Private William Jones (Company E, 8th Illinois Cavalry) rushed fifty yards into the field east of the Boonsboro Pike and bloodied up a Virginian in hand-to-hand combat when a bullet struck him in the left side of his body. The ball passed through his chest and stopped just under the skin on the opposite side of his body. The 8th Illinois found them after the engagement, side by side upon the field. Corporal Sewell Flagg (Company E) went down with a severe arm wound and Morris Stull (Company G) received a saber cut.[51]

The rear squadron of the 9th Virginia fell back to both sides of the Boonsboro Pike, leaving room for the other squadron, in column of fours, to countercharge the aggressive Westerners. As the two squadrons leap frogged south, they slammed into the narrow covered bridge which spanned the creek about one mile south of town.[52] In the retreat, Captain John F. Hughlett (Company D) lost his horse to Yankee carbine fire. Finding a riderless horse, he mounted up and continued down the pike.[53]

Sergeant George W. Beale (Company C, 9th Virginia Cavalry), whose father was the regiment's lieutenant colonel, panicked. Riders careened blindly into dust obscured telegraph poles along the road. Horses fell over one another, hurling their riders to the ground.[54] Colonel W. H. F. Lee's horse galloped into a pile up and crashed to the ground, knocking the officer senseless.[55] The hapless Captain Hughlett (D Co.), who was unhorsed again, this time by a collision with downed riders, hurled himself over the fence west of the Pike and hid himself in the corn.[56]

Lieutenant Colonel Robert Beale (9th Virginia Cavalry) wheeled about with a few of his men and led a sabre charge against the Illinois troops. A bullet dropped his horse in the road sixty feet in front of their column. Private Thomas Lewis (Company B) dismounted and handed his horse to the colonel, who remounted and escaped.[57]

On the southern end of the bridge, Captain Thomas Haynes (Company H) rallied his squadron and charged into the Westerners who had just run over Colonel Lee.[58] Private A. V. Teeple (Company H, 8th Illinois Cavalry) was unhorsed when his mount stumbled and threw him. A Rebel officer slashed his head with a sabre blow. The dazed trooper crawled into his saddle and was hurried to the rear with two other prisoners.[59]

At the same time, Captain Haynes dismounted and pulled Colonel Lee's riderless horse to its feet, while his men engaged the 8th Illinois in hand-to-hand combat. He yelled at the semiconscious Lee to get up. The badly bruised colonel could not move. When his Virginians were pressed back, the captain remounted and retreated to the southern end of the bridge, leaving the colonel in the road.[60]

The Confederates did not stop running until they reached the Keedysville Road intersection, some two miles farther south. General Fitzhugh Lee rallied a large part of his command there. They waited needlessly for the Yankee cavalry to pursue them. Later in the afternoon, when he realized he was not being aggressively pursued, he pulled his command east toward South Mountain to draw the Federals away from the rallying army at Sharpsburg.[61] [Refer to Map 70]

The fighting had cost both sides dearly. The 4th Virginia Cavalry lost its sergeant major—dead—and several wounded.[62] The 9th Virginia Cavalry left Lieutenants Armstreet E. Fowlkes (Company G) and Frank Oliver (Company F) dead upon the field. Another sixteen were killed or mortally wounded and ten more captured. Its colonel was missing.[63] In the fight at Boonsboro the 8th Illinois Cavalry lost one killed—Sergeant Robert MacArthur (Company M), fifteen wounded, among them the fearless Captain Elisha Kelley (Company E) and three captured.[64]

The Northerners won the day because they held the field. In all the Illinois cavalrymen netted about five hundred wounded, many of whom they captured in a large brick building along the National Pike which the Confederates had turned into a hospital. They also captured Lieutenant Bernard H. Carter, Jr. (Company D, 3rd Virginia Cavalry) from whose father they had stolen horses on the Peninsula.[65]

While the Federals lurched east and south toward the Antietam Creek, the Army of Northern Virginia regrouped around Sharpsburg and the captured garrison at Harpers Ferry. The Army of Northern Virginia, under Lee's command, had never lost any engagements prior to South Mountain. In addition, a large force of Federal cavalry, which escaped from Harpers Ferry the night before, had captured more than sixty ammunition wagons, a couple of hundred sick and wounded men, and Samuel Garland's body in a predawn raid near Williamsport, Maryland. Despite the loss of most of Longstreet's wagons, Lee would not acknowledge defeat in Maryland. He was a gambler, who had no intention of going into Virginia whipped.[66]

In retrospect, however, he had lost the battle but not the war. Ezra Carman correctly assessed the situation when he wrote, "Though tactically defeated in the two engagements at Crampton's Gap and Turner's Gap the Confederates were strategically successful and General D. H. Hill was correct in his statement that they had 'accomplished all that was required, the delay of the Yankee army until Harper's Ferry could not be relieved.' "[67]

Battles do not end when the shooting stops. The scars are left behind for everyone to live with. At Fox's Gap, the civilians scrounged the field upon the troops' departure. Young Frank P. Firey and his father meandered through Wise's field, carefully trying not to tread upon the Confederate bodies which the Yankees had not found the time to inter. In walking along Thomas Drayton's former position they discovered the corpse of a young Georgian. Mr. Firey estimated the fair haired boy was about eighteen years old. In his pocket they found a letter from his sister in which she wrote, "Hurry up and whip the Yankees and come home." She would never know that her brother had perished from a bullet in the forehead.

They found the stiff corpse of Lieutenant Colonel George W. James (3rd South Carolina Battalion) near where the 21st Massachusetts had spent the night. Mister Firey cut several of the officer's buttons from his tunic for souvenirs before burying the South Carolinian. (He kept the buttons to make ear bobs and a breastpin for his daughter.)[68]

Twenty-four-year-old George Moore, and his father, J. D. Moore, who lived near the stone wall where John Gibbon's Westerners won their famous nom de guerre—the Iron Brigade—, found a young North Carolinian sitting along the Old Sharpsburg Road. The sight of the boy gurgling blood and water through the hole in his chest with every breath brought tears to George's eyes. All the while, the Confederate moaned, "Oh, if only I could see my mother!"

On the wood road, between the Mountain House and Daniel Wise's he found a Confederate sitting upright with his rifle across his knees and his head lowered as if in sleep. The father and his son raised the corpse's chin. An ugly purple mark in his forehead explained his death. A short distance away they came across another fellow who had lost his head just above his ears. It was a clean cut, as precise as a surgeon's work. Mr. Moore speculated he was the victim of a shell. Sixty years later, George Moore, then eighty-four years old, wept when he recalled his visit to those fields of courage and endurance.[69]

Appendix

LIST OF ENGAGEMENTS
and
KNOWN CASUALTIES
for
SEPTEMBER 5 through SEPTEMBER 15, 1862

Key: KIA = Killed in Action
     WIA = Wounded in Action
     MIA = Missing in Action
     CIA = Captured in Action

SEPTEMBER 5, 1862

Poolesville, Md.
    squadron (100 men) 1st Mass. Cav.   9 WIA & CIA; 39 CIA
                         vs.
               5th Va. Cav.   3 KIA; 4 WIA

SEPTEMBER 6, 1862

Sugar Loaf Mountain, Md.
    (2 men) U.S. Signal Corps   2 CIA
               vs.
    (2 men) 1st N.C. Cav.

SEPTEMBER 6, 1862

Sugar Loaf Mountain, Md.
    Cos. D and E, 1st N.Y. Cav.   (no casualties reported)
    Cos. A and I, 9th Va. Cav.

SEPTEMBER 7, 1862

Poolesville. Md.
    4 cos., 3rd Ind. Cav.
    4 cos., 8th Ill. Cav.
           vs.
           7th Va. Cav.   2 CIA

SEPTEMBER 8, 1862

Poolesville, Md.
> Battery M,   2nd U.S. Horse Artillery
> > 3rd Ind. Cav.   1 KIA; 11 WIA
> > 8th Ill. Cav.   1 WIA
> > > vs.
> > 7th Va. Cav.   2 WIA
> > 12th Va. Cav.   2 KIA; 6 WIA
> > Chew's Va. Battery

SEPTEMBER 8, 1862

Monocacy Church, Md.
> 8th Ill. Cav.   1 WIA
> > vs.
> 2nd Va. Cav.

SEPTEMBER 8, 1862

Braddock Heights, Md.
> 50 men, 1st Md. Cav.
> > vs.
> 15 men, 1st Va. Cav.   14 CIA

SEPTEMBER 8, 1862

Hyattstown, Md.
> 1st N.Y. Cav.
> > vs.
> pickets, Hampton's brigade   3 CIA

SEPTEMBER 9, 1862

Hyattstown, Md.
> 1st N.Y. Cav.
> > vs.
> unidentified Confederate infantry (squad CIA)

SEPTEMBER 9, 1862

Monocacy Church, Md.
> Cos. K and M, 8th Ill. Cav.
> > vs.
> 12th Va. Cav.   2 KIA; 7 CIA

SEPTEMBER 9, 1862

Barnesville—Sugar Loaf Mountain—Barnesville, Md.
> several cos., 3rd Ind. Cav.
> > 8th Ill. Cav.
> section, 4th Maine Arty.
> > vs.
> > 9th Va. Cav.   2 KIA; 5 WIA; 19 CIA

SEPTEMBER 9, 1862

Barnesville, Md.
> 1 man, 8th Ill. Cav.
> > vs.
> 1 Confederate cavalryman   1 KIA

SEPTEMBER 10, 1862

Sugar Loaf Mountain, Md.
section,   4th Maine Arty.
          6th U.S. Cav.   1 KIA; 1 WIA
          3rd Ind. Cav.
          8th Ill. Cav.
              vs.
          2nd Va. Cav.
          12th Va. Cav.
2 cos., 9th Va. Cav.

SEPTEMBER 10, 1862

Boonsboro, Md.
20 men, A Co., 1st Md. Cav.   1 KIA; 3 WIA and CIA; 1 WIA
    vs.
10 men, H Co., 4th Va. Cav.
3 men, T. J. Jackson's staff

SEPTEMBER 11, 1862

Sugar Loaf Mountain, Md.
section,   4th Maine Arty.
          6th U.S. Cav.
          3rd Ind. Cav.
          8th Ill. Cav.
          8th Pa. Cav.
          Hancock's brigade, VI Corps
              vs.
          2nd Va. Cav.
          12th Va. Cav.
section, Stuart's Horse Arty.

SEPTEMBER 11, 1862

Hyattstown, Md.
2 cos.,   1st N.Y Cav.
2 cos.,   1st U.S. Cav.
              vs.
          2nd Va. Cav.
          12th Va. Cav.
section, Stuart Horse Arty.

SEPTEMBER 12, 1862

Frederick, Md.
Shambeck's Co., Ill. Dragoons   3 KIA; 12 WIA; 4 CIA
Abraham's Co., Va. Cav.   1 KIA; 7 WIA; 4 CIA
Kanawha Division, IX Corps
section, Simmonds' Ky. Btty.
    vs.
150 men, Wade Hampton's Cav. brigade   2 KIA; 5 WIA and/or CIA
Washington S.C. Arty.

SEPTEMBER 13, 1862

Braddock (Fairview) Pass, Md.
    1st Mass. Cav.
    8th Ill. Cav.   1 WIA
    3rd Ind. Cav.   1 KIA; 2 WIA
    Harland's brigade, IX Corps   2 WIA
        "M," 2nd U.S. Horse Arty.
    "B" & "L," 2nd U.S. Horse Arty.
    vs.
    Wade Hampton's Cav. brigade
    Washington S.C. Arty.

SEPTEMBER 13, 1862

Middletown, Md.
             1st Mass. Cav.
             8th Ill. Cav.
             3rd Ind. Cav.
        "M," 2nd U.S. Horse Arty.
    "B" & "L," 2nd U.S. Horse Arty.
    section, "C" & "G," 3rd U.S. Horse Arty.
             vs.
             1st N.C. Cav.   8 WIA; 3 CIA

SEPTEMBER 13, 1862

Bolivar Cross Roads, Md.
    Cos. D, E, & M, 8th Ill. Cav.   1 KIA; 2 WIA
        detachment, 3rd Ind. Cav.   2 WIA
        vs.
        skirmishers, Jeff Davis Leg.   2 CIA

SEPTEMBER 13, 1862

north of Frederick, Md.
             1st N.Y. Cav.
             12th Pa. Cav.
    section, "M," 2nd U.S. Horse Arty.
             vs.
             4th Va. Cav.
             9th Va. Cav.

SEPTEMBER 13, 1862

Jefferson, Md.
             6th Pa. Cav.   1 WIA
             9th N.Y.
    Irwin's brigade, VI Corps
    vs.
    Chew's Va. Btty.
             2nd Va. Cav.   5 CIA

SEPTEMBER 13, 1862

Quaker School House, Md.
    squadron, 8th Ill. Cav.   1 KIA; 8 WIA; 3 CIA
    Cos. E & F, 3rd Ind. Cav.   3 KIA; 8 WIA; 5 CIA
    vs.
    Cobb's Leg.   4 KIA; 9 WIA

SEPTEMBER 14, 1862

Turner's Gap between the Zittlestown Road and the Frosttown Road
    The Army of Northern Virginia   (1750 present)
        D. H. Hill's division
            Rodes' brigade   (1200 present)
                61 KIA   157 WIA   204 MIA   =   422 Total
                                                      35% casualties

            Stevens' (Evans') brigade   (550 present)
                23 KIA   148 WIA   45 MIA   =   216 Total
                                                      39% casualties

    The Army of the Potomac
    I Corps   (3247 present)
        Meade's division   (3247 present)
            Seymour's brigade
                38 KIA   133 WIA   0 MIA   =   171 Total

            Magilton's brigade
                25 KIA   63 WIA   1 MIA   =   89 Total

            Gallagher's brigade
                32 KIA   100 WIA   0 MIA   =   132 Total
                                            12% division casualties

Turner's Gap between the crest of the hill and the Frosttown Road
    The Army of Northern Virginia
    Longstreet's Corps   (1369 present)
        D. R. Jones' division
            Garnett's brigade   (407 present)
                35 KIA   142 WIA   19 MIA   =   196 Total
                                                      48% casualties

            Kemper's brigade   (400 present)
                11 KIA   57 WIA   7 MIA   =   75 Total
                                                      19% casualties

            Walker's (Jenkins') brigade   (562 present)
                 3 KIA   29 WIA   0 MIA   =   32 Total
                                                       6% casualties

    The Army of the Potomac
    I Corps   (5529 present)
        Hatch's (Doubleday's) division
            Staff
                 0 KIA   1 WIA   0 MIA   =   1 Total

            Phelps' brigade   (520 present)
                20 KIA   67 WIA   8 MIA   =   95 Total
                                                      18% casualties

            Wainwright's brigade   (968 present)
                 3 KIA   52 WIA   4 MIA   =   59 Total
                                                       6% casualties

            Patrick's brigade   (848 present)
                 3 KIA   19 WIA   1 MIA   =   24 Total
                                                       3% casualties

Ricketts' division
    Duryea's brigade   (1100 estimated present)
        5 KIA   16 WIA   0 MIA =   21 Total
                                         2% casualties
    Christian's brigade   (1087 estimated present)
        2 KIA   6 WIA   0 MIA =   8 Total
                                         1% casualties
    Hartsuff's brigade   (1006 present)
        2 KIA   4 WIA   0 MIA =   6 Total
                                         1% casualties

Turner's Gap at the National Pike Gorge
The Army of Northern Virginia
Jackson's Corps   (1429 present)
    D. H. Hill's division
        Colquitt's brigade   (1429 present)
          18 KIA   74 WIA   17 MIA =   109 Total
                                         8% casualties

The Army of the Potomac
I Corps
    Hatch's division
        Gibbon's brigade   (1346 present)
          37 KIA   251 WIA   30 MIA =   318 Total
                                     24% casualties

Fox's Gap
The Army of Northern Virginia   (6763 estimated present)
Jackson's Corps
    D. H. Hill's division
        Ripley's brigade (1061 present)
                                    (no casualties)
        G. B. Anderson's brigade   (1243 present)
          7 KIA   54 WIA   29 MIA =   90 Total
                                         7% casualties
        Garland's brigade   (945 present)
          37 KIA   168 WIA   154 MIA =   359 Total
                                       38% casualties
        Bondurant's battery
          0 KIA   3 WIA   0 MIA =   3 Total

Longstreet's Corps
    D. R. Jones' division
        G. T. Anderson's brigade   (507 present)
          0 KIA   3 WIA   4 MIA =   7 Total
                                         1% casualties
        Drayton's brigade   (650 present)
          49 KIA   164 WIA   176 MIA =   389 Total
                                       60% casualties
    Hood's division
        Wofford's brigade   (864 present)
          0 KIA   3 WIA   2 MIA =   5 Total
                                       1% casualties
        Law's brigade   (1493 present)
          3 KIA   11 WIA   5 MIA =   19 Total
                                       1% casualties

Stuart's cavalry division
  5th VA Cav. and Pelham's artillery
    27 casualties estimated
    Confederate casualties at Fox's Gap = 899

The Army of the Potomac
IX Corps (13,458 present)
  Staff
    1 KIA   0 WIA   0 MIA =   1 Total
  Willcox's division (3603 present)
    Christ's brigade
      26 KIA 136 WIA   0 MIA = 162 Total
    Welsh's brigade
      37 KIA 151 WIA   0 MIA = 188 Total
    8th MA Lgt Arty.
      1 KIA   4 WIA   0 MIA =   5 Total
                  division total   =   355
                  9.8% casualties
  Sturgis' division (3411 present)
    Nagle's brigade
      0 KIA   34 WIA   7 MIA = 41 Total
    Ferrero's brigade
      10 KIA 83 WIA 23 MIA = 116 Total
               division total =   157
                  4.6% casualties
  Rodman's division (2934 present)
    Fairchild's brigade
      2 KIA   18 WIA   0 MIA = 20 Total
    Harland's division (not engaged)
               division total =   20
                  6% casualties
  Kanawha division (3510 present)
    Scammon's brigade
      63 KIA 201 WIA   8 MIA = 272 Total
    Crook's brigade
      17 KIA 64 WIA   3 MIA = 84 Total
               division total = 356
                 10.1% casualties
                corps total = 889
                 6.6% casualties

SEPTEMBER 14, 1862

Crampton's Gap, Md.
  The Army of Northern Virginia (2441 estimated present)
    Stuart's cavalry division
      Munford's brigade (200 present)
        3 KIA   5 WIA   0 MIA =   8 Total
                   4% casualties
      Chew's Btty. (no casualties)

  Longstreet's Corps
    McLaws' division
      Cobb's brigade (1310 present)
        58 KIA 186 WIA 442 MIA = 686 Total
                 52% casualties

Semmes' brigade   (628 present)
    3 KIA   19 WIA   37 MIA =   59 Total
                                          9 % casualties

Manley's Btty.   (no casualties)
Macon's Btty.   (no casualties)
Troup Arty.   (31 present)
    1 KIA   3 WIA   0 MIA =   4 Total
                                    13 % casualties

R. H. Anderson's division
Parham's brigade   (322 present)
    5 KIA   74 WIA   124 MIA = 203 Total
                                    63 % casualties

The Army of the Potomac
VI Corps   (12,833 present)
Slocum's division
    Staff
        0 KIA   1 WIA   0 MIA =   1 Total

    Torbert's brigade
      38 KIA   134 WIA   0 MIA = 172 Total

    Bartlett's brigade
      50 KIA   167 WIA   0 MIA = 217 Total

Newton's brigade
    24 KIA   98 WIA   2 MIA = 124 Total

Smith's division
Hancock's brigade   (no casualties)

Brooks' brigade
    1 KIA   18 WIA   0 MIA =   19 Total

Irwin's brigade   (1707 present)
    0 KIA   1 WIA   0 MIA =   1 Total
                  corps' casualties   =   4 %

SEPTEMBER 15, 1862

Boonsboro, Md.
    8th Ill. Cav.   1 KIA; 15 WIA; 3 CIA
    3rd Va. Cav.   1 CIA
    4th Va. Cav.   1 KIA; several WIA
    9th Va. Cav.   18 KIA; 10 CIA

Endnotes

Chapter One

1. Richard L. T. Beale, *History of the 9th Virginia Cavalry in the War Between the States*, B. F. Johnson Publishing Company, 1899, p. 37.

2. Heros Von Borcke, *Memoirs of the Confederate War For Independence*, I, Morningside Bookshop, Dayton, Ohio, 1985, pp. 182-183.

3. New York *Times*, September 13, 1862, p. 1.

4. Von Borcke, I, p. 181.
   Augustus D. Dickert, *History of Kershaw's Brigade*, Morningside Bookshop, Dayton, Ohio, 1976, p. 152.
   Edward A. Moore, *The Story of a Cannoneer Under Stonewall Jackson*, J. P. Bell, Inc., Lynchburg, Va., 1910, p. 130.
   New York, *Times*, September 13, 1862, p. 1.

5. Von Borcke, I, pp. 181-182.

6. William W. Sherwood, Diary, September 6, 1862, Mss 51 shsp: 1, Virginia Historical Society, Richmond, Va.

7. John Shipp, Diary, September 5, 1862, Mss 2sh 64662, Virginia Historical Society, Richmond, Va.

8. Samuel D. Buck, *With the Old Confeds*, H. E. Houck & Co., Baltimore, Md., 1925, p. 59.
   Otis Smith, "Reminiscences," Thach Papers, Southern Historical Collection, University of North Carolina Library, Chapel Hill, North Carolina, p. 2.

9. W. A. Johnson, "Barbara Frietchie," *The National Tribune Scrap Book*, #1, *The National Tribune*, Washington, D.C., p. 3.

10. Harold B. Simpson, *Gaines Mills to Appomattox*, Texian Press, Waco, Texas, p. 101.
    Joseph B. Polley, *Hood's Texas Brigade*, Morningside Bookshop, Dayton, Ohio, 1976, p. 112.
    He wrote that the Texas Brigade crossed at Point of Rocks, which is up river from White's Ford.

11. John H. Worsham, *One of Jackson's Foot Cavalry*, James I. Robertson, (ed.), McCowat-Mercer Press, Jackson, Tenn., p. 136.

12. Polley, p. 112.
    Worsham, p. 135.
    William A. McClendon, *Recollections of War Times*, The Paragon Press, Montgomery, 1909, p. 128.

13. Worsham, p. 136.
    Maryland Civil War Centennial Commission, *Maryland Remembers*, Hagerstown, Md., 1961, p. 23.

14. Von Borcke, I, p. 181.
    Moxley G. Sorrel, *Recollections of a Confederate Staff Officer*, Bell I. Wiley, (ed.), McCowat-Mercer Press, Jackson, Tenn., 1958, p. 98.

15. Buck, p. 59.

16. McClendon, p. 128.

17. Buck, p. 59.

18. Ibid.

19. McClendon, pp. 128-129.

20. Ibid.

21. Kenneth E. Stiles, *4th Virginia Cavalry*, H. E. Howard Co., Inc., Lynchburg, Va., 1985, p. 19.

22. Worsham, p. 136.

23. Polley, p. 112.

24. George Michael Neese, *Three Years in the Confederate Horse Artillery*, Neale Publishing Co., N.Y., 1911, p. 11.
    William Miller Owen, *In Camp and Battle With the Washington Artillery of New Orleans*, Ticknor and Co., Boston, 1885, p. 134.

25. Von Borcke, I, p. 185.

26. James Steptoe Johnston, Letter to Mary M. Green, September 22, 1862, Mercer Green Johnston Collection, Manuscript Department, Library of Congress.

27. Charles F. Walcott, *History of the 21st Massachusetts Volunteers in the War for the Preservation of the Union, 1861-1865*, Boston, 1882, p. 191.

28. James L. Coker, *History of Company G Ninth S.C. Regiment Infantry, S.C. Army and of Company E, Sixth S.C. Regiment Infantry C.S. Army*, The Attic Press, Greenwood, S.C., p. 103.

29. Robert T. Hubard, Notebook 1860-1866, "Damnation of Vancouver," and "Turvey" Manuscripts, Acc. No. 10522, Manuscript Department, University of Virginia, Charlottesville, Va., p. 14.

30. Alexander Hunter, *Johnny Reb and Billy Yank*, The Neale Publishing Co., N.Y., 1905, pp. 273-274.

31. James B. Painter, Letter to Brother, Letters 1861-1863, October 5, 1862, Acc. No. 10661, Manuscript Department, University of Virginia, Charlottesville, Va.

32. W. A. Smith, *The Anson Guards*, Stone Publishing Co., Charlotte, N.C., 1914, pp. 153-154.

33. Nathaniel Wood, *Reminiscences of Big I*, McCowat-Mercer Press, Jackson, Tenn., 1956, pp. 33-34.

34. Sorrel, p. 96.

35. Ibid.

36. John B. Hood, *Advance and Retreat*, Richard N. Current, (ed.), Civil War Centennial Series, Indiana University Press, Bloomington, 1959, p. 38.
    Polley, pp. 113-114.

37. James V. Murfin, *The Gleam of Bayonets*, Bonanza Books, N.Y., 1965, p. 36.

38. Von Borcke, I, p. 186.
    Stiles, p. 19.
    Richard L. T. Beale, p. 37.
    William N. McDonald, *A History of the Laurel Brigade, Originally the Ashby Cavalry of the Army of Northern Virginia and Chew's Battery*, Bushrod C. Washington, (ed.), Sun Job Printing Office, Baltimore, 1907, p. 90.

39. Thomas Munford, "Recollections," Munford-Ellis Civil War Manuscript, 1861-1865, Box 1, Manuscript Department, Duke University, Durham, North Carolina.

40. Thomas Munford to Ezra Carman, December 10, 1894, Ezra Carman Correspondence, "The Maryland Campaign," Antietam National Battlefield, p. 159.

41. Dennis Frye, *12th Virginia Cavalry*, H. E. Howard Co., Inc., Lynchburg, Va., 1988, p. 16.

42. Von Borcke, I, p. 185.

43. J. B. V. Gilpin, Diary, September 5, 1862, E. N. Gilpin Collection, Manuscript Department, Library of Congress.

44. William B. Baker, Letter, September 6, 1862, William B. Baker Papers, Southern Historical Collection, University of North Carolina, Chapel Hill, North Carolina.

45. "General Pleasonton's Cavalry Division, in the Maryland Campaign, September, 1862," *Historical Magazine*, May 1969, p. 291.

46. Abner Hard, *History of the Eighth Cavalry Illinois Volunteers in the Great Rebellion*, Morningside Bookshop, Dayton, Ohio, 1984, p. 170.

47. Samuel J. B. V. Gilpin, Diary, September 5, 1862, E. N. Gilpin Collection, Manuscript Department, Library of Congress.

48. Stiles, p. 19.

49. Samuel J. B. V. Gilpin, Diary, September 5, 1862, E. N. Gilpin Collection, Manuscript Department, Library of Congress.

50. Ezra Carman, "The Maryland Campaign," V, Manuscript Division, Library of Congress, p. 3.

51. Benjamin W. Crowninshield, *A History of the First Regiment of Massachusetts Cavalry Volunteers*, Houghton, Mifflin and Company, Boston, 1891, p. 70.

52. *Massachusetts Soldiers, Sailors, and Marines in the Civil War*, VI, Norwood Press, Norwood, Mass., 1933, p. 129.

53. Crowninshield, pp. 70-71.

54. Ezra Carman, "The Maryland Campaign," V, Manuscript Division, Library of Congress, p. 4.
    Crowninshield, pp. 71-72.

55. Ibid.

56. Von Borcke, I, p. 186.

57. *Massachusetts Soldiers*, VI, pp. 129, 142, 145.
    Ezra Carman, "The Maryland Campaign," V, Manuscript Division, Library of Congress, p. 3.
    Ulysses Robert Brooks, *Stories of the Confederacy*, The State Co., Columbia, S.C., 1912, p. 78.
    Brooks did not identify the author of his article. I found the same story at the University of North Carolina, Chapel Hill.
    D. Rea, *Sketches From Hampton's Cavalry in the Summer, Fall and Winter Campaigns of '62 Including Stuart's Raid into Pennsylvania and Also in Burnside's Rear*, Strother and Co., Raleigh, N.C., 1863.
    Richard L. T. Beale, p. 37.
    Von Borcke, I, p. 186.

58. Stiles, p. 19.
    Samuel J. B. V. Gilpin, Diary, September 5, 1862, E. N. Gilpin Collection, Manuscript Department, Library of Congress.

59. Otis Smith, "Reminiscences," Thach Papers, Southern Historical Collection, University of North Carolina, Chapel Hill, North Carolina, pp. 3-4.

60. Pulaski Cowper, (comp.), *Extracts of Letters of Major-Gen'l Bryan Grimes to His Wife*, Edwards, Broughton & Co., Raleigh, N.C., 1883, p.19.

61. Von Borcke, I, p. 186.

62. Ibid., pp. 186-187.

63. Von Borcke, I, pp. 186-187.

64. Ibid., pp. 186-187.
    Richard L. T. Beale, p. 37.

65. James Steptoe Johnston, Letter to Mary M. Green, September 22, 1862, Mercer Green Johnston Collection, Manuscript Department, Library of Congress.

66. George T. Todd, *First Texas Regiment*, Texian Press, Waco, TX, 1963, p. 10.

67. Polley, p. 112.

68. Moore, p. 130.

69. James Steptoe Johnston, Letter to Mary M. Green, Mercer Green Johnston Collection, Manuscript Department, Library of Congress.

70. Otis Smith, "Reminiscences," Thach Papers, Southern Historical Collection, University of North Carolina, Chapel Hill, North Carolina, pp. 2, 4, 5.

71. George T. Todd, p. 10.

72. Samuel J. B. V. Gilpin, Diary, September 5, 1862, E. N. Gilpin Collection, Manuscript Department, Library of Congress.

73. James Wren, Diary, September 5, 1862, Manuscript, Antietam National Battlefield.

74. George T. Stevens, *Three Years in the Sixth Corps*, S. R. Gray Publisher, Albany, 1866, p. 134.

75. Robert Underwood Johnson and Clarence Clough Buel, (ed.), *Battles and Leaders of the Civil War*, II, part 2, Grant-Lee Edition, The Century Company, N.Y. 1888, p. 556.

76. Edward E. Schweitzer, Diary, September 1, 1862, Civil War Times Illustrated Collection, USAMHI.

77. Charles S. McClenthen, *Campaign in Virginia and Maryland of Tower's Brigade, Ricketts' Division, From Cedar Mountain to Antietam,* Masters and Lee, Printers, Syracuse, 1862, p. 28.

78. From a survey of rosters in Battles & Leaders, II, pp. 598-603.

79. William B. Baker, Letter, September 6, 1862, William B. Baker Papers, Southern Historical Collection, University of North Carolina, Chapel Hill, North Carolina.

80. Matthew J. Graham, *The Ninth Regiment New York Volunteers (Hawkins' Zouaves),* E. P. Coby & Co., Printers, N.Y., p. 254.

81. George Gordon Meade, *The Life And Letters of George Gordon Meade*, Charles Scribner's Sons, N.Y., 1913, I, p. 308.

82. Charles E. Goldsborough, "Graphic Description of Lee's Occupation of Frederick, Maryland in 1862." *The National Tribune*, October 14, 1886, p. 4.

83. Katherine S. Markall, Diary, September 5, 1862, Microfilm Room, C. Burr Artz Library, Frederick, Md., pp. 71-72.

Chapter Two

1. Ezra Carman, "The Maryland Campaign," V, Manuscript Division, Library of Congress, p. 5.

2. Ulysses Robert Brooks, p. 78.

3. Ezra Carman, "The Maryland Campaign," VII, Manuscript Division, Library of Congress, p. 187.

4.   J. Willard Brown, *The Signal Corps, U.S.A. in the War of the Rebellion*, U.S. Veteran Signal Corps Association, Boston, 1896, p. 241.

5.   Ibid., pp. 242-241.

6.   It is important to note that Lieutenant Miner died in 1871, and that the author of the unit history, J. Willard Brown, apparently, held Miner in high respect. It is, therefore, highly unlikely that he would have mentioned Miner's rendezvous with the young lady.
     Rea's account, because it was written in 1862 and immediately after the event occurred, is probably more accurate than Brown's story. Both confirm that the dispatch event actually transpired.

7.   Ulysses Robert Brooks, pp. 78-79.
     Von Borcke, I, p. 187.

8.   Samuel J. B. V. Gilpin, Diary, September 6, 1862, E. N. Gilpin Collection, Manuscript Division, Library of Congress.

9.   Otis Smith, "Reminiscences," Thach Papers, Southern Historical Collection, "University of North Carolina, Chapel Hill, North Carolina, p. 5.

10. J. M. Polk, *Memories of the Lost Cause*, Austin, Texas, 1905, p. 10.

11. John Shipp, Diary, September 6, 1862, Mss 2sh 64662, Virginia Historical Society, Richmond, Va.

12. William D. Henderson, *12th Virginia Infantry*, H. E. Howard Co., Inc., Lynchburg, Va., 1984, p. 32.

13. George S. Bernard, *War Talks of Confederate Veterans*, Fenn & Owen, Publishers, Petersburg, Va, 1892, pp. 20-21.

14. James Steptoe Johnston, Letter to Mary M. Green, September 22, 1862, Mercer Green Johnston Collection, Manuscript Division, Library of Congress.

15. Katherine S. Markall, Diary, September 6, 1862, Microfilm Room, C. Burr Artz Library, Frederick, Md., p. 72.

16. Charles E. Goldsborough, "Graphic Description of Lee's Occupation of Frederick, Maryland in 1862," *The National Tribune*, October 14, 1886, p. 4.

17. Osmun Latrobe, Diary, September 6, 1862, Osmun Latrobe Diary, Virginia Historical Society, Richmond, Va., p. 8.

18. Ezra Carman, "The Antietam Campaign," V, Manuscript Division, Library of Congress, p. 5.

19. Ezra Carman, "The Maryland Campaign," V, Manuscript Division, Library of Congress, p. 7.
     John E. Divine, *8th Virginia Infantry*, H.E. Howard, Inc., Lynchburg, Va., 1983.
     George T. Todd, p. 10.
     William D. Henderson, p. 32.
     William W. Sherwood, Diary, September 6, 1862, Mss51 shsp:1, Virginia Historical Society, Richmond, Va.

20. W. A. Johnson, pp. 3-4.

21. James Steptoe Johnston, Letter to Mary M. Green, September 22, 1862, Mercer Green Johnston Collection, Manuscript Division, Library of Congress.

22. William M. Owen, p. 130.

23. Otis Smith, "Reminiscences," Thach Papers, Southern Historical Collection, University of North Carolina Library, Chapel Hill, North Carolina, pp. 3, 6-7.

24. Samuel J. B. V. Gilpin, Diary, September 6, 1862, E. N. Gilpin Collection, Manuscript Division, Library of Congress.
     Historical Magazine, May, 1869, p. 290.

25. William H. Beach, *The First New York (Lincoln) Cavalry From April 19, 1861 to July 7, 1865*, Lincoln Cavalry Association, N.Y., 1902, p. 168.

Samuel J. B. V. Gilpin, Diary, September 6, 1862, E. N. Gilpin Collection, Manuscript Division, Library of Congress.

Ezra Carman, "The Maryland Campaign," V, Manuscript Division, Library of Congress, p. 4.

Historical Magazine, May, 1869, p. 291.

26. James H. Stevenson, *Boots and Saddles*, Patriot Publishing Co., Harrisburg, Pa., 1879, pp. 116-117.

Beach, p. 168.

Robert Krick, *9th Virginia Cavalry*, H. E. Howard Co., Inc., Lynchburg, Va., 1982, p. 10. The troops probably were Companies A & I, which were left to cover Sugar Loaf Mountain.

27. Stevenson, pp. 116-117.

Beach, p. 168.

28. Ulysses Robert Brooks, pp. 79-80.

29. Von Borcke, I, pp. 187-188.

William W. Blackford, *War Years With JEB Stuart*, Charles Scribner's Sons, N.Y., 1946, p. 140.

30. Henry Kyd Douglas, *I Rode With Stonewall*, Mockingbird Books, Atlanta, Ga., 1976, pp. 148-149.

31. Ezra Carman, "The Maryland Campaign," V, Manuscript Division, Library of Congress, p. 7.

32. W. A. Johnson, p. 6.

Douglas, p. 149.

33. Ibid.

Charles W. Squires, "The Last of Lee's Battle Line," W. H. T. Squires, (ed.), 1894, Civil War Times Illustrated Collection, USAMHI, p. 22.

34. Douglas, p. 149.

35. Worsham, pp. 136, 138.

Moore, p. 130.

36. Worsham, pp. 137-138.

37. W. A. Johnson, p. 6.

38. Otis Smith, "Reminiscences," Thach Papers, Southern Historical Collection, University of North Carolina Library, Chapel Hill, North Carolina, p. 6.

39. Curtis Pollock, Letter to Mother, September 10, 1862, Civil War Miscellaneous Collection, USAMHI.

40. Von Borcke, I, p. 188.

Blackford, p. 140.

41. Von Borcke, pp. 188-191.

42. Buck, p. 60.

43. New York *Times*, September 14, 1862, p. 1.

44. William M. Owen, p. 130.

45. Douglas, pp. 149-150.

46. Frank M. Myers, *The Commanches*, Kelly, Piet & Co., Baltimore, Md., 1871, pp. 107-109.

47. Thomas Munford, "Recollections," Munford-Ellis Civil War Manuscript, 1861-1865, Box 1, Manuscript Department, Duke University, Durham, North Carolina.

48.   Bernard, pp. 20-22.

49.   *Battles and Leaders*, II, p. 583.
      Martin L. Sheets, Diary, September 6, 1862, Civil War Times Illustrated Collection, USAMHI.
      Edward E. Schweitzer, "Memoir," September 6, 1862, Civil War Times Illustrated Collection, USAMHI.

50.   George T. Stevens, pp. 134-135.

51.   Henry C. Boyer, "At Crampton's Pass," August 31, 1886, Philadelphia *Weekly Press*, not paginated.
      Frederick D. Bidwell, (comp.), *History of the 49th Regiment New York Volunteers*, J. B. Lyons, Albany, N.Y., 1917, p. 18.

52.   Bidwell, p. 18.
      Robert S. Westbrook, *History of the Forty-Ninth Pennsylvania Volunteers*, Altoona Times Printer, Altoona, Pa., 1898, p. 123.

53.   McClenthen, p. 29.

54.   Wood, p. 35.

55.   Moore, p. 136.

56.   Worsham, pp. 138-139.

57.   James Steptoe Johnston, Letter to Mary M. Green, September 22, 1862, Mercer Green Johnston Collection, Manuscript Division, Library of Congress.

Chapter Three

1.   Thomas Munford, "Recollections," Munford-Ellis Civil War Manuscript, 1861-1865, Box 1, Manuscript Department, Duke University, Durham, North Carolina.
      Neese, p. 113.

2.   Westbrook, p. 123.
      Peter Augustus Filbert, Diary, September 7, 1862, Harrisburg Civil War Round Table Collection, USAMHI.

3.   Bidwell, p. 18.

4.   Peter Augustus Filbert, Diary, September 7, 1862, Harrisburg Civil War Round Table Collection, USAMHI.

5.   Henry C. Boyer, "At Crampton's Pass," August 31, 1886, Philadelphia *Weekly Times*, not paginated.

6.   Allen D. Albert, (ed.), *History of the Forty-Fifth Pennsylvania Volunteer Infantry 1861-1865*, Grit Publishing Co., Williamsport, Pa., 1912, p. 47.
      Curtis Pollock, Letter to Mother, September 10, 1862, Civil War Miscellaneous Collection, USAMHI.

7.   Samuel J. B. V. Gilpin, Diary, September 7, 1862, E. N. Gilpin Collection, Manuscript Division, Library of Congress.
      Hard, pp. 170-171.
      William N. Pickerill, *History of the 3rd Indiana Cavalry*, Aetna Printing Co., Indianapolis, 1906, p. 24.
      Ezra Carman, "The Maryland Campaign," V, Manuscript Division, Library of Congress, p. 5.
      Historical Magazine, May 1869, p. 290.

8.   Samuel J. B. V. Gilpin, Diary, September 7, 1862, E. N. Gilpin Collection, Manuscript Division, Library of Congress.

9. John A. Sloan, *Reminiscences of the Guilford Grays, Co. B, 27th N.C. Regiment*, R. O. Polkinhorn, Printer, Washington, D.C., 1883, p. 40.

10. William M. Owen, p. 132.

11. Charles W. Squires, "The Last of Lee's Battle Line," W. H. T. Squires, (ed.), 1894, Civil War Times Illustrated Collection, USAMHI, p. 22.

12. Douglas, p. 150.

13. Worsham, p. 139.

14. William M. Owen, p. 131.

15. Charles W. Turner, (ed.), *Captain Greenlee Davidson, C.S.A. Diary and Letters, 1851-1863*, McClure Press, Verona, Va., 1975, p. 46.

16. W. A. Johnson, pp. 4-6.

17. W. A. Smith, p. 151.

18. John Dooley, *Confederate Soldier*, Joseph T. Durkin, (ed.), Washington, D.C., 1945, p. 26.

19. Bernard, p. 24.

20. W. A. Johnson, p. 5.

21. Von Borcke, I, pp. 192-193.

22. William M. Owen, p. 131.

23. Douglas, p. 150.

24. Westbrook, p. 123.
    David Wright Judd, *The Story of the Thirty-third New York State Volunteers*, Benton and Andrews, Rochester, 1864, p. 179.
    Bidwell, p. 18.
    Charles C. Morey, Diary, September 7, 1862, Charles C. Morey Collection, USAMHI.
    Stevens, p. 135.
    Jacob Haas, Diary, September 7, 1862, Harrisburg Civil War Round Table Collection, USAMHI.

25. Douglas, p. 151.
    Katherine S. Markall, Diary, September 8, 1862, Microfilm Room, C. Burr Artz Library, Frederick, Md.

26. M. M. R. McLaughlin, January 1, 1863, Southern Historical Collection, University of North Carolina Library, Chapel Hill, North Carolina.
    Neese, p. 113.

27. James W. Overcash, Letter to Father, October 10, 1862, Joseph Overcash Papers, Manuscript Department, Duke University Library, Durham, North Carolina.

28. Neese, p. 113.

Chapter Four

1. McDonald, p. 91.

2. Neese, p. 113.

3. Ezra Carman, "The Maryland Campaign," V, Manuscript Division, Library of Congress, p. 51.

4. Thomas Munford Letter to Ezra Carman, December 10, 1894, 159/Correspondence, Antietam National Battlefield.

5. Ezra Carman, "The Maryland Campaign," V, Manuscript Division, Library of Congress, p. 6.

6. *Historical Magazine*, p. 291.

7. McDonald, p. 91.
    Frye, p. 14.

Historical Magazine, p. 291.
Hard, p. 171.

8.   Neese, pp. 113-114.

9.   Neese, p. 114.
     Historical Magazine, p. 291.
     Ezra Carman, "The Maryland Campaign," V, Manuscript Division, Library of Congress, p. 5.

10. Neese, p. 114.

11. *Historical Magazine*, p. 291.
     Hard, p. 171.
     Pleasonton stated clearly that the 3rd Indiana initiated the assault and that the 8th Illinois "mopped up" after it was over.

12. Neese, p. 114.

13. Frye, p. 14.

14. Ibid., pp. 14-15.
     Neese, p. 114.

15. Neese, p. 114.

16. Frye, p. 15.

17. Charles T. O'Ferrall, *Forty Years of Active Service*, The Neale Publishing Co., N.Y., 1904, pp. 51-52.

18. Frye, pp. 117, 153.

19. H. B. McClellan, *The Life and Campaigns of Major-General J.E.B. Stuart*, Houghton, Mifflin and Co., Boston, 1885, p. 111.
     Ezra Carman, "The Maryland Campaign," V, Manuscript Division, Library of Congress, pp. 5-6.
     Hard, p. 171.

20. Neese, p. 114.

21. Ibid., p. 115.

22. Frye, p. 15.

23. Samuel J. B. V. Gilpin, Diary, September 8, 1862, E. N. Gilpin Collection, Manuscript Division, Library of Congress.
     Hard, p. 171.
     Ezra Carman, "The Maryland Campaign," V, Manuscript Division, Library of Congress, p. 6.

24. Frye, p. 15.
     Hard, p. 171.

25. H. B. McClellan, p. 111.
     Ezra Carman, "The Maryland Campaign," V, Manuscript Division, Library of Congress, p. 6.
     Hard, p. 171.

26. Ezra Carman, "The Maryland Campaign," V, Manuscript Division, Library of Congress, p. 5.

27. Samuel J. B. V. Gilpin, Diary, September 8, 1862, E. N. Gilpin Collection, Manuscript Division, Library of Congress.

28. Neese, p. 115.

29. Hard, p. 171.

30. "Historical Sketch of Middletown Valley and Official Programme and Souvenir of the Boosters," Festival and Home Coming Week, September 13-19, 1914, files of Antietam National Battlefield.

OR, XIX, pt. 1, pp. 535, 545.

Valley News Echo, Potomac Edison Co., September 1862.

Antietam-South Mountain Centennial Association, Inc., "Battle of Antietam, Centennial and Hagerstown Bicentennial, Official Program and Historical Guide," August 31 through September 17, 1962, p. 20.

31. William M. Owen, p. 131.

32. John Shipp, Diary, September 7, 1862, Mss2sh 64662, Virginia Historical Society, Richmond, Va.

33. Dooley, pp. 26-27.

34. "Lee's Proclamation to the People of Maryland," Antietam National Battlefield.

35. Daniel Harvey Hill, *Bethel to Sharpsburg*, II, Edwards & Broughton Co., Raleigh, 1926, p. 339, fn 2.

36. Ibid, fn 4.

37. New York *Times*, September 14, 1862, p. 1.

38. Charles E. Goldsborough, "Graphic Description of Lee's Occupation of Frederick, Maryland in 1862," *The National Tribune*, October 14, 1886, p. 4.

39. Nicholas A. Davis, *The Campaign From Texas to Maryland*, The Steck Co., Austin, 1905, p. 88.

40. William A. McClendon, *Recollections of War Times*, The Paragon Press, Montgomery, Ala., 1909, p. 130.

41. Harold B. Simpson, *Gaines' Mills to Appomattox*, p. 102.

42. Von Borcke, I, pp. 193-194.
Blackford, p. 141.

43. Sloan, p. 40.

44. William W. Sherwood, Diary, September 8, 1862, Mss51 shsp:1, Virginia Historical Society, Richmond Va.

45. Jacob W. Haas, Diary, September 8, 1862, Harrisburg Civil War Round Table Collection, USAMHI.
Stevens, p. 135.
Judd, p. 179.

46. *Battles and Leaders of the Civil War*, II, p. 583.
Martin L. Sheets, Diary, September 8, 1862, Civil War Times Illustrated Collection, USAMHI.
Edward E. Schweitzer, "Memoir," Civil War Times Illustrated Collection, USAMHI, p. 13.

47. William J. Bolton, "War Journal," War Library and Museum, Philadephia, Pa., pp. 234-235.

48. William B. Baker, Letter, September 9, 1862, William B. Baker Papers, Southern Historical Collection, University of North Carolina, Chapel Hill, North Carolina.

49. Blackford, p. 141.

50. Von Borcke, I, pp. 194-195.

51. Blackford, p. 141.

52. Stevenson, p. 117.

53. Beach, pp. 167-168.
This is a reconstruction based upon Wilson's report to his sergeant.

54. Ibid., pp. 168-169.

55. Von Borcke, I, p. 195.

56. Blackford, p. 141.

57. Beach, pp. 168-169.

58. Blackford, p. 141.
     Von Borcke, I, p. 195.
     Beach, p. 169.
     Both Von Borcke and Blackford insisted that the skirmish was very brief. The Federals
     were driven back. Von Borcke waxed eloquent about the many Union casualties and
     the gallant charge. The charge probably did occur. It seems in keeping with Stuart's
     personal concept of the chivalrous role of the cavalry. The Federals, nevertheless, did
     not lose any men in this long range affair.

59. Von Borcke, I, p. 141.

Chapter Five

1.   Von Borcke, I, p. 196.
     Blackford, p. 142.
     Von Borcke established the time at around 1:00 A.M.

2.   Von Borcke, I, p. 196.

3.   Blackford, pp. 141-142.

4.   Von Borcke, I, p. 198.

5.   Ibid., pp. 197-198.
     Blackford, p. 142.

6.   Alfred N. Proffitt, Letter to Brother, September 9, 1862, Proffitt Family Papers,
     1850-1862, Southern Historical Collection, University of North Carolina, Chapel Hill,
     North Carolina.

7.   William W. Sherwood, Diary, September 8, 1862, Mss51 shsp:1, Virginia Historical
     Society, Richmond, Va.
     Sherwood got his dates mixed up. He should have entered the date as September 9,
     1862.

8.   Douglas, pp. 149-150.
     Katherine S. Markall, Diary, September 9, 1862, Microfilm Room, C. Burr Artz Diary,
     Frederick, Md., p. 74.

9.   W. A. Johnson, pp. 9-10.

10. Frye, p. 15.
     Historical Magazine, May 1869, p. 291.
     Richard L. T. Beale, p. 37.
     The reports indicate that perhaps Munford's brigade was scattered over a large area
     and that the 12th Virginia Cavalry was the only regiment of his at Monocacy Church
     crossroads. The rest of his brigade is not mentioned by any of the Federal or Con-
     federate participants as being present during the ensuing engagement. Munford cen-
     sured the 12th for its poor behavior upon the field on the day before, which possibly
     explains why it was the rear guard at the crossroads. The Federal reports mention
     an encounter with the 9th Virginia Cavalry at Barnesville, but do not mention meeting
     any of Munford's men there.

11. Stevenson, p. 117.

12. Richard L. T. Beale, p. 37.
     Frye, p. 15.
     Krick, p. 10.

13. Samuel J. B. V. Gilpin, Diary, September 9, 1862, E. N. Gilpin Collection, Manuscript Division, Library of Congress.

14. Hard, p. 171.
    This is an assumption based upon the regimental historian, who stated that the regiment was spread out in detachments. This regiment tended to function on squadron level — two companies per squadron. Company B approached Barnesville on a road about five miles to the right of Captain Elon J. Farnsworth. That road is the Barnesville-Gaithersburg Road. Company K advanced on the Poolesville Road, which placed it with Company M near the center of the regimental line. It is only logical that the rest of the regiment would have been spread out to the left in correct order. The Federals generally followed the "book" when deployed for combat. Such a deployment would have created the following regimental line from left to right by companies: A-D-F-H-K-M-C-L-I-G-E-B.

    T. Benton Kelley, "How I Captured Seven Johnnies," *The National Tribune*, December 12, 1889, p. 3.
    Kelley stated that Companies B and E were in the same squadron, which supports the above supposition concerning the regimental organization during the Maryland Campaign.

15. Hard, pp. 171-172.
    The author mistakenly recorded that Farnsworth's squadron attacked the 9th Virginia Cavalry.
    Historical Magazine, pp. 290-291.
    Frye, p. 15.
    Sergeant Samuel Morgan and Private John Colbert (Company A) died as a result of the skirmish at Monocacy Church. One of the two, probably, was mortally wounded, because the historian of the 8th Illinois Cavalry said his men killed one Confederate, wounded several, and captured eight.

16. Hard, p. 173.
    The author, in a mental slip, bragged that Roe captured three good horses and four Rebels when it should have been the other way around.

17. Ibid., p. 173.
    G. W. Beale, *A Lieutenant of Cavalry in Lee's Army*, The Gorham Press, Boston, 1908, p. 37.

18. Ibid., pp. 37-38.
    Krick, p. 10.

19. Hard, p. 173.

20. *Historical Magazine*, p. 291.
    G. W. Beale, p. 37.

21. Samuel J. B. V. Gilpin, Diary, September 9, 1862, E. N. Gilpin Collection, Manuscript Division, Library of Congress.
    The Hoosier Lieutenant referred to was probably Lieutenant Cassius Williams. He was the only lieutenant mentioned in Beale's 9th Virginia Cavalry as being killed and left upon the field. Lieutenant William F. King of Company I was wounded but no mention is made of him being captured.

22. *Historical Magazine*, p. 291.

23. Thomas Munford, "Recollections," Munford-Ellis Civil War Manuscript, 1861-1865, Box 1, Manuscript Dept., Duke University, Durham, North Carolina.
    Von Borcke, I, p. 198.
    Katherine S. Markall, Diary, September 9, 1862, Microfilm Room, C Burr Artz Library, Frederick, Md., p. 74.

24. Judd, p. 179.
    Westbrook, p. 123.
    Jacob W. Haas, Diary, September 9, 1862, Harrisburg Civil War Round Table Collection, USAMHI.
    Peter Augustus Filbert, Diary, September 9, 1862, Harrisburg Civil War Round Table Collection, USAMHI.

25. John Conline, "Recollections of the Battle of Antietam and the Maryland Campaign," *War Papers Read Before the Michigan Commandery of the Military Order of the Loyal Legion of the United States*, Vol. II, From December 7, 1893 to May 5, 1898, James H. Stone, Co., Printers, Detroit, 1898, p. 113.
Charles C. Morey, Diary, September 9, 1862, Charles C. Morey Collection, USAMHI.
Stevens, p. 135.
Surgeon Stevens mistakenly recalled that his regiment, the 77th New York, marched three miles and halted in Johnsville. It probably covered three miles and bivouacked somewhere else. Johnsville is about 28 miles northeast of Dawsonville.

26. John Conline, p. 113.

27. Jacob W. Haas, Diary, September 9, 1862, Harrisburg Civil War Round Table Collection, USAMHI.

28. Account after account from the Union regimentals and their diaries reflect this.
OR, XIX, pt. 1, p. 1007.
This report reads, in part, "The well-fed, well-clothed Union soldiers laid waste everything before them, plundering houses, hen-roosts, and hog-pens, showing an utter want of discipline."

29. William B. Baker, Letter to Mother, September 9, 1862, William B. Baker Papers, Southern Historical Collection, University of North Carolina, Chapel Hill, North Carolina.

30. James Wren, Diary, September 9, 1862, Manuscript, Antietam National Battlefield.

31. Committee of the Regimental Association, *History of the Thirty-Fifth Regiment Massachusetts Volunteers 1862-1865*, Mills, Knight & Co., Printers, Boston, 1884, p. 24.

32. Allen D. Albert, p. 47.

33. Ibid.
Edward E. Schweitzer, Memoir, Civil War Times Illustrated Collection, Manuscript Dept., USAMHI.
James Wren, Diary, September 9, 1862, Manuscript, Antietam National Battlefield.
Albert Augustus Pope, "Journal of the Southern Campaign, War of the Rebellion, August 27, 1862-June 9, 1865, Civil War Times Illustrated Collection, USAMHI.
Sturgis' division marched to Brookville in five to six hours, perhaps the best time set by a IX Corps unit that day. It averaged 1.3-2 miles per hour as compared with .8-1.2 miles per hour for the rest of the Corps. At ninety steps per minute, as required for the "common time," they could cover 3 miles per hour.
Thomas H. Parker, *History of the 51st Regiment P.V. and V.V.*, King and Baird Printers, Philadelphia, 1869, p. 223.
The author mistakenly credited his regiment with covering 18 miles in six hours. The regiment belonged to the same brigade as the 35th Massachusetts and probably marched 12 miles, instead.

34. James Wren, Diary, September 9, 1862, Manuscript, Antietam National Battlefield. His diary contains a detailed account of the IX Corps' role in North Carolina.

35. See Frederick Dyer, *A Compendium of the War of the Rebellion*, for sketches of each regiment.

36. Matthew J. Graham, pp. 256-257.
35th Mass., p. 23.

37. Ibid.

38. Matthew J. Graham, p. 256.

39. Thomas H. Parker, p. 223.

40. Matthew J. Graham, p. 257.

41. Edward E. Schweitzer, Memoir, Civil War Times Illustrated Collection, Manuscript Dept., USAMHI.

42. Matthew J. Graham, pp. 257-258.

43. Von Borcke, I, pp. 198-199.

44. Ibid., p. 199.

45. Samuel J. B. V. Gilpin, Diary, September 9, 1862, E. N. Gilpin Collection, Manuscript Division, Library of Congress.

46. Hard, p. 171.

47. Beach, p. 169.

48. Sloan, p. 41.

49. *Battles and Leaders*, Vol. II, p. 606.
     Sloan, p. 41.

50. Hard, p. 173.

Chapter Six

1. Samuel J. B. V. Gilpin, Diary, September 9-10, 1862, E. N. Gilpin Collection, Manuscript Division, Library of Congress.

2. *Historical Magazine*, p. 291.

3. Thomas Munford, "Civil War Manuscript 1861-1865," Munford-Ellis Collection, Box 1, Thomas T. Munford Division, Manuscript Department, Duke University Library, Durham, N.C.

4. R. L. T. Beale, p. 38.

5. Von Borcke, I, p. 199.

6. It is interesting to note that both Beale and Munford wrote extensively about the two days of fighting around Sugar Loaf Mountain. Lieutenant Colonel Beale concentrated on the skirmishing of September 10 and Munford on the fighting of September 11. H. H. Matthews of Pelham's Battery, in an article written for the Saint Mary's *Beacon*, Leonardtown, Md., January 19, 1905, credited Munford with the superior handling of his brigade against overwhelming numbers.

7. Turner, pp. 47-48.

8. McClendon, p. 131.
    Private McClendon erred when he recollected that A. P. Hill's men passed through Lawton's camp at 9:00 A.M.

9. Douglas, pp. 151-152.

    Conrad Reno, "General Jesse Reno at Frederick, Barbara Fritchie and Her Flag," *Civil War Papers*, II, MOLLUS, Boston, 1900, p. 560.

10. It would be impossible to reconstruct what Jackson was thinking as the army left Frederick. After he captured Harpers Ferry and the Army of Northern Virginia had lost at South Mountain, he met with Lee at Sharpsburg, Maryland on September 16. On that day, they decided to give battle rather than retreat across the Potomac defeated.

    Robert E. Lee, Letter to Mrs. T. J. Jackson, January 25, 1866, Letterbook of Robert E. Lee, Virginia Historical Society, Richmond, VA.

    For the army's route, see:
    Dorothy Mackay Quynn and William Rogers Quynn, "Barbara Frietschie," *Maryland Historical Magazine*, Vol. XXXVII, Sept., 1942, #3, pp. 238-240.
    Please, note the correct spelling of her name and not Whittier's Anglicized version.

11. Douglas, p. 152.
     Quynn, pp. 238-240.

     Freeman Ankrum, *Maryland and Pennsylvania Historical Sketches*, The Times-Sun, West Newton, PA, 1947, p. 65.

12. Turner, p. 48.

13. Reno, pp. 562-563.
     Ezra Carman, "Barbara Frietchie Romance," typed mss., Antietam National Battlefield, pp. 79-80.
     The girls on the doorstep were May Hopwood, Caroline Brengle, Harriet Fleming, and Mary and Laura A. Hitschen.
     Ibid., New York *Times*, June 7, 1897, "Hawkins' Zouaves."
     Local tradition had it that a Confederate knocked the flag from the hands of a small girl for which an officer reprimanded him. There was no reoccurrence.
     E. Y. Goldsborough, "Barbara Fritchie. The Truth about the Loyalty of That Brave Dame," *The National Tribune*, January 28, 1892, p. 5.
     He said an officer protected Mrs. Quantrell from the insults and advances of the enlisted men and after the officer left, a Confederate soldier knocked the flag from her hands.
     Joseph Walker, "Frederick Town," *The National Tribune*, June 6, 1888, p. 8.
     According to Walker, Mrs. Quantrell's son-in-law, the Confederate lieutenant cut the flag from Virginia's hands. She picked it up only to have it knocked away again. At this point, Mrs. Quantrell displayed a larger flag.
          The story in the text is a composite of the several sources cited, which I believe conveys the story more accurately than the individual accounts by themselves.

14. McClendon, pp. 131-132.
     Reno, pp. 553-556.
     Mr. Nixdorff noted the Rebels used the spring on her property quite often that day.

15. Reno, pp. 553-558.

16. William M. Owen, p. 133.

17. Ibid.

18. William Johnson, pp. 18-19.
     Lewis H. Steiner, p. 21.

19. William Johnson, p. 19.

20. Lewis H. Steiner, p. 21.

21. William Johnson, p. 20.

22. The troop dispositions in the column are drawn from Special Order 191, parts III, IV, and VII. The diaries of Private George Bernard (12th Virginia) and Corporal William Sherwood (17th Virginia) definitely established the order of march and the time it took to evacuate Frederick.

23. Osmun Latrobe, Diary, September 6, 1862, Osmun Latrobe Diary, Virginia Historical Society, Richmond, Va., p. 10.

24. William D. Henderson, p. 33.

25. Bernard, p. 24.

26. William Sherwood's diary is the most reliable source to establish the movements of Kemper's brigade. Unlike John Dooley's diary, which was rewritten after the war, and David E. Johnston's recollections of the 7th Virginia (1914), Sherwood's diary is in his own hand.
          It is interesting to note that he wrote not only the day of the week but also the date. On "September, Sunday, 13, 1862," he caught himself and corrected the date to September 14, while leaving the preceding dates unchanged. According to his entry for "Thursday, September 10" (September 11) the regiment (and one may therefore assume the brigade) prepared to march at 5:00 A.M. and marched 12 miles from Frederick that day.
          It appears researchers may have used his diary without catching the error. Ralph Gunn (*24th Virginia*), David Riggs (*7th Virginia*), and Lee Wallace, Jr. (*1st Virginia*) assert the brigade got as far as Boonsboro. Their works, unfortunately, are not footnoted to assist in verifying their statements.

Captain Osmun Latrobe on Longstreet's staff wrote the column halted two miles east of Middletown.

27. D. H. Hill, *Bethel to Sharpsburg*, II, pp. 343-344, fn. 4.

28. William Sherwood, Diary, September 10, 1862, Virginia Historical Society, Richmond, VA.

29. Dooley, pp. 28-29.

30. Turner, p. 47.

31. Douglas, p. 152.

32. Reno, p. 561.

33. Charles A. Cussel, *Durell's Battery in the Civil War*, Craig, Finley & Co., Philadelphia, 1900, p. 72.
     George H. Otis, *The Second Wisconsin*, Alan D. Gaff, (ed.), Morningside Bookshop, Dayton, Ohio, 1984, p. 59.

34. Albert A. Pope, "Journal of the Southern Campaign, War of the Rebellion, August 27, 1862-June 9, 1865," Civil War Times Collection, USAMHI.

35. Cussel, p. 71.

36. Archibald F. Hill, *Our Boys*, John E. Potter, Philadelphia, 1864, pp. 391-393.

37. Otis, p. 59.

38. Jacob D. Cox, *Military Reminiscences of the Civil War*, I, Charles Scribner's Sons, NY, 1900, p. 267.
     This is the general's personal reasoning.

39. Thomas F. Galwey, *The Valiant Hours*, The Stackpole Co., Harrisburg, Pa., 1961, p. 34.
     Thomas McCamant, "Personal Recollections of the Maryland Campaign of 1862," Pennsylvania Commandery, MOLLUS War Papers, 1866-1895, II, February 3, 1903, unpublished mss., MOLLUS Library, Philadelphia, Pa., p. 3.

40. Westbrook, p. 123.

41. Jacob Haas, Diary, September 9 and 10, 1862, Harrisburg Civil War Round Table Collection, USAMHI.

42. Westbrook, p. 123.

43. Jacob Haas, Diary, September 9 and 10, 1862, Harrisburg Civil War Round Table Collection, USAMHI.

44. Westbrook, p. 123.

45. Jacob Haas, Diary, September 10, 1862, Harrisburg Civil War Round Table Collection, USAMHI.

46. Hard, p. 174.

47. Samuel J. B. V. Gilpin, Diary, September 10, 1862, E. N. Gilpin Collection, Manuscript Division, Library of Congress.

48. Richard L. T. Beale, p. 38.

49. Thomas Munford, "Civil War Manuscript 1861-1865," Munford-Ellis Papers, Thomas T. Munford Division, Manuscript Department, Duke University Library, Durham, N.C.

50. H. H. Matthews, "The First Maryland Campaign," Saint Mary's *Beacon*, Leonardtown, Md., January 19, 1905, Carman Papers, Antietam National Battlefield, Part V.

51. *Historical Magazine*, p. 294.

52. OR, XIX, pt. 1, p. 535.
     Ibid., XIX, pt. 2, p. 249.

53. M. M. Green, "Saving Stonewall Jackson," from the Scrap Book of Henry Kyd Douglas, Antietam National Battlefield, not paginated.

54.   Worsham, p. 139.
        Worsham mistook the day. He cited it as September 11.
        Henry K. Douglas, "The Boonsboro Incident," Correspondence with the Baltimore *Sun*, Antietam National Battlefield.

55.   Ibid.

56.   OR, XIX, pt. 1, p. 536.
        Ibid., XIX, pt. 2, p. 249.
        Colonel Downey insisted his men killed 9 or 10 Confederates.

57.   Douglas, pp. 152-153.
        Turner, p. 48.
        L. Allison Wilmer, et al., *History and Roster of Maryland Volunteers, War of 1861-65*, I, Press of Guggenheimer, Weil and Co., Baltimore, Md., 1898, p. 702+.
        Interestingly enough, the 1st Maryland Cavalry recorded no casualties in the skirmish. The reporting of slightly wounded men, prisoners, and fatalities from such "insignificant" skirmishes depended upon the orderly and the commanding officer who were responsible for accounting for such incidents.

58.   Douglas, p. 153.

59.   Turner, p. 48.

60.   Douglas, p. 154.

61.   M. M. Green, "Saving Stonewall Jackson," p. 2.
        Henry Kyd Douglas took strong exception to Green's purported conversation with Jackson. He even drew Bassett French into the controversy. French insisted that he did not recall the conversation despite the fact that Private Green said that French published the matter in a magazine called the *Southern Literary Messenger*. It would be well to keep in mind that it is an enlisted man's word against that of two officers, both of whom idolized Jackson. French wrote to Douglas to support his fellow officer's claim that "no one would have had the hardihood to address Gen. Jackson in a public road." Further, French "thought" that Jackson's conversation was "Entirely foreign to his spirit and manner" and that Green, probably had accidentally mixed headquarters gossip into his recollection.

62.   D. H. Hill, *From Bethel to Sharpsburg*, I, fn 1, pp. 337, 347.

Chapter Seven

1.   Peter Filbert, Diary, September 11, 1862, Harrisburg Civil War Round Table Collection, USAMHI.

2.   William B. Baker, Letter, September 11, 1862, William B. Baker Papers, Southern Historical Collection, University of North Carolina, Chapel Hill, N.C.

3.   Charles J. Mills, "Through Blood and Fire: The Civil War Letters of Major Charles J. Mills," Gregory Coco Collection, Harrisburg Civil War Round Table Collection, USAMHI, pp. 32, 34.

4.   James Shinn, Diary, September 11, 1862, Edwin Augustus Osborne Papers, #567, Southern Historical Collection, University of North Carolina, Chapel Hill, N.C., p. 132.

5.   Calvin Leach, Diary, September 11, 1862, Calvin Leach Diary, Southern Historical Collection, University of North Carolina, Chapel Hill, N.C.
        James Shinn, Diary, September 11, 1862, Edwin Augustus Osborne Papers, #567, Southern Historical Collection, University of North Carolina, Chapel Hill, N.C., p. 132.

6.   *Report of Lewis H. Steiner, M.D.*, Inspector of the Sanitary Commission, Anson D. F. Randolph, N.Y., 1862, p. 22.

7.   Turner, p. 48.

8.   James S. Johnston, Letter to Mary Green, September 22, 1862, Mercer Green Johnston Collection, Manuscript Division, Library of Congress.

9. Walcott, p. 188.
   Walcott found the Rebels on the 13th, some two days later, as his regiment went into bivouac east of Middletown. The local people told him that Stonewall Jackson had ordered the men hanged for stealing and that was why the local orchards and chicken coops were still intact.

10. James Shinn, Diary, September 11, 1862, Edwin Augustus Osborne Papers, #567, Southern Historical Collection, University of North Carolina, Chapel Hill, N.C., p. 132.

11. William Sherwood, Diary, September 11, 1862, Virginia Historical Society, Richmond, Va.

12. James Shinn, Diary, September 11, 1862, Edwin Augustus Osborne Papers, #567, Southern Historical Collection, University of North Carolina, Chapel Hill, N.C., p. 133.

13. James Shipp, Diary, September 11, 1862, Virginia Historical Society, Richmond, Va.

14. Bernard, p. 24.

15. Ibid.

16. Westbrook, p. 123.

17. Hard, p. 175.

18. Ibid., p. 172.
    Westbrook, p. 123.

19. Ibid.
    There is no mention of artillery assisting the cavalry in this advance. Therefore it may be assumed that it did not participate.

20. Ibid.
    Samuel J. B. V. Gilpin, Diary, September 11, 1862, E. N. Gilpin Collection, Manuscript Division, Library of Congress.

21. H. H. Matthews, "The First Maryland Campaign," Saint Mary's *Beacon*, Leonardtown, Md., Jan. 19, 1905, Carman Papers, Antietam National Battlefield, Part V.

22. Ibid.
    Matthews, a Stuart/Pelham worshipper, insisted that Shanks' section forced the VI Corps to retire after suffering considerable losses.
    Westbrook, p. 123.
    The sergeant, a member of Hancock's Brigade, noted that the skirmishers became engaged about 9:00 A.M. and exchanged shots with the Confederates on the mountain.

23. Samuel J. B. V. Gilpin, Diary, September 11, 1862, E. N. Gilpin Collection, Manuscript Division, Library of Congress.

24. Von Borcke, I, p. 200.

25. Thomas Munford, "Civil War Manuscript 1861-1865," Munford-Ellis Papers, Box 1, Thomas T. Munford Division, Duke University Library, Durham, N.C.
    Von Borcke, I, p. 199.

26. Munford does not explain what he did after confronting Stuart, but someone had to give the command to withdraw.

27. Von Borcke, I, p. 200.

28. Hard, p. 175.

29. Westbrook, p. 123.

30. Jacob Haas, Diary, September 11, 1862, Harrisburg Civil War Round Table Collection, USAMHI.
    Peter Filbert, Diary, September 11, 1862, Harrisburg Civil War Round Table Collection, USAMHI.

31. Stevenson, p. 118.

32. Neese, p. 117.

33. Von Borcke, I, p. 201.
     McDonald, p. 38.
     Neese, p. 117.
     Von Borcke loved to elaborate on minor incidents. No Federal records substantiate
     the claim that they occupied Urbana. Contrary to Von Borcke's account, no Federal
     shells struck within the town. The Federals on their own admission had no artillery
     within five miles of the village.
           Munford's cavalry must have been the rearguard at Hyattstown. Lee's and Hamp-
     ton's brigades had passed through Urbana before noon. The only cavalry in the area
     was Munford's. They had to have been the troops which occupied Urbana after Stuart
     left. One can safely assume that Von Borcke did not linger to identify the uniforms
     of the "attacking" troops.
           Private Neese (Chew's Battery) states that the brigade retired on the Urbana Road
     to Monocacy Bridge without firing a shot — a point about two-three miles south of
     Frederick. Captain McDonald of the Laurel Brigade says they went into position on
     the Buckeystown Road three miles from Frederick. The Buckeystown Road intersects
     the Urbana Road about two miles south of Frederick. The Urbana Road is the only
     logical route that could have been used to cover Stuart's withdrawal from Urbana.
     It would not have made sense for Munford to have moved west on the Urbana-
     Buckeystown Road across the northern base of Sugar Loaf Mountain.
           It is useful to recall that after the war Von Borcke became a Stuart idolizer who
     contributed more than a fair share of myth to the Stuart image.

34. Martin L. Sheets, Diary, September 11, 1862, Civil War Times Illustrated Collection,
     USAMHI.

35. William Todd, *The Seventy-Ninth Highlanders, New York Volunteers in the War of the
     Rebellion 1861-1865*, 1905, p. 229.
     His diary is one day behind itself. His regiment arrived in Hyattstown around dark.
     J. H. E. Whitney, *The Hawkins' Zouaves: Their Battles and Marches*, by the author, N.Y.,
     1866, p. 125.

36. E. M. Woodward, *Our Marches*, John E. Potter and Co., Philadelphia, p. 193.
     M. H. France, (comp.), *The Conception, Organization and Campaigns of "Company H"
     4th Penn. Reserve Volunteer Corps, 33 Regiment in Line 1861-5*, Baldwin & Chapman,
     Publishers, Tunkhannock, Pa., 1885, p. 62.
     Archibald F. Hill, p. 393.

37. Franklin B. Hough, *History of Duryee's Brigade*, J. Munsell, Albany, 1864, p. 109.
     Isaac Hall, *History of the Ninety-Seventh Regiment, New York Volunteers*, L. C. Childs
     & Son, 1870, p. 85.
     Otis, p. 59.

38. Lyman C. Holford, Diary, September 11, 1862, Manuscript Division, Library of Congress.

39. Ezra Carman to Thomas T. Rosser, May 12, 1897, Fitzhugh Lee's Cavalry Brigade, D.
     H. Hill's Division, regimental information, Antietam Studies, National Archives.

40. Ezra Carman Notes, Antietam National Battlefield, pp. 200-202.

41. E. M. Woodward, *Our Marches*, p. 193.
     Woodward does not say what the farmers had lost but one may assume based upon
     the Confederate accounts that the crops were left in tact but the horses were taken.

42. E. M. Woodward, *Our Marches*, pp. 193-194.
     France, p. 62.
     Archibald F. Hill, p. 393.

43. Galwey, p. 34.

44. Charles Harrison Mills, "Through Blood and Fire," Gregory Coco Collection, Harrisburg
     Civil War Round Table Collection, USAMHI, p. 32.

45. Stevenson, p. 118.

    Beach, p. 170.

46. Martin L. Sheets, Diary, September 11, 1862, Civil War Times Illustrated Collection, USAMHI.

    I am referring to the West Virginia cavalry as West Virginians to clarify their allegiance to the Union. At the time, West Virginia had not seceded from the state of Virginia and the cavalry unit was therefore Virginian.

47. James Abraham, "With the Army of West Virginia 1861-1864," Evelyn A. Benson, (ed.), Publication No. 1, Lancaster, Pa., 1974, Civil War Times Illustrated Collection, USAMHI, p. 16.

48. John L. Parker, and Robert G. Carter, *History of the Twenty-Second Massachusetts Infantry*, Rand Avery Co., Boston, 1887, p. 184.

49. Edward E. Schweitzer, "Memoir," Civil War Times Illustrated Collection, USAMHI, p. 13.

50. Charles Mills, "Through Blood and Fire," Gregory Coco Collection, Harrisburg Civil War Round Table Collection, USAMHI, p. 33.

51. *35th Mass.*, p. 24.

52. Jacob Cox, pp. 268-270.

    T. Harry Williams, *Hayes of the Twenty-Third The Civil War Volunteer Officer*, Alfred A. Knopf, N.Y., 1965, p. 134.

    I considered Cox's date rather than the one stated by Williams as the more accurate one.

    I did not delete Reno's explicit language because it is what he said. His reference to "black" refers to the Old English word for evil.

53. Bernard, p. 24.

54. Dooley, p. 31.

    Osmun Latrobe, Diary, September 12, 1862, Osmun Latrobe Diary, Virginia Historical Society, Richmond, Va., p. 10.

55. Worsham, p. 139.

56. H. B. McClellan, p. 112.

57. Sloan, p. 41.

    Battles and Leaders, II, p. 613.

58. John Calvin Gorman, "Memoirs of a Rebel," George Gorman, (ed.), *Military Images*, Nov./Dec., 1981, p. 4.

Chapter Eight

1. James Abraham, "With the Army of West Virginia 1861-1864," Evelyn A. Benson, (ed.), Publication No. 1, Lancaster, Pa., 1974, Civil War Times Illustrated Collection, USAMHI, p. 16.

2. Cox, I, p. 268.

3. Osmun Latrobe, Diary, September 12, 1862, Osmun Latrobe Diary, Virginia Historical Society, Richmond, Va.

    Dooley, p. 31.

    Jackson's corps, which was moving in on Harpers Ferry, no longer played an active role on Maryland's soil until September 16, when Jackson reported to Lee with his men at Sharpsburg.

4. Ezra Carman, "The Maryland Campaign," VII, Manuscript Division, Library of Congress, p. 1.

5. Angela Kirkham Davis, "War Reminiscences," Antietam National Battlefield, p. 31.

    I changed the capitalization and the punctuation in the quote to give the description, according to Mrs. Davis, the correct emphasis.

348ENDNOTES — Pages 86 to 88

6. Ibid., pp. 31-32.
Mrs. Davis erred in her recollection of the day the Confederates passed through Funkstown. They entered the town on Thursday, September 12, and not Wednesday, September 11, as she recollected. All the diaries I have found to date, including that of Osmun Latrobe of Longstreet's staff, say that he entered Hagerstown on the 12th and not on the 11th.

7. Osmun Latrobe, Diary, September 12, 1862, Osmun Latrobe Diary, Virginia Historical Society, Richmond, Va.
Ezra Carman, "The Maryland Campaign," VII, Manuscript Division, Library of Congress, p. 1.

8. Owen, pp. 135-136.

9. Frank M. Mixon, *Reminiscences of a Private*, The State Co., Columbia, S.C., 1910, p. 27.

10. Angela Kirkham Davis, "War Recollections," Antietam National Battlefield, p. 32.

11. Dooley, p. 31.
At this point in the war slavery was not the real issue which justified the war to the rest of the world. As a rule, in the Army of the Potomac, blacks did not receive much better treatment than the slaves who traveled with the Army of Northern Virginia. In the Federal army, they did not receive arms to forage with and generally officers, not enlisted men, reserved the right to "adopt" stray "contrabands" as their personal servants or cooks. The Union officers meted out reward and punishment as swiftly as if they owned the freedmen.
"Civil War Letters of Francis Edwin Pierce of the 108th New York Volunteer Infantry." *Rochester In The Civil War*, The Rochester Historical Society Publications, XXII, p. 151.
Captain Francis E. Pierce (Company F) of the newly recruited 108th New York, who generally referred to his servant as his "shade" sometimes kicked his man to his feet and did not willfully share even his ground covers with the fellow.
John Williams Hudson, Letter to Sophia, October 16, 1862, vertical file, Western Maryland Room, Washington County Free Library, Hagerstown, Md.
Colonel Edward Ferrero, who commanded a New York-Massachusetts Brigade, picked up an apparently homeless child named Johnny and kept him as an unofficial attache'.
Edward O. Lord, (ed.), *History of the Ninth New Hampshire Volunteers*, Republican Press Association, Concord, 1895, pp. 125-126.
The 9th New Hampshire also adopted a stray child. They picked up a five year old boy named Jokum who followed them out of Washington. When the men tried return him, he refused to go. Rather than let him loose, they stole an old mule for him to ride and kept him as a "mascot." Adept at mimicry, he entertained the New Englanders for over a year before they let him go, on his own, in Washington.

12. Calvin Leach, Diary, September 12, 1862, Southern Historical Collection, University of North Carolina, Chapel Hill, N.C.

13. William Sherwood, Diary, September 12, 1862, Virginia Historical Society, Richmond, Va.

14. William D. Henderson, p. 34.

15. Neese, p. 117.
Thomas Munford, "Civil War Manuscript 1861-1865," Munford-Ellis Papers, Box 1, Thomas T. Munford Division, Manuscript Department, Duke University Library, Durham, N.C., p. 22.

16. Oliver C. Bosbyshell, *The 48th in the War*, Avil Printing Co., Philadelphia, 1895, p. 74.
Walcott, p. 187.
James Wren, Diary, September 12, 1862, Manuscript, Antietam National Battlefield, p. 99.
James Pratt, James and Charlotte Pratt Collection, USAMHI, p. 31.

Parker, p. 223.

Parker is the only IX Corps author who remembers the rain; his writing predates most of the other IX reports and therefore is considered a valid reference. The fact that the day became much hotter after the rain stopped is not the least bit unusual in the fall in Maryland.

17. Cox, I, p. 268.

18. *35th Mass.*, p. 24.

19. Thomas H. Parker, p. 223.

20. James Pratt, Letter to wife, September 13, 1862, James and Charlotte Pratt Collections, USAMHI, p. 21.

Oliver C. Bosbyshell, p. 74.

21. James Wren, Diary, September 12, 1862, Manuscript, Antietam National Battlefield, p. 99.

22. Archibald F. Hill, p. 392.

23. Marsena R. Patrick, *Inside Lincoln's Army*, David S. Sparks, (ed.), Thomas Yoseloff, N.Y., 1964, p. 142.

24. John H. Cook, Diary, September 11, 1862, State Historical Society of Wisconsin, Archives and Manuscript Dept., Vertical Files, Antietam National Battlefield.

25. George Fairfield, Diary, September 12, 1862, State Historical Society of Wisconsin, Archives and Manuscript Dept., Vertical Files, Antietam National Battlefield. 9/12/62.

26. Patrick, p. 143.

John H. Cook, Diary, September 12, 1862, State Historical Society of Wisconsin, Archives and Manuscript Dept., Vertical Files, Antietam National Battlefield.

George Fairchild, Diary, September 12, 1862, State Historical Society of Wisconsin, Archives and Manuscript Dept., Vertical Files, Antietam National Battlefield.

27. Benjamin F. Cook, *History of the Twelfth Massachusetts Volunteers (Webster Regiment)*, Twelfth (Webster) Regimental Association, Boston, 1882, p. 67.

Hough, p. 109.

Isaac Hall, p. 85.

28. Ulysses Robert Brooks, p. 81.

29. H. B. McClellan, p. 114.

30. Cox, I, p. 271.

31. *35th Mass.*, p. 24.

32. Von Borcke, I, pp. 202-203.

Blackford, p. 142.

Katherine S. Markall, Diary, September 12, 1862, Microfilm Room, C. Burr Artz Library, Frederick, Md., p. 76.

The flag waving incident occurred on top of the McPherson house, which was next door to the Calvin Page house.

33. Clark E. Goldsborough, "Graphic Description of Lee's Occupation of Frederick, Maryland in 1862," *The National Tribune*, October 14, 1886, p. 4.

34. James Abraham, "With the Army of West Virginia 1861-1864," Evelyn A. Benson, (ed.), Publication No. 1, Lancaster, Pa., 1974, Civil War Times Illustrated Collection, USAMHI, p. 17.

35. Von Borcke, I, pp. 203-204.

Von Borcke invented a much more heroic stand than actually occurred.

36. James Abraham, "With the Army of West Virginia 1861-1864," Evelyn A. Benson, (ed.), Publication No. 1, Lancaster, Pa., 1974, Civil War Times Illustrated Collection, USAMHI, p. 17.

37. Clark Goldsborough, "Graphic Description of Lee's Occupation of Frederick," *The National Tribune*, October 14, 1886, p. 4.

38. James Abraham, "With the Army of West Virginia 1861-1864," Evelyn A. Benson, (ed.), Publication No. 1, Lancaster, Pa., 1974, Civil War Times Illustrated Collection, USAMHI, p. 17.

39. Martin L. Sheets, Diary, September 12, 1862, Civil War Times Illustrated Collection, USAMHI.
    Cox, I, p. 271.

40. James Abraham, "With the Army of West Virginia 1861-1864," Evelyn A. Benson, (ed.), Publication No. 1, Lancaster, Pa., 1974, Civil War Times Illustrated Collection, USAMHI, p. 17.

41. Cox, I, p. 271.
    Lester L. Kempfer, *The Salem Light Guard, Company G, 36th Ohio Volunteer Infantry, Marietta, Ohio, 1861-1865*, Adams Press, Chicago, 1973, p. 86.

42. William R. Quynn, (ed.), *The Diary of Jacob Engelbrecht 1858-1878*, III, The Historical Society of Frederick County, Inc., Frederick, Md., 1976, p. 181.

43. James Abraham, "With the Army of West Virginia 1861-1864," Evelyn A. Benson, (ed.), Publication No. 1, Lancaster, Pa., 1974, Civil War Times Illustrated Collection, USAMHI, p. 17.
    D. Cunningham and W. W. Miller, *Report of the Ohio Antietam Battlefield Commission*, 1904, pp. 61, 77.
    Williams, p. 135.
    Cox, I, p. 271.
    Cox confused Moore's with Scammon's Brigade. Scammon's Brigade had the lead.

44. James Abraham, "With the Army of West Virginia 1861-1864," Evelyn A. Benson, (ed.), Publication No. 1, Lancaster, Pa., 1974, Civil War Times Illustrated Collection, USAMHI, p. 17.

45. Reno, p. 565.

46. Cox, I, p. 271.
    Cunningham and Miller, p. 87.

47. Clark E. Goldsborough, "Graphic Description of Lee's Occupation of Frederick," *The National Tribune*, October 14, 1886, p. 4.

48. James Abraham, "With the Army of West Virginia 1861-1864," Evelyn A. Benson, (ed.), Publication No. 1, Lancaster, Pa., 1974, Civil War Times Illustrated Collection, USAMHI, p. 17.
    Martin L. Sheets, Diary, September 12, 1862, Civil War Times Illustrated Collection, USAMHI.

49. Katherine S. Markall, Diary, September 12, 1862, Microfilm Room, C. Burr Artz Library, Frederick, Md., p. 76.

50. Clark E. Goldsborough, "Graphic Description of Lee's Occupation of Frederick," *The National Tribune*, October 14, 1862, p. 4.
    Steiner, p. 23.
    Goldsborough had no idea that Hospital Steward Fitzgerald of the Sanitary Commission had already crossed Stuart's path and had similarly piqued him by refusing to comply with the same request.

51. Reno, p. 565.

52. Cox, I, pp. 271-272.

53. Reno, p. 565.

54. Cox, I, p. 272.
    Martin L. Sheets, Diary, September 12, 1862, Civil War Times Illustrated Collection, USAMHI.

55. William R. Quynn (ed.) *The Diary of Jacob Engelbrecht 1858-1878*, III, The Historical Society of Frederick County, Inc., Frederick, Md., 1976, p. 181.

56. Ibid.

    H. B. McClellan, p. 114.

    OR, XIX, pt. 1, p. 823.

57. William R. Quynn, (ed.), *The Diary of Jacob Engelbrecht 1858-1878*, III, The Historical Society of Frederick County, Inc., Frederick, Md., 1976, p. 181.

    James Abraham, "With the Army of West Virginia 1861-1864," Evelyn A. Benson, (ed.), Publication No. 1, Lancaster, Pa., 1974, Civil War Times Illustrated Collection, USAMHI, p. 17.

58. Clark E. Goldsborough, "Graphic Description of Lee's Occupation of Frederick," *The National Tribune*, October 14, 1886, p. 4.

    Cox, I, p. 272.

    H. B. McClellan, p. 114.

    James Abraham, "With the Army of West Virginia 1861-1864," Evelyn A. Benson, (ed.), Publication No. 1, Lancaster, Pa., 1974, Civil War Times Illustrated Collection, USAMHI, p. 17.

    OR, XIX, pt. 1, p. 823.

    Von Borcke, I, p. 203.
    Von Borcke said the Federals had a 6 Pounder and that they were on the eastern side of the stone bridge.

    Martin L. Sheets, Diary, September 12, 1862, Civil War Times Illustrated Collection, USAMHI.
    Sheets said that the section consisted of a 20 Pound Parrott and a 12 Pound Napoleon.

    J. H. Horton and Solomon Teverbaugh, *A History of the Eleventh Regiment Ohio Volunteer Infantry*, W. H. Shuey, Printer and Publisher, Dayton, Ohio, 1866, p. 69.
    They said the Federals had two guns in the street.

    Edward E. Schweitzer, "Memoir," Civil War Times Illustrated Collection, USAMHI, p. 13.
    He stated that the Federals had only one gun present.

59. Ulysses Robert Brooks, pp. 81-82.

60. Ibid., p. 82.

    Von Borcke, I, p. 203.

    Blackford, p. 142.

61. Ibid.

62. Ulysses Robert Brooks, pp. 82-83.

63. Clark E. Goldsborough, "Graphic Description of Lee's Occupation of Frederick," *The National Tribune*, October 14, 1886, p. 4.

64. Reno, pp. 565-566.

65. William R. Quynn, (ed.), *The Diary of Jacob Engelbrecht 1858-1878*, III, The Historical Society of Frederick County, Inc., Frederick, Md., 1976, p. 181.

66. Horton and Teverbaugh, p. 69.

67. Clark E. Goldsborough, "Graphic Description of Lee's Occupation of Frederick," *The National Tribune*, October 14, 1862, p. 4.
    Goldsborough had the soldier's personal effects sent home to his widow in Michigan.

68. James Abraham, "With the Army of West Virginia 1861-1864," Evelyn A. Benson, (ed.), Publication No. 1, Lancaster, Pa., 1974, Civil War Times Illustrated Collection, USAMHI, p. 17.

69. James Abraham, Letter to Brother, September 20, 1862, Historical Society of Pennsylvania.

70. OR, XIX, pt. 1, p. 823.

    H. B. McClellan, p. 114.

71. Ulysses Robert Brooks, p. 82.

72. James Abraham, "With the Army of West Virginia 1861-1864," Evelyn A. Benson, (ed.), Publication No. 1, Lancaster, Pa., 1974, Civil War Times Illustrated Collection, USAMHI, p. 17.

73. William R. Quynn, (ed.), *The Diary of Jacob Engelbrecht 1858-1878*, III, The Historical Society of Frederick County, Inc., Frederick, Md., 1976, p. 181.

74. Horton and Teverbaugh, p. 69.

75. James Abraham, "With the Army of West Virginia 1861-1864," Evelyn A. Benson, (ed.), Publication No. 1, Lancaster, Pa., 1974, Civil War Times Illustrated Collection, USAMHI, p. 17.

76. Samuel Compton, Autobiography, Samuel Compton Papers, Manuscript Department, Duke University Library, Durham, N.C., p. 91.

77. Horton and Teverbaugh, p. 70.

78. Martin L. Sheets, Diary, September 12, 1862, Civil War Times Illustrated Collection, USAMHI.

79. Horton and Teverbaugh, p. 70.

80. Cunningham and Miller, p. 87.

81. Edward E. Schweitzer, "Memoir," Civil War Times Illustrated Collection, USAMHI, p. 14.

82. James E. D. Ward, *Twelfth Ohio Volunteer Infantry*, Ripley, Ohio, 1864, p. 57.

83. Samuel E. Compton, Autobiography, Samuel Compton Papers, Manuscript Department, Duke University Library, Durham, N.C., p. 92.

84. James E. D. Ward, p. 57.

85. William R. Quynn, (ed.), *The Diary of Jacob Engelbrecht 1858-1878*, III, The Historical Society of Frederick County, Inc., Frederick, Md., 1976, p. 181.

86. Horton and Teverbaugh, p. 69.

87. Reno, p. 566.
     Henry J. Spooner, "The Maryland Campaign with the Fourth Rhode Island," *Personal Narratives Sixth Series, No. 5, Soldiers and Sailors Historical Society of Rhode Island*, p. 14. Reno wrote that he met Colonel John Hartranft of the 51st Pennsylvania in the street. That is not likely, Hartranft's command did not cross the Monocacy that day. He further stated that he met Generals McClellan, Reno, and Burnside further down the road. That is also unlikely. McClellan did not enter Frederick until the next day. More than likely, he met Colonel William Steere, whose regiment overran the hospital and the Hessian Barracks and whom he later mistakenly remembered as John Hartranft. *The National Tribune* did not always carefully check its material before it printed it.

88. Reno, p. 567.

89. Steiner, p. 24.

90. *Historical Magazine*, p. 291.

91. Samuel J. B. V. Gilpin, Diary, September 12, 1862, E. N. Gilpin Collection, Manuscript Division, Library of Congress.

92. Beach, p. 170.
     Stevenson, p. 119.

93. Charles M. Smith, Letter to Parents, September 18-21, 1862, Smith Family Papers, Civil War Miscellaneous Collection, USAMHI.

94. James S. Brisbin, Letter to Wife, September 16, 1862, Civil War Times Illustrated Collection, USAMHI.

95. J. Graham, pp. 260-261.

96. Bosbyshell, p. 74.

James Wren, Diary, September 12, 1862, Manuscript, Antietam National Battlefield, p. 100.

97. *35th Mass.*, p. 24.

98. James Madison Stone, *Personal Recollections of the Civil War*, by the author, Boston, 1918, p. 83.

99. William Todd, p. 229.

100. Frederick Pettit, Letter, September 20, 1862, Civil War Times Illustrated Collection, USAMHI.

101. Galwey, p. 34.

102. Ernst Linden Waitt, (comp.), *History of the Nineteenth Regiment Massachusetts Volunteer Infantry 1861-1865*, Salem Press, Salem, Mass., 1906, p. 127.

103. John S. Weiser, Letter to Parents, September 12, 1862, Civil War Miscellaneous Collection, USAMHI.

104. Jacob W. Haas, Diary, September 12, 1862, Harrisburg Civil War Round Table Collection, USAMHI.

Peter A. Filbert, Diary, September 12, 1862, Harrisburg Civil War Round Table Collection, USAMHI.

Westbrook, p. 123.

105. Jacob Haas, Diary, September 12, 1862, Harrisburg Civil War Round Table Collection, USAMHI.

Peter Filbert, Diary, September 12, 1862, Harrisburg Civil War Round Table Collection, USAMHI.

Westbrook, p. 124.

Stevens, p. 135.

Judd, p. 179.

106. Jacob Haas, Diary, September 12, 1862, Harrisburg Civil War Round Table Collection, USAMHI.

107. Peter Filbert, Diary, September 12, 1862, Harrisburg Civil War Round Table Collection, USAMHI.

Filbert said he washed in the creek. The soldiers would have drunk from it also.

108. Montreville Williams, Diary, September 12, 1862, Museum Collection, Antietam National Battlefield.

109. Ezra Carman, "The Maryland Campaign," VII, Manuscript Division, Library of Congress, p. 3.

110. D. H. Hill, *From Bethel to Sharpsburg*, II, fn 2, p. 340.

111. Ulysses Robert Brooks, p. 83.

112. Blackford, p. 142.

Von Borcke, I, p. 205.

113. Neese, pp. 117-118.

Chapter Nine

1. *Historical Magazine*, p. 291.

Beach, p. 170.

Stevenson, p. 120.

Alfred Pleasonton said a section of artillery went with McReynolds' command. The regimental historian of the 1st New York Cavalry stated that Battery M, 5th U.S. Artillery accompanied the column. There was no Battery M, 5th U.S. in the Army at the time. There was a Battery M, 2nd U.S. which was assigned to the Cavalry Division. I suspect that the author of the regimental history wrote down the wrong regimental number.

2. *Historical Magazine*, p. 291.

3. Ibid.
    Samuel J. B. V. Gilpin, Diary, September 13, 1862, E. N. Gilpin Collection, Manuscript Division, Library of Congress.
    Benjamin W. Crowninshield, p. 73.

4. Pleasonton, p. 291.

5. Ibid.
    Pleasonton remarked that he sent a couple of sections of artillery from the two batteries mentioned here without specifying the number of guns. If, as I suspect, a section of Hains' Battery M went with the 1st New York Cavalry, that would have left two sections of Hains' and Robertson's four guns to support the cavalry.
    OR, XIX, pt. 1, p. 823;
    Worthington Chauncey Ford, (ed.), *A Cycle of Adams Letters 1861-1865*, Vol. I, Houghton Mifflin Co., Boston, Mass., 1920, p. 185.
    Charles F. Adams said he found the 1st Massachusetts Cavalry about three miles from town.
    Pickerill, p. 24.
    Pickerill stated that the regiment ran into Confederate artillery about one mile beyond their camp.

6. Samuel J. B. V. Gilpin, Diary, September 13, 1862, E. N. Gilpin Collection, Manuscript Division, Library of Congress.
    The batteries must have been split. They were the only artillery employed at Braddock Pass and when Gilpin noted that his regiment supported one battery on the south of the road then one to the north of the road, he implies that there were two distinct batteries involved.

7. Joseph Mills Hanson, "A Report on the Employment of the Artillery at the Battle of Antietam, MD," U.S. Department of the Interior, National Park Service, May 27, 1940, pp. 5-6.

8. Von Borcke, I, p. 205.

9. Crowninshield, p. 73.
    Samuel J. B. V. Gilpin, Diary, September 13, 1862, E. N. Gilpin Collection, Manuscript Division, Library of Congress.
    It is misleading to assume that the Federal cavalry deployed immediately. According to Private Samuel Gilpin, the 3rd Indiana dashed to the right to support some guns after being under fire for *"a few hours."* He then said that the regiment dismounted and fought up the mountainside as skirmishers.

10. Crowninshield, p. 74.

11. Charles M. Smith, Letter to Parents, September 18, 1862, Smith Family Papers, Civil War Miscellaneous Collection, USAMHI.

12. Crowninshield, p. 74.

13. Worthington C. Ford, pp. 185-186.

14. Von Borcke, I, p. 205.

15. Ulysses Robert Brooks, p. 83.
    Private Rea stated that Hampton's Brigade came up as a reserve to Lieutenant Colonel W. T. Martin's Jeff Davis Legion.

16. H. B. McClellan, p. 114.

17. Von Borcke, I, p. 205.
    Von Borcke made no mention of the general consulting with any of the field commanders.

18. H. B. McClellan, p. 114.
    Ulysses Robert Brooks, p. 83.

19. Ibid.

Carman Papers, Brigadier General Wade Hampton's cavalry brigade, 1st N.C. Cavalry, Reports of Cos. A and E, and Captain W. H. Cheek, Antietam Studies, National Archives.

20. Ulysses Robert Brooks, p. 84.

21. Von Borcke, I, p. 206.

Samuel J. B. V. Gilpin, Diary, September 13, 1862, E. N. Gilpin Collection, Manuscript Division, Library of Congress.

Ulysses Robert Brooks, p. 84.

The artillery duel lasted two hours.

H. B. McClellan, p. 115.

Worthington C. Ford, p. 185.

The regiment rested in the road for 3 hours. By comparing that with Rea's account the artillery skirmishing must have ended between 11:00 A.M. and noon.

22. Lyman C. Holford, Diary, September 13, 1862, Manuscript Division, Library of Congress.

23. Isaac Hall, p. 85.

Hough, pp. 109-110.

24. Westbrook, p. 124.

Bidwell, p. 18.

Judd, p. 180.

25. Charles C. Morey, Diary, September 13, 1862, Charles C. Morey Collection, USAMHI.

26. Montreville Williams, Diary, September 13, 1862, Museum Collection, Antietam National Battlefield.

The 3rd New Jersey covered about 8 miles in six hours — an average of 1.3 miles per hour.

Jacob Haas, Diary, September 13, 1862, Harrisburg Civil War Round Table Collection, USAMHI.

Peter Filbert, Diary, September 13, 1862, Harrisburg Civil War Round Table Collection, USAMHI.

The 96th Pennsylvania left camp at 10:00 A.M. and went into bivouac at Buckeystown at 2:00 P.M. According to Jacob Haas, they marched 8 miles — an average of 2 miles per hour. The regiment, apparently, was marching at the "Common Time" (90 steps/minute).

27. Richard C. Datzman, M.D., "Who Found Lee's Lost Dispatch," Monograph, February 3, 1973, Antietam National Battlefield, p. 9.

Dr. Datzman made the assumption that the IX moved out around 9:00 A.M. or 10:00 A.M., the approximate time that the XII wandered upon the field and were crowded on the right flank by IX Corps soldiers who were moving at a right angle to their northern flank.

Battles and Leaders, II, p. 603.

Silas Colgrove, commanding the 27th Indiana, recorded that the XII arrived in Frederick around noon.

To be on the safe side, I estimate the arrival of the order to march around 11:00 A.M. The first artillery shots were fired around 9:00 A.M. Time must be allotted for a courier to reach Frederick and find IX Corps Headquarters.

28. Charles M. Smith, Letter to Parents, September 18-21, 1862, Smith Family Papers, Civil War Miscellaneous Collection, USAMHI.

Smith wrote that the 11th Connecticut was the infantry regiment which came to their support. That implies that Harland's Brigade led the column which came to the regiment's assistance.

29. Carman Papers at Antietam, New York *Times*, June 7, 1897.

30. Whitney, p. 128.

31. Charles F. Johnson, *The Long Roll*, The Roycrofters, East Aurora, N.Y., 1911, (Reprint, Hagerstown Bookbinding and Printing, 1986), p. 182.

32. OR, XIX, pt. 1, pp. 449-450.

33. This is my estimation of the situation. The Army of the Potomac did not move out until after McClellan received the "Lost Order 191." It makes sense that at this stage of the campaign when he had no solid contact with Lee's army that McClellan might fear being flanked and overrun and therefore act with caution.

34. Albert A. Pope, "Journal of the Southern Campaign, War of the Rebellion, August 27, 1862-June 9, 1865, September 13, 1862, Civil War Times Illustrated Collection, USAMHI.
     James Pratt, Letter to Wife, September 13, 1862, James and Charlotte Pratt Collection, USAMHI, p. 22.
     Bosbyshell, p. 74.
     Frederick Pettit, Letter, September 20, 1862, Civil War Times Illustrated Collection, USAMHI.
     Daniel E. Hurd, "My Experiences in the Civil War," September 13, 1862, William Marvel Collection, USAMHI.
     Kempfer, p. 86.
     All of these sources cite the IX Corps' departure time as sometime in the late afternoon.

35. Otis, p. 60.

36. Datzman, p. 9.

37. Ibid.
     These are based on the statements of William H. Hostetter, David B. Vance, George W. Welch, Enoch G. Boicourt, and John Campbell all of whom were from Companies A and F of the 27th Indiana.
     Battles and Leaders, II, p. 603.
     In this article by Silas Colgrove, he said that Private (Cpl.) Mitchell found the letter and that the private and Sergeant Bloss brought the letter to him and that he took the letter to his division commander, Alpheus Williams. Colgrove wrote his article for the *Century Magazine* in response to an enquiry from Mitchell's son, William A. Mitchell, who was trying to obtain a posthumous pension for his father who had died in 1868.
         Hostetter and Vance both, in sworn affidavits, recalled that Bloss went to the reserve picket post alone. I believe that Colgrove's statement to the magazine included Mitchell in an attempt to alleviate the family's severely distressed financial situation.
         Corporal Barton W. Mitchell, who was born in 1816, suffered from rheumatism and heart trouble. Having been raised in Ohio and central Indiana, which between 1816-1840 were still considered to be part of the frontier, one can assume that he had little if any formal education. No mention of his schooling appears in the family history. The affidavits state that Mitchell never held the orders in his hand and he never read them. If he could not read, it makes sense that he would not embarrass himself, considering he was twenty years older than most of the men around him.

38. Ezra Carman, "The Maryland Campaign," VII, Manuscript Division, Library of Congress, p. 4.
     Ezra Carman, Colonel of the 13th New Jersey, wrote that the Corps arrived upon the field near noon and that Bloss erred in his estimation of the time.

39. Von Borcke, I, p. 209.

40. Ibid., I, pp. 206-207.

41. Samuel J. B. V. Gilpin, Diary, September 13, 1862, E. N. Gilpin Collection, Manuscript Division, Library of Congress.
     Samuel Gilpin wrote in his diary that the regiment supported a battery on the left of the road for about two hours before the regiment moved to the right to support a battery on the northern flank.
     Hard, 8th IL, p. 175.
     He did not state exactly where the regiment was but it makes sense that it probably deployed to the right after the 3rd Indiana debouched to the left.

42. Von Borcke, I, p. 207.

43. Samuel J. B. V. Gilpin, Diary, September 12, 1862, E. N. Gilpin Collection, Manuscript Division, Library of Congress.

44. *Historical Magazine*, p. 291.
     Pleasonton credited both the 3rd Indiana and the 8th Illinois with skirmishing up the mountainside.
     Von Borcke, I, p. 207.
     Von Borcke saw two skirmish lines advance, which indicates that two separate units were involved. Federals were notorious for following the rules. Skirmishers fought in extended order and in single lines. It is safe to assume that the 8th Illinois moved to the south side of the road.

45. Von Borcke, I, pp. 206-207.

46. Pickerill, p. 24.

47. Von Borcke, I, p. 207.

48. Ulysses Robert Brooks, p. 83.

49. Worthington C. Ford, p. 186.

50. Charles M. Smith, Letter to Parents, September 18-21, 1862, Smith Family Papers, Civil War Miscellaneous Collection, USAMHI.

51. Worthington C. Ford, p. 186.

52. Charles W. Smith, Letter to Parents, September 18-21, 1862, Smith Family Papers, Civil War Miscellaneous Collection, USAMHI.

53. Von Borcke, I, pp. 207-208.

54. Ulysses Robert Brooks, p. 84.

55. Pickerill, p. 24.

56. Von Borcke, I, pp. 208-209.

57. Von Borcke, I, p. 209.
     Ulysses Robert Brooks, p. 84.
     Pickerill, p. 24.
     H. B. McClellan, p. 114.
     Historical Magazine, p. 291.

58. H. B. McClellan, p. 115.
     Von Borcke, I, p. 209.
     Ulysses Robert Brooks, p. 84.

59. *Historical Magazine*, p. 294.
     The 8th Illinois Cavalry accounted for the other wounded man. He was hit somewhere near the outskirts of Frederick — I presume by a shell fragment.

60. Ezra Carman, "The Maryland Campaign," VII, Manuscript Division, Library of Congress, p. 5.

61. Special Orders 191, typed copy, Antietam National Battlefield.

62. Ezra Carman, "The Maryland Campaign," VII, Manuscript Division, Library of Congress, p. 6.

63. Ibid., p. 5.
     This is my personal assessment of McClellan's reason for writing the communique as he did. Being a school teacher and a former manager of personnel, I feel qualified to judge when a person is covering his rear and when he is trying to "butter up" a superior. McClellan goes so far as to include among the last lines of the cable, "....My respects to Mrs. Lincoln. ["She was" or "I was" — it is not clear but implied] Received most enthusiastically by the ladies...."

64. Ibid., p. 5.

James Pratt, Diary, September 13, 1862, James and Charlotte Pratt Collection, USAMHI, p. 22.

The regiment departed between 3:00-4:00 P.M.

Bosbyshell, p. 74.

The regiment left for Frederick at 3:30 P.M.

35th Mass., p. 25.

The regiment marched in the middle of the afternoon.

Kempfer, p. 86.

The 30th Ohio left its camp near Frederick about 3:00 P.M.

65. *Historical Magazine*, p. 292.

66. Worthington C. Ford, p. 186.

Adams mentioned only two ridges — the one his regiment was behind and the one to the west where the Confederate artillery was located. There are actually four ridges. Once the initial descent is made into Middletown Valley, there is a moderate incline, followed by a small swale with a valley beyond that ridge. The third ridge rises abruptly from that swale followed by a deep creek valley which rises sharply to the town of Middletown proper.

67. Pickerill, p. 25.

68. Von Borcke, I, pp. 209-210.

Ulysses Robert Brooks, pp. 84-85.

69. Charles M. Smith, Letter to Parents, September 18-21, 1862, Smith Family Papers, Civil War Miscellaneous Collection, USAMHI.

70. Ulysses Robert Brooks, p. 85.

Von Borcke, I, p. 209.

71. H. B. McClellan, p. 115.

72. Von Borcke, I, p. 209.

73. Worthington C. Ford, p. 186.

74. Pickerill, p. 25.

75. Ulysses Robert Brooks, p. 85.

Carman Studies, Archives, 1st NC, Co. E.

OR, XIX, pt. 1, p. 823.

76. Von Borcke, I, pp. 209-211.

Pickerill, p. 25.

77. Worthington C. Ford, p. 186.

Crowninshield, p. 74.

78. Von Borcke, I, p. 210.

Heros Von Borcke wrote:

"In my judgment our admirable General here betrayed a fault which was one of the few he had as a cavalry leader; and the repetition of the error on several occasions, at later periods of the war, did us material damage. His own personal gallantry would not permit him to abandon the field and retreat, even when sound military prudence made this clearly advisable."

79. Ulysses Robert Brooks, pp. 85-86.

Carman Papers, Brigadier General Wade Hampton's cavalry brigade, 1st N.C. Cavalry, Reports of Cos. A and E, Antietam Studies, National Archives.

80. *Historical Magazine*, p. 292.

81. Von Borcke, I, p. 211.

82. Worthington C. Ford, pp. 186-187.

83. OR, XIX, pt. 1, p. 824.

The North Carolinians lost three men captured.

Carman Papers, Brigadier General Wade Hampton's cavalry brigade, 1st N.C. Cavalry, Report of Co. E, Antietam Studies, National Archives.

Two of those casualties came from Company K of the 1st North Carolina Cavalry.

84. Hard, p. 176.

85. *Historical Magazine*, p. 292.

Ulysses Robert Brooks, p. 85.

86. OR, XIX, pt. 1, p. 824.

The 1st North Carolina Cavalry lost 8 wounded and 3 captured.

Carman Papers, Brigadier General Wade Hampton's cavalry brigade, 1st N.C. Cavalry, Report of Co. E, Antietam Studies, National Archives.

Company K lost Captain Siler, 2 sergeants, and 3 privates wounded and 2 captured. The remaining 3 casualties apparently came from Company E.

87. Pickerill, p. 25.

Hard, p. 176.

Companies A, B, C, F, G, H, I and M took part in the excursion. Companies G and I, H and F comprised official squadrons. Based upon the casualty returns from the skirmish at Quebec School House, all these companies had some troops present.

88. Worthington C. Ford, p. 187.

Charles M. Smith, Letter to Parents, September 18-21, 1862, Smith Family Papers, Civil War Miscellaneous Papers, USAMHI.

Pickerill, p. 25.

Hard, p. 176.

89. Worthington C. Ford, p. 188.

Charles M. Smith, Letter to Parents, September 18-21, 1862, Smith Family Papers, Civil War Miscellaneous Papers, USAMHI.

90. Worthington C. Ford, pp. 187-188.

The effects of the sunlight are based upon my observations of the lighting in the late afternoon from that same hill.

91. *Historical Magazine*, p. 292.

92. Hard, p. 177.

Historical Magazine, p. 294.

Pleasonton recorded 2 wounded for the 3rd Indiana but none for the 8th Illinois Cavalry.

93. H. B. McClellan, p. 115.

94. Letter, G. W. Beale to Ezra Carman, September 30, 1897, Fitzhugh Lee's Cavalry Brigade, Antietam Studies, National Archives.

Stevenson, pp. 120-121.

It is interesting to note that in the official history of the 1st New York Cavalry, the historian mentions they had a few men captured and they, in turn, captured a few Rebel cavalrymen.

The historian also said the regiment had no baggage with it and the men were on short rations.

Beach, p. 170.

Sergeant Beach stated the regiment captured a few straggling Rebs.

It does not make sense that a brigade would be sent on a 25 mile reconnaissance without any supplies. The Union army just did not function that way. I tend to believe Lee attacked the 1st New York and made off with some of its supplies, and the historian chose to not mention that point.

95. Stevenson, p. 121.

Once again, I assume that was McReynolds' decision. G. W. Beale, 9th Virginia Cavalry, makes no mention of a Federal pursuit. I believe McReynolds continued his line of march to verify the prisoners' statements.

96. Beach, p. 171.

97. Ibid.
     Stevenson, p. 121.

98. This is based upon an estimate of a rate of march of about 4 miles per hour.

99. Charles F. Johnson, p. 182.

100. Graham, pp. 264-265.
     Whitney, p. 128.

101. Neese, p. 118.

102. H. B. McClellan, p. 115.

103. Charles F. Johnson, p. 183.

104. H. B. McClellan, p. 115.
     OR, XIX, pt. 1, p. 825.

105. *Historical Magazine*, p. 294.

106. Charles Johnson, p. 183.

107. Whitney, p. 129.

108. Charles Johnson, p. 183.

109. Ibid.
     Graham, p. 264.

110. Charles Johnson, p. 183.

111. Graham, p. 265.
     Whitney, p. 129.

112. Charles F. Johnson, p. 183.
     When they called in their pickets, Johnson's section of Company I did not get the word.
     Company I must have been on picket duty.

113. Graham, p. 266.
     Whitney, p. 129.

114. Bernard, p. 25.
     William D. Henderson, p. 34.

115. Judd, p. 180.

116. Montreville Williams, Diary, September 13, 1862, Museum Collection, Antietam National Battlefield.
     Williams recorded that his division, Slocum's, reached the foot of the mountains by 3:00 P.M. That meant that Irwin's brigade would have crossed ahead of them.

117. Judd, pp. 180-181.
     Graham, p. 266.

118. Ibid.

119. OR, XIX, pt. 1, p. 825.

120. Judd, p. 181.

121. H. B. McClellan, pp. 115-116.

122. Neese, pp. 118-119.

123. N. Pickerill, p. 26.

124. Ulysses Robert Brooks, p. 85.
     The only explanation for all the cavalry mentioned by Pickerill of the 3rd Indiana is the presence of Hampton's brigade. The description given by Private Rea of the 1st N.C. Cavalry implies that the Cobb's Legion doubled back to attack the Federals.

125. Pickerill, 3rd IN Cav., p. 26.
     H. B. McClellan, p. 116.

126. OR, XIX, pt. 1, p. 824.

127. Charles Dawson, Letter to Mollie, October 11, 1862, John S. Derbyshire, Rocky Mount,
     N.C., Used with permission.
     He said the fire came in from two directions.
     OR, XIX, pt. 1, p. 824.
     According to the *Official Records*, Captain Wright's company led the attack.

128. Pickerill, p. 26.

129. OR, XIX, pt. 1, p. 824.

130. Charles Dawson, Letter to Mollie, October 11, 1862, John S. Derbyshire, Rocky Mount,
     NC, Used with permission.
     OR, XIX, pt. 1, p. 824.

131. Pickerill, p. 26.
     Charles Dawson, Letter to Mollie, October 11, 1862, John S. Derbyshire, Rocky Mount,
     N.C., Used with permission.

132. Hard, p. 176.

133. Pickerill, p. 26.
     He recorded the incident where both sergeants were found dead with the Federal on
     top of the Confederate. It is safe to assume that they probably shot each other in a
     way similar to what happened with Captain Fetterman and his lieutenant in the 1860's
     while fighting the Indians in Montana.

134. Charles Dawson, Letter to Mollie, October 11, 1862, John S. Derbyshire, Rocky Mount,
     N.C. Used with permission.

135. Hard, p. 176.

136. Ibid., pp. 359-366.
     This is a fairly accurate list of the casualties in that fight.
     Pickerill, p. 28.
     He recorded the Rebel casualties at 13. The 3rd Indiana lost 4 men captured and for
     some unaccountable reason, Alfred Pleasonton did not mention the action in his of-
     ficial reports, whereas the Confederates did.
     Samuel J. B. V. Gilpin, Diary, September 13, 1862, E. N. Gilpin Collection, Manuscript
     Division, Library of Congress.
     He noted that the Yanks lost 13 men and that the Rebs lost 37, including a colonel
     and lesser officers.
     H. B. McClellan, p. 116.
     The Rebs lost 13 men.
     OR, XIX, pt. 1, p. 824.
     The Rebels officially reported 13 men lost. They state that the Federals lost about 30
     men and that the Confederates captured 5 men.
     Historical Magazine, p. 294.
     Casualties from the engagement on the Harpers Ferry Road and at Middletown:
     8th Illinois: 1 Killed and 8 Wounded.
     3rd Indiana: 3 Killed, 8 Wounded, and 5 Missing.

137. Neese, p. 119.
     H. B. McClellan, p. 116.

138. Neese, p. 119.

139. Bernard, p. 25.

140. Kempfer, p. 86.

141. This is based upon the times mentioned by the various regimental historians.

142. Cox, I, p. 275.

143. *35th Mass.*, p. 25.

144. Walcott, pp. 187-188.

145. Stone, p. 84.

146. *35th Mass.*, p. 25.

147. Stone, pp. 83-84.

148. Ibid., p. 85.
     Private Stone said Mrs. Frietschie refused to sell Reno the flag.
     Conrad Reno, p. 569.
     Benjamin Franklin Reno, the general's brother, told Conrad, the general's son, that the old lady gave Jesse Reno the large bunting flag which she had flown from the window when the Rebel army marched through the city but she kept a smaller silk flag. Interestingly enough, she and the general each sipped a glass of sherry before ending the visit.

149. Daniel E. Hurd, "My Experiences in the Civil War," William Marvel Collection, USAMHI.
     Ezra Carman, "The Maryland Campaign," VII, Manuscript Division, Library of Congress, p. 6.
     The marching orders were timed at 6:20 P.M.

150. William J. Bolton, "War Journal," War Library Museum, p. 237.

151. *35th Mass.*, p. 26.

152. Stone, p. 85.
     Walcott, p. 188.

153. William J. Bolton, "War Journal," War Library Museum, p. 237.

154. Kempfer, p. 87.

155. Samuel Compton, Autobiography, Samuel Compton Papers, Manuscript Department, Duke University Library, Durham, N.C., p. 93.

156. *Proceedings of the 34th Annual Reunion of the 11th Ohio*, not paginated.

157. George M. Blackburn, (ed.), *With the Wandering Regiment, The Diary of Captain Ralph Ely of the 8th Michigan Infantry*, Central Michigan University Press, Mt. Pleasant, 1965, p. 42.

158. Willcox's "green" regiments were the 8th and 17th Michigan, 45th, 50th, and 100th Pennsylvania.

159. Frederick Pettit, Letter, September 20, 1862, Civil War Times Illustrated Collection, USAMHI.
     Albert, p. 47.

160. David G. Lane, *A Soldier's Diary*, privately printed, 1905, p. 10.

161. Ezra Carman, "Maryland Campaign," typed transcript of his handwritten notes, p. 237.
     William Todd, pp. 229-230.

162. Charles Johnson, pp. 183-184.
     Whitney, p. 129.
     He said the regiment returned to Frederick around 11:00 P.M.
     Graham, p. 267.
     Both Graham and Whitney said the detail was left behind by accident under the command of a Sergeant Jackson. Charles Johnson, who was a member of the detail griped that the men were left behind by the incompetence of his sergeant. The sergeant was Robert M. Johnston, Company H, 9th New York. Private Charles Johnson refused to enter why he was so upset with the NCO. He said it was not worth mentioning.
     David L. Thompson, Letter to Elias, Oct., 1862, Antietam National Battlefield.
     He wrote to his friend that the regiment returned at 10:00 P.M.

163. William R. Quynn, *Engelbrecht Diary*, III, p. 182.

      Graham, pp. 262-263.

      The lieutenant got his days mixed up. He says the fire occurred on September 12. Whitney, p. 130.

      David L. Thompson, Letter to Elias, October 1862, Antietam National Battlefield.

164. Bidwell, p. 18.

      Montreville Williams, Diary, September 13, 1862, Museum Collection, Antietam National Battlefield.

      Peter Filbert, Diary, September 13, 1862, Harrisburg Civil War Round Table Collection, USAMHI.

      Jacob Haas, Diary, September 13, 1862, Harrisburg Civil War Round Table Collection, USAMHI.

      Westbrook, p. 124.

      Stevens, p. 135.

      Charles C. Morey, Diary, September 13, 1862, Charles C. Morey Collection, USAMHI.

      Judd, p. 181.

      Ezra Carman, "The Maryland Campaign," VII, Manuscript Division, Library of Congress, p. 15.

165. Ezra Carman, "The Maryland Campaign," VII, Manuscript Division, Library of Congress, pp. 16-17.

166. Ibid., p. 15.
      The I Corps marched 16 miles on September 13, 1862.
      II Corps — 6 miles.
      IV (Couch's Div.) — 5 miles.
      V (Sykes' Div.) — 6 miles.
      VI Corps — 6 miles.
      IX Corps — 6 miles.
      XII Corps — 5 miles.

167. Bernard, p. 41.

      OR, XIX, pt. 1, p. 861.

      John M. Priest, *Antietam: The Soldiers' Battle*, White Mane, Shippensburg, Pa., 1989, pp. 318-319.

168. *Battles and Leaders*, II, p. 560.
      Hill recorded that he received the message in the forenoon. He must have received it later than that because Colquitt, whose brigade was in Boonsboro, did not reach Turner's Gap until sundown.

169. Von Borcke, I, p. 212.
      Von Borcke is probably right in saying Stuart had sent Hampton's command south when he reached Turner's Gap. I believe they took the mountain wood road (Appalachian Trail) across to Fox's Gap, one mile south of Turner's Gap.

170. George D. Grattan, "The Battle of Boonsboro Gap or South Mountain," *Southern Historical Society Papers*, XXXIX, 1914, pp. 33-35.

171. Ezra Carman, "The Maryland Campaign," VII, Manuscript Division, Library of Congress, pp. 20-21.

172. Letter, Ezra Carman to Thomas L. Rosser, May 12, 1897, Fitzhugh Lee's cavalry brigade, Antietam Studies, National Archives.

173. Grattan, p. 39.
      Hill and Stuart did not hold each other in high esteem. A great deal of the animosity probably occurred because of Stuart's mishandling of the situation. By informing Lee that the Army of the Potomac was on the march he could report that his scouts had done their job well. By informing Colquitt that he was being followed by a small cavalry force, he could not be faulted for lying. In the running fight from Middletown, I doubt if he ever saw the Kanawha Division coming over Catoctin Mountain.

Stuart strikes me as the kind of officer who felt above responding to those whom he considered to be inferior in status or rank. He seems to be the kind of man who preferred to deal with the "Top Brass" rather than the lower ranking officers. He seemed to prefer to play the cavalier but not the field commander in this campaign.

174. Ezra Carman, "The Maryland Campaign," VII, Manuscript Division, Library of Congress, pp. 21-23.

175. Cox, I, pp. 277-278.

Chapter Ten

1. Grattan, p. 36.

2. Ibid.
   Ezra Carman, "The Maryland Campaign," VIII, Manuscript Division, Library of Congress, pp. 66-67.

3. *Battles and Leaders*, II, p. 561.
   Grattan, p. 36.
   I believe that Grattan's account of the time of Hill's arrival at the Gap is more accurate than Hill's. As Colquitt's aide, Grattan probably had a more distinct recollection of what happened because he was on the scene much earlier than the general. He would have known when and where the troops were posted much better than Hill. If Colquitt had been at the foot of the mountain as the general stated, he would have believed the Federals had retired. The Yankee videttes were in the valley at the National Pike-Bolivar Road intersection well within view of the foot of the mountain. Grattan insisted the general did not relocate Colquitt's brigade but that the move had already been executed before the general arrived.

4. *Battles and Leaders*, II, p. 561.
   Grattan, p. 35.

5. *Battles and Leaders*, II, p. 562.

6. Letter, Stirling Murray to Ezra Carman, July 25, 1898, Stuart's Horse Artillery, Pelham's Battalion, Antietam Studies, National Archives.
   Rosser and Pelham were at Fox's Gap. Their exact position, however is not known. Having gone over the terrain with Dr. Jay Luvaas and a team from the U.S. Army War College and having surveyed the map of the area as it looked at the time, I believe I can safely surmise that Pelham placed his artillery in the same position that Bondurant's gunners used later in the day. From that corner of the field, along the wood road, a section had a clear field of fire of any traffic approaching the Gap by the woods or the road to the east and southeast.
   Cox, I, p. 281.
   He said the Confederate artillery, which was posted on the edge of the woods, opened fire upon Scammon at a distance of ½ mile.

7. Ezra Carman, "The Maryland Campaign," VIII, Manuscript Division, Library of Congress, p. 3.
   Cox, I, pp. 279-280.
   OR, XIX, pt. 1, pp. 435-436.
   Carman and Cox said Benjamin's and Gibson's batteries went into action before Scammon's brigade left camp. Lieutenant Benjamin in his official report said he reported to Pleasonton about 8:00 A.M.

8. Samuel W. Moore, Diary, September 14, 1862, Museum Collection, Antietam National Battlefield.
   Moore, who was in Frederick, heard the cannonading and recorded the time as 6:00 A.M.
   1862 Hagerstown Almanac.
   Sunrise was at 5:49 A.M.
   Battles and Leaders, II, p. 562.

9. Ezra Carman, "The Maryland Campaign," VIII, Manuscript Division, Library of Congress, p. 3.

10. *Battles and Leaders*, II, p. 562.

11. Cox, I, pp. 278-280.

12. Letter, R. B. Wilson to Ezra Carman, July 22, 1899, Ezra Ayers Carman Collection, Manuscript Division, Library of Congress.

    James Abraham, *With the Army of West Virginia 1861-1864*, Publication No. 1, Evelyn A. Benson, Lancaster, Pa., 1974, Manuscript Department, USAMHI, p. 17.

    Ezra Carman, "The Maryland Campaign," VIII, Manuscript Division, Library of Congress, p. 7.

    The order of march is based upon a combined description from these three sources of how the fighting at Fox's Gap unfolded.

13. Cox, I, p. 280.

14. Grattan, p. 35.

15. *Battles and Leaders*, II, p. 562.

16. Ezra Carman, "The Maryland Campaign," VIII, Manuscript Division, Library of Congress, p. 5.

17. Cox, I, p. 281.

18. *Battles and Leaders*, II, pp. 562-563.

19. John B. Hood, p. 40.

    The "pig path" John Hood described in his *Advance and Retreat* is not the road which the Official Atlas alleged was cut by the Confederates. Hood's men were at the Gap when ordered to move by the flank toward Garland's position. The wood road cuts south from the Mountain House and is still very narrow trail, i.e. not much more than a "pig path."

20. Ezra Carman, "The Maryland Campaign," VIII, Manuscript Division, Library of Congress, p. 6.

    I assumed that the 5th North Carolina led the advance of Garland's brigade because the regiment was the first one placed into position south of Fox's Gap.

    Grattan, p. 37.

21. William Woods Hassler, *Colonel John Pelham Lee's Boy General*, Garrett and Massie, Inc., Richmond, Va., 1960, p. 85.

    I am using this text because I could not find any other which gave even an inkling of detail about Pelham's role at Fox's Gap. Relying upon the reputation of the author as a professional historian, I decided to use the book, despite the fact that it is not footnoted.

22. Ezra Carman, "The Maryland Campaign," VIII, Manuscript Division, Library of Congress, p. 7.

    OR, XIX, pt. 1, p. 1040.

    Ezra Carman, "Battle of South Mountain Turner's Pass," Ezra Carman Papers, Antietam National Battlefield, p. 225.

    Letter, John Purifoy to Ezra Carman, August 7, 1900, Ezra Ayers Carman Collection, Manuscript Division, Library of Congress.

    All sources, Federal and Confederate, estimate or assert the fighting between the infantry regiments started at 9:00 A.M. John Purifoy in his letter to Ezra Carman recalled seeing the Federal skirmishers at least one half an hour before the main infantry firing. This means that the time of his observation approximately 8:30 A.M. It took some time to deploy; therefore the time of the initial cannon shot was about 8:00 A.M.

23. Ezra Carman, "The Maryland Campaign," VIII, Manuscript Division, Library of Congress, p. 7.

    Cox, I, p. 281.

24. Letter, R. B. Wilson to Ezra Carman, July 22, 1899, Ezra Ayers Carman Collection, Manuscript Division, Library of Congress.

25. James Abraham, *With the Army of West Virginia 1861-1864*, Publication No. 1, Evelyn A. Benson, Lancaster, Pa., 1974, Manuscript Department, USAMHI, p. 17.

26. Ezra Carman, "The Maryland Campaign," VIII, Manuscript Division, Library of Congress, p. 7.

27. *Battles and Leaders*, II, p. 5.

28. Ibid.
Ezra Carman, "The Maryland Campaign," VIII, Manuscript Division, Library of Congress, pp. 12, 13.

29. Letter, John Purifoy to Ezra Carman, July 15, 1899, Ezra Ayers Carman Collection, Manuscript Division, Library of Congress.

30. Letter, John Purifoy to Ezra Carman, July 21, 1900, Ezra Ayers Carman Collection, Manuscript Division, Library of Congress.

31. Letters, John Purifoy to Ezra Carman, July 15, 1899 and July 21, 1900, Ezra Ayers Carman Collection, Manuscript Division, Library of Congress.
In the 1900 letter, Purifoy readily admits, "If I were to visit the field now I do not know whether I could definitely settle it....I find it the most difficult thing to do in the world to find two or more participants in a battle who have the same recollection of the topography or location at which the battery did its shooting."

32. Ibid., 7/15/99.

33. Cox, I, p. 282.

34. Ezra Carman, "Battle of South Mountain Turner's Pass," Ezra Carman Papers, Antietam National Battlefield, pp. 224-225.

35. Williams, p. 137.

36. James Abraham, *With the Army of West Virginia 1861-1864*, Publication No. 1, Evelyn A. Benson, Lancaster, Pa., 1974, Manuscript Department, USAMHI, p. 17.

37. Ezra Carman, "Battles of South Mountain Turner's Pass," Ezra Carman Papers, Antietam National Battlefield, pp. 224-225.

38. James Abraham, *With the Army of West Virginia 1861-1864*, Publication No. 1, Evelyn A. Benson, Lancaster, PA., 1974, Manuscript Department, USAMHI, p. 17.

39. Letter, John Purifoy to Ezra Carman, July 15, 1899, Ezra Ayers Carman Collection, Manuscript Division, Library of Congress.

40. James Abraham, *With the Army of West Virginia 1861-1864*, Publication No. 1, Evelyn A. Benson, Lancaster, PA., 1974, Manuscript Department, USAMHI, p. 17.

41. Letter, R. B. Wilson to Ezra Carman, July 11, 1899, Ezra Ayers Carman Collection, Manuscript Division, Library of Congress.

42. Ezra Carman, "The Maryland Campaign," VII, Manuscript Division, Library of Congress, p. 7.
The National Tribune, August 23, 1883, p. 1.
James Abraham, *With the Army of West Virginia 1861-1864*, Publication No. 1, Evelyn A. Benson, Lancaster, Pa., 1974, Manuscript Department, USAMHI, p. 17.
It is interesting to note that Abraham, who left behind a very detailed description of the Frederick fight, writes about South Mountain that "...soon after commencing the ascent, encountered the rebel skirmishers in some fields and pushed them back." He gives no indication of rifle shots being exchanged or of combat of any type occurring to his front. It is fair to say that his men probably were the ones seen by the Alabamians and that he reported the battery's exact position to Cox. Companies A and F of the 12th Ohio came out of the woods almost directly opposite the battery because they knew where it was. They must have gotten the intelligence from someone who had seen the guns. That was most likely Abraham and his men.

43. Letter, John Purifoy to Ezra Carman, July 15, 1899, Ezra Ayers Carman Collection, Manuscript Division, Library of Congress.

44. Ezra Carman, "The Maryland Campaign," VIII, Manuscript Division, Library of Congress, p. 13.

45. Based upon the author's survey of the ground and the available maps.

46. Ezra Carman, "The Maryland Campaign," VIII, Manuscript Division, Library of Congress, p. 13.

47. Ibid., p. 14.

48. Walter Clark, (ed.), *Histories of the Several Regiments and Battalions From North Carolina in the Great War 1861-65*, II, E. M. Uzzell, Printer and Binder, Raleigh, N.C., 1901, pp. 219-220.

49. Williams, p. 137.

50. Ezra Carman, "Battle of South Mountain Turner's Pass," Ezra Carman Papers, Antietam National Battlefield, p. 225.

51. Ibid.

52. Robert B. Cornwell, Letter to Brothers and Sisters, October 3, 1862, Harrisburg Civil War Round Table Collection, USAMHI.

53. Letter, John Purifoy to Ezra Carman, July 15, 1899, Ezra Ayers Carman Collection, Manuscript Division, Library of Congress.

54. Letter, John Purifoy to Ezra Carman, August 7, 1900, Ezra Ayers Carman Collection, Manuscript Division, Library of Congress.

55. OR, XIX, pt. 1, p. 1040.
    Ezra Carman, "Battle of South Mountain Turner's Pass," Ezra Carman Papers, Antietam National Battlefield, p. 225.
    Williams, p. 137.
    Ezra Carman, "The Maryland Campaign," VIII, Manuscript Division, Library of Congress, p. 14.

56. Benjamin M. Collins, "Manuscript History of the Regiment," Southern Historical Collection, University of North Carolina, Chapel Hill, N.C., p. 8.

57. OR, XIX, pt. 1, p. 464.
    Letter, R. B. Wilson to Ezra Carman, July 11, 1899, Ezra Ayers Carman Collection, Manuscript Division, Library of Congress.

58. Walter Clark, II, p. 20.
    Ezra Carman, "The Maryland Campaign," VIII, Manuscript Division, Library of Congress, p. 15.

59. Letter, John Purifoy to Ezra Carman, July 15, 1899, Ezra Ayers Carman Collection, Manuscript Division, Library of Congress.
    John Purifoy wrote that the general ordered the battery to withdraw as he rode past their position from the north. This implies that Garland was near the crossroads. It must have happened before he consulted with Colonel McRae for the last time.
    OR, XIX, pt. 1, p. 1040.

60. OR, XIX, pt. 1, p. 1040.

61. Letter, John Purifoy to Ezra Carman, July 15, 1899, Ezra Ayers Carman Collection, Manuscript Division, Library of Congress.

62. Ezra Carman, "The Maryland Campaign," VIII, Manuscript Division, Library of Congress, p. 15.

63. OR, XIX, pt. 1, p. 1040.

64. Williams, p. 138.
    Ezra Carman, "Battle of South Mountain Turner's Pass," Ezra Carman Papers, Antietam National Battlefield, p. 225.

65. OR, XIX, pt. 1, p. 1040.

66. Ezra Carman, "The Maryland Campaign," VIII, Manuscript Division, Library of Congress, p. 15.

67. OR, XIX, pt. 1, p. 467.
    Ezra Carman, "Battle of South Mountain Turner's Pass," Ezra Carman Papers, Antietam National Battlefield, p. 226.

68. Ibid., p. 225.

368 ENDNOTES — Pages 145 to 151

69. Williams, p. 138.

70. Letter, John Purifoy to Ezra Carman, July 15, 1899, Ezra Ayers Carman Collection, Manuscript Division, Library of Congress.

71. *Battles and Leaders*, II, p. 587.

72. William W. Lyle, *Lights and Shadows of Army Life*, R. W. Carroll & Co., Cincinnati, Ohio, 1865, pp. 127-128.
Horton and Teverbaugh, p. 71.

73. Ezra Carman, "The Maryland Campaign," VIII, Manuscript Division, Library of Congress, p. 16.

74. A. B. Counnel, "Reno's Death," *The National Tribune*, August 23, 1883, p. 1.

75. Ezra Carman, "The Maryland Campaign," VIII, Manuscript Division, Library of Congress, pp. 16-17.

76. Ibid., p. 13.

77. A. B. Counnel, "Reno's Death," *The National Tribune*, August 23, 1883, p. 1.

78. Ezra Carman, "The Maryland Campaign," VIII, Manuscript Division, Library of Congress, p. 17.

79. OR, XIX, pt. 1, p. 469.
Cunningham and Miller, p. 77.

80. *Battles and Leaders*, II, pp. 563-564.

81. OR, XIX, pt. 1, p. 1041.
Walter Clark, II, pp. 220-221.

82. Harry Warner, "Notes on South Mountain' tells of Civil War Horrors," undated, newspaper, probably from Frederick.

83. OR, XIX, pt. 1, p. 1041.

84. Ezra Carman, "Battle of South Mountain Turner's Pass," Ezra Carman Papers, Antietam National Battlefield, p. 225.
Williams, p. 138.

85. Ezra Carman, "Battle of South Mountain Turner's Pass," Ezra Carman Papers, Antietam National Battlefield, p. 225.

86. Williams, p. 139.

87. Letter, R. B. Wilson to Ezra Carman, July 11, 1899, Ezra Ayers Carman Collection, Manuscript Division, Library of Congress.

88. Williams, p. 139.
Ezra Carman, "Battle of South Mountain Turner's Pass," Ezra Carman Papers, Antietam National Battlefield, p. 225.

89. Williams, p. 139.
Lyle, p. 130.

90. Letter, R. B. Wilson to Ezra Carman, July 22, 1899, Ezra Ayers Carman Collection, Manuscript Division, Library of Congress.

91. Samuel Compton, Autobiography, Samuel Compton Papers, Manuscript Department, Duke University Library, Durham, N.C., p. 93.

92. Ibid., pp. 93-94.

93. Ward, pp. 59-60.
Ward recalled seeing several officers who were drunk, much to the shame of the regiment.
Samuel Compton, Autobiography, Samuel Compton Papers, Manuscript Department, Duke University Library, Durham, N.C., pp. 95-96.
He remembered Colonel White carried two canteens — one was full of whiskey and that the other of brandy.
I am supposing it was during this first lull in the battle, just before noon, when the officers did much of their drinking. They had been fighting uphill in the full sunlight and had good reason to drink. Many of the enlisted men, like Samuel Compton in Company F emptied their canteens entirely and had no water during the attack which followed.

94.   Ward, p. 59.

95.   Ibid., p. 59.

96.   Cox, I, p. 281.

97.   Letter, R. B. Wilson to Ezra Carman, July 11, 1899, Ezra Ayers Carman Collection, Manuscript Division, Library of Congress.

98.   Walter Clark, II, p. 115.
      Ulysses Robert Brooks, p. 87.

99.   Lyle, p. 129.

100. Cunningham and Miller, p. 98.
      This source reported Crome was killed while reaching for the rammer.
      Walter Clark, II, p. 115.
      Ezra Carman, "The Maryland Campaign," VIII, Manuscript Division, Library of Congress, p. 18.
      Lyle, p. 129.

101. Letter, R. B. Wilson to Ezra Carman, July 22, 1899, Ezra Ayers Carman Collection, Manuscript Division, Library of Congress.
      OR, XIX, pt. 1, p. 464.

102. Walter Clark, II, p. 115.
      Ulysses Robert Brooks, p. 88.
      Ezra Carman, "The Maryland Campaign," VIII, Manuscript Division, Library of Congress, p. 18.

103. Letter, R. B. Wilson to Ezra Carman, July 22, 1899, Ezra Ayers Carman Collection, Manuscript Division, Library of Congress.
      OR, XIX, pt. 1, p. 464.

104. Horton and Teverbaugh, p. 71.
      The authors insisted they were fired on from three sides. The only way that could have happened was if they had run into an extended line. Logically Colonel Christie covered his flank with skirmishers in the woods where he had limited vision.

105. Horton and Teverbaugh, p. 71.
      Ezra Carman, "The Maryland Campaign," VIII, Manuscript Division, Library of Congress, p. 19.

106. Walter Clark, II, p. 220.

107. Ibid.

108. Horton and Teverbaugh, p. 72.
      Proceedings 33rd and 34th Annual Reunion of the 11th Ohio, 1905 and 1906, Letter, September 19, 1904, J. Hammer Smith, Company B, not paginated.

109. Ezra Carman, "The Maryland Campaign," VIII, Manuscript Division, Library of Congress, p. 19.

110. Walter Clark, II, p. 221.
      Ezra Carman, "The Maryland Campaign," VIII, Manuscript Division, Library of Congress, p. 19.
      Samuel Compton, Autobiography, Samuel Compton Papers, Manuscript Department, Duke University Library, Durham, N.C., p. 94.
      Ward, p. 58.
      Letter, R. B. Wilson to Ezra Carman, July 22, 1899, Ezra Ayers Carman Collection, Manuscript Division, Library of Congress.
      The 23rd Ohio, according to Carman, poured through a cornfield and an opening in the stone fence against the 23rd North Carolina and the 12th Ohio charged the 20th North Carolina frontally. Adjutant V. E. Turner (23rd North Carolina) said that Company E, on the left of the line, where the attack came from, did not receive the word to retreat and was enveloped. Samuel Compton (Company F, 12th Ohio) recalled that the regiment drove the Confederates from the stone wall then swung around behind a brigade [actually] a regiment of North Carolina conscripts [actually the 23rd North

Carolina]. James Ward (12th Ohio) said that his men used the bayonet frequently. Captain R. B. Wilson (Company F, 12th Ohio) saw the bayonet used as the regiment assaulted the 20th North Carolina. In the confusion of the general attack, it was quite possible for some men of the 12th Ohio to break to the south to flank and enfilade the 23rd North Carolina.

111. OR, XIX, pt. 1, p. 1046.
      Colonel Ruffin (13th North Carolina) said that his regiment had moved to the brow of the hill at Wise's field and then moved north, at Colonel McRae's order, to connect with the right of George B. Anderson's North Carolina brigade. He did not connect with Anderson as he said.
      Battles and Leaders, II, p. 564.
      In a letter to D. H. Hill after the war, Ruffin reminded Hill that Anderson did not come up until after the 13th had broken out of the Federal drive upon its right flank, after the 23rd and the 20th regiments were driven from the field.

112. Walter Clark, II, p. 221.

113. Ezra Carman, "The Maryland Campaign," VIII, Manuscript Division, Library of Congress, p. 19.
      Ezra Carman, "Battle of South Mountain Turner's Pass," Ezra Carman Papers, Antietam National Battlefield, p. 226.

114. W. F. Beyer and O. F. Keydel, (ed.), *Deeds of Valor*, I, Peerin-Keydel Co., Detroit, 1907, p. 71.

115. Ezra Carman, "The Maryland Campaign," VIII, Manuscript Division, Library of Congress, p. 19.
      Samuel Compton, Autobiography, Samuel Compton Papers, Manuscript Department, Duke University Library, Durham, N.C., p. 94.
      Letter, R. B. Wilson to Ezra Carman, July 22, 1899, Ezra Ayers Carman Collection, Manuscript Division, Library of Congress.

116. Letter, R. B. Wilson to Ezra Carman, July 22, 1899, Ezra Ayers Carman Collection, Manuscript Division, Library of Congress.
      Samuel Compton, Autobiography, Samuel Compton Papers, Manuscript Department, Duke University Library, Durham, N.C., p. 94.

117. Beyer and Keydel, I, pp. 71, 73.

118. Walter Clark, II, p. 115.

119. Samuel Compton, Autobiography, Samuel Compton Papers, Manuscript Department, Duke University Library, Durham, N.C., p. 94.

120. Walter Clark, II, p. 222.

121. Letter, R. B. Wilson to Ezra Carman, July 22, 1899, Ezra Ayers Carman Collection, Manuscript Division, Library of Congress.

122. Walter Clark, II, p. 221.

123. Samuel Compton, Autobiography, Samuel Compton Papers, Manuscript Department, Duke University Library, Durham, N.C., p. 95.

124. Lyle, pp. 129-130.

125. OR, XIX, pt. 1, p. 465.

126. Samuel Compton, Autobiography, Samuel Compton Papers, Manuscript Department, Duke University Library, Durham, N.C., pp. 95-96.

127. Ward, p. 59.

128. Horton and Teverbaugh, p. 72.

129. OR, XIX, pt. 1, p. 472.
      In the confusion of the battle, it appears the regiment had advanced behind the 23rd North Carolina and the 20th North Carolina and came under a cross fire from their own troops who were pressing the Confederates along the wood road.

130. OR, XIX, pt. 1, p. 467.

131. Letter, John Purifoy to Ezra Carman, July 21, 1900, Ezra Ayers Carman Collection, Manuscript Division, Library of Congress.

132. This is based upon an examination of the ground and subsequent Federal observations which reported many dead Confederates behind the stone wall at the summit. Colonel Ruffin of the 13th North Carolina and Colonel D. McRae, the brigade commander, do not mention exactly where the regiment was. It makes sense that if the artillery was facing south and southeast rather than east that friendly troops were in their line of fire in that direction.

133. OR, XIX, pt. 1, p. 465.
Colonel Carr B. White, 12th Ohio, said his regiment remained pinned for "some time under a sharp fire of canister and shell."

134. Joseph E. Walton, "At South Mountain," *The National Tribune*, October 10, 1898, p. 3.
Joseph E. Walton, "The 30th Ohio," *The National Tribune*, December 31, 1885, p. 3.
Horton and Teverbaugh, p. 72.
The authors implied that both batteries were in action at the same time.
Ezra Carman, "The Maryland Campaign," VIII, Manuscript Division, Library of Congress, p. 23.

135. Joseph E. Walton, "At South Mountain," *The National Tribune*, October 6, 1898, p. 3.

136. Ibid., p. 2.

137. OR, XIX, pt. 1, p. 459.
Cox said in the *Official Records* that the 36th Ohio supported the 12th Ohio.
Ezra Carman, "The Maryland Campaign," VIII, Manuscript Division, Library of Congress, p. 21.
Carman reported that the 36th was on the right of the 30th Ohio, which would have placed it across and north of the Old Sharpsburg Road.
Battles and Leaders, II, p. 564.
Ruffin, in moving north — to the left, was hemmed in by a Federal regiment to his left.
OR, XIX, pt. 1, p. 471.
George Crook reported that the 36th Ohio was sent to the right of the line, which would have placed it on the right of the 30th Ohio.
Cox evidently erred on this point in writing his report.

138. OR, XIX, pt. 1, p. 1042.

139. Ibid., p. 1042.

140. Ibid., p. 1042.
He said he rallied parts of the 20th and the 23rd regiments and shortly thereafter, Colonel Thomas Rosser (5th Virginia Cavalry) consulted with him and asked for infantry support on a hill behind the Mountain House. That implies he was in the hollow west of the wood road and the hill Rosser referred to was the one in Cox's memoirs almost 900 yards southwest of the Mountain House.
Battles and Leaders, II, p. 564.
Thomas Ruffin (13th North Carolina) made no mention of having any contact with Colonel McRae. His exclusion of the colonel's name from his letter to D. H. Hill speaks louder than the colonel's "official" account that "he" ordered Ruffin to connect with G. B. Anderson's North Carolina brigade.
John Calvin Gorman, "Memoirs of a Rebel," *Military Images*, Nov./Dec. 1981, p. 5.

141. Walter Clark, I, p. 245.

142. James Shinn, Diary, September 14, 1862, Edwin Augustus Osborne Papers #567, Southern Historical Collection at the University of North Carolina, Chapel Hill, N.C.

143. OR, XIX, pt. 1, p. 1042.

144. *Battles and Leaders*, II, p. 564.

145. Letter, John Purifoy to Ezra Carman, July 21, 1900, Ezra Ayers Carman Collection, Manuscript Division, Library of Congress.

146. *Battles and Leaders*, II, p. 564.

147. Joseph E. Walton, "At South Mountain," October 6, 1898, p. 3.

148. Letter, R. B. Wilson to Ezra Carman, July 22, 1899, Ezra Ayers Carman Collection, Manuscript Division, Library of Congress.

149. Samuel Compton, Autobiography, Samuel Compton Papers, Manuscript Department, Duke University Library, Durham, N.C., pp. 96-97.

150. Letter, R. B. Wilson to Ezra Carman, July 11, 1899, Ezra Ayers Carman Collection, Manuscript Division, Library of Congress.

151. Robert B. Cornwell, Letter to Brothers and Sisters, October 3, 1862, Harrisburg Civil War Round Table Collection, USAMHI.

152. Joseph E. Walton, "At South Mountain," *The National Tribune*, October 6, 1898, p. 2.

153. OR, XIX, pt. 1, p. 459.

154. *Battles and Leaders*, II, p. 564.

155. John Calvin Gorman, "Memoirs," *Military Images*, Nov./Dec. 1981, p. 5.

156. Andrew Wykle, "A Fighting Regiment," *The National Tribune*, January 9, 1902, p. 3.

157. Ezra Carman, "The Maryland Campaign," VIII, Manuscript Division, Library of Congress, p. 21.

158. D. H. Hill, *From Bethel to Sharpsburg*, II, p. 373.
     Ezra Carman, "The Maryland Campaign," VIII, Manuscript Division, Library of Congress, p. 22.

159. OR, XIX, pt. 1, p. 1042.

160. John Calvin Gorman, "Memoirs," *Military Images*, Nov./Dec. 1981, p. 5.

161. *Battles and Leaders*, II, p. 564.

162. Joseph E. Walton, "At South Mountain," *The National Tribune*, October 6, 1898, p. 2.

163. Files, 30th OH, Antietam National Battlefield, from the papers of Mrs. Ann R. Hunt.

164. Andrew Wykle, "A Fighting Regiment," *The National Tribune*, January 9, 1902, p. 3.

165. Letter, R. B. Wilson to Ezra Carman, July 11, 1899, Ezra Ayers Carman Collection, Manuscript Division, Library of Congress.

166. Horton and Teverbaugh, p. 269.

167. Letter, R. B. Wilson to Ezra Carman, July 22, 1899, Ezra Ayers Carman Collection, Manuscript Division, Library of Congress.

168. Horton and Teverbaugh, p. 269.

169. *Proceeding of the 33rd and 34th Reunion of the 11th Ohio, 1905 and 1906*, not paginated.

170. Horton and Teverbaugh, p. 269.

171. Letter, R. B. Wilson to Ezra Carman, July 22, 1899, Ezra Ayers Carman Collection, Manuscript Division, Library of Congress.

172. OR, XIX, pt. 1, p. 465.

173. James E. Ward, p. 60.

174. *Proceeding of the 33rd and 34th Reunion of the 11th Ohio, 1905 and 1906*, not paginated.

175. Robert B. Cornwell, Letter to Brothers and Sisters, October 3, 1862, Harrisburg Civil War Round Table Collection, USAMHI.

176. Horton and Teverbaugh, p. 131.

177. Samuel Compton, Autobiography, Samuel Compton Papers, Manuscript Department, Duke University Library, Durham, N.C., p. 97.

178. John Calvin Gorman, "Memoirs," *Military Images*, Nov./Dec. 1981, p. 5.

179. James Shinn, Diary, September 14, 1862, Edwin Augustus Osborne Papers #567, Southern Historical Collection at the University of North Carolina, Chapel Hill, N.C.

180. *Battles and Leaders*, II, p. 564.

181. Samuel Compton, Autobiography, Samuel Compton Papers, Manuscript Department, Duke University Library, Durham, N.C., p. 98.

182. Horton and Teverbaugh, p. 270.

183. Samuel Compton, Autobiography, Samuel Compton Papers, Manuscript Department, Duke University Library, Durham, N.C., p. 98.

   Compton also erred when he said the fighting around the Wise field lasted about 45 minutes. Crome's artillery was in battery by 11:00 A.M. which meant the infantry assault began several minutes later. In the *Official Records*, XIX, pt. 1, p. 459, Jacob Cox reported the fighting on the mountain top ended around noon. In the same volume, on p. 464, Captain James McMullin said he sent Crome forward around 11:00 A.M.

184. *Battles and Leaders*, II, p. 564.

185. D. H. Hill, *From Bethel to Sharpsburg*, II, p. 372.

186. Letter, John Purifoy to Ezra Carman, July 21, 1900, Ezra Ayers Carman Collection, Manuscript Division, Library of Congress.

   John Purifoy told Ezra Carman, "Bondurant's and Carter's were the only batteries in the first engagement, Carter's being in the gap just west of the Mountain House in the early part of it..."

   These guns must have come from Carter's battery. Lane's was further northeast supporting Colquitt. Carter's Battery had one 10# Parrott, two 12# Mountain Howitzers, and two 6# Smooth Bores. Hill would have used either the smoothbore section or the mountain howitzers for close support. Parrotts were too scarce in the Confederate Army to risk at close quarters.

   Following a conversation with Paul Chiles (ANB) on 12/16/89, I have concluded that the guns used were the Mountain Howitzers. Their light weight tube (220 lbs.) made them extremely mobile. They fired mainly 12# case shot. Their small powder charge could not hurl a 12# solid shot far enough to be effective in the gorge and their canister rounds, which consisted of packed musket balls rather than the standard 27 count cast iron shot, were too light weight to be effective.

   Kempfer, p. 87.

   John Palmer, Company D, 36th Ohio, mentions that they were shelled out.

187. *Battles and Leaders*, II, p. 566.

   Ezra Carman, "The Maryland Campaign," VIII, Manuscript Division, Library of Congress, p. 22.

   D. H. Hill, *From Bethel to Sharpsburg*, II, p. 372.

188. Based upon maps in:
   Cox, I, p. 279.
   Battles and Leaders, II, p. 568.
   OR, Maps.

189. Kempfer, pp. 87, 92, 94-97.
   Concerning the casualties, Private Augustus Ward wrote to his captain, Jewett Palmer, Jr. the following:
   "That damned Pete Hackenberry [sic]...was as sound as a buck till we got to Manassas Junction, and began to hear cannon their [sic] the cuse [sic] got sick suddenly and often got over that, that leg got lame again, so that he has not done a days duty since. He is now the devel [sic] knows where — I think he has deserted again God grant it!"

190. "List of Soldiers by Date of Death," Antietam National Battlefield Files.
   Andrew Wykle, "A Fighting Regiment," *The National Tribune*, January 9, 1902, p. 3.

191. OR, XIX, pt. 1, p. 459.

192. D. H. Hill, *From Bethel to Sharpsburg*, II, p. 373.
   Ezra Carman, "The Maryland Campaign," VIII, Manuscript Division, Library of Congress, p. 22.

193. OR, XIX, pt. 1, p. 459.
   Cox, I, pp. 284-285.
   Battles and Leaders, II, p. 587.
   Ezra Carman, "The Maryland Campaign," VIII, Manuscript Division, Library of Congress, pp. 23-24.
   In his research, Carman relied heavily upon *Battles and Leaders*, the *Official Records*,

and, apparently Cox's 1900 *Reminiscences*. Neither the *Reminiscences* nor Carman's interpretation of what happened agrees with the *Official Records* or *Battles and Leaders*. Carman had a separate action occurring after Garland lost the Gap, in which the 12th and the 36th Ohio regiments, in the center, drove back a Confederate counterattack, including Rosser's cavalry. In his *Reminiscences*, Cox asserted the 12th and the 36th Ohio regiments drove back a counterattack which included dismounted cavalry.

In his report, dated September 20, 1862, Cox did not include anything about dismounted cavalry, which implies that he did not see any. He said the 12th Ohio and the 36th Ohio did drive back a brief attack upon his center but he did not say, at that time, that the 36th regiment was in the center of the line.

In *Battles and Leaders*, II, Cox reported that the Rebel cavalry occupied a hill west of the Mountain House. He *did not* state that the attack of the 12th and the 36th Ohio regiments drove the cavalry to that point. That was an assumption either he or Carman made years later.

In writing about this supposed attack along the Old Sharpsburg Road Carman actually described the initial drive which carried the wood road south of Fox's Gap. In his rewriting of the accounts for all publications following the *Official Records*, Cox embellished them to make sense out of a battle which he did not observe in its entirety.

Carman, VIII, p. 22, ironically summarized the general's ignorance best when he wrote:

"...he knew nothing of the enemy's strength; did not know what he might encounter in the woods and dense thickets lying beyond the ridge road; naturally supposed that his enemy was in force to hold the position against his own division; was ignorant of the fact that he had thoroughly disposed of four regiments of Garland's brigade and that there was scarcely anything to oppose him."

194.   D. H. Hill, *From Bethel to Sharpsburg*, II, p. 373.
       Battles and Leaders, II, p. 587.
       OR, XIX, pt. 1, p. 459.
       Cox, I, p. 285.

Chapter Eleven

1.   OR, XIX, pt. 1, p. 1033.

2.   Calvin Leach, Diary, September 13 and 14, 1862, Southern Historical Collection, University of North Carolina, Chapel Hill, N.C.

3.   *Battles and Leaders*, II, p. 587.

4.   OR, XIX, pt. 1, p. 464.

5.   Frederick Pettit, Letter, September 20, 1862, Civil War Times Illustrated Collection, USAMHI.
     Lewis Crater, *History of the Fiftieth Regiment Penna. Vols., 1861-1865*, Coleman Printing House, Reading, Pa., 1884, p. 32.

6.   Frederick Pettit, Letter, September 20, 1862, Civil War Times Illustrated Collection, USAMHI.
     OR, XIX, pt. 1, p. 439.

7.   Gabriel Campbell, Letter to Ezra Carman, August 23, 1899, Antietam National Battlefield.

8.   Lewis Crater, p. 32.

9.   Frederick Pettit, Letter, September 20, 1862, Civil War Times Illustrated Collection, USAMHI.

10. Ezra Carman, "The Maryland Campaign," VIII, Manuscript Division, Library of Congress, p. 25.

11. Calvin Leach, Diary, September 13 and 14, 1862, Southern Historical Collection, University of North Carolina, Chapel Hill, N.C.

12. Ezra Carman, "The Maryland Campaign," VIII, Manuscript Division, Library of Congress, p. 46.

13. D. H. Hill, *Bethel to Sharpsburg*, II, pp. 373-374.

Ezra Carman, "The Maryland Campaign," VIII, Manuscript Division, Library of Congress, p. 25.

Battles and Leaders, II, p. 567.

William Todd, pp. 231-232.

Ripley could not have followed G. B. Anderson immediately. If he did not arrive upon the field until just before 3:00 P.M., as he implies then he did not follow quickly. Anderson probably was engaged between 1:00 P.M. and 3:00 P.M. William Todd of the 79th New York said that he saw the Confederates advance upon the abandoned guns shortly after they were abandoned. That would have made it about 1:00-2:00 P.M.

14. Lester Kempfer, p. 87.

15. William Lyle, pp. 130, 131, 132, 399.

16. This order is based upon the assumption that if the 79th New York shouldered the section into battery, it had to lead the column. The 17th Michigan deployed to its right. The 8th Michigan broke to the rear through the 50th Pennsylvania. It is interesting to note that Benjamin Christ in his Official Report did not mention, in detail, the actions of either the 8th Michigan or the 50th Pennsylvania, indicating that they might not have behaved as well as he would have expected. The 28th Massachusetts, he wrote, assisted later in the day, but not in a major capacity.

    By studying the casualty tabulations in the *Official Records*, one can estimate the degree of actual combat to which the regiments were exposed.

    28th Mass. —   7
    8th Mich. —   8
    17th Mich. — 132
    79th N.Y. —   12
    50th Pa. —   3

OR, XIX, pt. 1, pp. 186, 437-438.

William Todd, p. 230.

Gabriel Campbell, Letter to Ezra Carman, August 23, 1899, Carman Papers, Antietam National Battlefield, p. 214.

17. William Todd, pp. 230-231.

18. OR, XIX, pt. 1, p. 433.

19. William Todd, p. 231.

20. Ibid., pp. 231-232.

21. Albert, p. 53.

22. OR, XIX, pt. 1, p. 439.

23. Ibid., pp. 433-434.

24. *Massachusetts Soldiers, Sailors, and Marines in the Civil War*, V, pp. 446-449. Adams and Mellen died from their wounds. D'Arcy and Francis were discharged with disabilities.

25. OR, XIX, pt. 1, p. 434.
    Cussel, p. 73.

26. This is an assumption based upon the problem of maneuvering a 14 yard long column in a 360 degree turn in a very confined space. The ambulance drivers were not only confused but also hemmed in by the infantry and artillery columns in the road.

27. Albert, p. 48.

28. Gabriel Campbell, Letter to Ezra Carman, August 23, 1899, Carman Papers, Antietam National Battlefield, p. 214.

29. OR, XIX, pt. 1, p. 186.

30. Crater, pp. 32-33.

31. Frederick Pettit, Letter, September 20, 1862, Civil War Times Illustrated Collection, USAMHI.

32. Ibid.

33. This is based upon the distances probably occupied by the various regiments.

    Column of caissons occupied 14 yards (42 feet). Add 8 feet to that to allow for spacing between guns and Cook's six caissons each with a six horse team would have occupied approximately 300 feet. That would have put them in the Old Sharpsburg Road from the Martz cabin to the Hoffman house.

    The division numbered about 3600 effectives, which in column of fours, in close column, would have theoretically covered 1800 feet. The average regiment, excepting the 17th Michigan (700-800 men), Cook's Battery (about 100 men), and the 46th New York (287 men), numbered about 400 men.

    Cook's battery occupied about 300 feet of road.

    The 79th New York occupied about 100 feet.

    The 17th Michigan covered about 190 feet.

    The 8th Michigan, the 50th Pennsylvania, and the 28th Massachusetts each covered about 100 feet or road for a total of 300 feet.

    In all, Christ's brigade stretched from Martz's cabin to Henry Gross' home. Breaking off by regiments it would have placed the regiments as follows:

    79th N.Y. near Hoffman's.

    17th Mich. north of the road about 100 feet southeast of the 79th NY.

    8th Mich., 50th Pa., and 28th Mass. in the road from the western edge of the Gross property to the house.

    Ezra Carman, "The Maryland Campaign," VIII, Manuscript Division, Library of Congress, p. 27.

    Crater, p. 33.

    Gabriel Campbell, Letter to Ezra Carman, August 23, 1899, Carman Papers, Antietam National Battlefield, p. 212.

    Carman said Willcox formed his line parallel with the Old Sharpsburg Road and almost at right angles to Cox's line. The 79th N.Y. and the 17th Mich. faced west, and up hill. The other regiments faced north. Captain Gabriel said his regiment was enfiladed. To do that, the regiment had to face its flank to the Rebel artillery. Adjutant Crater (50th PA) said he saw artillery fire upon the regiment's left. That must have been Bondurant's, which meant the regiment must have had its left flank presented to the left.

34. Ezra Carman, "The Maryland Campaign," VIII, Manuscript Division, Library of Congress, p. 23.

    OR, XIX, pt. 1, p. 461.

35. Frederick Pettit, Letter, September 20, 1862, Civil War Times Illustrated Collection, USAMHI.

36. Lyle, pp. 130, 131, 132, 399.

37. Crater, p. 33.

38. Cox, I, p. 287.

39. OR, XIX, pt. 1, p. 437.

40. Lane, p. 30.

41. Gabriel Campbell, Letter to Ezra Carman, August 23, 1899, Carman Papers, Antietam National Battlefield, pp. 212, 214.

    Campbell said the Confederates were firing grape shot at his men. Grape shot was an antebellum naval projectile which contained very large cast iron shot. During the Civil War, infantry tended to confuse canister with grape shot and case shot with canister. I sincerely doubt the Rebels were using canister upon the 17th Michigan because Bondurant's Battery, near the Wise farm, would have had to have fired its canister through the woods east of the battery's position to hit the prone 17th Michigan. More than likely, the captain confused the grape shot with case shot. He would have been under fire from Lane's Battery, one mile to the north on the high ground north of the National Pike, because that battery had a clear line of sight of all the fields west of the Martz cabin and the cornfield which surrounded it.

42. Lyle, pp. 133-134.

43. Ezra Carman, "The Maryland Campaign," VIII, Manuscript Division, Library of Congress, p. 25.

44. These were the only Federal troops in the woods at that point.

45. Ezra Carman, "The Maryland Campaign," VIII, Manuscript Division, Library of Congress, p. 25.

46. William Todd, pp. 231-232.

47. "Statistics of South Mountain and Antietam," Massachusetts Military Society, Thomas Livermore, Carman Papers, Antietam National Battlefield, p. 217.

48. Ezra Carman, "The Maryland Campaign," VIII, Manuscript Division, Library of Congress, pp. 24-25.

49. OR, XIX, pt. 1, pp. 1031-1032.
     Ezra Carman, "The Maryland Campaign," VIII, Manuscript Division, Library of Congress, p. 25

50. Calvin Leach, Diary, September 13 and 14, 1862, Southern Historical Collection, University of North Carolina, Chapel Hill, N.C.

51. "Statistics of South Mountain," Massachusetts Military Society, Thomas Livermore, Carman Papers, Antietam National Battlefield, p. 218.
     His comment reads:
     "Ripley's Brigade insignificant if any"

52. David E. Johnston, The Story of a Confederate Boy in the Civil War, Commonwealth Press, Inc., Radford, Va., (Reprint, Leonard A. Parr, 1980), p. 139.
     Henry Tweatt Owen, "Recollections of Antietam," Henry Tweatt Owen Papers, Sec. 3, Virginia Historical Society, Richmond, Va., p. 3.

53. John Dooley, p. 34.

54. Henry T. Owen, "Recollections of Antietam," Henry Tweatt Owen Papers, Sec. 3, Virginia Historical Society, Richmond, Va., p. 4.
     Since Kemper arrived at the gap ahead of Garnett, Garnett had to have preceded him onto the Sharpsburg Road.

55. This is my assumption of the division's formation. Anderson reached the mountain before Drayton.
     Ezra Carman, "The Maryland Campaign," VIII, Manuscript Division, Library of Congress, pp. 26, 56.

56. Kempfer, p. 87.

57. Albert, p. 48.

58. OR, XIX, pt. 1, pp. 441-442.

59. Gabriel Campbell, Letter to Ezra Carman, August 23, 1899, Carman Papers, Antietam National Battlefield, p. 214.

60. Frederick Pettit, Letter, September 20, 1862, Civil War Times Illustrated Collection, USAMHI.

61. Gabriel Campbell, Letter to Ezra Carman, August 23, 1899, Carman Papers, Antietam National Battlefield, p. 214.

62. Cox, I, p. 289.

63. Gabriel Campbell, Letter to Ezra Carman, August 23, 1899, Carman Papers, Antietam National Battlefield, p. 212.

64. Ezra Carman, "The Maryland Campaign," VIII, Manuscript Division, Library of Congress, pp. 25-26.
     OR, XIX, pt. 1, pp. 1032, 1020.
     D. H. Hill, Bethel to Sharpsburg, II, p. 377.
     The author in this source cited the arrival time as about 3:00 P.M.
     Battles and Leaders, II, p. 569.
     Hill was apparently mistaken about the 3:30 P.M. arrival time of Drayton's and G. T. Anderson's brigades at the Mountain House. There is no way he could have taken the troops from there to Anderson and back within half an hour and also have received word that Ripley's advance was progressing well. More than likely, the two brigades

arrived at the Mountain House around 2:30 to 3:00 P.M. and were near Ripley's position by around 3:30 P.M. to 4:00 P.M.

65. Hood, pp. 39-40.

66. Polley, p. 114.
Hood did not know that as the Texans passed Lee, they swore they would not fight without him. Lee nodded, raised his hand, and said, "You shall have him, gentlemen."

67. Henry T. Owen, "Recollections of Antietam," Sec. 3, Virginia Historical Society, Richmond, Va., pp. 5-6.
Henry T. Owen, "South Mountain," Carman Papers, Antietam National Battlefield, p. 184. The manuscript is more detailed than the newspaper article which Carman collected. Both, however, fill in voids left by the other, so they complement each other.

"Boonsboro or South Mountain," Carman Papers, Antietam National Battlefield, p. 234.

68. Dooley, p. 35.
Dooley said the brigade arrived at the top of the mountain around 5:00 p.m. The brigade had to have been near the Sharpsburg Road-National Pike intersection at least an hour before, which allowed it time to get organized and to climb the mountain.

69. Henry T. Owen, C. Co., 18th Va., mss., pp. 6-8.

Henry T. Owen, "South Mountain," Carman Papers, Antietam National Battlefield, p. 185.

70. D. H. Hill, *Bethel to Sharpsburg*, II, p. 376.
Ripley did not approach the field by an obscure trail as asserted here. If you look at the map and put yourself in the position of D. H. Hill at the Mountain House, it is very unlikely that he directed Ripley to march back toward Boonsboro to outflank his own troops from the west. Ripley must have used the wood road because at that time it was, apparently, the only approach road which Hill knew existed.
    I believe, like the author of this work, Ripley did divert his command along an "even fainter trail" which skirted the western slope of the mountain, but that he did have contact with G. B. Anderson, at least initially. According to the *Official Records*, XIX, pt. 1, p. 1020, the three commanders were ordered to move south "until they came in contact with Rosser, when they should change their flank, march into line of battle, and sweep the woods before them."
    Ripley apparently did as ordered. He came to the intersection, which was southeast of Rosser's position. He marched the column by the right flank to the intersection, followed it south, then ordered it to move by the left flank, in line, into the woods which were then on its left.

71. OR, XIX, pt. 1, p. 908.

72. *Battles and Leaders*, II, p. 569.

73. Albert, p. 52.

74. Dickert, p. 174.

75. OR, XIX, pt. 1, p. 461.

76. Ibid., pp. 441-442.

77. Crater, p. 33.

78. William Todd, p. 232.

79. OR, XIX, pt. 1, p. 443.

80. Ibid., p. 443.

81. Dickert, p. 174.

82. Gabriel Campbell, Letter to Ezra Carman, August 23, 1899, Carman Papers, Antietam National Battlefield, p. 214.
Dickert in his history of Kershaw's brigade stated that the 3rd South Carolina Battalion was cut off from the rest of the brigade. Gabriel Campbell said the regiment came under fire from the wood stacks and the stone wall mentioned in the text, which means that some of Drayton's men pushed quite forward to the front.

Ezra Carman, "The Maryland Campaign," VIII, Manuscript Division, Library of Congress, p. 21.

83. Walcott, p. 189.
    Stone, p. 86.

84. *35th Mass.*, p. 27.

85. OR, XIX, pt. 1, p. 442.

86. Todd, p. 232.

87. Albert, pp. 48, 52.
    William J. Bolton, "War Journal," War Library Museum, Philadelphia, Pa., p. 239.

88. Gabriel Campbell, Letter to Ezra Carman, August 23, 1899, Carman Papers, Antietam National Battlefield, p. 214.
    It is my assumption the 17th Michigan fired from the "hollow" which Campbell described in his letter. It formed a natural breastwork and would have been an ideal place to return fire from prior to charging with the bayonet.

89. *Battles and Leaders*, II, p. 571.

90. Ezra Carman, "The Maryland Campaign," VIII, Manuscript Division, Library of Congress, p. 32.

91. Gabriel Campbell, Letter to Ezra Carman, August 23, 1899, Carman Papers, Antietam National Battlefield, p. 214.

92. Albert, pp. 48, 53.

93. Ibid., pp. 53-54.

94. Gabriel Campbell, Letter to Ezra Carman, August 23, 1899, Carman Papers, Antietam National Battlefield, pp. 212, 213, 214.

95. Cussel, p. 73.

96. Ibid., p. 73.

97. Joseph E. Walton, "The 30th Ohio — Some Reminiscences of the Battle of Antietam," *The National Tribune*, December 31, 1885, p. 3.

98. OR, XIX, pt. 1, pp. 908-909.

99. Ibid., p. 909.

100. Ibid., p. 909.
     G. T. Anderson reported Ripley was at least a quarter of a mile away from his right flank.

101. Walter Clark, II, p. 245.

102. *35th Mass.*, p. 27.
     Edward O. Lord, (ed.), *History of the Ninth Regiment New Hampshire Volunteers*, Republican Press Association, Concord, 1895, p. 72.

103. Ibid., p. 104.
     Walcott, p. 189.

104. William J. Bolton, "War Journal," War Library Museum, Philadelphia, Pa., p. 238.

105. Robert West, "Reno's Death," *The National Tribune*, August 9, 1883, p. 1.

106. *35th Mass.*, p. 27.
     Albert A. Pope, "Journal of the Southern Campaign, War of the Rebellion, August 27, 1862-June 9, 1865," Civil War Times Illustrated Collection, USAMHI.

107. Walcott, p. 189.
     Stone, p. 85.

108. Walcott, p. 189.

109. *Battles and Leaders*, II, p. 571.

110. Richard Alden Huebner, (comp.), *Merserve Civil War Record*, RAH Publications, Oak Park, Mich., 1987, p. 14.

111. Stone, pp. 85-86.

112. Albert A. Pope, "Journal of the Southern Campaign, War of the Rebellion, August 27, 1862-June 9, 1865," Civil War Times Illustrated Collection, USAMHI.

113.   OR, XIX, pt. 1, p. 443.

114.   Bosbyshell, p. 75.

115.   Lord, pp. 72, 83.

116.   Ibid., p. 127.

117.   Daniel Hurd, "My Experiences in the Civil War," William Marvel Collection, USAMHI, p. 4.
       Lord, p. 73.
       The regimental history said the men fixed bayonets after they charged.

118.   Edward O. Lord, p. 83.

119.   Frederick Pettit, Letters, September 20 and 21, 1862, Civil War Times Illustrated Collection, USAMHI.

120.   Bosbyshell, p. 75.
       Joseph Gould, The Story of the Forty-Eighth, Regimental Association, Mt. Carmel, Pa., 1908, p. 78.

121.   James Wren, Diary, September 14, 1862, Manuscript, Antietam National Battlefield, p. 102.

122.   Lord, pp. 73, 83-84.

123.   Daniel Hurd, "My Experiences in the Civil War," William Marvel Collection, USAMHI, p. 4.

124.   Gabriel Campbell, Letter to Ezra Carman, August 23, 1899, Carman Papers, Antietam National Battlefield, p. 215.

125.   Letter, John Purifoy to Ezra Carman, July 21, 1900, Ezra Ayers Carman Collection, Manuscript Division, Library of Congress.

126.   Bosbyshell, p. 75.
       James Wren, Diary, September 14, 1862, Manuscript, Antietam National Battlefield, p. 161.

127.   Albert, p. 54.

128.   Hagerstown Almanac, 1862.

129.   Albert, p. 54.

130.   Dickert, pp. 172, 175.
       Gabriel Campbell, Letter to Ezra Carman, August 23, 1899, Carman Papers, Antietam National Battlefield, p. 215.

131.   Albert, p. 54.

132.   OR, XIX, pt. 1, p. 442.

133.   James Wren, Diary, September 14, 1862, Manuscript, Antietam National Battlefield, p. 102.

134.   Ibid., p. 102.
       This is based upon Wren's statement that the old troops "lay quiet."
       Frederick Pettit, Letters, September 20 and 21, 1862, Civil War Times Illustrated Collection, USAMHI.
       He fired 11 shots. Most of his men fired 15. They had slight opposition.
       Gabriel Campbell, Letter to Ezra Carman, August 23, 1899, Carman Papers, Antietam National Battlefield, p. 215.
       The 17th Michigan flanked the lane and seems to have fired into it for a few minutes.

135.   Lord, p. 73.

136.   Ibid., p. 79.
       Daniel Hurd, "My Experiences in the Civil War," William Marvel Collection, USAMHI, p. 4.

137.   Ibid.

138. Walter Clark, II, p. 245.

139. Crater, p. 33.

140. Walter Clark, II, p. 245.

141. Crater, p. 33.

142. Ibid., pp. 33-34.

143. OR, XIX, pt. 1, p. 909.

144. James Wren, Diary, September 14, 1862, Manuscript, Antietam National Battlefield, p. 102.

145. Daniel Hurd, "My Experiences in the Civil War," William Marvel Collection, USAMHI, p. 4.
     Lord, pp. 78-79.

146. OR, XIX, pt. 1, p. 442.

147. James Wren, Diary, September 14, 1862, Manuscript, Antietam National Battlefield, pp. 102, 104.

148. Ibid., p. 103.

149. Walter Clark, II, p. 245.

150. OR, XIX, pt. 1, p. 909.

151. Lord, p. 75.

152. Frederick Pettit, Letter, September 20, 1862, Civil War Times Illustrated Collection, USAMHI.

153. Lord, p. 79.

154. Gabriel Campbell, Letter to Ezra Carman, August 23, 1899, Carman Papers, Antietam National Battlefield, p. 215.
     Lord, p. 79.
     OR, XIX, pt. 1, p. 442.

155. Gabriel Campbell, Letter to Ezra Carman, August 23, 1899, Carman Papers, Antietam National Battlefield, p. 4.
     Lord, p. 85.

156. OR, XIX, pt. 1, p. 909.

157. OR, XIX, pt. 1, pp. 442, 1032.
     Lord, p. 79.

158. Ibid., p. 79.

159. OR, XIX, pt. 1, p. 442.
     Gabriel Campbell, Letter to Ezra Carman, August 23, 1899, Carman Papers, Antietam National Battlefield, p. 215.
     Lord, p. 74.

160. Gabriel Campbell, Letter to Ezra Carman, August 23, 1899, Carman Papers, Antietam National Battlefield, p. 212.

161. Bosbyshell, p. 75.

162. James Wren, Diary, September 14, 1862, Manuscript, Antietam National Battlefield, p. 103.

163. Walter Clark, II, p. 247.

164. James Wren, Diary, September 14, 1862, Manuscript, Antietam National Battlefield, p. 103.

165. Crater, p. 34.

166. David Thompson, Letter to Elias, October 1862, Vertical Files, Antietam National Battlefield.

Johnson, p. 187.

Graham, pp. 271-273.

Graham, Thompson, and Johnson insisted the 103rd and the 9th were deployed first. Thompson and Johnson said the regiments were extended in a line. Thompson said the 9th New York held the center of the brigade with the 89th and the 103rd New York on the left and right, respectively. Johnson, in his diary, had the 103rd N.Y. and the 89th N.Y. to the left of the 9th N.Y. Graham had the brigade in an "L" as follows: 103rd N.Y., 89th N.Y., and the 9th N.Y. as the "base line."

The brigade numbered a little over nine hundred men. The distance along that portion of the field was around 1000 feet. I believe that the regiments were in a straight line initially with the 103rd on the left, 89th N.Y. in the center, and the 9th N.Y. on the right. It makes sense to secure the flanks first then fill in the center.

167.   James Wren, Diary, September 14, 1862, Manuscript, Antietam National Battlefield, p. 104.

168.   Graham, p. 272.
       Johnson, p. 186.

169.   Graham, p. 274.
       Johnson, p. 186.

170.   Graham, p. 272.
       The Lieutenant said the 103rd behaved itself after a moment's unsteadiness.

171.   Johnson, p. 186.

172.   John Calvin Gorman, "Memoirs of a Rebel," George Gorman, (ed.), *Military Images*, Nov./Dec., 1981, p. 5.

173.   Johnson, p. 186.

174.   David Thompson, Letter to Elias, October 1862, Vertical Files, Antietam National Battlefield.

175.   Johnson, p. 186.

176.   Ibid.

177.   David Thompson, Letter to Elias, October 1862, Vertical Files, Antietam National Battlefield.

178.   James Wren, Diary, September 14, 1862, Manuscript, Antietam National Battlefield, p. 104.
       Gould, p. 78.
       Bosbyshell, p. 76.
       Lord, p. 75.

179.   Bosbyshell, p. 76.
       Gould, p. 78.

180.   Walter Clark, II, pp. 245-246.

181.   Cussel, p. 74.

182.   Lord, p. 77.

183.   Walter Clark, II, p. 246.

184.   Ezra Carman, "The Maryland Campaign," VIII, Manuscript Division, Library of Congress, p. 37.

185.   James Wren, Diary, September 14, 1862, Manuscript, Antietam National Battlefield, p. 104.
       Bosbyshell, pp. 76-77.

186.   Ibid., p. 77.

187.   James Wren, Diary, September 14, 1862, Manuscript, Antietam National Battlefield, p. 104.

188.   OR, XIX, pt. 1, p. 186.

189. James Wren, Diary, September 14, 1862, Manuscript, Antietam National Battlefield, p. 104.

190. Gabriel Campbell, Letter to Ezra Carman, August 23, 1899, Carman Papers, Antietam National Battlefield, p. 215.

191. Huebner, p. 14.
    35th Mass., p. 27.

192. Ibid., p. 28.

193. Ibid.

194. Albert A. Pope, "Journal of the Southern Campaign, War of the Rebellion, August 27, 1862-June 9, 1865," Civil War Times Illustrated Collection, USAMHI.

195. *35th Mass.*, p. 29.

196. OR, XIX, pt. 1, p. 909.

197. Albert A. Pope, "Journal of the Southern Campaign, War of the Rebellion, August 27, 1862-June 9, 1865," Civil War Times Illustrated Collection, USAMHI.

198. Ezra Carman, "The Maryland Campaign," VIII, Manuscript Division, Library of Congress, p. 40.

199. William J. Bolton, "War Journal," War Library Museum, Philadelphia, Pa., p. 239.

200. Walcott, p. 188.

201. Jerome M. Loving, (ed.), *Civil War Letters of George Washington Whitman*, Duke University Press, Durham, N.C., 1975, p. 66.

202. A. B. Counnel, "Reno's Death," *The National Tribune*, August 23, 1883, p. 1.
    A. H. Wood, "How Reno Fell," *The National Tribune*, July 6, 1883, p. 1.
    Theodore Dimon, Letter to Fitz John Porter, June 15, 1883, Carman Papers, Antietam National Battlefield, p. 239.

203. Gabriel Campbell, Letter to Ezra Carman, August 23, 1899, Carman Papers, Antietam National Battlefield, p. 215.

204. *35th Mass.*, p. 29.

205. William J. Bolton, "War Journal," War Library Museum, Philadelphia, Pa., p. 240.

206. A. H. Wood, "How Reno Fell," *The National Tribune*, July 6, 1883, p. 1.

207. Gabriel Campbell, Letter to Ezra Carman, August 23, 1899, Carman Papers, Antietam National Battlefield, p. 215.

208. A. H. Wood, "How Reno Fell," *The National Tribune*, July 6, 1883, p. 1.
    J. E. Walton, "The 30th Ohio — Some Reminiscences of the Battle of Antietam," *The National Tribune*, December 31, 1885, p. 3.
    Theodore Dimon, Letter to Fitz John Porter, June 15, 1883, Carman Papers, Antietam National Battlefield, p. 239.

209. A. H. Wood, "How Reno Fell," *The National Tribune*, July 6, 1883, p. 1.

210. Gabriel Campbell, Letter to Ezra Carman, August 23, 1899, Carman Papers, Antietam National Battlefield, pp. 215-216.

211. This is not in Campbell's account. He implied it, however, when he wrote of "reaching the cover of the wood..." The general would not have needed cover, i.e. protection unless there was some fighting going on in the area.

212. Gabriel Campbell, Letter to Ezra Carman, August 23, 1899, Carman Papers, Antietam National Battlefield, p. 216.

213. A. H. Wood, "Reno's Death," *The National Tribune*, July 6, 1883, p. 1.

214. OR, XIX, pt. 1, p. 909.

215. Ezra Carman, "The Maryland Campaign," VIII, Manuscript Division, Library of Congress, p. 39.

216. Stephen Elliott Welch, Letter to Parents, September 22, 1862, Elliott Stephen Welch Papers, Manuscript Department, Duke University Library, Durham, N.C.

217. Ezra Carman, "The Maryland Campaign," VIII, Manuscript Division, Library of Congress, p. 39.

218. Albert A. Pope, "Journal of the Southern Campaign, War of the Rebellion, August 27, 1862-June 9, 1865," Civil War Times Illustrated Collection, USAMHI.

219. Walcott, p. 190.

220. *35th Mass.*, p. 30.
    William J. Bolton, "War Journal," War Library Museum, Philadelphia, Pa., p. 240.
    Thomas H. Parker, p. 226.

221. Loving, p. 66.

222. Harold Simpson, *Hood's Texas Brigade*, p. 167.

223. OR, XIX, pt. 1, p. 187.

224. William J. Bolton, "War Journal," War Library Museum, Philadelphia, Pa., pp. 239-241.

Chapter Twelve

1. E. M. Woodward, *Our Campaigns*, p. 195.
    E. M. Woodward, *History of the Third Pennsylvania Reserves*, MacCrellish & Quigley, Book and Job Printers, Trenton, NJ, 1883, p. 173.
    Benjamin F. Cook, p. 67.
    1st Lieutenant Samuel W. Moore, Diary, September 14, 1862, Museum Collection, Antietam National Battlefield.
    J. Harrison Mills, *Chronicles of the Twenty-First Regiment New York State Volunteers*, 21st Veteran Regiment Association, Buffalo, 1887, p. 278.

2. Archibald F. Hill, p. 394.

3. James H. McIlwain, Letter to Emma, September 14, 1862, Lewis Leigh Collection, USAMHI.

4. Samuel W. Moore, Diary, September 14, 1862, Museum Collection, Antietam National Battlefield.

5. Archibald F. Hill, p. 394.
    Samuel W. Moore, Diary, September 14, 1862, Museum Collection, Antietam National Battlefield.
    Moore wrote that his brigade, in Ricketts' division, had to wait for King's and McCall's (Meade) division to pass before it could get onto the National Pike. He said it was 8:00 A.M.

6. Samuel W. Moore, Diary, September 14, 1862, Museum Collection, Antietam National Battlefield.
    Ezra Carman, "Battle of South Mountain, September 14th, 1862," Manuscript, Antietam National Battlefield, p. 226.
    Warren Hargood Freeman, *Letters From Two Brothers Serving in the War for the Union*, privately printed, Cambridge, 1871, p. 50.

7. James B. Casey, (ed.), "The Ordeal of Adoniram Judson Warner: His Minutes of South Mountain and Antietam," *Civil War History*, September 1982, Vol. 28, #3, p. 217.
    The Pennsylvania Reserve division left for Frederick around 8:00 A.M.

8. E. M. Woodward, *Our Campaigns*, p. 195.

E. M. Woodward, *The Third Reserve*, p. 173.
Woodward served in both regiments: in the 2nd as sergeant major and adjutant, and in the 3rd as major. Both accounts are nearly identical, however, the minute variations require separate footnoting.

9. Archibald F. Hill, p. 394.

10. William Henry Locke, *The Story of the Regiment*, James Miller, Publisher, N.Y., 1872, p. 120.

11. Rufus R. Dawes, *Service With the Sixth Wisconsin Volunteers*, Morningside Bookshop, Dayton, Ohio, p. 79.

12. J. Harrison Mills, *Chronicles of the Twenty-first Regiment New York Volunteers*, 21st Regiment Veteran Association, Buffalo, 1887, p. 278.

13. McClenthen, p. 30.

14. John Gibbon to his wife, September 13, 1862, Box 1, John Gibbon Papers, Historical Society of Pennsylvania.

15. Hough, p. 111.
    Isaac Hall, pp. 85-86.

16. Samuel W. Moore, Diary, September 14, 1862, Museum Collection, Antietam National Battlefield.

17. Bates Alexander, "Pennsylvania Reserves, That Corps' Experience During the Late War," The Hummelstown *Sun*, August 9, 1895, not paginated.

18. Ibid.

19. Ibid.

20. E. M. Woodward, *Our Campaigns*, p. 195.
    William M. Owen, p. 134.
    No limbers or caissons were reported lost during the skirmish of September 13, 1862. The only existing report of any demolished ammunition chests comes from Lt. William M. Owen of the Washington Artillery. The rear chest of one of the caissons blew up on the National Pike because a private was smoking while riding the caisson. This occurred on September 10, 1862.

21. Rufus Dawes, p. 79.

22. Mills, p. 278.
    Patrick, p. 143.

23. Hough, p. 111.
    McClenthen, pp. 30-31.
    Isaac Hall, p. 86.

24. Hough, p. 111.

25. Bates Alexander, "Pennsylvania Reserves, That Corps' Experience During the Late War," The Hummelstown *Sun*, August 16, 1895, not paginated.

26. E. M. Woodward, *Our Campaigns*, p. 195.
    France, p. 62.

27. Frank Holsinger, "South Mountain and the Part the Pennsylvania Reserves Took in the Battle," *The National Tribune*, September 27, 1883, p. 7.
    OR, XIX, pt. 1, p. 267.

28. E. M. Woodward, *3rd Res.*, pp. 173-174.
    OR, XIX, pt. 1, p. 267.

29. Bates Alexander, "Pennsylvania Reserves, That Corps' Experience During the Late War," The Hummelstown *Sun*, August 16, 1895, not paginated.

30. E. M. Woodward, *3rd Res.*, p. 174.

31. Franklin Hough, p. 112.

32. Isaac Hall, p. 87.

33. Samuel W. Moore, Diary, September 14, 1862, Museum Collection, Antietam National Battlefield.

34. Rufus Dawes, p. 80.

35. Franklin Hough, p. 112.

36. Samuel W. Moore, Diary, September 14, 1862, Museum Collection, Antietam National Battlefield.

37. John W. Urban, *My Experiences Mid Shot and Shell and in Rebel Den*, published by the author, Lancaster, Pa., 1882, p. 204.
     E. M. Woodward, *3rd Res.*, p. 176.
     Martin D. Hardin, *History of the Twelfth Regiment Pennsylvania Reserve Volunteer Corps*, by the author, N.Y., 1890, p. 116.

38. Bates Alexander, "Pennsylvania Reserves, That Corps' Experience During the Late War," The Hummelstown *Sun*, August 16, 1895, not paginated.

39. E. M. Woodward, Our Campaigns, p. 198.

40. Worthington Chauncey Ford, pp. 188-189.
     Crowninshield, pp. 74-75.

41. Patrick, p. 143.

42. Patrick, p. 143.
     OR, XIX, pt. 1, p. 221.
     Mills, p. 279.

43. Samuel W. Moore, Diary, September 14, 1862, Museum Collection, Antietam National Battlefield.

44. This is based upon McClellan's boast to Lincoln about having Lee's plans in his grasp.

45. Bates Alexander, "Pennsylvania Reserves, That Corps' Experience During the Late War," The Hummelstown *Sun*, August 22, 1895, not paginated.
     E. M. Woodward, Our Campaigns, p. 198.

46. Josiah R. Sypher, *History of the Pennsylvania Reserve Corps*, Elias Barr & Co., Lancaster, Pa., 1865, p. 368.

47. OR, XIX, pt. 1, p. 1034.
     Ezra Carman, "The Maryland Campaign," VIII, Manuscript Division, Library of Congress, p. 46.

48. Had Rodes spread his men out to cover every inch of ground, he would have averaged one man every two to three feet.

49. OR, XIX, pt. 1, p. 1034.

50. This is based upon the misplaced location of the "Virginia Troops" on the Official Records' map and upon Robert Rodes' report of the action.
     OR, XIX, pt. 1, p. 1055.

51. Robert Emory Park, "Sketch of the Twelfth Alabama Infantry," Wm. Ellis Jones, Book and Job Printer, Richmond, 1906, p. 8.

52. OR, XIX, pt. 1, p. 1054.
     In his report, Robert Rodes commended Captain Carter and a lieutenant of Cutts' Battalion who came to his assist too late and therefore were not deployed. Rodes was too busy with his firing line to see every action. The single gun that fired upon the Reserves probably came from Lane's battery (Cutts Battalion) which was the only artillery on the south spur at the time.

53. Frank Holsinger, "South Mountain and the Part the Pennsylvania Reserves Took in the Battle," *The National Tribune*, September 27, 1883, p. 7.

54. Bates Alexander, "Pennsylvania Reserves, That Corps' Experience During the Late War," The Hummelstown *Sun*, August 22, 1895, not paginated.

    Bates Alexander, "One of Our Constituents; What a Pennsylvania Man Thinks of Our Paper," *The National Tribune*, p. 3.

55. E. M. Woodward, *The Third Reserve*, p. 176.

    E. M. Woodward, Our Campaigns, p. 198.

56. Bates Alexander, "Pennsylvania Reserves, That Corps' Experience During the Late War," The Hummelstown *Sun*, August 22, 1895, not paginated.

    Bates Alexander, "One of Our Constituents; What a Pennsylvania Man Thinks of Our Paper," *The National Tribune*, p. 3.

57. OR, XIX, pt. 1, p. 267.

    Archibald F. Hill, pp. 394-395.

58. OR, XIX, pt. 1, p. 267.

59. Ibid., p. 274.

60. Hardin, p. 117.

61. E. M. Woodward, Our Campaigns, p. 198.

    OR, XIX, pt. 1, p. 272.

    Samuel P. Bates, *History of Pennsylvania Volunteers 1861-5*, I, B. Singerly, State Printers, Harrisburg, 1869, pp. 584, 669, 698.

62. OR, XIX, pt. 1, p. 274.

63. Hardin, p. 117.

    OR, XIX, pt. 1, p. 273.

64. Bates Alexander, "One of Our Constituents: What a Pennsylvania Man Thinks of Our Paper," *The National Tribune*, December 12, 1889, p. 3.

65. Bates Alexander, "Pennsylvania Reserves, That Corps' Experience During the Late War," The Hummelstown *Sun*, August 22, 1895, not paginated.

66. Archibald F. Hill, p. 395.

67. Ezra Carman, "The Maryland Campaign," VIII, Manuscript Division, Library of Congress, pp. 47-48.

68. Otis D. Smith, "Reminiscences," Thach Papers, Southern Historical Collection, University of North Carolina Library, Chapel Hill, N.C., p. 7.

69. Ezra Carman, "The Maryland Campaign," VIII, Manuscript Division, Library of Congress, p. 48.

    John D. McQuaide, Letter to Thomas McQuaide, September 22, 1862, Civil War Times Illustrated Collection, USAMHI.

    Andrew J. Elliott, Diary, September 14, 1862, Pennsylvania "Save the Flags" Collection, USAMHI.

70. Otis D. Smith, "Reminiscences," Thach Papers, Southern Historical Collection, University of North Carolina Library, Chapel Hill, N.C., pp. 7-8.
    Smith described the Widow Main as an "old lady."

71. Ezra Carman, "The Maryland Campaign," VIII, Manuscript Division, Library of Congress, p. 49.

72. OR, XIX, pt. 1, pp. 274-275, 1035.

73. Sypher, pp. 374-375.

74. OR, XIX, pt. 1, pp. 274-275, 1035.

    Ezra Carman, "The Maryland Campaign," VIII, Manuscript Division, Library of Congress, p. 49.

75. OR, XIX, pt. 1, p. 1035.

    Ezra Carman, "The Maryland Campaign," VIII, Manuscript Division, Library of Congress, p. 49.

76. Casey, p. 217.
     Warner said he was sent by Meade to the right to intercept the Confederate push toward that flank. Meade had to have interpreted the 5th Alabama's move as a threat.

77. Woodward, *3rd Res.*, p. 173.

78. Samuel Bates, I, p. 549.

79. Ibid., p. 698.
     Contrary to Ezra Carman's construction, the accounts from the 1st, 2nd, 6th, and 13th Reserves seem to indicate they stayed north of the Zittlestown Road. The only regiment to deflect away from the line appears to have been the 5th Reserves.

80. Ezra Carman, "The Maryland Campaign," VIII, Manuscript Division, Library of Congress, pp. 48-49.
     James Casey, p. 217.

81. Samuel P. Bates, *History of Pennsylvania Volunteers, 1861-5*, B. Singerly, State Printers, Harrisburg, 1869, p. 369.
     OR, XIX, pt. 1, p. 1035.

82. Robert Park, p. 88.

83. Bates Alexander, "Pennsylvania Reserves, That Corps' Experience During the Late War," The Hummelstown *Sun*, August 23, 1895, not paginated.

84. Robert Park, p. 89.

85. Ezra Carman, "The Maryland Campaign," VIII, Manuscript Division, Library of Congress, p. 49.

86. Casey, p. 217.

87. Ezra Carman, "The Maryland Campaign," VIII, Manuscript Division, Library of Congress, p. 49.

88. James Monroe Thompson, *Reminiscences of the Autauga Rifles, C. Co., 6th Alabama Volunteer Regiment, C.S.A.*, William Stanley Hoole, (ed.), Prattville, Ala., 1879, p. 17.

89. H. N. Minnigh, *History of Company K 1st (Inft.) Penn'a Reserves*, "Home Print" Publisher, Duncansville, Pa.

90. Otis D. Smith, "Reminiscences," Thach Papers, Southern Historical Collection, University of North Carolina Library, Chapel Hill, N.C., pp. 8-9.

91. Ezra Carman, "The Maryland Campaign," VIII, Manuscript Division, Library of Congress, pp. 49-50.

92. Bates Alexander, "Pennsylvania Reserves, That Corps' Experience During the Late War," The Hummelstown *Sun*, August 22, 1895, not paginated.
     Archibald F. Hill, p. 395.

93. Bates Alexander, "Pennsylvania Reserves, That Corps' Experience During the Late War," The Hummelstown *Sun*, August 22, 1895, not paginated.

94. Archibald F. Hill, p. 395.

95. Ibid., pp. 395-396.

96. France, p. 63.

97. Ezra Carman, "The Maryland Campaign," VIII, Manuscript Division, Library of Congress, p. 54.

98. Archibald F. Hill, p. 396.

99. Bates Alexander, "Seventh Reserves," The Hummelstown *Sun*, August 30, 1895, not paginated.

100. Ezra Carman, "The Maryland Campaign," VIII, Manuscript Division, Library of Congress, p. 97.

101. Edward McCrady, Jr., "Heroes of the old Camden District, South Carolina, 1776-1861," *Southern Historical Society Papers*, Vol. XVI, January-December, 1888, p. 24.

102. Ezra Carman, "The Maryland Campaign," VIII, Manuscript Division, Library of Congress, p. 98.

103. W. J. Andrews, *Sketch of Company K, 23rd South Carolina Volunteers in the Civil War From 1861-1865*, Richmond, Whittet, and Shepperson, Printers, (Reprinted by Wilder and Ward Offset Printing, Sumpter, S.C., 1974), p. 14.

104. Ezra Carman, "The Maryland Campaign," VIII, Manuscript Division, Library of Congress, pp. 54, 98.

105. OR, XIX, pt. 1, p. 1035.

106. Ibid.
   Bates Alexander, "Seventh Reserves," The Hummelstown *Sun*, August 30, 1895, not paginated.
   This position is based upon Rodes' statement that the Yankees captured the high knoll on his left (Main's). Alexander noted a large field to the right of the regiment as it crested the ridge.

107. Bates, I, p. 698.
   OR, XIX, pt. 1, p. 1035.

108. Sypher, p. 370.

109. OR, XIX, pt. 1, p. 1035.
   Bates Alexander, "Seventh Reserves," The Hummelstown *Sun*, August 30, 1895, not paginated.

110. Archibald F. Hill, p. 397.

111. OR, XIX, pt. 1, pp. 1035-1036.
   Bates, I, p. 698.

112. Casey, pp. 217-218.

113. OR, XIX, pt. 1, pp. 1035-1036.

114. Isaac Hall, p. 87.

115. OR, XIX, pt. 1, p. 1036.

116. Ibid., p. 186.

117. Otis Smith, "Reminiscences," Thach Papers, Southern Historical Collection, University of North Carolina, Chapel Hill, N.C., p. 10.

118. Bates Alexander, "Seventh Reserves," The Hummelstown *Sun*, August 30, 1895, not paginated.

119. Archibald F. Hill, pp. 397-398.

120. John D. McQuaide, Letter to Thomas McQuaide, September 22, 1862, Civil War Times Illustrated Collection, USAMHI.

121. Frank Holsinger, "South Mountain and the Part the Pennsyvlania Reserves Took in the Battle," *The National Tribune*, September 27, 1883, p. 7.

122. Casey, p. 218.

123. Reuben Schell, Letter to Father, September 24, 1862, Robert Ulrich Collection.

124. Casey, p. 218.

125. James Monroe Thompson, p. 17.

126. Ezra Carman, "The Maryland Campaign," VIII, Manuscript Division, Library of Congress, p. 57.
   Carman reported Garnett's Confederate brigade got onto the field about sunset. Kemper had arrived shortly before him.

127. Patrick, p. 143.
   OR, XIX, pt. 1, p. 241.

128. Mills, p. 279.

129. OR, XIX, pt. 1, p. 242.
   Patrick said the regiment advanced rapidly without unslinging its knapsacks.
   Marsena Patrick, p. 143.

According to his diary, he personally led the regiment onto the field and apparently did not give it time to remove its gear.

130.   The only house east of the ridge and below the crest road is J. Shaffer's. It is the only house the 21st New York could have come across in its northwesterly approach.

131.   Mills, p. 280.
        Mills did not serve at South Mountain. His regimental history is based upon accounts provided by participants. He had no personal knowledge about how much time the movement consumed.
        Theodore B. Gates, *The Ulster Guard*, Benjamin H. Tyrrel, N.Y., 1879, pp. 295-296. Interestingly enough, Gates said the 35th and the 80th New York were sent over to the left flank to cover the National Pike and that they stayed there an hour. While Gates misstated the time as 2:00 P.M., the hour delay before joining the 21st New York makes sense.
        Marsena Patrick, p. 143.
        Patrick sent the 35th New York out with instructions to connect with the 21st New York and the National Pike and that the 80th New York was very slow coming up. The hour delay in getting deployed would place the 80th New York on line around dusk which coincides with the arrival of Phelps' and Doubleday's brigades.

132.   Patrick, p. 143.
        Gates, p. 296.

133.   Dooley, p. 35.

134.   Ibid.

135.   Ibid.
        Ezra Carman, "Boonsboro or South Mountain," Carman Papers, Antietam National Battlefield, p. 234.

136.   David E. Johnston, p. 140.

137.   Ezra Carman, "The Maryland Campaign," VIII, Manuscript Division, Library of Congress, p. 58.
        Carman did not make the connection necessary to explain why Kemper straddled the Frosttown Road (which he and so many of the Yankees mistook for the Old Hagerstown Road). Kemper could not have crossed it facing east because that would have presented his rear to the 8th Reserves. He faced north. The skirmishers of the 21st New York clearly saw his men forming along the fence which ran perpendicular to their position in the woods east of the road.

138.   Ezra Carman, "The Maryland Campaign," VIII, Manuscript Division, Library of Congress, pp. 58, 97.
        John M. Priest, *Antietam: The Soldiers' Battle*, White Mane Publishing Co., Inc., Shippensburg, PA, 1989, p. 321.
        By adding Carman's casualties to the number present at Antietam, I can account for all of the regiments but the 24th Virginia. If there were about 400 men and I subtract the known regimental strengths from 400 I can arrive at the approximate strength of the 28th Virginia.

139.   "Reports of the First, Seventh and Seventeenth Virginia Regiments in 1862," *Southern Historical Society Papers*, Vol. XXXVIII, 1910, p. 266.

140.   OR, XIX, pt. 1, pp. 241-242.

141.   Gates, p. 296.
        Mills, p. 280.
        Patrick, p. 143.

142.   OR, XIX, pt. 1, pp. 242, 246.

143.   Ibid., p. 221.

144.   OR, XIX, pt. 1, p. 231.
        Ezra Carman, "The Maryland Campaign," VIII, Manuscript Division, Library of Congress, p. 61.

145. Ezra Carman, "The Maryland Campaign," VIII, Manuscript Division, Library of Congress, p. 58.

146. "Reports of the First, Seventh and Seventeenth Virginia Regiments in 1862," *Southern Historical Society Papers*, Vol. XXXVIII, 1910, p. 266.

147. Mills, p. 281.

148. Henry T. Owen, "Recollection of Antietam," Henry Tweatt Owen Papers, Sec. 3, Virginia Historical Society, Richmond, p. 9.

149. Ezra Carman, "The Maryland Campaign," VIII, Manuscript Division, Library of Congress, p. 57.
     OR, XIX, pt. 1, p. 220.
     John Hatch's report clears up exactly where the Confederate line was established at the beginning of the action. He wrote: "The enemy was found posted behind a fence. [After] minutes of heavy firing, a charge was made by the First Brigade [Phelps], which succeeded in gaining and taking possession of the fence held by the enemy."

150. Mills, p. 281.

151. According to Webster's *Dictionary*, a pace is about 2.5-3 feet in length. At a halt every fifteen paces (15 × 2.5') one would have to stop about 48 times to cover 1800 feet.

152. OR, XIX, pt. 1, p. 232.

153. Marsena Patrick, p. 144.

154. Ezra Carman, "The Maryland Campaign," VIII, Manuscript Division, Library of Congress, p. 61.

155. Henry T. Owen, "Recollections of Antietam," Henry Tweatt Owen Papers, Sec. 3, Virginia Historical Society, Richmond, Va., pp. 9-10.
     The 80th New York and the 21st New York contained 289 effectives. In skirmish order, with three to six foot intervals between men, their line would have extended well past both flanks of Garnett's brigade.

156. Bates, p. 297.

157. OR, XIX, pt. 1, p. 232.

158. Ibid., pp. 231-231, 266,

159. Ibid., p. 232.

160. Ibid., pp. 220, 232.

161. Patrick, p. 144.

162. Henry T. Owen, "Recollections of Antietam," Henry Tweatt Owen Papers, Sec. 3, Virginia Historical Society, Richmond, Va., p. 10.

163. Ezra Carman, "The Maryland Campaign," VIII, Manuscript Division, Library of Congress, p. 96.

164. Henry T. Owen, "Recollections of Antietam," Henry Tweatt Owen Papers, Sec. 3, Virginia Historical Society, Richmond, Va., p. 10.

165. Ezra Carman, "The Maryland Campaign," VIII, Manuscript Division, Library of Congress, p. 57.
     Carman did not sort out his information in great depth. The cornfield was the second position held by those two regiments.

166. OR, XIX, pt. 1, p. 232.

167. Mills, p. 281.

168. Ibid.
     Patrick, p. 145.

169. Mills, p. 281.
     Patrick, p. 144.

170. Dooley, pp. 36-37.

171. "Reports of the First, Seventh and Seventeenth Virginia Regiments in 1862," *Southern Historical Society Papers*, Vol., XXXVIII, 1910, p. 266.

172. Henry T. Owen, "Recollections of Antietam," Henry Tweatt Owen Papers, Sec. 3, Virginia Historical Society, Richmond, Va., p. 11.

173. Abram P. Smith, *History of the Seventy-Sixth Regiment, New York Volunteers; What It Endured and Accomplished*, Courtland, N.Y., 1867, p. 152.

174. OR, XIX, pt. 1, pp. 237-238.
      Abram P. Smith, p. 152.

175. Edward L. Barnes, "The 95th New York at South Mountain," *The National Tribune*, January 7, 1886, p. 2.

176. Abram P. Smith, p. 152.

177. Ibid.
      Edward L. Barnes, "The 95th New York at South Mountain," *The National Tribune*, January 7, 1886, p. 2.

178. OR, XIX, pt. 1, p. 223.
      Mills, p. 283.

179. Wood, p. 36.

180. Abram P. Smith, p. 153.

181. Mills, p. 284.
      OR, XIX, pt. 1, p. 223.
      Captain Noyes did not credit himself for the quote. Abner Doubleday, however, cited him for leaping on top of the wall and cheering the men on.

182. Abram P. Smith, pp. 154-155.
      Mills, p. 283.

183. Ibid., p. 284.

184. Abram P. Smith, p. 154.

185. Wood, p. 35.

186. Mills, p. 284.

187. Edward L. Barnes, "The 95th New York at South Mountain," *The National Tribune*, January 7, 1886, p. 2.

188. Wood, p. 35.

189. Mills, p. 285.
      Abram P. Smith, p. 154.
      Wood, p. 35.

190. Ibid.

191. "Reports of the First, Seventh and Seventeenth Virginia Regiments in 1862," *Southern Historical Society Papers*, Vol. XXXVIII, 1910, p. 266.

192. Henry T. Owen, "Recollections of Antietam," Henry Tweatt Owen Papers, Sec. 3, Virginia Historical Society, Richmond, Va., pp. 12-14.

193. OR, XIX, pt. 1, p. 235.
      Mills, p. 284.
      Abram P. Smith, pp. 155-156.
      Smith left the service on May 2, 1862 and was not at South Mountain. George Noyes did serve there. Noyes' account and Smith's account are very similar. More than likely, Stamp used the captain's statement as the basis for his regimental history. In so doing, he appears to have placed the charges by Strange and Walker in the wrong order.

194. Patrick, p. 145.

195. "Reports of the First, Seventh, And Seventeenth Virginia Regiments in 1862," *Southern Historical Society Papers*, Vol. XXXVIII, 1910, p. 266.

196. Henry T. Owen, "Recollections of Antietam," Henry Tweatt Owen Papers, Sec. 3, Virginia Historical Society, Richmond, Va., p. 14.

197. Ezra Carman, "The Maryland Campaign," VIII, Manuscript Division, Library of Congress, p. 65.

198. Coker, p. 107.
Patrick, p. 145.
He noted the time as 8:00 P.M.
Samuel L. Moore, Diary, September 14, 1862, Museum Collection, Antietam National Battlefield.
He estimated the time as 8:30 P.M.

199. Mills, p. 284.
Abram Smith, p. 155.

200. Ezra Carman, "The Maryland Campaign," VIII, Manuscript Division, Library of Congress, p. 95.
Coker, p. 107.

201. McClenthen, p. 32.

202. OR, XIX, pt. 1, p. 246.

203. Ibid., p. 264.

204. Cook, p. 66.

205. OR, XIX, pt. 1, p. 185.

206. McClenthen, p. 33.

207. OR, XIX, pt. 1, p. 263.

208. Coker, p. 107.

209. Henry T. Owen, "Recollections of Antietam," Henry Tweatt Owen Papers, Sec. 3, Virginia Historical Society, Richmond, Va., p. 15.

210. John Cook, Diary, September 14, 1862, Vertical Files, Antietam National Battlefield.

211. Dawes, p. 81.

212. OR, XIX, pt. 1, p. 252.

213. Dawes, p. 81.

214. OR, XIX, pt. 1, p. 256.

215. Worthington C. Ford, pp. 188-189.
Crowninshield, p. 75.

216. OR, XIX, pt. 1, pp. 248, 252, 256.

217. The only house it could have been was the Mountain House. The colonel in his report said he then engaged the Rebels at close range, implying that the house was some distance off. He drove the Rebs ¾ miles which put him well within rifle range from the left flank.

218. OR, XIX, pt. 1, pp. 250, 256.

219. Dawes, p. 82.

220. Ibid.
George Fairchild, Diary, September 14, 1862, State Historical Society of Wisconsin, Archives and Manuscript Dept., copy, Antietam National Battlefield.

221. OR, XIX, pt. 1, p. 250.
Wendell D. Croom, *The War History of Company C (Beauregard Volunteers) Sixth Georgia Regiment*, Fort Valley, "Advertiser Office," 1879, p. 14.

222. Ezra Carman, "The Maryland Campaign," VIII, Manuscript Division, Library of Congress, p. 70.

223. Lyman C. Holford, Diary, September 14, 1862, Manuscript Division, Library of Congress. George Fairchild, Diary, September 14, 1862, State Historical Society of Wisconsin, Archives and Manuscript Dept., copy, Antietam National Battlefield.

224. Philip Cheek and Mair Pointon, *History of the Sauk County Riflemen*, 1906, p. 47.

225. Dawes, p. 83.

226. Alan T. Nolan, *The Iron Brigade*, MacMillan Co., N.Y., 1961, p. 129.

227. Ezra Carman, "The Maryland Campaign," VIII, Manuscript Division, Library of Congress, p. 70.

228. Dawes, p. 83.

229. OR, XIX, pt. 1, p. 257.

230. Dawes, p. 83.

231. Tully Graybill, Letter to Wife, September 26, 1862, John W. Kiely Collection, with permission.

232. Philip Cheek and Mair Pointon, p. 49.

233. Dawes, p. 97.

234. Ezra Carman, "The Maryland Campaign," VIII, Manuscript Division, Library of Congress, p. 71.

235. Ibid., p. 95.

Chapter Thirteen

1. Ezra Carman, "The Maryland Campaign," VII, Manuscript Division, Library of Congress, p. 398.

2. Henry C. Boyer, "At Crampton's Pass," The Shenandoah *Evening Herald*, August 31, 1886.
   Boyer did not say which companies were to accompany the command, but the corps had only two companies attached to it.
   Battles and Leaders, II, p. 599.

3. Jacob W. Haas, Diary, September 14, 1862, Hagerstown Civil War Round Table Collection, USAMHI.

4. Joseph J. Bartlett, "Crampton's Pass," *The National Tribune*, December 19, 1889, p. 1.

5. Montreville Williams, Diary, September 14, 1862, Museum Collection, Antietam National Battlefield.
   The 4th New Jersey reached Jefferson at 9:00 A.M.
   Peter A. Filbert, Diary, September 14, 1862, Hagerstown Civil War Round Table Collection, USAMHI.

6. Ezra Carman, "The Maryland Campaign," VII, Manuscript Division, Library of Congress, p. 387.

7. Joseph J. Bartlett, "Crampton's Pass," *The National Tribune*, December 19, 1889, p. 1.
   Jacob Haas, Diary, September 14, 1862, Harrisburg Civil War Round Table Collection, USAMHI.
   Peter A. Filbert, Diary, September 14, 1862, Harrisburg Civil War Round Table Collection, USAMHI.

8. Montreville Williams, Diary, September 14, 1862, Museum Collection, Antietam National Battlefield.
   The 4th New Jersey left Jefferson around 10:30 A.M.
   George T. Stevens, p. 135.
   He said the "Advance" sounded at 10:00 A.M.
   Robert S. Westbrook, p. 124.
   The order to march arrived at 9:00 A.M.

9. Joseph J. Bartlett, "Crampton's Pass," *The National Tribune*, December 19, 1889, p. 1.
    Henry C. Boyer, "At Crampton's Pass," The Shenandoah *Evening Herald*, August 31, 1886.

10. Ezra Carman, "The Maryland Campaign," VII, Manuscript Division, Library of Congress, p. 398.

11. Henry C. Boyer, "At Crampton's Pass," The Shenandoah *Evening Herald*, August 31, 1886.

12. Ezra Carman, "The Maryland Campaign," VII, Manuscript Division, Library of Congress, pp. 399, 403.
    OR, XIX, pt. 1, p. 874.
    Southern Historical Society Papers, XIII, p. 273.
    Ibid., XXXIII, p. 97.

13. Ezra Carman, "The Maryland Campaign," VII, Manuscript Division, Library of Congress, p. 404.
    Bernard, p. 24.
    Southern Historical Society Papers, XII, p. 521.
    Benjamin H. Trask, *16th Virginia Infantry*, H. E. Howard, Inc., Lynchburg, Va., 1986, p. 17.

14. Bernard, p. 25.
    Ezra Carman, "The Maryland Campaign," VII, Manuscript Division, Library of Congress, p. 403.
    William B. Henderson, *41st Virginia Infantry*, H. E. Howard, Inc., Lynchburg, Va., 1986, p. 30.

15. Neese, p. 120.

16. Henry C. Boyer, "At Crampton's Pass," The Shenandoah *Evening Herald*, August 31, 1886.

17. Jacob Haas, Diary, September 14, 1862, Harrisburg Civil War Round Table Collection, USAMHI.

18. Henry C. Boyer, "At Crampton's Pass," The Shenandoah *Evening Herald*, August 31, 1886.

19. Joseph J. Bartlett, "Crampton's Pass," *The National Tribune*, December 19, 1889, p. 1.

20. Henry C. Boyer, "At Crampton's Pass," The Shenandoah *Evening Herald*, August 31, 1886.

21. Neese, p. 121.

22. Henry C. Boyer, "At Crampton's Pass," The Shenandoah *Evening Herald*, August 31, 1886.

23. *Battles and Leaders*, II, p. 593.
    This is based upon William Franklin's report and the map in *Battles and Leaders*.

24. Neese, p. 121.

25. Henry C. Boyer, "At Crampton's Pass," The Shenandoah *Evening Herald*, September 2, 1886.

26. Neese, pp. 121-122.

27. Joseph J. Bartlett, "Crampton's Pass," *The National Tribune*, December 19, 1889, p. 1.
    Bartlett did not say where he was exactly, but implied that he was reconnoitering the ground to the northwest for a possible approach to the mountain. He was not with the 96th Pennsylvania. Henry C. Boyer did not see him with the regiment during the early stages of the battle.

28. Westbrook, p. 124.
    Stevens, p. 136.

29. Joseph J. Bartlett, "Crampton's Pass," *The National Tribune*, December 19, 1889, pp. 1-2.

30. Bernard, p. 25.

Southern Historical Society Papers, XII, p. 521.

Henderson, *12th Va.*, p. 35.

31. The meeting house is on the eastern face of the mountain near the top of the gap. It is a private residence today.

32. Ezra Carman, "The Maryland Campaign," VII, Manuscript Division, Library of Congress, p. 405.

33. Bernard, p. 41.

34. Ibid., p. 303.

35. Ezra Carman, "The Maryland Campaign," VII, Manuscript Division, Library of Congress, p. 405.

36. Joseph J. Bartlett, "Crampton's Pass," *The National Tribune*, December 19, 1889, p. 2.

37. OR, XIX, pt. 1, p. 393.

38. H. Seymour Hall, "Personal Experience Under General McClellan After Bull Run, Including the Peninsular and Antietam Campaign From July 27, 1862 to November 10, 1862," a Paper prepared and read before the Kansas Commandery of the MOLLUS, January 3, 1894, p. 20.

39. This description of the field is based upon Henry C. Boyer's description. To ascertain approximately where the fields were, I used the *Official Records'* Map to accompany XIX, 1, p. 36 and William B. Franklin's account in *Battles and Leaders*, II, pp. 595, 596.

   Franklin estimated his engaged force (Slocum's) at approximately 6500 officers and men and Smith's division (not as actively engaged) at 4500 effectives, which represents 89% of his paper strength.

   Henry Boyer's account, places two of the New Jersey regiment, Newton's four regiments, and the 96th Pennsylvania on the front line, with the rest of Bartlett's brigade (3 regiments), less the 121st New York, supporting the 96th Pennsylvania. The 96th Pennsylvania fielded about 500 effectives. Two of the New Jersey regiments supported the other two units in the Jersey brigade. The entire division consisted of 13 commands. 6500 men divided by 13 regiments equals 500 men per regiment.

   Regimental front equalled number of men present times 2' front per man, divided by the number of ranks (lines) of men. A group of 500 men in column of fours would be figured as 500 × 2 divided by 4 = 250' front when facing by the flank.

   In battle line the problem would read 500 × 2 divided by 2 = 500' front.

   A seven regiment front of 500 men each would cover at least 3500 feet.

   The distance between the Burkittsville Road and the northern most boundary of the field above the Widow Tritt's and the right flank of Newton's brigade in the *Official Records'* Maps is approximately 3700 feet. The Map incorrectly portrayed Bartlett's position. Bartlett's account of the battle as well as the descriptions left by Captain Newton M. Curtis (Company G, 16th New York, p. 170) and by Ezra Carman (VII, p. 408) clearly indicate that Newton's two right regiments relieved Bartlett's two front line regiments. Newton's right flank and Bartlett's right flank were approximately the same.

   Estimating the new 121st New York at 700-900 men (800 ave.) and removing them from the strength of the attacking force would give Slocum 5700 men. Deducting the 95th Pennsylvania's 500 men would reduce the number to 5200 men between 11 regiments. The average strength between regiments would amount to 473 effectives.

   6 regiments at 473 men = 2838 + 500 (PA) = 3338. 3700' − 3338' = 362' for spacing between regiments. The spacing between flanks would average 52'-60' with the space increasing as casualties increased.

40. Bernard, p. 41.

   He said Parham had 520 men in his three regiments. Munford had 200 cavalrymen. The 10th Georgia brought in 208 soldiers.

41. Bernard, p. 27.

42. Ezra Carman, "The Maryland Campaign," VII, Manuscript Division, Library of Congress, pp. 31, 33.

43. Bernard, p. 27.

44. Ezra Carman, "The Maryland Campaign," VII, Manuscript Division, Library of Congress, pp. 31, 43.
   This is an estimate based upon the overall losses sustained by the 5th Maine the 16th New York, and the 27th New York.
   Newton Martin Curtis, *From Bull Run to Chancellorsville*, G. P. Putnam's Sons, New York, 1906, p. 170.
   Lieutenant Colonel Joel Seaver (16th New York) said the regiments were engaged about 30 minutes or more.

45. Ezra Carman, "The Maryland Campaign," VII, Manuscript Division, Library of Congress, p. 33.
   Joseph J. Bartlett, "Crampton's Pass," *The National Tribune*, December 19, 1889, p. 2.

46. Henry C. Boyer, "At Crampton's Pass," The Shenandoah *Evening Herald*, September 2, 1886.

47. Ezra Carman, "The Maryland Campaign," VII, Manuscript Division, Library of Congress, p. 31.

48. Henry C. Boyer, "At Crampton's Pass," The Shenandoah *Evening Herald*, September 2, 1886.

49. Joseph J. Bartlett, "Crampton's Pass," *The National Tribune*, December 19, 1889, p. 2.

50. Ezra Carman, "The Maryland Campaign," VII, Manuscript Division, Library of Congress, pp. 31, 33.
   Joseph J. Bartlett, "Crampton's Pass," *The National Tribune*, December 19, 1889, p. 2.

51. Henry C. Boyer, "At Crampton's Pass," The Shenandoah *Evening Herald*, September 2, 1886.

52. Francis Boland, Letter, undated, probably September, 1862, John Breslin Letters, Harrisburg Civil War Round Table Collection, USAMHI, p. 6.

53. Conline, p. 113.

54. J. Shaw, "Crampton's Gap: Where the Boys Did Not Know but they were Firing Cordwood at Them," *The National Tribune*, October 1, 1891, p. 3.

55. Ibid., p. 3.
   Shaw erred when he said the New Jersey soldiers were only fifty yards from the Rebs. From his position, he could not have seen this incident if it were 250 yards to the front.

56. OR, XIX, pt. 1, p. 384.

57. Captain William H. Lessig, Company C, 96th Pa.

58. Henry C. Boyer, "At Crampton's Pass," The Shenandoah *Evening Herald*, September 2 and 3, 1886.
   Boyer did not mention who the officer was that ordered the charge. Bartlett, who commanded the 27th New York in 1861, was the only officer present in that area who would have had the authority to call up artillery support. Bartlett in his story for *The National Tribune* said he posted the 96th Pennsylvania before talking to Torbert.
   Joseph J. Bartlett, "Crampton's Pass," *The National Tribune*, December 19, 1889, p. 2.

59. Ibid.

60. Bernard, pp. 25-28.

61. Ibid., p. 44.

62. Conline, pp. 113-114.
   Daniel H. Hill, *Bethel to Sharpsburg*, II, p. 394.
   According to Hill, Macon used three guns and Manly one in the defense of Brownsville Gap. In a footnote on the same page, he inserted part of Manly's report in which Manly stated that he used his rifled guns.
   R. L. Lagemann, "Summary of the Artillery Batteries in postions to support the Infantry during the action at Bloody Lane, with a Map showing their locations," Monograph, Antietam National Battlefield Site, March 6, 1962, p. 15.

Manly had only one rifled gun in his battery and Macon had only two. Since Manly was the on site officer as opposed to Hill who was at Turner's Gap, several miles to the north, one may assume that Manly deployed only the three rifled pieces available.

63. Bernard, p. 43.

64. Ibid., p. 28.
OR, XIX, pt. 1, p. 394.
Colonel Henry Cake said his men reached the skirmish line about 5:30 P.M.

65. Ezra Carman, "The Maryland Campaign," VII, Manuscript Division, Library of Congress, p. 411.

66. John P. Beech, "Crampton Pass and the Part Taken by the 4th New Jersey in That Engagement," *The National Tribune*, May 8, 1884, p. 7.
Sergeant Beech (B Co., 4th NJ) mistakenly said Newton ordered the attack.
Henry C. Boyer, "At Crampton's Pass," The Shenandoah *Evening Herald*, September 3, 1886.

67. Ezra Carman, "The Maryland Campaign," VII, Manuscript Division, Library of Congress, p. 34.
Newton Martin Curtis, p. 170.
J. Shaw, "Crampton's Gap," *The National Tribune*, October 1, 1891, p. 3.
Carman did not have Henry Boyer's account of the battle. Quite typical of so many postwar studies he assumed that the brigades were formed as they were assigned. He never assumed that the *Official Record* Maps were inaccurate.

68. OR, XIX, pt. 1, p. 392.

69. Henry C. Boyer, "At Crampton's Pass," The Shenandoah *Evening Herald*, September 3, 1886.

70. Ezra Carman, "The Maryland Campaign," VII, Manuscript Division, Library of Congress, p. 35.

71. Henry C. Boyer, "At Crampton's Pass," The Shenandoah *Evening Herald*, September 3, 1886.

72. W. F. Beyer and O. F. Keydel, I, p. 73.

73. Henry C. Boyer, "At Crampton's Pass," The Shenandoah *Evening Herald*, September 3, 1886.

74. OR, XIX, pt. 1, pp. 395-396.

75. H. B. McClellan, p. 121.
In his report, Munford said those two regiments expended all their ammunition before retiring as the remaining two regiments of the brigade arrived at the crest of the gap. Supposing they had forty rounds of ammunition and were firing at the prescribed rate of 2-3 rounds per minute, it took approximately 13 to 20 minutes to fire away the contents of their cartridge boxes.
Henry C. Boyer, "At Crampton's Pass," The Shenandoah *Evening Herald*, September 3, 1886.
Boyer timed the advance of the New Jersey brigade and the 96th Pennsylvania to the Mountain Church Road at twenty-one minutes, more than enough time for the two regiments to expend their ammunition.
Ezra Carman, "The Maryland Campaign," VII, Manuscript Division, Library of Congress, p. 41.

76. Ezra Carman, "The Maryland Campaign," VII, Manuscript Division, Library of Congress, pp. 38-39.
McLaws tried to explain Cobb's poor performance when he wrote:
"Cobb was inexperienced enough not to realize, that as ranking officer, he was responsible for everything that might happen in the rear, where his inferiors in rank were stationed, unless they were under immediate orders of others superior to himself....If he had had more experience as to his responsibility which rank confers he would not have waited an hour in camp upon contingencies, but would have gone in person in advance to inform himself as to the best way to provide against misfortune."

OR, XIX, pt. 1, p. 861.

77. Conline, p. 114.
The Vermonters saw the Confederate right flank run before they reached the stone wall west of David Arnold's barn.

Joseph Lawton, "One of Kearny's Men. The First Troops That Crossed Long Bridge — On the Peninsula and at Crampton's Gap," *The National Tribune*, August 20, 1908, p. 7.
The Rebels did not make a stand until they reached the top of the mountain. They ran from the Mountain Church road before the Yankees reached them.

John P. Beech, "Crampton's Pass and the Part Taken by the 4th New Jersey in That Engagement," *The National Tribune*, May 8, 1884, p. 7.
Sergeant Beech said the Confederates fell back in a semi-circle, indicating that the regiments on the flanks gave way before the center.

78. W. F. Beyer and O. F. Keydel, I, pp. 73-74.

79. Bernard, pp. 28-29.

80. Westwood A. Todd, "Recollections," Westwood A. Todd Papers, in the Southern Historical Collection, University of North Carolina, Chapel Hill, N.C., pp. 60, 61.

81. Henderson, *12th Va. Inf.*, pp. 35, 119.
Bernard, p. 305.

82. Ibid., p. 43.
Bernard could not recall whether Jones shouted his tease at Stainback or at Johnson. He left it up to the reader to decide.

83. *Confederate Veteran*, XVI, 1908, pp. 48, iv.

84. Philip F. Brown, *Reminiscences of the War, 1861-1865*, privately printed, 1912, p. 27.

85. Jacob W. Haas, Diary, September 14, 1862, Harrisburg Civil War Round Table Collection, USAMHI.

86. OR, XIX, pt. 1, p. 396.

87. OR, XIX, pt. 1, p. 396.

88. Henry C. Boyer, "At Crampton's Pass," The Shenandoah *Evening Herald*, September 3, 1886.

89. John Shipp, Diary, September 14 and 15, 1862, Virginia Historical Society, Richmond, Va.

90. Henry C. Boyer, "At Crampton's Pass," The Shenandoah *Evening Herald*, September 3, 1886.

91. H. B. McClellan, p. 121.

92. Jacob W. Haas, Diary, September 14, 1862, The Harrisburg Civil War Round Table Collection, USAMHI.

93. Bernard, p. 29.

94. Conline, p. 114.

95. Ezra Carman, "The Maryland Campaign," VII, Manuscript Division, Library of Congress, p. 45.
OR, XIX, I, pt. 1, p. 826.

96. Conline, p. 114.

97. Bidwell, p. 18.

98. Bernard, p. 43.

99. Judd, p. 182.

100. John P. Beech, "Crampton Pass and the Part Taken by the 4th New Jersey in That Engagement," *The National Tribune*, May 8, 1884, p. 7.

101. Conline, p. 114.

102. Ezra Carman, "The Maryland Campaign," VII, Manuscript Division, Library of Congress, p. 42.

103. Bernard, p. 43.

104. Ibid., p. 42.
Ezra Carman, "The Maryland Campaign," VII, Manuscript Division, Library of Congress, p. 42.
John Conline, p. 114.
Trask, p. 17.

105. Conline, p. 114.

106. Bidwell, p. 19.

107. OR, XIX, pt. 1, pp. 386-388.

108. John F. Stegeman, *These Men She Gave*, University of Georgia Press, Athens, p. 61.

109. H. B. McClellan, p. 121.
Stegeman, pp. 61-62.

110. OR, XIX, pt. 1, pp. 387, 861.

111. H. B. McClellan, p. 121.

112. Stegeman, p. 62.
DeRossett Lamar, "About a Distinguished Southern Family," *Confederate Veteran*, VIII, 1900, p. 164.
OR, XIX, pt. 1, p. 387.
The 4th New Jersey captured Colonel Lamar of Cobb's Legion, who died in Burkittsville the next day.
    Cobb's brother-in-law died in Pleasant Valley on the opposite side of the mountain, the next day.

113. OR, XIX, pt. 1, pp. 392-401.

114. W. F. Beyer and O. F. Keydel, I, p. 74.

115. Curtis, p. 171.

116. Daniel H. Hill, *Bethel to Sharpsburg*, II, p. 395.

117. OR, XIX, pt. 1, p. 394.

118. Curtis, p. 170.

119. OR, XIX, pt. 1, p. 394.

120. Daniel H. Hill, *Bethel to Sharpsburg*, II, p. 395.

121. OR, XIX, pt. 1, p. 386.

122. W. F. Beyer and O. F. Keydel, I, p. 74.
Joseph J. Bartlett, "Crampton's Pass," *The National Tribune*, December 19, 1889, p. 2.

123. OR, XIX, pt. 1, p. 388.

124. J. Shaw, "Crampton's Gap, Where the Boys Did Not Know but they were Firing Cordwood at Them," *The National Tribune*, October 1, 1891, p. 3.
Joseph Lawton, "One of Kearny's Men. In the First Troops That Crossed Long Bridge — On the Peninsula and at Crampton's Cgap," *The National Tribune*, August 20, 1908, p. 7.

125. Stegeman, p. 62.

126. John P. Beech, "Crampton Pass and the Part Taken by the 4th New Jersey in That Engagement," *The National Tribune*, May 8, 1884, p. 7.

127. Joseph J. Bartlett, "Crampton's Pass," *The National Tribune*, December 19, 1889, p. 2.

128. J. Shaw, "Crampton's Gap, Where the Boys Did Not Know but they were Firing Cordwood at Them," *The National Tribune*, October 1, 1891, p. 3.

129. Stegeman, p. 62.

130. Ibid.

131. John P. Beech, "Crampton Pass and the Part Taken by the 4th New Jersey in That Engagement," *The National Tribune*, May 8, 1884, p. 7.

132. Conline, p. 114.
      Judd, p. 184.
      Stevens, p. 139.

133. Ezra Carman, "The Maryland Campaign," VII, Manuscript Division, Library of Congress, p. 41.
      Letter, Thomas Munford to Ezra Carman, December 10, 1894, Typed Correspondence, #159, Antietam National Battlefield.

134. Ezra Carman, "The Maryland Campaign," VII, Manuscript Division, Library of Congress, p. 46.
      Von Borcke, I, pp. 217-219.

135. OR, XIX, pt. 1, p. 861.

136. Montreville Williams, Diary, September 14, 1862, Museum Collection, Antietam National Battlefield.

137. Westwood A. Todd, "Reminiscences," Westwood A. Todd Papers, in the Southern Historical Collection, University of North Carolina Library, Chapel Hill, N.C., p. 62. In the quote, the officer said Newton was his corps commander.

138. Bernard, pp. 30-31.
      Bernard was quite fuzzy headed by this time. He did not recall exactly when he drank the tea nor did he recall exactly when he saw the doctor in relation to the time of his arrival at the hospital. The only doctor whom I know of being captured was Thomas Newton.

139. Westwood A. Todd, "Reminiscences," Westwood A. Todd Papers, in the Southern Historical Collection, University of North Carolina Library, Chapel Hill, N.C., p. 62.

140. Brown, pp. 27-29.

141. OR, XIX, pt. 1, p. 861.
      Ezra Carman, "The Maryland Campaign," VII, Manuscript Division, Library of Congress, p. 45.

142. Ezra Carman, "The Maryland Campaign," VII, Manuscript Division, Library of Congress, p. 43.
      Daniel H. Hill, *Bethel to Sharpsburg*, II, p. 394.

143. Bernard, p. 43.

Chapter Fourteen

  1. Bidwell, p. 19.
      According to Frederick Bidwell, the 49th New York started to advance toward Harpers Ferry, though not as far as the 2 or more miles claimed.
      Judd, p. 183.
      He said the VI Corps stood to arms.

  2. Von Borcke, II, p. 221.
      Von Borcke said Blackford, Dabney, and Farley rode up to him after Stuart heard the news of the surrender. It can be assumed they were all three together and not with Von Borcke when the news of Harpers Ferry arrived.

  3. Blackford, pp. 144-145.

  4. Von Borcke, II, p. 220.

  5. Blackford, p. 145.

  6. Judd, p. 183.

7. Westbrook, p. 124.

8. Jacob W. Haas, Diary, September 15, 1862, Harrisburg Civil War Round Table Collection, USAMHI.

9. Bernard, p. 31.

10. Westwood A. Todd, "Reminiscences," Westwood A. Todd Papers, in the Southern Historical Collection, University of North Carolina Library, Chapel Hill, N.C., p. 63.

11. Walcott, p. 191.

12. Ibid., p. 193.

13. *35th Mass.*, pp. 31-32.

14. *Confederate Veteran*, IV, 1896, p. 27.

15. Walcott, p. 193.

16. Albert, p. 55.
    Gould, p. 78.

17. Lord, pp. 89-92.

18. Bosbyshell, p. 77.

19. Ibid., pp. 107-108.

20. Gould, p. 78.

21. James Wren, Diary, September 15, 1862, Antietam National Battlefield Collection, p. 108.
    Gould, p. 78.

22. Walcott, p. 194.
    Samuel Compton, "Autobiography," Samuel Compton Manuscript, Manuscript Department, Duke University Library, Durham, N.C., pp. 99-100.
    William J. Bolton, "War Journal," War Library Museum, Philadelphia, Pa., p. 251.

23. Walcott, p. 194.

24. Ibid.
    Stone, p. 88.
    35th Mass., p. 26.

25. William J. Bolton, "War Journal," War Library and Museum, Philadelphia, Pa., p. 251.
    Thomas H. Parker, pp. 228-229.

26. William Todd, p. 236.

27. Walcott, p. 194.

28. William Todd, p. 236.

29. Lord, p. 90.

30. James Wren, Diary, September 15, 1862, Antietam National Battlefield Collection, pp. 105-106.
    I deliberately cleaned up Wren's spelling and punctuation to make Pleasants' conversation more intelligible.

31. *35th Mass.*, p. 36.

32. Andrew Wykle, "A Fighting Regiment Four Years' Service at the Front With the 36th Ohio," *The National Tribune*, January 9, 1902, p. 3.

33. Stone, pp. 88-89.

34. Whitney, pp. 132-133.

35. *35th Mass.*, p. 36.

36. William J. Bolton, "War Journal," War Library and Museum, Philadelphia, Pa., p. 252.

37. Jacob H. Cole, *Under Five Commanders*, News Printing Company, Patterson, N.J., 1906, pp. 80-81.

38. Abram P. Smith, p. 159.

39. John W. M. Long, "South Mountain Battle Events," Middletown *Valley Register*, July 7, 1922.

40. McClenthen, p. 33.

41. Bates Alexander, "Seventh Reserves," The Hummelstown *Sun*, September 13, 1895. Alexander mistakenly referred to the captured major as a colonel.

42. Lieutenant Samuel W. Moore, Diary, September 15, 1862, Antietam National Battlefield Museum Collection.
     Moore heard Strong's name as "Straine."

43. Bates Alexander, "Seventh Reserves," The Hummelstown *Sun*, September 13, 1895. There were no majors, healthy or otherwise, captured uring the battle in this end of the field. The only man of that rank had to have been the surgeon Lieutenant Samuel Moore mentioned. Surgeons did dress better than the average line soldier and could have been mistaken for a staff officer by an infantryman.

44. Hard, p. 178.

45. William A. Hill, Letter to Ezra Carman, July 18, 1898, Antietam Studies, National Archives, Washington, D.C.

46. Thomas P. Nanzig, *3rd Virginia Cavalry*, H. E. Howard Co., Inc., Lynchburg, Va., p. 21.

47. H. B. McClellan, p. 124.

48. G. W. Beale, p. 45.

49. William A. Hill, Letter to Ezra Carman, July 18, 1898, Antietam Studies, National Archives, Washington, D.C.

50. G. W. Beale, Letter to Ezra Carman, June 6, 1897, Antietam Studies, National Archives, Washington, D.C.

51. Hard, p. 179.

52. G. W. Beale, Letter to Ezra Carman, June 3, 1897, Antietam Studies, National Archives, Washington, D.C.

53. G. W. Beale, Letter to Ezra Carman, June 6, 1897, Antietam Studies, National Archives, Washington, D.C.

54. G. W. Beale, p. 45.

55. G. W. Beale, Letter to Ezra Carman, June 3, 1897, Antietam Studies, National Archives, Washington, D.C.

56. G. W. Beale, p. 45.

57. G. W. Beale, Letter to Ezra Carman, June 6, 1897, Antietam Studies, National Archives, Washington, D.C.

58. G. W. Beale, Letter to Ezra Carman, June 3, 1897, Antietam Studies, National Archives, Washington, D.C.

59. Hard, p. 181.
     Robert L. T. Beale, p. 140.

60. G. W. Beale, Letter to Ezra Carman, June 3, 1897, Antietam Studies, National Archives, Washington, D.C.

61. G. W. Beale, Letter to Ezra Carman, June 6, 1897, Antietam Studies, National Archives, Washington, D.C.
     H. B. McClellan, p. 126.
     G. W. Beale, in his June 3, 1897 letter to Carman, apparently plagiarized McClellan per vatim.

62. William A. Hill, Letter to Ezra Carman, July 18, 1898, Antietam Studies, National Archives, Washington, D.C.

63. G. W. Beale, p. 46.

64. *Historical Magazine*, May, 1869, p. 294.
     Hard, p. 179.

65. Ibid., p. 182.

    G. W. Beale, Letter to Ezra Carman, June 6, 1897, Antietam Studies, National Archives, Washington, D.C.

    Robert L. T. Beale wrote that the Confederate wounded were in a large building on the main street. It most likely was the U.S. Hotel.

66. Robert E. Lee, Letter to Mrs. T. J. Jackson, January 25, 1866, Letterbook of Robert E. Lee, Virginia Historical Society, Richmond, Va.

67. Ezra Carman, "The Maryland Campaign," VII, Manuscript Division, Library of Congress, p. 81.

68. Frank P. Firey, "On the Battle Field of South Mountain," *Confederate Veteran*, XXIII, 1915, pp. 71-72.

69. Harry Warner, "Notes on South Mountain," undated newspaper article from the files of George Brigham, Middletown Historical Society, Middletown, Md.

Bibliography

PUBLISHED PRIMARY SOURCES

Albert, Allen D., (ed.), (Co. D), *History of the Forty-Fifth Regiment Pennsylvania Veteran Volunteer Infantry, 1861-1865*, Grit Publishing Co., Williamsport, 1912.

Baquet, Camille, (Lt., Co. A, 1st N.J.), *History of the First Brigade, New Jersey Volunteers*, MacCrellish & Quigley, State Printers, Trenton, 1910.

Beach, William H., (Sgt., Co. B), *The First New York (Lincoln) Cavalry From April 19, 1861 to July 7, 1865*, Lincoln Cavalry Association, N.Y., 1902.

Beale, G. W., (9th Va. Cav.), *A Lieutenant of Cavalry in Lee's Army*, The Gorham Press, Boston, 1908.

Beale, Richard L. T., (Ltc.), *History of the Ninth Virginia Cavalry in the War Between the States*, B.F. Johnson Publishing Co., 1899.

Bennett, A. J., *The Story of the 1st Massachusetts Light Battery Attached to the Sixth Army Corps*, Deland and Barta, Boston, 1886.

Bernard, George S., (Co. I, 12th Va.), *War Talks of Confederate Veterans*, Fenn & Owen, Publishers, Petersburg, Va., 1892.

Beyer, W. F. and O. F. Keydel, (ed.), *Deeds of Valor*, Vol. I, Perrin-Keydel Co., Detroit, 1907.

Bidwell, Frederick D., (comp.), *History of the 49th Regiment New York Volunteers*, J. B. Lyons, Albany, N.Y., 1917.

Blackburn, George M., *With the Wandering Regiment, The Diary of Captain Ralph Ely of the 8th Michigan*, Central Michigan University Press, Mt. Pleasant, 1965.

Blackford, William W., *War Years With Jeb Stuart*, Charles Scribner's Sons, N.Y., 1946.

Bosbyshell, Oliver C., (Cpt., Co. G, 48th Pa.), *The 48th in the War*, Avil Printing Co., Philadelphia, 1895.

Brooks, Ulysses Roberts, (1st N.C. Cav.), *Stories of the Confederacy*, The State Co., Columbia, S.C., 1912.
  [This contains the following book: Rea, D., *Sketches From Hampton's Cavalry in the Summer, Fall and Winter Campaigns of '62 Including Stuart's Rain into Pennsylvania and Also in Burnside's Rear*, Strother and Co., Raleigh, 1863.]

Brown, J. Willard, *The Signal Corps, U.S.A. in the War of the Rebellion*, U.S. Veteran Signal Corps Association, Boston, 1896.

Brown, Philip F., (Pvt., Co. C, 12th Va.), *Reminiscences of the War 1861-1865*, privately printed, 1912.

Buck, Samuel D., (Lt., Co. H, 13th Va.), *With the Old Confeds*, H. E. Houck & Co., Baltimore, 1925.

Cheek, Philip and Mair Pointon, (Co. A, 6th Wis.), *History of the Sauk County Riflemen*, 1909.

Clark, Walter, (ed.), *Histories of the Several Regiments and Battalions From North Carolina in the Great War*, 5 Volumes, E. M. Uzzell, Printer and Binder, Raleigh, 1901.

Coker, James L., *History of Company G Ninth S.C. Regiment, Infantry, S.C. Army and of Company E, Sixth S.C. Regiment Infantry C.S. Army*, The Attic Press, Greenwood, S.C.

Cole, Jacob H., (Co. A, 57th N.Y.), *Under Five Commanders*, News Printing Co., Patterson, N.J., 1906.

Committee of the Regimental Association, *History of the 35th Regiment Massachusetts Volunteers, 1862-1865*, Mills, Knight & Co., Printers, Boston, 1884.

Conline, John, (Co. E, 4th Vt.), "Recollections of the Battle of Antietam and the Maryland Campaign," *War Papers Read Before the Michigan Commandery of the Military Order of the Loyal Legion of the United States*, Vol. II, From December 7, 1893 to May 5, 1898, James H. Stone Co., Printers, Detroit, 1898.

Cook, Benjamin F., (Cpt., Co. E, 12th Mass.), *History of the Twelfth Massachusetts Volunteers (Webster Regiment)*, Twelfth (Webster) Regimental Association, Boston, 1882.

Cowper, Pulaski, (comp.), (Col., 4th N.C.), *Extracts of Letters of Major Gen'l Bryan Grimes to His Wife*, Edwards, Broughton & Co., Raleigh, 1883.

Cox, Jacob Dolson, *Military Reminiscences of the Civil War*, Vol. I, Charles Scribner's Sons, N.Y., 1900.

Crater, Lewis, (Adj., 50th Pa.), *History of the Fiftieth Regiment Penna. Vols., 1861-65*, Coleman Printing House, Reading, 1884.

Crowninshield, Benjamin W., *A History of the First Regiment of Massachusetts Cavalry Volunteers*, Houghton, Mifflin and Co., Boston, 1891.

Curtis, Newton M., (Cpt., Co. G, 16th N.Y.), *From Bull Run to Chancellorsville*, G. P. Putnam's Sons, N.Y., 1906.

Cussel, Charles A., *Durrell's Battery in the Civil War*, Craig, Finley & Co., Philadelphia, 1900.

Davis, Nicholas A., *The Campaign From Texas to Maryland*, The Steck Co., Austin, 1905.

Dawes, Rufus, (Maj., 6th Wis.), *Service With the Sixth Wisconsin Volunteers*, Morningside Bookshop, Dayton, Ohio, 1984.

DePeyster, J. Watts, *The Decisive Battles of the Late Civil War, or Slaveholders' Rebellion*, MacDonald and Co., Printers, N.Y., 1867.

Dickert, D. Augustus, *History of Kershaw's Brigade*, Morningside Bookshop, Dayton, Ohio, 1976.

Eddy, Richard, (Chaplain), *History of the Sixtieth New York State Volunteers*, by the author, Philadelphia, 1864.

Everett, Donald E., (ed.), *Chaplain Davis and Hood's Texas Brigade*, Principia Press of Trinity University, San Antonio, 1962.

Ford, Worthington Chauncey, *A Cycle of Adams Letters 1861-1865*, Vol. I, Houghton Mifflin Co., Boston, 1920. (1st Mass. Cav.)

France, M. H., comp., *The Conception, Organization and Campaigns of "Company H" 4th Penn. Reserve, Volunteer Corps, 33 Regiment in Line 1861-5*, Baldwin & Chapman, Publishers, Tunkhannock, Pa., 1885.

Freeman, Warren H., (13th Mass.), *Letters*, privately printed, Cambridge, 1871.

Galloway, George N., "The Ninety-fifth Pennsylvania Volunteers," Philadelphia, 1884.

Galwey, Thomas F., (Sgt., Co. B, 8th Ohio), *The Valiant Hours*, The Stackpole Co., Harrisburg, Pa., 1961.

Gates, Theodore B., (Col., 20th N.Y.S.M.), *The Ulster Guard*, Benjamin H. Tyrrel, N.Y., 1879.

Goodhart, Briscoe, (Co. A), *History of the Independent Loudoun Virginia Rangers, U.S. Volunteer Cavalry Scouts 1862-1865*, Press of McGill and Wallace, Washington, D.C., 1896.

Gould, Joseph, (Q.M. Sgt., 48th Pa.), *The Story of the Forty-Eighth*, Regimental Association, Mt. Carmel, 1908.

Graham, Matthew J., (Lt., Co. F), *The Ninth Regiment New York Volunteers (Hawkins' Zouaves) Being History of the Regiment and Veteran Association from 1860-1900*, E.P. Coby & Co., Printers, N.Y., 1900.

Hadley, Amos, (ed.), *History of the Sixth New Hampshire Regiment in the War for the Union*, Republican Press Association, Concord, 1891.

Hall, Isaac, (Lt., Co. D), *History of the Ninety-Seventh Regiment, New York Volunteers*, L. C. Childs & Son, 1870.

Hall, H. Seymour, "Personal Experience Under General McClellan After Bull Run, Including the Peninsular and Antietam Campaign From July 27, 1861 to November 10, 1862," paper read before the Kansas Commandery of the MOLLUS, January 3, 1894.

Hard, Abner, (surgeon), *History of the Eighth Cavalry Regiment Illinois Volunteers in the Great Rebellion*, Morningside Bookshop, Dayton, Ohio, 1984.

Hardin, Martin D., *History of the Twelfth Regiment Pennsylvania Reserve Volunteer Corps*, N.Y., 1890.

Hill, Archibald F., (8th Pa. Res.), *Our Boys*, John E. Potter, Philadelphia, 1864.

Hill, Daniel Harvey, *Bethel to Sharpsburg*, Vol. II, Edwards & Broughton Co., Raleigh, 1926.

History of the 17th Virginia Infantry, C.S.A., Kelly, Piet & Co., Baltimore, 1870.

Horton, J. H., and Solomon Teverbaugh, (Co. F, 11th Ohio), *A History of the Eleventh Regiment Ohio Volunteer Infantry*, W. H. Shuey, Printer and Publisher, Dayton, Ohio, 1866.

Hood, John B., *Advance and Retreat*, Richard N. Current, (ed.), Civil War Centennial Series, Indiana University Press, Bloomington, 1959.

Hough, Franklin B., *History of Duryee's Brigade*, J. Munsell, Albany, 1864.

Huebner, Richard Alden, comp., *Merserve Civil War Record*, RAH Publications, Oak Park, Mich., 1987.

Hunter, Alexander, (Co. A, 17th Va.), *Johnny Reb and Billy Yank*, The Neale Publishing Co., N.Y., 1905.

Johnson, Charles F., (Co. I, 9th N.Y.), *The Long Roll*, The Roycrofters, East Aurora, N.Y., 1911. (Reprint, Hagerstown Bookbinding and Printing, Inc., 1986.)

Johnson, Robert U., and Clarence C. Buel, (ed.), *Battles and Leaders of the Civil War*, Grant-Lee Edition, Vol. II, Part 2, The Century Co., N.Y.

Johnston, David E., (7th Va.), *The Story of a Confederate Boy in the Civil War*, Commonwealth Press, Inc., Radford, Va. (Reprint, 1980, Leonard A. Parr).

Judd, David Wright, *The Story of the Thirty-third New York State Volunteers*, Benton and Andrews, Rochester, 1864.

Kempfer, Lester L., *The Salem Light Guard, Company G, 36th Ohio Volunteer Infantry, Marietta, Ohio, 1861-1865*, Adams Press, Chicago, 1973.

Lane, David, (Co. G, 17th Mich.), *A Soldier's Diary, The Story of a Volunteer, 1862-1865*, privately printed, 1905.

Life and *Letters of Wilder Dwight*, (Ltc., 2nd Mass.), Ticknor and Fields, Boston, 1868.

Locke, William H., (chaplain, 11th Pa.), *The Story of the Regiment*, James Miller, Publisher, N.Y., 1872.

Lord, Edward O., (ed.), *History of the Ninth Regiment New Hampshire Volunteers*, Republican Press Association, Concord, 1895.

Loving, Jerome M., (ed.), (Lt., Co. D, 51st N.Y.), *Civil War Letters of George Washington Whitman*, Duke University Press, Durham, N.C., 1975.

Lyle, William W., (chaplain, 11th Ohio), *Lights and Shadows of Army Life*, R. W. Carroll & Co., Cincinnati, 1865.

McClellan, H. B., *The Life and Campaigns of Major-General J. E. B. Stuart*, Houghton, Mifflin and Co., Boston, 1885.

McClendon, William A., (Co. G, 15th Ala.), *Recollections of War Times*, The Paragon Press, Montgomery, 1909.

McClenthen, Charles S., (Co. G., 26th N.Y.), *Campaign in Virginia and Maryland of Towers' Brigade, Ricketts' Division, From Cedar Mountain to Antietam*, Masters and Lee, Printers, Syracuse, 1862.

McKinsey, Folger and T. J. C. Williams, *History of Frederick County Maryland*, Vol. I, L. R. Titsworth & Co., 1910.

Mills, J. Harrison, (Co. D), *Chronicles of the Twenty-first Regiment New York Volunteers*, 21st Regiment Veteran Association, Buffalo, 1887.

Minnigh, Henry N., (Lt., Co. K, 1st Pa. Res.), *History of Company K, 1st (Inft.) Penn's Reserves*, "Home Print" Publisher, Duncansville, Pa.

Moore, Edward A., (Sgt., Poague's Va. Btty.), *The Story of a Cannoneer Under Stonewall Jackson*, J. P. Bell, Inc., Lynchburg, Va., 1910.

Myers, Frank M., (White's Bttn.), *The Commanches*, Kelly, Piet & Co., Baltimore, 1871.

Nagle, Theodore M., (C Co., 21st N.Y.), *Reminiscences of the Civil War*, Erie, Pa. 1923.

Neese, George Michael, (Chew's Va. Btty.), *Three Years in the Confederate Horse Artillery*, The Neale Publishing Co., N.Y., 1911.

Newcomer, C. Armour, *Cole's Cavalry*, Cushing & Co., Baltimore, 1895.

Norton, Henry, (Co. H), *History of the Eighth New York Volunteer Cavalry*, Chenango and Telegraph Printing House, Norwich, N.Y., 1889.

O'Ferrall, Charles T., (Cpt., Co. I, 12th Va. Cav.), *Forty Years of Active Service*, The Neale Publishing Co., N.Y., 1904.

Otis, George H., (Co. B), *The Second Wisconsin*, Alan D. Gaff, (ed.), Morningside Bookshop, Dayton, Ohio, 1984.

Owen, William Miller, (Wash. Arty.), *In Camp and Battle of the Washington Artillery of New Orleans*, Ticknor and Co., Boston, 1885.

Park, Robert Emory, (Cpt., Co. F, 12th Ala.), *Sketch of the Twelfth Alabama Infantry*, William Ellis Jones, Book and Job Printer, Richmond, 1906.

Parker, John L. and Robert G. Carter, *History of the Twenty-Second Massachusetts Infantry*, Rand Avery Co., Boston, 1887.

Parker, Thomas H., *History of the 51st Regiment of P.V. and V.V.*, King and Baird Printers, Philadelphia, 1869.

Patrick, Marsena R., (I Corps), *Inside Lincoln's Army*, David S. Sparks, (ed.), Thomas Yoseloff, N.Y., 1964.

Pickerill, William N., *History of the 3rd Indiana Cavalry*, Aetna Printing Co., Indianapolis, 1906.

Polk, J. M., (Co. I, 4th Texas), *Memories of the Lost Cause*, Austin, Texas, 1905.

Polley, Joseph B., *Hood's Texas Brigade*, Morningside Bookshop, Dayton, Ohio, 1976.

Proceedings of the Thirty-fourth Annual Reunion of the Eleventh Ohio, September 20, 1906.

Quynn, William R., (ed.), *Jacob Engelbrecht Diary*, Vol. III, The Historical Society of Frederick County, Frederick, Md., 1976.

Racine (Rosine), J. Polk, (Co. I, 5th Md.), *Recollections of a Veteran*, Bicentennial Commission of Cecil County, Reprint, 1987.

Report of Lewis H. Steiner, M.D., Inspector of the Sanitary Commission Anson D. F. Randolph, N.Y., 1862.

Report of the Ohio Battlefield Commission, Springfield Publishing Co., Springfield, Ohio, 1904.

Rich, Edward R., (Co. E, 1st Md. Cav., C.S.A.), *Comrades!*, S. E. Whitman, Easton, Md., 1898.

Sloan, John A., (Co. B, 27th N.C.), *Reminiscences of the Guilford Grays, Co.B, 27th N.C. Regiment*, R.O. Polkinhorn, Printer, Washington, D.C., 1883.

Smith, Abram P., (Q.M.), *History of the Seventy-Sixth Regiment New York Volunteers*, Courtland, N.Y., 1867.

Smith, W. A., (Co. C, 14th N.C.), *The Anson Guards*, Stone Publishing Co., Charlotte, N.C., 1914.

Sorrel, G. Moxley, (Longstreet's staff), *Recollections of a Confederate Staff Officer*, Bell I. Wiley, (ed.), McCowat-Mercer Press, Jackson, Tenn., 1958.

Spooner, Henry J., (Lt.), "The Maryland Campaign with the Fourth Rhode Island," Personal Narratives, Sixth Series, No. 5, Soldiers and Sailors Historical Society of Rhode Island.

Stevens, George T., (Surgeon, 77th N.Y.), *Three Years in the Sixth Corps*, S. R. Gray Publisher, Albany, 1866.

Stevenson, James H., (Lt., Co. C, 1st N.Y. Cav.), *A History of the First Volunteer Cavalry of the War*, Patriot Publishing Co., Harrisburg, Pa., 1879.

Stone, James Madison, (Co. K, 21st Mass.), *Personal Recollections of the Civil War*, by the author, Boston, 1918.

Sypher, Josiah R., *History of the Pennsylvania Reserve Corps*, Elias Barr & Co., Lancaster, 1865.

"The Annals of the War," Philadelphia *Weekly Times*, The Times Publishing Co., Philadelphia, 1879.

The Official Records of the War of the Rebellion, Vol. XIX, Part 1.

Thompson, James Monroe, *Reminiscences of the Autauga Rifles, G Co., 6th Alabama Volunteer Regiment, C.S.A.*, William Stanley Hoole, (ed.), Prattville, Ala., 1879.

Thompson, William M., *Historical Sketch of the Sixteenth Regiment New York State Volunteer Infantry April 1861-May 1863*, 1st Reunion, Pottsdam, N.Y., 1886.

Tobie, Edward P., *History of the First Maine Cavalry*, Press of Emery & Hughes, Boston, 1887.

Todd, George T., (Cpt., Co. A), *First Texas Regiment*, Texian Press, Waco, 1963.

Todd, William, (ed.), *History of the Ninth Regiment N.Y.S.M. (Eighty-Third N.Y. Volunteers)*, Veterans of the Regiment, N.Y., 1889.

Todd, William, (ed.), *The Seventy Ninth Highlanders, New York Volunteers in the War of the Rebellion 1861-1865*, Press of Brandow, Barton, & Co., 1886.

Turner, Charles W., (ed.), (Letcher's Va. Btty.), *Captain Greenlee Davidson, C.S.A. Diary and Letters 1851-1863*, McClure Press, Verona, Va., 1975.

Urban, John W., (Co. D, 1st Pa. Res.), *My Experiences Mid Shot and Shell*, Lancaster, 1882.

Vail, Enos B., (Co. E, 20th N.Y.S.M.), *Reminiscences of a Boy in the Civil War*, by the author, 1915.

Von Borcke, Heros, *Memoirs of the Confederate War for Independence*, Vol. I, Morningside Bookshop, Dayton, Ohio, 1985.

Waitt, Ernst Linden, (comp.), *History of the Nineteenth Regiment Massachusetts Volunteer Infantry 1861-1865*, Salem Press, Salem, Mass., 1906.

Walcott, Charles F., (Cpt., Co. B), *History of the 21st Massachusetts Volunteers in the War for the Preservation of the Union, 1861-1865*, Boston, 1882.

Ward, James E. D., *Twelfth Ohio Volunteer Infantry*, Ripley, Ohio, 1864.

Westbrook, Robert S., (Sgt., Co. B), *History of the Forty-Ninth Pennsylvania Volunteers*, Altoona Times Printer, Altoona, 1898.

Whitney, J. H. E., *The Hawkins Zouaves: Their Battles and Marches*, by the Author, N.Y., 1866.

Wood, Nathaniel, (Lt., Co. A, 19th Va.), *Reminiscences of Big I*, McCowat-Mercer Press, Jackson, Tenn., 1956.

Woodward, E. M., *History of the Third Pennsylvania Reserves*, MacCrellish & Quigley, Book and Job Printers, Trenton, N.J., 1883.

Woodward, E. M., SGM., 2nd PA Res.), *Our Marches*, John E. Potter and Co., Philadelphia.

Worsham, John H., (Co. F, 21st Va.), *One of Jackson's Foot Cavalry*, James I. Robertson, Jr., (ed.), McCowat-Mercer Press, Jackson, Tenn., 1964.

PUBLISHED SECONDARY SOURCES

Cree, Lemoin, *A Brief History of South Mountain House*, The Valley Register, Middletown, Mitchell H. Dodson, 1963.

Divine, John E., *8th Virginia Infantry*, H. E. Howard Co., Inc., Lynchburg, 1983.

Fields, Frank E., Jr., *28th Virginia Infantry*, H. E. Howard Co., Inc., Lynchburg, 1985.

Frye, Dennis, *12th Virginia Cavalry*, H. E. Howard Co., Inc., Lynchburg, 1988.

Gunn, Ralph White, *24th Virginia Infantry*, H. E. Howard, Inc., Lynchburg, 1987.

Hassler, William Woods, *Colonel John Pelham Lee's Boy General*, Garrett & Massie, Inc., Richmond, Va., 1960.

Henderson, William B., *41st Virginia Infantry*, H. E. Howard, Inc., Lynchburg, 1986.

Henderson, William D., *12th Virginia Infantry*, H. E. Howard Co., Inc., Lynchburg, 1984.

Jordan, Erwin L., Jr., and Herbert A. Thomas, Jr., *19th Virginia Infantry*, H. E. Howard Co., Inc., Lynchburg, 1987.

Krick, Robert, *9th Virginia Cavalry*, H. E. Howard Co., Inc., Lynchburg, 1982.

Maryland Civil War Centennial Commission, Maryland Remembers, Hagerstown, 1961.

Nanzig, Thomas P., *3rd Virginia Cavalry*, H. E. Howard, Inc., Lynchburg, Va., 1989.

Simpson, Harold B., *Gaines' Mills to Appomattox, Waco and McLennan County in Hood's Texas Brigade*, Texian Press, Waco, 1963.

Simpson, Harold B., *Hood's Texas Brigade: Lee's Grenadier Guard*, Texian Press, Waco, Texas, 1970.

Stegeman, John F., *These Men She Gave*, University of Georgia Press, Athens.

Stiles, Kenneth E., *4th Virginia Cavalry*, H. E. Howard Co., Inc., Lynchburg, 1985.

Trask, Benjamin H., *16th Virginia Infantry*, H. E. Howard, Inc., Lynchburg, Va., 1986.

Williams, T. Harry, *Hayes of the Twenty-Third*, Alfred A. Knopf, N.Y., 1965.

Manuscripts

Historical Society of Pennsylvania

Abraham, James, (Lt., 1st W. Va. Cav.), Letters:
Letter to Brother, September 20, 1862.
Letter to Friends, September 23, 1862.

Gibbon, John, (brigadier general, U.S.A.), Letter to Wife, September 13, 1862, Box 1, John Gibbon Papers.

Antietam National Battlefield:

"Antietam Relic Lists, Photograph Lists, Bibliography and Human Interest Stories," manuscript.

"Barbara Frietchie Romance," Ezra Carman typed transcript, pp. 79-82.

Batchelder, Albert A., (Co. C, 6th N.H.), Letter to Father, not dated. (Vertical Files).

"Battle of South Mountain, September 14th, 1862," Ezra Carman typed transcript, pp. 224-232.

"Boonsboro or South Mountain," (1st Va.), Ezra Carman typed transcript, p. 234.

Bresnahan, John, (Co. A, 27th Ind.), "Battle of Antietam," Ezra Carman typed transcript, pp. 103-104.

Campbell, Gabriel, (Cpt., Co. E), "The 17th Michigan at South Mountain Sep. 14, 1862," Letter to Ezra Carman, August 23, 1899, typed transcript, pp. 212-217.

Campbell, Gabriel, (Cpt., Co. E), Letter to Ezra Carman, August 1899, Carman Papers, 100 107/Corr.

Carman, Ezra, "Maryland Campaign," typed transcript of his handwritten notes.

Christen, William, et al., (17th Mich.), "Stonewall Regiment, A History of the 17th Michigan Volunteer Infantry Regiment," Michigan Volunteer Infantry Regiment, Detroit, 1986. (secondary)

Coffin, Charles C., "Saving the Nation," Ezra Carman typed transcript, pp. 148-157.

"Confederate Casualties," 101, Carman Papers, 105/Transcript.

Cook, John H., Diary, (Co. D., 6th Wis.), State Historical Society of Wisconsin, Archives and Manuscript Dept. (Vertical Files).

Datzman, Richard Carroll, "Who Found Lee's Lost Dispatch?", monograph, February 3, 1973. (secondary)

Davis, Angela Kirkham, manuscript, *War Reminiscences: A Letter to My Nieces.*

Dimon, Theodore, (2nd Md.), Letter to Fitz John Porter, June 15, 1883, Ezra Carman typed transcript, pp. 239-241.

Douglas, Henry Kyd, "The Boonsboro Incident," Correspondence with the Baltimore *Sun.*

Fairfield, George, (Cpl., Co. C, 6th Wis.), State Historical Society of Wisconsin, Archives and Manuscript Dept. (Vertical Files).

Green, M. M., (1st Va. Cav.), "Saving 'Stonewall' Jackson," Extract from Scrap Book of General Henry Kyd Douglas.

"Harper's Ferry," Ezra Carman typed transcript, pp. 161-163.

"Hawkins' Zouaves," New York *Times*, June 7, 1897, Ezra Carman Papers.

"Lee's Proclamation to the People of Maryland."

Livermore, Thomas L., "Statistics of South Mountain and Antietam," Ezra Carman typed transcript, pp. 217-221.

Matthews, H. H., (Pelham-Breathed Battery), "The First Maryland Campaign, Saint Mary's *Beacon*, Leonardtown, Md., January 19, 1905, Ezra Carman transcripts, pp. 177-182.

Owen, H. T., (Co. C, 18th Va.), Ezra Carman typed transcript, pp. 183-189.

"Reunion of Army Veterans," Ezra Carman typed transcript, pp. 202-205.

"79th New York at South Mountain," Ezra Carman typed transcript, pp. 237-238.

"South Mountain: The Seventy-Sixth Regiment New York Volunteers," Ezra Carman typed transcript, pp. 221-224.

"Special Orders No. 191."

(35th Mass.), Item 110, Ezra Carman Papers.

"35th Mass. at South Mountain," Ezra Carman typed transcript, pp. 232-233.

"Where Armies Contended," typed transcript of the Ezra Carman Papers, pp. 193-202. (Vertical Files).

Williams, Albert B., (Co. I, 122nd N.Y.), AC# AW69, Letter to Father, October 14, 1862, Albert B. Williams Papers, University of Rochester, N.Y. (Vertical Files).

Williams, Montreville, (Chief Musician, 3rd N.J.), Diary, Museum Collection.

Wilson, Martin L., (Sgt., Co. A, 122nd N.Y.), Letter to John, September 19, 1862. (Vertical Files).

Wren, James, Diary, (Cpt., Co. B, 48th Pa.), manuscript.

Special Collections Department, Duke University Library, Durham, N.C.:

Compton, Samuel, (Co. F, 12th Ohio), Autobiography, Samuel Compton Papers. Library, Durham, NC.

Jackson, Ashbury Hull, (Cpt., Co. C, 44th Ga.), Letter to Mother, September 23, 1862, Edward Harden Papers.

Munford, Thomas, (2nd Va. Cav.), Recollections, Munford-Ellis Civil War Manuscript, 1861-1865, Box 1.

Overcash, James W., (Co. G, 6th N.C.), Letter to Father, October 10, 1862, Joseph Overcash Papers.

Untitled Sketch of the 23rd N.C., Raleigh *News and Observer*, Sunday, April 11, 1897, C.S.A. Archives, Box 16, Army Units Ga.-N.C. file, H. C. Williams.

Welch, Stephen Elliott, (Hampton's Legion, S.C.), Letter to Parents, September 22, 1862, Stephen Elliott Welch Papers.

Antietam Studies, National Archives, Washington, D.C.:

D. H. Hill's Division, Regimental information.
Fitzhugh Lee's Cavalry Brigade
    Ezra Carman's notes on Fitz Lee's Brigade.
    Letter, G. W. Beale to Ezra Carman, June 3, 1897.
    Letter, G. W. Beale to Ezra Carman, June 6, 1897.
    Letter, R. B. Lewis to Ezra Carman, May 8, 1897.
    Letter, Ezra Carman to T. L. Rosser, May 12, 1897.
    (Rosser's response on the back.)
    Letter, William A. Hill to Ezra Carman, July 18, 1898.
Stuart's Horse Artillery—Pelham's Battalion
    Letter, Stirling Murray to Ezra Carman, July 25, 1898.
    Letter, Stirling Murray to Ezra Carman, March 10, 1900.
Col. Thomas T. Munford's Cavalry Brigade
    Letter, Thomas Munford to Ezra Carman, April 7, 1896.
    Letter, Thomas Munford to Ezra Carman, December 12, 1894.
Brigadier General Wade Hampton's Cavalry Brigade
    "Records of Events on Muster Roll of Field, Staff and Band of the 9th Regt. N.C. State Troops, or 1st Cavalry, C.S.A.
    1st North Carolina Cavalry Co. A.
    W. H. Cheek, (1st N.C. Cav.), June 14, 1897.
    1st North Carolina Cavalry Co. E.
    1st North Carolina Cavalry.

University of North Carolina, Southern Historical Collection, Chapel Hill, N.C.:

Baker, William B., (Co. D, 1st Maine Cav.), Letters to Family, September 6, 9, 11, 13, 14, 1862, William B. Baker Papers.

Collins, Benjamin M., (Cpt., Co. C, 12th N.C.), Manuscript History of the Regiment.

Leach, Calvin, Diary, (Co. B, 1st N.C.).

McLauchlin, M. M. R., (Cpt., 38th N.C.), entry, January 1, 1863.

Proffitt, Alfred N. and Andrew J. Proffitt, (both Co. D, 18th N.C.), Letter to Brother, September 9, 1862, and Letter to Father, not dated, Proffitt Family Papers, 1850-1862.

Shinn, James Shinn, (Orderly Sgt., Co. B, 4th N.C.), Diary, Edwin Augustus Osborne Papers #567.

Smith, Otis D., (6th Ala.), "Reminiscences," Thach Papers.

Todd, Westwood A., (12th Va.), "Recollections," Westwood A. Todd Papers.

United States Army Military Institute, Carlisle Barracks, Pa.:

CWRT = Civil War Round Table

CWTI = Civil War Times Illustrated

Barrow, Atwell J., (Winchester Btty. and Alleghany Arty.), Diary, Civil War Misc. Collection.

Benson, Evelyn Abraham, *With the Army of West Virginia 1861-1864*, (LT James Abraham, W. Va. Cav.), Publication No. 1, Evelyn A. Benson, Lancaster, Pa., 1974, CWTI Collection.

Boland, Francis, (Co. K, 96th Pa.), undated letter, Harrisburg CWRT Collection.

Brisbin, James S., 6th U.S. Cav., Letter to Wife, September 16, 1862, CWTI Collection.

Cornwell, Robert B., (Co. A, 23rd Ohio), Letter to Brothers and Sisters, October 3, 1862, Harrisburg CWRT.

Elliott, Andrew J., (Co. A, 8th Pa. Res.), Diary, Pennsylvania "Save the Flags" Collection.

Filbert, Peter Augustus, (Cpt., Co. B, 96th Pa.), Diary, Harrisburg CWRT Collection.

Haas, Jacob W., (Cpt., Co. G, 9th Pa.), Diary, Harrisburg CWRT Collection.

Heirs, William Andy, (3rd Ala.), Letter to Cousin, September 7, 1862, CWTI Collection.

Hurd, Daniel Emerson, (Co. G, 9th N.H.), "My Experiences in the Civil War," William Marvel Collection.

McIlwain, James H., (11th Pa. Res.), Letter to Emma, September 14, 1862, Lewis Leigh Collection.

McQuaide, John D., (Co. C, 8th Pa. Res.), Letter to Thomas McQuaide, September 22, 1862, CWTI Collection.

Mills, Charles J., (Adj., 2nd Mass.), *Through Blood and Fire: The Civil War Letters of Major Charles J. Mills*, Harrisburg CWRT, Gregory Coco Collection.

Morey, Charles C., (Sgt., Co. E, 2nd Vt.), Diary, Charles C. Morey Collection.

Morton, John, (Co. F, 17th Mich.), Letter to Mother, September 24, 1862, CW Misc. Collection.

Pettit, Frederick, (Co. C, 100th Pa.), Letters September 19, 21, and 23, 1862, CWTI Collection.

Pope, Albert Augustus, LT, Co. I, 35th Mass.), "Journal of the Southern Campaign, War of the Rebellion, August 27, 1862-June 9, 1865," CWTI Collection.

Pratt, James, (Co. H, 35th Mass.), James and Charlotte Pratt Collections.

Smith, Charles M., (Co. E, 1st Mass. Cav.), Letter to Parents, September 18, 1862, Smith Family Papers, CW Misc. Collection.

Smith, Jason, Letter to Mother, September 8, 1862, Alonzo and Jason Smith Papers, 35th Mass.. Infantry Regt., Correspondence.

Squires, Charles W., (Wash. Arty.), "The Last of Lee's Battle Line," W. H. T. Squires, (ed.), 1894, CWTI Collection.

Weiser, John S., (130th Pa.), Letter to Parents, September 12, 1862, CW Misc. Collection.

Wesson, Silas D., (8th Ill. Cav.), Diary, CWTI Collection.

Private Collections:

Dr. Richard A. Sauers:

Alexander, Bates, (7th Pa. Res.), "Pennsylvania Reserves," Hummelstown *Sun*, August 9, 16, 22, 30, September 6, 13, 1895.

John S. Derbyshire, Rocky Mount, N.C.:

Dawson, Charles, (Co. F, 3rd Ind. Cav.), Letter to Mollie, October 11, 1862.

John W. Kiely Collection:

Graybill, Tully, (Maj., 28th Ga.), Letter to Wife, September 26, 1862.

Daniel Toomey Collection:

Keeler, Samuel B., (Co. I, 4th N.J.), Letter to Brother, Clifford, September 16, 1862.

Robert Ulrich Collection:

Shell, Reuben and Beneville, (7th Pa. Res.), Letters to Parents, September 24 and 29, 1862.

Manuscript Division, Library of Congress, Washington, D.C.:

Carman, Ezra Ayers Collection, Library of Congress. E.B. White (12th Ohio) to Carman, July 11, 1899. John Purifoy (Bondurant's Ala. Btty.) to Carman, July 15, 1899, July 21 and August 7, 1900.

Carman, Ezra, "The Maryland Campaign."

Gilpin, Samuel J. B. V., (Co. E, 3rd Ind. Cav.), Diary, E. N. Gilpin Collection.

Holford, Lyman C., (Co. A, 6th Wis.), Diary.

Johnston, James S., (11th Miss.), Letter to Mary M. Green, September 22, 1862, Mercer Green Johnston Collection.

Manuscript Department, University of Virginia, Charlottesville, Va.:

Hubard, Robert T., (Lt., Co. K, 3rd Va. Cav.), Notebook 1860-1866, "Damnation of Vancouver" and "Turvey" Manuscripts, Acc. No. 10522.

Johnson, Samuel S., (1st Mass. Indpt. Light Arty.), Diary, 1862, March 10-1864, August 29, Acc. No. 8493.

Painter, James B., (Co. K, 28th Va.), Letters, 1861-1863, Letters to Family, October 5, 1862, Acc. No. 10661.

Virginia Historical Society, Richmond, Va.:

Latrobe, Osmun, (Longstreet's staff), Diary, Osmun Latrobe Diary.

Owen, Henry Thweat, (Cpt., Co. C, 18th Va.), Papers, Sec. 3, "Recollections of Antietam."

Sherwood, William W., (Cpl., F Co., 17th Va.), Diary, Mss51 shsp:1.

Shipp, John, (G Co., 6th Va.), Diary, Mss2sh 64662.

PRIMARY SOURCES:

Newspapers/Periodicals:

Boyer, H.C., (Co. A, 96th PA), "At Crampton's Pass," August 18, 1886, Philadelphia *Weekly Press.*

Casey, James B., (ed.), "The Ordeal of Adoniram Judson Warner: His Minutes of South Mountain and Antietam," *Civil War History*, Vol. 28, #3, September, 1982, p. 217 + . (10th Pa. Res.)

Confederate Veteran

Confederate Veteran, (Fox's Gap), IV, 1896, p. 27.

Confederate Veteran, (12th Va.), XVI, 1908, p. 48 iv.

Confederate Veteran, (24th Va.), XXXV, 1927, p. 211.

Confederate Veteran, (8th Va.), XXXVII, 1929, p. 105.

Firey, Frank P., "On the Battle Field of South Mountain," XXIII, 1915, p. 71.

Lamar, DeRossett, "About a Distinguished Southern Family," VIII, 1900, p. 164.

Historical Magazine

"General Pleasonton's Cavalry Division, in the Maryland Campaign, September, 1862," May, 1869, p. 291 + .

Military Images

Gorman, John Calvin, (Cpt., Co. B, 2nd N.C.), "Memoirs of a Rebel," George Gorman, (ed.), Nov./Dec., 1981, pp. 4-6.

Southern Historical Society Papers

XII, Jan-Dec., 1884, (12th Va. Cav.).

Grattan, George D., (D. H. Hill's staff), "The Battle of Boonsboro Gap or South Mountain," Vol. XXXIX, 1914, p. 31 + .

Hill, D. H., "Address at the Reunion of the Virginia Division of the Army of Northern Virginia Association, Vol. XIII, 1885, p. 267 + .

McCrady, Edward, Jr., (Col.), "Heroes of the Old Camden District, South Carolina, 1776-1861," XVI, Jan-Dec., 1888, p. 24.

"Reports of the First, Seventh and Seventeenth Virginia Regiments in 1862," Vol. XXXVI, 1910, p. 262 + .

The National Tribune, Washington, D.C.

Alexander, Bates, (Sgt., Co. C, 7th Pa. Res.), "One of Our Constituents: What a Pennsylvania Man Thinks of Our Paper," December 12, 1889, p. 3.

Alsley, J. B., (Cpt., Co. H, 27th Ind.), "Lee's Lost Order," March 26, 1908, p. 7.

Barnes, Edward L., (Adj., 95th N.Y.), "The 95th New York at South Mountain," January 7, 1886, p. 2.

Bartlett, Joseph J., "Crampton's Pass," December 19, 1889, p. 1.

"Battlefields Revisited," October 13, 1892, p. 4.

Beech, John P., (Sgt., Co. B, 4th N.J.), "Crampton's Pass and the Part Taken by the 4th New Jersey in That Engagement," May 8, 1884, p. 7.

Bingham, Charles H., (13th Mass.), "Easy, Loafing Straggler's Life," April 19, 1928, p. 5.

Counnel, A. B., (Co. F, 30th Ohio), "Reno's Death," August 23, 1883, p. 1.

Goldsborough, Clark E., "Graphic Description of Lee's Occupation of Frederick, Maryland in 1862," October 14, 1886, p. 4.

Goldsborough, E. Y., "Barbara Fritchie. The Truth About the Loyalty of That Brave Dame," January 28, 1892, p. 5.

Holsinger, Frank, (Co. F, 8th Pa. Res.), "South Mountain and the Part the Reserves Took in the Battle," September 27, 1883, p. 7.

Kelley, T. Benton, (Co. E, 8th Ill. Cav.), "How I Captured Seven Johnnies," July 15, 1909, p. 7.

Lawton, Joseph, (Cpl., Co. B, 4th N.J.), "One of Kearny's Men," August 20, 1908, p. 7.

P.P.C., (8th Ill. Cav.), "A Private's View of Antietam," March 19, 1908, p. 7.

Shaw, J., (Co. H, 95th Pa.), "Crampton's Gap," October 1, 1891, p. 3.

"The 22nd N.Y.," September 24, 1885, p. 3.

Vernon, George W., (LTC, Cole's Cav.), "Cole's Maryland Cavalry," January 16, 1908, p. 7.

Walton, Joseph E., (Co. I, 30th Ohio), "At South Mountain," October 6, 1898, p. 2.

Walton, J. E., "The 30th Ohio—Some Reminiscences of the Battle of Antietam," December 31, 1885, p. 3.

West, Robert, (Bugler, Co. H, 51st N.Y.), "Reno's Death," August 9, 1883, p. 1.

Wood, A. H., (Co. L, 6th N.Y. Cav.), "How Reno Fell," July 6, 1883, p. 1.

Wykle, Andrew, (Co. K, 30th Ohio), "A Fighting Regiment," January 9, 1902, p. 3. 1884, p. 7.

Maryland Historical Magazine

Quynn, Dorothy Mackay and William Rogers Quynn, "Barbara Frietschie," Vol. XXXVII, September, 1942, #3, p. 227 + .

New York *Times*, September 9 and 14, 1862, p. 1.

References

Massachusetts Soldiers, Sailors, And Marines in the Civil War, Six Volumes, Norwood Press, Norwood, Mass., 1933.

Wilmer, L. Allison, et al., *History and Roster of Maryland Volunteers, War of 1861-65*, Vol. I, Press of Guggenheimer, Weil and Co., Baltimore, 1898.

Index